IFIP Advances in Information and Communication Technology 362

IFIP – The International Federation for Information Processing

IFIP was founded in 1960 under the auspices of UNESCO, following the First World Computer Congress held in Paris the previous year. An umbrella organization for societies working in information processing, IFIP's aim is two-fold: to support information processing within ist member countries and to encourage technology transfer to developing nations. As ist mission statement clearly states,

> *IFIP's mission is to be the leading, truly international, apolitical organization which encourages and assists in the development, exploitation and application of information technology for the benefit of all people.*

IFIP is a non-profitmaking organization, run almost solely by 2500 volunteers. It operates through a number of technical committees, which organize events and publications. IFIP's events range from an international congress to local seminars, but the most important are:

- The IFIP World Computer Congress, held every second year;
- Open conferences;
- Working conferences.

The flagship event is the IFIP World Computer Congress, at which both invited and contributed papers are presented. Contributed papers are rigorously refereed and the rejection rate is high.

As with the Congress, participation in the open conferences is open to all and papers may be invited or submitted. Again, submitted papers are stringently refereed.

The working conferences are structured differently. They are usually run by a working group and attendance is small and by invitation only. Their purpose is to create an atmosphere conducive to innovation and development. Refereeing is less rigorous and papers are subjected to extensive group discussion.

Publications arising from IFIP events vary. The papers presented at the IFIP World Computer Congress and at open conferences are published as conference proceedings, while the results of the working conferences are often published as collections of selected and edited papers.

Any national society whose primary activity is in information may apply to become a full member of IFIP, although full membership is restricted to one society per country. Full members are entitled to vote at the annual General Assembly, National societies preferring a less committed involvement may apply for associate or corresponding membership. Associate members enjoy the same benefits as full members, but without voting rights. Corresponding members are not represented in IFIP bodies. Affiliated membership is open to non-national societies, and individual and honorary membership schemes are also offered.

Luis M. Camarinha-Matos
Alexandra Pereira-Klen
Hamideh Afsarmanesh (Eds.)

Adaptation and Value Creating Collaborative Networks

12th IFIP WG 5.5 Working Conference
on Virtual Enterprises, PRO-VE 2011
São Paulo, Brazil, October 17-19, 2011
Proceedings

Springer

Volume Editors

Luis M. Camarinha-Matos
Universidade Nova de Lisboa
Campus de Caparica, 2829-516 Monte Caparica, Portugal
E-mail: cam@uninova.pt

Alexandra Pereira-Klen
Axia Value Chain
Av. Nações Unidas, 12551, 04578-903 São Paulo, SP, Brazil
E-mail: alexandra.klen@axiavaluechain.com

Hamideh Afsarmanesh
University of Amsterdam
Science Park 904, 1098 XH Amsterdam, The Netherlands
E-mail: h.afsarmanesh@uva.nl

ISSN 1868-4238 e-ISSN 1868-422X
ISBN 978-3-642-23329-6 e-ISBN 978-3-642-23330-2
DOI 10.1007/978-3-642-23330-2
Springer Heidelberg Dordrecht London New York

Library of Congress Control Number: 2011936663

CR Subject Classification (1998): H.5.3, C.2, H.4, J.1, D.2, H.5

Typesetting: Camera-ready by author, data conversion by Scientific Publishing Services, Chennai, India

Printed on acid-free paper

Springer is part of Springer Science+Business Media (www.springer.com)

Preface

Collaborative networks (CNs) emerged more than a decade ago as a key element of economic growth and a very active area of scientific production. Dynamic collaborative organizations properly respond to the increasing need of strong adaptability to the constantly changing economic context. Several collaborative forms such as virtual organizations, virtual enterprises, professional virtual communities, industry clusters and business ecosystems are now supported by large research and business practice communities. These new organizational forms require the development of a new theoretical base. In recent years, many international projects have contributed to these needed scientific advances. The accumulated body of empiric knowledge and the size of the involved research community has provided the basis for the foundation of what is now a well-established scientific discipline on "collaborative networks". This discipline is strongly multidisciplinary and thus the PRO-VE Working Conference is designed to offer a major opportunity to gather contributions from engineering, economics, management, and socio-human communities, among others.

Value creation is a major challenge for organizations in times of economic turbulence and rapid societal changes. CNs represent a determinant inductor of value creation, not only for business communities, but also for other entities in society. Understanding and modeling the process, assessing, and developing methods and tools to support value creation in CNs is an R&D challenge requiring a multidisciplinary approach. The capability of generating value in a networked society requires high self-adaptation capacity, both from the participating entities in order to adhere to a collaboration culture, as well as from the CN as a whole to dynamically adjust to the needs, constraints, and opportunities posed by a rapidly changing environment. The main focus of PRO-VE 2011 was thus on the crucial aspects that can empower CNs as a main actor of change in society.

PRO-VE 2011 held in São Paulo, Brazil, was the 12th event in a series of successful conferences, including PRO-VE 1999 (Porto, Portugal), PRO-VE 2000 (Florianopolis, Brazil), PRO-VE 2002 (Sesimbra, Portugal), PRO-VE 2003 (Lugano, Switzerland), PRO-VE 2004 (Toulouse, France), PRO-VE 2005 (Valencia, Spain), PRO-VE 2006 (Helsinki, Finland), PRO-VE 2007 (Guimarães, Portugal), PRO-VE 2008 (Poznan, Poland), PRO-VE 2009 (Thessaloniki, Greece), and PRO-VE 2010 (St. Etienne, France).

This book includes a number of selected papers from the PRO-VE 2011 Conference, providing a comprehensive overview of recent advances in various CN domains and their applications, with a particular focus on adaptation of the networks and their value creation. With this focus, this edition of the conference specifically emphasizes CN topics related to: evolution from social networking to CNs, social capital, value chains, co-creation of complex products, performance management, behavioral aspects in CNs, CNs planning and modeling, benefit analysis, sustainability issues etc., as well as including important technical and scientific challenges in applying CNs to areas such as advanced logistics networks, business processes modeling, service orientation, and other emerging application domains, for example, ageing, tourism, crisis, and emergency scenarios, among others.

Similar to previous editions of PRO-VE, this book itself is the result of cooperative and highly distributed work among the authors of its articles and the input from the International Program Committee members who contributed to paper evaluations. It therefore represents a valuable tool for those interested in research advances, emerging applications, and future challenges for R&D in CNs. We would like to thank all the authors both from academia/research and industry for their contributions. We also appreciate the dedication of the PRO-VE Program Committee members who helped with the selection of articles and contributed with their valuable comments to help authors improve the quality of their work.

July 2011

Luis M. Camarinha-Matos
Alexandra Pereira-Klen
Hamideh Afsarmanesh

Organization

PRO-VE 2011 - 12th IFIP Working Conference on Virtual Enterprises

São Paulo, Brazil, October, 17–19, 2011

Program Committee Chair

Luis M. Camarinha-Matos (Portugal)

Organizing Committee Co-chairs

Alexandra Pereira-Klen (Brazil)
Ricardo J. Rabelo (Brazil)

Program Committee

Antonio Abreu (Portugal)
Hamideh Afsarmanesh (The Netherlands)
Cesar Analide (Portugal)
Samuil Angelov (The Netherlands)
Dario Antonelli (Italy)
Dimitris Assimakopoulos (France)
Vincent Augusto (France)
Américo Azevedo (Portugal)
Panagiotis Bamidis (Greece)
Ron Beckett (Australia)
Frederick Benaben (France)
Peter Bertok (Australia)
Xavier Boucher (France)
Jean Pierre Bourey (France)
Carlos Bremer (Brazil)
Jeremy Bryans (UK)
Patrick Burlat (France)
Luis M. Camarinha-Matos (Portugal)
Aline Cauvin (France)
Wojciech Cellary (Poland)
Sophie D'Amours (Canada)
Rob Dekkers (UK)
Alexandre Dolgui (France)
Schahram Dustdar (Austria)
Jens Eschenbaecher (Germany)
Elsa Estevez (Argentina)
Erastos Filos (Belgium)
John Fitzgerald (UK)
Myrna Flores (Switzerland)
Rosanna Fornasiero (Italy)
Cesar Garita (Costa Rica)
Ted Goranson (USA)
Paul Grefen (The Netherlands)
Jairo Gutierrez (Colombia)
Tarek Hassan (UK)
Tomasz Janowski (Macau)
Toshiya Kaihara (Japan)

Eleni Kaldoudi (Greece)
Iris Karvonen (Finland)
Alexandra Pereira-Klen (Brazil)
Bernhard Koelmel (Germany)
Kurt Kosanke (Germany)
Adamantios Koumpis (Greece)
Andrew Kusiak (USA)
István Mézgar (Hungary)
Paulo E. Miyagi (Brazil)
Arturo Molina (Mexico)
Ovidiu Noran (Australia)
Paulo Novais (Portugal)
Adegboyega Ojo (Macau)
Eugénio Oliveira (Portugal)
Angel Ortiz (Spain)
Luis Osório (Portugal)
Hervé Panetto (France)
Iraklis Paraklakis (Greece)
Adam Pawlak (Poland)
Sophie Peillon (France)
Keith Phalp (UK)
Willy Picard (Poland)
Ricardo Rabelo (Brazil)
João Rosas (Portugal)
Hans Schaffers (The Netherlands)
Raimar Scherer (Germany)
Jens Schütze (Germany)
Weiming Shen (Canada)
António L. Soares (Portugal)
Jorge P. Sousa (Portugal)
Chrysostomos Stylios (Greece)
Klaus-Dieter Thoben (Germany)
Lorna Uden (UK)
Antonio Volpentesta (Italy)
Lai Xu (UK)
Peter Weiß (Germany)

TECHNICAL SPONSORS:

ifip

IFIP WG 5.5 COVE
Co-Operation infrastructure for Virtual Enterprises and electronic business

SoCol net

Society of Collaborative Networks

Other sponsors:

FIA FUNDAÇÃO INSTITUTO DE ADMINISTRAÇÃO

ORGANIZATIONAL CO-SPONSORS

Axia Value Chain

UFSC

New University of Lisbon

UNINOVA

University of Amsterdam

Table of Contents

Part I: From Social Networking to Collaborative Networks

Part II: Social Capital and Collaborative Networks

Part III: Value Chain for Enhancing Collaborative Networks

Part IV: Co-creation of Complex Products

Part V: Performance Management - I

Part VI: Performance Management - II

Part VII: Active Ageing and Tourism Networks

Part VIII: Knowledge Transfer and Innovation Networks

Part IX: Advanced Logistics Networks

Part X: Behavioral Aspects

Part XI: Collaborative Networks Modeling and Theory

Part XII: Business Processes Modeling

Part XIII: Mining Approaches in Collaborative Networks

Part XIV: Service Orientation

Part XV: Collaborative Networks Planning

Part XVI: VO Formation

Part XVII: Networks in Crisis and Emergency Scenarios

Part XVIII: Benefits Analysis

Part XIX: Sustainability Issues

Part I

From Social Networking to Collaborative Networks

Multi-level Social Networking to Enable and Foster Collaborative Organizations

Youakim Badr[1], Noura Faci[2], Zakaria Maamar[3], and Frédérique Biennier[1]

[1] INSA de Lyon, F-69621, Villeurbanne, France
[2] Université Lyon 1, F-69622, Villeurbanne, France
[3] Zayed University, U.A.E.
{youakim.badr,frederique.biennier}@insa-lyon.fr,
noura.faci@univ-lyon1.fr, zakaria.maamar@zu.ac.ae

Abstract. Recent interest in capitalizing on the social network phenomenon has shown some relatively successful benefit to the business world. Social networking can sustain large-scale collaborative strategies between people and organizations. However, the main challenge remains the smooth weaving of social networks into organizations daily operations. In this paper we extend the reach and scope of social networks for an entire organization and show how they provide benefit to the business as a whole. We introduce a multi-layered social network model where people may play simultaneously one or more roles (e.g., suppliers, competitors, and customers) and participate in providing products, supporting services, and/or consuming them in sustainable collaborative environments. The experiments demonstrate both the widespread interest and possibilities of online social communities to foster collaboration among organizations.

Keywords: Social network, collaboration, business model, virtual organization.

1 Introduction

Web 2.0, one of the latest buzzwords in information and communication technologies domain, encourages people to break the isolation barrier so they can engage over the Internet in various activities that usually lead into creating knowledge (e.g., blogs and wikis), sharing information (e.g., mashups and folksonomies), and establishing contacts (e.g., social networking sites). Capitalizing on people's positive experiences about Web 2.0, many organizations consider that improving their product quality and service delivery can, also, happen through Web 2.0. Employees are these days invited to embrace social networks such as Facebook to establish and foster contacts with their colleagues, customers, and suppliers. Organizations aim at streamlining their business processes with their strategic plans and adapting their best practices in response to the opportunities that these applications offer [2]. Gearing organization-flavored social networks towards the specific needs of customers, suppliers, partners, and competitors organizations look forward to establishing new partnerships with their different stakeholders to effectively undertake joint business activities including resource co-design, co-marketing, co-production, co-development, and sharing. These

L.M. Camarinha-Matos et al. (Eds.): PRO-VE 2011, IFIP AICT 362, pp. 3–10, 2011.

new business conditions lead in significant structure and behavior changes within and cross organizations, such as focusing on core processes and promoting interoperability. To support organizations in their new endeavors, one can think of taking advantage of Internet-based social networks to build "trusted business communities". In these communities, people with different backgrounds and from different locations collaborate to co-create new value-added services. In addition, each member of a business community may play simultaneously one or more roles (e.g., provider, worker, and customer) and participate in providing products, supporting services and/or consuming them in sustainable and economical environments. This human-centric community leads in the development of human networks, spanning across organizational boundaries.

After presenting the background and motivation in section 2, we propose a multi-layer social network model to design a collaborative organization in section 3. The capitalized collaborative relationships are illustrated in the experimental results section and used to facilitate and enrich business collaboration to co-create new services and / or improve the partnership / service discovery and adaptation processes. Weaving social networks into the organization information systems will open up new business opportunities and transform organizations into socio-technical ecosystems driven by collaboration and information exchange.

2 Background

Due to market trends and fast-changing conditions, organizations should be more flexible, adapt to business changes and increase customer satisfaction, leading in new product-service collaborative organizations [3]. This induces significant organizational and strategic adaptations within organizations, such as focusing on their core business and looking for new collaboration strategies. Such business strategies raise the importance of developing outsourcing policies and promoting inter-enterprise collaborative business leading to alliances or network-based organizations. Several works have addressed the way collaborative organizations are set, paying attention on the firms collaboration “maturity” leading to set “collaborative breeding environments” gathering firms that “could collaborate” or paying more attention on trust and personal relationships factors to set collaborative trusted communities [10].

Roughly speaking, networked collaborative organizations consist of nodes and edges. The nodes refer to any type of object or entity such as individuals or organizations, and the edges refer to relationships between these nodes such as the degree of friendship between two persons or distance between two cities. Relationships are sometimes directional, bidirectional, with weight, or a mixture of all of these. Social networks are known to be tacit, informal, and intangible. This can hinder their identification and proper use. In previous work [1] [2], we focused on the importance of acknowledging their existence in organizations, so they can be structured to become formal and tangible representations. In an organization, we have identified four types of inter-related social networks [1]: customer, supplier, competitor, and partner.

1. Customer-centric social network states the nature of relationships between an enterprise's customer and the acquaintances of this customer in the network, such as friendship and kinship.
2. Supplier-centric social network states the nature of relationships between an enterprise's supplier and the acquaintances of this supplier in the network, such as supplier-of-supplier and competition.
3. Competitor-centric social network states the nature of relationships between an enterprise's competitor and the acquaintances of this competitor in the network, such as spontaneous-collaboration and competitor-of-competitor.
4. Finally, partner-centric social network states the nature of relationships between an enterprise's partner and the acquaintances of this partner in the network such as add-on and alliance.

These relationships bring to light the importance of corporate social networking. The use of social networks is reported in different domains such as social sciences, artificial intelligence, and business sciences. Ethier notes that ``*the study of social networks is important since it helps us to better understand how and why we interact with each other, as well as how technology can alter this interaction. The field of social network theory has grown considerably during the past few years as advanced computing technology has opened the door for new research*" [4]. Raab and Milward note that social networks are either bright or dark [5]. The former occur when the outcomes of socializing turn out beneficial for individuals, groups, businesses, and society at large. Contrarily, the latter occur when the outcomes of socializing are obtained at great cost to individuals, groups, businesses, and social welfare. Research reveals that social networks operate at many levels, from families up to the level of nations, and play a role in determining first, how problems are solved and organizations are run, and second, the degree to which individuals succeed in achieving their goals. Facebook, MySpace, and LinkedIn offer a glimpse of today's social applications that help people deploy and manage their own Web-based social networks. Social networking brings a new dimension to the Web by offering novel communication channels between people and between communities [7]. Connolly states that "*since social Web applications are built to encourage communication between people, they typically emphasize some combination of the following social attributes: identity, reputation, presence, relationships, groups, conversations, and sharing*" [8].

3 Towards Social Organizations

To deal with the large-scale collaboration challenge among organizations, we propose to take advantage of social networking to discover potential partners to fit new business opportunities. This involves coupling the functional and non functional description of business or industrial services offered by the different firms including, for example, partner profile and competencies, product offer, industrial and business process specifications to corporate social networks so that business or industrial offers can be discovered, selected, and composed to set collaborative organizations [9]. This selection process integrates both "production knowledge", namely partner competencies and capabilities, environmental constraints such as trusted environment,

IT support interoperability, sustainability and partner, and "social behaviour" in order to capitalize partner's collaborative activities and to evaluate partner's ability to set successful collaboration. It is for sure that embracing social networks in the world of work would raise important human issues such as privacy, confidentiality and trustworthiness requiring a legal framework to address these issues as well as new community models to integrate corporate and business knowledge.

To deal with this challenge, we define a multi-level social network model as a hyper graph showing the connection between employees, customers, suppliers, partners, and competitors. Participants in a multi-level social network connect to each other through different relationships representing multiple types of networks overlaid on top of one another. Each relationship, which is ranging from information sharing to social bindings, refers to a particular role played by the participants.

3.1 Value-Added of Social Networks to Organizations

We model the multi-layered social network as a *hyper graph* structure with *d*-layers: where the first layer is the physical network and each layer connects subset of nodes playing same role and binding to various relationships. As an example, we focus on a multi-layered social networks consisting of customers, suppliers, competitors, and partners. These social networks should be woven into the organization of day-to-day operations so that socio-economical factors as competitiveness level between customers and fairness selection of providers are taken into account. Each social network has a value-added to this operation implementation as follows (Fig. 1):

1. Customer social network permits to identify potential relationships between customers such as competition, referral, and collaboration so that new business opportunities can be identified by the enterprises to fit better the customer needs and improve its competitiveness level:
   - **Competition relationship.** captures the number of times that a group of customers had to compete over specific products and services offered by the organization and the customers who won the competitions. This should allow the organization to guarantee a fair competition by strengthening its ability to identify appropriate business opportunities with the whole of its customers like adjusting the nature of products and services to offer in response to these customers' demands.
   - **Referral relationship.** captures the number of times that a group of customers dealt with the organization based on the recommendation of other customers and how relevant these recommendations were for the organization. This should allow the organization identify business opportunities in response to customers' expectations.
   - **Collaboration relationship.** captures the number of times that a group of customers got together to form collective groups when requesting products and services from the organization and how fruitful these collaborations were for the organization. This should enable the organization increase its productivity and benefits and as a result improve its competiveness level.
2. Supplier social network permits to identify potential relationships between suppliers:

- **Competition relationship** captures the number of times that a group of suppliers had to compete over specific calls for proposals generated by the organization and the suppliers that won the competitions. This should enable the organization exploit better the economic value that suppliers can provide by adjusting the calls for proposals.
- **Referral relationship** captures the number of times that a group of suppliers dealt with the organization based on the recommendation of other suppliers when they cannot participate in a competition and how relevant the recommendations were for the organization. Therefore, suppliers can recommend other suppliers for keeping their competitiveness level with their respective competitors. Based on past recommendation experiences, the organizations can trust or not their suppliers.
- **Collaboration relationship** captures the number of times that a group of suppliers got together when providing the products for the suppliers of the organization. This should enable the organization guarantee fruitful collaboration by identifying the suppliers of suppliers to solicit.

3. Partner social network captures partnerships experiences:
   - **Collaboration relationship** captures the number of times a partner provides the customers with satisfactory services. This should allow the organization secure the loyalty of the customers.
   - **Referral relationship** captures the number of times a group of partners support the organization based on the recommendations of other partners when they cannot participate in collaborations and how relevant the recommendations were for the organization.

4. Competitor social network permits to identify potential relationships between the organization's competitors such as competition and referral.

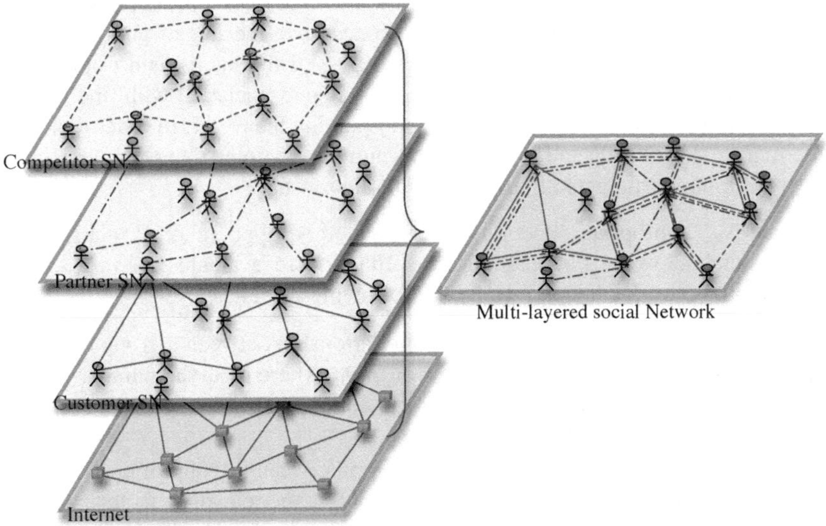

Fig. 1. A Multi-layered Social Network including Competitors, Partners and Customers

- Competition relationship captures the number of times that the organization and a group of competitors compete in global marketplace and who won the competitions. This should enable the organization improve its competitiveness level by adjusting the Partner-centric SN and Supplier-centric SN (e.g., add new partners/suppliers and release old ones).
- Referral relationship captures the number of times that a group of competitors compete with the organization based on the recommendation of other competitors when they cannot participate in competition and how negative the recommendations were to the organization.3.2. Formal Representation of the Multi-layered Social Network.

We define the multi-layered social network, *M*, of a given Organisation, *O*, as a tuple (*Nodes*, *Roles*, *SocialRelationships*), where:

- *Nodes* denotes the set of nodes constituting the whole social community of *O* and *n* the cardinality of *Nodes*.
- *Roles* denotes the set of available roles the nodes can play and *r* the cardinality of Roles. Each role defines a particular layer in the multi-layered social network among any subset of *Nodes*. For example, an organisation can build its social community by focusing on specific roles such as customers, suppliers, competitors, and partners just to mention. In this case, *Roles* = {customer, supplier, competitor, partner}. We also denote by $P_{role \in Roles}$ the set of all possible relationships among nodes of *role* and *m* the cardinality of P_{role}. For example, an organisation may focus on relationships, such as competition, referral and collaboration with its customers. In this case, the relationship set is defined as $P_{customer}$={competition, referral, collaboration}.
- *SocialRelationships* denotes the matrix of social relationships for any node with respect to all its peers and all its possible roles. The matrix has (*n* x *n* x *r*) dimension. We assume that the matrix (*n* x *n* x *1*) defines a basic physical network *I*, such as Internet, connecting all nodes by means of information and communication technologies. Each element w_{ijk} of the matrix is a t-uple $<V^1, V^2, ..., V^m>_{ijk}$ where V^q is the quantitative value associated with the qth social relationship in P_k between the nodes *i* and *j* playing the role *k*. In order to normalize the matrix, we introduce T^q_{ik} is the total number of times that the node *i*, playing the role *k*, has participated in the qth social relationship.

To update w_{ijk}, appropriate functions are suggested per type of social relationship and type of social network. For example, the function to evaluate w_{ijk} in a customer-centric social network can be given by the following formulas:

- The value $V^{competition}_{i,j}$ of the competition relationship between a group of customers c_i and c_j is computed as $V^{competition}_{ci,cj} = \omega_{ij} / \Theta_{ij}$, where ω_{ij} is the number of times c_i won the competition against c_j, Θ_{ij} the number of times c_i and c_j compete, and $T^{competition}_{ci,\, customer} = \sum_{l=1,n} \Theta_{il}$.
- The value $V^{referral}_{i,j}$ of the referral relationship between a group of customers c_i and c_j is computed as $V^{referral}_{ci,cj} = O_{ij} * \sigma_{ij}$, where O_{ij} is the relevance factor given by the organization in terms of subsequent business opportunities, σ_{ij} is the number of times c_i recommends c_j, and $T^{referral}_{ci,\, customer} = \sum_{l=1,n} \sigma_{il}$.

- The value $V^{collaboration}_{i,j}$ of the collaboration relationship between a group of customers c_i and c_j is computed as $V^{collaboration}_{ci,cj} = \Phi_{ij} * \pi_{ij}$, where Φ_{ij} is the fruitfulness factor given by the organization in terms of productivity and π_{ij} the number of times c_i collaborates with c_j, and $T^{collaboration}_{ci,\ customer} = \sum_{l=1,n} \pi_{il}$.

4 Experimental Results

To measure the value-added of multi-layered social networks to an organization, we apply social network analysis to measure interactions between people. We consider a real case study related to advertising of a new perfume. The marketing department leads the study by contacting perfume retailers and negotiating with their customers exhibition stands, discount rates and whether they accept to recommend the new perfume to their clients by sending them messages on twitter. These "digital community relationships" are used to build the user centric community model: each node in our model is associated to an user identified by his/her email address and We build our social data from customer emails, twitter usernames respectively. However, edges reflect exchange between users, either by twitter, such as if available, and a twitter hash tag to mark the new perfume and categorize its related messages in a Tweet or by email to identify collaborations between users. We also exploit the open source software Gephi [6] to visualize our customer social networks respectively with respect to the collaboration relationship based on exchanged emails and the referral relationship based on twit messages. In addition, we use the spigot plug in to analyze email contacts with customers. Figure 2 (left) displays the collaboration relationship network as a directed acyclic graph of 332 nodes and 693 edges. Moreover, the spigot plug in allows us to built a network about customers who follow each other and who search or mention the new perfume hash tag. Figure 2 (right) displays a network based on the referral relationship of customers who twit the new perfume. The network is a directed graph of 174 nodes and 590 connections. Since the marketing department has a list of customer emails and their twitter usernames, it becomes possible to study the customer social network with respect to collaboration and recommendation relationships and evaluate their impact on social network metrics (Average Path Length, Average Degree, Network Diameter, Graph Density, etc.).

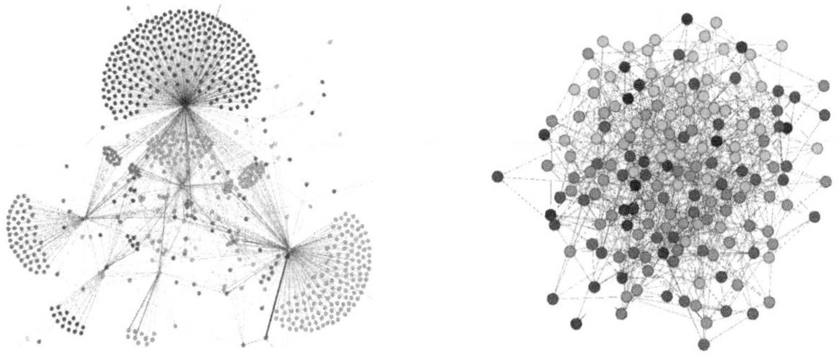

Fig. 2. Customer social network based on collaboration and referral relationships

5 Conclusion

In this paper we presented a multi-layered social-network-based architecture to support business collaboration. This architecture consists of four layers referring to social networks that respectively include consumers, providers, partners and competitors of an organization and ensure their connection through different relationships like collaboration, competition, and referral. The value-added of each social network to organizations was also discussed per layer. The implementation of "this model was illustrated with customers social networks based on twitter and emails through and based on collaboration and referral relationships. The experimental results show customers' behavior during collaboration and their influence on each other.

Acknowledgement. This work is a part of the project PROCESS 2.0 (2010-2012) and generously funded by the "Direction Générale de la Compétitivité, de l'Industrie et de Services" of the French Ministry of Economy and supported by the Midi-Pyrénées Region.

References

[1] Badr, Y., Maamar, Z.: Can Enterprises Capitalize on their Social Networks? The Cutter IT Journal, Issue on Measuring the Success of Social Networks 22(10) (2009)

[2] Maamar, Z., Badr, Y.: Social Networks as a Service in Modern Enterprises. In: The International Conference on the Current Trends in Information Technology (CTIT 2009), Dubai, United Arab Emirates (2009)

[3] Elhabib, N., Boucher, X., Peillon, S.: Collaborative Networks for a sustainable world. In: Camarinha-Matos, L.M., Afsarmanesh, H., Boucher, X. (eds.) PRO-VE 2010. IFIP AICT, vol. 336. Springer, Heidelberg (2010)

[4] Ethier, J.: Current Research in Social Network Theory, `http://www.ccs.neu.edu/home/perrolle/archive/Ethier-SocialNetworks.html` (visited September 2008)

[5] Raab, J., Milward, H.B.: Dark Networks as Problems. Journal of Public Administration Research and Theory 13(4) (2003)

[6] Bastian, M., Heymann, S., Jacomy, M.: Gephi: An Open Source Software for Exploring and Manipulating Networks. In: The International AAAI Conference on Weblogs and Social Media (2009)

[7] Vossen, G.: Web 2.0: A Buzzword, a Serious Development, Just Fun, or What? In: Proceedings of the International Conference on Security and Cryptography (SECRYPT 2009), Milan, Italy (2009)

[8] Connolly, S.: 7 Key Attributes of Social Web Applications, `http://connollyshaun.blogspot.com/2008/05/7-keyattributes-of-social-web.html` (visited April 2010)

[9] Biennier, F., Aubry, R., Maranzana, M.: Integration of Business and Industrial Knowledge on Services to Set Trusted Business Communities of Organisations. In: Camarinha-Matos, L.M., Boucher, X., Afsarmanesh, H. (eds.) PRO-VE 2010. IFIP AICT, vol. 336, pp. 420–426. Springer, Heidelberg (2010)

[10] Afsarmanesh, H., Camarinha-Matos, L.M.: A Framework for Management of Virtual Organizations Breeding Environments. In: Proceedings of PRO-VE 2005 – Collaborative Networks and their Breeding Environments, Valencia, Spain, September 26-28, pp. 35–48. Springer, Boston (2005)

Corporate Social Networking as an Intra-organizational Collaborative Networks Manifestation

Álvaro Albuquerque[2] and António Lucas Soares[1,2]

[1] INESC Porto, Campus da FEUP, Rua Dr. Roberto Frias, 378, 4200-465 Porto, Portugal
[2] DEI, FEUP, University of Porto, Rua Dr. Roberto Frias, sn 4200-465 Porto, Portugal
alvaro.jorge.albuquerque@gmail.com, asoares@inescporto.pt

Abstract. This paper describes and discusses the results of an empirical study about social-networks/microblogging adoption in a financial institution. Social networking at the workplace literature is overviewed and then presented the methodology and hypothesis of the study. Interviews, a survey and a experimental pilot were used as data collection methods. An extract of the results related with the experimental pilot are discussed and some conclusions derived from them.

Keywords: corporate social networks, collaborative networks, value creation.

1 Introduction

New manifestations of intra-organization collaborative networks are being fostered by the adoption of social-networking/microblogging enterprise platforms. There are signs that the adoption of the paradigm of social networks in the workplace can create new forms of communication and collaboration [1][2]. Microblogging, a fairly new phenomenon of Social Computing, is promising in corporate environments because it facilitates informal communication, sharing knowledge and finding solutions together [3]. However the benefits of adopting social-networking/microblogging in companies is still unclear. Nor is it clear how companies should adopt it and which factors influence the adoption of microblogging. This paper describes the results of an empirical study in a portuguese financial institution. The research questions were the following: (1) The introduction of social-networking/microblogging can create value for the Bank[1] (2) What are the critical success factors in the adoption of social-networking/microblogging by the Bank? As it is an exploratory study of a complex subject about which little or nothing is known, it was deemed appropriate the use of multiple methods of data collection: (a) interviews, (b) a departmental survey and (c) an experimental pilot of a corporate social-networking/microblogging tool. This paper is organized as follows: first we give an overview of past research work about this topic, then we describe the methodology adopted; and an overview of the results, and finally we discuss the results and derive conclusions applicable in the more general field of collaborative networks.

[1] The term "Bank" will be used as a short name to refer the financial institution.

L.M. Camarinha-Matos et al. (Eds.): PRO-VE 2011, IFIP AICT 362, pp. 11–18, 2011.

2 Social Networking in the Workplace

Social-networking and microblogging are relatively new phenomena in business therefore there is still little research to find out how its use can improve knowledge sharing and social interaction in the workplace. However there is a body of research on the use of social networks in companies, both the use of public social networks in the workplace as the use of internal social networks.

Skeels and Grudin [4] found a number of benefits arising from use of these technologies. LinkedIn was useful to create and maintain professional networks. Facebook was useful in the workplace to maintain contact with colleagues and build and strengthen working relationships. On the other hand has been found concerns in many employee about the legitimacy of the activity at these sites in the workplace. In particular there were questions about waste of time and security, particularly concerned with the disclosure of confidential information. There were also other problems, of a more practical nature for employees, about the mixing of personal and professional life, related to the management of links, the boundaries of hierarchy, status and power.

DiMicco [5] found that in a closed corporate environment, employees can use a social network platform to meet new people instead of just connecting with those who already know (different attitude from that observed in the use of Facebook). When using such a platform to maintain links with known contacts (either on their workplace or in their network of contacts) people reported: increased ties with their immediate network; a greater sense of corporate citizenship (will to serve the business asset), greater access to specialists within the company. The more intensely you use the social network (which means more frequent visits and stronger associations with the community) the most users report increased their social capital in the company: report closer ties in their network and greater propensity to contribute to the company, they feel more interested in connecting globally and also greater ability to access specialists.

According to Zhao and Rosson [6], informal exchanges in timely conversations (e.g. in "hallway conversations") among employees play an important role in the success of organizations and contain a variety of potential benefits of fostering collaboration in the workplace. The beneficial consequences arising from informal communication, are organized into two classes: Relational Benefits and Personal Benefits. *Relational Benefits* are the effects that informal communication can have in the relationship of two people and their interpersonal activities, such as collaborative work. *Personal Benefits* are related to informal communication with people in the workplace (work related or not) may lead to the acquisition of beneficial information for the purposes of personal work. For example, you can gain different perspectives on the work of both and can generate new opportunities for collaboration.

The literature review showed that current scientific understanding of social networking in the workplace is somehow limited. Empirical studies, and in particular case study research is needed to increase our knowledge of an, apparently, important emergent socio-technical behaviour. The following pages describe an empirical study that contributes to increase our knowledge about the value of informal communication in general in modern organizations.

3 Research Hypothesis and Methodology

A qualitative singular embedded case study with multiple methods of data collection was designed: an interdepartmental survey, interviews and a pilot using a microblogging enterprise tool. The units of analysis underlying the analysis of results, the analytical framework adopted in the Case Study, contains collaboration as the main concept which, according to the research questions, we want to evaluate and maximize. The first research question asks to what extent the adoption of microblogging enhances collaboration among users in order to generate value to the organization. The second research question is about the factors that influence the maximization of the collaboration. Thus, collaboration is seen in the study as a central concept. The dimensions are the viewpoints within an organization: Employee, Organization, Technology. The indicators in each perspective were the themes identified in interviews and must be considered in the analysis: Privacy, Performance, Motivations, (Emplowee); Productivity, Information Quality, Security, Governance (Organization); Maintenance, Facilitating Conditions (Technology).

Two groups of hypotheses were considered according to the research questions: *Value Hypotheses (Hypotheses related to Value): h*ypotheses regarding the Microblogging practice in the Bank and *Factors Hypotheses (Hypotheses related to Factors)*: hypotheses taken from the Microblogging evaluation model (Gunther *et al.*, 2009).

The data collection methods were 1) interviews, 2) a departamental survey and 3) a social networking/microblogging pilot.

Table 1. Units of Analysis

	Perspectives	Indicators
Value	Employee	EVH1-It contributes to bringing people together and forging stronger links. EVH2-Contributes to raising the awareness of what is going on around EVH3-There is a natural predisposition to use of social networks
	Organization	OVH1-Only makes sense in the organization if it is assumed to be informal OVH2-Represents a means to complement existing communication channels OVH3-It constitutes a useful tool for collaborative work
	Technology	TVH1-It helps to reduce email
Factors	Informal communication	FH1-Communication Benefits are positively related to Performance Expectancy
	Norms and Organizational Culture	FH2-Collaborative Norms is positively related to Intention to use microblogging
	Information Quality/Noise	FH3-Beliefs regarding the Signal-to-Noise Ratio are negatively related to Performance Expectancy
	Reputation	FH4a-Reputation is positively related to Performance Expectancy FH4b-Reputation is positively related to Intention to use microblogging
	Facilitating Conditions	FH5-Facilitating Conditions has a positive effect on intention to use Microblogging
	Privacy	FH6-Privacy Concerns have a negative effect on Intention to use Microblogging
	Codification Effort	FH7-Beliefs regarding Codification Effort are negatively related to Performance Expectancy

1) *Interviews*: 17 interviews were conducted with people in the bank selected to collect arguments from the perspectives of employee, organization (management and business perspective) and technology. The questions focused on potential benefits and risks. During the interviews, in order to generate discussion, a mockup of an Internal Social Networking site, with an interface inspired on Facebook, on which each employee may subscribe channels of information (institutional entities or project groups) was presented.

2) DSI *Survey*: An anonymous survey was conducted to all 442 employees of the Information Systems Department (DSI) and obtained 177 responses, a participation rate of 40%. With 17 closed questions and a research question of free opinion, it was intended to gather opinions on the perceived usefulness of social networks as collaborative practice, the internal perception of risk, and to measure the willingness to use an internal social network. Also has been questioned about the pattern of utilization of public social networks and attractiveness for the phenomenon of social networks.

3) *Yammer Pilot*: An important tool used in this investigation to collect primary data in participant observation mode was a pilot trial using the software Yammer at work. Yammer[2] is an enterprise social network/microblogging platform, provided as as service, that is specifically designed for use by businesses.

Yammer has not been officially adopted by the bank. The pilot was initiated by the researcher as an employee of the bank, within a team with experimental features (DSI-Innovation), and with the explicit purpose of providing a pilot experiment in this investigation. The experiment began on 27 January 2010 and the period of observation was four months. Initially only 10 invitations were sent to DSI-Innovation team members. The use of Yammer was not promoted or even mentioned in official channels of corporate communication. The network of Yammer users of the bank grew spontaneously by email invitations sent by the free initiative of the users (using a feature on Yammer). At the end of the experiment there were 94 registered users. All users were from DSI (Information Systems Dep.) with the exception of one. Throughout the observation period, were placed in total 1123 messages. Exploratory analysis on the use of the pilot is based on the following types of information: Yammer Data (registered users and messages posted); and a Survey to assess the experience of using the pilot. Although the pilot did not have a set of users representative of the universe of study that is the Information Systems Department, it contains a representative subset of an entire team adopting Yammer in the workplace, the DSI-Innovation team. Thus, we analyzed in detail the 381 posts made in Innovation private group to study the collaboration within the team. On the final phase of the pilot, a survey by questionnaire was conducted to all 94 users who registered in Yammer. We called it Pilot User Experience Evaluation (PUEE) and it was not anonymous to get a maximum number of responses. We obtained 65 responses, a participation rate of 69%. With 17 closed questions and a open question for free opinion, it was aimed to collect the following information: understanding of the tool, type of use, perceived usefulness and demographic profile.

Due to space limitations, in the next section we present the results that concern to the experiment pilot only.

---

[2] `http://www.yammer.com`

4 Results

The pilot was a rich experience that illustrated the potential of collaborative networks implementation based on social networking/microblogging. This experience had a positive impact in the study either by direct observation of the phenomenon in the workplace and to have contributed to a more enlightened view of the people surveyed (both in interviews and in survey). For a user to join the private network of the bank on Yammer, known as "Bank Network", she just needs to have an email address of the bank. Thus, any user of the bank who can access the Internet in the workplace could join, just on their own initiative, the private network of the bank on Yammer. At the end of May there were 94 registered users. The graph in Figure 1 shows the growth of the Bank Yammer network in terms of the number of registered users.

As noted above, the use of Yammer was not promoted or even mentioned in official channels of corporate communication. The initial idea, on 27 January, was to create a pilot experiment limited for use by the team members of investigator, the DSI-Innovation team. So after creating the "Bank Network" at Yammer, the researcher made only nine invitations, which corresponds to the number of people on his team. The team leader was the first to join stating explicitly, in a first message, his collaboration in the pilot. Other team members joined during the following days and the last one joined on 8 February, 12 days later. On that day also joined the first user outside the DSI-Innovation team and from that day the "Bank Network" started to grow spontaneously from invitations sent by free initiative of users. This level of acceptance favors the EVH3 hypothesis. According to the Pilot User Experience Evaluation (PUEE), 80% of users of the pilot were non-directors, 14% were intermediate level directors and only 6% were director or higher. On the DSI-Innovation organic division, the team which is part of the researcher, all its members were registered and used the Pilot. In total 1123 messages were posted on Yammer being the first two months of most intense use. In Figure 1, where a steepening of the curve corresponds to higher intensity of messages, we see clearly a slowdown after the ini

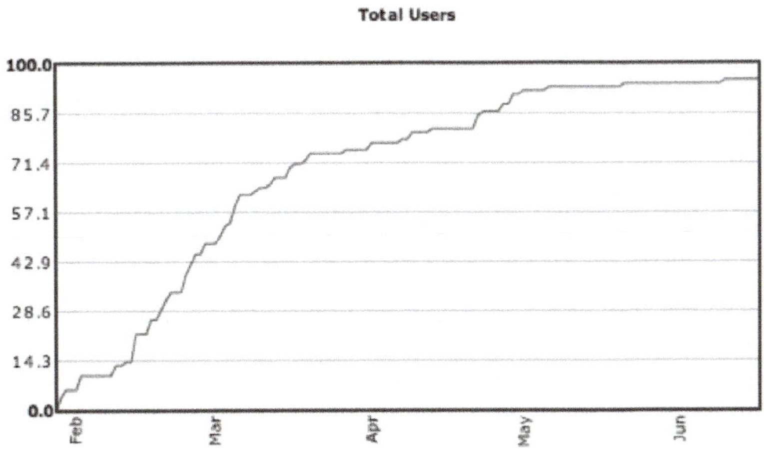

Fig. 1. Evolution of registered users

tial trial period. Although there have been 94 registered users yammer on, only 50 users have posted messages. Among the registered users, 47% did not put any messages and some justifications were collected on the PUEE survey: 34% referred time constraints; 32% think there was no subjects of interest; 28% just wanted to watch and learn; and 12% did not recognize value.

5 Discussion

The following is an analysis of the risks and benefits of adopting social-networks/microblogging from three perspectives which are the units of analysis of the Case Study.

Employee perspective: benefits
According to Zhao and Rosson [6] the benefits of informal communication have two dimensions: relational benefits and personal benefits. It is in the relational benefits class that fits the feeling of closeness among geographically dispersed teams that observed in the pilot Yammer. The proximity, which has positive impact on cooperation, is obtained from the increased awareness of what is going on around. At the survey held 77% of participants agreed that the social network makes it possible to get to know the activity shared by the colleagues. The personal benefits that result from informal communication in the workplace, work related or not, may lead to the acquisition of beneficial information for the purposes of personal work. For example, to be aware of different perspectives on the work of others, can lead to new opportunities for collaboration. Still on personal benefits, 64% consider social networking in the workplace, an opportunity to give their opinion and show their value in the organization. For these reasons, both personal benefits and the benefits that come out of informal relational promote productivity. In an interview to pilot users of Yammer, microblogging has been viewed as a productivity factor because it replaces informal contacts through other channels, telephone, email or "hallway conversation" and thus minimize interruptions to work. One director noted that there was an user satisfaction. Another advantage pointed out in the interviews by the employees is the equal opportunities in participation. DiMicco *et al.* [5] also identify the advantages of social networks the possibility to access to specialists, increased ties with their immediate network of people and an interest to interconnect with each other. A benefit for the employee who observed the pilot Yammer, is its potential to reduce email. This possibility was perceived by the community that used the pilot transmitted on interviews and confirmed by the survey user experience of the pilot.

Employee perspective: risks
The issue of privacy has been widely referred throughout all the interviews as a potential disadvantage of social networking. A view taken from a blog of a community of interest in Enterprise 2.0, argues that it makes no sense to speak of privacy in a business context. According to some authors opinions, "the strength in these tools lies in the transparency and the openness in communication, not in creating additional little silos next to your IM history, personal Emails and others technologies that may be available. If you want or need privacy, you can create 1-on-1 conversations in other places. After all this is a tool that is inside of a controlled user group (all employees, R&D department, Marketing, etc.)".

Organization Perspective: benefits
The benefits that come from the perspective of employees are reflected in benefits to the organization by increasing individual and collective productivity. The pilot demonstrated that microblogging practice promotes communication in a team. This idea is confirmed in the survey DSI where 77% of participants agree that the creation of an internal social networking can improve collaboration among work teams. The pilot Yammer has also demonstrated the usefulness of the practice of microblogging in the creation of thematic forums for example Harvest group established under the pilot, but that according to its creator, is already a common practice. In the interviews, there were suggested some themes to create groups based on the logic of thematic forums freely subscribed by anyone: Workers Committee, the Sports Group, DSI-Quality. There were identified two cases in the bank's real needs that potentially configure social networks use cases. The Asset Management area and also the Stocks Department. Both want a communication software in the restricted environment that allows them to share short pieces of information, without much formalism, and the possibility of retaining comments.

Organization Perspective: risks
Concerns about the quality of information within a social network in the working environment was shown by all the directors interviewed. The content featuring an informal channel microblogging may entail excessive noise or, as stated in the literature, a low value of signal to noise ratio [7]. This concern has two motivations. On the one hand the fear that employees may waste time communicating and the consequent dispersion of attention with a negative impact on productivity; Moreover fears of poor quality of the information posted on the channel. According to a director in an interview, there is a risk of malicious use.

The experiment conducted in the pilot, particularly in respect of use in a team, revealed a reduced risk of problems of information quality and noise. A detailed analysis of the messages exchanged in the team revealed that 87% of the messages were about work and only 9% of the messages were considered "hallway conversation". The typical solution of microblogging tools for the noise problem is the possibility that each person must choose the content they are interested in receiving. So has the option to "follow" people, or to subscribe to your posts, and subscribe to group participation. That is, the organization of communication in public or private groups helps to minimize the noise problem of information.

A consensual solution to the problem of information quality, widely discussed in the interviews, is to promote an organizational culture through the publication of explicit rules on the use of the channel. In the DSI survey, 91% of respondents agree with the creation of a code of conduct and rules of practice as a way to mitigate security risks, information quality and productivity loss.

The issue of security is a crosscutting concern among the various perspectives involved, employees, organization and technology. The solution to security problems also involves the organizational culture, the adoption of rules and norms of use. A question was asked on the Survey about possible ways to mitigate extreme scenarios for the use of risk by employees. 75% agree that there should be some control mechanism in the bank about the information their employees post in the Internal Social Network. If necessary, the bank must have ways to delete messages that may threaten the organization.

The informal nature of a microblogging communication channel seems to be a disadvantage to its use as a channel of communication between the company and its employees. However, DSI Survey put the question about the possibility of a an internal social networking channel to be used a means of communication between the bank and its employees. 61% said they agree. But when the question is aked again and there is a focus on the institutional character of the messages, 53% agree.

6 Conclusion

Social networking in corporate environments is, to say the least, raising curiosity mainly as a tool for improving communication and social interaction for work purposes. If this leads to better collaboration or to the enhancement of the intra-organizational collaborative networks is something that needs to be studied. The case study presented in this paper is a contribution to our knowledge about these phenomena. Although current corporate social networking platforms can convey value creation through communication and interaction, this is likely to be not enough for a significant adoption of this paradigm by most organizations. Our current research is looking at ways of how to combine advanced information organization, classification and retrieval with social networking. The goal is to leverage the potential value of these two important dimensions of an organization. We are extending this research to collaborative networks of organizations (inter-organizations).

References

1. Parameswaran, M., Whinston, A.B.: Social Computing: An Overview. Communications of the Association for Information Systems 19, 762–780 (2007), http://crec.mccombs.utexas.edu/attachments/105_Social_Computing_An_Overview.pdf
2. Bente, S., Karlay, J.: Enterprise Social Network Platforms as a Managment Tool in Complex Technical Systems. In: Proceeding, paper 545, Americas Conference on Information Systems, AMCIS 2009 (2009), http://aisel.aisnet.org/amcis2009/545
3. Passant, A., Hastrup, T., Bojars, U., Breslin, J.: Microblogging: A semantic web and distributed approach. In: 4th Workshop Scripting For the Semantic Web (SFSW 2008) Co-located with ESWC 2008 (2008), http://www.semanticscripting.org/SFSW2008/papers/11.pdf
4. Skeels, M., Grudin, J.: When Social Networks Cross Boundaries: A Case Study on Workplace Use of Facebook and LinkedIn. In: Proceedings of the 2009 International Conference on Supporting Group Work. ACM Press, Sanibel Island (2009), http://portal.acm.org/citation.cfm?id=1531674.1531689
5. DiMicco, J.M., Millen, D.R., Geyer, W., Dugan, C.: Research on the Use of Social Software in the Workplace. In: Proc. CSCW 2008 Workshop Social Networking in Organizations, San Diego, California, November 8-12 (2008), http://www.joandimicco.com/pubs/dimicco-millen-geyer-dugan_cscw08_workshop.pdf
6. Zhao, D., Rosson, M.B.: How and Why People Twitter: The Role that Micro-blogging Plays in Informal Communication at Work. In: Proceeedings of the ACM Group 2009, Florida, USA, pp. 243–252 (May 2009), http://portal.acm.org/citation.cfm?id=1531710
7. Gunther, O., Krasnova, H., Riehle, D., Schondienst, V.: Modeling Microblogging Adoption in the Enterprise. In: Proceeding of 15th Americas Conference on Information Systems (ACIS), San Francisco, USA (2009), http://warhol.wiwi.hu-berlin.de/aigaion2/index.php/attachments/single/1

Communication and Power in Collaborative Networks: The Hypothesis of Technology as Confidence Enhancer

Ana Gomes[1] and Maria Cristina Maneschy[2]

[1] Socius/ISEG – Universidade Técnica de Lisboa, R. Miguel Lupi, 20, 1249-078, Lisbon, Portugal
acalapez@estgp.pt
[2] Universidade Federal do Pará, Campus Universitário do Guamá, R. Augusto Corrêa, 1, CEP 66075-110, Belém, Pará, Brasil
cristina@ufpa.br

Abstract. Since the eighties of the 20th century that the social and organizational sciences are interested in networks as organizational configuration and the identification of the dimensions that determine or influence the effectiveness of their performance, their adaptability and resilience. Communication and power are two of these core dimensions, because they strongly influence the degree of trust latent in the network, and trust is the key ingredient of human systems optimization. Very often a third, as neutral perceived party, plays a determinant role in the systematic negotiation process, which is inherent to collaborative networks [10] dynamics. We argue that computer platforms, perceived as a neutral and transparency enhancer device, may play an important role as trust promoter, namely in strong uncertainty avoidance contexts.

Keywords: Collaborative networks, cooperation, communication, power, trust.

1 Introduction

This paper has as main objective the presentation and discussion of the hypothesis we propose, and which is the basis of our present research agenda, and simultaneously the innovative contribution of our work. We hypothesise the possibility of developing a computer collaborative platform, which may enhance trust in strong uncertainty avoidance contexts, by playing the role of a neutral perceived partner. We base our hypothesis both on theoretical thinking and empirical data collected in previous case studies carried out in different geographical and social contexts, and using different methodologies [1] [2] [3], such as half-structured interviews submitted to thematic content analysis, surveys and social-network analysis. Regardless of methodology and context[1], the studies highlight some commonalities, such as power centralization, and a coordination and cross-communication deficit. In both the Brazilian[2] and the

[1] The referred studies concern two different geographical and national spaces, namely Portugal and Brazil, and also different activity areas, namely industry, agriculture and fisheries.
[2] http://www.geert-hofstede.com/hofstede_brazil.shtml

L.M. Camarinha-Matos et al. (Eds.): PRO-VE 2011, IFIP AICT 362, pp. 19–26, 2011.

Portuguese[3] case, we are dealing with high Power Distance[4] (PDI) and high Uncertainty Avoidance[5] (UAI) contexts, which condition an environment of potential distrust towards the out-group and simultaneously the attribution of total responsibility to leadership. These in turn reinforces both power centralization and mistrust. An extended report about collaborative networks in the north of Portugal [3] emphasizes precisely the relevance of leadership and the need for collaborative devices which enhance extended information exchange and promote common work. We propose the development of a collaborative technological platform, which shall be designed integrating social and cultural dimensions in order to help institutionalize[6] leadership, promote wide information sharing and common work. The advantage of using a technological device, not as a substitute of human interaction or human will, but as a support mechanism, lies on two aspects: first, the speed and extent of sharing possibilities, and second and perhaps even more important, technology tends to be socially perceived as a neutral player, which means that people frequently consider that technological devices have no will of their own and therefore no hidden agenda. As perceived neutral players they may contribute to build up confidence inside the system, for instance promoting the social rewarding of cooperative attitudes and action through game like devices.

In short, we may consider as innovative contributions of our proposition the intentional integration of context bond social and cultural dimensions in the design of a collaborative platform and the deliberate use of its neutrality perception as network confidence enhancer.

2 A Collaboration Unfriendly Context

It is broadly consensual that during the last two decades of the 20th century the conditions for a deep transformation of organizational structures emerged. During the 80's the extension and strengthening of global competition and its immediate consequences, generated a significant pressure on production costs which dictated the need for radical rationalization [4] and innovation [5], [6], namely process innovation [7]. During the 90's the massive proliferation of ICT use inevitably imposed the need to perform in network organised teams [8] [9] [10]. If on the one hand, this kind of organization has become an imperative, on the other hand, it puts the problem of the need for cooperation, which is not an evident issue [11] [3]. Its quality depends

---

[3] http://www.geert-hofstede.com/hofstede_portugal.shtml

[4] As defined by Hofstede, the Power Distance Index (PDI) shows "the extent to which the less powerful members of organizations and institutions (like the family) accept and expect that power is distributed unequally. This represents inequality (more versus less), but defined from below, not from above. It suggests that a society's level of inequality is endorsed by the followers as much as by the leaders" [12]

[5] As defined by Hofstede, the Uncertainty Avoidance Index (UAI) "deals with a society's tolerance for uncertainty and ambiguity; it ultimately refers (...) to what extent a culture programs its members to feel either uncomfortable or comfortable in unstructured situations. Unstructured situations are novel, unknown, surprising, different from usual. Uncertainty avoiding cultures try to minimize the possibility of such situations". [12]

[6] Decentralize across the organizational network.

largely on contextual dimensions, namely the degree of perceived insecurity, and how the involved actors deal with it.

Regardless of the context, it is clear that the network organizational form increases the insecurity of social relations in that it broadens the range of potential and effective interactions and destroys the security of traditional organisational borders. But the way in which this insecurity is perceived and dealt with is contextual bond. In contexts where high PDI and UAI coexist [12], like in Brazil and Portugal collaboration became a very difficult exercise.

Collaboration involves necessarily a high level of communication, which itself implies the act of making something in common and accordingly there must be a certain degree of trust. We may define trust as the social belief about the predictability of actions [13], or the suspension of doubt [14]. In the absence of trust, Uncertainty Avoidance increases. The combination of high PDI and high UAI scores results in bad quality[7], mostly downward vertical communication. Horizontal communication is generally almost exclusively informal, based on personal affective ties [15], and as such contingent and risky [16]. Simultaneously, the very relationship with power is ambiguous and contradictory, since ties with power holders are of course sought, but simultaneously suspicion loaded. The difference between personalised and socialised power [17] is hardly perceived, and personal power is mostly regarded as free of any activity inhibition (self-control) [17], so that leaders are perceived to act exclusively motivated by self-interest, not hesitating to sacrifice in the process the interests of the larger community. This situation configures a paradox insofar as the social need for security leads to the acceptance of power and responsibility transfer to the person of a leader, but the leader itself is mistrusted. The centralization of power also implies the concentration of information access, if only because it diminishes and devalues horizontal communication.

A network of organizations involves continuous negotiation and therefore implies the existence of mediating factors, in order to keep conflict in manageable levels. A mediator, by definition, must be perceived as a neutral part of the game. Our hypothesis is that collaborative computer interfaces may play the role of the perceived neutral part, not so much as conflict mediator, but as conflict preventer, in that it may contribute for the improvement of communication quality, through higher transparency and the fulfilling of an "automatic" role of social control, which rewards and punishes behaviours, namely cooperative and non-cooperative behaviours.

3 Empirical Evidence

Two empirical studies relating to networks of rural producers were conducted, in very different environments (Portugal and Brazilian Amazonia), using different methodologies (half-structured interviews and social network analysis respectively), and both reveal high power distance, preponderance of vertical communication, mistrust and occasional extension of the network based on personal and family relations without any apparent middle or long-term strategic thinking [2] [1].

---

[7] Scarce, ambiguous and often redundant and inadequate communication, which does not transmit the effectively needed information.

3.1 Rural Associations in the Amazonia

In 2005 a preliminary study was undertaken about the rural associations in the north-east of Pará State, Brazilian Amazonia [2]. External pressures for associating, namely public development programs, technical assistance, access to land and training possibilities stimulated the formation of peasant associations [18] [19]. Overall, the emergence of these local associations has been linked to concerns about popular participation and decentralization of state functions [20]. The analysis of the characteristics of the networks of associations was carried out using Ucinet and Netdraw, [21].

Here are briefly presented the main features of the networks of the 36 associations studied. Their contacts comprised other similar associations, social groups, individuals, organizations and public institutions. The main nodes, those exhibiting more links, are banks and the technical and funding assistance agency.

Most of the fishermen and farmers associations' contacts tended to be homogeneous and more geographically limited. Their main contacts were: firstly, the banks and the above referred agency and, secondly, the politicians. Some central associations, located in more dynamic areas of the municipalities featured numerous and different links, while the majority had relatively few and homogeneous contacts and lacked alternative information sources in the network. The local associations appeared to be linked primarily through common links, i.e., indirectly rather than directly, especially via the unions, the bank, and a few government agencies and NGOs. Fieldwork found that associations in different municipalities were not interacting in a manner that allowed sharing concerns and ways of dealing with them. The structure of contacts reflected these limits. The same applied to the limited exchange of experiences of income generation that some of the local groups were implementing. A thicker and more varied horizontal contact structure would be expected to contribute to influence the agenda of the powerful nodes, notably decision-making institutions and the unions.

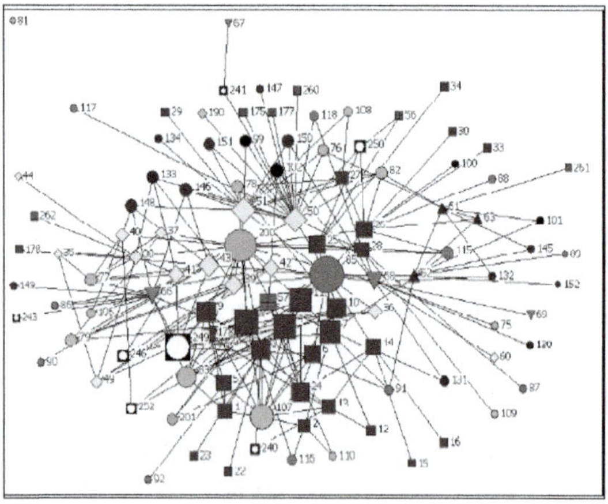

Fig. 1. Exploratory graphic representation of the social relations network involving 36 rural associations in the Pará State. Brazilian Amazonia. Source: [2]

3.2 The "Rocha Do Oeste" Network

In 2008 a network of Portuguese rural producers was studied using qualitative methodologies, namely half-structured interviews and thematic content analysis [1]. Like in the Brazilian case, the constitution of the producers associations were externally induced by public and supra-national organizations, like the EU. The associative organizational mode was imposed as a form of accessing project funding. The case analyzed concerns the cultivation and commercial distribution of the "Rocha do Oeste" pear, and its transformation in a kind of "identity product" [22]. The network has proven to be very effective with regard to the quantitative growth of the production area as well as a significant improvement of the organoleptic quality of the fruit, but failed in the aim of turning it into an" identity product". Some of the main reasons for this partial failure where diagnosed, and are here presented using passages from the direct discourse of some local social players. The detected problems relate precisely to high power distance[8], which prevents communication, namely horizontal communication; generalized mistrust[9], which prevented the consolidation of a common trademark, and lack of strategic thinking[10], which

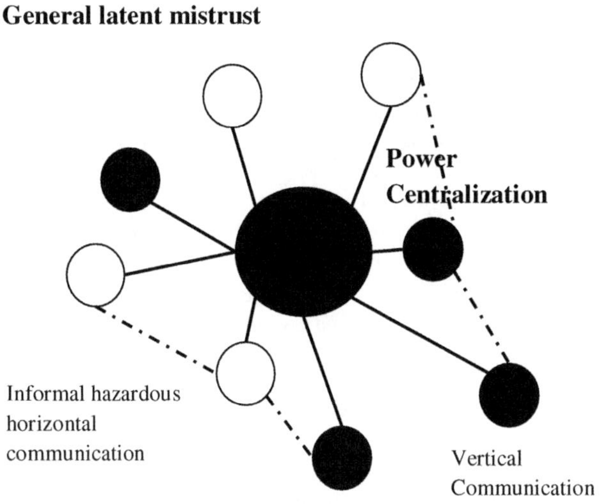

Fig. 2. Network cooperation ineffectiveness dimensions

[8] No. They command. They prescribe the treatments we pour in... Everything is done according to their orders. That's all, according to their command. They give the orders. The technicians command us, they tell us what to do. So, it must be precisely as they tell us. (Excerpt of farmer's discourse).

[9] The elite is much more involved in their own projects than with the region. The elite are usually inclined to politics and unfortunately politics degenerate into district perspectives which cut the region into pieces. (Excerpt of a local development's agent discourse).

[10] The Oeste, historically this region is based on a *casaleiro* logic. The *casaleiro*...he has a little cottage and he imitates his neighbour's cottage. And he does everything alone. His property has no size of a farm. (Excerpt of a local development's agent discourse)

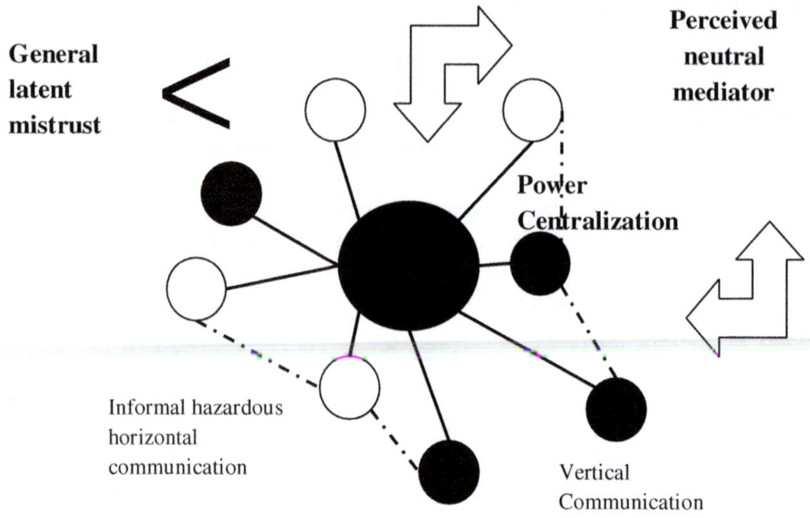

Fig. 3. The hypothesis of the perceived neutral mediator

prevented the diversification of economic and cultural activities around agricultural production[11]. Moreover it also prevented the extension and strengthening of the network in all domains, inclusive the financial, thus perpetuating the dependence upon the original funding institutions[12].

The high complexity of interrelated factors and dimensions present in both the explained cases may be graphically simplified, in order to abstract the general lines of network structuring of former "isolated" entities. The schemes (Figure 2 and 3) introduce the main ineffectiveness and suggest process improvement possibilities, namely recurring to collaborative software devices.

4 Discussion and Conclusion

Considering the fact that technology is often perceived as a neutral factor, we hypothesize that the building of a collaborative computer platform, which takes in account socio-cultural and political dimensions in its development, could contribute to enhance the quality of communication, and therefore the effectiveness of cooperation. Its building requires interdisciplinary effort, flexibility and mutual learning and

---

[11] I don't know, I really don't know. There's a cook or a craftswoman, I don't know if you'd call her a cook or craftswoman and her name's ...if I'm not mistaken...Zira. Isn't it? Who also...who also makes some products using pears. I don't know her....but I think there's already been some cooperation with her here. A long time ago....(Excerpt of the discourse of producer's association coordinator revealing ignorance about network members).

[12] Due to political issues, the Community Support Framework which should have started in January 2007, along with brute disorganisation, the fact is that not a single item of the new community support framework has yet been spent.. Not a single project has been approved. (Excerpt of the discourse of the main producer's association general coordinator).

monitoring processes. The latter are especially relevant in very heterogeneous networks in order to capitalize the diverse nodes' resources, notably knowledge, skills and experiences. In a context of high UAI and PDI the platform might routinely record and track the members' activities and contacts related to the network objectives and values; moreover, it may produce periodical graph representation of the ties, indicating centrality, density areas and accessibility to embedded resources. Such information might translate into objective assessment criteria, quantitative and qualitative ones. Also, the framing of rewards and sanctions perceived as fair due to the perceived neutrality of the "controller". Expected consequences are: (a) communication transparency able to counteract the historical paradox of leader centrality and mistrust; (b) growing awareness of the balance between constraints and opportunities from membership to the network; (c) more trust based relations between peripheral and central nodes; (d) higher density of the links at lower costs of nurturing them, costs partly covered by the platform data; (e) stimuli for structural and behavioural adjustments; (f) network adaptability to changing environments via real time information and assessment devices.

Such functionalities do not replace consensus-building occasions. They also do not replace strategies oriented to the institutionalization of group relations [23], such as meetings, ceremonies, and rituals.ïThe platform is a step towards the participatory management of collaborative networks; its inputs should encourage the mutual recognition of members, their shared concerns and resources, as well as the value of their collaborative actions. Well-informed agents about the network utility and outcomes are supposedly more committed to its rules and success.

References

1. Gomes, A.: The "Rocha do Oeste": the bourgeoning of a regional identity in the shade of pear orchards. In: Ghent: Proceedings of the 8th European Social Science History Conference (2010), http://www2.iisg.nl/esshc/programme.asp?selyear=10&
2. Maneschy, M., Klovdahl, A.: Redes de associações de grupos de camponeses na Amazônia Oriental (Brasil): fontes de capital social? Redes – Revista hispana para el análisis de redes sociales 12(4) (2007)
3. Carneiro, L., Soares, A.L., Patrício, R., Alves, A., Madureira, R., Sousa, J.P.: Redes Colaborativas de Elevado Desempenho no Norte de Portugal. INESC, Porto (2007)
4. Hammer, M., Champy, J.: Reenginiering the corporation: a manifesto for business revolution. Harper Business, New York (1993)
5. Freeman, C.: The economics of business innovation. Frances Pinter, London (1982)
6. Drucker, P.: Innovation and entrepreneurship. Elsevier, Burlington (1985)
7. Hammer, M.: Deep change: how operational innovation can transform your company. Harvard Business Review 82(4), 84–93 (2004)
8. Castells, M.: A galáxia Internet: reflexões sobre, Internet, negócios e sociedade. Fundação Calouste Gulbenkian, Lisboa (2004)
9. Castells, M.: A sociedade em rede: a era da informação, economia, sociedade e cultura. Paz e Terra, São Paulo (1999)
10. Camarinha-Matos, L.M., Afsarmanesh, H.: Collaborative Networks: a new scientific discipline. Journal of Intelligent Manufacturing 16, 439–452 (2005)

11. Rosas, J., Camarinha-Matos, L.M.: An approach to assess collaboration readiness. International Journal of Production Research 47(17), 4711–4735 (2009)
12. Hofstede, G.: Culture's consequences: Comparing Values, Behaviors, Institutions, and Organizations Across Nations. Sage, Thousend Oaks (2001)
13. Fukuyama, F.: Trust. Penguin, London (1995)
14. Möllering, G.: Rational, institutional and active trust:just do it!?, `http://www.mpifg.de/people/gm/downloads/Moellering_CH2inBijlsma2005_Elgar.pdf`
15. Gomes, A.C., Lopes, C.B.: Comunicação e eficácia numa equipa virtua. In: Gomes, A.C., Gonçalves, I.L., Maneschy, M.C. (eds.) Dos dois lados do Atlântico: trabalhadores, organizações e sociabilidades, UFPA/ Paka Tatu, Belém, Pará (2011)
16. Luhmann, N.: Trust and power. Wiley, Chichester (1979)
17. Mc Clelland, D.C.: Power: the inner experience. Irvington, New York (1975)
18. Moreira, E.: Mouvement social pour la défense d'un territoire traditionnel à Porto de Moz (Amazonie Brésilienne): une participation "par le bas". In: Teisserenc, P. (ed.) La mobilisation des acteurs dans l'action publique locale: au Brésil, en France et en Tunisie, pp. 59–72. L'Harmattan, Paris (2006)
19. Hébette, J.: Participation municipale en milieu rural dans l'Etat du Pará: ouverture institutionnelle et contraintes sociopolitiques. In: Teisserenc, P. (ed.) La mobilisation des acteurs dans l'action publique locale: au Brésil, en France et en Tunisie, pp. 33–48. L'Harmattan, Paris (2006)
20. Szreter, S., Woolcock, M.: Health by association? Social capital, social theory and the political economy of public health. International Journal of Epidemiology 33, 650–667 (2004)
21. Borgatti, S., Everett, M., Freeman, L.: Ucinet for Windows: software for Social Network Analysis. Analytic Technologies, Harvard (2002)
22. Pesteil, P.: Au carrefour de l'économique et du culturel: la filière castanéicole corse comme marqueur de l'identité. Études Rurales 157-158, 221–228 (2001)
23. Portes, A.: Social Capital: Its Origins and Applications in Modern Sociology. Annual Review of Sociology 24, 1–24 (1998)

Part II

Social Capital and Collaborative Networks

An Approach to Measure Social Capital in Collaborative Networks

António Abreu[1,2] and Luis M. Camarinha-Matos[2]

[1] ISEL, Polytechnic Institute of Lisbon, Portugal
[2] CTS – Uninova and Faculdade de Ciências e Tecnologia, Universidade Nova de Lisboa, 2829-516 Caparica, Portugal
ajfa@dem.isel.ipl.pt, cam@uninova.pt

Abstract. The characterization and assessment of the social capital of a collaborative network is an important element to help promoting the success of collaboration. The development of indicators of social capital can help enterprise managers not only to analyze and measure their social capital but also to support the decision-making processes. However, models and mechanisms to measure the social capital in collaborative contexts are lacking. Starting with a brief discussion about the nature of social capital and applying some concepts from social networks theory this paper introduces some perspectives and criteria to identify and measure the value of social capital of a member of a Virtual organization Breeding Environment.

Keywords: Social Capital, Social Network, Collaborative Networks.

1 Introduction

In recent years, the business environments have faced dramatic challenges, which combined with the enabling role of the advances in the information and communication technology, are leading to the emergence of a large variety of collaborative network (CN) forms.

As frequently mentioned by several authors on (e.g. Collaborative Networks), as well as reports from a growing number of practical case studies, when an enterprise is a member of a long-term networked structure, such as a supply chain or a Virtual organizations Breeding Environment (VBE), there is the assumption that such involvement brings valuable (potential) benefits to the involved entities [1, 2], [3]. These benefits include an increase of the "survival capability" in a context of market turbulence, but also the possibility to better achieve common or compatible goals. On the basis of these expectations are, among others, the following factors: joining of complementary skills and capacities, access to new / wider markets and new knowledge, etc [4].

However, it is important to realize that when an enterprise is a member of a long-term networked structure, for instance a Virtual organizations Breeding Environment, its value is not only given by its tangible assets – economic capital (e.g. cash, resources, and goods). In this context, the existence of cooperation agreements, norms, reciprocal relationships, mutual trust, common infrastructures and common

L.M. Camarinha-Matos et al. (Eds.): PRO-VE 2011, IFIP AICT 362, pp. 29–40, 2011.

ontologies, allows members to operate more effectively in the pursuit of their goals. In other words, there is an intuitive assumption that a VBE structure represents a group of organizational entities that have developed intangible assets of "social capital" that bring added value to its members. As a result, in a VBE context the social capital works as a complement to tangible assets, and may have a leveraging effect to increase the value of others assets, and vice versa.

However, although social capital is not a new concept, its definition is not consensual among the various main disciplines that have addressed this topic (e.g. economy, sociology) and therefore several definitions can be found in the literature [5]. This situation results in part from the fact that the social capital needs to be analyzed from a multi-dimensional perspective which has not been considered in previous works. For instance, the diversity of the understandings of social capital varies according to the authors being focused on: the relationships that an actor has with other actors, the structure of relations among actors within a network, or both types of relationships [6].

Social capital metrics tailored to collaborative networks or even an adequate conceptual basis for social capital analysis is not available yet and might be an obstacle for a wider acceptance of this paradigm. According to Stone [7] the tools available for measuring social capital are not enough and further research is required.

Nevertheless, in recent years some preliminary studies have explored the importance of social capital in the context of networked organizations [8], however none of them has proposed methods, approaches or support tools to help managers of enterprises to analyze and measure their social capital in the context of Virtual organizations Breeding Environments.

This paper introduces a brief discussion of the nature of social capital in order to support a model to analyze social capital which is inspired on the Social Networks Analysis area and proposes a set of indicators that are deemed suitable for collaborative networks.

2 Some Background

As mentioned above, social capital has been defined according to multiple and separated perspectives or for different purposes. From a sociological perspective, Bourdieu [9] defined social capital as "the aggregate of the actual or potential resources which are linked to possession of a durable network of more or less institutionalized relationships of mutual acquaintance and recognition," while for Portes [10] social capital is "the ability of actors to secure benefits by virtue of membership in social networks or other social structures". On the other hand, from an economic perspective Nahapiet and Ghoshal [11] defined social capital as "the sum of the actual and potential resources embedded within, available through, and derived from the network of relationships possessed by an individual or social unit. Social capital thus comprises both the network and the assets that may be mobilized through that network". For Fukuyama [12] "social capital can be defined simply as the existence of a certain set of informal values or norms shared among members of a group that permit cooperation among them".

Taking into account the above definitions, it is possible to conclude that social capital is a valuable (intangible) asset which has some typical characteristics of economic capital such as: It can be invested with the expectation of future benefits [13] and is convertible [9]. But, on the other hand, it is different, since its existence lies in the relationships that are established within the network while economic capital can exist at the member level [14]. In other words, social capital cannot be traded by entities on an open market like economic capital, but exclusively within a network [15].

3 A Model to Analyze Social Capital

In order to analyze the social capital of each member in a collaborative network, it is necessary to develop a model that supports the analysis of the relationships among members and the assets that may be accessed through the network of contacts.

Therefore, as a first approach, these relationships can be modeled using graphs, as illustrated in Fig. 1. The proposed model [16] considers elementary-maps and aggregate-maps. The elementary maps are:

- Map of business contacts - a graph showing the network of formal relationships with the purpose to provide services or goods to satisfy a request among members belonging to the network. In this case, the link's width represents the level of relationship between two enterprises in a defined time interval, and its value is given by the following equation:

$$LR_{ij} = w_1 \times SRFC_{ij} \times SRIC_{ij} + w_2 \times PRFC_{ij} \times PRIC \times VS_{ij}$$

$$\sum_{j=1}^{2} w_j = 1 \text{ and } w_j > 0 \tag{1}$$

Where:

LR_{ij} - Level of relationship between enterprise i and enterprise j, in a defined time interval. It has a value over the interval $[0,+\infty[$.

$SRFC_{ij}$ - Frequency of contacts between enterprise i and enterprise j, based on subordinate relation, in a defined time interval. It has a value over the interval $[0,+\infty[$.

$SRIC_{ij}$ - Intensity of contacts between enterprise i and enterprise j, based on subordinate relation, in a defined time interval. It has a value over the interval $[0,1]$.

$PRFC_{ij}$ - Frequency of contacts between enterprise i and enterprise j, based on peer relation, in a defined time interval. It has a value over the interval $[0,+\infty[$.

$PRIC_{ij}$ - Intensity of contacts between enterprise i and enterprise j, based on peer relation. It has a value over the interval $[0,1]$.

VS_{ij} - Value systems alignment between enterprise i and enterprise j, in a defined time interval. It has a value over the interval $[0,1]$.

However, the main difficulty is naturally the determination of each of the five components mentioned above. To collect and record those values without being intrusive in the network members' "life" requires further research and development.

- Map of enterprises' assets - a graph that shows the assets held by each enterprise and how they are shared. In this case, there are two sets of nodes: enterprises and assets. The nodes are connected by ownership/access relations.

The aggregate-maps show how an enterprise may have access to assets held by another enterprise. It results from the aggregation of the map of business contacts and the map of enterprises' assets. Based on this map, it is now possible to analyze the social capital of each enterprise through a visual representation of the assets that are held by an enterprise.

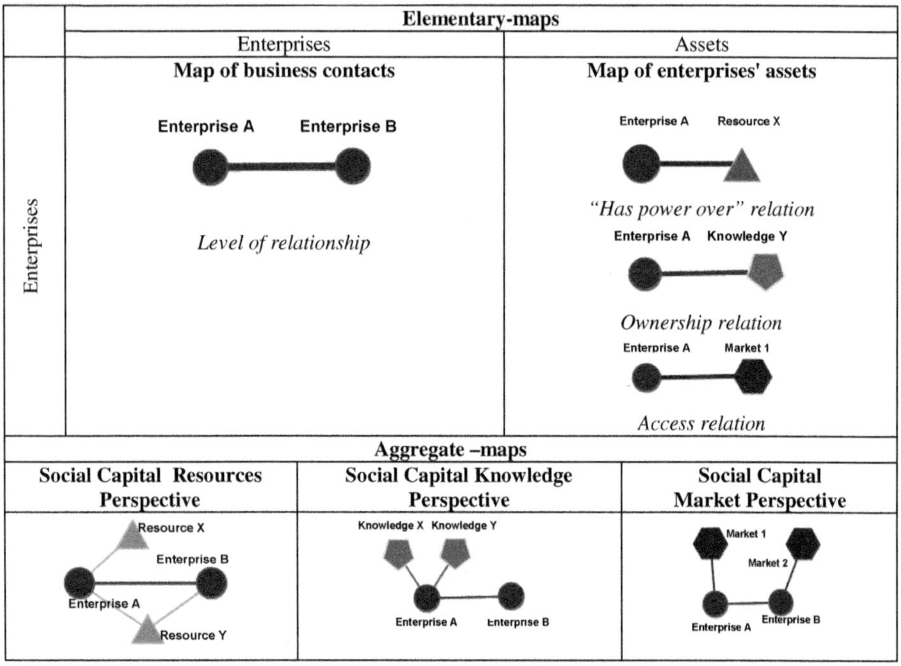

Fig. 1. Simple model to analyze Social Capital in CNs

Combining these concepts with elements from the Social Network Analysis area, a set of basic indicators tailored to collaborative networks is proposed as shown in Table 1 and Table 2. Table 1 includes a list of indicators to analyze in detail the level of relationships between enterprises and Table 2 shows a set of indicators to evaluate the level of expertise of an enterprise and how the assets are shared in the network.

Table 1. Indicators for relationship analysis

Indicator	Short Description	Expression
Individual Business Contacts (IBC_i)	**Definition** This indicator measures the number of distinct business contacts / "collaborative processes" that an enterprise has established with other enterprises. In terms of social network analysis, it corresponds to the node degree **Potential Use** • Assessment of the level of collaboration • Assessment the prestige/popularity of an enterprise	IBC_i = Number of contacts connected to node e_i e_i - enterprise i
Apparent Individual Business Contacts Index ($AIBCI_i$)	**Definition** This index represents the ratio between the individual business contacts of an enterprise and the total of enterprises involved in the network. **Potential Use** This index gives an apparent and simple to compute measure of accessibility of an enterprise to the assets that can be mobilized through the network. An enterprise with an AIBCI close to zero means that such enterprise might not have access to the assets available within the network.	$AIBCI_i = \frac{IBC_i}{N}$ N –Number of nodes involved in the network
Individual Business Contacts Index ($IBCI_i$)	**Definition** This index measures the ratio between the individual business contacts of an enterprise and the sum of the individual business contacts of all enterprises involved in the network. **Potential Use** • Normalization of the level of involvement of an enterprise in relation to other members of the network. • Benchmarking with enterprises involved in other networks.	$IBCI_i = \frac{IBC_i}{\sum_{j=1}^{N} IBC_j}$ N – Number of nodes involved in the network
Individual Level of Relationship (ILR_i)	**Definition** The sum of the level of the relationships that an enterprise achieved as a result of its performance in collaborative process. **Potential Use** • Evaluate the behaviour of an enterprise. An enterprise with a low level of ILR means that such enterprise might exhibit a non-collaborative behaviour. • Evaluate the prominence level of an enterprise, assuming that prominent enterprises are those that are extensively involved in relationships with other enterprises.	$ILR_i = \sum_{j=1}^{N} LR_{ij}$ LR_{ij} – Level of relationship between actor i and actor j. N – Number of nodes involved in the network
Individual Level Relationship index ($ILRI_i$)	**Definition** This index represents the ratio between the individual level of relationship of an enterprise and the sum of the individual level of relationship of all enterprises involved in the network. **Potential Use** • Normalization of the level of relationships of an enterprise in relation to other members of the network. • Benchmarking with enterprises involved in other networks.	$ILRI_i = \frac{ILR_i}{\sum_{j=1}^{N} ILR_j}$ N – Number of nodes involved in the network
Individual Level of Accessibility (ILA_i)	**Definition** This indicator measures for each enterprise the ratio between the individual level of relationship and the individual business contacts. **Potential Use** This indicator measures the level of accessibility or ability of an enterprise to access the assets that can be mobilized through the network.	$ILA_i = \frac{ILR_i}{IBC_i}$
Individual Accessibility Index (IAI_i)	**Definition** This indicator measures, for each enterprise, the ratio between the individual level of accessibility of an enterprise and the sum of the individual levels of accessibility of all enterprises involved in the network. **Potential Use** • Normalization of the level of accessibility of an enterprise in relation to other members of the network. • Benchmarking with enterprises involved in other networks.	$IAI_i = \frac{ILA_i}{\sum_{j=1}^{N} ILA_j}$ N – Number of nodes involved in the network

Table 2. Indicators for assets analysis

Indicator	Short Description	Expression
Total of Assets (M)	**Definition** This indicator counts the number of distinct assets held by the network. **Potential Use** This indicator measures the level of versatility/polyvalence of the network.	$M = \sum_{j=1}^{A} m_j$ A – Number of distinct assets involved in the network m_j – asset j
Total of enterprise Owned Assets (TOA_i)	**Definition** This indicator measures the number of distinct assets held by an enterprise. In terms of social network analysis, it corresponds to the enterprise's node degree **Potential Use** This indicator measures the level of expertise or capacity of an enterprise.	TOA_i = Number of ownership relations connected to enterprise e_i
Apparent Owned Assets Index ($AOAI_i$)	**Definition** This index represents the ratio between the number of assets that belong to an enterprise and the number of the assets that can be mobilized through the network. **Potential Use** This indicator measures the potential level of dependence that an enterprise might have in relation to the assets that can be mobilized through the network. An enterprise with an AOAI close to one means that this enterprise is the owner of nearly all assets available within the network.	$AOAI_i = \frac{TOA_i}{M}$ M – Number of assets held by the network
Owned Assets Index (OAI_i)	**Definition** This index represents the ratio between the number of assets that belong to an enterprise and the sum of the number of distinct assets held by all enterprises involved in the network. **Potential Use** • Normalization of the number of assets held by an enterprise in relation to other members of the network. • Benchmarking with enterprises involved in other networks.	$OAI_i = \frac{TOA_i}{\sum_{j=1}^{N} TOA_j}$ N – Number of enterprises involved in the network
Partial Owned Assets (POA_{ik})	**Definition** This indicator accounts for the number of distinct assets held by an enterprise according to perspective k for instance: innovation, capacity and market. In terms of social network analysis, it corresponds to the enterprise's node degree for perspective k. **Potential Use** This indicator measures the level of expertise of each enterprise according to perspective k.	POA_{ik} = number of ownership relations according to perspective *k* connected to enterprise e_i
Apparent Partial Specialization Index ($APSI_{ik}$)	**Definition** This index measures the ratio between the number of assets according to perspective *k* that belong to an enterprise and the total of the assets according to perspective *k* that can be mobilized through the network. **Potential Use** This indicator gives an indication of the level of specialization of an enterprise according to perspective k. An enterprise with an APSI close to one means that such enterprise within the network is specialized in this perspective *k*.	$APSI_{ik} = \frac{POA_{ik}}{M_k}$ M_k – Number of assets held by the network according to perspective *k*.
Partial Specialization Index (PSI_{ik})	**Definition** This indicator measures, for each enterprise, the ratio between the Apparent Partial Specialization of an enterprise and the sum of the Apparent Partial Specialization of all enterprises involved in the network. **Potential Use** • Normalization of the level of specialization of an enterprise according to perspective *k* in relation to other members of the network. • Benchmarking with enterprises involved in other networks.	$PSI_{ik} = \frac{APSI_{ik}}{\sum_{j=1}^{N} APSI_{jk}}$ N – Number of enterprises involved in the network

Table 2. (*Continued*)

Assets Abundance (AA_i)	**Definition** This indicator counts the number of distinct ownership relations of an asset. In terms of social network analysis, it corresponds to the node´s degree. **Potential Use** This indicator measures the level of abundance of an asset inside the network. An asset with an AA close to one means that it is exclusive because it is owned by few enterprises of the network.	AA_i = Number of ownership relations connected to asset a_i
Apparent Assets Exclusivity Index ($AAEI_i$)	**Definition** This index measures the ratio between the level of proliferation of an asset and the number of enterprises involved in the network. **Potential Use** This index gives a simple to compute measure of exclusivity of an asset. An asset with an AAEI near to zero means that such asset belongs to few enterprises. On the other hand, an asset with an AAEI close to one means that such asset is owned by all enterprises in the network.	$AAEI_i = \frac{AA_i}{N}$ N –Number of enterprises involved in the network
Assets Exclusivity Index (AEI_i)	**Definition** This index measures the ratio between the level of proliferation of an asset and the sum of the number of distinct assets held by all enterprises involved in the network **Potential Use** • Normalization of the level of exclusivity of an asset in the network. • Benchmarking with other networks.	$AEI_i = \frac{AA_i}{\sum_{j=1}^{M} AA_j}$ M – Number of assets held by the network
Partial Owned Assets Worth ($POAW_{ik}$)	**Definition** The sum of the worth of the assets that are held by an enterprise according to perspective k. **Potential Use** The purpose of this indicator is to measure the worth of the assets that are held by an enterprise according to perspective k.	$(POAW_{ik}) = \sum_{m=1}^{M} v_{Am,i,k}$ M – Number of assets held by the network $v_{Am,i,k}$ - Value assigned to asset *Am* held by enterprise *i* according to perspective k.
Total of Owned Assets Worth ($TOAW_i$)	**Definition** The sum of the worth of the assets that are held by an enterprise. **Potential Use** The purpose of this indicator is to measure the total worth of the assets that are held by an enterprise.	$(TOAW_i) = \sum_{k=1}^{K} POAW_{ik}$ K – number of distinct perspectives
Partial Owned Assets Worth Index ($POAWI_{ik}$)	**Definition** This index measures, for each enterprise, the ratio between the worth of the assets that are held by an enterprise according to perspective k, and the sum of the worth of the assets that are held by all enterprises involved in the network according to perspective k. **Potential Use** • Normalization of the assets worth of an enterprise according to perspective *k* in relation to other members of the network. • Benchmarking with enterprises involved in other networks.	$POAWI_{ik} = \frac{POAW_{ik}}{\sum_{i=1}^{N} POAW_{ik}}$ N –Number of enterprises involved in the network
Total of Owned Assets Worth Index ($TOAWI_i$)	**Definition** This index measures, for each enterprise, the ratio between the worth of the assets that are held by an enterprise, and the sum of the worth of the assets that are held by all enterprises involved in the network. **Potential Use** • Normalization of the assets worth of an enterprise in relation to other members of the network. • Benchmarking with enterprises involved in other networks.	$TOAWI_i = \frac{TOAW_i}{\sum_{i=1}^{N} TOAW_i}$ N –Number of enterprises involved in the network

4 Example Application

In order to analyze and measure the social capital of members of a collaborative network, the following example illustrates how the proposed indicators can be used.

For this scenario, the existence of a VBE is considered, which contains seven enterprises identified as E1 to E7. Let us suppose that at the VBE management level there are records of the enterprises' past involvement in collaboration activities, which makes it possible to quantify the level of relationships between enterprises (LR_{ij}) as illustrated in Table 3.A, and there are also records of the type of assets, value of each one of those assets that can be mobilized through the network, and how the assets are held by each enterprise, as illustrated in Table 3.B.

Table 3. a) Record of the level of relationships. b) Record of the assets worth

A

	E1	E2	E3	E4	E5	E6	E7
E1	0	0	0	0	0	0	30
E2	0	0	90	50	50	50	0
E3	0	90	0	0	0	90	0
E4	0	50	0	0	20	0	0
E5	0	50	0	20	0	10	10
E6	0	50	90	0	10	0	0
E7	30	0	0	0	10	0	0

B

	Knowledge				Market			Resources			
	K1	K2	K3	K4	M1	M2	M3	R1	R2	R3	R4
E1	10	0	0	0	20	0	0	0	0	0	0
E2	0	20	20	0	20	0	0	30	0	0	0
E3	10	20	20	0	20	0	0	30	0	0	0
E4	0	0	0	0	0	10	0	0	40	0	0
E5	0	20	20	0	0	10	0	0	0	50	0
E6	10	0	0	0	0	10	0	0	0	50	0
E7	0	0	0	50	0	10	50	0	40	0	50

Table 4. Indicators for relationships analysis

	IBC	AIBCI	IBCI	ILR	ILRI	ILA	ILAI
E1	1	14%	6%	30	4%	30	10%
E2	4	57%	22%	240	30%	60	20%
E3	2	29%	11%	180	23%	90	29%
E4	2	29%	11%	70	9%	35	11%
E5	4	57%	22%	90	11%	23	7%
E6	3	43%	17%	150	19%	50	16%
E7	2	29%	11%	40	5%	20	7%

Based on the data of the level of relationships presented in Table 3.A, and applying the equations defined in Table 1, the Table 4 shows some examples of indicators for this network.

Analysing the value of the indicators in Table 4, it is possible to verify, for instance, according to the apparent individual business contact index (AIBCI), that enterprises E2 and E5 are the most involved in collaboration with other enterprises and both have relationships with 57% of the members of this network. However, in terms of individual level of accessibility (ILA), the highest value belongs to enterprise E3.

Table 5. Indicators for assets analysis

A – Knowledge	POA	APSI	PSI	POAW	POAWI
E1	1	25%	10%	10	5%
E2	2	50%	20%	40	20%
E3	3	75%	30%	50	25%
E4	0	0%	0%	0	0%
E5	2	50%	20%	40	20%
E6	1	25%	10%	10	5%
E7	1	25%	10%	50	25%
Total		4		200	

B – Market	POA	APSI	PSI	POAW	POAWI
E1	1	33%	13%	20	14%
E2	1	33%	13%	20	14%
E3	1	33%	13%	20	14%
E4	1	33%	13%	10	7%
E5	1	33%	13%	10	7%
E6	1	33%	13%	10	7%
E7	2	67%	25%	50	36%
Total		3		140	

C – Resources	POA	APSI	PSI	POAW	POAWI
E1	0	0%	0%	0	0
E2	1	25%	14%	30	10%
E3	1	25%	14%	30	10%
E4	1	25%	14%	40	14%
E5	1	25%	14%	50	17%
E6	1	25%	14%	50	17%
E7	2	50%	29%	90	31%
Total		4		290	

D – Global	TOA	AOAI	OAI	TOAW	TOAWI
E1	2	18%	8%	30	5%
E2	4	16%	16%	90	14%
E3	5	20%	20%	100	16%
E4	2	8%	8%	50	8%
E5	4	16%	16%	100	16%
E6	3	12%	12%	70	11%
E7	5	20%	20%	190	30%

E – Assets	AA	AAEI	AEI
K1	3	43%	12%
k2	3	43%	12%
K3	3	43%	12%
K4	1	14%	4%
M1	3	43%	12%
M2	4	57%	16%
M3	1	14%	4%
R1	2	29%	8%
R2	2	29%	8%
R3	2	29%	8%
R4	1	14%	4%

Taking into account this example, let us now suppose that enterprises E3 and E5 need to have access to some assets in order to accomplish a business opportunity. In this case, if the assets are held by enterprises with which both have business contacts, the enterprise that has more chances of being successful is the enterprise E3.

Based on the data on the type of assets, value of each asset, and how the assets are held by each member, presented in Table 3.B, and applying the equations defined in Table 2, the Table 5 shows some examples of indicators to evaluate the level of expertise of an enterprise and how the assets might be shared within this network.

Based on these data, it is possible to verify, for instance, that according to the knowledge perspective (see Table 5.A), in terms of assets worth (see POAW), enterprises E3 and E7 have identical values despite the enterprise E3 having more assets than the enterprise E7 (see POA).

Using graphs to analyze social capital. The adoption of quantified indicators combined with a graphical visualization provides a tool to analyse in detail the 'sub-structures' that may be present in a collaborative network. Divisions of members into cliques, i.e. sub-structures of a network in which the members are more closely and intensely linked to one another than they are to other members of the network, can be important to understand how social capital flows within the network.

On the other hand, at micro level the knowledge of how a member is embedded in a sub-structure within a network may be important to understand how it can increase its social capital. For instance, some members can act as 'bridges' between groups. In Fig. 2, the enterprise E5 acts as a bridge between the sub-structure made by enterprise E7 and enterprise E1 and the other enterprises of the network. Furthermore, the node's size in Fig. 2 represents the proportion of assets that are held by each enterprise, and the link's width represents the value of the level of relationship between enterprises. Hence, the enterprises that hold more assets are enterprises E7 and E3. On the other hand, if we look at the links between enterprises, we can easily identify a clique, for instance, among enterprises E2, E3 and E6 with a high level of accessibility among them.

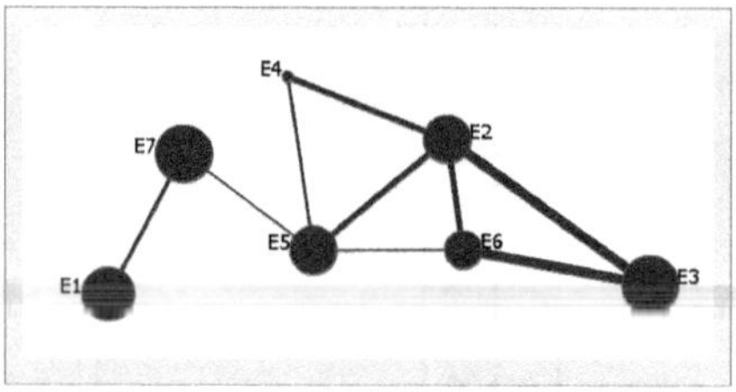

Fig. 2. Owner Assets Index

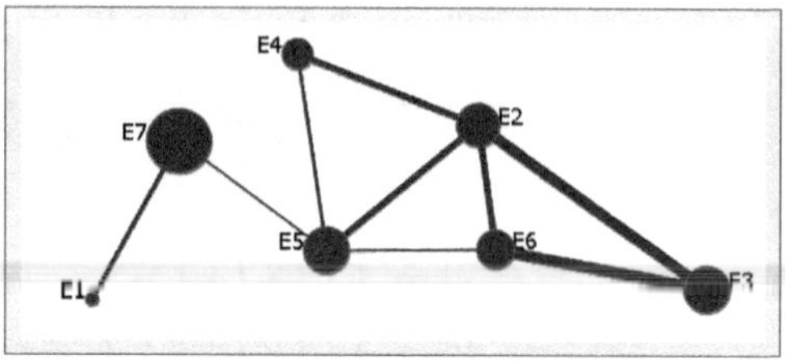

Fig. 3. Total of Owner Assets Worth

The nodes' size in Fig. 3 represents the worth of the assets hold by each enterprise, and the link's width represents the value of the level of the relationship between them. Hence, in this network, the enterprise that holds more social capital is enterprise E7. However, as enterprise E7 has a low level of accessibility, the links around enterprise E7 are narrow, which can act as an obstacle to increase the social capital of this network.

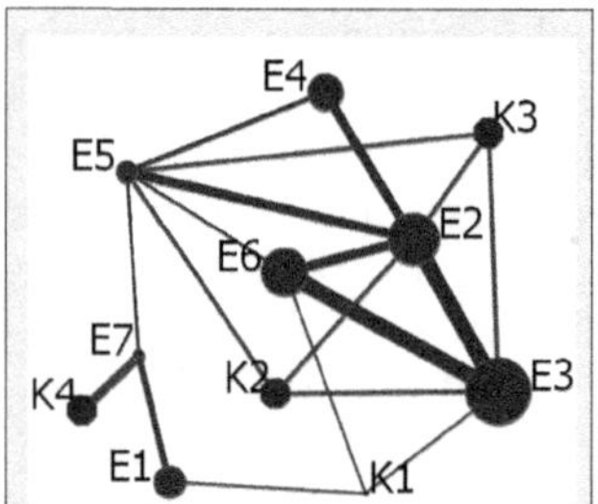

Fig. 4. Individual Level of Accessibility and assets worth

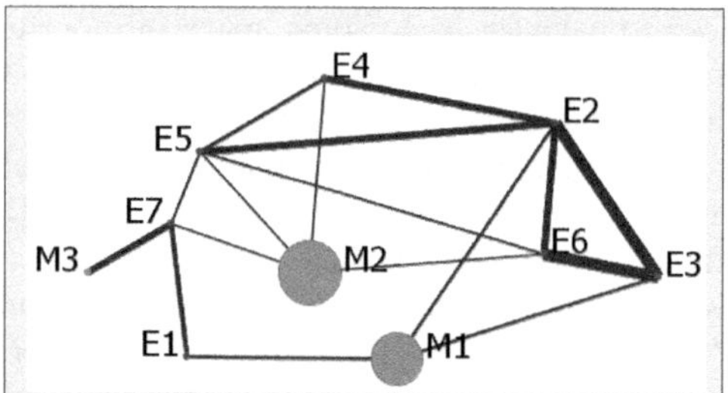

Fig. 5. Apparent Assets Exclusivity index and "level of health" of the relationships

Fig. 4 illustrates the advantage of this model in the use of multiple indicators. In this example, the nodes' size of the enterprises represents the individual level of accessibility (ILA) of each enterprise. The link's width between enterprises represents the value of the level of relationship among them, and the link's width between an enterprise and an asset represents the worth of that asset. In this case, the nodes' size of the assets is identical because they have no associated metrics.

Hence, according to the knowledge perspective, it is possible to verify that the most valuable asset is K4, and it is an exclusive asset that is hold by enterprise E7. Furthermore, the enterprise E7 has the lowest level of accessibility. In this context, despite the asset K4 belongs to the bag of network's assets, only a small group of enterprises is likely to be successful in accessing to this asset through the network of business contacts. For instance, in this case, although enterprise E3 holds the highest value in terms of individual level of accessibility, based on this analysis it hardly can access to the asset K4.

On the other hand, Fig. 5 illustrates an example of analysis of the abundance of the assets by the members of the network. In this case, the nodes' size of the assets represents the level of abundance of each asset in this network. The link's width between enterprises represents the value of the level of relationship among them, and the link's width between an enterprise and an asset represents the worth of that asset. The nodes' size of the enterprises is identical because they have no associated metrics. In this case, the most common asset is the asset M2, and the asset M3 is the most valuable one, which is also an exclusive asset that is hold by enterprise E7.

5 Conclusions

Reaching a better characterization and understanding of the role of social capital in collaborative processes is an important element for a better understanding of the behavioral aspects in the collaborative networks paradigm in its various manifestation forms.

The definition of a set of indicators to capture and measure the social capital can be a useful instrument to support the promotion of collaborative behaviours, and for a VBE member a way to extract the advantages of belonging to a network.

Using simple calculations as illustrated above, it is possible to extract some indicators. Some preliminary steps in this direction, inspired by the Social Networks Analysis, were presented, although it is necessary to do a more extensive experimental validation. The main difficulty is naturally the determination of the "level of health" of the relationships and the worth corresponding to each asset. In order to collect and record those values without being intrusive in the network member's 'life' requires further research and development. It is also important to rank the indicators according to their practical usefulness. Such ranking should encompass the vision and strategy defined for the collaborative network.

The proposed model, although simplistic, has the advantage of providing a visual/graphical representation which is easy to understand. The development of a system to monitor and keep track of the changes over time is particularly useful here.

Acknowledgments. This work was supported in part by the FCT-MCTES – "Fundação para a Ciência e Tecnologia" (CTS multiannual funding) through the PIDDAC Program funds", and the European Commission through GloNet project.

References

1. Beckett, R.C.: Perceptions of value that sustain collaborative networks. In: Camarinha-Matos, L.M., Afsarmanesh, H., Ortiz, A. (eds.) Collaborative Networks and Their Breeding Enviroments. Springer, Heidelberg (2005)
2. Afsarmanesh, H., Marik, V., Camarinha-Matos, L.M.: Challenges of collaborative networks in Europe. In: Camarinha-Matos, L.M., Afsarmanesh, H. (eds.) Collaborative Networked Organizations: A Research Agenda for Emerging Business Models. Kluwer Academic Publishers, Dordrecht (2004)

3. Tenera, A., Abreu, A.: A TOC perspective to improve the management of collaborative networks. In: Camarinha-Matos, L.M., Picard, W. (eds.) Pervasive Collaborative Networks, pp. 167–176. Springer, Boston (2008)
4. Camarinha-Matos, L.M., Abreu, A.: A contribution to understand collaboration benefits. In: Camarinha-Matos, L.M. (ed.) Emerging Solutions for Future Manufacturing Systems. Springer, Heidelberg (2004)
5. Bankston, C.L., Zhou, M.: Social Capital as a Process: The Meanings and Problems of a Theoretical Metaphor? Sociological Inquiry 72(2), 285–317 (2002)
6. Adler, P.S., Kwon, S.-W.: Social Capital: Prospects for a new concept. The Academy of Management Review 27, 17–40 (2002)
7. Stone, W.: Measuring social capital: Towards a theoretically informed measurement framework for researching social capital in family and community life. Family Matters Autumn 38 (2001)
8. Francis, J., Mukherji, A., Mukherji, J.: Examining relational and resource influences on the performance of border region SMEs. International Business Review 18(4), 331–343 (2009)
9. Bourdieu, P.: The Forms of Capital. In: Richardson, J.G. (ed.) Handbook of Theory and Research for Sociology of Education, pp. 241–258. Greenwood Press, New York (1986)
10. Portes, A.: Social Capital its origins and applications in modern sociology. Annual Review of Sociology 24, 1–25 (1998)
11. Nahaiet, J., Ghoshal, S.: Social Capital, Intellectual Capital, and the organizational advantage. Academy of Management Review 23(2), 242–266 (1998)
12. Fukuyama, F.: Social Capital and the modern capitalist economy: Creating a high trust worplace. Stern Business Magazine (1997)
13. Camarinha-Matos, L.M., Abreu, A.: Performance indicators based on colaborative benefits. In: Camarinha-Matos, L.M., Afsarmanesh, H., Ortiz, A. (eds.) Collaborative Networks and Their Breeding Enviroments. Springer, Heidelberg (2005)
14. Robison, L.J., Schimid, A., Siles, M.E.: Is social capital really capital? Review of Social Economy 60, 1–24 (2002)
15. Gant, J., Ichniowski, C., Shaw, K.: Social capital and organisational change in high involvement and traditional work organisations. Journal of Economics and Management 11, 289–328 (2002)
16. Abreu, A., Camarinha-Matos, L.M.: Understanding Social Capital in Collaborative Networks. In: Bas, Á.O., Franco, R.D., Gasquet, P.G. (eds.) BASYS 2010. IFIP AICT, vol. 322, pp. 109–118. Springer, Heidelberg (2010)

A Review on Intellectual Capital Concepts as a Base for Measuring Intangible Assets of Collaborative Networks

Raul Rodriguez-Rodriguez, Juan-Jose Alfaro-Saiz, and Maria-Jose Verdecho

Universitat Politècnica de Valencia, Departamento de Organización de Empresas,
Camino de Vera sn, 46022 Valencia, Spain
{raurodro,jalfaro,mverdecho}@cigip.upv.es

Abstract. This work presents a revision of the main definition and significances of the term Intellectual Capital, as it is an important issue of study. Once the main scientific works related to Intellectual Capital are presented and their main contributions highlighted, this work shows how it has been attempted to measure the Intellectual Capital at both individual enterprises and collaborative networks, as a source of meaningful information to make decisions. The paper evidences the lack of works that have successfully dealt with measuring Intellectual Capital at the collaborative networks level, highlighting the main barriers and what a proper measuring framework should address at this level.

Keywords: Intellectual capital, collaborative networks, measurement.

1 Introduction

A company's capability to create value depends on its ability to implement strategies that respond to market opportunities by exploiting their internal resources and capabilities [1]. Therefore, managers need to understand what the key internal resources and drivers of performance in their organisations are. Traditionally, those resources were physical, such as machines and equipments, and financial capital. In today's economy traditional tangible assets seem to become increasingly transient and rarely provide a long-term competitive advantage. This reflects the belief that intangibles assets are a fundamental resource of corporate growth and organizations need to put into work procedures for managing their intangible assets. In the last years, the concept of Intellectual Capital (IC) has emerged as a key to analyse and evaluate the intangible assets of organizations.

2 Literature Review

In the last two decades, several models have been developed for managing the IC. All of them attempt to identify, classify, measure and manage the company's IC. Some models are focused on the global IC of the company such as the Skandia Navigator [2], the Intangible Assets Monitor [3]. On the other hand, other frameworks are focused on the intangibles related to the defined strategies such as [4] or the Intellectual Capital Management System. However, none of these models implement

L.M. Camarinha-Matos et al. (Eds.): PRO-VE 2011, IFIP AICT 362, pp. 41–47, 2011.

or suggest the integration within a performance measurement system, which would contribute the advantages of its use.

In the literature, the concept of IC has been defined from different management perspectives as shown in Table 1. For instance, accounts prefer to talk about intangibles and according to [5], define them as "non-financial fixed assets that do not have physical substance but are identifiable and controlled by the entity through custody and legal rights". From a human resource (HR) perspective, IC refers to skills, knowledge, and attitudes of employees. From a marketing perspective, intangibles such as brand recognition and customer satisfaction are at the heart of business success, whereas from at the information technology (IT) perspective, intangibles are seen as being software applications and network capabilities (for an in-depth discussion of the different perspectives on IC please refer to [6]). As shown by the above definitions, there is no agreement upon what constitutes a good or sufficient definition of IC. Finally, IC is an important theme in different disciplines and is looked at from different perspectives such as economics, strategic management, finance, accounting, reporting and disclosure, human resources, and marketing and communication. However, there are few works developed related to the IC in the field of performance measurement.

Table 1. Main definitions of Intellectual Capital

References	Definition
[7]	It is set up by intangible property and intangible resources.
[8]	It is knowledge that can be converted into value.
[9]	It is the result of four main components, which are the market assets, human-centred assets, intellectual property assets and infrastructure assets.
[3]	It is related to three categories of intangible assets: internal structure, external structure and human competence.
[10]	It is composed of (and generated by) a thinking part, i.e. the human capital, and a non-thinking part, i.e. the structural capital.
[11]	It is an intellectual material that has been formalised, captured and leveraged to produce a higher-valued asset.
[2]	It is the sum of human and structural capital. In more detail it involves applied experience, organizational technology, customer relationships and professional skills that provide an organization with a competitive advantage in the market.
[12]	It is a concept under which are classified all organization intangible resources as well their interconnections

The Intellectual Capital Management Models are focused on the establishment of one definition of IC, the components or dimensions of its structure, the intangible assets that belong to each component or dimension, and the indicator used to measure the identified intangible assets. Some models, as result of their activities, elaborate one report with two proposals, one as internal management tool and the second as external spreading tool of information for informing to the stakeholders about the real value of the company and not only about its financial value. Only some of the recently developed models of IC identify the need of linking the intangible assets with the strategy of the company, such as [4]. Such a project was the first model that proposed the identification of the strategic objectives of the company and the critical intangible assets related to each of these strategic objectives as one of the main steps of this project. Moreover, the RICARDA project establishes that the first step to create a report of Intellectual Capital for Regional Networks o Clusters is the definition of the regional network or cluster's objectives in medium and long term and the second step is concerning to the identification of each intangible assets that affect them.

3 Measuring Intellectual Capital

3.1 Enterprise Level

Nowadays, IC has become a determinant resource for enterprise to retain and improve competitive advantages. Because of its abstract nature, the IC is very difficult to measure, having become a challenge for business managers to evaluate the performance of IC effectively.

[13] identified as benefits of IC measurement firstly the identification and mapping of intangible assets, which allows the company knowing its resources of competitive advantages on the future. Secondly, the recognition of knowledge flow patterns within the company. The last two benefits drive to the prioritization of critical knowledge issues, which allow the acceleration of learning patterns within the company thanks to the best practice identification and diffusion across the company, by presenting a strong business case for the best practice. Besides, the measurement of the IC permits a constant monitoring of asset value as well as to find ways of increasing the value of the company and the understanding of how knowledge creates interrelationships and increases innovation. From the point of view of the employees, the benefits are with regard to the increasing of collaborative activities and a knowledge sharing culture as a result of increased awareness of the benefits of knowledge management. Also the employee self-perception of the organization and their motivation are increased. Finally, it creates a performance-oriented culture.

Measurement of IC will result in significant benefits to the organization that will help to determine business strategy, process design as well providing competitive advantage.

Additionally, [12] carried out an exhaustive literature review in which he highlighted the following main limitations in the existing measurement systems:

- The existing approaches relate to the organization as a whole and do not account for individual departments or knowledge workers.
- They do not balance past-orientation with future predictions, or quantitative financial measures with qualitative perceptual and process measures.
- Behavioural dynamics and its impact on organizational economics are not measured.
- There is no system for measuring process effectiveness in capturing tacit knowledge transfer.

At present, measuring a company's Intellectual Capital is quite common. According to Nordic survey, two thirds of Finnish companies measure their Intellectual Capital regularly. Despite the fact that measuring Intellectual Capital is considered important, only 35 percent of the companies know how Intellectual Capital should be measured and reported [14]. Although different measurement systems for measuring Intellectual Capital have been developed, none of them has been accepted for common use. According to [3] the approaches for measuring intellectual capital fall into four categories: Direct Intellectual Capital Methods (DIC), Market Capitalization Methods (MCM), Return on Assets Methods (ROA) and Scorecard Methods (SC). The methods offer different advantages and disadvantages.

Scorecard Methods in particular have been developed as a tool for management and although all the scorecard methods have many similarities, they can be categorized into two different types: the (traditional) balanced performance measurement methods and Intellectual Capital measurement methods. The balanced performance measurement frameworks, e.g. the Balanced Scorecard [15] and the Performance Pyramid [16], have been developed for measuring and managing an organization's performance from several perspectives. IC is often related to one or more of these perspectives. However, in the IC measurement methods, e.g. the Skandia Navigator [2] and the Intangible Assets Monitor [3], the main rationale is the measurement of IC. Financial and other physical assets are not paid as much attention as the Intellectual-Capital-related factors.

Kaplan y Norton [17] indicated that the intangible assets are hard for competitors to imitate, which makes them a powerful source of sustainable competitive advantage. The Learning and Growth Perspective of the Balances Scorecard has long been considered its weakest link, and Kaplan and Norton admitted it . To improve this the authors included in this perspective the intangibles assets essentials for implementing any strategy, which are classified in three categories: Human Capital (the skills, talent and knowledge that a company's employees possess), Information Capital (the company's database, information systems, networks and technology infrastructure) and Organizational Capital (the company's culture, its leadership, how aligned its people are with its strategic goals and employee's ability to share knowledge). Additionally, and to link these intangible assets to the company's strategy and performance, these authors developed a tool called "strategic map".

Although the terminology used to describe and categorize intangible assets is far from being cohesive at the detailed level, there has recently been a general convergence towards a three-pronged framework consisting of Human Capital, Organizational (or Structural) Capital and Relational Capital [4]. Therefore, it is not clear why Information Capital is considered by Kaplan and Norton separated from Organizational Capital as most of the researches on this field agree.

As well, the concept of Relational Capital is completely missing from Kaplan and Norton's definition of intangible assets. The Balanced Scorecard includes a Customer Perspective and it could be argued that customer relationships could be included into this perspective. In fact, Kaplan and Norton [17] argue that this perspective should contain the customer value proposition. Even if relationships might be included the issue remains that according to Kaplan and Norton's definition of intangibles assets, Relational Capital is not included, which defies the views of most researchers working in this field.

At this point, several gaps have been identified in the above literature review such as the lack of consensus among the researchers and the practitioners about the definitions of IC, the IC components and the IC indicators. Many and various have been the attempts to measure the intangible assets of the companies through different IC models. Kaplan and Norton, instead of creating a new model to measure the intangible assets, have integrated the measurement of the intangible assets within their Balanced Scorecard. Several researchers have criticized this attempt, having being identified several gaps in the way they have done such a merge.

3.2 Collaborative Network Level

On the other hand, and looking at the collaborative networks ambit, all these research gaps are present, among others. Collaboration implies factors such as trust, equity, coherence, visibility, contradictory objectives, or communication issues that are beyond the individual enterprise's problems [18]. This fact makes much more difficult to measure performance of collaborative networks from both a tangible and intangible point of view. Measuring intellectual capital is still in its early steps, as highlighted above and, at the collaborative ambit, even more.

Some authors have recently dealt with the issue of measuring performance at collaborative contexts [18, 19, 20, 21, 22]. However, none of these works have deeply stated how to measure IC at collaborative networks levels. However, by bringing up the main conclusions together, it is possible to affirm that it is still lacked a method that should:

- Establish the linkage between the tangible and the intangible assets of the CN. This is such a difficult task but it needs to be done in order that CN decision-makers will be able to clearly know to what extent the achievement of a certain degree of IC within the CN is impacting over the fulfillment of the CN's strategic objectives. This could be done by applying either subjective (surveys, Multi-Criteria Decision-Aid Techniques) or objective techniques (statistical techniques analyzing historical data from the CN).
- Consider the specific requirements of IC in CN as compared to individual enterprises. Nowadays, individual enterprises take part in several supply chains/CNs and, therefore, it is very likely that some of these CNs will have contradictory objectives. Then, the decision-making mechanisms of each individual enterprise are internal and not known to a single CN. Such a lack of knowledge of how the individual enterprise is going to decide can be a serious barrier. Besides, contradictory objectives will lead to discussions within the CN and ways that will lead to consensus should be waved. Some collaborative factors have been mentioned above and these are of particular relevance to CN. How to deal with them in different scenarios and regarding IC is still lacked.
- From the last one, it would be desirable to find out to what extent are linked together both different IC intensity degrees and the achievement of one or more important collaborative factors. For instance, to study how different levels of IC in two enterprises of a CN affects to their cycles of trust-distrust.

To sum up, it is possible to affirm that, as result of the analysis of the identified gaps on the measurement of the intangible assets, a new approach is necessary at both the individual enterprise and the collaborative network context with the aim of improving this research field.

4 Conclusions

Recently, the thematic of Intellectual Capital has emerged as a key issue to analyse and evaluate the intangible assets of organizations. Both practitioners and academics agree on the fact that before to measure Intellectual Capital, it is necessary to find a common definition of what Intellectual Capital is. Then, this paper firstly presents the main Intellectual Capital definitions. Then, it highlights the main advantages of measuring Intellectual Capital in organisations and, extensively, in collaborative networks, concluding that there is still a huge research field to be filled in on this area.

References

1. Penrose, E.T.: The theory of the growth of the firm. John Wiley, New York (1959)
2. Edvinsson, L., Malone, M.S.: IC: the Proven Way to Establish Your Company's Real Value by Measuring Its Hidden Values. Piatkus, London (1997)
3. Sveiby, K.E.: The New Organizational Wealth: Managing & Measuring Knowledge-Based Assets. Berrett-Koehler Publishers, Inc., San Francisco (1997)
4. MERITUM Guidelines. Guidelines for Managing and Reporting on Intangibles, Madrid (2002)
5. International Accounting Standards Board (IASB). Intangible Assets, International Accounting Standards No. 38 revised. IASB, London (2004)
6. Marr, B.: Perspectives on IC: Multidisciplinary Insights into Management, Measurement, and Reporting. Elsevier, Boston (2005)
7. Hall, R.: The strategic analysis of intangible resources. Strategic Management Journal 2, 135–137 (1992)
8. Edvinsson, L., Sullivan, P.H.: Developing a model for managing intellectual capital. European Management Journal 14, 356–365 (1996)
9. Brooking, A.: IC: Core Assets for the Third Millennium Enterprise. Thompson Business Press, London (1996)
10. Roos, J., Roos, G., Dragonetti, N.C., Edvinsson, L.: IC: Navigating the New Business Landscape. Macmillan, London (1997)
11. Stewart, T.A.: IC: The New Wealth of Organisations. Doubleday/Currency, New York (1997)
12. Bontis, N., Dragonetti, N.C., Jacobson, K., Roos, G.: The knowledge toolbox: a review of the tools available to measure and manage intangible resources. European Management Journal 17, 391–402 (1999)
13. Kannan, G., Aulbur, W.G.: IC: Measurement effectiveness. Journal of IC 5, 389–413 (2004)
14. Nordika Project. Measuring and Reporting IC: Experiences, Issues, and Prospects. OECD, Paris (2002)
15. Kaplan, R.S., Norton, D.P.: The Balanced Scorecard – Measures that Drive Performance. Harvard Business Review, 71–79 (January/February 1992)

16. Lynch, R.L., Cross, K.F.: Measure Up! The Essential Guide to Measuring Business Performance. Mandarin, London (1991)
17. Kaplan, R.S., Norton, D.P.: Measuring the Strategic Readiness of Intangible Assets. Harvard Business Review 82, 167–176 (2004)
18. Alfaro Saiz, J.J., Rodriguez-Rodriguez, R., Ortiz Bas, A., Verdecho, M.J.: An information architecture for a performance management framework by collaborating SMEs. Computers in Industry 61, 676–685 (2010)
19. Busi, M., Bititci, U.S.: Collaborative performance management: present gaps and future research. International Journal of Productivity and Performance Management 55, 7–25 (2006)
20. Angerhofer, B.J., Angelides, M.C.: A model and a performance measurement system for collaborative supply chains. Decision Support Systems 42, 283–301 (2006)
21. Gaiardelli, P., Saccani, N., Songini, L.: Performance measurement of the after-sales service network – Evidence from the automotive industry. Computers in Industry 58, 698–708 (2007)
22. Gruat, F.A., La Forme, V., Campagne, J.P.: A Framework to analyse Collaborative Performance. Computers in Industry 58, 687–697 (2007)

Social Capital and Knowledge Sharing – Lessons Learned

Gunilla Widén

Information Studies, School of Business and Economics at Åbo Akademi University, Fänriksgatan 3 B, 20500 Åbo, Finland
gunilla.widen@abo.fi

Abstract. Social capital is put forward as a suitable theoretical framework to explain knowledge sharing mechanisms in organizations. The aim of this paper is to summarize lessons learned from different contexts where the social capital dimensions have been used to explain information and knowledge sharing. The contexts studied are mainly within business organizations, virtual worlds, and higher education. The dimensions of social capital have been found useful when exploring knowledge sharing practices. The studies illuminate important aspects on how the combination of structures, relations and contents support sharing. The different cases also underline the importance of the *contextual dimension*, the role of the social capital dimensions are focused differently depending on context.

Keywords: Social capital, Knowledge sharing, Knowledge Management, Business organization, Virtual worlds, Higher education.

1 Introduction

Social capital has been put forward to explain knowledge sharing and has been used as a theoretical framework to illuminate motives and enablers of information and knowledge sharing [1, 2, 3, 4]. Social capital provides a framework explaining knowledge sharing mechanisms through the dimensions of structures, relations, and contents. This perspective illuminates how social and information phenomena are anchored in each other [4]. A larger research project at Åbo Akademi University has focused social capital and information behaviour [5] and has resulted in a number of empirical studies where social capital dimensions have been used to study knowledge sharing from an information science perspective.

The aim of this paper is to summarize lessons learned so far from the project and in collaboration with other researchers in the field. Also other relevant studies and literature on social capital and knowledge sharing is included. The contexts studied are mainly within business organizations, virtual worlds, and higher education. The dimensions of social capital have been found useful when exploring knowledge sharing practices. The studies bring important aspects to our attention on how the combination of structures, relations and contents support sharing.

2 The Social Capital Framework

Social capital is associated with benefits coming from and changing with social relations and networks [6]. According to a often cited definition by Nahapiet and Ghoshal [7, p 243] social capital is

L.M. Camarinha-Matos et al. (Eds.): PRO-VE 2011, IFIP AICT 362, pp. 48–57, 2011.

"The sum of actual and potential resources embedded within, available through, and derived from the network of relationships possessed by an individual or social unit. Social capital thus comprises both the network and the assets that may be mobilized through that network".

Social capital is mainly studied on a society level [8] and refers to enablers like networks, norms, and trust that help individuals to act together more effectively towards common aims [9]. In the organizational context social capital focuses on information as a resource and e.g. inter-unit resource exchange [10]. Social capital is also studied on an individual level, underlining what individuals gain from networks like status and opportunities [11]. Connected to information and knowledge sharing social capital is relevant while information behaviour patterns are anchored in the individual and organisational structures where people interact. Information seeking takes often place in collaborative settings and therefore the social aspects play an important role. Contextual and social factors affect group members' physical activities and their cognitive and emotional experiences with relevance to information sharing [12]. Therefore, empirical studies on information seekers within their social context focus on practices rather than on the individuals' information behaviour. The analysis shift from cognitive to social, looking at the information seekers within their social context where connections and interacting with sources are underlined [13, 14]. The social capital perspective helps us to explore the context in which information sharing takes place. It provides us with a framework for the hidden motives of information sharing, giving information behaviour its social context. In order to manage multiple aspects on knowledge sharing mechanisms the dimensions of social capital are suitable tools while they describe structures, relations, and contents (see table 1).

Table 1. Dimensions of social capital according to the definition by Nahapiet and Ghoshal [7]

Dimensions of social capital and aspects focused in the different dimensions		
Structural dimension	**Cognitive (content) dimension**	**Relational dimension**
Network ties	Shared codes, language	Norms
Network configuration	Shared narratives	Trust
Appropriable organization		Obligations
		Identification

The *structure dimension* is about the access to other actors, individual and corporate [15]. This structure is necessary for information sharing and development and use of social capital in an organization. The structure influences the two other dimensions of social capital [7, 15]. Social interaction in structures are channels for information and resource flows [10]. This dimension reflects the impersonal properties of the network relations and a network tie is the fundamental structural concept, the basic element of communication networks [16].

The *relational dimension* is about expectations and obligations where trust is the most important relational feature [15]. Trust is needed in order to share what you know. This dimension influences access to other parties in the structure, it underlines the expected value through exchange, and the motivation of parties to engage in knowledge creation [7, 15]. Trust is the most studied concept of social capital [17]. As trusting relationships develop inside a network, actors build up reputations of trustworthiness. There are different levels of trustworthiness which result in different levels of resource exchange and combination [10].

Finally, the *cognitive (or content) dimension* is both the foundation for social capital as well as a key mechanism in generating further organizational goals like intellectual capital [15]. This dimension is a visible condition necessary for formation and utilization of social capital. Communication is the mechanism whereby the available stock of social capital can be accessed and utilized to further organizational goals and objectives [15].

In the following the dimensions of social capital are studied in three different contexts; business, virtual, and higher education in order to illuminate information and knowledge sharing mechanisms.

3 Social Capital and Knowledge Sharing in Business Organizations

There is a wide repertoire of studies on social capital in corporate research. The interest in social capital lies in the rise of the knowledge-based organization [18]. Social capital and social networks are seen as giving financial advantage. Firms benefit from social capital because it facilitates cooperation and coordination, which minimize transaction costs [19]. Social capital unifies shared resources which are accessed based on relationships [20]. This is the main aspect of research concerned with social capital in the business organisation literature.

Social capital affects business organizations internally, promoting greater coordination among people and collaboration between units. Further, trust is the foundation for cooperation internally as well as externally. Companies that are working together in a joint effort and that have established trustful relationships are able to develop deeper relationships with one another, which can be accessed in the future for other business projects. However, managing social capital explicitly is complicated while social capital formation is more a local process and involves social practices [2].

In a study in two Finnish companies [21] it is shown how the structural and relational dimensions of social capital interplay supporting knowledge sharing for common aims. The studied companies are different where one case is a claims handling department in insurance business involving routine-based work and the other case is a biotechnology firm defined as an expert organization. Studying the social capital dimensions in these cases show that building a common knowledge base is better realised in the claims handling unit where the personal knowledge and expertise is brought to the group systematically through weekly meetings and a functioning personal network structure. The group has a high level of trust within their structures and information and knowledge has become a collective resource. This group has however better circumstances to develop the structures that are needed. The biotechnology field is a hectic environment and the importance of communicative ability and trust is more highlighted. Trust has another role where information and knowledge are typically personal resources that are brought to a collective attention on demand. The individuals must trust that they get crucial information from each other whenever needed.

This is also shown in business online environments. In a case study by Hall and Widén-Wulff [22] it was clear that the exchange of information in online environments is highly dependent on social relationships. Effective sharing of information contents is not happening without trusting relationships although there are technical infrastructure and financial rewards on offer.

Knowledge Management initiatives must be brought to the local context where the human and social processes underpin the formal structures enabling information sharing. These are important insights in the management of organisations and especially in the management of expert organisations where the individual knowledge base is important to bring into the common awareness. The online perspective put additional challenges to Knowledge Management and underlines the importance of the relational dimension of social capital even more.

4 Social Capital and Knowledge Sharing in Virtual Worlds

Using the social capital framework to study information and knowledge sharing in virtual communities and contexts is useful while social capital is the basis for collective action and it helps to understand what the motivations are to participate in the community and what it is that people get for their participation. Social capital has been studied in different kinds of virtual communities, such as virtual learning communities [23, 24] and social networking sites [25]. According to Blanchard and Horan [26] social capital can increase in virtual communities that are based on existing physical communities. Boundaries that have separated real and virtual are fading and the social actors move more and more within and among different domains, converting forms of capital into one another [27].

Södergård [24] has studied young people's use of the Internet during their free time and participation in virtual community (Lunarstorm). In this case possible tools for developing social capital in that context were studied. It was shown that the virtual community is of importance for young people's social capital. The structural dimension describes the pattern of interaction between the players. Social structures are more obvious in virtual context than in real life. Trust was developed through entries in the so called guestbooks in the community and had an impact on relationships between friends in reality. The young persons interacted with their friends in real life also in the virtual community. In the content/cognitive dimension the common language was underlined. Here the young persons experienced that they could use their own language. The knowledge base created in the virtual community is of value in that it is embedded in a social structure and accessible to those who are members of the structure. The virtual community offered additional aspects to all three dimensions of social capital that is not available in real life. Based on this study it can be concluded that a virtual community can be seen as a complement and tool for developing social capital among young people [24].

In a study by Huvila et al. [28] it was shown that the virtual world Second Life clearly had key elements for generating and fostering social capital although the existence of social capital in Second Life and real life respectively do not completely match. Socialising is an important motivation for participating in Second Life and Second Life is an environment, which fosters the accumulation of social capital. Most of the activities the respondents mentioned were meetings, get-togethers, conferences or informal meetings with people and colleagues. Individuals in Second Life form networks and have friends they meet in the virtual world and the more they engage in 'production', the more they have social capital. There are clear codes of conduct and behaviour expressed in form of positive and negative experiences of behaviour. The mechanisms of trust are mostly based on judgments made on social behaviour rather than on Second Life specific indicators such as the type of the account of the other resident. Second Life gives access to extended social networks beyond the real life and as the findings indicate, increases both the amount and quality of these connections. Any further conclusions may not be done based on this study [28] while it is limited by the relatively small sample with an unknown bias. A larger study and case studies on considerably different samples of Second Life residents are needed to get a deeper understanding of the nature of social capital in Second Life.

In an interview study of players in the multiplayer online game (World of Warcraft) it was shown how players formed different kinds of social networks in the game where rules, boundaries, and norms were formed. It was clear that social capital was created in the process where the players formed these social networks with different kinds of goals in mind (a wide range of practical benefits for accomplishing game goals). For players who knew each other from before the online game was an important way to maintain and pursue their relationships. For others it was also an possibility to bridging social capital [29].

In summary, the research conducted so far shows that virtual communities and virtual worlds foster social capital among the members of the world or community. The emergence of social capital in virtual communities has implications from the information sharing point of view. Social capital has been shown to be important in engaging users to make significant contributions in virtual communities. Existence of social capital can be seen as an indicator of a success of information sharing online, and simultaneously the understanding of social capital and its formation can be used to understand why some collaborative efforts of sharing information and constructing common knowledge resources succeed and other fail. Again the relational dimension is heavily defined through trust, identity, and roles. In the relational dimension the underlying motives for sharing are stressed. In earlier studies it has been shown that exchange of information in online environments is highly dependent on social relationships. Although social infrastructure often starts in the face-to-face environment, online techniques and Web platforms support the development of relational ties through structures and shared codes [22].

5 Social Capital and Knowledge Sharing in Higher Education

Social capital in the context of higher education has not been studied very much. The studies are mainly looking at social aspects of learning which of course touches upon the same interest. How students interact in their networks and how social capital can be beneficial in students work has been of interest lately especially in online environments. There are a number of studies looking at blogs, wikis and social networks as important tools of support for learning in different environments [30].

Hall and Widén-Wulff [22] have studied social aspects of information sharing in two cases in the context of higher education. They underline that it is clear that the exchange of information in online environments is highly dependent on social relationships. Studying a group of undergraduate students it was shown that time spent in shared classes accounted for friendship ties (social capital). These, in turn, yielded the highest levels of online information exchange. In the other case, master students attending a distance course, showed that trust between the students in the online environment was first established and grew from face-to-face interactions. In addition, students were unwilling to share the benefit of their strong relationships with group outsiders. Further evidence of the importance of social factors is underlined in the power of social incentives to information share, as opposed to hard rewards, such as the expectation of the straightforward award of a mark in the case of undergraduate students. Social factors affecting information sharing behaviour in online environments in higher education depends on a complex mix of factors. These include the social capital shared amongst actors, the level of trust on which this is based, the potential for reciprocal transactions, and the management of incentives structures. In a later study on university students in blogging communities where blogs were used as a tool to encourage the interaction between students Hall et al. [31] showed that social reward is a key to sharing, a kind of gift economy, and therefore an important part of how the social network structures are built among students. Blogs increased the reflective engagement with teaching material and there was also a higher level of shared peer support between class members [32].

Tötterman [33, 34] has studied social capital and information sharing on an organizational level in a university context (Finnish university faculty). In this study, the main focus was on the interdepartmental information sharing, i.e. the interviewees' communication with their faculty colleagues from other departments. The university system - both internationally and in Finland - is undergoing some rather great changes (e.g. educational, financial, and organizational), and the effects from social capital, e.g. synergy, reduced transaction costs and intellectual capital, could be seen as crucial to handling these changes efficiently. In the study it was shown that a lack of organizational social capital within the faculty's interdepartmental relations had effects on the faculty's information sharing climate. The findings from this study indicated that information sharing tends to work more efficiently within the departments, the local bounded networks and the faculty external networks. The interviewees themselves stressed some important incentives for a successful information sharing climate, such as working in the same building, personal friendship and scholarly closeness. Most interviewees tended to underline the existence of formal and informal network structures, trust and an open communication climate within one's own department and in some cases with one's closest neighboring departments. In these environments, the signs of active collaborative information sharing are most obvious.

Lessons learned from the context of higher education show that social capital is a useful framework to gain insights into information sharing mechanisms. The framework of social capital sheds light and characterizes the incentives for information sharing in a very distinct manner. The findings show that in the studied university faculty that there existed many different forms of cultures with their own kinds of social capital, which in turn affects their information sharing activities. The relational dimension is highlighted in this context.

6 Discussion and Lessons Learned

The role of social capital in knowledge sharing is clear. Social construction of knowledge is crucial and is depending on the environment. The organizational environment is a combination of structures, relations, and contents supporting knowledge sharing in different ways. How these dimensions interplay and support sharing is illuminated through three main contexts studied through several cases, that is business organizations, virtual communities and virtual worlds, and higher education and university context. This overview underlines that the *contextual perspective* in information and knowledge sharing is very important. The dimensions of social capital put forward especially the roles of structures and relations which are promoted differently depending on context.

In table 2 we can see that different dimensions of social capital are underlined and a challenge depending on the studied contexts.

Studying cases of business organizations it was clear that depending on the nature of work and work tasks different dimensions of social capital are promoted and therefore affecting information and knowledge sharing. Knowledge on an organizational level is created in conversations, collaboration, and different social contexts [35]. One of the problems of knowledge work and knowledge management is the content dimension, that is the difficulty in getting people to share their tacit knowledge. The awareness of the importance of functioning network structures and relational factors is an important prerequisite for sharing also tacit knowledge. Accessibility and common language also motivates people to contribute. In this context new social and interactive tools can support sharing, enabling people to create ideas, accumulate knowledge, create networks, share and manage information [36, 37].

The virtual community context offered additional aspects to all three dimensions of social capital that is not available in real life. This is a complement and tool for developing social capital. Open source technologies give the sharing visible structures, underlining the structural dimension in this context. The content dimension is defined as shared goals, common experience, language and knowledge. Shared meaning and collective knowledge are key aspects. The relational dimension is seen as a challenge where interaction between virtual and real life seems important for the development of trust.

Table 2. Social capital dimensions in the studied contexts

Studied context	Most focused dimension	Challenge
Business	Relational and Structural	Content dimension
Virtual	Structural	Relational
Higher education	Relational	Structural

In the higher education context the findings show that in the studied university faculty that there existed many different forms of cultures with their own kinds of social capital, which in turn affects their information sharing activities. Local contexts and local networks are stronger places for knowledge sharing. Social factors affecting information sharing behaviour among students in online environments in higher education depends on a complex mix of factors. These include the social capital shared amongst actors, the level of trust on which this is based, the potential for reciprocal transactions, and the management of incentives structures. In a later study on university students in blogging communities where blogs were used as a tool to encourage the interaction between students Hall et al. [31] showed that social reward is a key to sharing, a kind of gift economy, and therefore an important part of how the social network structures are built among students which is a challenging task.

Understanding how social capital works is crucial when creating new intellectual capital in an organization. Social capital refers to both norms and networks as facilitating collective action and encouraging cooperative behaviour. Especially the relational and structural dimensions interplay with emphasis on relation dimension as a key enabler of sharing. Structures give access but relations are needed to actually share. This is also underlined by Wilson [38] who points out that sharing happens more likely where the individual experience benefits from sharing and trusts the person sharing with. It is crucial to be aware of the contextual perspective, how social capital is nurtured, while it directly affects how information and knowledge is accessed and shared. For effective information and knowledge sharing to happen there is a need to know the network, how to access it and what kinds of benefits there are within the network. KM initiatives must be brought to the local context where the human and social processes underpin the formal structures enabling information sharing. These are important insights in the management of organisations and especially in the management of expert organisations where the individual knowledge base is important to bring into the common awareness. These insights are further discussed in combination of suitable tools for supporting information and knowledge sharing in a business organisation.

7 Conclusions

Social capital has been suggested as a suitable theoretical framework to explain knowledge sharing mechanisms in organizations. This paper has summarized lessons learned from different contexts where the social capital dimensions have been used to explain information and knowledge sharing. The studies illuminate important aspects on how the combination of structures, relations and contents support sharing. The different cases also underline the importance of the *contextual perspective*, the role of the social capital dimensions are focused differently depending on context. Especially the relational dimension is underlined in all three contexts, both as a prerequisite and a challenge. The importance of trust can't be neglected when discussing knowledge sharing. Also the aspects of benefits and social rewards have been pointed out in several cases underlining that knowledge sharing is a kind of gift economy. Managing social capital and knowledge sharing is a complex task but the awareness of the different dimensions of social capital underpinning information sharing is prerequisite for effective knowledge management.

Acknowledgements. This work has been supported by a grant from the Academy of Finland.

References

[1] Davenport, E., et al.: Managing social capital as knowledge management - some specification and presentation issues. In Humanizing information technology: from ideas to bits and back. In: Todd, R.J. (ed.) Proceedings of the 66th ASIST Annual Meeting, Humanizing Information Technology: from Ideas to Bits and Back, pp. 101–108. Information Today, Medford (2003)
[2] Davenport, E., Snyder, H.W.: Managing social capital. Annual Review of Information Science and Technology 39, 517–550 (2005)
[3] Ginman, M.: Social capital as a communicative paradigm. Health Informatics Journal 9(1), 57–64 (2003)
[4] Widén-Wulff, G., Ginman, M.: Explaining knowledge sharing in organizations through the dimensions of social capital. J. of Information Science 30(5), 448–458 (2004)
[5] Widén-Wulff, G., et al.: Information behaviour meets social capital: a conceptual model. Journal of Information Science 34(3), 346–355 (2008)
[6] Adler, A., Kwon, S.: Social capital: prospects for a new concept. Academy of Mangement Review 27(1), 17–40 (2002)
[7] Nahapiet, J., Ghoshal, S.: Social Capital, Intellectual Capital, and the Organizational Advantage. Academy of Management Review 23(3), 242–266 (1998)
[8] Putnam, R.D.: Bowling alone: the collapse and revival of American community. Simon & Schuster, New York (2000)
[9] Baron, S., Field, J., Schuller, T.: Social capital - critical perspectives. Oxford U.P., Oxford (2000)
[10] Tsai, W., Ghoshal, S.: Social capital and value creation: the role of intrafirm networks. Academy of Management Journal 42(4), 464–476 (1998)
[11] Burt, R.S.: Social capital: theory and research. De Gruyter, New York (2001)
[12] Hyldegård, J.: Collaborative information behaviour: exploring Kuhlthau's information search process model in a group-based educational setting. Information Processing & Management 42(1), 276–298 (2006)
[13] Mackenzie, M.L.: Information gathering revealed within the social network of line-managers. In: Proceedings of the 66th Annual Meeting of the American Society for Information Science and Technology, pp. 85–94. Information Today, Medford (2003)
[14] Hyldegård, J.: Collaborative information behaviour - exploring Kuhlthau's Information Search Process model in a group-based educational setting. Information Processing & Management (2004) (in press)
[15] Hazleton, V., Kennan, W.: Social capital: reconceptualizing the bottom line. Corporate communications 5(2), 81–86 (2000)
[16] Upadhyayula, R.S., Kumar, R.: Social capital as an antecedent of absorptive capacity of firms. In: DRUID Summer Conference 2004: Industrial Dynamics, Innovation and Development, Elsinore, Denmark (2004)
[17] Portes, A.: Social capital: its origins and applications in modern sociology. Annual Review of Sociology 24, 1–24 (1998)
[18] Lesser, E.L.: Leveragning social capital in organizations. In: Lesser, E.L. (ed.) Knowledge and Social Capital: Foundations and Applications, pp. 3–16. Butterworth Hernemann, Butterworths (2000)

[19] PovertyNet, Social capital and firms (2004), `http://www.worldbank.org/poverty/scapital/sources/firm1.htm`
[20] Tymon, W.G., Stumpf, S.A.: Social capital in the success of knowledge workers. Career Development International 8(1), 12–20 (2003)
[21] Widén-Wulff, G.: Challenges of Knowledge Sharing in Practice: a Social Approach. Chandos Publishing, Oxford (2007)
[22] Hall, H., Widén-Wulff, G.: Social exchange, social capital and information sharing in online environments: lessons from three case studies. In: Huotari, M.-L., Davenport, E. (eds.) From Information Provision to Knowledge Production, pp. 73–86. University of Oulu, Oulu (2008)
[23] Daniel, B., Schwier, R.A., McCalla, G.: Social capital in virtual learning communities and distributed communities. Canadian Journal of Learning and Technology 29(3) (2003)
[24] Södergård, P.: Virtuell gemenskap: ett informationsvetenskapligt perspektiv på ungdomars cyberkultur. Åbo Akademi U.P., Åbo (2007)
[25] Ellison, N.B., Steinfield, C., Lampe, C.: The benefits of Facebook "Friends": social capital and college students' use of online social network sites. Journal of Computer-Mediated Communication 12(4) (2007)
[26] Blanchard, A., Horan, T.: Virtual communities and social capital. Social Science Computer Review 16(3), 293–307 (1998)
[27] Malaby, T.: Parlaying value: capital in and beyond virtual worlds. Games and Culture 1(2), 141–162 (2006)
[28] Huvila, I., et al.: Social Capital in Second Life. Online Information Review 34(3), 295–316 (2010)
[29] Williams, D., et al.: From tree house to barracks: the social life of guilds in World of Warcraft. Games and Culture 1(4), 338–361 (2008)
[30] Craig, E.M.: Changing paradigms: managed learning environments and Web 2.0. Campus-Wide Information Systems 24(3), 152–161 (2007)
[31] Hall, H., Widén, G., Paterson, L.: Not what you know, nor who you know, but who you know already: examining online information sharing behaviours in a blogging environment through the lens of social exchange theory. Libri 60, 117–128 (2010)
[32] Hall, H., Davison, B.: Social software as support in hybrid learning environments: the value of the blog as a tool for reflective learning and peer support. Library & Information Science Research 29, 163–187 (2007)
[33] Tötterman, A.-K., Widén-Wulff, G.: What a social capital perspective can bring to the understanding of information sharing in a university context. Information Research: an International Electronic Journal 12(4) (2007)
[34] Tötterman, A.-K.: Kommunikationsdimensionen i socialt kapital: en studie av informationsdelning, förtroende och social identitet vid en universitetsfakultet. Meddelanden från Ekonomisk-statsvetenskapliga fakulteten vid Åbo Akademi Åbo Akademi, Åbo (2008)
[35] Avram, G.: At the crossroads of Knowledge Management and Social Software. The Electronic Journal of Knowledge Management 4(1), 1–10 (2006)
[36] Brady, M.: Blogging: personal participation in public knowledge-building on the web. University of Essex, Chimera Institute for Social & Tech. Research, Colchester (2005)
[37] Hasan, H., Pfaff, C.C.: The Wiki: an environment to revolutionise employees' interaction with corporate knowledge. In: OZCHI, Sydney, Australia (2006)
[38] Wilson, T.D.: Information sharing: an exploration of the literature and some propsitions. Information Research: an International Electronic Journal 15(4) (2010), `http://informationr.net/ir/15-4/paper440.html`

Establishing Knowledge Management as an Important Factor to Develop Social Capital for Collaborative Networks

Rolando Vargas Vallejos, Janaina Macke, and Kadígia Faccin

University of Caxias do Sul, Graduate Program in Business Administration
95070-560 Caxias do Sul, Brazil
rvvallej@ucs.br, jmacke@terra.com.br, kadigia@msn.com

Abstract. Collaborative Networked Organizations are being considered a response to the economic market pressures. Some research projects try to identify the key factors that enable the growth and survival of these collaborative networks. One strategy is to create Virtual Organization Breeding Environments in order to prepare organizations and persons to rapidly respond to a collaboration opportunity. In those breeding environments is possible to develop endogenous resources that permit collaborative practices, like social capital. The present paper discusses the importance of Social Capital and its relationship with Knowledge Management for Virtual Organization Breeding Environments. Knowledge is created during the processes of collaborative networks that rarely are documented and reused. Implementing an effective Knowledge Management method will motivate to increase Social Capital. The present work points out that knowledge sharing is important to develop Social Capital in three Brazilian collaborative networks called VIRFEBRAS, APROVALE and APROBELO.

Keywords: Collaborative Networked Organization, Virtual Organization Breeding Environment, Social Capital, Knowledge Management.

1 Introduction

Collaborative Networked Organizations (CNOs) are considered a key issue for economic growth. CNOs are new organizational forms of collaboration such as Virtual Organizations, Virtual Enterprises, Professional Virtual Communities and other emergent forms of collaboration, which are regarded as the answer to the increasing need of strong adaptability to a constantly changing economic context.

In recent years, many international projects have contributed to this scientific discipline. In one of these international projects, called ECOLEAD, the Virtual Organization (VO) creation process is considered to happen in the context of a VO Breeding Environment (VBE). A VBE is a long-term collaborative network composed of organizations and specialists prepared to collaborate and thus rapidly respond to a collaboration opportunity or necessity. Camarinha-Matos and Afsarmanesh [1] affirm that VBE creation and VO creation are different processes, triggered by different motivations. A VBE is created as a long-term association and

L.M. Camarinha-Matos et al. (Eds.): PRO-VE 2011, IFIP AICT 362, pp. 58–65, 2011.

its members are recruited from the universe of organizations according to certain criteria. According with Romero et al. [2], a VBE is a long-term strategic alliance of organizations aimed at offering the necessary conditions to support the rapid configuration of a VO. For that reason, VBE focuses on creating an adequate environment for the establishment of cooperation agreements, common operation principles, common interoperable infrastructures, common ontologies, and mutual trust among others.

This paper presents a proposal to focus the implementation of Knowledge Management as a strategic action to form and consolidate a VBE. A Knowledge Management method will create an environment to develop Social Capital between the VBE members. That affirmation is the result of two research projects developed by the Social Theory Research Group (TSO) of the University of Caxias do Sul. In both research projects the objective was to analyze the influence of Social Capital in CNOs. One project studied a mould and die CNO called VIRFEBRAS, and the other project studied a Brazilian wine cluster, two CNOs called APROVALE and APROBELO.

2 Collaborative Networked Organizations

The concept of networked organizations is not new, but its use has been influenced by changes in politics, economy and society. Some strong arguments may explain the dissemination of the use of the network concept. In an economical perspective, a networked organization may be an answer because of the intense competition caused by a globalized economy [3], [4]. In a political perspective, a networked organization seems to be an answer to the fiscal crisis and to the erosion of the contemporaneous Government supremacy [3].

In the last two decades a special attention has been given to Collaborative Networked Organization (CNO), considered as one of the emergent models of networked organizations. A CNO is constituted by several entities (e.g., organizations and specialists) that are autonomous, geographically distributed, and heterogeneous in terms of their operating environment, culture, social capital, and goals. These entities collaborate to achieve common goals, and their interactions are supported by Information and Communication Technologies. Unlike other networked organizations, in CNOs collaboration is an intentional property that derives from the shared belief that together the network members can achieve goals that would not be possible or would have a higher cost if attempted by them individually [5].

Some examples of CNOs are Virtual Organizations, Virtual Enterprises, and Professional Virtual Communities. Camarinha-Matos and Afsarmanesh [1] state that the Virtual Organization (VO) creation process is considered to happen in the context of a VO Breeding Environment (VBE). For the authors a VBE is a long-term collaborative association that is composed of organizations prepared to collaborate and thus rapidly respond to an opportunity or necessity. VBE creation and VO creation are different processes, triggered by different motivations. A VBE is created as a long-term association and its members belong to the universe of organizations according to certain established criteria. A VO is a temporary organization triggered by a specific business/collaboration opportunity and its members are primarily selected from the VBE.

Collaborative environments are traditionally established within a geographic region, as industrial districts, with the advantage of having a common business culture and a sense of community, but this restriction may be overcome by VBEs. VBEs incorporate the involvement of geographically distributed organizations, and this assumption overlooks some important obstacles as: How to quickly establish an inter-operable collaboration infrastructure? How to build trust among organizations, which is the base for any collaboration? How to develop and agree on the common principles of sharing and working together? [5]. Noticeably, most of these obstacles are related to human behaviour.

A large number of research projects in CNOs are carried out worldwide, and a growing number of practical cases have been reported. CNOs are complex systems, emerging in many forms in different application domains, and require the contribution from multiple disciplines. Camarinha-Matos and Afsarmanesh [6] have raised the need of modelling for understanding, managing, simulating/ predicting the behaviour of CNOs. As a first attempt to reach a comprehensive modelling framework for CNO, the authors propose four dimensions, which are: structural, componential, functional and behavioural.

The structural dimension addresses the CNO composition considering its constituting elements (participants and their relationships), the roles performed by those elements. The componential dimension focuses on the individual tangible/intangible elements in the CNO's network, e.g. the resource composition such as human elements, software and hardware resources, information and knowledge repositories. The functional dimension addresses the execution of time-sequenced flows of operations (processes and procedures) related to the operational phase of the CNO's life cycle. The behavioural dimension addresses the principles, policies, and governance rules that drive or constrain the behaviour of the CNO members.

Following the same line of work, Romero and collaborators [2] propose a VBE reference model and its instantiation methodology considering two sub-spaces: endogenous elements (VBE inside) and exogenous interactions (VBE outside). The authors identify the key business processes required to support and facilitate the VBE management activities needed to be performed during the VBE lifecycle, considering VBE fundamental processes and VBE background processes. One of these VBE fundamental processes is "Trust Management", which refers to Social Capital.

3 Social Capital as a Key Factor for VBE

Social Capital is a component of the Social Theory that is being considered as a key element for the development of human and economic communities. Social Capital can be understood as a set of informal norms and values, common to the members of a specific group, which allows cooperation among them.

Social Capital produces socio-cultural goods in the form of emotions, feelings and relationships [7]. High levels of Social Capital enable better use of development opportunities, due to increased information flows that facilitate the action [8], [9]. Thus, confidence, stability, durability of relationships and the network density are key elements to high levels of trust and cooperation. These qualities also influence the clarity and visibility of mutual obligations [10], [8].

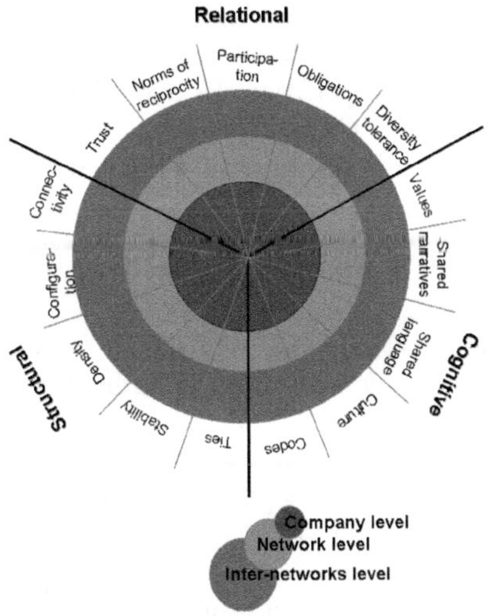

Fig. 1. Social Capital dimensions and their elements [13]

Studying Social Capital and its importance in the creation of intellectual capital, Nahapiet and Ghoshal [11] proposed three Social Capital dimensions, which are: structural, relational and cognitive. The structural dimension analyzes the presence or not of relationships between the actors, the configuration or morphology of the network, describing the standards of connections, through variables as density, connectivity network configuration, stability and ties. The relational dimension describes the kind of personal relationship, developed through a history of interactions [12]. This dimension focuses on aspects that influence behaviour, such as respect and friendship, which are crucial for sociability, acceptance and prestige. Two actors can occupy similar positions in a network, however if their emotional and personal attitudes differ, their actions will be different in many aspects. Therefore it involves a behavioural component, which is revealed through facets as trust and distrust, norms, obligations and expectations, participation and diversity tolerance [10], [11], [9]. The cognitive dimension of Social Capital refers to the resources that emanate shared visions, interpretations and systems of meaning, mainly codes and narratives, shared values and other cultural elements. Figure 1 represents these three Social Capital dimensions and their essential elements.

For Macke and collaborators [13], increasing the Social Capital level in a CNO will facilitate member's access to opportunities, and initiatives for collaborative action. Therefore, Social Capital can be considered the basic resource for a competitive strategy based on cooperation. For the Social Capital flow between organizations, four main conditions are necessary, which are: time, interaction, interdependence and closure [11].

A CNO can be more competitive and have success when investing in two key elements, which are organizational culture and relationship among persons. Elements as trust, networks of relationship and sharing norms are topics that have been discussed by researchers from different areas. The concept became known from Robert Putnam's studies of two decades ago. Putnam relates the results of more than twenty years study about Italian society, in which the initial topic was to understand the differences of development of north and south Italy. The author concludes that the disparities between institutional performance and development of the regions result from a major presence of Social Capital. The author's conclusion had a strong impact on the scientific community, and was later corroborated by other studies [9], [14].

4 Research Projects Evaluating Social Capital in CNOs

The Social Theory Research Group (TSO) of the University of Caxias do Sul, Brazil developed two research projects analyzing the influence of Social Capital in CNOs. One project studied a mould and die CNO called VIRFEBRAS, and the other studied a Brazilian wine cluster, two CNOs called APROVALE and APROBELO.

In both research projects were developed instruments (surveys) to evaluate the inter-organizational Social Capital within a CNO. In order to develop those instruments, in an exploratory phase, semi-structured interviews, direct observation and document analysis of the CNO's members were carried out. Thus, Social Capital elements that influence the dynamics of the network were analyzed, and local aspects related to the network competitiveness, considering the Social Capital classification of Nahapiet and Ghoshal [11] were identified, which are cognitive, relational and structural.

The VIRFEBRAS CNO is a group of small and medium enterprises that work in the mould and die sector. The idea to form the CNO started in 1998, supported by the University of Caxias do Sul, with the objective to join competencies in combination with common goals, keeping the members' own identities, in order to raise more competitiveness and new business opportunities.

The results of the research project were published by Macke and collaborators [13], and one important contribution was the identification and classification of competitive CNOs variables related to the Capital Social dimensions, which is showed in Table 1.

In the second research project, the Serra Gaúcha wine cluster was studied, specifically two CNOs called APROVALE and APROBELO. Although the Serra Gaúcha cluster's production is responsible for 80% of the national wine production, the Brazilian wine industry is going through some difficulties, and for that reason collaborative networks are being created.

In order to evaluate the inter-organizational Social Capital and its relations with competitiveness of those CNOs, it was applied the survey developed in the first research project. The information was submitted to factor analysis using PCA (Principal Component Analysis), with varimax rotation and pairwise treatment (all valid observations of each variable considered) for the missing data [15].

In the case of the Brazilian wine cluster, the Social Capital is represented mainly by the relational dimension, which explains 25.60% of the total variance; the structural dimension represents 25.28% and, the cognitive dimension explains 16.48% of it [15]. The results show that the Social Capital levels are very similar, ranging from 2.40 to 3.74. Similarly, average factors were close: for the cognitive dimension, 3.37; for the structural dimension, 3.33, and for the relational one, 3.41. Therefore, we concluded that there is a high level of Social Capital in the APROVALE and APROBELO CNOs, and thus a general balance among the three dimensions.

Table 1. Inter-Organizational Social Capital items of VIRFEBRAS

Dimension	Items
Relational	When I need help, I can count on other members of the network.
	Within the network you need to be aware that no one takes advantage of the situation.
	In the formal activities of the network, I do feel part of a group.
	I feel a member of the network.
	Similarities between participants facilitate the dynamics of the network.
	Differences within the group do not affect the network.
	The members of the network always seek to work together through ideas, resources and information.
	Within the network, the members think and act in accordance with the interests of all.
	Most members of the network participate on events proposed (meetings, exhibitions, lectures, seminars, trips, etc.).
	Even if my opinion is contrary to that of most of the other members of the network, I feel comfortable to discuss it.
	The more different ideas within the network, the better.
Structural	If I need some information to take a decision, I know where to find it on the network.
	Within the network there are several opportunities to exchange information.
	The network is connected to other entities, as other networks of businesses, unions, government agencies, among others.
	The network has a hierarchical structure (president, directors and other members).
	I have contact with members of the network at least once a week.
	I also have contact with members of the network outside formal activities.
	I consider the members of the network my friends.
Cognitive	Most members know and agree with the objective of the network.
	The objective of the network is also clear to those not participating in the network.
	I participate in the network because I agree with the purpose for which it was created.
	The members of the network always share information among themselves.

Based on these results, Macke and collaborators [15] established and measured the relationship between Social Capital level and competitiveness. The Relational Social Capital showed higher correlation with Endogenous Resources Appropriation. This indicates that a better use of local characteristics comes from the existence of ties among network participants. These results confirm the initial thesis that Social Capital is closely linked to competitiveness improvement, and the resource-based view defends that resources clearly provide competitive opportunities and high returns.

Something relevant that appears in both research projects was the relationship between knowledge creation and Social Capital. As detected by Macke and collaborators [15], the continuous and dynamic process of knowledge exchange enhances to increase the level of Social Capital in CNOs. Noticeably, all three dimensions of Social Capital (cognitive, structural and relational) are based on information and knowledge sharing as a mediator for use of resources that generate improvements. This is why we understand that the implementation of a Knowledge

Management method is one of the most important actions for the success of a CNO. During the different processes of a CNO relevant knowledge is created, especially tacit knowledge. The idea is to transform tacit into explicit knowledge in order to maximize the capitalization and dissemination of it.

5 Conclusions

The research projects results support the theoretical foundations that information and knowledge sharing is one of the key benefits of Social Capital, because that information and knowledge sharing contributes to the increase of CNOs' business performance. The knowledge combination contributes to Social Capital creation through incremental or radical changes. We agree with Macke and collaborators [15] when they point out four conditions for the combination and exchange processes: (i) the opportunity to make the combination or exchange; (ii) the worthwhile interactions; (iii) the motivation (receptivity to learning and new knowledge creation); and (iv) the combination capabilities (capacity to combine knowledge and best practices).

Based on the research projects results, we conclude that:

i) developing Social Capital is fundamental for the CNOs success;
ii) in order to have higher levels of Social Capital in CNOs, it is recommended to set up VBEs;
iii) in the CNOs' four dimensions of the framework proposed by Camarinha-Matos and Afsarmanesh [6] (structural, componential, functional and behavioural), the presence of Social Capital is transversal. Observe that most of the examples of the endogenous elements in the four dimensions concern to Knowledge Management (Figure 2). The effectiveness of the CNO life cycle is going to be powered with Knowledge Management.

For that reason, we conclude that Knowledge Management is an important factor to increase the Social Capital level in CNOs. By increasing the Social Capital in a VBE, the effectiveness of the VO/VE life cycle will be more efficient.

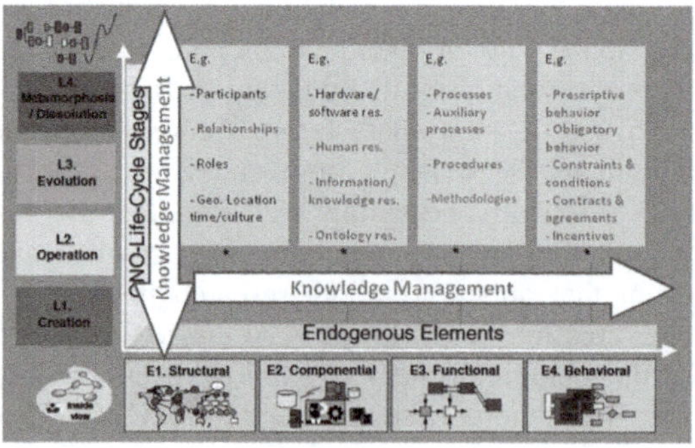

Fig. 2. The presence of Knowledge Management in the proposed framework considering the crossing of CNO life cycle and the endogenous elements perspective [6]

Acknowledgments. This work is being supported by the University of Caxias do Sul.

References

1. Camarinha-Matos, L.M., Afsarmanesh, H.: A framework for virtual organization creation in a breeding environment. Annual Reviews in Control 31(1), 119–135 (2007a)
2. Romero, D., Galeano, N., Molina, A.: A virtual breeding environment reference model and its instantiation methodology. In: Camarinha-Matos, L.M., Picard, W. (eds.) Pervasive Collaborative Networks, vol. 283, pp. 43–52. Springer, Boston (2008)
3. Castells, M.: Aera da informação: economia, sociedade e cultura. Paz e Terra, São Paulo (1998)
4. Loiola, E., Moura, S.: Análise de redes: uma contribuição aos estudos organizacionais. In: Fischer, T. (ed.) Gestão Contemporânea – cidades estratégicas e organizações locais. Fundação Getúlio Vargas, Rio de Janeiro (1996)
5. Camarinha-Matos, L.M., Afsarmanesh, H.: Collaborative Networks: A new scientific discipline. Journal of Intelligent Manufacturing (16), 439–452 (2005)
6. Camarinha-Matos, L.M., Afsarmanesh, H.: A comprehensive modeling framework for collaborative networked organizations. Journal Intelligent Manufacturing 18, 529–542 (2007b)
7. Robison, L., Flora, J.: The social capital paradigm: bridging across disciplines. American Agricultural Economics Association 85(5), 1187–1193 (2003)
8. Coleman, J.S.: Social capital in the creation of human capital. American Journal of Sociology 94, 95–120 (1988)
9. Fukuyama, F.: The great disruption: human nature and the reconstitution of social order. London Profile Books (1999)
10. Putnam, R.D., Leonardi, R., Nanetti, R.Y.: Making democracy work: civic traditions in modern. Princeton University Press, Princeton (1993)
11. Nahapiet, J., Ghoshal, S.: Social capital, intellectual capital and the organizational advantage. Academy of Management Review 23(2), 242–266 (1998)
12. Granovetter, M.S.: The strength of weak ties. American Journal of Sociology 78, 60–80 (1973)
13. Macke, J., Vallejos, R.V., Toss, E.: Building inter-organizational social capital instruments to evaluate collaborative networks. iBusiness 2, 67–71 (2010a)
14. Onyx, J., Bullen, P.: Measuring social capital in five communities. The Journal of Applied Behavioral Science 36(1), 23–42 (2000)
15. Macke, J., Vallejos, R.V., Faccin, K., Genari, D.: The impact of inter-organizational social capital in collaborative networks competitiveness: an empirical analysis. IFIP AICT, vol. 336, pp. 517–526. Springer, Boston (2010b)

Part III

Value Chain for Enhancing Collaborative Networks

Customer-Oriented and Eco-friendly Networks for Health Fashionable Goods – The CoReNet Approach

Américo Azevedo[1], João Bastos[1], António Almeida[1], Carlos Soares[1], Nicola Magaletti[2], Enrico Del Grosso[2], Dieter Stellmach[3], Marcus Winkler[3], Rosanna Fornasiero[4], Andrea Zangiacomi[4], and Andrea Chiodi[5]

[1] INESC Porto & Faculdade de Engenharia da Universidade do Porto, Rua Doutor Roberto Frias S/N, 4200-465 Porto, Portugal
{ala,joao.bastos,antonio.henrique}@fe.up.pt, csoares@fep.up.pt
[2] TXT e-Solutions SPA, Via Frigia 27, 20126 Milano, Italy
{nicola.magaletti,enrico.delgrosso}@txt.it
[3] DITF Denkendorf – Centre for Management Research, Koerschtalstrasse 26, 73770 Denkendorf, Germany
{marcus.winkler,dieter.stellmach}@ditf-denkendorf.de
[4] ITIA-CNR -Institute of Industrial Technologies and Automation -National Council of Research, Via Bassini 15, 20133 Milano, Italy
{rosanna.fornasiero,andrea.zangiacomi}@itia.cnr.it
[5] SYNESIS – Viale Fulvio Testi, 128, Cinisello Balsamo, Milano, Italy
andrea.chiodi@synesis-consortium.eu

Abstract. The design, production and distribution of small series of health fashionable goods for specific target groups of wide impact in terms of market for the European industry as elderly, disables, diabetics and obese people represents a challenging opportunity for European companies which are asked to supply the demand with affordable price and eco-compatible products. Added to this challenge, textile, clothing and footwear manufactures seek for innovative collaborative networking solutions that could provide an entire digital life-cycle for the products and services required by the market. Aligned with this need, the EU CoReNet project aims to design and develop a new smart collaborative consumer-driven framework with the related services and components. This paper addresses the multidisciplinary complexity of customer-oriented and eco-friendly networks for health fashionable goods in particular addressing business requirements analysis, value chain issues, co-planning production and co-design topics in collaborative business processes tailored for high variability of the consumers demand and expectations.

Keywords: Collaborative Networks, Value Chain, Business Intelligence, Collaborative Framework.

1 Introduction

In recent years it is emerging at industrial level an adoption of collaborative strategies addressing the small series production of high-customized complex products. This is particularly relevant for health fashionable goods for specific target groups. In fact,

L.M. Camarinha-Matos et al. (Eds.): PRO-VE 2011, IFIP AICT 362, pp. 69–76, 2011.

consumer needs and expectations of specific target groups - such as elderly, obese, disabled, or diabetic persons- are arising as challenging opportunities for European companies which are asked to supply small series of innovative and fashionable goods of high quality, affordable price and eco-compatible. In order to design, develop, produce and distribute such products, a new framework and related components of collaborative networking are need to be developed, enabling the product to stay as long as possible digital to produce on-demand.

Research is necessary in many topics like: a) consumer integrated collaborative eco-oriented design, b) a radical renewal by the adoption of Rapid Manufacturing and Business Intelligence technologies; and c) the overall integration and co-ordination of business processes and information exchange by a set of new (web)services for network design and ad-hoc (re-)configuration, for real-time planning, forecasting and replenishment, and for tracking and tracing of ecology and quality.

This paper addresses the multidisciplinary complexity of customer-oriented and eco-friendly networks for health fashionable goods in particular concerning main collaborative business processes tailored on customized environment as well as able to respond to the high variability of the consumers demand and expectations.

2 Foundations and Research Topics

The emergence of global markets has forced the European Manufacturing Industry, SMEs in particular, to adapt to a new competitive environment in order to proactively respond to challenging market requirements with increased responsiveness and flexibility. This reality is intensified by the fact that consumer goods, in particular fashion products as clothing and footwear have in the last years been facing an increased number of seasonal collections. Moreover the mass customization paradigm requires that companies are ready to produce small batches (till one-of-a-kind product for mass market) to satisfy customer requirements.

Other related aspects are not only connected with social phenomena's such as ageing, increased obesity and disabled people but also with the growing sensitivity towards eco-friendly products. All these issues pose a challenge for TCFI (textile, clothing and footwear industry) manufacturers: how they can address consumers demand for personalization and value adding of harmonized products not only in terms of aesthetics, but also in terms of health, innovative functionalities and environmental impact?

Nowadays there is a clear need for health fashionable consumer goods, since customers want to be fully satisfied both under the point of view of their look and their health. This need generates a very distinctive type of demand, based on small lot series and fast delivery, forcing companies to change their manufacturing philosophy. It is no longer possible to deal with long transportation times of materials and components or extended lead times in manufacturing services to face this new demand paradigm.

Indeed, addressing this new type of customer demand groups as main target, it is necessary to develop new collaborative supply chain solutions based on cost effective, social compliant and eco-efficient design and production of customized products that fully satisfy the customers considering their health issues as well as their desire for fashionable products.

2.1 Value Chain Issues

As previously underlined, once products are becoming less standardized as customers are demanding custom-tailored options, one of the major challenges faced by TCFI organizations is the demand for increasingly levels of value in terms of responsiveness and shorter cycle times for production and delivery of newly developed products at lower prices. This calls for a supply chain that is quick, accurate, and provides top-quality products and customer support at different levels and steps.

As a consequence products are becoming more complex, presenting a greater variety of configurable options and must be tailored to a greater number of smaller market "niches". Therefore, in many market segments, only those firms that present the ability to "mass-customize" are able to success.

The traditional view of the customer as a passive actor in the value chain is rapidly changing. The continuous transfer of power in the supply chain, from the producer to the consumer, is forcing the conventional approach to become less and less appropriate. As Christopher argues: "in the present, instead of designing supply chains from the 'factory outwards' the challenge is to design them from the 'customer backwards'" [1]. With this new reality, the consumer should not be at the end of the supply chain but at its start, forcing to a change of philosophy from supply chain management to demand chain management. In this new vision, there is a philosophical difference between supply chain management and what Christopher call 'demand chain management'. This new concept is focused in creating a market-driven supply chain and starts by fully understanding the value that customers seek in the market in which the firm competes. This customer perception will enable the identification of the market segments and subsequently the value proposition by translating customer requirements into an offer of customized product and services. The final step is to integrate the customer value with an effective supply chain network strategy that addresses the demand with intelligent approaches.

2.2 Business Intelligence in Collaborative Networks

To be able to quickly respond to changes in the demand, companies must be able to continuously monitor the behavior of their customers. This can be done with Business Intelligence tools [2]. These tools use data that represent the behavior and preferences of customers obtained not only from transactional systems (e.g., orders) but also from other sources where they express their opinions (e.g., social networks).

These data are then stored in a Data Warehouse (DW) [3], which is a database designed for decision support and not for operational purposes. From these technologies, designers can automatically extract patterns from the behavior of customers using OLAP (OnLine Analytical Processing) tools, dashboards as well as Data Mining (DM) techniques [4]. From the DM methods, that can be useful for designers, two main approaches can be identified: clustering, to identify subgroups of customers with homogeneous behavior, and association, to identify emerging trends (e.g. recently, shirts with classic design typically also have single cuffs).

Models supported by these methods can be applied to improve production planning and supply chain management (e.g., anticipating trends in product demand and, consequently, in raw material needs), to design new products (e.g., anticipating what product features may be most successful in the coming seasons) as well as sales and marketing (e.g., customizing catalogs and websites for different customer profiles).

2.3 Co-planning Production in Collaborative Networks

Small series and customized products require totally different supply networks structures, where each company is specialized in a specific manufacturing phase of a product or a market segment. In this context, and following the approach described, a supply network should be configured for each customer order and tend to include a small number of skilled companies. The key selection criteria should be the ability to perform the required operations for the desired delivery date, with the expected cost. In practice these scenarios will be characterized by a very large number of small orders, each of them having different partner companies, based on their availability and capabilities. In this context co-planning and control will be required to optimize the production plans that result, on a first iteration, from the configuration (or set up) of the supply network for each order.

For those companies, at the end of the design and development process, where all the items belonging to a specific collection and the related basic elements have been defined (for example, 2D/3D models, Part Programs for cutting, printing and any other automation step), the products are ready to be proposed for sales.

For the addressed consumer categories, a "configuration space" may be provided to define the final version of product, without including the "critical" components (for example the fabrics and yarns for garments, the last and sole for the shoes, etc.) that must be kept absolutely standard for the higher number of different models, since this level of personalization would imply costs not acceptable for small series.

Beside the early phases for the design and development of the collection, once the sales have been closed and the product completely defined and configured, along with the measures, quantities and due dates, all the complete set of information required for the actual production can be finally defined (final BOM, accessories, etc.) and the production orders (PO) can be generated for a specific customer order. During this phase it is possible to identify the Supply Chain specification (design and formation) for a specific customer order, that implies to have identified all the suppliers and partners in charge of carry out all the external activities, assigned the whole set of operations associated to a specific product and finally obtained all the information and data needed for the planning activities.

One of the most critical aspects during the PO execution is the management of the external activities that may be strongly different for each product. Therefore, during the PO execution is strongly required that manufacturer and partners could interact and share information, exchange documents and take decisions.

For this specific purpose, this paper addresses the importance of flexible IT services supporting collaborative planning that should engage the manufacturer and any partner to be involved on specific order basis. The main objective is to enable the planning of POs assigned to any partner and support the related info and document management.

2.4 Co-design and Sustainability

Collaborative design tools empowers the consumers to design their own products by providing them the ability to collaborate in an informed design process not only regarding aesthetics, prices and delivery times, but also resources consumption and social responsibility. In line with this, to implement sustainability parameters in the design phase rely on the synchronization of the design along the supply chain. In product (co-)design commercial tools, the product design stage is seen as a unique phase to be performed by designer, eventually based on some indications/sketches defined by the consumer and the consumer interaction always take place only in terms of product configuration. However due to the change of power from companies to customers, co-design should not only be supported through the usual consumer-designer interaction, providing the consumer with dedicated mechanisms for indications on product style and for simplified direct modification of product design, but also through co-design collaborative mechanisms along the supply chain.

Indeed, nowadays stakeholders collaborating to product definition (especially shoes) are today acting in a fragmented supply chain, counting more than 20 steps including materials and components subcontractors. In such a context, product engineering is spread between different actors and interoperability is still an open issue. Therefore, in this paper it will be addressed such a gap by providing interoperability mechanisms to collect internal CAD data, orientate them and exchange product design information with PDM systems of component suppliers along the chain and recollect then intermediate part engineering in the central CAD.

Concerning sustainability aspect, first of all it has to be underlined that garments and shoes are complex products in terms of their environmental impacts. Therefore a pressing matter related with this issue involves the track and trace retrieval of information related to each product and its production process (to any level of depth along the supply chain) by relevant stakeholders, along the whole product life cycle to enable products and related components traceability.

3 CoReNet Approach

The proposed CoReNet (Customer-Oriented and Eco-friendly Networks for Health Fashionable Goods) approach [5], intends to support textile, clothing and footwear companies in the implementation of new models for small series production for health and fashionable goods following the Competitive Sustainable Manufacturing (CSM) paradigm [6] and current initiatives of European Technological Platforms like Manufuture [7] and Footwear. The project intends to support the whole value chain to get and manage consumer data to investigate its needs; involve consumer into design and product configuration phases; exchange consumer data through adequate data models and secure systems; manage the collaboration with suppliers in order to plan and distribute on time; implement innovative manufacturing technologies; deliver timely the product to customer; and monitor the quality and sustainability of products.

Sustainability issues will be assured by the exploitation and implementation of technologies able to exploit the emergent and pervasive infrastructure of the Semantic Web, joined to an effective adoption of state of the art RFID and sensor technologies.

With this approach, consumers and the whole distribution system will be able to verify the quality of products before their purchase and during their utilization. On the other side, designers will be allowed to model their product after a precise connotation of all the chosen product's components and producers will be able to verify such characteristics along each step of production and supply.

3.1 Consumer Target Group Analysis

In the case of CoReNet project the target is mainly on specific market segments where it is necessary to find the right trade-off between healthy and fashionable features of products for disabled, diabetic, obese and elderly people. As previously underlined, products should be based not only on fashion trends but may cover different kind of requirements coming from customers, both based on aesthetic and on functional and on health needs.

The analysis of the target groups' requirements which is part of this work is based on existing literature and on field questionnaires made to European people belonging to these categories. What turned out is that these target groups represent a share of the market which is getting larger and larger, asking for products to fulfill their requirements in terms of improved comfort and wearability, like to protect the body from regular environmental impact (e.g. heat, cold, water, humidity) in a high comfort and high quality. This means for TCFI companies to refocus design and production of their clothing and shoe models based not only on fashion requirements but also on other features which need to be taken into consideration from the design phase changing the approach to product conception.

3.2 Business Requirements Analysis

The CoReNet project aims at enterprise interoperability with a special focus on the development of a new holistic framework, consisting of a set of methods, tools and technologies to support collaborative networks addressing consumer-oriented market segments demand for sustainable small series of fashionable products. In order to identify the functional requirements for this framework, a set of business requirements analysis was performed in key industrial players of TCFI supply chain. This comprehensive analysis allowed the identification of functional requirements (see fig. 1) and use case scenarios (overlapping both the footwear and clothing scenarios) relevant to the definition of the CoReNet proposed reference model.

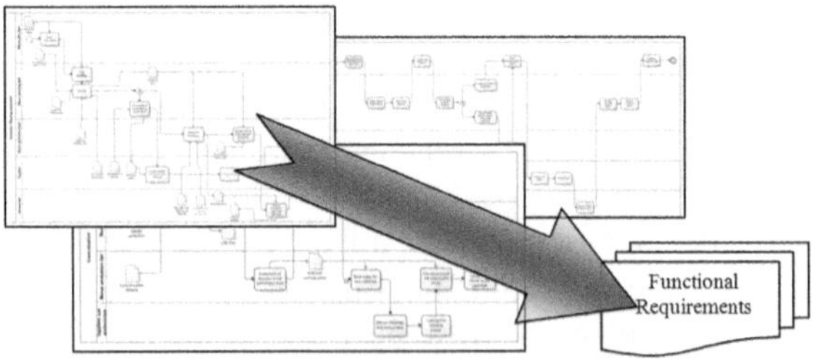

Fig. 1. Business Requirements gathering

3.3 Proposed Reference Model

The Reference Model proposed is based on mapping TCFI processes at three levels: strategic, tactic and operative according to three perspectives (cf. Fig.2):

Organizational Perspective: Through the proposal of innovative production paradigms based on new concepts that go beyond-lean approaches addressing the agile manufacturing concept. The process planning and configuration of the supply networks is achieved through collaboration mechanisms generating a virtual organization model fit to provide the required productive resources. Also the formalization of interaction processes with customer requirements and needs will complete the design of the value chain.

ICT Perspective: It is related with the required infrastructure that supports the services, methods and tools necessary for the network operation. This infrastructure maps the information and ICT services necessary for networking management during the different processes identified (from design, to product configuration, to production planning, to production to delivery).

Knowledge Perspective: The knowledge perspective of the reference model highlights both the available knowledge and business intelligence in the network and the required knowledge at other places along the network. This covers all different kinds of knowledge from partner competences to knowledge about material properties or machinery availability and process capabilities.

In this context, the specific objective of new research shall be to increase significantly the sustainability of value creation of small series health fashionable consumer goods and in particular of footwear and accessories, for emerging social niches like elderly, obese, diabetics and disable people, by systemic/coordinated intra- and inter-sector networking of producers/service providers using cutting-edge (digital and) production technologies as well as innovative organizational models based on cross-supply network integration through the major breakthrough innovations which are complementary each other.

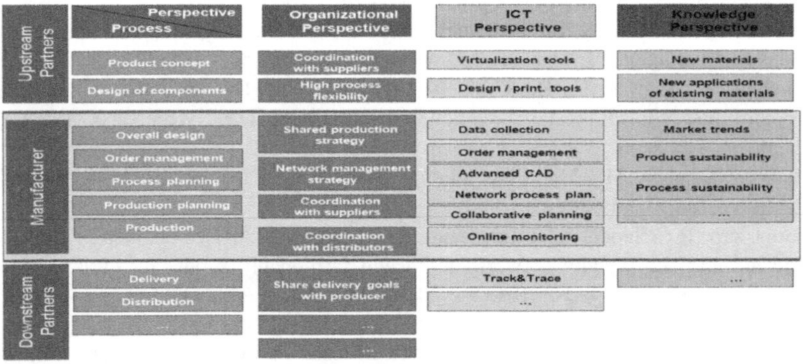

Fig. 2. CoReNet Proposed Reference Model

The proposed Reference Model will be applicable both to companies producing customized goods according to the traditional framework where most of the production is kept internally (i.e. only minor processes are externalized like production of components) and to companies doing their business on online sales, externalizing most of the other processes. This requires different levels and means of collaboration in the three different perspectives (organizational, ICT and knowledge) which need to be investigated.

4 Conclusions and Further Research

The ongoing European project "Customer-oriented and eco-friendly networks for healthy fashionable goods (CoReNet)" aims to provide TCFI companies with the tools and methods to face the challenge of working in demand-driven and customer oriented collaborative networks.

Until now the project research work allowed the definition of a Reference Model that set up the foundations for the development of future technologies and tools that support network operation. The following phases include the instantiation to specific companies' requirements of the reference model according to their business model in order to support them in the path to small series production of healthy products. The model will be evaluated and improved in the CoReNet project together with the industry partners and the customers.

Acknowledgments. The research leading to these results has received funding from the European Union's Seventh Framework Programme (FP7/2007-2013) under grant agreement n° [260169].

References

1. Christopher, M.: Logistics and supply chain management - Creating Value-Adding Networks, 3rd edn. Prentice Hall, Englewood Cliffs (2005)
2. Lo, W., Hong, T., Jeng, R.: A framework of E-SCM multi-agent systems in the fashion industry. International Journal of Production Economics 114, 594–614 (2008)
3. Kimball, R., Reeves, L., Ross, M., Thornthwaite, W.: The Data Warehouse Lifecycle Toolkit, 2nd edn. Practical Techniques for Building Data Warehouse and Business Intelligence Systems. Wiley, Chichester (1998)
4. Han, J., Kamber, M.: The Data mining: concepts and techniques. Morgan Kaufmann Publishers Inc., San Francisco (2000)
5. Fornasiero, R., Chiodi, A., Carpanzano, E., Carneiro, L.: Research issues on Customer-oriented and eco-friendly networks for health fashionable goods. In: Ortiz, Á., Franco, R.D., Gasquet, P.G. (eds.) BASYS 2010. IFIP AICT, vol. 322, pp. 36–44. Springer, Heidelberg (2010)
6. FoF-PPP: Factories of the Future: Public, Private Partnership, Strategic Multi-annual Roadmap (2009)
7. Manufuture, Strategic Research Agenda (2006)

Value Network of Amazon Non Timber Forest Products: A Mapping Tool to Support a Complex Network Strategic Planning

Jeferson Straatmann, Mateus Cecílio Gerolamo, and Luiz Cesar Ribeiro Carpinetti

School of Engineering of São Carlos, University of São Paulo, Av. Trabalhador Sancarlense, 400, São Carlos – SP, CEP.: 13566-590, Brazil
jstraatmann@gmail.com

Abstract. The Non Timber Forest Products (NTFP) value chains are viewed as an alternative for the forest conservation and for the improvement of life conditions of Traditional Communities. These products are part of different chemical, cosmetic, food and pharmaceutical industries, which are trying to improve the sustainability of their supply chains. For the improvement of inter-organizational NTFP network in the Amazon region, an adapted value chain map was structured to map the Value Network and foster the strategic planning process. The mapping tool brought the whole scenario view for planning process, helping to integrate knowledge, values and perspectives, resulting in a common view for the NTFP Value Network future.

Keywords: Value Chain Mapping, Inter-organizational Network, Collaborative Network, Value Network Mapping, Non Timber Forest Products, Rural and Forest SMEs.

1 Introduction

The market demand for organic products and for social-environmental safe products is increasing worldwide and companies are no longer ignoring these issues [1]. To deliver the quality demanded for those products the companies must take deeply care of their value chain, with a good traceability process implemented and, in some cases, to work closely with suppliers. That is especially relevant in the Non Timber Forest Products (NTFP) scenario.

In Brazil, mainly in the Amazon Forest, the NTFP are usually not domesticated species, collected directly from the forest by Traditional Population/Communities[1] (Indigenous, Riverside, Maroons) [3]. The harvesting of these products demands a huge effort from the population, being made in a rudimentary/low technology mean and commercialized to different levels of middlemen [4]. Due to the dispersion in the

[1] According to the Brazilian government law for Traditional Population / Community, Traditional Population are: culturally diverse groups that are recognized as such, with their own forms of social organization, which occupy and use lands and natural resources as a condition to its cultural, social, religious, ancestral and economic, knowledge, innovations and practices, generated and transmitted by tradition [2].

L.M. Camarinha-Matos et al. (Eds.): PRO-VE 2011, IFIP AICT 362, pp. 77–84, 2011.

Amazon territory, the seasonality, the infrastructure issues and low volume of production it is difficult for companies to have only one supplier, requiring a network of suppliers. This process requires a great coordination effort from companies that usually prefer to purchase their forest raw material from middlemen.

After the ECO 92 conference the attentions for the NTFP value chains and for the Traditional Communities start to grow, increasing the government investments in the creation of new sustainable use protected areas, increasing, also, the number of Non Governmental Organizations (NGO), international agencies and government environmental institutions [5]. That has promoted a strong socio-environmental network, with many inter-dependent institutions, generally with a low coordination level in different regions. Usually these institutions participate directly or indirectly in the promotion of NTFP value chains, but with low contact with market reality, technology, and enterprises demand.

The Brazilian Amazon Forest is a traditional source of raw materials for food, cosmetics and pharmaceutical enterprises, which have usually two possibilities: *i)* buy NTFP from the "exploiting" supply chain [4, 6]; or, *ii)* promote specific agreements and partnerships with Traditional Communities [6, 7]. The agreement between The Body Shop Company and Kayapó Indigenous Communities in Brazilian Pará State, for purchasing Brazilian Nut Oil, is an example of a dyadic relationship between a cosmetic enterprise and a Traditional Community [6, 7]. The agreement was continuously supported by The Body Shop and FUNAI (the Brazilian government indigenous agency), but it did not work properly for a number of not well considered factors, specially: *i)* the Kaypó traditional way of life (social organization, subsistence agriculture, volumes, forest multiple use) and, *ii)* the involvement of important regional institutions, that could have provided support, added value and transparency to the partnership. To escape from those simple dyadic "business" relationships the companies, institutions and Traditional Communities must start to see the Product Value Chain as a Product Value Network, which sees more than just the chain relations but specially add value through the horizontal network perspective.

The value added in the product network may appear to the market in terms of a better communication between the chain "direct/productive" actors (Traditional Communities, traders, enterprises), and the "indirect" actors (government agencies, NGOs, sponsors), increasing knowledge, trust, trade transparency, quality, traceability for the whole network and consumers.

The organization and visualization of the Value Network data for a regional NTFP strategic planning process - involving different actors (some analphabets) - is a complex and challenge activity. The paper brings the adaptation made in two value chain mapping process to structure a Value Network Map (VNM), and a case description of a NTFP Value Network strategic planning process at Altamira region in the Brazilian Amazon.

This specific tool provides a simple graphical display of the vertical network (between the value chain links), also presenting information about the horizontal network (Traditional Communities networks and support institutions networks). A scenario analysis combining the mapping tool with network and planning methods were used for the strategic planning process. The methods used, its adaptation for the local reality, the process and the results obtained are described.

This paper is organized as follows: section 2 presents a review of Value Stream Mapping, Value Links and describes the adaptation in the methods to satisfy the Network demand; section 3 presents and discuss the application of the tool for a specific Network Strategic Plan in the Amazon region; section 4 conclude this work.

2 Value Chain Mapping and Analysis

Different processes mapping tools can be used for mapping the value chain of a product. The Value Stream Mapping (VSM) was developed and is being used for improvement of internal and external streams or chains of industries (mainly auto-parts) [8, 9]. Its visual characteristics were designed to be easily understandable for the whole company, from the shop floor employees to the company CEOs. This specific aspect of the VSM is particularly appropriated to NTFP chains context that involves: Traditional Communities (high illiteracy rate), social institutions, government and enterprises.

Because of the original use, oriented for manufacture enterprises, the VSM is able to well organize productive, logistics, market and production methods data and indicators [8, 9]. This tool competence provides a well structured mean to organize and see the chain in detail, with different information and comparing one process or chain operator with the others. The VSM is oriented for the improvement of selected product chains, not being able to provide the visualization of the Network as a whole (value chain operators, stakeholders and support actors).

This Stakeholders complementation is better organized in the *ValueLinks* Mapping (VLM) tool, developed by GTZ (German Agency for Technical Cooperation) to promote specific micro and small-sized enterprises, small farmers, agribusiness, handicraft or manufacturing sub-sectors by promoting the value chains they are operating in [10]. But, nevertheless, the methodology focus continues in the analysis of a specific chain.

The *ValueLinks* method is oriented to promote diverse kinds of rural value chains, considering the Micro level (the value chain operators and the operational service providers) and the Meso level (includes all chain-specific actors providing regular support services or representing the common interest of the value chain actors) [10]. The analysis is grouped in three main tasks, being the mapping of the value chain the most essential one: *i)* Value chain mapping; *ii)* Quantifying and describing value chains in detail; *iii)* Economic analysis of value chains and benchmarking.

The organization and visualization of the VLM is done mainly by boxes structures, linked by arrows and oriented by the value chain processes. The graphical standard is basically the same for the different operators, not providing a clear picture for logistics issues and the processes itself. The Meso level visualization of the VLM (inferior part of the map - Fig. 1) and the participative methodology brings a good complementation to the VSM.

An integration of both methods (Fig. 1) allows a good graphic quality of the chain, with easy understandability, a participative analysis of the process and the visualization of the stakeholders. This integration can be strengthened with the vision of the inter-organizational network as a whole, which reinforce the necessity of a perspective change: from a value chain to a value network, defined as a set of relatively autonomous units, managed independently, operating together in a framework of common principles and service level agreements [11, 12], including the chain operators, the support institutions and stakeholders.

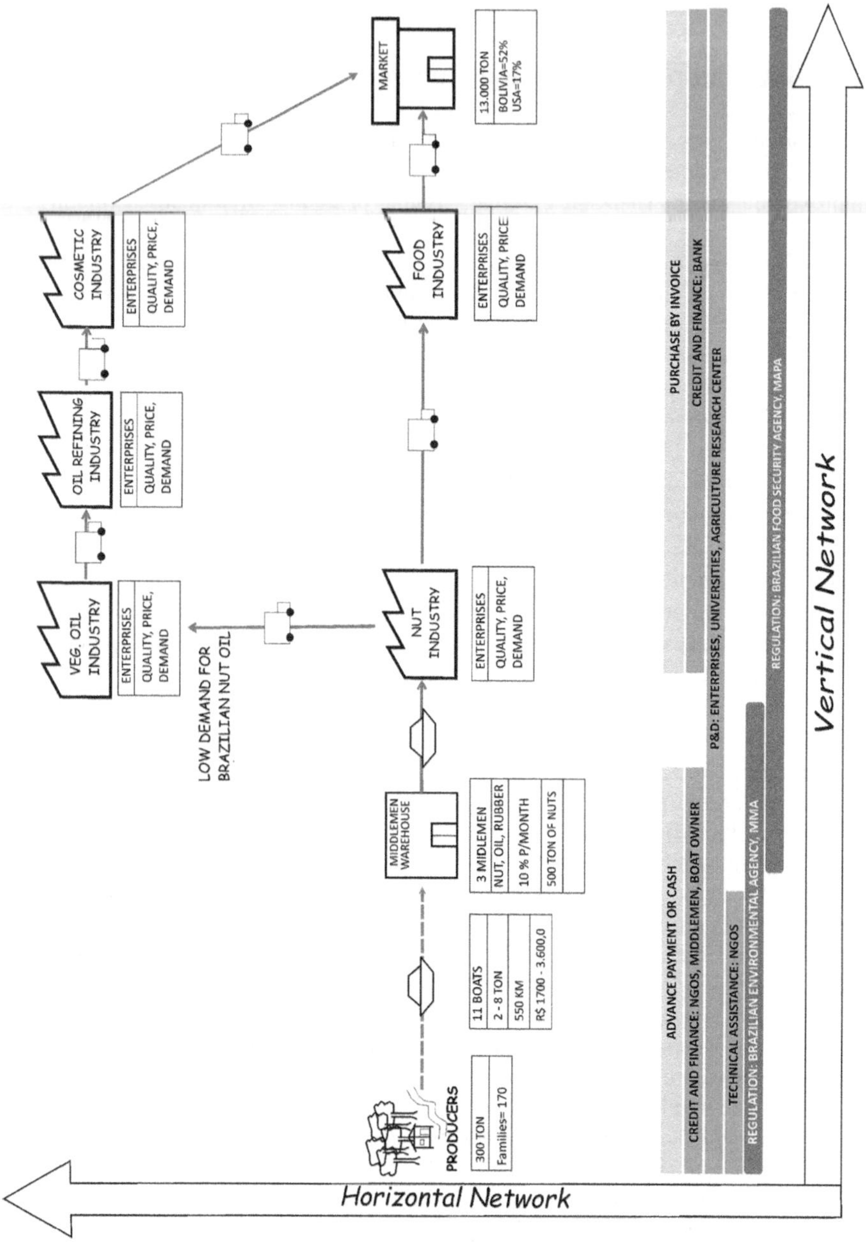

Fig. 1. Brazilian Nuts Value Network Map

For the Amazon NTFP, the perspective change from value chain to value network is a gain of quality in action, due to different regional bottlenecks, like: the disperse and informal network of Traditional Communities; the lack of communication forms in the region; the bad logistics infrastructure; the "preference" for "exploratory" commercialization chains to reduce purchasing costs; and, the lack of coordination between governmental agencies, enterprises and NGOs.

Other tools should be used concomitantly to support the VNM, the planning process and the common future statement, specially: market, logistics, infrastructure and statistics data, Wenn diagram, SWOT analysis, World Café and Appreciative Inquiry. The last two methods are centered in the persons (experiences and perspectives), searching individual and common group goals/visions for cooperation in the specific work environment (enterprise, network, etc.).

3 NTFP Collaborative Network Strategic Planning

The Altamira municipality is located in the Pará state, inside the Brazilian Amazon. Most of the region is surrounded by protected areas, created mainly in the last decade (2000 – 2010) to protect the forest and the Traditional Communities of the region (mainly riverside communities and indigenous communities) as a result of different inter-organizational work. The use of these areas are restricted, some of which are full protected areas (only scientific research is allowed) and some are intended for living and for sustainable use. That directs the regional potential for forest entrepreneurship, specifically NTFPs for the Traditional Communities.

There are different kinds and levels of networks in the region, structuring, sharing knowledge and labor force in different scenarios. Inside the sustainable use protected areas the social organization are structured in familiar and social networks, that change knowledge about the best practices of managing the forest, change work force for the bottlenecks activities and provides assistance for emergency issues. These networks are connected to a formal organization that represents the protected area population. Usually these formal organizational standards do not represent the population organizational forms, which complicate its management.

The regional institutions, including the Traditional Communities ones, are organized in an informal network, to dialog, plan and act in a more coordinated way. This network was formed in 2008 to organize the diverse organizations in the regions to face the social, environmental and economics regional challenges. The network has specific cliques or sub-networks of institutions that are focused in their specific goals, being the NTFPs clique an important part of it.

The Wenn Diagram in Fig. 2 illustrates the organizational scenario of the region regarding the NTFPs. The proximity to the center illustrates the activeness and importance of the player, classifying actors as: *i)* with Veto power (V); *ii)* first, second and third layer player; and, *iii)* Enterprise, Government and NGO player. The lines qualifies the kind of relationship between the actors: *i)* continuous line - stable relationship; *ii)* dashed line - weak relationship; *iii)* double line - strong relationship; *iv)* lightning – conflict; and, *v)* continues line with stroke - relationship stopped.

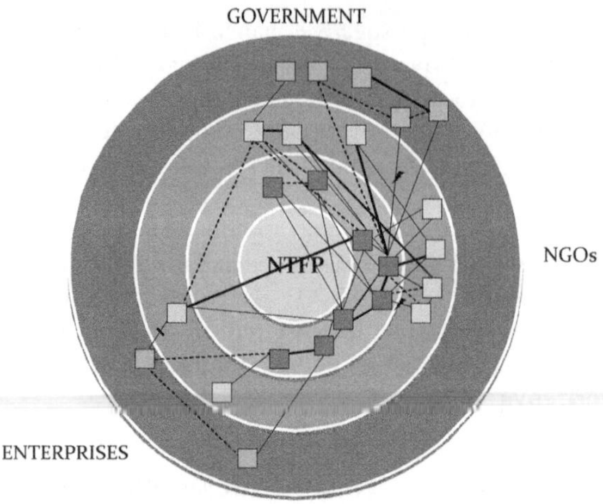

Fig. 2. Wenn Diagram for NTFP in the studied region

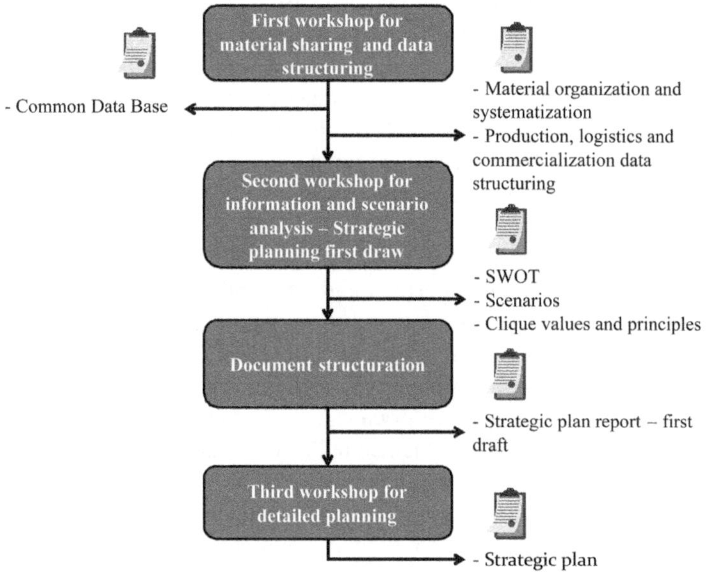

Fig. 3. Planning process and results

This NTFP clique is improving the network organization, promoting a strategic planning process to guide the clique actions and influencing the regional political scenario. The process were structured in four planning phases, mainly focused in: *i)* knowledge sharing and structuring; *ii)* scenario and SWOT analysis and common values, principles and goals statement; *iii)* information and documentation structuring; and *iv)* detailed planning (Fig. 3).

The whole strategic plan process was oriented by the Value Network Map structured as showed in section 2 of this paper. The map promoted a better understanding of the whole network (vertical and horizontal actors), facilitating the dialog between Traditional Communities, supporting institutions and partner enterprises. The production, logistics and commercialization data (gathered in the first phase) was structured in the map and additional support worksheets and maps was prepared. The tool brings a better understanding of the current scenario of NTFPs in the region, helping to answer some questions about cooperation and improvement of value networks: how are the relationships between the actors of the chain (producers, middlemen, local retailers, industrial partner)? What public polices could be accessed and what is missing for that happens? What are the fair prices for NTFP in different situations? How does the commercialization processes works for the communities and for the industrial partners? What arrangements should be done for improvements? How to improve the Traditional Communities networks exchanges (knowledge, process standards, processing tools and equipments)? What strategy should be followed to add value to the NTFP and when (outsource production? attract companies to the region? organize business partnerships? Etc.)?

The SWOT analysis was developed just after the map construction and explanation, resulting in different evaluations of the current scenario. A scenario analysis using the Value Network Map and the SWOT results was performed thereafter, revealing the cooperation necessity within the different actors, resulting in different collective actions such as: common data base of materials; common plan for NTFPs; land regularization processes; institutions technicians join training process; NTFPs quality processes standards; regional socio-environmental quality label for NTFPs; public policies for production and commercialization shared actions; and, mapping of the existing Traditional Communities networks and relationships.

An important result and input for the process was the creation of common values, principles and goals for the network clique. This perspective arrives to solve dialog issues between the actors, which were too much focused in their own institutions goals, creating barriers for the planning processes. The common values were important to align the perspectives of the participants/organizations and foster productive and shared dialogs.

Aiming the improvement of the relationships and the commitment with the plan, the final workshop was structured with the combination of two common future statement methodologies: Appreciative Inquiry and World Café. These methodologies improved the understanding of the proposals, reinforced the common goals, values and principles of the clique and fostered the individual commitment with the collective plan. The final workshop reviewed the decisions taken in the scenario analysis, prioritized the actions, and determined the responsible parties, resources and deadlines.

4 Conclusion

The combination of the VSM and *ValueLinks* tools to map the Value Network provided good results for the NTFPs planning process, providing in terms of representation: a structured data organization, especially for the chain operators in the dialog box; a better understanding of the connection and ties between the chain operators; the position of the stakeholders (support, credits, technical and regulatory institutions in the chain). Concerning the planning process the tool provided:

knowledge exchange; the whole network understanding; a better analysis of the current and future scenarios; commitment; and, a clearer definition of bottlenecks, roles, common goals, collective actions and future vision.

The improvement/adaptation of the mapping tool, a reorganization of the process and the utilization of complementary planning tools are recommended, according to the inter-organizational network context. For the specific case of NTFPs it is strongly recommended to adopt a Value Chain and/or Value Network Mapping Tool to organize the vertical and horizontal cooperation data, allowing actors to see the whole instead of their limited organizational scope.

Future research may be conducted especially concerning: *i)* Full Development/ Improvement of the Value Network Mapping Tool and detailed framework; *ii)* research over inter-organizational collaborative meetings methodologies for common future statement, like World Café and Appreciative Inquiry; and, *iii)* research over network planning frameworks.

References

1. Butler, R., Laurance, W.F.: New strategies for conserving tropical forests. Trends in Ecology & Evolution 23(9), 469–472 (2008)
2. Brasil: Decreto No 6.040, de 7 de fevereiro de 2007. Institui a Política Nacional de Desenvolvimento Sustentável dos Povos e Comunidades Tradicionais (2007)
3. Homma, A.K.O.: The dynamics of extraction in Amazonia: A historical perspective. In: Nepstad, D.C., Schwartzman, S. (eds.) Non-timber Products from Tropical Forests: Evaluation of a Conservation and Development Strategy. Advances in Economic Botany, vol. 9, pp. 23–32 (1992)
4. Belcher, B., Schreckenberg, K.: NTFP Commercialization: A Reality Check. Development Policy Review 25(3), 355–377 (2007)
5. Fearnside, P.M.: Conservation Policy in Brazilian Amazonia: Understanding the Dilemmas. World Development 31(5), 757–779 (2003)
6. Ros-Tonen, M.A.F., Andel, T.V., Morsello, C., Otsuki, K., Rosendo, S., Scholz, I.: Forest-related partnerships in Brazilian Amazonia: There is more to sustainable forest management than reduced impact logging. Forest Ecology and Management 256, 1482–1497 (2008)
7. Morsello, C.: Company–community non-timber forest product deals in the Brazilian Amazon: A review of opportunities and problems. Forest Policy and Economics 8(4), 458–494 (2006)
8. Rother, M., Shook, J.: Learn to See: Value Stream Mapping to Add Value and Eliminate MUDA. Lean Enterprise Institute, Cambridge (1999)
9. Jones, D., Womack, J.: Seeing the Whole: mapping the extended value stream. Lean Enterprise Institute, Cambridge (2002)
10. Springer-Heinze, A. (ed.): ValueLinks Manual - The Methodology of Value Chain Promotion. GTZ, Eschborn (2007), http://www.value-links.de/manual/distributor.html (Access at: April 11, 2011)
11. Ehret, M.: Managing the trade-off between relationships and value networks. Towards a value-based approach of customer relationship management in business-to-business markets. Industrial Marketing 33, 465–473 (2004)
12. Peppard, J., Rylander, A.: From Value Chain to Value Networks: Insights for mobile operators. European Management Journal 24(2-3), 128–141 (2006)

Flexible Integration of Service Suppliers in Collaborative Service Procurement Networks

Maik Herfurth[1], Thomas Schuster[1], and Peter Weiß[2]

[1] FZI Forschungszentrum Informatik, Haid-und-Neu-Str. 10-14,
76131 Karlsruhe, Germany
{herfurth,schuster}@fzi.de
[2] ISS International School of Service Management, Hans-Henny-Jahnn-Weg 9,
22085 Hamburg, Germany
weiss@iss-hamburg.de

Abstract. A new conceptual design for service procurement networks may surpass existing limitations and bottlenecks. Thereby efficiency can be improved and transaction costs be reduced. To overcome existing limitations a design approach is presented that supports enterprise application integration based on master data and company-wide business process integration. Master data is harmonized with standardized data types and service-oriented architectures (SOA). eBuS-XML is introduced, in the proposed solution it serves as service-specific XML-based library for transaction data types, storage and integration of service e-procurement order processing.

Keywords: Collaborative Procurement Networks, Service Procurement, B2B Integration, Service-Oriented Architecture (SOA), eBuS-XML.

1 Introduction

Service e-procurement is an important subject in the field of e-business. Service suppliers and service supplicants cooperate in collaborative networks [1] [2] as part of service supply chains. In service supply chains, the major characteristics of services – intangibility, interaction and individuality - have most influence on service e-procurement practice. E-business solutions and standards today merely reflect specific elements and variables of services. Despite of recent advancements and innovations in ICT, electronic service procurement solutions are often lacking efficiency. Typical observations are [3]:

i) service procurement processes are not fully integrated in current IT systems
ii) electronic data exchange is only supported partially and
iii) integration solutions are often not adequately aligned with peculiarities of service processes and logic being tailored primarily to the needs of material procurement.

Consequently, collaborative service processes suffer from various media breaks and are thus source of increasing costs, occurring failures and manual error handling. Service procurement is a niche market of specialized IT vendors offering

L.M. Camarinha-Matos et al. (Eds.): PRO-VE 2011, IFIP AICT 362, pp. 85–92, 2011.

individualized, highly specialized IT tools supporting service-related business logic and transactions [4]. In this paper, we conceptualize the design and flexible solutions based on flexible service-oriented architectures.

2 Service Procurement and Collaborative Networks

Service procurement processes are still a source of high costs to companies due to its perceived complex and heterogeneous purchasing processes. Service procurement networks consist of service consumers, service producers and intermediate parties. Service producers (contractors) are mostly small and medium-sized companies. Service consumers (ordering party) are bigger companies while intermediate parties are supporting medium-sized companies for service consumers and producers. Standards are seen as "[...] valuable basis for networking within individual industry sectors" [5]. A companies' value is more and more determined through its ecosystem and ability to interact with business partners on the basis of electronic services or machine-to-machine transactions [5]. Companies trading with each other use often similar software, or vendors determine formats and often industry sector standards. Service procurement requires specific collaborative services which are not adequately supported by IT applications and electronic services yet. Large companies typically support up to now service-related business processes through individually customized web-based information systems [6].

2.1 Collaborative Business Processes

Collaborative business processes have a major influence on the conceptual design of service e-procurement.

Service procurement processes seem to have the same phases as material processes. But a major difference of service procurement processes is in process

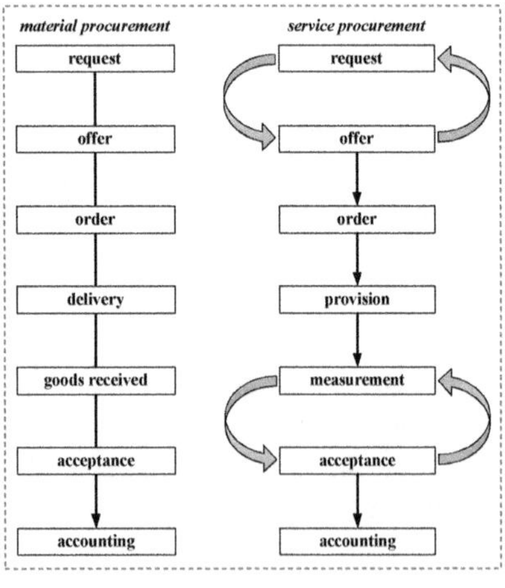

Fig. 1. Interaction Cycles of Service Procurement

phases *offer* and *measurement*, which are characterized by a differing logic through more interactions between actors that result in process cycles [3] (see fig. 1). Process cycles derive from the interaction of service consumers and service producers during the *offer phase*: both actors have to agree on the specification of the service provision. In the *measurement phase*, the service consumer and the service producer negotiate the bill of quantities for the accounting. The degree of business process integration influences significantly effectiveness and efficiency of service-related procurement transactions. The effective integration of company-wide business processes along the service value chain is still immature. This motivates the development of a flexible enterprise application integration solution. Large enterprises have started to standardize collaborative business processes with their suppliers, often using purchasing platforms (Supplier Self Services) which are highly integrated in their ERP systems [5].

3 Solution and Evaluation Approach

In order to surpass the described problems and challenges for service e-procurement, service procurement networks were evaluated by looking at a set of real life use cases (18 in total). Internal and company-wide processes were analyzed with regard to document and data flow, as well as used IT-systems. For the conceptual design of electronic services for service procurement networks, two essential elements were identified: (1) service business processes (supporting required interaction phases) and (2) flexible IT systems. The designed solutions support service-oriented transactions through standardized interfaces, data integration and harmonized service master data. Master data is seen to "[…] bring a strong competitive advantage" [5]. The analyzed use case scenarios represent typical sector-specific value chain constellations from the area of industrial maintenance services and are related to facility management, industry waste disposal, asset management, cleaning and renewable energies (photovoltaic plants). For analysis of the selection of use cases a systematic approach was applied (see fig. 2).

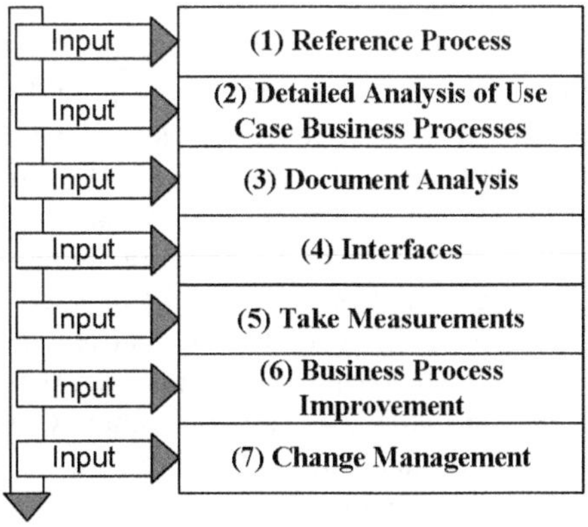

Fig. 2. Systematic Analysis Approach

A detailed analysis of the business processes starts with reference process modeling (1) in order to realize mayor differences and discrepancies of process instances of selected use cases. The reference process model was presented in [4]. The reference process model defines typical collaborative interfaces between contractors and ordering parties. In a detailed analysis of use cases (2), the business processes are analyzed, media breaks are marked and scrutinized, redundant activities like repeated manual input of business data in company's IT-system. An analysis of documents (3) aims at better understanding of information flows in the service network. Existing interfaces (4) connecting the various IT-systems were looked at and data flows were analyzed in depth. Internal and company-wide processes were assessed to measure processing time of transactions and processes, total cycle time for processing service orders and required amount of man-hours and days (5). Finally, the results of analysis of realized measurement leads to re-engineering of value or business processes (6) which need to be accompanied by an appropriate change management to achieve required sustainability (7). As a major result yielding from our analysis, a tool box was developed including universal e-business formats and features to be considered and implemented by service procurement systems. The following elements are contained in the tool box: reference modeling of service-related procurement processes, standardized e-business interfaces and transaction formats [3], service classification system [4] and universal service master data (data types in typical transactions) in electronic document exchange and data flow. In the remainder, the support of business process by EAI and SOA are in focus.

4 Support of Company-Wide Business Processes by EAI and SOA

Service-oriented Computing (SoC) is emerging as a promising paradigm for enabling flexible interconnection of autonomously developed and operated components within and across organizational boundaries [7]. SoC is a distributed application integration paradigm in which the functionality of existing components is described in a declarative way, new applications can be built by reuse of given functionality. The latter does allow an improved support of changed business processes. Main associated enabling technologies are currently the so called WS-technologies such as SOAP, WSDL, WS-Security and WS-BPEL. These technologies enable declarative service descriptions, publication of these descriptions, description-based service discovery and service reuse. Integration of services can foster the execution of distributed business processes and enhanced business-to-business integration. Major business-to-business integration types are *point-to-point integration*, *process based integration* and *mature B2B integration*. Process based integration support process management functionality by use of management systems to broke message exchange. The mature B2B integration provides connectivity to trading partner networks, examples are RosettaNet [8], EDI [9] or ebXML [10]. Collaborative networks of services suppliers and services consumers lack the support of flexible company–wide business processes for the planning, specification and the e-procurement of services. A service-specification support for the company's application integration and service-specification support of business processes is not support by today's solutions Especially the specification of interaction cycles (see fig. 2) is not supported.

4.1 Service Master Data Management

In procurement networks, a high flexibility in terms of business processes and changing market conditions are decisive for successful trading. IT-Solutions strive concurrently for advanced flexibility and a high level of integration to reduce transaction costs. The service oriented paradigm (SOA) fulfills both criteria. The loosely coupling replaces complex interfaces of individual technologies. Web services offer business functions of applications and hide system specific specifications. SOA defines network-based applications by describing their offered functions with WSDL and using XML for the exchange of XML documents. To enable harmonized document exchange and data flow, the description and specification of industrial services and transaction types need standardization. *eBuS-XML* was developed, an XML based format facilitating standardized transaction data to overcome ambiguous semantics and heterogeneous data type definitions.

Table 1. Requirements for implementing Electronic Procurement Solutions, Business Process Integration and Standardization

Requirements	Description	a	b	c	d	e	f
modularity	modularity of service position definitions	x					x
hierarchy support	hierarchy of service positions	x			x		x
linking	linking of service positions		x		x		x
hybrid structure	linkage between service positions and material						x
order sequence	free order sequence of service positions				x		x
classification	classification of material and services		x	x			x
position types	service position and material position		x	x			x
contracting	contract references	x					x
service identifiers	service identifier concept for different roles	(x)					x
external factor	description and specification of external factor						x
document types	specific document types for document exchange	(x)	(x)		(x)		x
electronic product catalogue	service positions specification in electronic product catalogues			x			x
service specifications	service specification format support	x					x
interfaces	definition of interfaces between procurement systems						x
message types and interfaces	binding of flexible architectures						x

eBuS-XML can be understood as an XML-based library of service transaction specific data types for the definition and description of order processing elements especially data transactions, service description and data and application integration. Data transaction elements are transaction documents, service description elements are definitions of service specifications. Electronic catalogues and enterprise application integration is supported through WSDL-based interfaces and message types.

eBuStrans defines the specific document types for the document exchange between business partners in the ecosystem. Service specifications contain all data required for describing and specifying service positions. The *service specification* data format enables interoperable and portable service specifications. *eBuScat* specifies data structures in conformity with existing standards such as BMEcat [11]. *eBuSWSDL* specifies interfaces and message types for a service-oriented interaction and integration of software packages and IT systems. The format allows and supports interactions of various business scenarios. New product-based services can be offered through third party service suppliers such as condition monitoring, preventive maintenance, spare parts management, etc. based on frame contracts and standardized service catalogues [5]. We analyzed existing standards like GAEB 90, 2000 and GAEB DA XML (a) [12], openTRANS (b) [13], BMEcat (c) [11], (d) UBL [14], ebXML (e) [9]. eBuS-XML (f) tends to overcome existing gaps and weaknesses. In table 1, requirements are defined for relevant data exchange in the context of industrial services. Differences of underlying business data and exchange standards were analyzed for electronic procurement solutions like e-catalogue standards and transaction standards. Based on our defined requirements, *eBuS-XML* defines all data types to fulfill derived requirements. *eBuS-XML* focuses on two parts of business communication: *harmonized data exchange of service procurement data for transactions* and *integration of application systems.*

5 Flexible Integration of Supplier and Customers in Collaborative Added Value Networks

For a flexible integration of suppliers and customers, different integration scenarios can be applied. In a *buy side* solution scenario, the ordering party provides a portal solution for the interaction and communication for the order processing. Contractors are enabled for login and interact with the ordering party by submitting order processing data and business documents. In most cases, after submitting data, the contractor receives a pdf-document as confirmation. Business processes are characterized by repetitive manual data input into respective IT systems. Electronic market places can be seen as further alternative solution scenario, these are often implemented by portal solutions that offer capabilities for distributive trading. In contrast to *buy side* solution scenarios, contractors offer their services with *sell side* solution systems. Based on a buy side solution we developed a service oriented approach to support and improve the integration and interaction with contractors. Based on our reference process model [3], five different services were identified. Four services are directly derived from the reference process and cover different process phases (see table 2). *eBuSWSDL* is presented as a defined part of the data type library of *eBuS-XML* and is partially covered by *eBuStrans*. It also inherits from *eBuScommontypes*. *eBuSWSDL* defines message types based on the transaction-oriented document types. The *eBuS-XML* library is shown in figure 4.

In a next step, WSDL specifications for Web Services and the exchange of message types have been defined. Service interfaces and message types are described. Interfaces define *portTypes*, *binding*, *ports* and *services*. Message types are based on our service specific XML library *eBuS-XML*.

Table 2. Web Service types for supporting the Reference Process Model

Web Service	Reference Process Phase	Description
Service Specification	Specification of services Requisition definition	Configuration and specification of services and aggregated services
Request for Quotation	Offer request Offer creation Offer comparison Offer negotiation	The specification is used for an offer request and creation of an offer. Offers can be compared and negotiated between parties.
Purchase Order	Order creation Order confirmation Order Measurement Order acceptance	Orders can be created and confirmed. Measurement data can be defined, created and accepted.
Invoicing	Invoice and debit note creation Payment confirmation	Invoice or debit note can be defined and exchanged. Payment to be confirmed.
Information	Supporting all phases	Defines additional service operations for continuous and complete data exchange

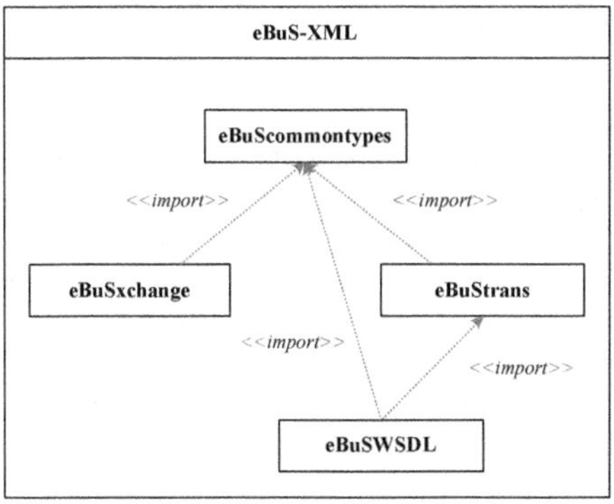

Fig. 3. eBuS-XML library

6 Conclusion and Outlook

In this paper, we presented a systematic approach for service procurement in collaborative service procurement networks. In total we analyzed 18 use cases which allowed us to validate the achieved results. Conceptual design for service e-procurement networks with two essential elements could be developed: service business processes and flexible IT systems which adequately support service-oriented transactions through standardized interfaces, data integration and harmonized service master data. A flexible web service architecture designed on basis of specific service business documents for message exchange was proposed. The integration of business processes and master data results in increased efficiency and effectiveness of service-related transactions such as order processing. Derived new features of enterprise application solutions fitting requirements of service procurement networks were introduced. We presented XML-based data types called *eBuS-XML* aiming at standardization of service-related business transactions as well as flows of data and documents. Furthermore, sell side scenario was presented and validated. The paper introduced *eBuSWSDL* and described WSDL document types and services. Next steps will foresee evaluating the different integration scenarios in real life procurement networks. Yielded results from our research need further validation and will be implemented in pilot applications. Several industry partners indicated their interest to evaluate and validate proposed solution approach and data format based on real life uses cases.

References

1. Herfurth, M., Meinhardt, A., Schumacher, J., Weiß, P.: eProcurement for industrial maintenance services. In: Camarinha-Matos, L.M., Paraskakis, I., Afsarmanesh, H. (eds.) PRO-VE 2009. IFIP AICT, vol. 307, pp. 361–368. Springer, Heidelberg (2009)
2. Camarinha-Matos, L.M., Paraskakis, I., Afsarmanesh, H. (eds.): PRO-VE 2009. IFIP AICT, vol. 307. Springer, Heidelberg (2009)
3. Herfurth, M., Kern, R., Rudolf, C., Weiß, P.: Reducing the complexity of Services: a new Approach to Service e-Procurement. In: Proceedings of the Multikonferenz Wirtschaftsinformatik MKWI 2010, Göttingen/Germany (2010)
4. Herfurth, M., Weiß, P.: E-Procurement for Industrial Maintenance Services. In: eChallenges 2009, Istambul/Turkey (2009)
5. Kagermann, H., Oesterle, H., Jordan, J.M.: IT-driven Business Models: Global Case Studies in Transformation. Wiley, New Jersey (2011)
6. myOpenFactory, DIN PAS 1074: myOpenFactory 4.0 (2009), `http://myopenfactory.com/products-myopenfactory.html`
7. Alonso, G., Casati, F., Kuno, H., Machiraju, V.: Web Services - Concepts, Architectures and Applications. Springer, Heidelberg (2004)
8. GS1: RosettaNet (2011), `http://www.rosettanet.org`
9. United Nations Economic Commission for Europe: UN/Edifact (2011), `http://www.unece.org/cefact/`
10. UN/CEFACT, OASIS: ebXML (2011), `http://www.ebxml.org/`
11. BME: BMEcat (2011), `http://www.bmecat.org/deutsch/index.asp?main=Start&pid=`
12. GAEB: GAEB DA XML (2011), `http://www.gaeb-da-xml.de/`
13. Fraunhofer IAO: openTRANS (2011), `http://www.opentrans.de/`
14. OASIS: ebXML (2011), `http://www.oasis open.org/committees/tc_home.php?wg_abbrev=ubl`

Part IV

Co-creation of Complex Products

Collaborative Networks in Support of Service-Enhanced Products

Luis M. Camarinha-Matos[1], Hamideh Afsarmanesh[2], and Bernhard Koelmel[3]

[1] Faculty of Sciences and Technology, Universidade Nova de Lisboa / Uninova, Portugal
cam@uninova.pt
[2] Informatics Institute, University of Amsterdam, The Netherlands
h.afsarmanesh@uva.nl
[3] CAS Software AG, Germany
bernhard.koelmel@cas.de

Abstract. The development and support of highly customized and service-enhanced products requires new organizational structures, involving the manufacturers, customers and local suppliers in a process of co-creation. This requires the implementation of the glocal enterprise notion with value creation from global networked operations and involving global supply chain management, product-service linkage, and management of distributed manufacturing units. An approach based on cloud-computing and advanced collaboration spaces is proposed for such contexts. As application scenario the manufacturing and life cycle support of solar parks is considered.

Keywords: Collaborative networks, Service-enhanced products, Collaborative Ecosystems, Cloud computing.

1 Introduction

There is a growing trend in manufacturing to move towards highly customized products, ultimately one-of-a-kind, which is reflected in the term *mass customization*. In fact, mass customization refers to a customer co-design process of products and services which meet the needs/choices of each individual customer with regard to the variety of different product features [2], [4]. Important challenges in such manufacturing contexts can be elicited from the requirements of complex technical infrastructures, like security infrastructures, alternative energy, or illumination systems in large public buildings or urban equipments, but also in more traditional complex products such as customized kitchens:

- These products typically require a variety of competencies and resources, hardly available in a single enterprise, which calls for collaboration among several companies and individuals.
- In many cases operations are performed within a fixed solution space, characterized by stable but still flexible and responsive processes, which can highly benefit from ICT support. As a result, the costs associated with customization allow for a price level that does not imply a switch in an upper market segment.

L.M. Camarinha-Matos et al. (Eds.): PRO-VE 2011, IFIP AICT 362, pp. 95–104, 2011.

- A complex multi-supplier product with a high degree of customization would benefit from associated services (e.g. maintenance support, assistance wizard, etc.) leading to the notion of service-enhanced products, which are more difficult to plan and arrange than with standardized mass products.
- Customization demands that the recipients of the customized goods transfer their specific needs and desires into a concrete product specification. This calls for customers' integration into the value creation process to detailed defining, configuring, matching, and/or modifying an individual solution. Different from a do-it-yourself setting this is done in close interaction between the manufacturers and the customer, who will contribute to co-creating the product/service with the manufacturer (or provider) responsible for providing the customized solution.

From a strategic management perspective, mass customization is a differentiated strategy. Customers gain from the customization of the increment of utility and variation of a good that better fits to their needs than the best standard product attainable. The larger the heterogeneity of all customers' preferences, the larger is this gain in utility and variation. From a managerial point of view, customization can be carried out with regard to fit, style, functionality, etc. Matching the level of customization offered by a manufacturer with the customers' needs becomes a major success factor. Providing European SMEs with adequate ICT support environments for mass customization therefore gives them a leading edge over other competitors from others regions that are more competitive in mass production of standardized products.

Overcoming the economic crisis requires companies to focus on exporting, namely to act in emerging markets such as the BRIC (Brazil, Russia, India, China), which is difficult for SMEs to compete in, if working alone. In this context, many enterprises are struggling to survive in the currently turbulent markets, whilst some become leaders in gaining new markets and effectiveness by targeting their future in terms of new products and services, or some other emerging technologies, having their focus already on technical innovation and strong customer-orientation. When focusing on customizable complex products, a domain where European companies might have an opportunity, it is important to be aware of the socio-economic, traditional, cultural, and perhaps even religious context surrounding the customer. A collaborative network involving not only a network of European manufacturers, but also the customer and some local suppliers is thus beneficial and necessary. Since the main customers of complex products and technical infrastructures are public entities, it is even frequently the case that the collaboration with local suppliers is a contractual requirement.

This paper introduces the base concepts and preliminary results of the GloNet project which aims the development of the required support platforms interlinked with the development of adequate organizational and governance models to facilitate the rapid formation and effective operation of the described partnerships.

2 A Motivating Case

The industry-driving use case in GloNet is in the Solar Park construction sector. The norm of operation in this industry is that of one-of-a-kind production and delivery of products (e.g. infrastructure, photovoltaic panels, and control systems). The results (products and services) are typically delivered through complementary competences sharing between different project participants. Such operational modes naturally have implications on the way the Product Lifecycle Management (PLM) is organized between the participating organizations.

As energy costs continue to rise, businesses need smarter energy management strategies. Advances in control technology give the benefits of energy management and control systems in a single, sustainable, and flexible networked infrastructure. During a product development process, it is essential to identify the critical components, critical suppliers and also the proportion of commodities to be outsourced to each supplier, thereby deciding on the structure of a virtual enterprise of involved companies.

The *Infranet Partners* is a network of SMEs specializing in the control technology solutions based on production and provision of advanced control technologies. This network was established in 1999 with 4 founding members and today there are some 20 partners in this network. In photovoltaic solutions around the world, products from the Infranet Partners are used to monitor and control solar park units and their related processes.

Solar parks include a number of subsystems — security, lighting, elevators, power, safety, and HVAC (Heating, Ventilating, and Air Conditioning) — that are crucial to a well-run system. But most of them operate separately or, at best, are connected through a series of costly, hard-to-maintain gateways to a single human-machine interface. The Infranet Partners invested on the concept of open control systems, where manufacturers follow independently maintained interoperability guidelines that create a single, unified automation system. Embedded technology and infrastructure products are at the heart of these open systems.

Aiming at a new generation of systems, integrating remote support services, and in order to better serve customers, the Infranet Partners aim to improve their current operation as a collaborative network, through:

- Creating a comprehensive pool of Technology and Application resources.
- Serving the customers as a single organization, offering locally adapted solutions from this shared pool.
- Answer the demand for holistic user-centered solutions (customers demand „complete" solutions out of one hand).
- Focusing on core competencies of each partner in the virtual enterprise: delegating the process of value generation into the supply chain.
- Combining their products range under the Infranet Partners brand and providing services associated to the products along their life cycle.
- Providing a comprehensive product range and support backed by frequent cross training.
- Sharing technical support and knowledge of different markets to provide solutions for customers.
- Sharing marketing information using an advanced dynamic groupware marketing tool to enable them to act faster to meet customer requirements.
- Reaching a smooth collaboration environment involving customers and local suppliers in their target market locations (e.g. India).

Example services associated to the product life cycle include:

- Remote monitoring and diagnosis
- Remote supervision
- Predictive maintenance
- Product usage: training, assistance, interaction.

Market drivers in complex industrial infrastructures like solar plants come with increased usage of controlling software and electronics as a distinguishing feature, coupled with changes in manufacturing such as globalization, increased competition, higher safety needs and faster serviceability. This has led to challenging new requirements for content-rich and price-competitive products. In this domain, the latest product developments incorporate new intelligent features with increasing complexity and the use of services, electronics and software as differentiators in the marketplace. These features require added manufacturing know-how along the value chain to drive the next level of operational efficiency and performance. The development of these complex interlaced systems over the entire product lifecycle represents an increasing challenge for all manufacturers and their suppliers.

As such, the following are some challenges faced by the manufacturers within the planned GloNet Virtual Enterprise:

- Mechanical, construction, electrical, and software product development have traditionally grown up as separate silos of expertise and technology that need to be brought together early in the development lifecycle of the product. Furthermore clients of such one-of-a-kind production industry demand user-centred customised products and services that a single organisation may not be able to deliver. GloNet is developing a platform, tools and governance principles to support effective creation and operation of the virtual enterprise and its interaction with the customer.
- There is no single management system for capturing product data at network level. Mechanical, electrical, and software data are often handled in separate document management systems with no automated sharing of data between the systems or links between data. With GloNet, all relevant documents can be stored centrally and called upon via web-service APIs, providing a single source of all product-related information along its life cycle.
- There is no commercial system design environment currently available for this application field. At the moment home-grown systems are patched together, which are expensive to develop and maintain. GloNet allows for a suitable extension.
- Due to the growing number of product variants and increasingly short lifecycles, costs for developing physical prototypes have become increasingly prohibitive, therefore the knowledge of the engineers have to distributed within projects, but limited to one project. GloNet provides role-based and differentiated authentication mechanisms to support this requirement. Furthermore, all requests are tracked.
- The Infranet partners are realizing embedded software in an area of competitive differentiation and are investigating how to improve and streamline their software processes along the value chain. There are no commercially available systems for keeping the software version synchronized with the mechanical and electrical product data. GloNet allows for a suitable extension.

- Due to the increased electronic content and provision of value added services like services associated to the product (solar park) along its life cycle (i.e. service design, decentralised support, proactive maintenance). Managing the supply chain without the basic Virtual Enterprise and tying to deal with as-shipped product structure is a growing challenge. GloNet provides a collaborative solution.

Within GloNet we envision a best practice in Virtual Enterprise management for complex industrial units like solar plants that will address these challenges.

3 The Conceptual Approach

GloNet adopts a cloud-based approach [5] for the development of such support environment so that its supporting services can dynamically upgrade without influencing the nodes and stakeholders in the environment. As such the environment stakeholders procure the use of upgraded services, which are always available through the cloud, rather than buying static products which typically need to be installed and maintained by the stakeholders on adequately supporting computing facilities. Specifically, over the *cloud* two **virtual spaces** are considered (Fig. 1):

- Collaborative solution space – where manufacturers, local suppliers and customers meet to co-design the product (and associated services).
- Service provision space – a "registry" of the products, along their life-cycle, where the customer can have access to the specific services associated to the customized product.

Fig. 2 illustrates the key concepts involved in GloNet and main relationships among these concepts.

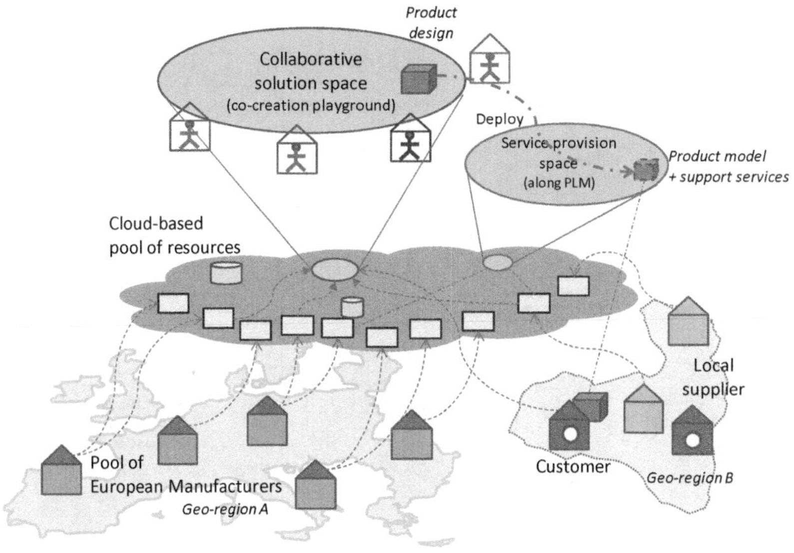

Fig. 1. Virtual spaces in GloNet

Organizational structures. Taking into account the possibilities offered by emerging technologies for collaboration support, including adaptive business process and business services modelling, participative environments, and social software, GloNet envisions a dynamic business ecosystem where interconnections between players and their roles are dynamically adjusted to the business opportunities. Therefore the project considers:

- Inter-play of long-term and short-term networks, i.e. Virtual enterprise Breeding Environments (VBE) and dynamic goal-oriented virtual enterprises (VE) [1].
- Interplay of manufacturers' network with customers and local suppliers (implementing the *glocal* enterprise and co-creation notions).
- Development phase network and PLM support network, in other words, a virtual enterprise might be organized for the product development and dissolve after the product is delivered, while another virtual enterprise, eventually sharing some members with the first one, might be organized to support the product along its life cycle.

In order to properly design the organizational structures, GloNet is starting with matching needs (analysis of current practices) with state of the art and emerging organizational models as identified in the disciplines of collaborative networks and organizational ecology and also briefly pointed out in the FInES roadmap [6].

Particularly in what concerns the involvement of the customers (and local suppliers) in an open innovation process, GloNet goes beyond the traditional process in which customer inputs are collected at the end of the process. Through the proposed *collaboration space*, GloNet exploits the synergies created by the involvement of the customer and local suppliers in all phases of the product development and life cycle support.

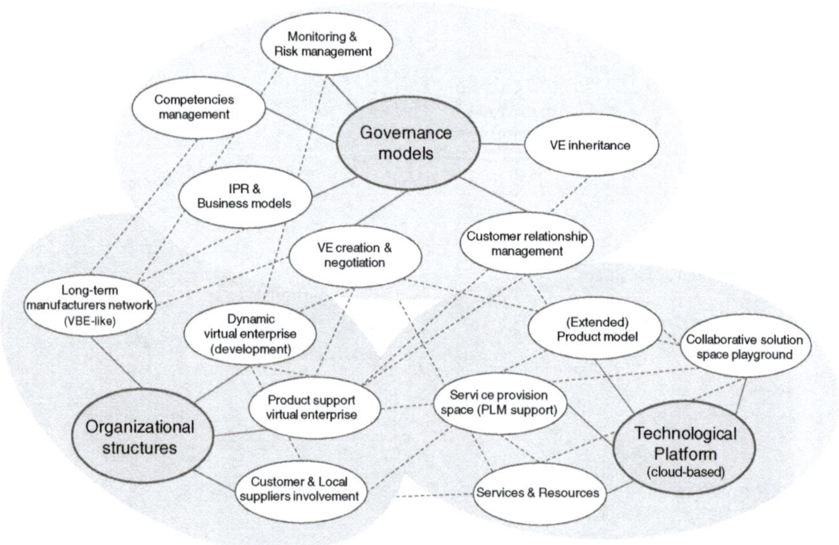

Fig. 2. Main supporting concepts

Technological platform. Regarding the base platform the following main characteristics are planned:

- Cloud-based infrastructure, based on open-source technologies, adopting relevant standards and based on OSGi.
- Incremental pool of services, knowledge, and other resources (scalability characteristic).
- Supporting the notion of extended product - combination of physical product with a set of linked support services (e.g. maintenance, remote diagnosis, remote user assistance, training, ...). A product model will become available in the *Service Provision Space* as a single entry point for product-related information and services along its life cycle. The product support virtual enterprise will naturally be linked to this product model.
- Besides the cloud-based platform, the environment includes two main (virtual) spaces: (i) *Collaborative solution space* - where new products are developed / customized (co-creation/mass customization) through the interplay of the various stakeholders (product development virtual enterprise); (ii) *Service provision space* - where models of products and associated services are kept along the product life cycle, supported by the product support virtual enterprise.

Governance models. Under this pillar the following main concepts and support functionalities are developed:

- Competencies management and competencies gap analysis (business intelligence).
- IPR & business models for co-created products.
- VE creation & negotiation principles, including readiness assessment and value systems alignment analysis.
- Performance monitoring and risk assessment, including aspects of "collaboration emotional health".
- Customer relationship management ("who owns the customer", brokerage services, etc.).
- VE inheritance - transition from product development VE to PLM support VE.

The chosen real industry pilot scenario, on the other hand, serves not only the demonstration and validation purposes, but also helps focusing on the requirements elicitation and system design and development.

4 Cloud Based Platform

GloNet base platform is based on the Cloud Development Stack model CAS OPEN [3], which is a standardized objective framework for cloud-offerings. CAS OPEN has a set of broad-based and deep capabilities that enable cost-effective development in the *Cloud*. The main objective that is addressed by the base GloNet architecture is the provision of a platform that allows for extensive customization and extensibility of SaaS for virtual enterprise functionalities offerings without compromising reliability and security. The architecture is intended not only to guide the software development but also to provide a technology-independent model of the platform. A base framework is assumed, providing the basis for interoperability, incremental service addition, security, and privacy mechanisms.

In order to increase the interoperability and consistency of engineering and manufacturing solutions with efficient collaboration approaches, the GloNet System will be built on top of an open service platform compliant with the OSGi framework.

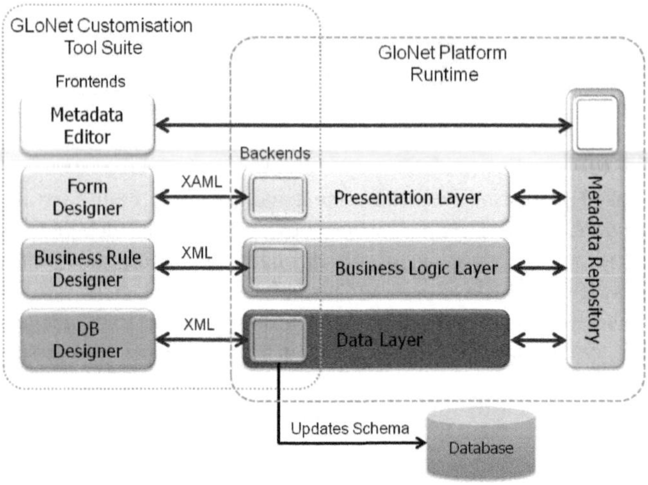

Fig. 3. GloNet base platform architecture

The system will consist of two major components: The Glo Net-Server, conceived as a central open cloud service infrastructure, consisting of basic functions and components, which are responsible for the business logic, the virtualization of "on premise solutions" as well as for interlinking and aggregating information sources of software services running on the platform. As a consequence of the SaaS customization scenario, development tools consist of two parts: (i) a *backend,* which is an integral part of the corresponding layer (data, logic, or presentation) and is available not only during the development of a solution, but also during runtime of a GloNet platform instance, (ii) a *designer* (design-time tool), which is used to create the configuration specifications that are accepted by the corresponding backend. Because a layer's behavior must be adaptable during runtime of a GloNet platform instance, the truly challenging part of the customization mechanism is actually the backend. Since almost all concepts and logic that are needed to support a SaaS customization are part of the backend, the latter will be the focus of the customization tools being developed in the course of the GloNet project.

The ability to use Web services enables the developers of solutions and customizations to leverage already existing (and tested) solutions for particular highly-specialized tasks within their apps, instead of having to reinvent the wheel. For example, an app or app extension for collaborative contact management could invoke an external service to perform a check if a pre-product is available within the value chain. This will be also the approach for integration with legacy systems found within some tenant's organization. An example would be to use a Web service to integrate a tenant's legacy ERP system. Naturally external services are expected to come with a variety of programming interface design conventions (atomic invocations, complex protocol-based conversations, etc), and different implementation technologies (SOAP-based and REST-based). For reasons of completeness and flexibility, the GloNet platform must support the integration of apps with any type of external service. On the other hand, for reasons of facilitating configuration-based integration of external services as an alternative (but not replacement) to programming-based integration, which should still be possible to do, the GloNet platform also needs to set some constraints on service design conventions and implementation technologies.

The ubiquity of the cloud helps overcome the previous need to house all the members of the team under one roof. The cloud places communications and coordination within the affordable reach of every SME.

5 Advanced Functionalities

On top of the cloud-based platform a set of advanced functionalities are designed:

Customized service-enhanced product specification. GloNet addresses ordering complex multi-supplier products which require high degree of customization, and tailoring to varied set of customer's criteria. One of the aims is thus to facilitate detailed specification of such complex customized products, when also enhanced with their required business services, e.g. to support their maintenance, insurance, etc. To achieve this, the development of the following supporting tools and intelligent user-based interfaces is going on:

- Services for customers/local suppliers to iteratively specify product details - starting with the semi-open data platform of all sub-product alternatives, the system will facilitate the iterative process of achieving the exact specific final selection of required sub-products, agreed by the customer to be ordered.
- Dynamically customizable set of business services enhancing the product - based on the customer profile established dynamically in the previous services, here we focus on the development of a recommendation tree for offering to customer all alternatives of enhancing services around the ordered product. An adaptive dialogue structure is also designed on top of the recommendation tree that uses service reputation for promoting the services to the customer.

Consortia formation and operation support. These functionalities are intended to support the networked multi-stakeholder organizational structures involved in the service-enhanced product development and support. Thus they include the elaboration of models, development of support tools (services) and governance principles regarding: (i) Long-term base networks (manufacturers), (ii) Dynamic goal-oriented virtual enterprises (also involving the customer and local suppliers), (iii) Virtual enterprises for product life cycle support. Furthermore, process monitoring, risk forecasting, and management are also included. Thus the main services here include:

- Services for management of long-term base network - to support the management of long-term alliances of manufacturers, which typically assume the form of a VBE (Virtual organizations breeding environment) with flexible boundaries (different levels of membership). Support services include partners' profiling and competency management, competencies gap analysis, collaboration readiness assessment, value systems alignment assessment, trust management, incentives and assets management.
- Services for dynamic consortia formation and order work plan - a collection of

software services for dynamic consortia formation and monitoring involvement of customers and local suppliers.

- Services for consortium risk forecasting and management - concerned with identification and characterization of risks in a collaborative context as well as their forecasting, monitoring and launching of preventive / corrective actions. The relationships between risks and competencies and expectations are analyzed. Since emotional / affective aspects play a critical role in the levels of commitment and performance of network members, attention is also devoted to monitoring and promotion of the collaboration "health" at network level.

6 Conclusions and Further Work

In support of complex service-enhanced products along their life cycle, the approach followed in GloNet aims to: (**i**) develop a novel way to commonly represent/provide information and knowledge which needs to be shared/exchanged among different stakeholders in the collaborative environment as dynamic software services that may upgrade in time; (**ii**) generate user-customized interfaces which dynamically adjust to different stakeholders, supporting their access and visualization needs; (**iii**) provide these services through the *cloud*, to be available to anybody, at any time, from anywhere, (**iv**) demonstrate how a broker in very close contact with the customer who gives an order, can iteratively retrieve all needed information to step by step design the customer order and finally presenting the solution that is accepted by the customer, (**v**) support the negotiation among all involved parties, (**vi**) generate a workflow from the accepted/negotiated solution, which will then be automatically monitored, while also available for monitoring by the involved stakeholders, during its execution, (**vii**) the automatic monitoring aims will forecast potential risks, and will suggest prevention measures to the broker during the execution of the order.

A preliminary system and exemplary services have been designed based on the needs identified in the context of solar plants. Next phases involve the field validation of the approach and tools as well as the assessment of their potential applicability to other contexts.

Acknowledgments. This work was funded in part by the European Commission through the GloNet project.

References

1. Camarinha-Matos, L.M., Afsarmanesh, H.: Collaborative Networks: Reference Modeling. Springer, Heidelberg (2008)
2. Cox, H., Mowatt, S.: Consumer-driven innovation networks and e-business management systems. Qualitative Market Research: An International Journal 7(1), 9–19 (2004)
3. Koelmel, B.: Enable secure access - CAS Open - SaaS Framework. Heidelberg Innovation Forum (2008)
4. Ogawa, S., Piller, F.T.: Collective Customer Commitment: Reducing the risks of new product development. MIT Sloan Management Review 47 (2006)
5. Ommeren, E., Duivestein, S., de Vadoss, J., Reijnen, C., Gunvaldson, E.: Collaboration in the Cloud. Microsoft and Sogeti (2009) ISBN 978 90 75414 24 0
6. FInES, Research Roadmap. European Commission, FInES Cluster (June 2010)

Collaborative Customization Strategy for Complex Products – Prospects for Engineer-to-Order and Customize-to-Order Production Scenarios

Ahm Shamsuzzoha[1], Timo Kankaanpaa[1], Luis Carneiro[2], and Petri Helo[1]

[1] Department of Production, University of Vaasa, P.O. BOX 700, FI-65101, Finland
{ahm.shamsuzzoha,timo.kankaanpaa,petri.helo}@uwasa.fi
[2] INESC Porto, Campus da FEUP, Rua Dr. Roberto Frias, 378, 4200-465, Porto, Portugal
luis.carneiro@inescporto.pt

Abstract. To compete in globalized business environments, manufacturing firms, especially small and medium enterprises (SMEs), need to be collaborative with respect to their total product life cycle. In this research, a focus on complex products is proposed and a new approach to structure collaboration in design and operational activities is suggested. A complete framework and guidelines for collaborative product design, development and manufacturing is proposed with respect to two product development scenarios: Engineer-to-Order (ETO) and Customize-to-Order (CTO). The ETO scenario, which is project-based, and the CTO scenario, which is platform-based, are employed to respond to individualized and market driven production strategies respectively. The CTO scenario is developed using the platform-based product family concept, following a new approach that uses a product configurator and white boxes to assure sustainable customization. The research also explains how the transition from ETO to CTO can be implemented, aiming at improving the customization level and profitability of SMEs. The overall results, lessons learned and future research directions conclude the paper.

Keywords: Business collaboration, product design and engineering, collaborative bill-of-materials (BOM), engineer-to-order (ETO), customize-to-order (CTO).

1 Introduction

The business potential resulting from collaborative environments is receiving more attention from industrial organizations than ever before [1]. Today's market competition is forcing companies, especially small and medium enterprises (SMEs), to be collaborative in order to differentiate their products and gain advantage over larger firms globally. The increasing level of product variety, shorter product life cycle, unpredictable demand levels, unprecedented number of features and user-selected preferences are exerting extra pressure on SMEs. To cope with this situation, geographically scattered design teams are needed to work collaboratively on a virtual basis [2]. This collaboration can be enhanced by intra and inter-enterprise participants to work together from any geographic location.

L.M. Camarinha-Matos et al. (Eds.): PRO-VE 2011, IFIP AICT 362, pp. 105–114, 2011.

Collaboration can start early in finding the immediate business opportunities and end up with taking advantage of those opportunities successfully. The business opportunities are ultimately the demand for specific products or product families which need to be designed and manufactured according to the customers' specifications and required features. In a networked business environment, the partners collaborate in the early conceptual phase of product development, where the necessary design and engineering are done with the objective of manufacturing the target product. During the conceptual design phase, the business partners communicate with each other and iterate various design options before choosing the best one. The conceptual design phase is followed by the detailed design and engineering stages, where the required design features are reviewed in terms of capacity, lead-time and costs.

The presented research defines the basic steps in developing both the ETO and CTO production scenarios in a collaborative business environment and also proposes a new approach to the customization of complex products based on transition strategy from ETO to CTO scenarios. In the ETO scenario, the customer suggests an idea/concept, time frame and budget, which are not just an updating of an existing solution but require specific functionalities. For complex products, the most challenging activity in this approach is to manage the long lead time. In ETO, detailed cost calculation and order specific engineering services are required.

On the other hand, in a CTO scenario, the development of a platform-based product family (PBPF) creates the possibility to offer the customer a wide variety of products with competitive costs. In this scenario, the product platform concept and a detailed business plan are needed to allow the business partners to comfortably decide the investment in such project. This research work proposes a CTO strategy, including all the methodological aspects, to manage the life cycle for such a PBPF and makes clear the differences and evolution paths from ETO to CTO strategies.

The rest of the paper is organized as follows: Section 2 presents a review of the existing literature on business collaboration with respect to product design and engineering, while Section 3 highlights the collaborative definition of BOM, which is necessary to structure the planning and control of operations. Section 4 and Section 5 present the scope of business collaboration in ETO and CTO production scenarios respectively. The transition of business scenario from ETO to CTO according to market opportunity is illustrated in Section 6. The basic outcomes from this research are discussed and concluded with future research directions in Section 7.

2 Literature Review

The growing concern with customer-tailored products creates tremendous challenges for product manufacturers in terms of costing and profitability. To achieve the solution for such challenges, manufacturing firms are focused on the joint development of product and process strategies for specific market needs [3]. This business strategy allows the identifying of ways to reduce the development cost and time for target products through sharing knowledge and resources. Distributed design, engineering and manufacturing provide the expected value chain integration among business partners, which opens new opportunities for collaborative work improvement [4].

Collaborative product development supports design innovation and increased productivity [5]. Moreover, design collaboration facilitates complicated interactions among multidisciplinary and globally distributed design teams through cooperation, coordination and communication [6]. Enhanced customization is enabled by business collaboration, where partners share their valuable knowledge and resources to be competitive in the market segment [7]. This strategic vision requires a distributed information network among partner organizations in order to facilitate up-to-date product and process architecture throughout the product's lifecycle.

In the complex product development process collaborative design and manufacturing also have influence over the customer order decoupling point, in the case of both ETO and CTO scenarios [8]. It provides practical benefit for achieving true customization through individualized product and/or offering product variants [9]. The demand for more personalized products forces manufacturing companies to evolve from an ETO to CTO production scenario to gain wider market segments. In order to be successful in collaboration for both ETO and CTO scenarios, the network partners need to ensure integration among engineering data management (EDM), product data management (PDM), product information management (PIM), technical document management (TDM), and technical information management (TIM) [10].

3 Collaborative Definition of BOM

In collaborative product design, engineering and manufacturing in the network, the most critical aspect is to create a BOM of the target product. The development of the BOM can be started as soon as the conceptual design is done and can be expanded or updated according to further design improvement. Usually, in the early stages of a new product design and engineering, the network partners' design teams create the first BOM, which is also known as product structure or engineering BOM.

The detailed level of the final BOM is confirmed after securitizing the multiple BOMs created and iterated within the partner organizations. Along with the component hierarchy, the detailed BOM usually contains a component hierarchy along with the required interfacing and materials. This BOM helps to allocate essential tooling, and defines the manufacturing processes that include routing, scheduling, and resource planning. This ensures an identical view of the target product and process definition among the cross-functional design teams of the network partners. It also contributes to promoting true collaborative engineering in the early stages of design, and optimizing the work between design and manufacturing.

The definition of the BOM is critical for all operations after the product design, including collaborative budgeting, operations planning and control. During the BOM definition, component suppliers can be searched for by browsing partners or giving search criteria and comparing with potential partners. In such an environment, the collaborative partners might develop their own substructures, thus maintaining their own BOM data in the same context.

The definition of collaborative BOM (CBOM) can be stated as the structure of components that are designed and developed among distributed partner organizations with the objective to assemble to the end product. This CBOM guides the individual partners in essential planning in terms of operational routings, parts sequences, product coding, selection of potential supplier, etc., as presented in Figure 1. The ICT-based CBOM also supports the required modification of the operational sequences and/or production routings in real time according to the production requirements. This real time information update is made visible to the other partners with a view to adjusting their production processes if needed. The semantic model for CBOM as displayed in Figure 1 saves on production quantity and cost along with the description of the product/operation/part, too. This information management approach to the product structure enables the defining and creating of high level production batches comfortably within the collaborative business network.

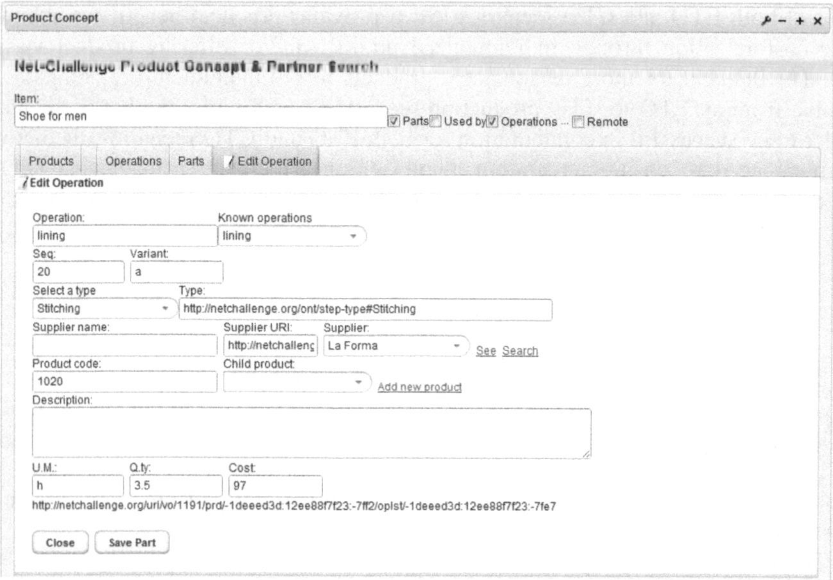

Fig. 1. Display of manufacturing operations of an example collaborative BOM

4 Business Collaboration in the ETO Scenario

The basic concept of the ETO production scenario is to develop and manufacture one-of-a-kind products, where the customer expectations for an individual product are fulfilled. The motivation behind the ETO scenario is to develop and manufacture a custom-made product collaboratively, where Virtual Organization (VO) partners participate in the complete product development process starting from the conceptual design phase to the final product design and development phase. The collaboration enables partners to fulfill more challenging business opportunities such as sharing costly resources, time consuming workloads, fatal risks and replying faster to customer requests. This approach is project-based, where the individual customer order is initiated after consulting with the customer in terms of his/her desires, emotional needs and requirements of the end product.

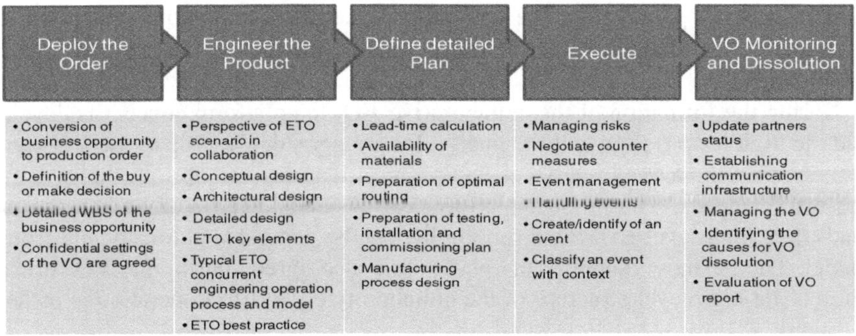

Fig. 2. High level operational sequence of collaborative ETO scenario

In this approach, the partners collaborate to define the product concept and quotation and form a VO after the customer order confirmation. After forming the VO, the VO enters the operation phase, where the customer order is deployed to the involved partners, followed by detailed product engineering and detailed collaborative planning. The required product specification, drawings and BOM are done at the product engineering sub-phase, while in detailed collaborative planning essential routings for the production processes are defined in order to achieve the confirmed delivery date of the final product. In this sub-phase, required calculation for the delivery lead time is performed. After confirming the delivery date, the process continues with the production execution and monitoring. In the production execution process, any abnormality or unforeseen events in the operational processes are monitored and managed in order to avoid unnecessary problems or risks.

Figure 2 presents the high level phases of the ETO VO Operation. In this phase, the VO partners monitor the production process and update the operational activities. A communication infrastructure is established in order to manage the entire VO. During this phase, possible causes for dissolving the VO are identified and a time frame is confirmed for dissolution. When the objective of developing collaboratively a one-of-a-kind product is achieved, the next stage is dissolving the VO as it was developed temporarily within a predefined timeframe. Before dissolving the VO, overall evaluation reports are sent to the collaborative partners.

5 Business Collaboration in the CTO Scenario

The result of the CTO production scenario is the collaborative development of a product platform, from where a stream of product variants can be specified and manufactured efficiently and economically, as required to meet customers' expectations. The main idea is to create a family based product platform, defining the common sets of components or modules to be used for delivering different product variants [11]. The platform offers cost efficient and enhanced customization features by adding and/or replacing customized components and/or modules within it. The variants created on the platform should be optimized from the manufacturing and logistics point of view and it should not be possible to generate incompatible combinations of parameters. The possibility to define special requirements for some components or functionalities (white spots) provides enlarged customization possibilities.

During the formation of the collaborative VO, the platform concept is developed and the high level design and the main rules are agreed. The role of the VO partners is to support the agreed interfaces and propose features and options that will fulfill the market needs. The product platform can be considered ready when the price, lead-time, high-level BOM and routing list can be generated automatically from the model. The business model of the platform is also agreed during the VO formation phase. The high level structure of the collaborative CTO VO operation is presented in Figure 3.

From Figure 3, it can be seen that the CTO scenario starts with the detailed development of a product platform, which is the prerequisite to successfully configure a product variant in accordance with a customer enquiry. The second phase of the CTO life cycle is to identify the platform architecture. This phase starts with the generic concept of the product platform architecture. The most important and time-consuming phase during the platform architecture definition is the interface management among the modules. The interfaces may have technical (dimensions), feature-based (material or color) or non-tangible relations (drivers). The platform can be initially designed as feature or component-based.

The consecutive stage after indentifying the platform architecture is to make a product variant. This phase starts with the identification of specific customer requirements to create a customized product variant.

The last phase of the CTO life cycle is the specification of special requirements (white spots). In this phase, special requirements from the prospective customers are collected. In order to fulfill such special requirements, the VO broker (initiating partner) consults with the collaborative partners for developing a specific module or component termed as 'white spot' that could satisfy such unique customer requirements. If there is a possibility to produce the specific module or white spot, the broker proceeds by defining the necessary price, lead-time, etc., with a view to preparing the updated quotation.

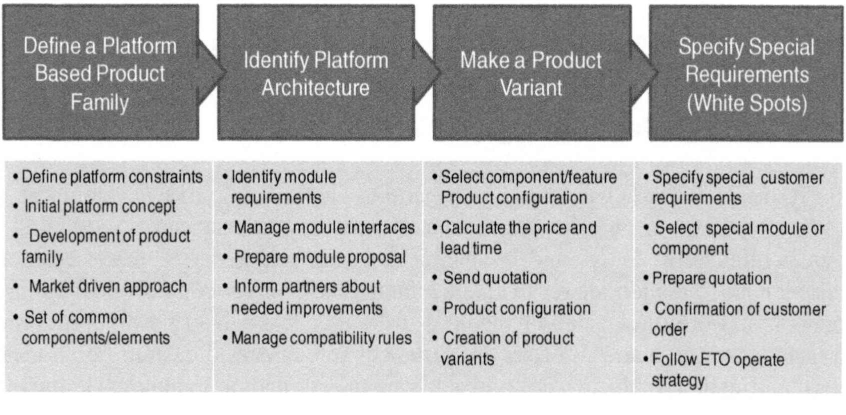

Fig. 3. High level operational sequences of collaborative CTO scenario

The proposed approach is revealed to be very powerful, as it can be implemented from an IT point of view with a product configurator, with the capability to manage white spot.

6 Transition from ETO to CTO Scenario

In this section, the scope and usability of the transition from ETO to CTO scenarios is demonstrated with respect to business potential and fulfilling customers' needs. In general, the ETO scenario is customer-driven or project-based, where a specific type of product or product group is developed in terms of unique design and specification. The CTO scenario is market-driven, as it responds to a broad business opportunity and customers are given the possibility to customize an existing solution and the output is a stream of products resulting from a configuration process with optional white spots.

Most SMEs do not have a strong product strategy and structured approach to product customization. Inconsequence, they become dependent on subcontracting and often are forced to compete on price. European SMEs have strong technical skills and are able to follow an ETO strategy more easily than a CTO one. It is therefore considered an important need to make a transition from ETO to CTO scenarios, which allows SMEs to enable and to manage overall competitiveness and sustainability. The detailed transition from ETO to CTO is presented in Figure 4.

In Figure 4, it can be observed that when a business opportunity is identified, the business partners need to check out its possible consequences. If the identified opportunity is highly customized, the business partners need to follow the ETO production scenario. In this approach, the collaborative partners form a specific VO

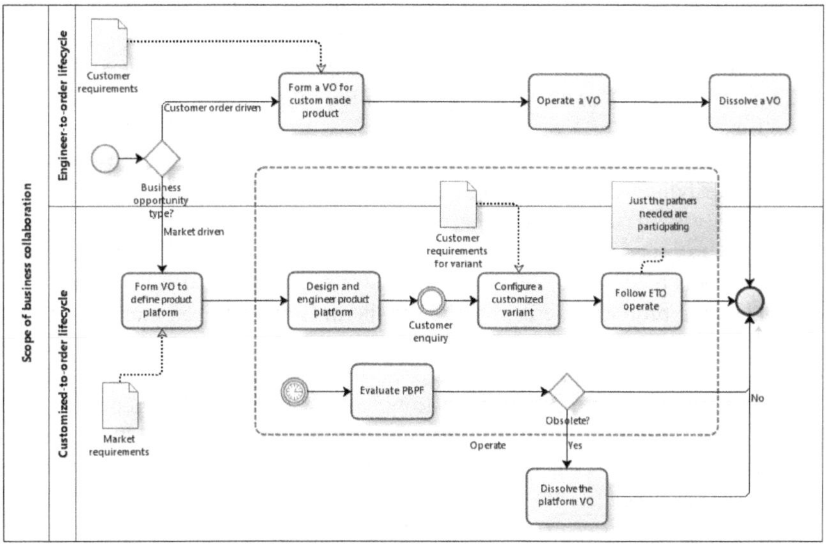

Fig. 4. Generic scope of the VO life cycle in a collaborative business environment

with the objective of developing and delivering a custom-made or one-of-a-kind product. After forming the VO the next available step is to operate the VO in terms of detailed designing, engineering, scheduling, routing and manufacturing the expected product. When the specific customer requirements are fulfilled through VO operation the last step is to dissolving the VO. At this stage, the partners are evaluated with respect to fulfilling the business targets as set during the VO formation.

Also in Figure 4 it can be noted that when the business opportunity is assessed to be market-driven the business partners move forward to accept the CTO production scenario. The objective of adopting this scenario is to develop a platform-based product family from where a stream of product variants can be customized. To adopt the CTO approach according to market demand, the collaborative partners form the necessary VO with the view to defining the product platform. In the operational phase of the VO the necessary detailed design and engineering of the platform is done. At this stage, the possibility of the individual customer's need for a variant is checked out for configuration purposes. When there is a possibility to configure an individualized product within the CTO scenario, the ETO operational steps are followed.

This ETO operational strategy within the CTO environment requires partners experienced in the ETO scenario, which in any case is the most common for SMEs. This operating environment develops the possibility to define a new module or component (known as white spot) according to the customer needs. If the new module or component (white spot) attracts an increasing level of interest from potential customers it can be merged to the platform for future use. During the VO operational phase, the developed platform is evaluated with respect to its outcomes and might be dissolved when it is considered obsolete over time. After fulfilling the objective of platform-based product family (PBPF), the necessary steps are taken to dissolve the previously formed VO. During the VO dissolution process, generic assessment is done in terms of performance evaluation of the partners, assessing the general liabilities of the partners and terminating the contractual agreements. The performance evaluation and the knowledge achieved from forming and operating the VO is stored for future use that will allow the enrichment of the business community.

The presented transition scenario from ETO to CTO supports the collaborative partners in designing and developing their products according to market demands. From the analysis, it is clear that the product development strategy can be changed according to customers' requirements. If the customer asks for an individualized (one-of-a-kind) product, then the developmental strategy should be ETO-based. On the other hand, if the products are developed for the mass customized market, it has to be then the CTO approach, where the product variants are created from the basic platform. In business collaboration, the partners decide whether the production scenario is market-driven (CTO) or customer order-driven (ETO) depending on the future business opportunities. However, on some occasions, the CTO approach can be merged with the ETO scenario when there are options for the customer to tailor his/her choice of product. This combined approach supports business organizations in adjusting their production processes according to the level of customization offered by them.

7 Conclusions

Business collaboration creates ample opportunities for manufacturing firms to survive healthily in today's competitive markets. This collaboration can emerge by forming virtual organizations that might be shorter or longer term. The VO duration depends on the business opportunity type and the commitment from the partner organizations. These networked businesses are especially important for SMEs, where there are often shortages of available and valuable resources and knowledge, which are the deciding factors for business sustainability. There is also a lack of proper communication infrastructures among SMEs which might allow them to be collaborative and enjoy the benefits of collaboration. The success of business collaboration depends not only on suitable qualified partners but also on the proper selection of the right ICT tools necessary for seamless information processing and to act in dynamic business environments [12].

In this research the fundamental requirements for collaborative business environments are presented with respect to product design and development, starting from the conceptual design phase and ending with manufacturing and control processes. The collaborative definition of the BOM is presented as a key step in this business collaboration.

To enable the long-term sustainability of SMEs two scenarios for the development and delivery of custom-made and customized products were developed, namely the ETO and CTO scenarios. The transition from an ETO to a CTO scenario was developed in this study, to allow the competitive delivery of customized products by SMEs. The very common situation with developing customized products is that the number of final products with an individual BOM will increase dramatically. The proposed concept makes the component commonality higher and the manufacturing of the customized final product more cost efficient.

The presented approach was validated with pilot companies from the textile and footwear sectors. An extension of these research results can be implemented in other real life industrial case networks in order to verify and validate the approach. The outcomes from such case applications might reduce the limitations of the presented approach and can be useful to fine tune these research results.

Acknowledgements. The authors would like to acknowledge the co-funding of the European Commission in NMP priority of the Seventh RTD Framework Programme (2007-13) for the Net Challenge project (Innovative Networks of SMEs for Complex Products Manufacturing), Ref. CP-FP 229287-2. The authors also acknowledge the valuable collaboration provided by the project team during the research work.

References

1. Camarinha-Matos, L.M., Afsarmanesh, H., Ollus, M.: Ecolead and CNO Base Concepts. In: Methods and Tools for Collaborative Networked Organizations. Springer Science+Business Media, LLC (2008)
2. Carneiro, L., Almeida, R., Azevedo, A.L., Kankaanpää, T., Shamsuzzoha, A.H.M.: An innovative framework supporting SME networks for complex product manufacturing. In: Camarinha-Matos, L.M., Boucher, X., Afsarmanesh, H. (eds.) PRO-VE 2010. IFIP AICT, vol. 336, pp. 204–211. Springer, Heidelberg (2010)

3. Shen, W.: Editorial of the special issue on knowledge sharing in collaborative design environments. Computers in Industry 52(1), 1–3 (2003)
4. Liandong, Z., Qifeng, W.: Integrated collaborative manufacturing management system for complex product. In: Second International Conference on Future Information Technology and Management Engineering, Sanya, Chine, December 13-14 (2009)
5. Shamsuzzoha, A.H.M., Helo, P.: Information dependencies within product architecture: prospects of complexity reduction. Journal of Manufacturing Technology Management 22(3), 314–329 (2011)
6. Shen, W., Norrie, D.H., Barthes, J.P.: Multi-Agent Systems for Concurrent Intelligent Design and Manufacturing. Taylor & Francis, London (2000)
7. Squire, B., Cousins, P.D., Brown, S.: Collaborating for customization: an extended resource-based view of the firm. International Journal of Productivity and Quality Management 1(1-2), 8–25 (2006)
8. Rudberg, M., Wikner, J.: Mass customization in terms of the customer order decoupling point. Production Planning & Control 15(4), 445–458 (2004)
9. Haug, A., Ladeby, K., Edwards, K.: From engineer-to-order to mass customization. Management Research News 32(7), 633–644 (2009)
10. McIntosh, K.G.: Engineering Data Management: A Guide to successful Implementation. McGraw-Hill, New York (1995)
11. Meyer, M.H., Lehnerd, A.P.: The Power of Product Platforms: Building Value and Cost Leadership. The Free Press, New York (1997)
12. Imtiaz, A., Hauge, J.B.: IFIP International Federation for Information Processing. In: Camarinha-Matos, L.M., Picard, W. (eds.) Pervasive Collaborative Networks, vol. 283, pp. 567–576. Springer, Boston (2008)

Integrating Co-development and Fit Coordination

Edmilson Rampazzo Klen and Luiz Salomão Ribas Gomez

EGR – Graphic Expression Department,
UFSC – Federal University of Santa Catarina, Florianópolis-SC, Brazil
{erklen,salomao}@cce.ufsc.br

Abstract. In the last recent years the globalized world has experienced its most amazing and rapid technological evolution. The repercussions and consequences of this (re-)evolution are many and can be seen and felt in the behavior of the enterprises and the consumers. For enterprises, new organizational structures are taking place contributing even for the emergence of the scientific discipline called Collaborative Networks. For consumers, a more active - and less reactive - role is gaining evidence and being directly influenced by the advances on information and communications technologies. The new web generation is participating in a silent movement of creation of prosumers[1]. As a consequence of this change in the behaviour of the enterprises and the consumers, a new space comes up with a high potential to be exploited. This space is seen as: products co-design or co-development environment. However, to lead the organizations in this collaborative relationship is necessary a fit coordination with specific competences to each case.

Keywords: Co-development, Competences, Fit coordination.

1 Introduction

Nowadays, consumers are dominating the Information and Communicate Technologies (ICT) advances, where, through them, their wishes became more transparent and available.

This is possible because their wishes are also discussed in the social nets, like communities, where producers can also participate to recognize these wishes of these (future) customers. In some cases, it is possible to observe in this kind of communities, discussion about a specific product that the consumers use or what they would like to use.

This scenario persuades towards a production addressed to these communities and, in some cases, in an individual form.

But is not enough to know what the market wishes, it is necessary to recognize the adequate organizations those will work together to attend the market.

The discipline Collaborative Network appears like a fundamental part to support this new evolutionary relationship among consumers and the organizations facilitating the joint of competences through new organizational structures, putting together appropriate organizations to attend the wishes of the consumers that arise by social nets of communities.

---

[1] Prosumer is the result of the contraction of the words: producer + consumer, Toffler [1]

L.M. Camarinha-Matos et al. (Eds.): PRO-VE 2011, IFIP AICT 362, pp. 115–122, 2011.

Authors like Thomas Friedman and John Gattorna take account the value related to the new globalization and the persons.

Successful companies agree that the person behind the transaction must also be considered. Such customer-focused and more flexible configurations are actually fundamental components of different supply chains. We are foreshadowing a new understanding of the way enterprises will work in the future [2]. Based on revolutions like the internet, cell phone, optic fiber, and so on, not just enterprises but also the individuals can act in an extended environment [3].

Is growing in this moment, a large volunteer business net shaping the prosumer concept also seen like talent pools. The smart enterprises have been using this potential to develop new and strong business models and systems [4].

This scenario (Figure 1) based on ICT is then composed by: 1) Customers or future customers creating social nets of communities that exchange ideas among them about new products or about improvements of products that already are in the market (i.e. Prosumer Communities). 2) Organizations supported by Collaborative Network always interested to know the wishes of the market. 3) The interaction between these parts that will facilitate the ideas exchange among producer and consumers to better know the market wishes and will also facilitate the choice of organizations that will work together (i.e. Virtual Organizations-VO) to attend the market more accurately (Toward Production). This ideas exchange environment will be here called Co-development Environment.

To complete this scenario is necessary an adequate management, an adequate coordinator. This person should be prepared to work with this market evolution related to the technological development of the production systems as well as of the information technology. The coordinator search & suggestion methodology proposed for this scenario is here called fit coordination.

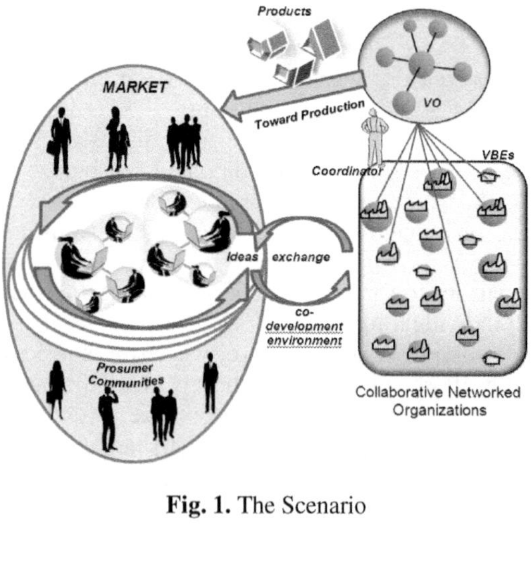

Fig. 1. The Scenario

2 The Co-development Environment

The fact is that functional organization, which have served us so well for so long, together with matrix and partnership variants, are being rapidly marginalized. This is happening as increasing competitive intensity in many industry-market combinations drives customers towards more aggressive and demanding buying behaviors [2]. These new organizational structures are been shaped in the last years based on the Collaborative Networked Organizations concepts [5].

In the case of the consumers a more active role — and less reactive — can be observed in the last years, where this behavior change is directly influenced by the facility of the access of new tools based on ICTs (Fig. 1). Environments, where there are ideas changes about a product or service (available on the market) support the mass collaboration.

The prosumers potentiate the co-development process in a very effective way mainly about their suggestions of design and usability. This is possible nowadays with a "home technology" — like the available in a social relationship — where is also possible to be applied with more details through the use of free CAD systems available on the internet, i. e. Google SketchUp [6].

The enterprises can now be integrated in this social net to find out new business opportunities. Some collaborative networked structures can help this interaction in a more organized form, i.e. Virtual Breeding Environment (VBE) and Virtual Teams (VT).

The VBE, that represents an association of organizations that share resources and skills to achieve a goal [7], has now the possibility to acquire new opportunities through this near contact with the prosumer communities. The ideas exchange with these future customers give a more detailed way to the wishes/necessities of the market providing a co-design and/or co-development environment.

The VT is a temporary group of professionals that work together towards a common goal such as realizing a consultancy job, a joint project, etc, and that use computer networks as their main interaction environment [8]. VT could be created with some personal competences to know and to evaluate the ideas/necessities/wishes in different viability aspects (technological, economics, social, etc). Professionals from different enterprises previously prepared to develop new ideas of new products can now work together just to evaluate these ideas coming direct from consumers or group of consumers. Moreover, the VT could also help the VBE administration staff to select the more appropriated enterprises — in a Virtual Organization (VO) structure — to attend a selected idea.

The VO would be a similar structure like the VT but, in this case, shaped with organizations/enterprises. The definitions of a VO often assume that it behaves and can be managed in some way like a single organization [9]

This co-design and/or co-development environment enables a "toward production", in other words, a product would come to the market incorporating strong feelings of a large group of persons with more chance to be a success in the market. In a virtuoso cycle this product would be continuously analyzed by this kind of consumers to other improvements enabling a long life in the market.

3 Fit Coordination

A good idea and an appropriate infrastructure are very important to the production of a new product but, to the work with collaborative structures – with different organizations with different visions, technologies, cultures, and so on, – a competent coordination of this structure is also essential.

Many organizations use the concept of competence to both measure and improve employee development as well as during their recruitment process.

The terminology of "competence" can be confusing because each organization normally has its own interpretation and understanding for the term.

Along the time many researchers have been studying competence. One of the well-established definitions on competence is provided by Durand [10] who states that competence is the ability to coordinate activities to the standards and rules required in the organization using an appropriate mix of knowledge, skill and attitude. According to him, these three dimensions must be present if someone wants to be effective in the coordination place. This understanding of competence is the one that will be used in this work.

As the VO coordinator has to deal with a distributed, dynamic and – sometimes - complex organizational environment one of his/her main attributes should be to adequately balance these dimensions of knowledge, skill and attitude in order to contribute to the achievement of the VO goals. As a direct consequence for all competences, Individual Competences - based on individual needs-, should always have a special attention.

Some essential Competencies of a VO Coordinator can be selected, extended and detailed according to the interest of a VT (composed, i.e, by experts from the VBE members) with the supervision of the VO Planner and the VBE Administrator for instance.

These competencies data can be gathered in a Competence Map where the data can be classified in the three dimension in an integrated form (Knowledge, Skill and Attitude) (Fig. 2), aiming to facilitate the recognition of an adequate candidate in the search and suggestion process.

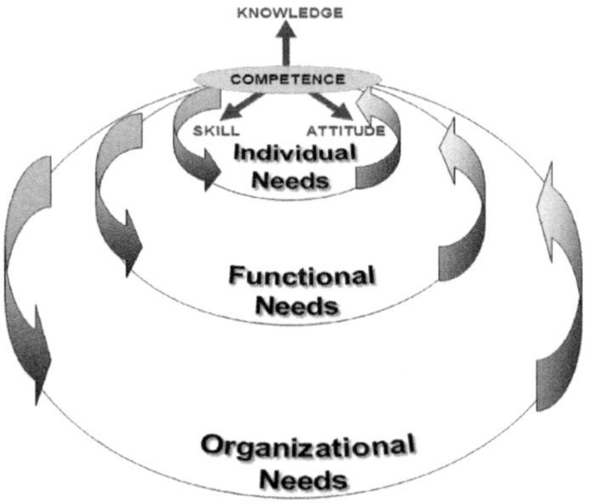

Fig. 2. Competence Cycle

A very crucial issue for the elaboration of the Competence Map is the use of an adequate Competence Common Ontology as well as the proposition of mechanisms necessary for using and evolving this ontology during the VBE/VO management. It is not the scope of this work to go deeper on this subject. However, given its relevance for the accuracy of this work, the scenario here presented (Fig. 3) is considered deterministic i.e. it is assumed that an ontology exits and is in use.

This competence cycle integrates three complementary competencies types: Individual Competences (the ones related to each individual person), Functional Competences (the ones required by the role to be performed – in this case the VO coordinator) and Organizational Competences (the ones necessary to achieve the objectives of the VO). The synergy among these competences potentializes the latent capacity of the individuals and contributes to leverage the results that can be achieved for the identified needs. The competences serve to fulfil the needs; and the needs serve to instigate competences.

3.1 A Methodology for a Coordinator Search and Suggestion

The coordinator(s) search and suggestion is a very important step in the VO life cycle, occurring normally in the Creation phase and – sometimes – in the Evolution phase. This step can be taken making use of the human resources available in the VO environment. The VBE can be an inexhaustible source for this kind of resources. Its members are organizations that have the knowledge of how to work in a Collaborative Network and, in some cases, already have persons with the required competences to manage a VO. Besides tangible goods or the traditional support services offered in the VBE, it is also possible to find this specific service for VO coordination. In some cases organizations may be elected/selected to act in a business "just" as VO coordinator. Furthermore the trust environment in force in the VBE cares for the quality and the accuracy of the information provided by the VO candidates.

This new "role" of VO Coordinator will most probably require in the near future specific training and educational programmes focusing on the VO management requirements. This will enlarge the universe of choices and will certainly contribute to a more sustainable VO management. This coordination should not be done essentially by a member belonging in the production process but must be a person with adequate competence for this specific VO and also has the acceptance of the VO members.

Based on Klen [11] an appropriated VO coordinator it is suggested the use of a methodology for searching and suggesting like the detail in Figure 3 that works with the 3-Steps:

- *STEP 1* - would be the register of VO Coordinator candidates where, these potential candidates, belong to the VBE or belong to a related PVC (Professional Virtual Communities) or are professionals outside of the VBE but indicated by VBE members. Organizations belonging to a VBE may be represented by more than one candidate. In this case the candidates must respect the non-conflict of interest agreement with its own employer.

- *STEP 2* - would be the Information Management where the VO candidates' Competence Maps are stored in a Data Base for future use by the VT (supported by VBE Administrator and/or by the VO Planner).

- *STEP 3* - would be the VO Coordinator search (and suggestion). This methodology normally takes place during the Creation (or Evolution) phase. For each business opportunity a different VO is created. Consequently each VO has its own specific needs and requirements which are identified and analysed by VT, always supported by the VBE Administrator and the VO Planner. Based on the VO needs some organizational competences are mapped. These ones constitute the basis for the VBE Administrator/VO Planner to search for specific VO Coordinator competences. In this methodology this step is a human-based one but it can also be performed in an automatic or semi-automatic way provided by an applied intelligence technique. Additionally the VBE Administrator/VO Planner can also set some preferences and/or constraints (e.g. they can apply filters and look for candidates from just a given organization).

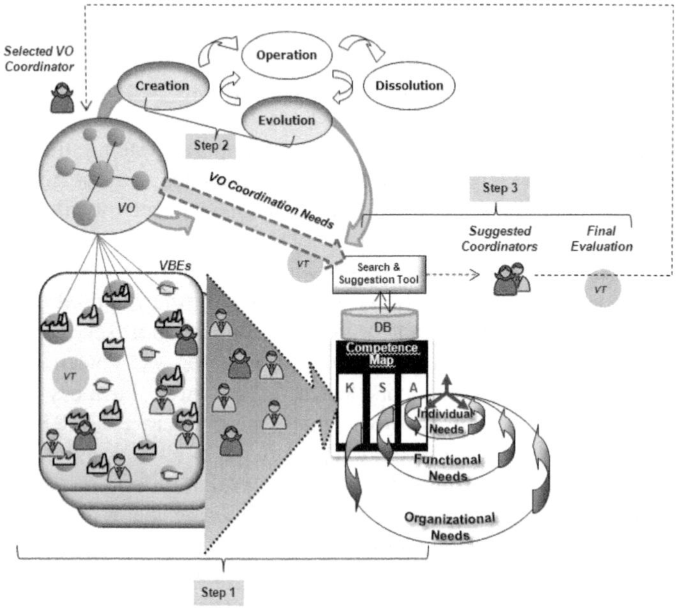

Fig. 3. Methodology for a Coordinator Search & Suggestion

4 Integrating Co-development and Fit Coordination

In a summarized vision, when a good idea is observed during the ideas exchange, the VBE can quickly form a VO, with adequate organizations, to produce i.e. a new product. With the methodology for a coordinator search & suggestion a coordinator can be also quickly selected based on the best competencies to lead this specifically VO to the success.

These different collaborative environments could be put together to facilitate the relation between the market and the producers (Fig. 4).

The market wishes/necessities would be appreciated by experts (VT) in different areas (technical, marketing, economy, etc.). Based on this analysis, the VT would indicate the best enterprises to compose the VO to produce the selected idea(s) and, based on the VO coordination needs, could also select an appropriated VO coordinator through the search&suggestion tool/methodology. This selection could, again, be analyzed by the VT based on the competencies of a person related on the VO coordination needs. This fit coordination would support the collaborative environments to make viable towards a production enabling for these new products (or services) a longer live and more success in the market.

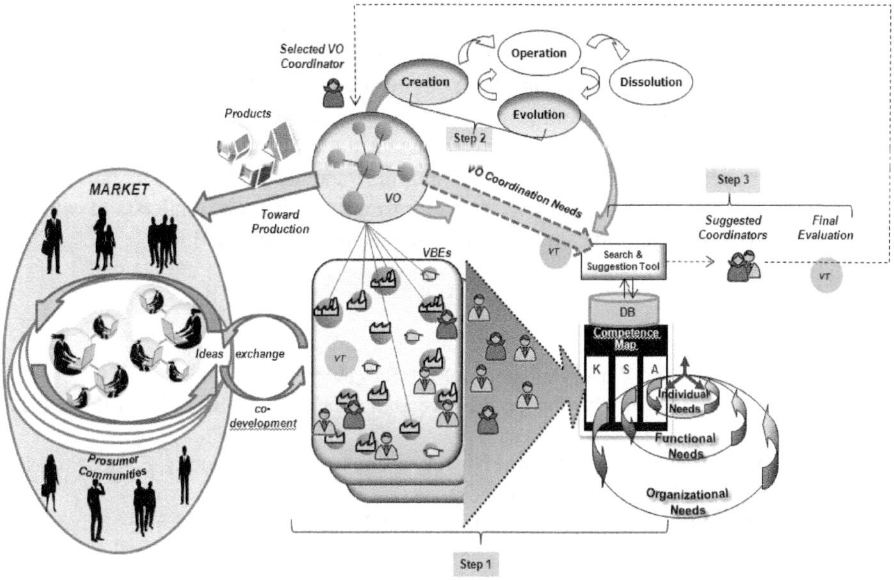

Fig. 4. Collaborative design/development environment supported by a fit coordination

5 Conclusion

The new mass collaboration is changing the way how enterprises and societies use the knowledge and the innovation capacity to create value [4].

The quick and close contact with the prosumers' necessities and wishes will demand changes in the work style of the enterprises in the production chain (i.e. VO) pressing them to an expressive collaborative work mainly in the information aspects.

All business areas should be prepared to attend this new market based on customers that want to collaborate. Information previously handled just by members from a production chain (i.e. marketing, production, logistics, development, etc.) can be also influenced by customer. In this new scenario, customers want collaborate not just about a specific product but, more beyond, expressing opinion about the hole product life cycle.

VBE members can, in this case, use this potential to develop new and stronger business models.

The customer evolution has a tendency to be amplified in future mainly in sustainability and in innovation aspects but, to better observe the customer necessities and wishes, proceedings should also be implemented in the VBE to guarantee the information quality.

If we are sensitive to customer needs and buying preferences, it will be obvious what we have to do, we won´t have to worry so much about our competitors – they´ll be worrying about us [2].

A good idea isn´t qualified just by its creativity and engineering but also by the viability, in other words, an adequate coordination is an essential part of the success of a product in the market and for the collaborative work.

The scenario presented in this paper, is based on the knowledge of the authors on the Collaborative Network area and on the work of the project Ecolead [12]. As a second step, this scenario will be adequate to be used in a new project, in the area of "Design for All", understood as an intervention on environments, products and services with the aim that everyone, including future generations, regardless of age, gender, capabilities or cultural background, can enjoy participating in the construction of our society, with equal opportunities participating in economic, social, cultural, recreational and entertainment activities while also being able to access, use and understand whatever part of the environment with as much independence as possible [13].

References

1. Toffler, A.: The Third Wave. Bantam Books, USA (1980) ISBN 0-553-24698-4
2. Gattorna, J.: Living Supply Chains. Prentice Hall, Englewood Cliffs (2006) ISBN 0-273-70614-4
3. Friedman, T.: The world is flat: a brief history of the twenty-first century. Farrar, Straus and Giroux, USA (2005) ISBN 0-374-29288-4
4. Tapscott, D., Williams, A.D.: Wikinomics – How Mass Collaboration Changes Everything. Penguin Books (2006) ISBN 978-1-59184-138-8
5. Camarinha-Matos, L.M., Afsarmanesch, H.: Collaborative Networked Organizations. Kluwer Academic Publishers, Dordrecht (2004) ISBN 1-4020-7823-4
6. Google, SketchUp, `http://sketchup.google.com` (access: May 26, 2010)
7. Camarinha-Matos, L.M., Afsarmanesh, H.: The Virtual Enterprise Concept. In: Infrastructures for Virtual Enterprises – Networking Industrial Enterprises. IFIP, Kluwer Academic Publishers, Dordrecht (1999) ISBN 0-7923-8639-6
8. Ecolead Project, IST-506958, European Collaborative Networked Organizations Leadership Initiative, D52.2 - Rough reference model for Collaborative Networks (2005), `http://ecolead.vtt.fi/`
9. Camarinha-Matos, L.M., Afsarmanesh, H., Ollus, M., Ecolead: A Holistic Approach to Creation and Management of Dynamic Virtual Organizations. Springer, Heidelberg (2005) ISBN 0-387-28259-9
10. Durand, T.: Strategizing for innovation: competence analysis in assessing strategic change. In: Sanchez, R., Heene, A. (eds.) Competence-based Strategic Management. John Wiley & Sons, Chichester (1997)
11. Klen, E.R.: Methodology for Virtual Organizations Managers Search and Suggestion based on Individual Competences. 216p. Thesis (Doctor in Production Engineering) in Portuguese – Post-Graduate Program in Production and Systems Engineering, UFSC, Brazil, Florianópolis – SC (2007)
12. Ecolead Project, IST-506958, European Collaborative Networked Organizations Leadership Initiative, `http://ecolead.vtt.fi/`
13. Design for All Foundation, published dossier (2011), `http://www.designforall.org`

Part V

Performance Management - I

Towards a More Effective Interoperable Solution through an A-Priori Performance Measurement System

Matthieu Lauras[1], François Galasso[1], Carine Rongier[1], Didier Gourc[1], and Yves Ducq[2]

[1] University of Toulouse, Mines Albi, Campus Jarlard, Route de Teillet, 81013 Albi, France
{matthieu.lauras,francois.galasso,carine.rongier, didier.gourc}@mines-albi.com
[2] University of Bordeaux 1 – IMS – UMR 5218 CNRS – 351 cours de la Libération – 33405 Talence cedex, France
yves.ducq@u-bordeaux1.fr

Abstract. Enterprises today face many challenges related to lack of interoperability. But several business and technical solutions are available to bridge this gap. This paper presents a structured and tooled methodology to help decision-makers to quantitatively assess interoperability solutions for their networked enterprise. Practically, this research work proposes an a priori performance measurement system that is able to model and simulate different interoperability solutions. Through a bi-dimensional analysis (stakes and accessibility), the system allows comparing all the potential solutions in order to choose the best one for the network. This scientific proposition is finally implemented on a real application case extracted from the French ISTA3 research project.

Keywords: Collaborative Network, Interoperability, Performance Measurement System, Decision Support System, Modelling and Simulation.

1 Introduction

There is a growing interest in solutions enabling companies to work together more effectively. A wide variety of collaborative systems exists and addresses different aspects of this complex problem while providing different benefits to networked enterprises. Thus, enterprise interoperability is crucial for companies and especially in decentralized, flexible and networked manufacturing system environment [1].

Enterprise applications and software systems need to be interoperable in order to achieve seamless business across organizational boundaries and thus realize virtual networked organizations. But interoperability should not only be considered a property of informatics systems. The diversity, heterogeneity, and autonomy of software components, application solutions, business processes, and the business context of an enterprise must also be considered [2].

But in practice, networked business encounters recurrent difficulties and only very limited success has been made due to the ongoing evolution of systems, the speed of market changes and growing complexity [1], [3]. Facing this huge complexity,

L.M. Camarinha-Matos et al. (Eds.): PRO-VE 2011, IFIP AICT 362, pp. 125–132, 2011.

decision-makers are confronted to the difficulty of choosing an accurate and relevant interoperability solution for their networked enterprises.

As for any decision-making, such a choice depends on the capacity of the decision maker to assess: (i) the current situation – What happened until today? What is the current progression (in a broader sense)? – and (ii) the possible evolution of the interoperability solution (information systems, business processes, organizational…) – What will happen and what are the consequences for the network?

Performance evaluation appears as a natural tool to design/modify/improve the interoperable solution of a networked enterprise. But judging an interoperability solution's performance in practice is very situation-specific and so complicated.

In accordance with the above, a complete and systemic methodology is proposed in this research work in order to help decision-makers for the selection of the best interoperability solution for their businesses at the scale of the network. Concretely, the purpose of this paper consists in designing a novel Performance Measurement System (PMS) able to evaluate and compare the performance of different interoperability solutions in a networked enterprise. This research work is a part of the French ISTA3 project (3rd generation Interoperability for Aeronautics Sub-contracTors). This is a research-oriented project, meaning it produces and uses research results, which target is to produce prototypes; industrially tested, for which one or several companies showed some interests to obtain a competitive advantage. It tries to integer the best of current research in Enterprise Interoperability: EM/ BPM (Enterprise Modeling / Business Process Modeling), Performance Evaluation, MDI (Model-Driven Interoperability), SOA (Service-Oriented Architecture) and Ontology.

The paper is divided into three main parts. First, literatures related to performance measurement systems in general and to performance for interoperability are discussed. From this background, our research statement is explained. Then we develop our scientific contributions in order to evaluate and compare interoperability solutions in a networked enterprise by exposing a performance-analyzing framework in one hand, and a modeling and simulation approach on the other hand. Next, a real case application relating to an aerospace network is presented.

2 Literature Selection

Interoperability is a keyword in many of the last decade's articles. It is defined by European projects INTEROP and ATHENA as "property referring to the ability of diverse systems and organizations to work together (inter-operate)" (www.interop-vlab.eu). This property should be obtained following four complementary dimensions: Business, Knowledge, Applications and Communications. In this paper we focus on the Business dimension.

Panetto and Molina [1] have identified five research challenges for enterprise integration and interoperability: (i) Collaborative Networked Organizations; (ii) Enterprise Modelling and Reference Models; (iii) Enterprise and Processes Models Interoperability; (iv) Validation, Verification, Qualification and Accreditation of Enterprise Models; (v) Model Reuse and Repositories.

About the second challenge, the authors pointed out the need for the community and practitioners to develop accurate and relevant performance measurement approaches able to support decision-making in interoperable environment. However, for many years, specialists [4], [5], [6] have highlighted the limitations at the networked scale of solutions based on the PMS in use today. Very important enterprise network features, like collaborative business processes, information partner heterogeneities, limited accessibility to information, and interoperability solutions for example, have been underestimated or, in some cases, not considered at all. These authors point out that there is little knowledge available on PMS and the use of Key Performance Indicators (KPI) in the open literature on network environments [4]. More recently, other authors [5], [6], [7], have confirmed that academics and practitioners are still in need of a new PMS which can handle the requirements of the new enterprise networks.

Progress on performance measurement requires an outlook encompassing the extended enterprise, a state of mind that emphasizes a collaborative win-win policy between respective partners. [7], [8], stress that the first step in developing an efficient collaboration is to improve the performance of disparate internal systems and processes responsible for managing and coordinating the interactions in the value chain. They show that interfacing activities locally, without a systematic overview, may result in failure, as it will be dependent on an exclusive use of internal measurements. [9] note effectively that the development of disparate measurement systems may result in superfluous and incompatible performance evaluation.

Consequently, a PMS dedicated to interoperability should measure locally and globally the performance of the network.

PMS are used either (i) to design a new system (or to modify an existing system), or (ii) to control an existing system referred hereinafter to (i) a priori or (ii) a posteriori. The objective of this work is to compare the performance of several interoperability solutions. Thus, the a priori performance evaluation is retained.

A priori performance evaluation consists in anticipating the future performance of the system (in our case, of the networked enterprise). This includes three main steps: (1) Innovation: explanation and objectives; (2) Implementation: variables and indicators choosing; (3) Observation: simulation through a model.

These steps are represented on Figure 1. This kind of performance evaluation is based on an enterprise model and on a simulation approach to evaluate the probable future results of each KPI (local and global in our case). One main difficulty relates to the design of the model and the link to the simulation approach.

Consequently, a PMS dedicated to interoperability should be based on accurate and relevant enterprise models (that is to say, a business process model able to focus on interoperability components of the network) on one hand, and based on a associated simulation tool (that is to say, a tool able to simulate the previous enterprise modelling and to measure the different KPI) on the other hand.

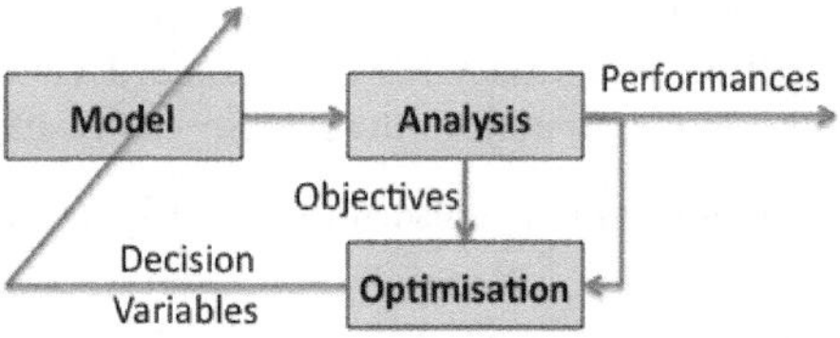

Fig. 1. A priori performance evaluation principle

Finally, this literature selection on interoperability highlights that several levels of interoperability exist [2], [10], and should be considered:

- Independent: these are organizations that would normally work without any interaction other than that provided by personal contact;
- Collaborative: these are organizations where recognized frameworks are in place to support interoperability and shared goals are recognized and roles and responsibilities are allocated as part of on-going responsibilities however the organizations are still distinct;
- Combined or Integrated: these are organizations where there are shared value systems and shared goals, a common understanding and a preparedness to interoperate;
- Unified: these are organizations in which the organizational goals, value systems, command structure/style, and knowledge bases are shared across the system.

Of course, each level requires different technologies, different skills and different level of maturity in terms of collaboration. But all the networks do not need the same level of interoperability to be competitive.

Consequently, a PMS dedicated to interoperability should be able to evaluate the ratio between the investments (costs, skills, technical...) needed to reach one level of interoperability and the expected potential performance results.

3 Scientific Proposition

Our proposition is based on two main assumptions. First, all partners of the network are considered to have already get their own dashboards or at least, they have KPI able to measure their local performance. Otherwise, they can use specific methods to define and to implement PMS such as ECOGRAI [12] or Balanced Score Card [13]. Second, decision-makers are able to define and model several options to support their interoperability needs. For instance, they could envisage and describe a collaborative solution, a combined solution and a unified solution (see. section 2). In order to compare the different solutions and to support decision-making, we propose a three steps methodology based on the results of the literature review:

1. Modelling the collaborative processes and the different interoperability options (this is the Innovation part);
2. Evaluating the accessibility of each option (this is the Implementation part);
3. Simulating each option in order to measure the associated performance (this is the Observation part).

Concerning the first step, a business process modelling language enabling to describe the different interoperability solutions is selected. Based on surveys done by [11], the Business Process Modelling Notation (BPMN) standard (www.bpmi.org) has been chosen. This standard presents two major interests for our research work:

- This modelling language allows describing clearly all the interfaces between partners of the network.
- BPMN is a language that is relatively easy to simulate by classical tools of Discrete Event Simulation (native in the majority of simulation software) (see. Figure 3).

Concerning the second step, the accessibility dimension aims to assess efforts that each interoperability solution (modelled in step 1) requires to be implemented in order to represent the different solutions on a common axis (from the least accessible solution to the most accessible one). This aggregated effort is evaluated through a multi-criteria analysis (not developed in this paper) that includes variables such as: project costs and/or duration, technical and business skills, investments, etc. Consequently, for one interoperability model, there is one accessibility level.

The third step consists in simulating the BPMN diagrams by using Discrete Event Simulation software such as Witness® or Arena®. The simulation models must include KPI defined by decision-makers as representative of the interoperability impact. Then, for each KPI, it is possible to measure the performance of each interoperability solution. Consequently, for a given model, there is a set of measures called “scenarii”. It is important to underline that the KPI's must be common to all solutions for comparison purpose. These KPIs are representative of the main interoperability stakes [1], [2], such as adaptability, integrity, security, time saving, or flexibility.

Finally, the different evaluations following the two dimensions discussed before - stake (for each KPI and for each potential solution) and accessibility (for each potential solution) - are represented on a same graph as described in Figure 2.

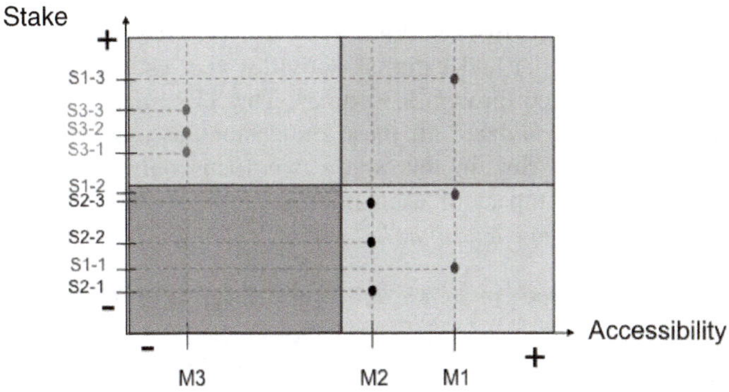

Fig. 2. Comparison graph for stake and accessibility of scenarii

4 Application Case

The problem statement discussed in this paper is particularly sensitive for the product development cycle. Taking time and money out of the product development cycle can pay big dividends for companies. Distributed teams of engineers are creating products and nowadays OEMs often delegate significant design responsibilities to their key suppliers.

In Aerospace industry, the strategy of the main aircraft manufacturers is to outsource more and more sub-assemblies. Thus, level 2 Subcontractors (STR2) develop more complex relationships and high value-added with level 1 sub-contractors (STR1) and their own subcontractors (STR3 and following ranks STRn). These relationships, as part of the design and manufacture of composite parts, use different methods of work and are handled through various tools for Design, Product Lifecycle Management (PLM), Technical Data Management, Production

Management... These tools must be interoperable in a flexible (fast adaptation to new cooperation) and economical way. In this application we focus on informational system interoperability.

In this application, extracted and voluntarily simplified from the ISTA3 French project, relationships between level 2 and 3 subcontractors are studied. In the purpose of this article, the illustration is done on a process dedicated to the validation of an estimate given by STR3 in an order at STR2 level and shown in Figure 3. It can be viewed from Figure 3 that the simulation model is based on BPMN concepts (pools, activities, message flows…). Indeed, this model is the only presented here.

In this process, a STR1 subcontractor sends a CAD model of a part to be manufactured by STR2. STR2 needs STR3 in order to create the necessary tools and thus, requests an estimate from STR3. Then STR3 writes (i.e. elaborates) the estimate that is sent back to STR2. The following steps are internal to STR2 and consist of an evaluation of the estimate and, if the estimate is correct, it is converted into an order sent to STR3 that finally receive the order. The elaboration of the tool concerns another process that is not described in this paper. The resources needed at STR2 are finally the Commercial Service, The Technical Service and the Project Leader. At STR3, the needed resource is the Project Leader.

Both internal and external performance linked to interoperable activities for each company needs to be assessed. Both internal activities (i.e. request estimate, write estimate, estimate evaluation…) and external activities (i.e. estimate request send, estimate send, …) are modelled through lead times. The STR2 and STR3 experts of the concerned process have validated all these dimensions as representative of the interoperability performance. But, in this study, we focus only on a KPI that is representative of the global impact of each interoperability solutions. Experts and authors have chosen the "*average lead-time*".

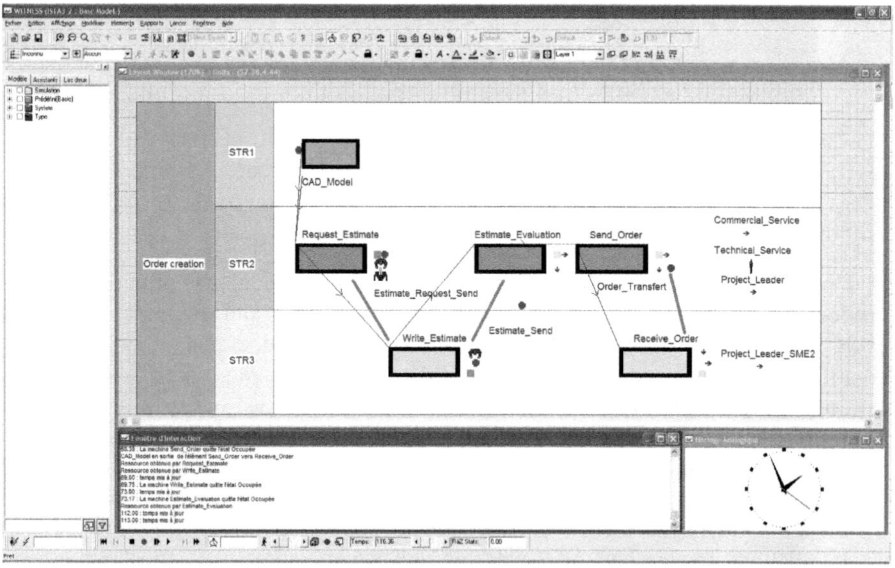

Fig. 3. Caption of Witness® model for process simulation

Three scenarii (interoperability solutions) are evaluated:

1. As-is simulation;
2. Improvement of STR2 internal activities through the use of an estimate management system;
3. Improvement of information transfer through the use of a collaborative platform such as Mediation Information System: this stimulates an improvement of interactions.

The stake of each scenario is given according relatively to the scenario 1 results, (i.e. the existing performances) and the results of the considered scenario, (i.e. future performances). Accessibility is given for each scenario according to the difficulty to set up such a scenario over a scale from 0 (very low accessibility) to 5 (very high accessibility). Obviously, an accessibility of 5 is given to the first scenario as it is the current situation. The results of the simulation are given in Table 1.

Obviously, these results are only available considering data given in the simulation. An extraction of real temporal values for each activity will be assessed in the frame of the ISTA3 project. Nevertheless this example shows clearly how our proposition can help decision-makers to compare objectively different interoperability levels for their network. In this example, the recommendation could consist in privileging the second scenario if the objective is to obtain a good compromise between accessibility (not too many efforts to produce) and stake (almost 20 % of lead-time reduction). But if the objective is to divide the lead-time by two then the decision-makers have to assume an important effort to upgrade their interoperability solution (IT, skills, project costs, collaborative protocols…) and could select the third scenario. The figure 4 shows the scenarios positions according to the matrix presented in previous part.

Table 1. Performance assessment for each scenario

Scenario	Average lead time	Stake	Accessibility
1	27,28	0	5
2	22,34	4,94 (18%)	3
3	15	12,28 (45%)	0

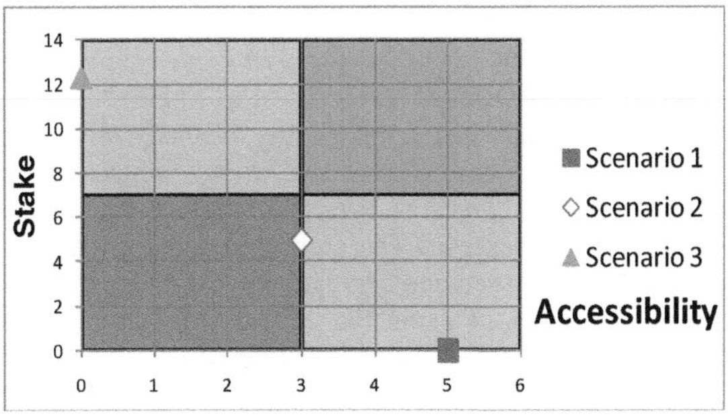

Fig. 4. Position of each scenario

5 Conclusion and Future Works

This research work aims at designing a Performance Measurement System (PMS) able to evaluate and compare the performance of different interoperability solutions in a networked enterprise using a three steps approach: (i) Modelling the collaborative processes and the different interoperability options; (ii) evaluating the accessibility of each option; (iii) simulating each option in order to measure the associated performance. This proposition is implemented on a real case study (aerospace industry) extracted from the French ISTA3 research project.

Though our proposition constitutes a significant step towards more effective interoperable solutions, several perspectives arise. Particularly, some complementary works are in progress to aggregate properly on a unique dimension on one hand the performance of all interoperability stakes (adaptability, integrity, security, time saving and flexibility) and, on the other hand, of all interoperability accessibility dimensions. Other studies should also be developed in order to define concretely the accessibility dimensions for an interoperability solution. Finally, further research should also include more practical insights on how managers can adjust and adapt the model to their own strategies.

References

1. Panetto, H., Molina, A.: Enterprise integration and interoperability in manufacturing systems: Trends and issues. Computers in Industry 59(7), 641–646 (2008)
2. Chen, C., Dassisti, M., Elvesaeter, B.: Interoperability Knowledge Corpus, Deliverable DI.1b, Workpackage DI, INTEROP NoE (2006), http://interop-vlab.eu/backoffice/ei_public_deliverables/
3. Jochem, R.: Enterprise Interoperability Assessment. In: 8th International Conference of Modeling and Simulation MOSIM 2010, Conference, Hammamet (2010)
4. Beamon, B.M.: Measuring Supply Chain Performance. International Journal of Operations and Production Management 19(3), 275–292 (1999)
5. Gunasekaran, A., Kobu, B.: Performance measures and metrics in logistics and supply chain management: a review of recent literature (1995 – 2004) for research and applications. International Journal of Production Research 45(12), 2819–2840 (2007)
6. Akyuz, G.A., Erkan, T.E.: Supply chain performance measurement: a literature review. International Journal of Production Research 48(17), 5137–5155 (2010)
7. Alfaro, J.J., Rodriguez-Rodriguez, R., Verdecho, M.J., Ortiz, A.: Business process interoperability and collaborative performance measurement. International Journal of Computer Integrated Manufacturing 22(9), 877–889 (2009)
8. Al-Mudimigh, A.S., Zairi, M., Ahmed, A.M.M.: Extending the concept of supply chain: the effective management of value chains. International Journal of Production Economics 87(3), 309–320 (2004)
9. Folan, P., Browne, J.: A review of performance measurement: towards performance management. Computers in Industry 56(7), 663–680 (2005)
10. Clark, T., Jones, R.: Organisational Interoperability Maturity Model for C2. In: Proceedings of the Command And Control Research And Technology Symposium, USA (1999)
11. Touzi, J.: Aide à la conception de Système d'Information Collaboratif support de l'interopérabilité des entreprises, PhD Thesis, INP Toulouse (2007)
12. Ducq, Y., Vallespir, B.: Definition and aggregation of a Performance Measurement System in three Aeronautical workshops using the ECOGRAI Method. International Journal of Production Planning and Control 16(2), 163–177 (2005)
13. Kaplan, R.S., Norton, D.P.: The balanced scorecard: Translating strategy into action. Harvard Business School Press, Boston (1996)

Performance Management in Collaborative Networks: Difficulties and Barriers

Juan-Jose Alfaro-Saiz, Raul Rodríguez-Rodríguez, and María-José Verdecho

Centre d'Investigació de Gestió i Enginyeria de Producció,
Universitat Politècnica de València, Camí de Vera s/n, 46022 València, Espanya
jalfaro@omp.upv.es

Abstract. Global competitiveness obliges to enterprises to collaborate in many processes such as new product and services development in order to shorten the lifecycle, development and commercialization. Therefore, the competence has drifted from an individual focus to a supply chain management one and, from some years, to a collaborative enterprises network approach. It is common to find frameworks for measuring/managing the performance within extended enterprises, supply chains, virtual enterprises, etc. However, few authors deal with a higher level: the collaborative networks one. This concept of enterprises management set up bigger difficulties regarding not only from a conceptual and structural point of view but also considering both the design and posterior development of systems capable of managing the performance achieved in this type of organizations. This work describes both the main difficulties and barriers when trying to apply performance management concepts to collaborative networks. In this sense, it is highlighted the weaknesses of the existing intra-organizational frameworks that cannot be projected, as they are conceived, to manage performance within collaborative networks.

Keywords: Performance management system, Collaborative enterprise networks.

1 Introduction

One of the strategies used to compete and adapt to global market needs is cooperation among organizations. Thus, searching for new business opportunities reaches a dimension of shared effort and responsibility in order to improve the quality of the products and services. Competitiveness has shifted from an individual factor to be dependent on the whole value chain of the product and/or service offered. Several authors affirm the importance of this thematic, [1] affirms, "the battleground of the next decade will be Supply Chain versus Supply Chain. Are you measuring the right things to win this battle?".

Nevertheless, today, it is not even enough to deal with the complexity of supply chains but more complex environments such as collaborative enterprise networks, which may embed to one or more supply chains. Thus, complex inter-organizational environments are composed of enterprises that are not only sharing flows of information, materials, etc. upstream and downstream (concept of supply chain) but

L.M. Camarinha-Matos et al. (Eds.): PRO-VE 2011, IFIP AICT 362, pp. 133–139, 2011.

these flows may also be without a lineal reference of products under a more or less common strategy. In this type of contexts, various enterprises and/or supply chains participate in the development of products where the customer differs that is to say the same enterprise is involved in several supply chains with different objectives, strategies, etc.

This type of inter-organizational contexts has a higher level of complexity that the one of the supply chains, and then, their performance management should be dealt with management systems able to integrate all the necessary elements to measure-manage them efficiently and effectively. Although a few years ago the interest of different forums (managers, researchers, etc.) was focused on performance measurement related to the Supply Chain, it is possible in the coming years will see a clear trend regarding Collaborative Enterprise Networks (CEN).

However, it is observed a lack of works regarding elements for measuring and managing relevant factors of the Collaborative Enterprise Networks, such as collaborative activities, inter-organizational relationships, common or global objectives of the Supply Chain, etc. Collaborative relationships will require suppliers and consumers to support multiple simultaneous business models and communication media in order to fully realise the benefits of collaborative business.

The research followed a constructivist approach, based on the following activities: recompilation, analysis and study of scientific knowledge, acquisition of main postulates and construction of initial classification [2]. The initial elements considered in the present constructivist approach were the following:

- The performance measurement/management evolution.
- The difficulties/barriers to performance management in CEN.
- The analysis of performance management systems within collaborative networks domain.

After this introduction, this paper describes the evolution of the performance measurement-management from individual contexts to Collaborative Enterprise Networks contexts. Then, difficulties and barriers to performance management in Collaborative Enterprise Networks are enumerated. Next, performance management systems in this context are analyzed. Finally, conclusions are exposed.

2 Performance Measurement/Management Evolution: Frameworks

Performance measurement-management systems have evolved in order to adapt to complexity of organizations. Initially, they were developed for intra-organizational contexts (individual level). Then, systems for dealing with supply chains (inter-organizational level) appeared. Recently, systems that try to manage CEN under an integrated approach have been developed. The intra-organizational domain has been widely studied in the literature, with various classifications and different models and frameworks such as the works by [3], [4], [5] and [6]. Later, at the end of 1990's, many concepts developed for intra-organizational performance measurement-management domain were adapted to inter-organizational domains in order to deal with supply chains. In this sense, in the literature, many works were developed; some of them from a theoretical point of view due to the difficulty of apply them in real contexts. Finally, some works have appeared that try to deal with domains that are more complex that supply chains. Thus, the works developed define complex frameworks to amplify performance measurement-management to enterprise networks that are more sophisticated. It is important to note the works by [7], [8], [9] and [10].

In addition, there are other types of works that describe performance measurement systems to measure some collaboration aspects ([11], [12], [13]) or virtual organizations ([14] and [15]) that may be included with some nuances in the domain of CEN.

3 Difficulties/Barriers to Performance Management in CEN

Performance management in CENs is not an easy task. As it cannot be managed what has not been measured before, the first aspect that has to be done is measuring its performance so that it can be managed.

CEN present a set of special characteristics that are difficulties for performance measurement systems that were not developed for this type of structures. After the analysis of the different works in the literature ([7], [16], [17], [18], [19], etc.) initially focused on structures more simple than CENs, a summary has been performed of the main difficulties/barriers that come up to this type of organization. In the next paragraphs, it is exposed the main difficulties/barriers to performance management in CENs distinguishing into four groups: A) Dynamicity and flexibility, B) Global vision, C) Broadness and D) Information systems role: intra-inter-organizational interface.

A) Dynamicity and Flexibility: enterprises have to adapt to all types of changes that occur (technological, organisational, economical, social, commercial, etc.). This circumstance affects production and organisational structures from both intra and inter-organisational points of view. This is a highly sensitive factor for CEN as any change in an enterprise may influence the global performance of the whole CEN without evidence of its appearing. From a point of view of CEN performance management, it is very important an adequate adaptation of each enterprise belonging to the CEN. There are many implications to consider:

- The CEN global performance management has to be flexible and sensitive to detect dysfunctionalities that these changes may involve and has to have mechanisms that allow modifying easily the performance measurement elements if necessary (it is usually necessary). In this sense, it is a common situation to re-define objectives and/or strategies and their corresponding performance indicators. Modifying the performance measurement-management elements is quite delicate (it has to be taken into account the priorities of the CEN, a perfect coherence among elements and maintain equity within the CEN) due to the high interaction among enterprises.
- The possibility of being affected any member of the CEN without the knowledge of its existence may oblige to re-make a part of the performance measurement system which involves time, effort and loss of control of the organization during that period.
- The incorporation or disappearance of members within the CEN also affects performance measurement systems in the same way as previously stated. In

addition, this circumstance may obligate to establish new equity and trust relationships among their members and, consequently, reaching of consensus which involves new mechanisms of coordination and organization. If equity does not exist among the enterprises participating within the CEN, it is practically impossible to create an environment of trust that enables the information exchange necessary to reach an adequate degree of efficiency from a global point of view. Performance measurement systems may include structured mechanisms highly automated to deal with these situations.

B) Global vision: CEN performance management also means to provide a global vision. This vision is related to the use of performance measurement-management elements (objectives, strategies, key performance indicators, etc.) that aid to measure and manage not only dyad inter-enterprise efficiency and effectiveness but also the whole CEN. This is complex requirement due to CEN dimensions.

This implies that global indicators are to be defined and those indicators should correspond to global CEN objectives and strategies. The use of global indicators should be a consequence of a clear structure of relationships that give response to various basic questions:

- What measurement elements have been specifically defined to measure-manage the global vision of the CEN?
- Are the global measurement-management elements related to partial measurement-management elements (intra-organizational level)? How do they influence each other?
- What has been each KPI defined at the global level for?
- What is improved in the CEN through its measurement-management?

CEN competitiveness is not only dependent on the interaction of the processes within enterprises. It is also needed to design and implement mechanisms that allow managing the whole CEN within performance measurement-management systems. This circumstance affects the phase of the design as well as the phase of implementation and management of the indicators and the rest of performance measurement elements used.

C) Broadness: The concept of CEN broadness makes reference to the number of partners that belongs to the CEN. The bigger the number of partners, the higher effort is needed to manage the global performance and obviously, the scalability requirements should be taken into account. This fact may be translated into the following consequences:

- Higher difficulty to establish common objectives and strategies for all the organizations that participate in the CEN. If enterprises are to be competitive and its relationship is to be sustainable, it is needed that all the members focus on strategic aspects of the business and that they have been established by consensus.
- Higher difficulty to select partial and global indicators.
- Increase in the quantity of information to be managed from a global point of view and higher difficulty in maintaining trust among the partners so that information is shared with the rest of partners.

- Higher difficulty in establishing linkages and equity relationships that sustain trust in order to collaborate and distribute benefits proportionally among all CEN partners. This element (equity) is very important to create a conscious and trust climate that provides the necessary information to manage CEN from a global perspective with an adequate degree of efficiency.

D) Information Systems role: intra and inter-organizational interface: Another important element for CEN performance management is the use of integrated management tools that support CEN members.

It is usual that when defining performance measurement-management elements (that derivate from the performance measurement system) needed to CEN management, it is also defined the data needed to compute them and the source of that information, that is: who will provide each piece of information? How is he/she going to provide it? And at what time he/she will do it? Precisely, in this moment, discrepancies among the CEN members may appear as some of them may have difficulties to provide such data due to several reasons: information treatment (lack of resources), being unable to provide it in the right time (lack of resources) or not being able to obtain the data (lack of resources). The quantity of needed information to manage CEN is large and demands that the performance management system used provide a structure (information architecture) able to support all the data. This circumstance is vital as if common platforms are not used for uploading, transmitting and managing the data, it is practically unfeasible, from a practical point of view, that the system survives.

Currently, the use of internal information systems (based on ERs and other tools) and Web Services facilitates information management but also data homogenization and standardization mechanisms are needed. In addition, privacy policies should be established through controlled access, especially on that information sensitive to third party.

4 Analysis of Performance Management Systems within Collaborative Networks Domain

In this section, the most relevant performance management systems for CENs are reviewed. As explained en section two, there are four systems that stand out: [7], [8], [9] and [10]. Then, those systems are analyzed (see Table 1) regarding to the degree of consideration of the difficulties/barriers identified in section 3.

Table 1. Analysis of PMS for CEN

	Difficulty / Barrier			
PMS	Dynamicity - Flexibility	Global vision	Broadness	I.S. role
Bititci et al. (2005) [7]	**	***	***	*
Folan & Browne. (2005) [8]	*	**	***	*
Gaiardelli et al. (2007) [9]	*	*	*	
Alfaro et al. (2005) [10]	**	***	***	*

- If the PMS does not deal with the barrier/difficulty, it is represented by ( ).
- If the PMS deals with the barrier/difficulty weakly, it is represented by (*).
- If the PMS deals with the barrier/difficulty moderately, it is represented by (**).
- If the PMS deals with the barrier/difficulty widely, it is represented by (***).

The main strengths of the EE PM model [7] are: that it makes explicit within the structure of the PMS the definition of performance indicators for measuring coordination through the interorganisational processes at both strategic and operational levels; makes explicit coordination measurement within the whole inter-organisational processes that take part in the PMS structure. Folan & Browne [8] developed a PMS for Extended Enterprise including mechanisms that measure the degree of contribution of each partner to the partnership (common interorganisational strategy), moreover, CEN broadness is very well treated. Gaiardelli et al. [9] develop a PMS (for the automotive after-sales service network) that is composed of four functional levels: business, process, activity and organisational unit, and development and innovation. Its strength lies in the connection made on interorganisational processes, although not seen a common strategy for the global network. Finally, Alfaro et al. (2007) provide a PMS that follows a top-down methodology from strategy to core process decomposition and ends with the stage of follow-up and monitoring. Emphasized in the ability to measure intra and inter-aspects and defining common performance measurement elements for all CEN. On the other hand, has an acceptable architecture to address certain dynamism in the CEN.

As can be observed in Table 1, none of the relevant PMS is a soundness system that deals with the main difficulties/barriers of CEN. The aspects that are less considered are those related to dynamicity-flexibility as well as the role of Information Systems and its integration.

5 Conclusions

Collaborative enterprise networks are a typology of organizational structure that currently is used to deal with the competitive requirements of global market. Thus, this structure has to be analyzed and studied broadly in order its reaches efficiency. One of the challenges is the development of performance management systems able to meet the complexity associated to this type of structure which can be observed under various perspectives. The existence of this complexity presents a set of difficulties/barriers that prevent current PMS deal with its tasks properly. In this work, the main difficulties/barriers and their implications in performance measurement-management have been described by grouping them into four types: A) Dynamicity/Flexibility, B) Global vision, C) Broadness and D) Information systems role: intra and inter-organizational interface.

In addition, it has been provided a brief review of PMS evolution from the individual enterprise domain to CEN domain in order to perform later an analysis of the PMS within CEN domain regarding the four difficulties/barriers. After the analysis, it is observed that it is still necessary to study further this type of structures in order to define PMS able to adapt to these contexts.

References

1. Hausman, W.H.: Supply chain performance metrics. The practice of supply chain management: Where theory and application converge. Kluwer Academic Publishers, Dordrecht (2003)

2. Coughlan, P., Coughlan, D.: Action research: action research for operations management. International Journal of Operation and Productions Management 22(2), 220–240 (2002)
3. Kaplan, R.S., Norton, D.P.: The balanced scorecard. Measures that drive performance. Harvard Business Review, 71–79 (January/February 1992)
4. Bourne, M.: Designing and implementing a balanced performance measurement system. Control - Official Journal of the Institute of Operations Management, 21–24 (July/August 1999)
5. Neely, A., Adams, C.: Perspectives on Performance. The Performance Prism' Web Site of Neely A (2001), http://www.som.cranfield.ac.uk/som/cbp/adn.htm
6. Hronec, S.M.: Vital Signs. Amacom, New York (1993)
7. Bititci, U.S., Mendibil, K., Martinez, V., Albores, P.: Measuring and managing performance in extended enterprises. International Journal of Operations & Production Management 25(4), 333–353 (2005)
8. Folan, P., Browne, J.: Development of an extended enterprise performance measurement system". Production Planning & Control 16(6), 531–544 (2005)
9. Gaiardelli, P., Saccani, N., Songini, L.: Performance measurement systems in the after-sales service: an integrated framework. International Journal of Business Performance Management 9(2), 145–171 (2007)
10. Alfaro, J.J., Ortiz, A., Rodríguez, R.: Performance measurement system for Enterprise Networks. International Journal of Productivity and Performance Management 56(4), 305–334 (2007)
11. Romero, D., Galeano, N., Molina, A.: A conceptual Model for Virtual Breeding Environments Value System. In: Camarinha-Matos, L., Afsarmanesh, H., Novais, P., Analide, C. (eds.) Establishing the Foundation of Collaborative Networks. Springer, Heidelberg (2007)
12. Msanjila, S.S., Afsarmanesh, H.: Trust analysis and assessment in virtual organization breeding environments. International Journal of Production Research 46(5), 1253–1295 (2008)
13. Bititci, U., Turner, T., Mackay, D., Kearney, D., Parung, J., Walters, D.: Managing synergy in collaborative enterprises. Production Planning & Control 18(6), 454–465 (2007)
14. Chalmeta, R., Grangel, R.: Performance Measurement Systems for Virtual Enterprise Integration. International Journal of Computer Integrated Manufacturing 18(1), 73–84 (2005)
15. Francisco, R.D., Azevedo, A.: Dynamic Performance Management In Business Networks Environment. In: Digital Enterprise Technology. Springer, US (2007)
16. Busi, M., Bititci, U.S.: Collaborative performance management: Present gaps and future research. International Journal of Productivity and Performance Management 55(1), 7–25 (2006)
17. Rodriguez, R., Ortiz, A., Alfaro, J.: Fostering collaborative meta-value chain practices. International Journal of Computer Integrated Manufacturing 22(5), 385–394 (2009)
18. Rodriguez, R.R., Gomez, P., Franco, D., Ortiz, A.: Establishing and keeping inter-organisational collaboration: Some lessons learned. International Federation for Information Processing 1, 214–222 (2007)
19. Leseure, M., Shaw, N., Chapman, G.: Performance measurement in organisational networks: an exploratory case study. International Journal of Business Performance Management 3(1), 30–46 (2001)

An Approach to Performance Management in Collaborative Networks Based on Stakeholders' Key Success Factors

Pedro S. Ferreira[1], Pedro F. Cunha[1,2], Luís Carneiro[3], and André Sá[3]

[1] CENI – Centro de Integração e Inovação de Processos, Portugal
{psf,pcunha}@ceni.pt
[2] EST/IPS – Escola Superior Tecnologia / Inst.Politécnico Setúbal, Portugal
[3] INESC Porto, Portugal
{luis.carneiro,andre.sa}@inescporto.pt

Abstract. Performance management in collaborative networks requires approaches suitable to deal with a larger domain than in traditional organisations, including new processes, new stakeholders and a less clear border between internal and external. The proposed approach addresses objectives and strategies setting, performance measurement and evaluation, monitoring, learning and improvement. It relies on the identification of key stakeholders and on their key success factors which provide the external perspective driving the performance evaluation and improvement. The work starts from the consideration of different natures and life times of Business Communities and Virtual Organisations, analyses the stakeholders' relations and emphasises the clear identification of value creation for stakeholders as an essential component to align organisations.

Keywords: Performance management, collaborative networks, virtual organisations, framework for performance management.

1 Introduction

As new forms of organisation emerge and develop to cope with the new challenges, companies lack the support to fully understand them, their implications and their benefits and to make the path towards them. That path is mostly a continuous process of adjustment concerning trust, sharing, collaboration, agility and competency.

Through collaborative networks (CN), participating organisations aim at delivering higher value and higher performance to their stakeholders and at sustaining competitive advantage, by sharing knowledge and resources. Performance management, essential to the success of collaborative networks, requires approaches suitable to the type and objectives of this type of networks. The change of previous organisational models, e.g. companies with sharp boundaries, formal relationships with other companies and a focus on internal efficiency and effectiveness, to networks has a profound impact upon performance management practices [1]. Though the single organisation performance management concepts and recommendations have been applied to networks and are to great extent valid, the new challenges require

L.M. Camarinha-Matos et al. (Eds.): PRO-VE 2011, IFIP AICT 362, pp. 140–147, 2011.

dealing with a larger domain, including new processes, new stakeholders and a less clear concept of internal and external to virtual and real organisations. Other specific issues of networks to deal with are the duration of their life and their virtual nature.

The concepts of virtual organization (VO) and virtual organization breading environment (VBE) [2] were used by the Net-Challenge project [3]. A Business Community (BC), according to the Net-Challenge project, is similar to a VBE, mainly composed of SME in the same industry, usually in a geographic proximity, that may be open or closed, depending on the restrictions to membership.

Performance management is very important also in CN to assure the delivery of value to its stakeholders and to strive to beat the competition. Moreover, performance management should contribute to trust development in CN, which is a fundamental enabler of collaboration, by delivering objective information on performance of CN and of their members. In this context, several contributions can be found for performance measurement considering it a way to demonstrate the benefits of participating in CN and to promote the acceptance of these organisational forms [4] and aiming at achieving equity among partners [5].

In the CN, performance management calls for suitable approaches and processes to identify critical factors and indicators, to formulate actions to take advantage of opportunities or overcome weaknesses and improve the system's performance as it defined by the stakeholders [6]. Performance management covers objectives, strategies, performance measurement and evaluation, monitoring, learning and improvement [7]. The following activities are part of a performance management process:

1. Definition of objectives and strategy formulation;
2. Definition of what to measure and targets setting;
3. Setup of a measurement system;
4. Measurement and analysis of performance;
5. Decision and carrying out of actions in order to achieve the targets.

Activity 1 of the previous list is concerned with what the organisation wants to be good at and what strategy it chooses to get there. The activities 2 to 4, which are part of the performance measurement process, receive inputs from the first one and deliver outputs to the last one. In the current context, performance measurement is about collecting data about the past so that a projection into the future can be done and improvement actions can be decided.

Performance management is tightly integrated with process design. Processes are designed and tuned for specific objectives, related to the organisation's strategy. A challenge is the alignment of processes and organisations and the development of suitable performance indicators that provide objective and explicit representation of performance and benefits within a collaborative network. Approaches like the Supply Chain Operations Reference (SCOR) model developed by Supply Chain Council that proposes performance indicators for supply chains are not oriented towards collaborative processes throughout the supply network [8], cannot cope with the dynamics of CN and cannot measure performance on soft factors related to the collaboration [9].

In the following sections of this paper the Net-Challenge approach to performance management based on stakeholders' key success factors is presented. This approach is part of the framework for performance management developed in the Net-Challenge project.

2 CN's Stakeholders and Their Key Success Factors

Performance cannot be objectively defined and it can only have a clear definition within each specific context [10]. In fact, the definition of performance lacks knowing to whom is performance delivered [7]. The base principle in this approach is that performance is determined by the stakeholders.

A key stakeholder is an entity with an interest in the organisation's activity or in its outcomes, which has the power to influence them considerably. Knowing who the key stakeholders are and what they are expecting from the organisation is the starting point to fulfil their expectations. The key stakeholders of the BC are BC Member, VO, Customer and Society. The VO's key stakeholders are Broker, Partner, Customer, BC and Society. Fig. 1 represents the stakeholders and their relations.

It is considered that the broker is the organisation holding the business opportunity and that it represents the customer at the same time it is a partner in the VO. However, taken into consideration the importance of having the VO oriented to the creation of value and to the customer, and with the purpose to emphasise its KSF and to keep the specific role of the broker clear, the customer is considered a VO's stakeholder.

The Business Community is a VO's stakeholder since it only fulfils its potential and its mission through the VO. The VO is a BC's stakeholder by definition, since the BC must provide the conditions for the formation and success of VO. The society is a key stakeholder of both BC and VO but with different perspectives related with their different time horizons and purposes.

Stakeholders are the ones who ultimately evaluate the performance of an organisation. So, it is fundamental to know what are the attributes they value most (in the product, service, job or whatever kind of deliverable) and that they expect the organisation and its competitors can provide them i.e., the success factors. The key success factors (KSF) are the most important success factors for the key stakeholders, the ones the organisation will concentrate on. The difficulty about determining the KSF lies in identifying the few things that will drive the organisation's strategy and its success [11].

The distinction of success factors (stakeholder centred) from factors internal to the organisation (organisation or process centred), which are the factors that drive or affect the success factors and that will be called performance factors, is important. The key success factors have to be known by asking the stakeholders. The way an organisation satisfies the KSF will determine its competitive advantage and for that reason they are in the base of a strategy formulation.

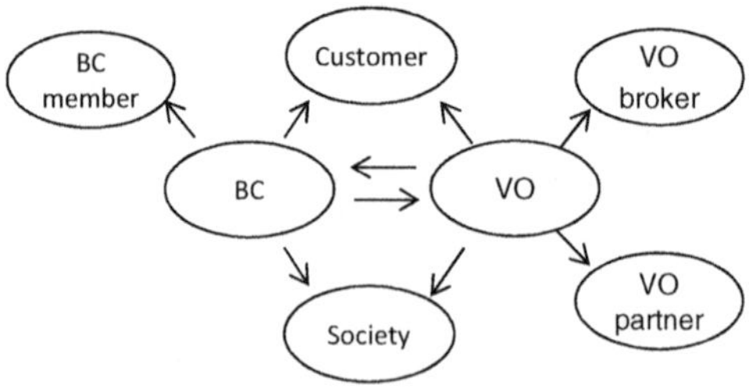

Fig. 1. BC's and VO's stakeholders

There is no consensus concerning this terminology. The concept of KSF is used with this name [8] and is also named key strategic factor [12]. A related concept in the SCOR model is the value proposition statement which identifies the KSF for types of customer in segmented markets [13]. Many authors do not distinguish the external and internal perspectives, using the names critical success factor [14] and key performance factor [11], among others.

The benefit concept is central in the approach to performance measurement of ECOLEAD project [4], since it is the driver of the collaborative network (CN) behaviour. The goal in a CN is the maximization of a benefit which is an attribute of its specific value system.

Since the KSF are related with competitiveness, it should be noted that competition and the possibility to choose alternatives exist both in BC and in VO and the choice will be determined by the performance on the KSF. As an example, an organisation may decide to participate or not in a BC and may be or not allowed to participate.

3 Performance Management in Collaborative Networks

The proposed approach to performance management aims at guaranteeing the alignment and achievement of strategic and operational business objectives in the Virtual Organisation and in its supporting Business Community environments. It relies on establishing a strategy based on key success factors (KSF) and on identifying and cascading them internally in alignment with the strategy. Fig. 2 depicts the Net-Challenge performance management framework.

The main components of the Net-Challenge framework for performance management are:

- a stakeholder's perspective of value which defines what performance is (external environment);
- the interlinked factors in the CN which can be acted upon in order to change performance (internal environment);
- the reference performance management processes aiming at making the strategy succeed;
- the information system;
- the process' resources;
- the communication processes (internal and with stakeholders).

Performance can be acted upon in the two environments, which means in two time horizons. In the VO, depending on its lifetime and in the BC, where members develop their capabilities, sharing knowledge whenever possible and try to know each other. In the BC, a management process can improve the instruments related to membership and those made available to VO to support their formation and operation, such as the standard processes, templates and specific ICT tools. Also a BC management process for strategy revision ponders the actual performance and the environment changes and adjusts strategy if necessary.

Two reference processes for performance management in the BC and in the VO are part of the Net-Challenge framework, which interface with the reference collaboration processes as briefly explained. In order to expedite the processes, particularly in VO,

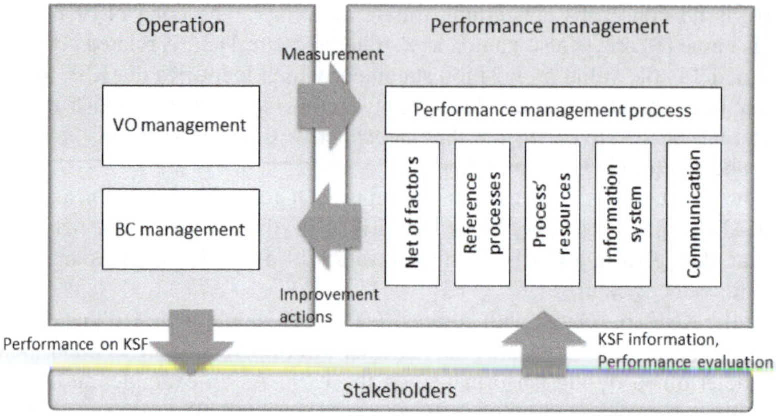

Fig. 2. Components and interactions in the Net-Challenge framework for performance management

some resources are provided – scenario templates which characterise typical business scenarios and propose sets of KSF and lists of success factors, the corresponding KPI and the definitions.

The information system collects data from VO partners and BC members for KPI, conveys evaluation of performance and feeds a central repository of information (BC member and VO profiles). Aggregated and disaggregated data allows analysing performance of VO, VO partners and of the whole BC. This system supports search of partners based on claimed capabilities, qualified processes and actual performance.

Internal and external communication of performance is essential to mobilise organisations to improvement, to convey the BC strategy and to reward the members.

In order to speed up and guide organisations in the analysis process and in the identification of KSF and also to clarify the concepts of the performance management framework, the framework contains examples of KSF to BC's and VO's stakeholders which are presented in Table 1 and Table 2, respectively. To find the KSF the key question is "what are most important requirements that the stakeholder wants from the organisation (and from other competing organisations) that will determine his evaluation or ultimately that will make him decide for one organisation?". Since it is important that a clear and common understanding of the meaning of each KSF exists, a KSF glossary is a required process resource.

The BC's KSF to the VO consider both the formation of the VO and its operation. During the formation, the VO does not exist formally but the KSF demanded are specific and distinct from those asked by a member to the BC.

The KSF listed are potential KSF and only some of them will apply in each scenario. It should also be noted that the BC also wants some of the VO's KSF to customer, meaning that those KSF are related with its mission statement and main goals (such as supporting the supply of complex, high added value products for demanding customers). By analysing the performance of all VO formed, the BC can determine its own success.

Table 1. List of some examples of BC's KSF to its stakeholders

Stakeholder	KSF	
BC member	• Business opportunities • Knowledge	• Reputation in the market • Economies of scale and scope
Virtual Organisation	• Preparedness of members • Information about members • Capacity	• Supporting instruments • Complementary capabilities
Customer	• Suppliers development	• Suppliers selection effort
Society	• Social responsibility	• Ethical behaviour

Table 2. List of some examples of VO's KSF to its stakeholders

Stakeholder	KSF		
Partner (not broker)	• Sales • Margin	• Payment terms • Capacity utilisation	• Knowledge • Reputation in the BC and in the market
Broker	• Cost and risk sharing • Responsiveness • Expertise	• KSF for Partner (not Broker)	• KSF for Customer (when the Broker represents the Customer)
Customer	• Price • Quality of the product • Innovative solutions / differentiation	• Location of partners • Technical support • Delivery time reliability • Delivery time	• Technical features • Confidentiality • Turnkey solutions • Customer service • Product mix
BC	• VO Sales • Margin • Turnkey solutions	• Delivery time • Quality of products • Technical features	• Knowledge • BC rules compliance • Reputation in the market
Society	• Ethical behaviour	• Tax compliance	• Environmental compliance

The identification of the most important factors that affect the key success factors – the key performance factors (KPF) – enables to act on the processes and measure them in alignment with the strategy. The process of identification and definition of KSF and KPF contribute to create a common language in the Business Community.

Key performance indicators (KPI) allow monitoring the performance of the organisations on the selected key factors (success and performance factors). However a performance factor may require more than one performance indicator to be fully measured. KPI are the (few) selected ones to measure the overall performance of a system or organisation. Some KPI are proposed with the main objective to speed up the analysis during formation of BC and VO.

Although quantitative indicators were preferred, for some factors only qualitative indicators could be found. Some are measured periodically others are measured once, which is the case of qualitative measures obtained at the VO's dissolution phase in a review of performance.

4 Validation

The Net-Challenge framework for performance management will be tested in a pilot application led by one industrial partner, in the textile and garment sector. In this sector, supply chains are hierarchical; many companies are very small and have a very informal approach to performance management. It will be mostly focused the validation of the process resources (KSF, KPF, KPI and business scenarios) and of the sub-processes to negotiate them and setup the performance management processes.

Interviews with key people in the participating organisations will enable an initial validation and adjustment and to determine the needs and requirements for training and assistance. Information will be acquired through inquiries about the initial conditions and the effectiveness of process execution. It will also be examined the contribution of the performance management processes to the alignment of strategies and to customer orientation. Both the validation and the specific requirements will enrich the framework.

5 Conclusions

The identification of CN's key stakeholders, of their relations and roles and the identification of their key success factors enables a comprehensive approach to performance management, from strategy setting to improvement decisions and monitoring. The paper focus the identification and definition of key success factors, i.e., of value creation for stakeholders as an essential component for the analysis and control of performance factors and thus to support the collaboration processes in CN.

As argued in this paper, performance measurement and particularly the selection of KPI require the existence of the sound base provided by the analysis of KSF or otherwise may be arbitrary and generate confusion, resources waste and lack of confidence on CN potential. The practical approach and the KSF presented can guide CN to develop their performance management systems in a logic way, contribute to fill the gaps found in this area and may stimulate organisations to get involved in CN.

Acknowledgments. The authors would like to acknowledge the co-funding of the European Commission within NMP priority of the Seventh RTD Framework Programme (2007-13) for the Net Challenge project (Innovative Networks of SMEs for Complex Products Manufacturing), Ref. CP-FP 229287-2. The authors also acknowledge the valuable collaboration provided by the project team during the research work.

References

1. Folan, P., Browne, J.: A review of performance measurement: Towards performance management. Computers in Industry 56, 663–680 (2005)
2. Camarinha-Matos, L.M., Afsarmanesh, H.: Elements of a base VE infrastructure. Computers in Industry 51(2), 139–163 (2003)

3. Carneiro, L., Almeida, R., Azevedo, A., Kankaanpaa, T., Shamsuzzoha, A.: An Innovative Framework Supporting SME Networks for Complex Product Manufacturing. In: Camarinha-Matos, L., Boucher, X., Afsarmanesh, H. (eds.) PRO-VE 2010. IFIP AICT, vol. 336, pp. 204–211. Springer, Heidelberg (2010)
4. Camarinha-Matos, L.M., Abreu, A.: Performance indicators for collaborative networks based on collaboration benefits. Production Planning & Control 18(7), 592–609 (2007)
5. Alfaro, J., Rodriguez, R., Ortiz, A.: A performance measurement system for virtual and extended enterprises. In: Camarinha-Matos, L.M. (ed.) Proceedings of the Sixth IFIP Working Conference on Virtual Enterprises, New York, vol. 186, pp. 285–292 (2005)
6. Cunha, P.F., Ferreira, P.S., Macedo, P.: Performance evaluation within cooperate networked production enterprises. International Journal of Computer Integrated Manufacturing 21(2), 174–179 (2008)
7. Otley, D.: Performance management: a framework for management control systems research. Management Accounting Research 10, 363–382 (1999)
8. La Forme, F.-A.G., Genoulaz, V., Campagne, J.-P.: A framework to analyse collaborative performance. Computers in Industry 58, 687–697 (2007)
9. Camarinha-Matos, L.M., Afsarmanesh, H.: Related work on reference modeling for collaborative networks. In: Camarinha-Matos, L.M., Afsarmanesh, H. (eds.) Collaborative Networks: Reference Modeling, pp. 15–28. Springer Science, Heidelberg (2008)
10. Lebas, M.J.: Performance measurement and performance management. International Journal of Production Economics 58, 23–35 (1995)
11. Kaydos, W.J.: Operational performance measurement: increasing total productivity. St. Lucile Press, Boca Raton (1999)
12. Kenny, G.: Strategic Planning and Performance Management: Develop and Measure a Winning Strategy. Elsevier/Butterworth-Heinemann, London (2005)
13. Bolstorff, P., Rosenbaum, R.: Supply chain excellence: a handbook for dramatic improvement using the SCOR model. American Management Association (2003)
14. Kaplan, R.S., Norton, D.P.: The Balanced Scorecard. Harvard Business School Press, Boston (1996)
15. Gunasekaran, A., Patel, C., McGaughey, R.E.: A framework for supply chain performance measurement. Int. J. Production Economics 87, 333–347 (2004)

Part VI

Performance Management - II

A Structured Methodology to Implement Performance Measurement Systems in Collaborative Networks

María-José Verdecho, Raúl Rodríguez-Rodríguez, and Juan-José Alfaro-Saiz

Department of Business Organization, CIGIP (Research Centre on Production Management and Engineering), Universitat Politècnica de València, Camino de Vera, s/n, 46022, Valencia, Spain
{mverdecho,jalfaro,raurodro}@cigip.upv.es

Abstract. Collaboration is one of the most commonly used strategies in the business environment. Enterprises that collaborate need reliable and efficient performance information. However, many collaborative enterprises fail to implement a common performance measurement system in an adequate manner due to the lack of sound mechanisms that connect all the elements within a performance measurement system. The purpose of this paper is to provide a methodology based on a multi-criteria decision method that aids to implement the different elements that compose a performance measurement system for collaborative networks. With this methodology enterprises have a tool to define all the aspects involved in the performance measurement system and to implement it. This approach has been applied to a collaborative enterprise network belonging to the automotive sector.

Keywords: performance measurement systems, collaborative networks, performance management.

1 Introduction

Collaboration is one of the business models that enterprises adopt to remain competitive. Companies collaborating share the responsibility of exchanging common planning, management, execution, and performance measurement information [1]. In addition, collaboration requires the commitment of human, financial or technical resources to build and sustain a more competitive business model [2]. For that reason, it is necessary to manage the evolution of the collaborative relationship by defining performance measurement systems (PMS) that aid to collect the necessary information in order to manage the activities of the collaborative association. In the literature, there has been an increasing interest in the development of PMS for inter-organizational contexts [3-6] and recently some PMS were developed for specific collaborative contexts [7-9]. This is because, as collaborative relationships present specific characteristics that need to be managed such as trust, commitment, cooperation, etc. [10-11]. Then, PMS developed for inter-organizational contexts should present specific characteristics to be useful for these contexts. One of this characteristic is related to the need that the design and implementation phases of PMS are coordinated in order to build them adequately. In this sense, decision makers

L.M. Camarinha-Matos et al. (Eds.): PRO-VE 2011, IFIP AICT 362, pp. 151–158, 2011.

usually deal with other important issues such as the prioritization of performance objectives in order to know which the most strategic objectives are and, therefore, in which aspects enterprises should be focused and allocate resources. Despite the importance of these activities, the inter-organizational PMS developed in the literature present some limitations for providing weights [12]. Then, PMS should incorporate methods for solving these issues in order to get an adequate PMS design and implementation.

In order to prioritize objectives, it is useful to define weights for the different objectives which can be stated as a multi-criteria problem involving different actors. In the same vein, structuring and consolidating data may also be solved as a multi-criteria problem. Therefore, multi-criteria methods can contribute to the elaboration and establishment of the performance measurement systems. The main goal of this paper is to propose a novel methodology to design and implement PMS in collaborative networks by using a multi-criteria decision-making approach. With this methodology, enterprises will have a tool that describes the steps to be followed by all the collaborating enterprises in order to define, reach agreement and manage the evolution of the collaborative enterprise network. Then, this methodology is developed to manage the performance of the association of enterprises instead of the individual enterprises. Evolution is managed by analyzing the performance reached by the whole association at the different periods and deriving, defining and implementing actions plans when performance is not achieved.

The structure of this paper is as follows. First, a literature review of inter-organizational PMS and multi-criteria decision analysis methods are presented focusing attention on the Analytic Hierarchy Process (AHP) method. Then, the methodology proposed to implement performance measurement systems is presented. Next, a case study of a collaborative enterprise network belonging to the automotive sector is described. Finally, conclusions are exposed.

2 Literature Review

Collaborative enterprise networks involve that different partners are working together for mutual benefits. Therefore, the definition of PMS for managing its activity is a task that has to be made by all the collaborative partners. There are several PMS developed in the literature for inter-organizational contexts such as the works [3-9]. These PMS are useful structures for defining and structuring performance measurement information from the strategic level to the process level by deploying linkages among the performance elements. However, they lack of mechanisms to prioritize the performance measurement elements data so that performance can be analyzed under an assessment making preference to those aspects that are more relevant for the sustainability of the collaborative enterprise network.

On the other side, there are many multi-criteria methods. In fact, multi-criteria methods are classified into two groups [13]: Multiple Objective Decision Methods (MODM) and Multiple Attribute Decision Methods (MADM). The main difference between both methods is that in MODM, decision makers need to reach multiple objectives that are in conflict of interest and the number of alternatives is elevated. However, MADM problems focus on obtaining a preference ranking on the alternatives characterized by multiple attributes that are in conflict and the number of alternatives is limited. In our problem, the number of performance objectives is limited and discrete so that MADM techniques are to be used. There are several MADM methods such as Multiple Attribute Utility Theory, (MAUT) [14], ELECTRE (ELimination Et Choix Traduisant la REalité) [15], PROMETHEE (Preference Ranking Organization METhod for Enrichment Evaluations) [16] and the Analytic Hierarchy Process, AHP [17].

AHP aims at integrating different measures into a single assessment for ranking decision alternatives which is the case of our problem. Also, ranking of objectives involves both tangible and intangible aspects and AHP deals with both types of aspects. This is because overall assessment should not only consider quantitative performance data but also some other criteria that are critical for successful parnerships and are not directly quantifiable, e.g. trust and commitment [18]. In addition, AHP has been used for many applications involving performance measurement criteria such as selecting a supplier [19-21], selecting performance indicators for supply chain management [22], evaluating performance of IT department in the manufacturing industry in Taiwan [23], and selecting ERP systems in textile industry [24]. However, there is not an application of AHP for supporting PMS design and implementation within inter-organizational contexts. For this reason, the purpose of the remaining of this paper is to present a methodology that uses AHP method to support the prioritization of the objectives within a PMS and the composition of an assessment for the whole collaborative network that fills this research gap.

3 The Proposed Methodology to Support the Implementation of PMS in Collaborative Contexts

In [19], the COL-PMS framework for managing performance within collaborative contexts is presented. The COL-PMS framework integrates the social side of collaboration within an integrated and solid PMS structure. The main purpose of this PMS is to support the decision-making process of the enterprises and entities that collaborate. For that reason, it is necessary that the PMS considers two levels: inter-organizational level (where collaboration takes place) and individual enterprise level. Fig. 1 shows the phases of the methodology proposed to implement the COL-PMS framework by using AHP which is composed of seven phases. In the phase 1, the performance elements of the PMS are defined. In this work, the PMS structure used is the COL-PMS but other PMS structures may be used. Then, the AHP method is applied to build a model (phase 2). The AHP method structures the decision problem in a hierarchy of levels. These levels are linked by unidirectional dependence relationships. In the upper level of the hierarchy, it is defined the ultimate goal of the decision problem. Then, the criteria that contribute to achieve the goal stand in the second level. In the next levels, intermediate sub-criteria and attributes that compose the hierarchical structure are located. Finally, in the last level, the decision alternatives are established. Using levels allows decision makers to focus on a small set of decisions [17]. The AHP method provides relative weights to each element within a level depending on its contribution to an element linked to it that is located on the immediate upper level. In our case, as we use the AHP model to obtain the weights of the performance objectives, we will have three levels (see Fig. 2): PMS vision (main goal), perspectives (criteria) and, finally, performance objectives (alternatives).

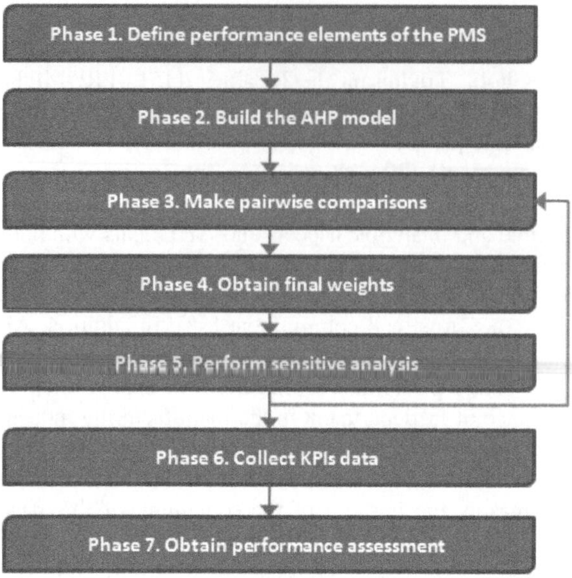

Fig. 1. Methodology for implementing a PMS by using AHP

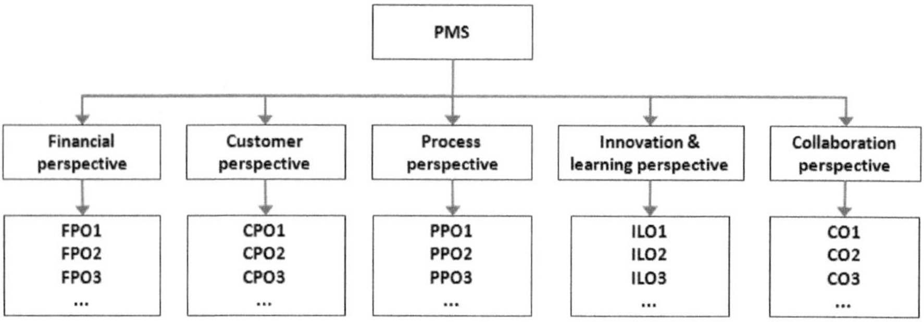

Fig. 2. AHP model

Once the model is built, it is needed to make pairwise comparisons in each level using the fundamental scale of Saaty [17], in order to obtain the pairwise comparison matrices (phase 3). After pairwise comparisons matrices are completed, the local priorities of the compared elements (priority vector) are calculated and consistency of judgements checked following the procedure described in [17]. Once all priority vectors are obtained and consistency verified, the final weights for the alternatives are calculated (phase 4). For that purpose, priorities of decision alternatives are combined together with the sets of priorities of the criteria. Then, in phase 5, it is performed a sensitive analysis to check how changes in the local weights of one of the criteria or alternatives affect the final priorities previously obtained. The purpose of this phase is to verify that the solution obtained as the preferred alternative is robust enough. In case that the solution is not robust, it is needed to go back into the phase 3 to analyze the pairwise comparison matrices defined. In phase 6, the data regarding the performance indicators is collected. Finally, phase 7, it is obtained the overall performance evaluation by multiplying the priority of every performance objective (given by the normalized priority) and the value reached in its corresponding performance indicator.

4 Case Study

The methodology has been applied to a collaborative enterprise network belonging to the automotive industry in Spain which is composed raw material suppliers, design centres and manufacturing plants (of a plastic injection moulding leading group) working for main OEMs. Due to the success of a new product launched, and the new market needs regarding this new product, the corporation pursued to change the policy and orientation towards collaborative working in order to agree the terms, commitment, money investments and resource and information sharing. One of the components of this product is critical as the technology and know-how required to design it and manufacture it is not a core capability of the manufacturer therefore collaborative working seem reasonable.

The first phase of the methodology consists of the definition of the PMS elements. Managing directors of the different enterprises assessed were in charge of the decision making of the different phases of the methodology. It took several meetings to reach an agreement on the strategic aspects of the relationship as the enterprises come with different backgrounds and understand in a different way the main components for the business vision. Once the global performance elements were defined, the different enterprises performed some adjustments into their performance indicators at the local level to accommodate all the relevant performance information coherently. Table 1 shows the performance elements (objectives and KPIs) defined for the collaborative enterprise network level. It consists of fourteen objectives and KPIs (divided into the five performance perspectives) which seems a reasonable number. These KPIs have been defined by the enterprises based on the objectives that they want to reach. It took two meetings to define these KPIs.

In the phase 3, in order to fill in the pairwise comparison matrices it was necessary to establish an initial meeting for explaining the AHP method. As this phase involves decision makers of all the enterprises, several possibilities can be used to obtain a final solution such as voting, aggregation methods on individual preferences or reaching consensus [17]. The companies agreed to use the aggregation on individual preferences if the initial judgement was equal or similar for all of them. However, if there was a large difference of judgement, this point needed to be dealt with in meetings for reaching consensus or a closer point of view. In order to reach consensus, the managing directors discuss the preferences until a better understanding is achieved. Therefore, a combined solution was applied in order to get an approximate common view of the problem. Then, enterprises meet several times in order to fill in the pairwise comparison matrices. In other cases, if consensus is not reached, other methods can be used such as voting.

Table 1. Performance elements of the collaborative enterprise network

Perspect.	Objectives	KPIs
Financial	FO1 Increase sales	KPI1 = sales (monthly)
	FO2 Increase high quality product margins	KPI2 = average of high quality products margin variation (monthly)
Customer	CPO1 Increase market share	KPI3 = market share variation (quarterly)
	CPO2 Increase customer loyalty	KPI4 = number of old customer purchases/ total purchases (quarterly)
	CPO3 Increase customer satisfaction	KPI5 = number of claims/complaints (weekly)
Process	PO1 Decrease production lead time	KPI6 = production lead time variation (monthly)
	PO2 Decrease new product development lead time	KPI7 = new product development lead time variation (per project)
	PO3 Implement initiatives for production performance improvement	KPI8 = number of performance improvement initiatives implemented (semester)
	PO4 Decrease non-conforming parts	KPI9 = number of non-conformance parts send to customer (weekly) (by customer)
Learning & Growth	LGO1 Increase innovation capability	KPI10 = Number of innovative products proposed (annual)
	LGO2 Improve engineering knowledge	KPI11 = number of common engineering development training sessions performed (semester)
Collaboration	CO1 Increase commitment	KPI12 = Number of agreements failed (monthly)
	CO2 Increase coordination	KPI13 = number of times that information is sent delayed (monthly)
	CO3 Maintain equity	KPI14 = meetings to discuss perception of equity after agreement (quarterly)

In the phase 4, the weights of the objectives are obtained. Results showed that the most important objectives representing more than 70% of the total weight were: FO1 Increase sales (with normalized weight of 0,16), CPO1 Increase market share (0,12), FO2 Increase high quality product margins (0,11), CPO3 Increase customer satisfaction (0.09), PO4 Decrease non-conforming parts (0,09), LGO1 Increase innovation capability (0.08) and CO3 Maintain equity (0,08). It can be observed that the relevant objectives belong to all the performance perspectives but the importance of the perspectives differ, being the financial perspective the most relevant followed by the customer perspective. It is to be noted that the objective CO3 Maintain equity reaches a weight of 0,08. This fact notes the importance of social climate aspects for sustaining collaboration in the long time.

In the last phase it is obtained the final results. The analysis showed that performance was mainly achieved by some of the most relevant objectives (those objectives with highest weight). However, financial objectives were not accomplished in the desired level (accomplished around 20%) and decision makers have to reassess what is expected in current market conditions. Another objective that is not achieved is the decreasing of non-conforming parts (accomplished around 50%). For those objectives that have not reached the expected results, actions plans are to be developed which allows reassessing the current targets or reaching them properly. It has to be noted that performance achievement was only reached at the 60% what was under the initial expectations (70%). However, results showed that performance measurement implementation has provided performance knowledge to the collaborative network as well as a tool for monitoring performance from now on.

From an information systems point of view, it has to be said that a web-based tool is being built in order to make possible to implement the system. Some of the next steps involve completing the tool and testing it, training further the people that are going to use it, move the data into the application and feed the system with updated data in order to analyze how the performance of the collaborative enterprise network evolves.

5 Conclusions

The literature counts with inter-organizational PMS that are useful structures for defining performance measurement systems. However, they lack of mechanism to prioritize the performance measurement elements data. This paper introduces a structured methodology supported by a multi-criteria method to aids to implement PMS for collaborative networks aiming to fill this research gap. Adaptations of this methodology can be made to manage other inter-enterprise relationships such as supply chains, etc. Further research work will involve the full development of the web tool in order to not only provide the storage of data and calculation of the results but also deals with the report analysis settings. In addition, it is needed to further testing the web tool and observe its evolution as well as the evolution of the PMS and the performance of the collaborative enterprise network in the long time. Other interesting research line is the validation of the proposed methodology in other contexts as well as the adaptation of other PMS and MADM techniques.

Acknowledgments. This work has been developed within the framework of a research project funded by the Polytechnic University of Valencia, titled "Design and Implementation of Performance Measurement Systems within Collaborative Contexts for aiding the Decision-making Process", reference PAID-06-08-3206.

References

1. Anthony, T.: Supply chain collaboration: success in the new internet economy (online). ASCET, http://anthony.ASCET.com
2. Bowersox, D.J., Closs, D.J., Stank, T.P.: How to master cross-enterprise collaboration. Supply Chain Management Review 7(4), 18–27 (2003)
3. Brewer, P.C., Speh, T.W.: Using the Balanced ScoreCard to measure supply chain performance. Journal of Business Logistics 21(1), 75–93 (2000)
4. Bititci, U.S., Mendibil, K., Martinez, V., Albores, P.: Measuring and managing performance in extended enterprises. Intern. J. of Operations & Production Management 25(4), 333–353 (2005)

5. Folan, P., Browne, J.: Development of an Extended Enterprise Performance Measurement System. Production Planning and Control 16(6), 531–544 (2005)
6. Alfaro, J., Ortiz, A., Rodríguez, R.: Performance measurement system for Enterprise Networks. International Journal of Productivity and Performance Management 56(4), 305–334 (2007)
7. Romero, D., Galeano, N., Molina, A.: A conceptual Model for Virtual Breeding Environments Value System. In: Camarinha-Matos, L., Afsarmanesh, H., Novais, P., Analide, C. (eds.) Establishing the Foundation of Collaborative Networks. Springer, Heidelberg (2007)
8. Msanjila, S.S., Afsarmanesh, H.: Trust analysis and assessment in virtual organization breeding environments. International Journal of Production Research 46(5), 1253–1295 (2008)
9. Westphal, I., Thoben, K.D., Seifert, M.: Measuring collaboration performance in virtual organizations. In: Camarihna-Matos, L., Afsarmanesh, H., Novais, P., Analide, C. (eds.) Establishing the Foundation of Collaborative Networks. Springer, Boston (2007)
10. Verdecho, M.J., Alfaro, J.J., Rodriguez-Rodriguez, R.: Foundations for collaborative performance measurement. Production Planning and Control 20(3), 193–205 (2009)
11. Verdecho, M.J., Alfaro, J.J., Rodriguez-Rodriguez, R.: COL-PMS: a collaborative performance measurement system. In: Ortiz, Á., Franco, R.D., Gasquet, P.G. (eds.) BASYS 2010. IFIP AICT, vol. 322, pp. 56–67. Springer, Heidelberg (2010)
12. Yüksel, I., Dagdeviren, M.: Using the fuzzy analytic network process (ANP) for Balanced Scorecard (BSC): A case study for a manufacturing firm. Expert Systems with Applications 37, 1270–1278 (2010)
13. Barba-Romero, S., Pomerol, J.: Decisiones Multicriterio: fundamentos teóricos y utilización práctica. Editorial: Universidad de Alcalá de Henares. Alcalá de Henares (1997)
14. Fishburn, P.: Independence in utility theory with whole product sets. Operations Research 13, 28–45 (1965)
15. Roy, B.: Classement et choix en présence de points de vue multiples: la méthode ELECTRE. Revue Française d'Informatique et de Reserche Opérationnelle 8, 57–75 (1968)
16. Brans, J., Vincke, P., Mareschal, B.: How to select and how to rank projects: the PROMETHEE method. European Journal of Operational Research 24, 228–238 (1986)
17. Saaty, T.L.: The Analytic Hierarchy Process. McGraw-Hill, New York (1980)
18. Mohr, J., Spekman, R.: Characteristics of partnership success: Partnership attributes, communication. Strategic Management Journal 15(2), 135–152 (1994)
19. Verdecho, M.J., Alfaro, J.J., Rodriguez-Rodriguez, R.: A multi-criteria approach to select suppliers based on performance. In: Ortiz, Á., Franco, R.D., Gasquet, P.G. (eds.) BASYS 2010. IFIP AICT, vol. 322, pp. 47–55. Springer, Heidelberg (2010)
20. Masella, C., Rangone, A.: A contigent approach to the design of vendor selection systems for different types of co-operative customer/ supplier relationships. International Journal of Operations & Production Management 20(1), 70–84 (2000)
21. Ghodsypour, S.H., O'Brien, C.: A decision support system for supplier selection using an integrated analytic hierarchy process and linear programming. International Journal of Production Economics 56-57, 199–212 (1998)
22. Bhagwat, R., Sharma, M.K.: Performance measurement of supply chain management using the analytical hierarchy process. Production Planning & Control 18(8), 666–680 (2007)
23. Lee, A.H.I., Chen, W.C., Chang, C.: A fuzzy AHP and BSC approach for evaluating performance of IT department in the manufacturing industry in Taiwan. Expert Systems with Applications 34(1), 96–107 (2008)
24. Cebeci, U.: Fuzzy AHP-based decision support system for selecting ERP systems in textile industry by using balanced scorecard. Expert Systems with Applications 36, 8900–8909 (2009)

Using Key Alignment Indicators for Performance Evaluation in Collaborative Networks

Roberto da Piedade Francisco, Américo Azevedo,
João Bastos, and António Almeida

INESC Porto - Institute for Systems and Computer Engineering of Porto,
Faculty of Engineering of the University of Porto, Porto, Portugal
{roberto.piedade,ala,joao.bastos,antonio.henrique}@fe.up.pt

Abstract. This paper aims to explore the performance alignment in collaborative network environments. It has been stated that performance management based on data collection and the evaluation of key performance indicators (KPIs) may not be effective due to the different indicators and measurement systems in place for the various participants in a collaborative network (CN). Therefore, measuring the strategic and inter-organizational alignment based on key alignment indicators (KAIs) can be an excellent alternative to improve performance evaluation systems. This approach has led to the exploration of the performance prediction paradigm and develops tools to estimate a performance and evaluate the degree of alignment by creating instances of a future performance in collaborative networks.

Keywords: Collaborative networks, performance management, alignment measurement.

1 Introduction

Constant changes in business environments force organizations to address the challenge of the growing demands of increasingly mature and saturated markets. This then obliges organizations to focus on achieving high levels of responsiveness and flexibility in the development, production and delivery of their products or services [1].

Performance evaluation in collaborative networks (CN) is a significant management function for supporting a successful business [2]. The different systems and performance indicators used by each partner can present difficulties when standardizing measurements. Therefore, an alignment measure is proposed to instantiate the overall performance of a CN.

This paper aims to highlight the relevant aspects of performance management and promote inter-organizational alignment in CNs, which is explained in the second section. The third section introduces theory, focusing on the performance prediction paradigm. This is followed by an outline of the alignment measurement in CNs, the related conceptual framework and the supporting mathematical tools are presented in section four and conclusions are outlined in section five.

L.M. Camarinha-Matos et al. (Eds.): PRO-VE 2011, IFIP AICT 362, pp. 159–166, 2011.

2 Performance Management and Alignment in Collaborative Networks

Performance measuring and management are crucial in order to improve processes and implement solutions that will improve the efficiency and effectiveness of organizational processes [3]. Furthermore, Seifert [4] has argued that "performance is the degree of target achievement of a process regarding pre-determined and application-dependent criteria". Complementing this definition, Seifert [4] also explains that performance measurement can be "understood as the measuring, analyzing and communication of the performance of business processes" and yet, if implemented efficiently it can have a significant and positive impact on organizations [5]. However, Taticchi [6] states that a performance measurement and management system is a broader system which is developed to collect, integrate and analyze performance measures to enhance decision-making processes while also evaluating strategies and promoting alignment.

Furthermore, Camarinha-Matos and Abreu [7] state that if the CN is able to simultaneously measure the individual performance of each member and the overall CN performance, then this will encourage participants to understand the benefits of this new paradigm.

The term alignment, although it has other connotations, is usually defined as an arrangement of groups or forces in relation to one another [8]. Thus, in order to contextualize this concept within the scope of collaborative networks it is possible to generalize that this term can be applied as a fit relationship between the participants of a CN. If an organization's strategy does not coincide with the targets, organizations should be aware of the need for adaptive systems in order to improve their level of effectiveness [9]. Kathuria, Joshi and Porth [10] state that alignment is important for formulating strategies, defining processes, supporting decision-making and, in particular, fitting key processes.

However, significant factors can have a negative or positive impact on alignment within a CN, for instance: trust, reliability, competence (skill level) and experience (know how). For example, according to Msanjila and Afsarmanesh [11], inter-organizational trust is not subjective like interpersonal trust and it is not always possible to know the values or past actions of potential partners in a collaborative relationship, particularly in the formation phase of a CN. Furthermore, the level of technological and commercial maturity of each participant could alter reliability which may lead to the exclusion of participants or the dissolution of the CN. Therefore, competence can be seen as the combination of knowledge, skills, technologies, physical systems, management and values and it gives organizations a competitive advantage in creating distinctive value that is recognized by customers [12].

It is therefore possible to determine that measuring and evaluating the behavior of the alignment factors is relevant in order to assess the overall network arrangement [13]. Furthermore, it is important to measure this alignment in the agreement moment and during the operation of the CN in order to verify whether a large gap in the alignment between partners appears.

3 A Predictive Approach in Performance Management

This new model of collaborative management can help organizations follow strategies that enable them to be more flexible and agile. The interval between analysis and evaluation and the time taken to react to process failures and develop solutions must be reduced in order to improve organizations' responsiveness.

Therefore, due to constant changes in organizational processes and their requirements, this work recommends a conceptual framework supported by a practical tool for performance estimation in order to support a proactive approach. Indeed, with a proactive performance prediction approach it is possible to foresee that the performance model will be based on the current status. Therefore, contrary to the reactive approach, that is not able predict what the module will become unless a trigger is detected, this approach will proactively react once a system concept/model change has been identified [14]. Consequently, this paper proposes a tool that learns the behavior of the system in order to anticipate the performance reaction to the changes made, and not only using data history analysis.

3.1 Feedforward Alignment

Having established that alignment can be measured using key alignment indicators (KAIs) estimation and performance classification tools were then developed and implemented in order to materialize this concept. In this innovative approach, a combination of feedfoward and feedback analysis, supported by leading and lagging performance measures, respectively, can establish a predictive approach to measuring alignment in collaborative networks (Figure 1).

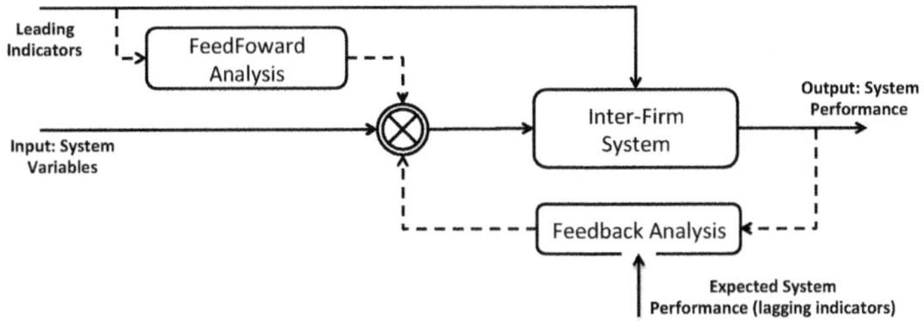

Fig. 1. Feedfoward and Feedback Control System

Thus, according to Busi and Bititci [15],

> *"Feedforward control involves the development and deployment of plans and objectives based on leading measures of real-time performance, while feedback control involves the measurement of performance against those objectives through historical lagging measures. Proactive performance management based on both feedforward and feedback control is based on the premise that a balanced set of leading and lagging performance measures should anticipate and not only correct bad performance."*

The proposed approach will be crucial to supporting the subsequent development of the alignment and measuring toolset proposed in this research.

3.2 Decreasing Reaction Time

Since the success and effectiveness of performance measurement depends on the time taken by organizations to react and make improvements, it is critical not only to reduce the reaction time but, more importantly, anticipate it [4]. Therefore, modeling complex manufacturing systems, using a predictive tool through data fusion, which is not only concerned with statistical data, but also with factors that may influence the future of the CN, can present real benefits for industry nowadays.

With this in mind, it is important to extract knowledge on statistical analysis and data mining tools that are collecting information and knowledge from data in order to use this to predict future patterns of behavior. A predictive model consists of a series of predictive indicators and variables that are likely to influence future behavior.

According to Seifert [4], reaction time consists of two stages: the feedback time and the implementation time (Figure 2). The first stage is represented by the "time span between the evaluated period and the calculation of the KPIs" during the performance measurement process. The second stage is represented by the "time span between detection and elimination of the performance deficit" closing the cycle of performance management.

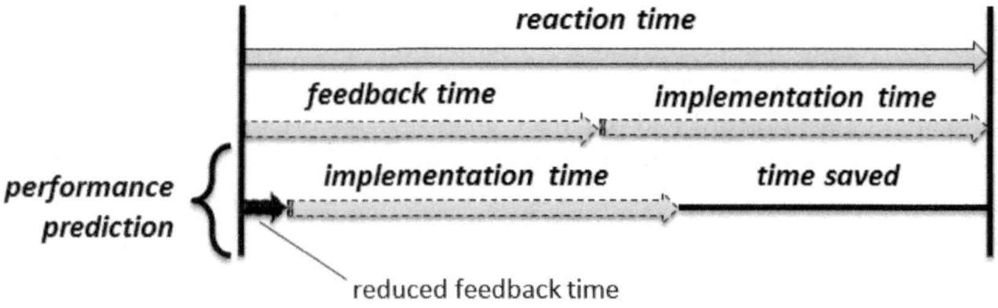

Fig. 2. Performance prediction benefits (adapted from Seifert [4])

Another important aspect related to the performance prediction concept is the definition of appropriate and relevant performance indicators. This is critical for the success of the organization, both individually and in a network environment. Performance measurement and performance management systems should be designed to support proactive management based on both feedback and feedforward operation control.

4 Proposed Alignment Measurement Framework

As part of the research conducted, an explanatory and exploratory investigation was developed within a set of SMEs in collaborative networks in Brazil. During this research, a conceptual framework called CNPMS [16] was adopted for performance management in collaborative networks and an estimation tool was applied to provide predictive measures. Thus, developments were performed to verify if the fit between the CN's strategy and inter-organizational processes could be measured using an alignment measure.

4.1 Key Alignment Indicators

Important questions regarding the 'fit' concept were raised by Venkatraman [17] within the scope of strategic management. Indeed, this is a process geared to deducing not only whether the business environment and organizational structure are aligned (external fit) but also whether the structure and processes of the organization are aligned (internal fit). The 'fit' concept, as outlined in the literature, represents the alignment or configuration of the organizational strategy and takes contingencies faced by the organization within its business environment into account [17]. The internal fit is usually related to the performance improvements [18], to ensure a higher level of alignment, and once calculated it can represent the state of internal fit of a CN.

Since alignment can be measured using KAIs, this led to the exploration of the performance prediction paradigm and the development of tools to estimate and evaluate the performance of the future degree of alignment or fit. The KAIs were then chosen from the predictive KPIs that best represent the effectiveness of inter-organizational processes (Figure 3). Subsequently, the KAIs were used to evaluate the degree of compliance with the established goals. Thus the KAI values are compared with their target values and then each participant is classified. Using these individual values it calculates the Fit Degree where the overall alignment is classified by a fuzzy logic in order to outline future alignment for the period stipulated.

The criteria for selecting the KAIs are derived from the CN decision makers' expectations based on the strategy and the inter-organizational scope. Therefore, initially it is important to perform a survey on each of the participants with the main KPIs used as well as linking each of them following an independent axis: cost, time and quality. Depending on the complexity of the expected KAIs, the CN manager must not only select the independent axis that must be included in the KAI calculation, but also the corresponding KPIs, as each KAI can only be composed of one specific KPI or a combination of KPI's. Subsequently, it is possible to define measurable alignment indicators that are capable of instantiating the overall CN performance state, according to the strategy defined for the entire network.

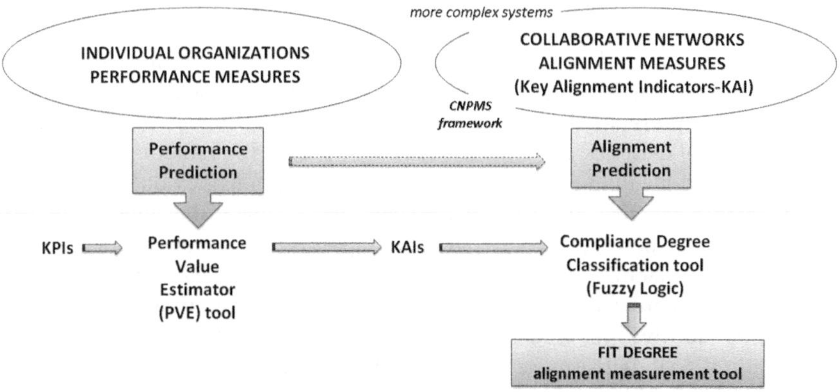

Fig. 3. Using KAIs for performance evaluation in collaborative networks

4.2 Fit Degree Supporting Tools

Since this research aims to develop tools that improve the reaction time in CNs, it is crucial to develop a tool to predict and estimate the performance of nonlinear systems. This approach is based on the leading and lagging factors that can influence the system's behavior. In order to fulfill these requirements, the so-called Performance Value Estimator (PVE) tool was used as a predictive control to monitor, learn and imitate the behavior of complex nonlinear systems that do not require profound knowledge of mathematics [19]. This tool, however, does require a thorough knowledge of the system that it will monitor and emulate. Indeed, this tool consists of Neural Networks and a Kalman Filter, two well-known mathematical tools that are currently used in the areas of automation and robotics.

The fact that Neural Networks (NN) is a non-linear tool with data-driven self-adaptive capabilities makes it a powerful tool for supporting the system's modeling tasks since it allows for the approximation of any continuous function with the desired accuracy. In reality, because the NN tool is able to model non-linear systems without prior knowledge of the relationship between the input and output variables, it can support companies with limited resources and emulate the system's behavior using non-complex past examples. Hence, it is easier to predict future performance using this modeling approach and considering the factors that can be anticipated and envisaged.

Indeed, with the NN modeling approach it is possible to emulate and anticipate the expected performance of a complex system. Nevertheless, one must be cautious with the use of the NN tool since there are a lot of causes and factors that can affect its performance. Therefore, the Kalman Filter was used in order to eliminate possibility of non-controllable errors (where possible) that can originate from the modeling system or from the leading and lagging factors measure. Due to the fact that this filter is capable of supporting estimations for past, present and future states even when the system modeling accuracy is unknown, this tool is normally applied to optimize the estimation of state models. In a higher mathematical layer of abstraction, the Kalman Filter can be seen as a tool that is used to estimate the instantaneous "state" of a dynamic system perturbed by white noise (random factors). Consequently, by incorporating these two significant approaches it was possible to develop a tool that is able to predict the evolution of the behavior of complex systems, minimizing the different errors and noises that can disturb the normal assessment of the performance of the system as presented by Azevedo and Almeida [19].

The PVE tool assumes an important role in this area in predicting the KPI values for the short and medium-term. Nevertheless, since alignment evaluation can be seen as a subjective exercise, in order to calculate and evaluate the inter-organizational alignment it was necessary to use a fuzzy approach. This approach informs the manager of the system's overall performance and takes the key alignment indicators into account and how these indicators will affect the overall performance of the collaborative network. As a result, a Fuzzy Logic System capable of evaluating the inter-organizational performance was included within the framework. The Fuzzy Logic was mainly developed to help decision makers solve classification problems when there is little knowledge and certainty about the system that will be controlled.

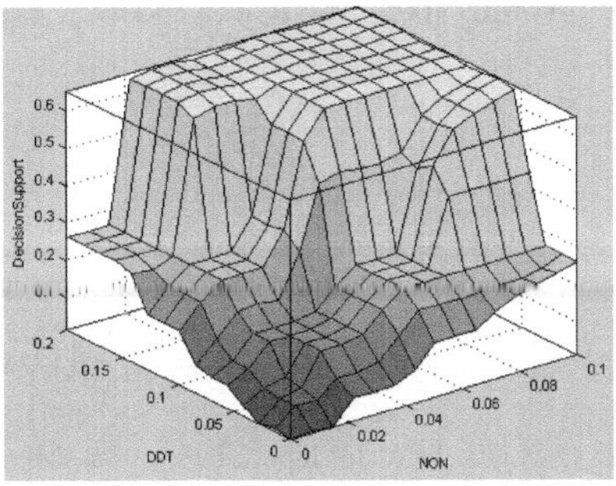

Fig. 4. 3D fuzzy decision surface

Therefore, in a Brazilian industrial supply chain collaborative network called G3, it was possible to define the 3D fuzzy decision surface based on the following KAIs: the delay in the delivery time (DDT), and the percentage of orders delivered with non-conformities (NON). It is then possible to visualize the 3D graph that represents the non-linearity desired for this system (Figure 4). For example, as the KAI values increase, the reliability of the partner decreases, as expected. The dark blue color in this figure represents "fits very well" and the yellow color represents "fits very badly".

Therefore, based on the methodologies explored in the previous section it is possible to integrate the PVE tool and the Fuzzy expert system, in order to build a framework capable of grasping and learning the normal behavior of the non-linear system in study. This framework predicts the future CN performance, using the KAIs as global performance indicators and, finally, evaluates the alignment measure according to the priorities and requirements of the collaborative network in analysis.

5 Discussion and Conclusions

This paper presents a new approach to performance management in collaborative networks (CNs) by measuring the inter-organizational alignment. A collaborative performance forecasting framework was developed and implemented to verify this approach. This alignment evaluation toolset presents both merits and potential advantages for CNs. A major benefit comes from its simplicity and robustness in providing managers with relevant information with regard to network alignment assessment in present and future states to support decisions. Another benefit comes from the fact that prediction results are provided more quickly and in a more proactive way than in other approaches, providing the manager with relevant information to make decisions and manage situations effectively.

In the practical application of the G3 collaborative network, the expert manager reported that the gains obtained by using the tool to predict the future performance of the CN included: being able to specify the sales and production goals with higher accuracy and being able to implement improvement solutions using priority criteria. Therefore, it encourages the CNs to implement solutions to promote alignment in the inter-organizational processes.

Acknowledgments. We would like to thank INESC Porto for supporting this research.

References

1. Chituc, C.M., Azevedo, A.L.: Multi-Perspective Challenges on Collaborative Networks Business Environment. In: Camarinha-Matos, L.M., Afsarmanesh, H., Ortiz, A. (eds.) Collaborative Networks and their Breeding Environments. LNCS, pp. 25–32. Springer, New York (2005)
2. Gibbons, P.M., Burgess, S.C.: Introducing OEE as a Measure of Lean Six Sigma Capability. International Journal of Lean Six Sigma 1, 134–156 (2010)
3. Sobotka, M., Platts, K.W.: Managing without Measuring: a Study of an Electricity Distribution Company. Measuring Business Excellence 14, 28–42 (2010)
4. Seifert, M.: Collaboration Formation in Virtual Organisations by Applying Prospective Performance Measurement. Verlagsgruppe Mainz, Aachen (2009)
5. Spitzer, D.R.: Transforming Performance Measurement: Rethinking the Way We Measure and Drive Organizational Success. Amacom, New York (2007)
6. Taticchi, P.: Business Performance Measurement and Management: New Contexts, Themes and Challenges. Springer, Berlin (2010)
7. Camarinha-Matos, L.M., Abreu, A.: Performance Indicators for Collaborative Networks Based on Collaboration Benefits. Production Planning and Control 18, 592–609 (2007)
8. Merriam-Webster Dictionary, `http://www.merriam-webster.com/dictionary/alignment`
9. Shimizu, T., Carvalho, M.M., Laurindo, F.J.B.: Strategic Alignment Process and Decision Support Systems: Theory and Case Studies. IRM, Hershey (2006)
10. Kathuria, R., Joshi, M.P., Porth, S.J.: Organizational Alignment and Performance: Past, Present and Future. Management Decision 45, 504–517 (2007)
11. Msanjila, S.S., Afsarmanesh, H.: On Hard and Soft Models to Analyse Trust Life-cycle for Mediating Collaboration. In: Camarinha-Matos, L.M., Paraskakis, I., Afsarmanesh, H. (eds.) Leveraging Knowledge for Innovation in Collaborative Networks. LNCS, pp. 381–392. Springer, Heidelberg (2009)
12. Hamel, G., Prahalad, C.K.: Competing for the Future. Harvard Business School Press, Boston (1994)
13. Faria, L., Azevedo, A.: Strategic Production Networks: the Approach of Small Textile Industry. In: 7th IFIP Working Conference on Virtual Enterprises, pp. 609–616. Springer, New York (2006)
14. Yang, Y., Wu, X.: Mining in Anticipation for Concept Change: Proactive-Reactive Prediction in Data Streams. Data Mining and Knowledge Discovery 13, 261–289 (2006)
15. Busi, M., Bititci, U.S.: Collaborative Performance Management: Present Gaps and Future Research. Int. J. of Productivity and Performance Management 55, 7–25 (2006)
16. Francisco, R.D., Azevedo, A.: An SSM-Based Approach to Implement a Dynamic Performance Management System. In: Camarinha-Matos, L.M., Paraskakis, I., Afsarmanesh, H. (eds.) Leveraging Knowledge for Innovation in Collaborative Networks. LNCS, pp. 476–483. Springer, Heidelberg (2009)
17. Venkatraman, N., Camillus, J.C.: Exploring the Concept of 'Fit' in Strategic Management. Academy of Management Review 9, 1–23 (1984)
18. Silveira, G.J.C., Sousa, R.S.: Paradigms of Choice in Manufacturing Strategy: exploring performance relationships of fit, best practices, and capability-based approaches. International Journal of Operations & Production Management 30, 1219–1245 (2010)
19. Azevedo, A., Almeida, A.: Factory Templates for Digital Factories Framework. Robotics and Computer-Integrated Manufacturing 27, 755–771 (2011)

On the Management of Virtual Organizations' Dissolution (in Virtual Business Networks)

Nicolás Hormazábal[1] and Josep Lluís de la Rosa[2]

[1] Tecnalia, Paseo Mikeletegi, 7 - Parque Tecnológico E 20009, San Sebastián, Spain
nicolash@eia.udg.edu
[2] Agents Research Lab, Edifici PIV, Campus de Montilivi, 17071. Girona, Spain
peplluis@eia.udg.edu

Abstract. The dissolution of Virtual Organizations is not just a stage where the commitments between the partners take to an end, but an issue that is worth considering through all the life cycle in Virtual Organizations. This paper gives further light to the model of Virtual Organizations split in several phases, detailing their roles and significance, and explaining from previous experiences why the dissolution has to be carefully planned fairly in advance. The key elements for managing the dissolution of virtual organizations are described, and further evidence on how they can have positive influence to the performance of Virtual Organizations, are contributed highlighting the phase's significance.

Keywords: Virtual Organization, Dissolution, Business Communities, Business Networks.

1 Introduction

Business Communities (BC) as non-hierarchical collaborative environments allow companies to create new Virtual Organizations (VO) as new business opportunities arise, providing tools for knowledge and resources sharing, a trusted network of companies and means for collaboration among the BC members in order to respond the market needs for competing with larger companies. Collaboration and knowledge sharing is of high added value that is key in these collaborative environments as companies can benefit from the knowledge and lessons learned from past experiences when creating new VOs.

In the state of the art, typically three main different phases have been defined in the VOs' lifecycle: Form, Operate and Dissolve [1], with a fourth additional one, Evolve [2] where the VO can modify its infrastructure and cooperation agreements in order to better respond to environmental changes or performance issues. The formation and operation phases have been extensively studied among the current literature, but the dissolution phase has been addressed in a superficial way. Dissolution is a phase that is performed only during the last steps of the VO lifecycle, but its significance ranges the whole lifecycle in different ways yet to be understood that deserve further study.

L.M. Camarinha-Matos et al. (Eds.): PRO-VE 2011, IFIP AICT 362, pp. 167–174, 2011.

Part of this work is included in the methodology design created for the Net-Challenge European project[1] [Ref.: FP7-CP-FP229278-2]. The paper is organized as follows: Section 2 focuses on the dissolution phase's significance by itself, section 3 emphasizes the significance of the dissolution among the other phases and section 4 concludes and explains the future work.

2 Dissolution Phase

During the dissolution phase, some issues must be addressed such as the management of results from the collaboration process made through the VO lifecycle like the intellectual property rights over the production, liabilities towards the customer (warranties), and financial results. Most of this should have been already defined and regulated in the cooperation agreement made during the formation phase, but within a BC environment, there should be also some other issues to be considered for the dissolution.

The dissolution phase represents a unique opportunity to retrieve, store and share the lessons learned from the cooperation and interaction between the different companies that participated in the VO, providing valuable information for future VO creation and operation.

2.1 Information Sharing during Dissolution

When creating a new collaboration network for VOs such as a Business Community (BC), one of the basic concepts that must be considered to assure collaboration and knowledge sharing is a common information and data structure properly modeled and organized [4] for facilitating the access to the information. One of the most valuable pieces of information is the one retrieved at the moment of reviewing past performed activities (it is usually named "post-mortem" in software projects), as a way to learn lessons from the experience. The lessons learned the *hard way* (by empirical failures), can be opportunities in future projects [5]. Creating a context that makes organizational learning possible from the past experiences represents a powerful tool for better future decision making.

The information stored during the VO dissolution as a way for future reference can be divided into two groups: Performance Review and Dissolution Cause Review.

Performance Review: Some of the information that should be modeled when creating a Business Community is the Key Performance Indicators (KPI), which must be defined before any VO should be created to allow comparing performance indicators from different organizations. The assessment of the KPIs is certifying the status of a VO, whether it is on the right track or not. The possible KPIs for a VO can be varied from the one VO to another VO but some are commonly used as lead-time, time-to-market, resource utilization, annual turnover, customer satisfaction level, business growth, etc. The KPI can have different values in respect to business strategy such as KPI for BC, VO, marketing, manufacturing, supply chain management, etc.

---

[1] http://www.netchallenge.org/

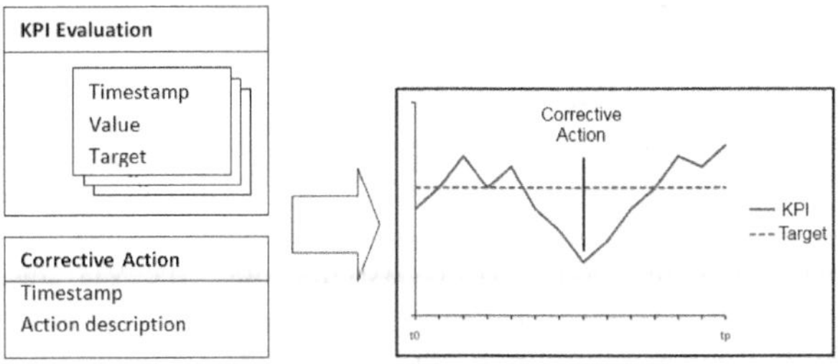

Fig. 1. KPI Evaluations: KPIs are evaluated and compared against the target value

Most of the KPI should have been evaluated during the VO operation as part of a VO performance monitoring process, but there are others that can only be evaluated after the collaboration has finished. These indicators are related to the individual assessment of the VO made by each partner, and may be subjective depending on their expectations, such as the partners' commitment evaluation, collaboration level or communication. This information should help to better define the success or failure of the overall VO, as it goes beyond of the fact whether the VO has achieved its main objectives or not. A VO that has achieved its goals but has gone through major internal problems and has needed many corrective actions should not be considered as equally successful as a VO that has achieved its goals without significant issues.

The KPI's historical data should be compiled along the stream of corrective actions executed, if any. This will help for future reference about the efficiency on the actions taken on the VO based on its impact to the performance indicators.

Each action should be documented as it will be useful for the future VOs in case they find similar cases; it is an important asset regarding the lessons learned point of view. So the evaluation for each KPI should contain a timestamp of the evaluation, the value and the desired target defined by the initial VO commitments and goals. The corrective actions (if any) should also include a timestamp to help establishing a connection among the actions and the KPIs performance changes. From Figure 1, it is observed that the performance level for each KPI can be measured by its deviation from its target value: If a VO has failed to achieve target product delivery deadline (KPI) corrective actions can be to revise the production strategy collaboratively in terms of resource reallocation, possible penalty for delayed partner(s), increasing the level of trust and networking among VO partners, improve partners' capability, etc.

Dissolution Cause Review: Usually, the dissolution is triggered when the VO has fulfilled its goals, or the business opportunity the VO was created for, no longer exists. But there are other causes that could make a VO dissolve, such as performance problems, environmental changes, internal VO members' decisions or resources shortage [3].

As additional information to the performance review, the dissolution cause should be included. It is expected that it puts in context the dissolution cause (why this cause was triggered, in case there were related KPIs), helping to detect in the future what consequences could be derived from performance deviations.

2.2 Product Support After Dissolution

VOs usually are created having a product or service development as an objective (after a business opportunity has been detected). The support tasks like after-sales actions, warranties and liabilities over components or process are not always part of the main VO goals. In the cooperation agreement the liabilities over the VO results should be defined, and these have to be assigned once the VO starts its dissolution process for assuring support towards the customers once the VO has been dissolved.

Some approaches suggest that the liabilities of each component of a product should be related to the component's suppliers [2], but the problem here is that the connection between the customer and the support organization goes from a *one to one* relation (the customer and the VO) to a *one to many* (the customer and each one of the suppliers). This could be a problem in terms of information management and product/technical support tracking as the support actions and liabilities are scattered among the different suppliers.

Another approach would be to provide support during the VO lifespan (mainly in the operation phase), and thus the VO should be kept active until no support is any longer needed. But this means to keep active a VO even if the business opportunity no longer exists and no production or activity of any kind is being performed besides the occasional support tasks, having members and resources assigned that wouldn't be needed, as not every partner should have been involved in production operations that would need further support.

Finally, as a way to keep the relation between the customer and the support team as a *one to one* relationship, allowing to each former VO member to be in knowledge of the support actions, the partners can create a new organization only focused on providing after-sales and technical support. Some approaches suggest having a specific virtual organization for after-sale services which should also provide quick services activities [6].

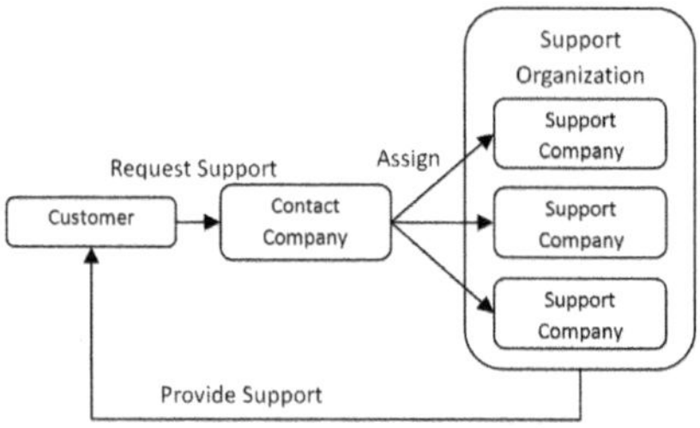

Fig. 2. Example of a support organization

Using this last approach as reference, the VO can define a "contact" company which will be the one who will be facing the customer inquiries and support requests, and will then delegate them to the respective partners (Fig 2); we will name this structure "support organization". This way, the relationship towards the customer remains almost equal than when the VO was active. This support organization should have less resources assigned, allowing the BC to count on more free resources to face new business opportunities and the components liabilities are still remaining with their suppliers (only there is a proxy between the customer and the companies now). The support organization's structure and activities should be simpler than a VO, as no production is needed but only coordination between its members for the support actions, and the resources committed from every company towards the support tasks should be significantly lower than the committed towards the dissolved VO.

This support organization should be kept active until no longer support is needed (for example, when warranties periods have expired).

2.3 Additional Dissolution Tasks

Additional tasks, more related to the initial commitments made during the VO formation should be performed during the dissolution. These tasks include sharing out the assets and financial results, intellectual property rights assignment and formalization, and the identification and performing of additional pending tasks that could be left from the operate phase (in case the VO has been dissolved unexpectedly and commitments towards external entities, such as suppliers, are left open).

During VO dissolution, the information access rights must be defined, specifying which information each partner can access to, and the security measures that will be used for protecting this information (encryption, passwords, etc.). The access rights level should specify if partners could use this information for forming and operating future VO in case a third party is involved.

3 Dissolution and the Other VO Life-Cycle Phases

The dissolution phase has an important role on the other VO life-cycle's phases, mainly from the knowledge acquired during the dissolution phase, but also as an issue to be considered when performing the task related to each of these phases.

The dissolution phase should provide information that could be used during the other life-cycle phases, but also is a key phase that needs to be considered from the beginning of a VO for avoiding further difficulties when reaching the final life-cycle's phase. The VO's cooperation agreement must include some key elements that are needed for the dissolution, which mainly are:

- **Conditions and guidelines for the final financial statement:** Detailing the initial assets, agreed liabilities, share out conditions, etc.
- **Intellectual property rights:** When creating the VO, the IPR of each partner must be decided over the results from the organization.
- **Dissolution conditions:** If a VO is created with a fixed lifespan (e.g. if it provides a service for a limited season), it must be defined at the initial cooperation agreement. The needed votes for VO dissolution (in case there is no dissolution agreement) and other dissolution conditions must be detailed.
- **Privacy over the shared information:** The members must decide at which level of detail the information will be shared with the BC (e.g. in the case of the performance evaluations some VOs would prefer to detail only the percentage over the target KPI value, instead of absolute values).

- **Dissolution process agreement**: Any other needed step, which depends on each VO's scope, for the dissolution must be detailed, creating the partners' agreement for dissolution.

Most of these elements depend on the BC, which could restrict them or provide a template for the cooperation agreement including standard dissolution elements. These elements could change if the VO is modified with the agreement of the VO partners. On the other side, the dissolution's results (performance reports, dissolution cause identification), support in different ways the other VO life-cycle phases.

3.1 Form Phase

When creating a new VO, at the form phase companies select partners that fit better the needs of the business opportunity using mainly the information each company gives about itself, its capabilities such as resources, availability or knowledge and expertise. One of the main benefits of a BC as an environment for creating new VOs, is that the companies that belong to it usually have already been profiled and their competencies identified at the moment of joining the community [7] (i.e. within a qualification process). A qualification process verifies the capabilities of the companies before joining a BC, but the information obtained from this process does not necessarily reflect the cooperation capacities of a company in a real performing VO. In cases that the BC has been active for a large period of time, it is likely that companies already had previous interactions with other BC members (and thus they have empirical knowledge about their performance in different situations).

The performance reports made during the dissolution phase provide information from real interaction within a VO. This information represents not only quantitative information about the member's performance, but also qualitative information that should be able to generate a list of trusted candidate partners in different ways, ranked by trust, reliability and other information from previous interactions. In order to take advantage of this information, BC members should have a set of visibility rights to the information related the other members' capacities when creating a new VO [4].

3.2 Operate Phase

One critical task related to the dissolution during the operate phase, is the identification of a dissolution cause. Dissolution not always happens when a business opportunity does not exist anymore, but other causes must be considered, such as unexpected events based on environmental changes, or internal problems in the VO: A key VO member could leave the VO and thus reducing the resources to a point that maybe the objectives could not be achieved, or unexpected environmental changes that affect the business opportunity could happen among other situations. Any unexpected cause that could lead the VO to its dissolution should be considered for future reference in order to better respond to future events or observed performance decreases [3]. If a dissolution cause is not properly detected, it could end in an underperforming VO that maybe wouldn't be available to achieve its goals. In this case, the VO should decide if it needs a reconfiguration (or evolution) to better respond, or in the worst case, dissolve itself.

BCs have an overall capacity that should be enough to respond to the market demands and position itself in the desired market position, based on the total capabilities of each of its members. When new business opportunities arise, new VOs are created and their members' resources are committed to it, reducing the BC available resources. Properly timed dissolution causes identification could free valuable resources for the whole BC that in other cases could be committed to an underperforming VO [8].

The knowledge acquired during the dissolution phase should also support the evolution of the VO. Once performance issues are detected in the different measured KPIs, the knowledge base should be able to provide information from past performance reports and the actions taken back then with their results. The identification of similar past cases is out of the scope of this paper, and please refer to tools using methodologies like case based reasoning [3] which is a good example of an automated tool for recommending actions for performance issues based on past experiences, or even recommending the dissolution if the results show that probably none of the VO objectives can be achieved given its current status. The dissolution phase should be able to provide enough information to support these kinds of tools.

4 Conclusions and Future Work

Dissolution represents a phase in the VO life-cycle and other collaboration forms that usually is overlooked, being for a long time mentioned as the least studied phase of the life-cycle [9], [10].

In this paper we tried to give arguments to show the dissolution phase as an opportunity to create better VOs in the future, which should be prepared to better respond to unexpected issues and situations in the future by providing past experiences knowledge. Plus, at a higher level, a dissolution cause identified at the right time, could help the whole BC by freeing inactive resources assigned in low performing VOs. The dissolution phase then, besides finishing the formal actions for closing the commitments between the VO partners, must collect and store information about the VO performance in a reusable, structured way in order to have it available for future reference.

In this paper we have identified the contributions of the dissolution phase such as:

- Support for VO partners search and selection.
- Support for VO performance improvement.
- Reference for past VO actions for performance improvement.

Plus, we identified where the dissolution must be considered and planned:

- During the formation phase for the definition of the dissolution conditions.
- VO evolution, in case the VO has changed its initial commitments, or added new partners.

And what should be considered during the dissolution phase:

- VO dissolution causes identification for future reference.
- Support organizations creation after VO dissolution.
- Creation of Performance Reports.

Future work is focused mainly on the complete formalization of the dissolution process and its steps (as well the formalization of a support organization creation and structure), and detailing further the significance of this phase by providing more proofs through experimentation and simulation environments.

Acknowledgments. The authors would like to acknowledge the co-funding of the European Commission within NMP priority of the Seventh RTD Framework Programme (2007-13) for the Net Challenge project (Innovative Networks of SMEs for Complex Products Manufacturing), Ref. CP-FP 229287-2.

References

1. Strader, T.J., Lin, F.-R., Shaw, M.J.: Information infrastructure for electronic virtual organization management. Decision Support Systems 23(1), 75–94 (1998)
2. Camarinha-Matos, L.: Infrastructures for virtual organizations – where we are, vol. 2, pp. 405–414 (2003) (presented at the ETFA 2003 - 9th Int. Conf. on Emerging Technologies and Factory Automation, Lisboa, 2003)
3. Hormazábal, N., Cardoso, H.L., De La Rosa, J.L., Oliveira, E.: An approach for virtual organisations' dissolution. In: Padget, J., Artikis, A., Vasconcelos, W., Stathis, K., da Silva, V.T., Matson, E., Polleres, A. (eds.) COIN@AAMAS 2009. LNCS, vol. 6069, pp. 70–85. Springer, Heidelberg (2010)
4. Afsarmanesh, H., Camarinha-Matos, L.M.: A Framework for Management of Virtual Organization Breeding Environments. In: Proceedings of IMP Group Conference, pp. 35–48 (2005)
5. Collier, B., DeMarco, T., Fearey, P.: A defined process for project post mortem review. IEEE Software 13(4), 65–72 (1996)
6. Hartel, I.: Virtual Organization of After-Sales Service in the One-Of-A-Kind Industry. In: Proceedings of the IFIP TC5/WG5.5 Third Working Conference on Infrastructures for Virtual Enterprises: Collaborative Business Ecosystems and Virtual Enterprises, PRO-VE 2002, p. 656 (2002)
7. Camarinha-Matos, L.M., Afsarmanesh, H., Ollus, M.: ECOLEAD: A holistic approach to creation and management of dynamic virtual organizations. In: PRO-VE 2005 - Collaborative Networks and their Breeding Environments, vol. 186, pp. 3–16. Springer, Boston (2005)
8. Hormazábal, N., De la Rosa, J.L.: Virtual Organisations Dissolution. In: Proceedings of the Distributed Computing and Artificial Intelligence, Advances in Soft Computing, vol. 79, pp. 139–146 (2010), doi:10.1007/978-3-642-14883-5_18
9. Muntaner-Perich, E., De La Rosa Esteva, J.L.: Towards a formalisation of dynamic electronic institutions. In: Sichman, J.S., Padget, J., Ossowski, S., Noriega, P. (eds.) COIN 2007. LNCS (LNAI), vol. 4870, pp. 97–109. Springer, Heidelberg (2008)
10. Camarinha-Matos, L.M., Afsarmanesh, H.: Tendencies and General Requirements for Virtual Enterprises. In: Proceedings of the IFIP TC5 WG5.3 / PRODNET Working Conference on Infrastructures for Virtual Enterprises: Networking Industrial Enterprises, pp. 15–30 (1999)

Part VII

Active Ageing and Tourism Networks

Collaborative Ecosystems in Ageing Support

Luis M. Camarinha-Matos[1] and Hamideh Afsarmanesh[2]

[1] Faculty of Sciences and Technology, Universidade Nova de Lisboa / Uninova, Portugal
cam@uninova.pt
[2] Informatics Institute, University of Amsterdam, The Netherlands
h.afsarmanesh@uva.nl

Abstract. New integrated and technology-supported services are needed to face the challenges of rapidly ageing societies. Collaborative networks provide a promising framework for the development of such services, which require the involvement of multiple stakeholders. In this direction, a roadmapping initiative is addressing the implementation of a new vision for technological support to ageing. To support this vision, a strategic research plan focused on four life settings - independent living, healthy living, occupation in life, and recreation in life - is introduced. A large number of stakeholders coming from different backgrounds contributed to the design and validation of this roadmap.

Keywords: Collaborative networks, ICT and Ageing, Collaborative Ecosystems, Roadmap.

1 Introduction

The rapidly increasing proportion of the elderly in western societies is creating a demographic unbalance, which raises serious social and economic concerns. It is thus timely to reassess the understanding of such terms as ageing and retirement, and questioning the common assumptions associated with work, personal fulfillment, leisure, community involvement etc. with respect to old age.

The current common association of senior citizens with a dependent stage of life does no longer match the way the European society is developing. The adoption of the concept of **"active ageing"** provides a more appropriate understanding of the later phases of life, given both the social and technological trends and outlook for the future [1]. Furthermore, the notion of **"productive ageing"** [2] has opened new perspectives for a change in the way society often perceives older people.

At present, most elderly citizens, following retirement, quickly become marginalized as they feel discarded by the society which often fails to even recognize their worth, instead of appreciating it and benefiting from it. Elderly is often seen as a cost burden rather than a resource, capable of value creation. This feeling of exclusion creates a vacuum in the life of the elderly citizens which can affect their health and well being. Even when remaining active at work, nowadays when a person gets older, his/her position becomes increasingly fragile in society, especially in moments of economic crisis when the competition for jobs intensifies. A critical challenge for society in respect to active ageing process is to create an environment in which the

L.M. Camarinha-Matos et al. (Eds.): PRO-VE 2011, IFIP AICT 362, pp. 177–188, 2011.

elderly citizens do not feel excluded, rather have a chance to use their knowledge and expertise in a fruitful way, by making a valued contribution to the communities in which they live [3], [4], [5].

ICT, and particularly high-speed pervasive broadband connectivity and web-based technologies, combined with intelligent robotics, smart homes, intelligent sensor networks and related technologies, offer new opportunities to provide care and assistance, create new ways of working, facilitate social interaction, and reduce limitations imposed by physical and mental conditions, location and time, thus increasing personal control. Nevertheless the sensitivity of the area, the dependency on the interplay between the introduction of new organizational and service models and creation of a new culture in society, the lessons learned with the limited success of past experiences, the risk of continuously developing technology that is not taken-up by target users, among others suggest the need for a careful analysis and a better planned approach towards what concerns new developments.

The creation of adequate support environments for the ageing citizens requires the involvement and effective coordination of multiple stakeholders. The concept of *collaborative ecosystem*, which can be seen as a particular case of a VBE and gets some inspiration on the principles and mechanisms of biological ecosystems, provides a promising conceptual framework to guide new conceptual and technological developments. Such support environments can also be seen as a materialization of the notion of *Services Society*, i.e. going beyond the concept of service ecology by considering not only the services and the actors affected by them, but also the context, organizational structures, and their governance principles, namely constituting the logical part of a service oriented architecture.

Nevertheless, such notions have emerged in enterprise-related business contexts and have not yet been explored in this domain. As such, *roadmapping* needs to play a fundamental role in the identification of a strategic research agenda and prioritization of needed actions. This paper introduces first results of the ongoing European roadmapping initiative BRAID.

2 Towards a Strategic Research Agenda

Realizing the critical issues of our ageing society, the European Commission has made a considerable investment in e-inclusion, ICT and ageing in its Framework Programmes. A number of related initiatives and experimental approaches have also emerged in other geographical regions, e.g., Australia, Canada, Japan and the United States. As a result, good progress has been made in various aspects of e-inclusion and particularly with regard to assistive technologies. A set of good practices and identified gaps is also available. Further research needs to build on these results and be guided by a strategic roadmap which provides an extended look at the future of active ageing and ageing well as a result of the knowledge and imagination of stakeholders, including experts, visionaries and drivers of change in this field. A well conceived roadmap needs to be drawn on the basis of an inspiring *vision* of what society wants to achieve in future [6], [7]. Vision-building is a mechanism to *define* the future that we wish to reach.

In addition to a number of RTD projects, particularly in FP7, four recently finished roadmapping projects – AALIANCE, CAPSIL, ePAL, SENIOR – have addressed different and complementary perspectives of ICT and ageing. Collectively, they covered major aspects of care and assistance, health care, extension of professional life and active ageing, and the related socio-economic and ethical issues. Furthermore, each one of these four projects developed efforts to organize communities of stakeholders. It is now urgent to **proceed to the next level of ambition,** towards a comprehensive *vision* and *strategic roadmap*, through the integration of these partial results and combination of perspectives, thus overcoming the fragmentation that has plagued the previous era of ICT and ageing. In addition to integration and consolidation of recent results, BRAID is exploring new synergies resulting from a holistic consideration of ageing, analyzing the trends and potential impacts of new disruptive technologies, and investigating a number of plausible scenarios of socio-economic crisis that might have a profound impact on the life of senior citizens.

Perspectives of analysis. ICT and Ageing represents indeed a complex area that can be analyzed from multiple perspectives and requires the contribution of multiple disciplines. In this work four perspectives or life settings are considered particularly relevant and selected as the basis for focused consideration in the various phases of the roadmapping process:

- *Independent living* - how technology can assist in normal daily life activities e.g. tasks at home, mobility, safety, agenda management (memory help), etc.
- *Healthy living* - how technology can assist in health monitoring, disease prevention, and compensation for disabilities.
- *Occupation in life* - how technology can support the continuation of professional activities along the ageing process.
- *Recreation in life* - how technology can facilitate socialization and participation in leisure activities.

The next sections introduce the vision and plan of actions for each setting.

3 Independent Living

This life setting addresses how technology can assist in normal daily life activities e.g. tasks at home, mobility, safety, agenda (memory help), etc. Main developments under this perspective are focused on assistance at home, namely for elderly living alone, which goes hand-in-hand with developments on smart homes. It includes services such as living status monitoring, with connection to care providers in case of any emergency, agenda manager to compensate for memory losses, companion and service robots, integration of intelligent home appliances, etc. Support outside home, namely in terms of mobility assistance, shopping assistance, and other daily life activities, is also considered.

Taking into account the current baseline, identified driving forces (technological, societal, organizational, economic, and regulatory driver), and major trends, as well as ideas emerging in numerous future scenarios developed in various research projects, the following vision (Table 1) is proposed for the independent living setting.

Table 1. Vision for Independent Living

In the coming decade, senior citizens will be empowered to live long, fulfilling, and independent lives through support from technological, societal, organizational, economic, and regulatory mechanisms. This includes ensuring security, safety, mobility and transport, facilitating access to relatives, carers and the community, and assisting with daily life activities, such as house-keeping, buying food, and personal hygiene care among others, to be equipped to live independently.
Main desired facets:
VI1. Established infrastructure and networks as the base for the support of independent living by technology
VI2. Assistive technology and support services that facilitate independent living
VI3. Monitoring devices and technologies supporting ambient intelligence solutions
VI4. Supporting tools and environment that foster the development of technologies for independent living
VI5. Advanced set of organized and commercial services aiming to enhance diminishing abilities of seniors and caring for seniors so that they can live independently
VI6. Tools to ensure security, ethics, rights, and privacy on data and used services
VI7. Mechanisms to increase knowledge dissemination, training and learning through sharing, both for seniors and all other stakeholders.

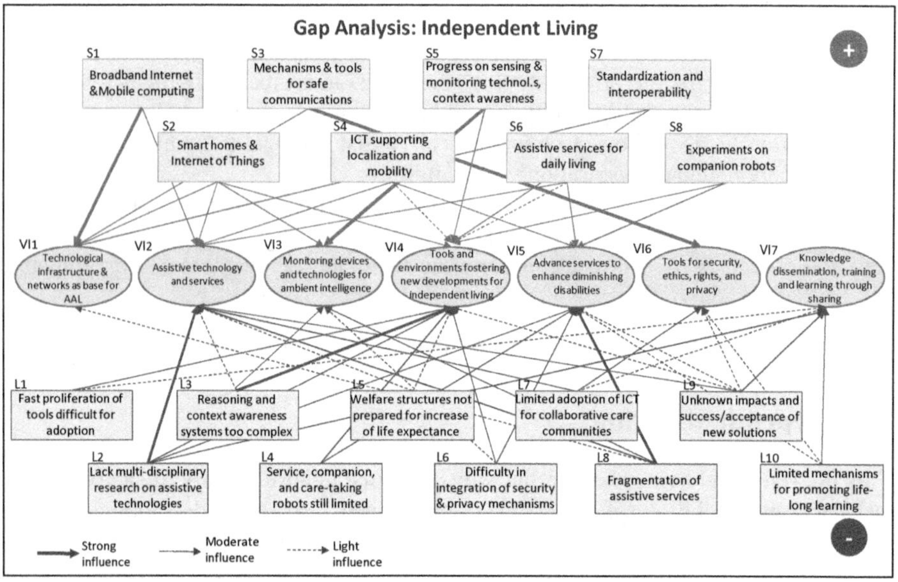

Fig. 1. Gap analysis – independent living example

Comparing this vision with the current situation, a systematic gap analysis was conducted, as illustrated in Fig. 1. As a result of an extensive brainstorming, group discussion and consensus building among a variety of stakeholders, a set of strategic research actions (AI1-AI6 in Table 2) are proposed. These actions are chosen in order to cover all stated facets of the vision (not necessarily a one-to-one correspondence between facets and actions), while being feasible considering the current situation(baseline) and trends, and taking into account the results of the gap analysis.

Table 2. Strategic research actions for Independent Living

AI1	***Monitor well-being.*** *Design, develop and integrate open and scalable sensor network environments both home-centered and human-centered, with intelligent monitoring, including new levels of security, safety, and privacy.*
AI2	***Extend capabilities.*** *Investigate, develop and integrate intelligent functionalities to compensate diminishing cognitive and physical capabilities and to design and develop intelligent, context-aware and self-adapting tools for personal assistance in planning and performing daily activities and facilitating societal participation.*
AI3	***Build supportive environments.*** *Design, develop, and validate preventive and responsive interventions based on situational awareness.*
AI4	***Establish collaborative environments.*** *Design and develop novel collaborative environments, combining social networking and collaborative networks of care provision stakeholders to facilitate support, companionship, and community participation*
AI5	***Assist mobility.*** *Integrate and customize methods and tools to assist mobility, including services for localization, trip planning, navigation, orientation in complex environments, driving assistance, and inter-modal transportation, focusing elderly needs.*
AI6	***Align independent and sustainable living.*** *Explore the alignment of ICT for Independent Living with smart grid and sustainable development technologies.*
RI1	***Assess impacts.*** *Promote integrative studies on the sociological, economic, ethical, and quality of life impacts of introducing services and technologies for independent living.*
RI	***Training for new environments.*** *Define new community-based training programs leveraging the potential of new technology-based assistive environments.*

further to the research actions, policy recommendations or socio-economic research actions are also included (RI1-RI2 in Table 2).

Collaborative aspects. As it can be observed in the proposed action plan, there is an aim to evolve towards more integrated services, involving multiple stakeholders, through well coordinated collaborative communities / ecosystems. As such, and beyond the "traditional" approaches followed in ICT and Ageing, the discipline of collaborative networks is likely to bring an important contribution to the development of future ageing support systems. This can be addressed at community level - social networking, re-enforcing community links, reducing loneliness, exchanging support through time banks, etc. - or at the specialized care provision level through collaboration among diverse stakeholders - care providers, health care centers, ambulance services, social security departments, NGOs, etc.

At the mobility assistance level, and in alignment with current trends in advanced transport infrastructures, collaboration among multiple stakeholders is also needed - e.g. transport operators, traffic management entities, toll operators, parking lot operators, and other service providers. Finally, at the home infrastructure level, and as we progress towards more intelligent appliances and subsystems, collaborative networks principles and mechanisms can provide a better framework for systems integration (a new perspective for *systems of systems*).

4 Healthy Living

This life setting addresses how technology can assist in health-related activities (remote health monitoring, emergency assistance, sensing environments, exercise assistance, prescription reminding, etc). Similarly to the previous case, the following vision (Table 3) and plan of actions (Table 4) are proposed.

Table 3. Vision for Healthy Living

In the coming decade, as a part of the ageing well paradigm, support for healthy living will become a high priority strategy across Europe. The emerging health care technologies and services will be used in new ways in the society, across a distributed infrastructure focusing on decentralized models, while sensible to the ethical consequences of the introduced innovations and providing mechanisms for the protection of individual rights. Both business-based and societal organizations supporting healthcare will adapt to this new environment.

Main desired facets:

VH1. Regulatory and technological infrastructure to support consumer driven healthcare (supporting data privacy, standards)

VH2. Advanced devices, robots, and tools supporting interventions for monitoring and provision of health care

VH3. Information based assistive services supporting the health care of seniors and involvement of other stakeholders

VH4. Appropriately designed home based interventions and support systems, based on seniors' cognitive and emotional status, which adapt whilst they age

VH5. Mechanisms to raise awareness on the formation of values, ethics, rights, and privacy on health related data and advanced ICT tools to ensure data security

VH6. Organized logistics and commercial networks of health care providers in the society, adapted to demographic change

VH7. Sensor based technologies, which are context aware, for healthcare support.

Table 4. Strategic research actions for Healthy Living

AH1	***Develop health monitoring systems.*** *Design, develop and integrate sensorial systems for health conditions monitoring, combined with intelligent diagnosis functionalities, understanding of the environment and other context factors, and smoothly adaptable to the needs of each senior individual.*
AH2	***Establish safe infrastructure.*** *Develop a safe and adaptable infrastructure, aligned with relevant standards in e-health, to support the provision of consumer-driven healthcare services.*
AH3	***Design integrated assistive services.*** *Create a multi-stakeholder framework for the emergence of integrated information-based assistive health care services, with particular emphasis on quality of service, recipient's quality of life.*
AH4	***Develop interventions.*** *Design, develop and assess advanced devices, intelligent robots, and intelligent tools to support home-based interventions and associated support systems, which are self-adapting to the cognitive, emotional, and physical status of the senior and respect the established safety and ethical principles.*
AH5	***Establish healthcare ecosystem.*** *Define new organizational and business models and develop support tools for the establishment of collaborative healthcare ecosystems involving healthcare providers, social security and regulatory authorities, forming the backbone for the emergence of new services for healthy living support.*
AH6	***Introduce innovative therapeutic approaches.*** *Exploring ICT to create novel therapeutic environments and support palliative care.*
RH1	***Develop regulatory framework.*** *Promote studies to elaborate and assess new organizational forms, legal structures and business models for healthcare provision to ageing population from a multi-sectoral collaboration perspective.*
RH2	***Establish organizational and business models.*** *Identify critical elements in ICT-based support services for healthy living.*
RH3	***Raise ICT awareness and skills in health and care.*** *Launch actions and develop mechanisms to increase the potential of ICT support for "healthy living environments" and to form a consensus on values, ethical principles, rights, safety, and privacy issues.*

Collaborative aspects. Also for this life setting, the role of collaborative networks can be identified in some of the proposed actions:

- Actions AH3 and AH5 clearly indentify the need for collaborative healthcare ecosystems as enablers for the emergence of novel integrated healthy living support services. This should be complemented with appropriate regulatory frameworks and business models (RH1 and RH2).
- Principles and mechanisms developed in the collaborative networks area can also bring important contributions to the safe infrastructures supporting health monitoring (AH1 and AH2).

5 Occupation in Life

This life setting addresses how technology can support the continuation of professional activities. The life setting of occupation in life can look very different for individuals, depending on the background work structure, sector, individual goals, capabilities, flexibility, opportunities, and functional ability. It covers both pre-retirement and post-retirement activities. In fact, in face of economic crisis and the growing pressure on the pension systems, it is likely that the notion of retirement as an abrupt even will change in the coming years. This setting includes both voluntary and paid work.

The following vision (Table 5) and plan of actions (Table 6) are proposed for this life setting.

Table 5. Vision for Occupation in Life

In the coming decade, due to the ageing population in Europe, an opportunity will arise to create a new framework for a model of work selected by seniors and adapted as they age, enabling them to earn a living through continued employment or have some form of continued work engagement. This framework will require support for its technological, socio-organizational, legal and political aspects. The aimed vision capitalises on the talents and expertise of senior workers, facilitating value creation through the use of ICT for the benefit of the individual, the economy and European society as a whole.
Main desired facets:
VO1. Established technological infrastructure (including support for connectivity, mobility and cloud computing) as the base for senior professionals' activities
VO2. Mechanisms to build associations of senior professionals and actively engage them, and support services for formation / management of teams of professionals
VO3. Advanced software environments to support seniors with adaptive personalized interfaces and affective interactions (within a context-aware and configure-yourself enriched environment)
VO4. Organized support for training and continued life-long learning for seniors
VO5. Increased social awareness about the value of senior professionals and their social cohesion and knowledge transfer (facilitating active involvement through networking, with emphasis on cross-generational and gender issues)
VO6. New business models for involvement of seniors within existing economical system
VO7. New policies and regulations for employment and protection of rights of senior professionals, particularly those who fall into other vulnerable groups (e.g. as a result of ethnicity, sexual orientation, gender, etc).

Table 6. Strategic research actions for Occupation in Life

AO1	***Build collaboration platforms and systems.*** *Design and develop open ICT collaboration platforms, support, and systems aimed at facilitating value creation, addressing the specific needs of communities of senior professionals, and which promote inter-generational interaction and socialization, which are enhanced by affective computing, context awareness, and trust establishment.*
AO2	***Generate adaptive solutions and services.*** *Develop and integrate self-adaptive and configurable technology solutions and services in ICT environments, applying principles of e-accessibility, design for all, and usability in order to facilitate technology acceptance and enable customization for/by seniors.*
AO3	***Leverage legacy.*** *Develop environments that empower and enable seniors to create a legacy capitalizing on their invaluable and transferable personal / professional knowledge and experience.*
AO4	***Create a model framework.*** *Develop approaches, models, and reasoning methods related to older people's occupation life cycle and their participation in the economic system, including value systems, behaviors, and issues of physical, cultural and emotional health.*
AO5	***Create trusted knowledge network.*** *Create a trusted knowledge network that provides an integrative framework to enable seniors within their occupation in life, whether professional or voluntary.*
AO6	***Join online and offline collaboration.*** *Develop integrative framework for identity management which effectively and seamlessly joins online and offline collaboration, for seniors, to create invaluable connections between virtual and real-world aspects of their occupation in life.*
RO1	***Improve working practices.*** *Investigate new models of working practices and related reward and taxation models for seniors, taking account of work-life balance, aging well and gender, and promote the findings to positively influence societal perception of older workers.*
RO2	***Enhance policy and legislation.*** *Identify and assess current national and European policy, legislation and incentives relevant to active participation of seniors in the socio-economic system and recommend new approaches that lower barriers and promote and support active aging.*
RO3	***Guide career transition.*** *Define new life-long training programmes and realistic practices that prepare for and guide the successful transition of senior knowledge holders from full employment to occupation in life.*

Collaborative aspects. The creation of collaborative networks to facilitate the continuation of the involvement of seniors in the socio-economic system and to leverage their value creation potential is explicitly addressed in actions AO1, AO5, and AO6. In particular, the integration of existing communities of senior professionals with other existing networks (e.g. SME networks) constituting some novel forms of hybrid collaborative networks need to be explored. The lack of such integration has led to some *ghettization* of associations of senior professionals.

Furthermore, new working practices, policy and legislation facilitating and promoting flexible continuation of professional life and inter-generational collaboration are needed.

6 Recreation in Life

This life setting addresses how technology can facilitate socialization and participation of ageing citizens in social, leisure, learning, and even religious, cultural and political activities.

The following vision (Table 7) and plan of actions (Table 8) are proposed for this life setting.

Table 7. Vision for Recreation in Life

In the coming decade, ageing citizens will increase their pursuit of active recreational lifestyles that suit their abilities and preferences, which creates new opportunities for innovative supporting products and services. Recreation is seen as a broad set of activities involving peoples' participation and enjoyment in cultural life, craft, hobbies, sport and physical activity, entertainment, socialising, travel & leisure, political engagement, spiritual and faith groups, life-long learning, passing on personal wisdom, history and experience, keeping pets, and playing games. Active recreational interests and lifestyles may improve mental well-being, and have a positive effect on the physical health and well-being of seniors. New technology solutions can support communications between seniors, families, friends, and peers, strengthening community participation and forming new communities and social networks with similar interests.
Main desired facets:
VR1. Infrastructure and required technological platforms (connectivity, communications and networking infrastructures and pervasive applications and services that are universally accessible)
VR2. Adequate features and training support to enable seniors to access and use ICT safely (free from harm) and with security (free from threat or intrusion)
VR3. Appropriately designed software services to support seniors with personalized interfaces and affection-based interactions, that can adapt to users' sensory, cognitive and physical capabilities (within a context-aware and configure-yourself enriched environment)
VR4. Mechanisms to increase social cohesion, access to community and networking of seniors (including support for transport and mobility)
VR5. Growth and development mechanisms to increase knowledge dissemination and learning through sharing
VR6. Established associations of seniors and communities of interest, allowing active engagement (physically and virtually).

Collaborative aspects. Although many elderly social networks, focused on their socialization, have emerged in the last years, the proposed action plan (Table 8) aims at promoting the development of participatory, and thus collaborative, communities. Through these networks senior citizens can actively engage in community activities, inter-generational interactions and joint recreation initiatives.

Collaborative gaming is another relevant direction, focused both on novel games for seniors - aiming at stimulating and preserving their cognitive capabilities - and games designed for inter-generational interaction and re-enforcement of family links.

These actions require both novel models and technology development, as well as new policies and regulatory frameworks.

Table 8. Strategic research actions for Recreation in Life

AR1	***Build recreational platforms, solutions and services.*** *Design and develop open, secure, interoperable, flexible, customizable and affordable ICT recreational platforms, solutions and services for senior citizens.*
AR2	***Build novel interfaces.*** *Develop novel human-machine interfaces with high quality of usability and applying design for all principles, oriented towards seniors' active engagement in recreational activities, considering their cognitive and physical capabilities, and including augmented reality, affective computing, companion artifacts, pervasiveness, etc.*
AR3	***Find new recreational channels.*** *Elaborate innovation portfolio of new ICT-supported recreational activities for seniors, exploring tele-presence, remote participation in cultural events, collaborative gaming, intelligent urban environments, etc.*
AR4	***Build participatory communities.*** *Design, develop and implement local and regional participatory communities that combine online and offline participation through social networking, inter-generational interaction, and local government involvement, focusing participatory recreational life and wellbeing.*
AR5	***Create and promote gaming.*** *Design, develop and promote novel physical, recreational and cognitive games for seniors, with a holistic focus on recreation, wellbeing, socialization, and inter-generational collaboration.*
RR1	***Assess recreation impact.*** *Promote multi-disciplinary studies on the impact of physical and cognitive recreational activities for seniors.*
RR2	***Train for digital lifestyle.*** *Create and deploy training programs and mechanisms oriented to help senior citizens enter and explore new lifestyles in the digital age, with particular attention to rural areas.*
RR3	***Promote studies in recreation.*** *Promote studies on all aspects of ICT-enabled/induced social innovation oriented to participatory involvement of elderly in recreational, cultural and social life.*

7 Roadmap Validation

The proposed vision statements and strategic actions plan resulted from a multi-stage construction and validation process. An initial formulation was prepared by the BRAID consortium following a series of consultation workshops and brainstorming sessions. Once a set of strategic actions emerged as a result of the brainstorming exercise, it was then necessary to proceed with a verification of those actions. The adopted verification process, at the early stages of the roadmapping process, comprised two main activities [6], [7]: (i) Verify that the proposed actions adequately cover all facets of the vision. (ii) Assess the feasibility of each action considering the results of the gap analysis. Fig. 2 illustrates the first step of validating the roadmap results for the action AI4 under the independent living perspective.

Regarding the second step of validation, related to feasibility, the adopted approach was to consider how the supporting and limiting elements at European level identified in the gap analysis facilitate or make difficult the implementation of each action. Fig. 3 illustrates the assessment of the feasibility of action AI4 under the Independent Living perspective. This verification needed to be conducted by experts and depends on the perception of each individual according to his/her background knowledge. Therefore a qualitative scale (scale: Moderate, Hard, Very Hard) was adopted.

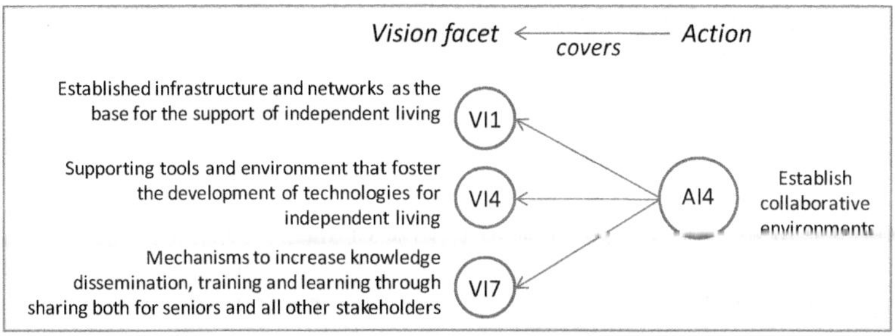

Fig. 2. Covering the vision facets – an example

	S1 - Broadband Internet &Mobile computing	S2-Smart homes & Internet of Things	S3-Mechanisms & tools for safe communications	S4-ICT supporting localization and mobility	S5-Progress on sensing & monitoring technologies,	S6-Assistive services for daily living	S7-Standardization and interoperability	S8-Experiments on companion robots	L1-Fast proliferation of tools difficult for	L2-Lack multi-disciplinary research on	L3-Reasoning and context awareness	L4-Service, companion, and care-taking robots	L5-Welfare structures not prepared for increase	L6-Difficulty in integration of security &	L7-Limited adoption of ICT for collaborative care	L8-Fragmentation of assistive services	L9-Unknown impacts and success/acceptance	L10-Limit. mechanisms to promote life-long	FEASIBILITY
AI4 Establish collaborative environments																			Hard

Fig. 3. Assessing feasibility – an example

The current phase of the project is focused on the refinement and **consensus-building** among relevant stakeholders. For this purpose, a number of *Consensus Building Events* are organized in different regions of Europe. This is a ongoing activity and until the current phase more than 60 stakeholders and experts have been involved in the validation process.

After the validation phase, and once a wider consensus is achieved on the appropriateness of the proposed vision and list of actions for each life setting, a more detailed description of the actions and the involved research challenges will be prepared. Furthermore, and in order to allow the development of an implementation plan, each strategic action will be decomposed into a number of more focused sub-actions. The last phase of the roadmapping process will focus on the development of the implementation plan for the proposed research agenda. Three modalities of implementation are considered:

- R&D – focusing on fundamental research and prototype development / proof of concept, aimed at addressing longer term challenges.
- Trials – oriented towards the development of pilots and validation scenarios that allow verification and refinement of the results of previous phase with the objective of facilitating the development of innovative products and services.
- Broad deployment and continuous improvement – aiming at large scale validation – large pilots – of new technologies and services, as a mechanism to facilitate their take-up by society.

The implementation schedule and inter-dependencies among actions will be established at this stage. Finally the main stakeholders, their roles in the implementation plan, and suitable organizational structures will be identified.

Since a roadmap is not a static plan, principles for implementation monitoring and roadmap revision / updating need to be included in the implementation plan.

8 Conclusions and Further Work

The increase in the percentage of aged population is a critical issue in most Western countries. Together with a number of other big changes in society, this creates large challenges, such as the need for society to care for a much bigger number of elder people than before, but also many new opportunities, as e.g. the possibility to make use of a bigger accumulation of wisdom and knowledge than before.

ICT can play an important role in the provision of support services, and many research projects have developed partial solutions. It is now time to pursue more integrated solutions, combining contributions from multiple stakeholders, an area where collaborative networks can provide an encompassing framework. In order to support further developments in this area, a strategic research roadmap is being developed, which covers the perspectives of independent living, healthy living, occupation in life, and recreation in life. Interim results in the form of a vision and research agenda are now available and going through a consensus building process.

The systematic roadmapping process behind the proposed roadmap as well as the extensive validation process involving a large community of stakeholders, are important factors for providing confidence in the adequacy of the proposed roadmap. Nevertheless, as normal in any "futures planning" initiative, a roadmap is a dynamic construct that needs to be periodically revised alongside its implementation, taking into account new trends as they inevitably emerge.

Acknowledgments. This work was funded in part be the European Commission through the BRAID project. The authors also thank the contribution of their partners as well as the multiple stakeholders involved in the consensus building workshops.

References

1. Active Aging: A Shift in the Paradigm – Denver Summit of Eight (Industrial Countries) (May 1997)
2. Hank, K.: Societal Determinants of Productive Aging: A Multilevel Analysis Across 11 European Countries. European Sociological Review (May 2010)
3. Garlick, S., Soar, J.: Human capital, innovation and the productive ageing: Growth and senior aged health in the regional community through engaged higher education. In: Annual AUCEA Conference, Alice Springs, Australia, July 2-4 (2007)
4. Aging and Work Life Balance in the EU, Llmarinen, Juhani (June 2006)
5. HSBC Insurance. The future of retirement – The new old age (May 2007), http://www.hsbc.com/1/PA_1_1_S5/content/assets/retirement/gender_perspective_eurasia_africa_1.pdf
6. Camarinha-Matos, L.M., Afsarmanesh, H.: A roadmapping methodology for strategic research on VO. In: Collaborative Networked Organizations – A Research Agenda for Emerging Business Models, ch. 7.1. Springer, Heidelberg (2004)
7. Camarinha-Matos, L.M., Afsarmanesh, H.: Active Ageing Roadmap – A Collaborative Networks Contribution to Demographic Sustainability. In: Camarinha-Matos, L.M., Boucher, X., Afsarmanesh, H. (eds.) PRO-VE 2010. IFIP AICT, vol. 336, pp. 46–59. Springer, Heidelberg (2010)

Active Ageing: Using an ARCON Framework to Study U3A (University of the Third Age) in Australia

Ronald C. Beckett[1] and Michael Jones[2]

[1] Centre for Industry and Innovation Studies, University of Western Sydney, Australia
rcb@reinvent.net.au
[2] School of Management and Marketing University of Wollongong, Australia
mjones@uow.edu.au

Abstract. There are more than 200 U3A groups in Australia where senior citizens collaborate to provide recreational learning opportunities to more than 60,000 other senior citizens. The movement continues to grow through the efforts of thousands of volunteers with very limited government support. We chose to use a collaborative network organisation modelling framework, ARCON, to both guide questions we asked in our research and to represent data from different instances in a consistent way. This provided a coherent view of the status quo, but supplementary questions were needed to consider the future viability of U3A groups. Spinoff network activities associated with some U3A groups were noted, suggesting the U3A model might be adapted for a variety of purposes. In such cases, it is hoped that the structured view provided by the ARCON framework might inform their design.

Keywords: Active Ageing, Collaborative Networks, ARCON, U3A, Volunteering.

1 Introduction

Many governments are supporting notions of active ageing in both the physical and intellectual sense to keep older members of the population healthy and stimulated. Individual intellectual stimulation may come from problem-solving, game-playing and lifelong learning. Community benefits [3] can be realised by accessing the collective experience of this older demographic, known as of the Third Age population, and providing stimulating learning opportunities [7]. In Australia, the primary government focus is on physical wellbeing, but large numbers of people (around 60,000) are engaged in local learning activities embracing an international initiative known as the University of the Third Age (U3A). These U3As operate with minimal, if any resources, yet they still achieve their stated goals. A question thus arises: how do they do it? Can an operating model be discerned? A recognised framework – ARCON – is used to characterise the U3A operations. This research extends a coherent understanding of how this arrangement works. We aim to see if the U3A example provides a substantive model for extension into other initiatives.

L.M. Camarinha-Matos et al. (Eds.): PRO-VE 2011, IFIP AICT 362, pp. 189–196, 2011.

2 Background on the University of the Third Age (U3A)

The University of the Third Age (U3A) began in 1973 when Professor Pierre Vellas organized a summer program for retired persons at the Universite des Sciences Socialies, Toulouse, France. The French model centred on a weekly public lecture on a major topic of concern for older persons. Supporting these were discussion groups, seminars, and recreational facilities, each taking advantage of the university facilities. Since 1973, the U3A concept has been implemented in many countries around the world [10]. China has the largest group. In 2002 there were reported to be 19,300 U3As and 1.81 million members [14].

Some countries have followed the French model. Others, including Australian U3A's, have followed a model that Midwinter [5] calls *Tutorial Cooperatives of the Elderly*. This latter derivative emerged in the UK in 1981 with 20 U3A's having 2,500 members being established in the first year. In this model, 'university' is given its original and intended meaning "… of people coming together to share and pursue learning in all its forms" [9]. The British model was first adapted by Peter Laslett – an academic from Cambridge University [15]. In 1981 he wrote the objects and principles of the British U3A [16]:

> *The pleasure of learning is a driving force in the work of U3As. U3As neither require nor award any qualifications. By sharing their learning, U3A members help one another to develop their knowledge, skills and experience. U3As arrange and support their own programmes as appropriate to their chosen learning activities. U3A members regard themselves as both learners and teachers.*

3 The Research Approach

Data were collected from interviews with some Australian U3A group leaders and from web pages plus some site visits. One Australian researcher, Rick Swindell [14], has been engaged with Australian U3A initiatives for around twenty years. We have been able to draw heavily on his documented work and on interactions with him.

We have used a collaborative organisation model framework (ARCON) that emerged from a large European study [1, 2] to try and characterise the U3As in Australia. The ARCON framework assumes that both internal and external interactions influence the operation of a Collaborative Network Organisation (CNO). Each of these is characterised at three levels of detail as follows:

- Internal (endogenous) elements having structural (who is involved and how), componential (tangible/intangible assets utilized), functional (processes and procedures) and behavioural (governance rules and values) dimensions. Each of these dimensions has four subsidiary categories: the active entity, passive entities, action and concepts.
- External (exogenous) elements having market (who are the customers or potential beneficiaries), support (services provided by third parties), societal (the broader community) and constituency (potential new participants and supporters) dimensions. Each of these dimensions has three subsidiary categories: network identity, interaction parties and interaction types

We developed four top-level questions related to each part of the model, with subsidiary questions stimulating discussion of further detail, again based on the model. These questions were:

- *How can we broadly categorize this Cooperative?* (Extent of collaboration, duration and focus)
- *Why did the cooperative start and why are you involved?* (Strategic intent and participant expectations)
- *Tell us how this Cooperative works.* Endogenous elements
- *Tell us where this Cooperative fits in to the bigger picture.* (Exogenous elements)

We found that whilst this provided information about the status quo, two supplementary questions were needed to explore the future prospects of the U3As:

- *What helps this Cooperative to prosper and grow?*
- *What do you see as the potential risks to the continuing operation of the Cooperative?*

4 About U3A in Australia

Australia adopted the British model, opening first in Melbourne in 1984, and then expanding throughout Australia. There are now over 211 U3A groups in Australia with 64,535 members [13]. According to a review by Swindell et al [8], the U3A groups in Australia range in size from a low of 24 members to a high of 5500 members (Sydney U3A). Nine groups have more than 1000 members. The median U3A Australian membership is 414. Australian U3As do not appear to limit membership numbers. The number of males participating has increased in recent years. The female/male ratio is now about 3:1. Providing intellectually stimulating opportunities and social networking are seen as the two major accomplishments of U3As. There is reported to be strong support for continuation of a laissez faire approach to teaching and learning in which course leaders come from any walk in life and teach in their preferred style. There was little enthusiasm for academic courses. Teaching takes place in any suitable community venue like rented premises, free or subsidized community facilities or private homes. Favoured ways of maintaining course quality were feedback from participants and “market forces”.

4.1 The Local U3A Groups

Local U3A groups are set up as self-standing entities, generally registered as unincorporated not-for-profit associations with a volunteer governing board and administrative staff. Most office bearers have a professional or business background. Volunteers may be teachers on one occasion and learners on another, but the focus is on sharing knowledge. Drawing on experience gained over many years, course delivery is commonly via a series of two-hour face-to-face sessions. Teaching facilities may be provided by other charitable organisations or by local government. Some U3As ask members to commit to a few hours of voluntary work each month on joining. *One large U3A (ACT) reported attracting a healthy flow of recent retirees as well as retaining a relatively high proportion of old members. One quarter of its 3700 members were aged 65 or less; 14% were aged 80 and older. The success or failure of a U3A group is strongly related to the skills and energy of its leadership [13].*

Our interviews suggested that *whilst many seniors groups tend towards the social rather than the intellectual needs of older people, U3A attracts people who want more and who in many instances can give more, because of their past experience as teachers, lecturers, historians, lawyers etc, as well as other walks of life. Its members have an enthusiasm for lifelong learning, and can share experience and knowledge as well as learn new things themselves. ---- Put simply, U3A is an educational movement, not just a senior's organization (a regional U3A leader).* A scan of contact data of 160 local groups in two States indicated about 60% of U3A groups maintain a website. Swindell et al [13] report the following: *more than a third of U3As use the Internet as a teaching/learning resource.*

4.2 Regional Coordination Groups

The largest regional group, U3A Network Victoria, represents 97 U3As having about 25,000 members. It is recognized by the Adult, Community and Further Education Board of Victoria as an education Peak Body. This makes it eligible for some funding consideration. Such funds are used to help engage a small number of paid employees. Governance is through a council of nominated representatives from members and an elected executive committee. Further sub-committees are instituted in the areas of finance, publicity and promotion. Its role is to promote the U3A movement, fostering the creation of new U3As and the further development of existing U3As; serving as a reference body, acting as a central resource facility, providing publicity, promotion and profile to the general public and to government and other public bodies. Information is disseminated through a Quarterly newsletter, a website and meetings of member representatives. The newsletter also presents opportunities available across local groups, such as special interest study tours.

4.3 U3A on Line

The Following observations have been provided by Rick Swindell [14]: *U3A Online, was set up in 1998 with a global focus from the outset. The administration and teaching in U3A Online is carried out by about 100 volunteers. Governance and administration occurs through regular virtual meetings. Discussion and voting takes place by electronic forum, email and Skype. It is commonplace for the majority of volunteers to work closely together for many years but never physically meet.*

Since 2002, Griffith University in Brisbane, Australia has hosted the entire operation free of charge on university servers, as part of its service to the wider community. In 2011 39 courses were available to U3A Online members with others in various stages of completion. For an additional fee, a further 13 courses are available to members through a cooperative arrangement with the Third Age Trust in the UK, which has provided online courses for its UK members since 2000. Depending on the availability of volunteer tutors, members may opt to pay an additional fee to join tutor-led discussions, during which participants interact with the leader and with others in the course by online forum and email. Site licenses are an additional service available to any U3A-style organization in any country. The course notes have all been written and illustrated by expert volunteers in their fields and in some cases these run to more than 100 pages when printed. All courses and resources are in English. In 2008, about 35% of Australian U3As were using on-line courses.

5 Discussion

We now consider the characteristics of the U3As studied in relation to attributes of the ARCON reference framework. The on-line and local Australian U3As are coalitions of individuals with a common interest in learning. They regard themselves as both learners and teachers with an emphasis on collaboration. In the ARCON framework this *extent of collaboration* implies - *communication & exchange for mutual benefit plus a complementarity of goals - aligning activities for mutual benefit, plus compatible goals with individuals working apart (with some coordination) plus having joint goals, joint identities and joint responsibilities (creating together) and (participant) teams.* This describes U3A working arrangements quite well. The regional U3A's are coalitions of organisations that deliver services with an emphasis on cooperation. In the ARCON model, this implies - *communication & exchange for mutual benefit plus a complementarity of goals - aligning activities for mutual benefit, plus compatible goals with individuals working apart (with some coordination).* Again a good description. The common themes are communications, exchange for mutual benefit and complementarity of goals. The primary communication tools are newsletters and word-of-mouth, but internet use is increasing. U3As are long-term strategic networks consistent with the ARCON definition of a professional virtual community: *is an alliance of professional individuals, and provides an environment to facilitate the agile and fluid formation of virtual teams.* This describes the local U3A arrangements for establishing and running courses quite well. Virtual teams are established at the regional level for a variety of purposes.

The ARCON framework *requirements for collaboration* include a number of things. *A clear purpose* – This is well enunciated in the British U3A model that is incorporated in the individual Australian U3A formation documents, as are some basic requirements like *processes* for defining structures and policies. At the personal level, the primary interest is in recreational learning (as compared with vocational learning). However, some individuals participate in courses for a specific purpose, such as learning a language prior to visiting a foreign country or learning about IT to be able to use e-commerce or to communicate with grandchildren. One of the *preconditions for collaboration* in the ARCON model is that parties must know each other's competencies. In the U3A case, this seems to have been established by social networking prior to formation and subsequently during operation as people volunteer to undertake different tasks. Another ARCON requirement is for a *collaboration space.* For most U3As this is a physical space, but both the U3A NSW regional group and the on-line U3A group seem to function quite well in a virtual space. Other ARCON requirements are concerned with *ownership and sharing of resources* and of equitable distributions of *commitments and rewards.* The U3As own almost no resources except for modest member funds, as they hire facilities or have them provided by external supporters. Most of the work is done by volunteers, where doing a job well is its own reward. However Mitchell et al [11] reported other benefits from a survey of 975 members - that *members of U3A had better-than-average general, physical and mental health, and that membership of U3A can, even in the very elderly, assist in conferring a much more positive perception of well-being.*

The ARCON framework provides a tructural view that helps us understand how Australian U3As work, but not why they are sustainable or why they continue to grow. It has been observed that the individual U3As value their independence. A survey of 122 U3As [13] reported that most would prefer to decline external assistance due to potential loss of autonomy (60%), increased bureaucracy (30%) and contrary to self-help ethos (25%). Important considerations for the immediate future were seen as maintaining or increasing membership, offering a wider range of courses, and seeking more permanent accommodation. When asked about the longer-term future, the most strongly supported suggestions were: 1) technical demands on the Third Age population will increase, 2) there is an expectation that retirees will need to do more to support themselves, and 3) a national communication network will assist local U3As to better meet the needs of a changing society. Anecdotal evidence also suggests that *U3As need to become far more professional and organised to attract baby boomers or they could slip into quiescence.*

Most data used in developing the ARCON framework related to collaboration between a modest number of enterprises, whereas the power behind the U3A network comes from a large number of individual volunteers. 60,000+ participants in Australia might sound like a lot but it represents only 0.85% of the total demographic group that could potentially participate, suggesting that these people have something special that drives them. It is suggested that this is an attribute of all successful collaborative network organizations – there is something special about the core participants.

We wanted to explore U3A operations as a potential model for other activities. Along the way, some spinoff activities were identified, suggesting this is a practical proposition. Timewitnesses [12] is an *example of the Internet opening up cooperative ventures for U3A members around the world. Timewitnesses is a "living archive" which allows people from any country who have childhood or adult memories of World War II, to preserve their stories for everyone. Many of the stories have been translated into German and French and in a number of cases school children assisted with the translations. [12]*

U3A Online has sponsored a number of research/development studies of U3A operations that have been carried out in association with appropriately trained member researchers. *The fundamental strength of the constituency research approach is that it entails research "with" rather than research "on" older people. The difference between "with" and "on" may not matter too much in large scale tick-a-box surveys. However, if much richer findings are needed, these are more likely to arise from interviews carried out by peers who are perceived to have primary empathy with the participants, rather than by younger researchers whose appearance, manner of dress, language, general persona, and time constraints may create barriers to in-depth communication [6]. "A voice worth listening to" is an example of a novel constituency research project undertaken exclusively by third agers. In this project a retired journalist visited and interviewed people aged 80 and older in Australia and New Zealand who were continuing to do remarkable things within their communities. The purpose of the research was to debunk the ageist and damaging mindset that advanced chronological age inevitably implies that an older person has become a burden on society. The lead researcher was in her mid 70s.*

6 Concluding Remarks

This paper makes two contributions to the literature. Firstly, it describes an instance of a self-supporting active ageing network driven by users for users. Secondly, it explores the utility of a collaborative network model, ARCON, in helping to understand the characteristics of the case study network.

U3As in Australia are formed by groups of individuals in local communities, not organisations like many collaborative network organisations. They want a stimulating, participative recreational learning network for seniors, not a senior's social network that may provide learning. Both conventional and on-line learning modes are available. The focus is on long-term collaboration. Whilst each group operates as a separate entity, most choose to contribute to a regional virtual or physical office to cooperate in acquiring services as a group, sharing information on courses, interacting with governments and facilitating membership growth. Some coherent structures are provided in that each local group is formally constituted, generally as a not-for-profit unincorporated association, and its constitution includes common foundation principles from a British model. Some spin-off activities that contribute to the broader community were also observed, indicating the practicality of alternative applications of the U3A model, which is similar to a professional virtual community arrangement.

The ARCON framework provided a good foundation for checking that the right questions were asked about the extent and style of collaboration in the research phase and for positioning U3A operations in the very broad spectrum of Collaborative Network Organisation possibilities during analysis. It was found however that supplementary questions about the future directions and possible risks to U3A sustainability were needed in the case of this long-term collaboration. Parallel consideration of human factors (individual actor attitudes and contributions) linked to literature on volunteering was also necessary. The real U3A drivers are the thousands of volunteer administrators and tutors who share their time and knowledge in an environment where these contributions are valued. It is reported that both this group and the student group experience increased self-esteem and feelings of wellbeing. There is some evidence that networking within and between U3As can provide a foundation for knowledge capture and research activities. There is also anecdotal evidence of entrepreneurial behaviour in establishing courses and marketing a U3A that will be the subject of a follow-on study.

References

1. Camarinha-Matos, L.M., Afsarmanesh, H., Ollus, M.: ECOLEAD: A holostic approach to creation and management of virtual organizations. In: Camarinha-Matos, L.M., Afsarmanesh, H., Ortiz (eds.) Collaborative Networks and their Breeding Environments, pp. 3–16 (2005) ISBN 0-378-28259-0
2. Camarinha-Matos, L.M., Afsarmanesh, H., Ermilova, E., Ferrada, K.A., Jarimo, T.: ARCON reference models for collaborative networks. In: Camarinha-Matos, L.M., Afsarmanesh, H. (eds.) Collaborative Networks: Reference Modeling. Springer, New York (2008)
3. Healy, J.: The Benefits of an Ageing Population The Australia Institute (2004) ISSN 1322-5421

4. Midwinter, E.: How many people are there in the third age. Ageing and Society 25, 9–18 (2005)
5. Midwinter, E.: The University of the Third Age in Britain. Higher Education Quarterly 38, 9–15 (1983)
6. Mayhew, C., Swindell, R.: Some Pleasures and Pitfalls of Working with Older Research Assistants. Australasian Journal on Ageing 15, 164–166 (1996)
7. Clarke, A., Warren, L.: Hopes, fears and expectations about the future: what do older people's stories tell us about active ageing? Ageing and Society 27, 465–488 (2007)
8. Swindell, R.: Characteristics and Aspirations of older learners in an Australian University of the Third Age Program: Part 1 – Survey Results. Educational Gerontology 16(1), 1–13 (1990)
9. U3A Trust, UK, http://u3a.org.uk/ (last accessed March 31, 2011)
10. World U3A, http://worldu3a.org/ (last accessed March 31, 2011)
11. Mitchell, R.A., Legge, V., Sinclair-Legge, G.: Membership of University of the Third Age and perceived well-being. Disability and Rehabilitation 19(6), 242–248 (1997)
12. Timewitness, http://timewitnesses.org/ (last accessed March 31, 2011)
13. Swindell, R.F., Vassella, K., Morgan, L., Sayer, T., Browne, R., Stewart, J., Waddington, J., White, B.: U3As in Australia and New Zealand 2008: The Successful Ageing organizations. Griffith University (2009), http://www3.griffith.edu.au/03/u3a/u3aonline/ (last accessed March 31, 2011)
14. Swindell, R.: Successful Ageing and International Approaches to Later Life Learning (in publication)
15. Peter Laslett, http://courses.u3a.org.uk/about-u3a/history-of-u3a.html?start=1 (last accessed March 31, 2011)
16. Objects and Principles, http://www.u3a.org.uk/index.php?option=com_content&task=view&id=160&Itemid=52 (last accessed March 31, 2011)

Tourism Breeding Environment: Business Processes Applied to Collaborative Networks in Tourism and Entertainment Sector

Leandro Loss[1] and Servane Crave[2]

[1] Axia Value Chain,
Av. Nações Unidas - 12551, CEP 04578-903,
São Paulo – SP, Brazil
leandro.loss@axiavaluechain.com
[2] Orange Labs R&D,
905, rue Albert Einstein, 06921,
Sophia Antipolis Cedex, France
servane.crave@orange-ftgroup.com

Abstract. This paper introduces the concepts related to Distributed Business Processes (DBPs) associated to collaborative networks when applied to tourism and entertainment sector. These concepts are framed by the coordination activities and services orchestration to be used by tourism and entertainment providers. It brings to light the investigation about the needs associated to the tourism and entertainment areas when working collaboratively. There is a lack of ability for the service providers to recognize customers' wishes in order to address their loyalty. Tourism and entertainment services are characterized as temporary arrangements that are well served by the arrangements provided in collaborative networks. This paper presents the enablers and the uncertainties related to the area in order to provide alternative solutions to cover the emergent needs, facilitate the enablers, and mitigate the uncertainties identified so far.

Keywords: Tourism, Entertainment, Distributed Business Process, Tourism Breeding Environment, Virtual Tourism Organization.

1 Introduction

A business process can be understood as a representation of what an organization is going to do in a given business, regardless of its complexity, size and quantity. It can involve manufacturing processes, services, shipment, storage and many other activities [1]. Business processes are therefore seen as a collection of activities that are performed daily or hourly or by the minute within an organization. Some of these activities are performed automatically while some require a high degree of human interaction. It is believed that formalizing key processes through business processes can support competitiveness, innovation, and allow a fast reconfiguration in order to react to market's changes and fluctuations.

New ways of thinking the enterprises structures have been observed on the opposite of the centralized and isolated activities [2]. The organizational

L.M. Camarinha-Matos et al. (Eds.): PRO-VE 2011, IFIP AICT 362, pp. 197–204, 2011.

reconfiguration has been changing since Taylor and Ford's ideas, when organizations were hierarchical and bureaucratic. New approaches by which organizations work have evolved from an entirely competitive environment among the actors to a collaboration environment in order to act in response to customers' wishes.

It is therefore possible to argue that in many organizations a shift occurs from a supply chain perspective where "products definitions and customer needs of enterprises are stable and well defined" [3] to a value network where "it is considered any web of relationships that generates tangible and intangible values through complex dynamics between two or more individuals, groups or organizations" [4]. It requires an evolution in the way business processes are seen and performed. Business processes shall not only evolve from a centralized and internal perspective, but also consider the increase of activities being done by other partners. As a result, the concept of Distributed Business Process (DBPs) has risen. According to [1], a DBP is "*a dynamic and temporary set of business processes which jointly gives rise to the end product or service*".

This paper describes how DBPs can be associated to the concepts of collaborative networks and be used for coordination activities and services orchestration in the tourism and entertainment providers. The paper is structured as follows: section 2 brings to light the main requirements to the shift from a centralized business to a DBP perspective. Section 3 investigates the tourism and entertainment main needs. Section 4 presents the enablers and uncertainties related to the tourism and entertainment sector while section 5 introduces how the concepts of collaborative networks associated to DBPs can provide alternative solutions to cover emerging needs, facilitate the enablers and mitigate the uncertainties identified so far. Section 6 reports the results with potential customers and brings the final considerations of this work.

Table 1. Requirements to move from Business Processes to DBPs

Requirements	Moving from Business Process to DBPs
Communication	When joining people from two or more organizations, it is possible that they do not speak the same language. It may create barriers for the business development. There are cases in which people speak the same language, but there may occur problems of synonymy and polysemy. The former refers to different words and phrases that express the same concept, while the latter refers to words that can have multiple meanings.
Data Interchange / Interoperability	There is a necessity of structured transmission of data between organizations by electronic means. It requires the use of standards like XML, ebXML, or WS-BPEL.
Real time response	It refers to issues related to time constraints. Partners need to provide information about availability and resources in a strict deadline.
Cooperation and collaboration	Cooperation and collaboration involves not only information exchange and adjustments of activities, but also sharing resources for achieving compatible goals.
Coordination	Aligning and altering activities so that results can be achieved efficiently.
Traceability	Modifications of requirements specifications affect other partners and even the final customer.
The Long Tail	To provide strategies to sell a large number of unique items in relatively small quantities.

2 Approaching Distributed Business Process

When moving from business processes to DBPs and collaborative approaches, organizations should take into account the value network perspective (Table 1). The business sector that benefits from the potential and the efficiency DBPs is the tourism and entertainment . Customers are getting more and more connected and looking for dynamic and easy composition offers as well as new experiences [5]. It has been observed that individual preferences are not fully taken into consideration by all actors in this sector in order to maximize customers' satisfaction.

3 Tourism and Entertainment Needs

According to the World Tourism Organization [5], tourism has become a popular global leisure activity. The tourism and entertainment service industries include a wide range of actors (Table 2).

Table 2. Classification of actors in tourism and entertainment sector

Area	Actors
Transportation services	Airline companies; Cruise ships; Trains; Buses; Taxis; Car rental agencies; among others.
Hospitality services	Hotels; Hostels; Resorts; Guest houses; Camping; Bed & breakfast; among others.
Entertainment venues	Amusement parks; Casinos; Shopping malls; Music venues; Theatres; Cinemas; Museums; Galleries; Operas; Night clubs; Restaurants; Kart club; Golf club; among others.
Others	Tourism offices; Tourist guides; Weather forecast; Guides (on-line, paper-based); Voyage agencies; among others.

These actors are usually working either isolated or in a low level of integration without taking advantage of the value network which they are part of. Service providers do not fully investigate the potential of this market and usually do not take into consideration the customers' personal wishes and previous experiences when proposing a new offer. The few situations whenever it happens, customers have to fill up their profiles in different websites. There is a lack of ability for service providers to recognize customers' wishes in order to address their fidelity.

Joint efforts shall provide new and innovative offers. Providing options to customers, and exploring the potential of a distributed approach add value to the network of service providers. Most of the service providers act in a reactive and not in a proactive fashion. It means that they wait for customers to contact them, and only then, trigger an action. They are still attracting customers through traditional market campaigns. Acting proactively implies in direct offers that fit to what customers are looking for or expecting. An alternative is to identify the customers' desires through the analysis of their profiles. Tourism and entertainment services are characterized as temporary arrangements (they do not last forever). These dynamic and temporal characteristics are well served by the arrangements provided in collaborative networks, such as Virtual Organization Breeding Environments and Virtual Organizations (see section 5).

The interaction with or among customers starts earlier and earlier in the purchasing phase. Years ago, buying a trip meant a physical meeting in a travel agency. Travel agents were tour planners, as well as sales agents, for travel suppliers. This situation no longer exists, and the tourism and entertainment sector has been changing dramatically. There is an opportunity to improve productivity by encouraging customers to use self-service. The structure is currently acquiring more decentralized market characteristics where each buyer/consumer has direct access to each seller/provider [6]. When a tourist "on his/her own" needs to find information from different providers, it is extremely difficult to know where to find the proper information. Besides that, customers are increasingly demanding personalized offers of travel products and services.

4 Enablers and Uncertainties

Trends affecting the tourism and entertainment industry generally include changing customer's demands, increased expectations in terms of value and convenience, and increasingly knowledgeable consumers who are themselves users of IT [6]. [7] argue that the widespread use of **Internet** and **electronic market places** together with increased competition and changing customer needs have fundamentally transformed the travel and entertainment service industry. Competitors have undermined their traditional business models. A large number of travel transactions and services have moved to the Internet.

By Observing this trend, [8] coined the term "cybermediaries". They have leaner cost structures, by reaching a global perspective and supplying technologically enabled economies of scale (large volumes at low transaction costs). Service providers in tourism and entertainment have to reposition their value propositions and provide greater value-added services based on the integration of Internet technologies and new marketing strategies.

There is the need not only for differentiated product strategies, but also for service level strategies. One example is the provision of highly personalized product and service packages involving high quality information and advisory services [7]. This trend is also supported by the idea of *prosumption* (production/consumption). [9] refer to the creation of products and services by the same people who will ultimately use them. The tourism and entertainment sector may use and get involve with end-users in order to adapt services to what customers are looking for. This kind of adaptation is then supported by good DBPs structures.

Interaction among customers is highly valuable as well. By putting a natural language question to a travel community the customer not only gets relevant answers for a vaguely formulated need, but also obtains additional relevant information, which he/she had not realized as part of his/her information need before this experience [7].

According to [3], "Web 2.0 encompasses a seemingly unlimited range of services, these services do have a number of common features": a) Internet is used as a low cost delivery platform; b) they involve the direct participation and tap into the creativity of a huge community of end users; c) they "emerge" rather than being " pre-defined". Moreover, there are no pointers to an integrated solution, based on Web 2.0 to join different services. On the other hand, Internet information is fragmented. It takes a significant amount of time to find good information, even for experienced travelers. The configuration of highly personalized products is extremely time-consuming, and the trustworthiness of many sources can still not be verified [7].

Nowadays customers are also looking for a better use of available technologies, lower costs, transparent and real-time transactions. The challenge is to develop and provide customers with rich experiences before and during their tourism and entertainment activities, so that customers can actively participate during the entire process (*do it yourself!*). The ways of interacting with the customers may range from simple SMS messages, posts in blogs, social networks, e-mails and also the advent of the new phenomenum called micro-blogging, like Twitter.

It is important to provide new and innovative services for tourism and entertainment so that each customer can be seen as unique. It means that each service is one-of-a-kind and fits to each specific customer's requirement or profile. In order to offer this kind of unique service for the customers, it is necessary to combine and organize multiple actors in order to add value to the service being provided. Modeling DBPs among multiple actors shall speed up the answers to potential customers.

5 Framing Tourism and Entertainment into Collaborative Networks

One suggestion to support the shift from a traditional business process perspective that is intra-organizational (centralized and isolated) to a DBPs perspective that is inter-organizational (distributed and collaborative) is the concept of *Tourism Breeding Environment*. A *Tourism Breeding Environment* is defined here as a set of organizations, usually service providers that agree cooperating with each other while adopting common operating principles and infrastructures. The *Tourism Breeding Environment's* main goal is to provide high quality tourist and entertainment services in a seamless and transparent way to the customer[1]. The actors previously identified in Table 3 are the ones to potentially populate the *Tourism Breeding Environment*.

Service providers organized like a *Tourism Breeding Environment* may easily achieve the basic requirements necessary in order to establish their DBPs than the ones that are not working in a collaborative way. *Tourism Breeding Environment* provides common communication channels, up-to-date information, coordination mechanisms, as well as support for the definition of distributed business to ensure that the customer will be satisfied with a set of service providers.

On the other hand, in order to offer better and adapted services, customers shall keep their profiles and their preferences updated. Customers' profiles shall contain their general information, main interests, time and budget availability, and other additional information that may be relevant, allowing an interface with the customers and providing suggestions when planning a trip and/or last minute tips.

[1] The definition of *Tourism Breeding Environment* is an adaptation of the *Virtual Organization Breeding Environment* definition coined by [10].

Not all service providers will interact with one single customer. Only a set of selected (either by the customer, or by an automatic composition of service, or any other criteria) service providers will work together. The selection of specific service providers opens space to the creation of a Virtual Organization that is being called *Virtual Tourism Organization*. The *Virtual Tourism Organization* emerges from the *Tourism Breeding Environment* as a temporary service provider. A *Virtual Tourism Organization* is seen as a temporary alliance among tourism and entertainment service providers that come together to deliver one-of-a-kind offer and value-added services. The *Virtual Tourism Organization* is set up during the customer's offer proposition and it is dismantled as soon as the service is provided. It is worth to highlight the importance of DBPs in this stage in order to harmonize interactions between service providers and their fast reaction to attend the customers' expectations. The *Virtual Tourism Organization* is then completely transparent to the customers. It means that the customer interface is always the same, but the service providers may change according to the customers' preferences.

The concept of *Virtual Tourism Organization* matches the dynamicity and reactivity that customers increasingly expect especially when using mobile and internet when they are traveling. Table 3 presents how a *Virtual Tourism Organization* fits the tourism and entertainment needs:

Table 3. Tourism and Entertainment Needs

Tourism needs	Virtual Tourism Organization
Temporary	They are created in order to supply a, usually short, time-frame offer.
One-of-a-kind services	A *Virtual Tourism Organization* allows a dynamic organization of service providers and resources that fits with customers' specific requirements. Customers do not need to adapt themselves to pre-defined tourism and entertainment packages. It is the *Virtual Tourism Organization* that is adapted to the customer.
Push and Pull information / offers	New services and suggestions can be offered to the customers. Information or offer of services shall be provided to the customers either according to their profiles or according to contextual data (weather, traffic, location-based services, and so on).
Real time	*Virtual Tourism Organizations* can be built and reconfigured "on the fly" in order to attend the customers' wishes (supported by DBPs).
Flexibility and dynamic arrangement	A *Virtual Tourism Organization* can adapt itself in case of unforeseen events by providing new offers to the customers.
Co-creation	Customers may provide suggestions to the *tourism breeding environment* and influence in the arrangement of the *Virtual Tourism Organization*, as well as evaluate the quality of the service being provided.
Pricing	Most of the customers look for lower prices and better services. The *Virtual Tourism Organization* may provide a combination of services that allows discounts and high quality services.

It is possible to cross-compare the tourism and entertainment needs to the requirements to move from a business process to a DBP perspective (Table 4). Many of the *Tourism Breeding Environment* needs can be supported by DBP and leveraged by their usage through a *Virtual Tourism Organization* environment.

Table 4. Cross-comparison: DBPs requirements vs. Tourism and Entertainment Needs

T&E Needs / DBP Requirements	Tempo-ray	One-of-a-kind	Push and pull informa-tion / offers	Dyna-micity	Flexibi-lity and dynamic arrange-ments	Co-creation	Pricing
Communication	√	√	√	√	√	√	√
Data Interchange / Interoperability	√	√	√	√	√	√	
Real-time response	√	√		√	√		
Cooperation & collaboration		√	√	√	√		
Coordination		√	√	√	√	√	√
Traceability		√			√	√	
Long Tail		√		√	√	√	

6 General Considerations

A preliminary study was elaborated in order to evaluate the concept behind the *Tourism Breeding Environment* and *Virtual Tourism Organization* concepts to support a value network for the tourism and entertainment sector. The main objective was to collect from potential end-users' their opinion. Users were requested to answer about the opportunity of receiving a pack of services related to tourism and entertainment. It was explained that services would be offered through the customer's mobile phone in a one-of-a-kind fashion. It was made clear that in order to avoid being intrusive or to disturb customers' daily life, the offers would be sent only if the customer had authorized them.

The questionnaire was made available on-line during two months. During this period invited people provided their opinions and their comments. A close look to the numbers showed that 46% of the replies were provided by men and 54% of the replies were provided by women. When considering the age of the responders, it was observed that people aged between 25 and 45 years old composed most of them (68%). These people represent the customers that are able to spend more money in tourism and entertainment activities. It also shows that the questionnaire did not approach the so-called "Y generation" and a future study shall consider this target population. “Y generation" importance appears as the new consumers to come and their power in adapting themselves to new and innovative solutions must be kept in mind. The questionnaire also showed that most of the responders were married or living in couples. It provided a hint that couples tend to better program their tourism and entertainment activities in advance, while single people look for possible options "on-the-fly". It also demonstrated the responders´ preference to choose/pick a pack of services composed by restaurants and cultural activities, like cinema, theater and so forth. It was observed that, when traveling, most of the people prefer staying in a hotel while traveling than staying in a friends' house or at their relatives´. Low-cost alternatives for accommodation complete the list. Most of them also book their accommodation by using a website, showing a tendency that privileges on-line services over the other traditional approaches (phone, physical).

Other important factors include *quality*, *price*, and *originality* of the service. As a result, *Tourism Breeding Environment* partners aligned by DBPs can mobilize their efforts to offer better services (quality) by integrating their activities, while a dynamic service composition can also bring original alternatives with special discounts and promotions. Despite the fact that most of the responders stated that they prepare their activities 2 days in advance or more, last-minute offers were welcome to overcome unpredictable events like delays and/or weather changes.

This work has provided a flavor about the potential of *tourism breeding environment* and *virtual tourism organization* concepts. It is important for the next steps to investigate the reaction of small-size service providers in tourism and entertainment to collect their opinions regarding collaborative work in a value network. Technical issues, like how to organize the payment of the pack of services, electronic identifiers, and a business model for the TBE are issues that shall not be underestimated and open new fields of research.

References

1. Pereira-Klen, A.P., Rabelo, R.J., Spinosa, L.M., Ferreira, A.C.: Distributed Business Process Management. In: PROVE 1999 Working Conf. on Infrastructures for VEs (1999)
2. Drucker, P.F.: Classic Drucker – The new society of organizations, pp. 127–138. Harvard Business School Press, Boston (2006)
3. Li, M., Crave, S., Grilo, A., van den Berg, R.: Unleashing the Potential of the European Knowledge Economy: Value Proposition for Enterprise Interoperability. European Commission: Info. Society and Media, Luxemburg (2008)
4. Allee, V.: A Value Network Approach for Modelling and Measuring Intangibles. In: Proceedings Transparent Enterprise, Madrid (November 2002)
5. World Tourism Organization (WTO 2009), Web page (2009), `http://www.unwto.org/index.php` (accessed in May 01, 2009)
6. Ammi, C.: International Scientific and Technical Encyclopedia. Global Consumer Behavior. International Scientific and Technical Encyclopedia (2007)
7. Novak, J., Schwabe, G.: Designing for reintermediation in the brick-and-mortar world: Towards the travel agency of the future. Electron Markets 19, 15–29 (2009)
8. Giaglis, G.M., Klein, S., O'Keefe, R.: Disintermetiation, reintermediation, or cybermetiation? The future of intermediaries in electronic marketplaces. In: Proceedings of the 12th Bled International Commerce Conference, Slovenia, Bled, June 7-9, pp. 389–407 (1999)
9. Tapscott, D., Williams, A.D.: Wikinomics: How Mass Collaboration Changes Everything, p. 320. Penguin, New York (2007)
10. Afsarmanesh, H., Camarinha-Matos, L.M.: A framework for management of virtual organizations breeding environments. In: Collaborative Networks and their Breeding Environments, pp. 35–48. Springer, Heidelberg (2005)

Part VIII

Knowledge Transfer and Innovation Networks

Prospecting of Opportunities in Innovation Networks for Technology Transfer

Juliana Sayuri Kurumoto, Angelita Moutin Segoria Gasparotto, and Fábio Müller Guerrini

São Carlos Engineering School (USP) – Production Engineering Department, Trabalhador São-Carlense Avenue, 400, Zip Code 13566-590 São Carlos, Brazil
{kurumoto,guerrini}@sc.usp.br, segovia_74@yahoo.com

Abstract. Studies present the importance of networks for SMEs, but few of them show the opportunities for technology transfer. The paper systematizes the goals that involve innovation networks as tools for prospecting opportunities for technology transfer in SMEs. It was conducted a case study in a high-tech company located in the state of São Paulo - Brazil. The goals were organized based on the objective model of the EKD (Enterprise Knowledge Development) methodology. As a result, it was possible to identify the problems, causes, constraints and opportunities influencing the environment and the collaboration. The paper contributes to future research to improve the network management.

Keywords: Prospecting of opportunities, Innovation networks, Technology transfer.

1 Introduction

The discussion on Collaborative Networks Organizations (CNO) has been gaining attention in the literature because of the importance that this phenomenon has presented the experiences of socioeconomic development in many countries over recent decades. This phenomenon is justified due to shorter development cycles, product research, requiring universities, research centers, businesses, government agencies and professionals, greater dynamism and flexibility in the production of goods and services. So, the term collaborative networks have been used to describe an alliance consisting of geographically distributed and heterogeneous agents in relation to their operating environments, cultural capital, but who see in collaborative work, a way to increase revenue, competitiveness, and share resources and knowledge [1].

Thus, innovation becomes a differential, which can ensure standards and rules that only later other companies should take in order to participate in the competitive environment. With innovation a key variable for achieving and sustaining competitive advantage, it becomes difficult development within the borders of small businesses, because competing directly with multinational corporations and, in most cases, has deficiencies such as lack of capital, scarcity of marketing, vulnerability to macroeconomic instability and lack of managerial training. The purpose of this paper therefore is to systematize the goals that involve innovation networks as tools for exploring opportunities to transfer technology to small and medium enterprises.

L.M. Camarinha-Matos et al. (Eds.): PRO-VE 2011, IFIP AICT 362, pp. 207–214, 2011.

2 Literature Review

2.1 Opportunities on Collaborative Networks Organizations

The more traditional definition of opportunities concerns the chance to introduce products, services or processes on the market [2]. There are two types of opportunities in a network [3]: (a) opportunities which may arise through the company or market: fruit of the relationship between members of the CNO with the external environment the market or society; (b) opportunities which may arise within the network of collaboration between the entities involved, by sharing lessons learned and expertise.

Different authors report on "Opportunities ", describing some phases:

- Perception: involves looking at the market in relation to their needs and trends; Discovery: involves the selection of a promising slice of the market, through a critical analysis before starting a new business or expand an existing market, based on perceived opportunity; Creation: involves the redirection of resources in order to create or improve a product /service already available [4].
- Preparation: involves a concise effort to develop expertise in a particular field of interest; Incubation: involves the maturing of an idea or problem, based on lessons learned; Insight: when there is actually identifying the opportunity; Evaluation: involves checking whether the concepts developed in the discovery phase are feasible. It may involve feasibility analysis of the opportunity identified, which are put to the test through various mechanisms, such as test marketing or financial analysis; Development: involves the establishment of the business from the viable opportunities. Whereas the business idea is feasible after the evaluation stage, the stage of development includes the detailed planning of activities in order to reduce uncertainty [5].
- Discovery: it involves the interpretation of opportunity recognized. It is a dynamic phase that depends directly on the sources of opportunities and lessons learned; Evaluation: involves applying a set of criteria to critically examine the feasibility of the chance discovery; Exploration: involves the management of resources for achieving the goals of the chance discovery [6].

One must consider that some of these opportunities are the result of a process where the solitary entrepreneur conceives an idea and give it its proper meaning. These authors believe that entrepreneurs and managers who prospect opportunities, are well-informed, strongly influenced by previous experiences and also by environmental conditions that surround them [7].

2.2 Innovation Networks

According to the Oslo Manual, the term innovation is defined by the implementation of products (goods and services) and processes technologically new or significantly improved [8]. Is characterized by constant evolution and incorporation of knowledge processes and products, innovation has become the main ingredient for competitiveness. There are five main forms of innovation [9]: (a) introduction of a new asset: a well that consumers are not yet familiar with, or a new quality of a well; (b) introduction of a new production method, a method that has not yet been tested by experience in the manufacturing industry itself, in any event must be based on a discovery scientifically new; (c) opening a new market: that the particular branch of manufacturing industry in the country concerned has not yet come, whether that market has existed or not; (d) gain a new source of supply of raw materials or semi-manufactured goods; and (e) establish a new organization of any industry, such as creating a monopoly or fragmentation of a monopoly position.

The innovation networks is a linkages between enterprises, research organizations, universities and government, working together with the common goal of creating, acquiring and integrating the different skills and knowledge required to develop complex technologies and product or process and bringing them to market [10]. This reduces the chaos in the innovation process and increase the likelihood of developing a successful innovation [10], [11].

Among the reasons for a network is being formed: (a) access to knowledge and information, (b) organizational learning, (c) reducing technological uncertainties, and risks of individual investments in the development of new knowledge, (d) exploitation of complementarities and synergy by merging of different skills, (e) seeking economic scales of production, (f) reducing the difficulty of market entry, (g) reducing the development time of new products, (h) unfamiliarity with the pace at which technology is considered of strategic importance for business [12].

Studies indicate that the collaborative networks for innovation are common in technologically intensive sectors, which dominates the complexity of knowledge and high uncertainty [13]. Recent researches are placing the topic of innovation networks in the context of SMEs, highlighting its importance for these firms [14], [15].

The networks offer advantages for SMEs, such as the sharing of skills in technology transfer, technological expertise, know-how, on regulatory issues, reduces the resource constraint, limiting the ability to innovate [16].

Sharing the same idea [17], [18] identified important relationships between inter-firm cooperation with intermediary institutions, cooperation with research organizations and the innovation performance of SMEs. The study also showed that the vertical and horizontal cooperation with customers, suppliers and other companies have a distinct role in the innovation process of SMEs compared to horizontal cooperation with institutions research, universities and government [19].

2.3 Technology Transfer

The term technology is used for various areas of knowledge, with different meanings [20]. In general, technology is regarded as something tangible, for example, machinery, equipment and intangible assets like skills and knowledge [21].

Definitions of [22] and [23] discuss the technology as the body of knowledge, tools and techniques, product or process, physical equipment or method of action arising out of or creation science or practical experience, which are used in the development, design, production and application of products, processes, systems and services.

In this work, we adopt the concept presented by [24], who consider technology as a technical knowledge or know-how that can be applied to a physical artifact improving the company's ability to offer products and services. The process of managing the acquisition, handling and incorporation of technology between entities is called technology transfer [25]. Entities can be countries, company, or individuals [26], [27].

This is an iterative process that not only transfers existing knowledge, but also facilitates the creation of new knowledge and product solutions [28].

Networks help to reduce insecurity in the development and use of new technologies. Therefore, SMEs should relate to other organizations, forming a dense network of innovation, possibly sharing knowledge and skills to improve their performance in technology transfer [29]. The transfer of network technology, the collaborative effort of learning seems most effective when SMEs participate [30].

3 Research Methodology

This research was conducted in three stages. The first, a survey was conducted in bibliographic databases to find articles in journals related to the objects of this study.

The databases used were the Web of Science, Science Direct, and Emerald. The keywords considered to start the search were innovation networks, technology transfer and prospecting of opportunity. The papers were selected based on the analysis of the impact factor of the journals that is published in the Journal Citation Report (JCR) indexed by the Institute for Science Information (ISI) and the abstracts to identify the main articles that could contribute to this research.

In the second stage, it was carried out a case study with a high tech firm. The use of this method is appropriate when seeking a greater understanding of contemporary facts researched [31], which in this case refers to the networks. As an instrument of data collection it was used the semi-structured interview with open questions. It was interviewed the project management office manager allocated in the department of research and development. The questionnaire aimed to understand the characteristics of the company, the difficulties and benefits of conducting collaborative activities which allowed the development of a model to systematize the goals that involve innovation networks as tools for exploring opportunities for technology transfer.

The last stage was the development of an organizational modeling based on the EKD (Enterprise Knowledge Development) methodology. The EKD provides a clear vision of how the business functions, facilitates learning and organizational communication, provides a structured description of the business, allows us to identify changes and assess the impact of the decision making. This is possible because the six models that consist of this methodology, as follows: concepts model, goals model, business rules model, actors and resources model, business processes model, requirements and technical components model [32].

Considering the purpose of this study, it was represented only the goals model that describes the goals of the enterprise along with the issues associated with achieving these goals. This model is related to the organization and its reason to exist. The components of the goals model are: (a) goal: refers to the desired state of the business to be achieved and is expressed through visions, directions, goals, intentions, needs, requirements, among others; (b) problem: it expresses that the environment is or may be in an undesirable state that hinders the achievement of goals; (c) cause: it expresses explanations or reasons for the problems. Causes are usually states or situations outside the control of the project, process, or organization; (d) restriction: it expresses business constraints, laws, rules or policies of the external world; (e) opportunity: it expresses resources that can make certain goals easier to achieve.

4 Case Study

It was carried out a case study with a technology based firm that operates in the field of optoelectronics in the state of Sao Paulo who is 25 years in the market. Besides the plant, the company has commercial and technical department in the state capital and laboratories in Sao Paulo, Fortaleza, Porto Alegre and Brasilia and overseas units.

The product lines are directed to the medical, industrial and defense areas, which the main products are the laser for ophthalmology, camera, satellite and defense equipment. The firm is considered medium-sized has according to the criteria of [33] with 450 employees. The capital is of domestic origin and primarily serves the domestic market, with approximately 90% of sales destined for the Brazilian market.

The firm has partnership with universities to develop sub-modules for software, research centers for technology development of materials and processes, and with companies that provide technologies and sometimes they are co-development partner. However, their relationships with other companies are to a lesser extent due to concerns about intellectual property. The Fig.1 presents the motivations for firm to collaborate represented by the goals model.

One of the main objectives of the firm is to grow and development innovations (Goal 1) in order to be competitive, becoming knowledge and high technology into benefits for society. Thus, to achieve these objectives, the firm needs to lower costs (Opportunity 1), managerial qualification (Opportunity 2), and to establish collaborative activities (Goal 2), with Universities (Entity 1), Research Centers (Entity 2), and Enterprises (Entity 3). In addition, laws enacted by the government as the Law of good (Policy 1), the Innovation law (Policy 2), and the Informatics law (Policy 3) has encouraged the firm to seek partners to develop new products and processes because they offer tax incentives and facilitate interaction between universities, research institutions and industry.

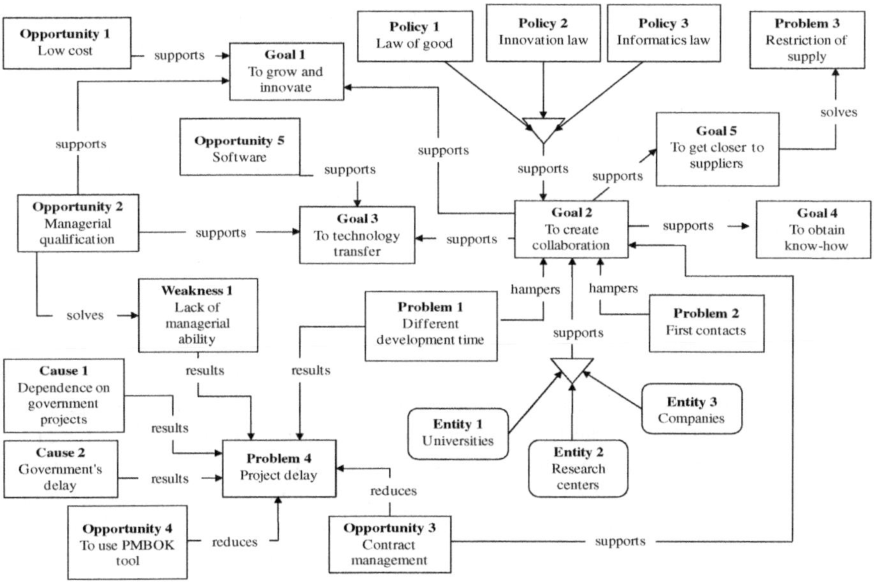

Fig. 1. Goal model

The company faces some difficulties with the cooperation (Goal 2) as the different development time (Problem 1) between universities and industry that result in delays in the project (Problem 4). Furthermore, it is difficult to establish the first contacts (Problem 2) to carry out a partnership because there is no trust between the people.

The establishment of a collaborative relationship aims to get closer to suppliers (Goal 5), allowing to solve the problem of restricted supply (Problem 3). Furthermore, it is possible to acquire know-how (Goal 4) by means of complementary competences and technology transfer (Goal 3), which may be in the form of information, knowledge or hardware. In the case of information and knowledge, this transfer can be supported by software such as CATIA (Computer Aided Three-dimensional Interactive Application), PDM (Product data management), among others.

The technology transfer (Goal 3) is supported by managerial qualification (Opportunity 2), because it allows the firm to identify and exploit opportunities to deepen their knowledge of science and technology when in contact with the external environment. With qualified staff (Opportunity 2), the firm reduces the lack of managerial capacity (Weakness 1) that often interferes with the progress of the project resulting in delays (Problem 4).

Late projects (Problem 4) occur as a result of internal forces such as lack of managerial capacity (Weakness 1) and also by external forces that are beyond the control of the organization as dependence on government projects (Cause 1) or delays government (Cause 2). Two solutions to avoid delays (Problem 4) are identified. The first refers to the application of a tool that assists in managing projects that is known as a manual of good practice PMBOK (Opportunity 4). The second is the contract management (Opportunity 3), because if the contract is clear, accompanied by control procedures, record and documentation of tasks and incidents becomes an important tool to avoid potential problems, and become a support to establish the collaboration (Goal 2).

It was noted that the firm knows the benefits of collaboration, but it has resistance due to intellectual property issues and problems in conducting projects. This occurs because of different social, cultural, organizational and economic characteristics [34].

To overcome these differences [35] points out the need to adapt the way of working with network needs, aligning different strategies to create a common vision of problem solving, acquiring competence in accordance with the individual capabilities of the partners, among others. The networks help to reduce insecurity, but since it is structured and managed properly.

5 Conclusions

Innovation is a key variable to achieve and sustain competitive advantages, its development is difficult within the borders of SMEs due to the scarcity of human and financial resources, vulnerability to macroeconomic instability and lack of managerial training. Thus, one of the mechanisms used to overcome these challenges is through the collaborative work with universities, research centers, companies and customers. This collaboration with various actors allows the sharing and transfer of knowledge, skills and information that contribute to the development of new technological solutions. This happens mostly when the company participates in a net horizontal and vertical. This work has contributed to the companies to understand factors that influence and help in the process of exploring opportunities in technology transfer and that reflects the innovations developed in networks. As ideas for future work should be noted that once the economic lever of Brazil is represented by small and medium enterprises, an issue to be undertaken by networks of innovation might involve the socio-economic aspects of the country. The problems of national industrial network can help in the training of human resources with a more realistic view of the market with a clear understanding of the business itself, with the field of information technologies and communication and increased power to generate innovations.

References

1. Camarinha-Matos, L.M., Afsarmanesh, H.: Classes of Collaborative networks. In: Putinik, G.D., Cunha, M.M. (eds.) Encyclopedia of Networked and Virtual Organizations. Idea Group, USA (2008)
2. Gaglio, C., Katz, J.: The psychological basis of opportunity identification: entrepreneurial alertness. Small Bus. Econ. 16, 95–111 (2001)
3. Camarinha-Matos, L.M., Afsarmanesh, H.: A framework for virtual organization creation in a breeding environment. Journal Annual Reviews in Control (Elsevier) 31(1), 119–135 (2007)
4. Ardichvili, A., Cardozo, R., Ray, S.: A Theory of Entrepreneurial Opportunity Identification and Development. J. Bus. Venturing 18, 105–123 (2003)
5. Lumpkin, G.T., Hills, G.E., Shrader, R.C.: Entrepreneurial Opportunity Recognition. In: Welsch, H. (ed.) Entrepreneurship: The Way Ahead, pp. 73–90. Routledge, London (2004)
6. Sarason, Y., Deant, T., Dillard, J.F.: Entrepreneurship as the Nexus of Individual and Opportunity: a Structuration View. J. Bus. Venturing 21, 286–305 (2006)
7. Zahra, S., Korri, J., Yu, J.: Cognition and International Entrepreneurship: Implications for Research on International Opportunity Recognition and Exploitation. Int. Bus. Rev. 14, 129–146 (2005)
8. Manual, O.: Guidelines for Collecting and Interpreting Innovation Data. In: OECD/EUROSTAT, 3rd edn., p. 166. OECD Publishing (2005)
9. Schumpeter, J.A.: The "Crisis" in Economics – Fifty Years Ago. J. Econ. Lit. 20, 1049–1059 (1982)
10. Rampersad, G., Quester, P., Troshani, I.: Managing Innovation Networks: Exploratory Evidence from ICT, Biotechnology and Nanotechnology Networks. Ind. Market. Manag. 39, 793–805 (2010)
11. Ojasalo, J.: Management of Innovation Networks: a Case Study of Different Approaches. European Journal of Innovation Management 11, 51–86 (2008)
12. Tsai, K.-H.: Collaborative Networks and Product Innovation Performance: Toward a Contingency Perspective. Res. Policy 38, 765–778 (2009)
13. Kelley, D.J., Nakosteen, R.A.: Technology Resources, Alliances, and Sustained Growth in New, Technology-Based Firms. IEEE T. Eng. Manage. 52, 292–300 (2005)
14. DeBresson, C., Amesse, F.: Networks of Innovators: a Review and Introduction to the Issue. Res. Policy 20, 363–379 (1991)
15. Hewitt-Dundas, N.: Resource and Capability Constraints to Innovation in Small and Large Plants. Small Bus. Econ. 26, 257–277 (2006)
16. Street, C.T., Cameron, A.-F.: External Relationships and the Small Business: A Review of Small Business Alliance and Network Research. J. Small Bus. Manage. 45, 239–266 (2007)

17. Chesbrough, H.: Open Innovation: The New Imperative for Creating and Profiting from Technology. Harvard Business School Press, Boston (2003)
18. Nieto, M.J., Santamaría, L.: The Importance of Diverse Collaborative Networks for the Novelty of Product Innovation. Technovation 27, 367–377 (2007)
19. Zeng, S.X., Xie, X.M., Tam, C.M.: Relationship between Cooperation Networks and innovation performance of SMEs. Technovation 30, 181–194 (2010)
20. Freddi, D.: The Integration of Old and New Technological Paradigms in Low- and Medium- Tech Sectors: The Case of Mechatronics. Res. Policy 38, 548–558 (2009)
21. Murmann, J.P., Freken, K.: Toward a Systematic Framework for Research on Dominant Design, Technological Innovation, and Industrial Change. Res. Policy 35, 925–952 (2006)
22. Schon, D.: Technology and Change. Pergamon, London (1967)
23. Abetti, P.A.: Technology: A Key Strategic Resource. Management Review 78, 37–41 (1989)
24. Kaplan, S., Tripsas, M.: Thinking about Technology: Applying a Cognitive Lens to Technical Change. Res. Policy 37, 790–805 (2008)
25. Trott, P.: Innovation Management and New Product Development, 3rd edn. Prentice Hall, Harlow (2005)
26. Autio, E., Laamanen, T.: Measurement and Evaluation of Technology Transfer: Review of Technology Transfer Mechanisms and Indicators. Int. J. Technol. Manage. 10, 643–664 (1995)
27. Autio, E., Hameri, A.P., Vuola, O.: A Framework of Industrial Knowledge Spillovers in Big-Science Centers. Res. Policy 33, 107–126 (2004)
28. Aragon-Correa, J.A., Garcia-Morales, V.J., Cordo'n-Pozo, E.: Leadership and Organizational Learning's Role on Innovation and Performance: Lessons from Spain. Ind. Market. Manag. 36, 249–359 (2007)
29. Lin, J.L., Fang, S.-C., Fang, S.-R., Tsai, F.-S.: Network Embeddedness and Technology Transfer Performance in R&D Consortia in Taiwan. Technovation 29, 763–774 (2009)
30. Albors, J., Sweeney, E., Hidalgo, A.: Transnational Technology Transfer Networks for SMEs. A Review of the State-of-the Art and an Analysis of the European IRC Network. Prod. Plan. Control 16, 413–423 (2005)
31. Yin, R.K.: Case Study Research: Design and Methods. SAGE Publications, Inc., Thousand Oaks (2003)
32. Bubenko, J., Persson, A., Stirna, J.: EKD User Guide, Research Report (2001)
33. SEBRAE - Brazilian Service Support for Micro and Small Enterprises, `http://www.sebrae.com.br`
34. Saad, M., Cicmil, S., Greenwood, M.: Technology transfer projects in developing countries – furthering the project management perspectives. Int. J. Project Manag. 20, 617–625 (2002)
35. Bullinger, H.-J., Auernhammer, K., Gomeringer, A.: Managing innovation networks in the knowledge-driven economy. Int. J. Prod. Res. 42, 3337–3353 (2004)

Networked R&D Units: Case Studies on Knowledge Transfer Processes

Paula Urze

FCT/UNL – Faculdade de Ciências e Tecnologia da Universidade Nova de Lisboa
SOCIUS – Centro de Investigação em Sociologia Económica e das Organizações, Lisbon, Portugal
pcu@fct.unl.pt

Abstract. This paper aims at identifying the knowledge transfer processes developed among R&D units and the competencies that are locally created to earn power by knowledge within these global innovation networks. Te paper's empirical section is grounded on two multinationals with R&D units in Portugal, one from a Norwegian electronic multinational and another from a Spanish automotive component multinational. Crossing the theoretical debate with the empirical results we expect to offer an insight on the understanding of knowledge transfer processes.

Keywords: knowledge flows, R&D units, innovation, automotive components and electronics industries.

1 Introduction

In the last few decades important transformations have been emerging in the society and in the economy, leading to the development of a new economic and social structure. The new concept of knowledge-based economy comes from the acknowledgement of the importance of knowledge for economic growth (Soete, 2000). Knowledge is recognized as a crucial source of economic rent and the effective management of organizational knowledge has increasingly been linked to competitive advantage and considered critical to the success of the business firm. In this way, a crucial challenge for multinationals is to combine the unique location-bound resources found in local clusters with the global resources of the firm to generate valuable and rare capabilities (Lundan, 2002). In this sense, they should assure that competencies from the different units are diffused throughout the group (Andersson et al, 2002). The aim of this paper is to analyze the knowledge transfer processes in two multinational networks (MNC) and the transfer mechanisms created to earn power by knowledge within these global value chains. The paper is structured as follows: firstly, we review the literature on knowledge accumulation and transfer in the context of MNCs. Secondly, the empirical analysis is reported, including methodology and discussion of results considering the theoretical contributes presented above. Conclusions make up the latter part.

L.M. Camarinha-Matos et al. (Eds.): PRO-VE 2011, IFIP AICT 362, pp. 215–224, 2011.

2 Knowledge Transfer Processes in Global Networks

2.1 Knowledge and Competencies as Strategic Resources: The Subsidiaries Absorptive Capacity

The last decade evidenced a significant concern about the study of how big corporations manage knowledge and, in particular, about the process in which they are transferred (Sölvell and Birkinshaw, 2000). Multinationals that are able to teach, as well as learn, can combine the unique location-bound resources found in local clusters with the global resources of the firm to generate valuable and rare capabilities. In this way, to learn and share knowledge and competencies become essential mechanisms to the company (Caraça e Simões, in: Simões et al, 2002: 139). Therefore, a crucial challenge for multinationals is to avoid that subsidiaries become isolated from other parts of the multinational and assure that competencies from the different units of the multinational are diffused throughout the group (Andersson et al, 2002: 116). According to Andersson, Björkman e Furu (2002), the development of competencies depends on the capacity of subsidiaries to recognize the value of external knowledge, incorporate it and apply it, in other words their absorptive capacity. Absorptive capacity is the organization's current readiness and accumulated knowledge, which enable it to identify and grasp new valuable knowledge outside the organization, and to use knowledge in value-creating processes. The higher the subsidiary's absorptive capacity, the more extensive its competence development, and consequently, the more it may contribute to the competence development of the whole MNC. In this manner, to recognize and absorb knowledge, subsidiaries must establish connections with local and external networks and be able to use the acquired knowledge as an important ground for the development of new competencies. Actually, integrating the capabilities and knowledge of the dispersed subsidiaries and making use of them in other MNC units represent a special advantage of the multinational and thus are an essential task for corporate management (Andersson, 2003: 426). In fact, is MNC management task to try to exploit capabilities developed within different subsidiaries in such a way that the MNC as a whole can benefit from them. To accomplish this, Andersson (2003) emphasizes the importance of the assigned role and responsibilities given by the MNC to subsidiaries. According to the author, the assignation of a specific role to a subsidiary will mean that its capabilities, developed in the intense and deep relations with local actors (especially costumers and suppliers), will be used and may also be integrated into other units. Besides the simple diffusion of competencies and capabilities is the diffusion of "good practices" in MNCs. Sölvell and Birkinshaw (2000) argue that the ability to manage and transfer good practices on a worldwide basis is what separates the successful MNCs from the less successful. In this sense, MNCs will gain if the good practices of a subsidiary are exported to other subsidiaries of the network and, consequently, one important goal for a MNC is to develop successful practices, standardized them and diffuse them in all the subsidiaries of the multinational group.

2.2 Knowledge Transfer Process: Barriers and Support Organizational Mechanisms

There are a number of obstacles to transfer competence in the MNC, which are associated with the competence itself and the characteristics of the sender, the recipient and the relationship between them. One of the biggest problems of knowledge transfer is to know how to solve the issue of transmission of tacit knowledge. Actually, tacit knowledge is a part of knowledge of hard appropriation and divulgation, because it is a non-specified, personal and contextual knowledge. This kind of knowledge has been considered an important component of innovation, having a fundamental role in the developments of science and technology. Accordingly, tacit knowledge can be converted in explicit knowledge trough a codification process, which makes the incorporation or diffusion of knowledge easier. However, this process evolves lost of information, due to the fact that part of the knowledge will stay only in the head of the people who have the knowledge. The other barrier is related to internal competition between subsidiaries. Subsidiaries tend to have different goals and often-limited incentives to transfer know-how to other units, particularly if it involves the time of their best people or proprietary technology that might leak out. By diffusing knowledge to other MNC units, the focal subsidiary may also lose some of its uniqueness, thus loosing bargaining power within the MNC. Another barrier refers to the interaction between the subsidiary and its local context. These competencies cannot easily be used in other corporate units' business contexts. This is because the absorptive capacity required to understand and apply the competence is developed within the unique context-specific, or even relation-specific (Forsgren et al, in: Andersson et al, 2002: 117). Once more, the local context is determinant, this time to understand knowledge transfer between MNCs' units. Related to the previous barrier is the socio-cultural and institutional context emphasized by Pedersen, Petersen and Sharma (2003: 74). According to the authors, knowledge transfer is influenced by the socio-cultural institutional distance between the foreign country and the home country of the MNC. Knowledge in firms is contingent on their socio-cultural environment; what is appropriate knowledge in one country may not suit the needs of firms in other countries. In turn, this may cause problems to the knowledge transfer process. Nevertheless, it is responsibility of the multinational group to take measures that stimulate the information flows between the different units of the group. In this manner, a crucial task for corporate management will be to recognize the absorptive capacity of the subsidiaries and in particular to coordinate the diffusion of the learning outcomes of the subsidiaries, i.e., to establish integration mechanisms that engender knowledge flows from one affiliate to others. Pedersen, Petersen and Sharma (2003) also consider that MNCs should develop mechanisms to facilitate knowledge transfer between its units, but these mechanisms have to suit the specific knowledge characteristics. Tacit and non-codified knowledge is harder to transfer and requires specific organizational mechanisms. Therefore, the choice of transfer mechanism has to be related to the characteristics of the particular knowledge.

The authors conclude that in general tacit knowledge is transferred though "rich communication", which comprises face-to-face communication and informal interaction, and explicit knowledge through "written media", which, by its turn, involves manuals, database, written instructions and blueprints. According to Pedersen, et al (2003: 69), the use of unsuitable transfer mechanisms may cause loss of knowledge in the process of transmission or may involve unnecessarily high communication costs, both with potentially negative effects on the performance of the MNC.

3 Case Studies

3. 1 Methodology

The empirical component of this paper is grounded on one extended case study (MNC A) and one local case study (MNC B). The extended case study, is based in an electronic multinational, involves an R&D subsidiary located in Portugal, a R&D subsidiary located in the Netherlands and also the headquarters, located in Norway. The local case study has been performed on a subsidiary of a Spanish multinational of the automobile industry located in Portugal. Two techniques were combined to carry out the empirical research: in-locu observation of the work processes and semi-directive interviews addressed to key actors belonging to different departments and hierarchical levels of the firms.

In Trondheim, the headquarters of MNC A, 11 interviews have been conducted with Top Management, Operation, R&D and Sales. In the second R&D unit, located in Beilen (Netherlands), recently acquired by network A, 6 interviews where conducted and other 5 within the Portuguese subsidiary.

In the local case study, 8 interviews were conducted with professionals of the product-engineering department and 4 with professionals of the processes engineering department. We focused our interviews on those two departments, as they are central in terms of R&D product and process development.

3.2 Case Study A

MNC A is a company from the electronics industry. The company has presently 270 employees in 12 locations and representatives in 6 other countries. The headquarters, with 110 workers and the Dutch subsidiary with 28 employees are the only units with strong R&D departments. The other subsidiaries, like the one in Malaysia with 17 workers, Australia with 13 and Thailand with 10, have local development activities. The other subsidiaries have less than 10 workers and their main activity is sales. However, there are subsidiaries with just a few workers, like in Portugal (with 5 workers) and in Brazil (with 7 workers), which have engineers performing product development.

Indeed, the relations established locally are crucial to the development of MNCs (Dunning, 2000). The contacts with the customers and the local market are essential, as the gathered information from theses contacts may be determinant to design the business future goals. As underlined by the vice-president for business development, the main motivation to create local units is to be closer to the customers and to the local market. "The main concern is to be able to understand what the customers really want, that's why we have these offices around them."

Another relevant aspect is the contribution local Universities and research centres could bring to firms R&D activities through researchers and high skilled workers interactions. According to the R&D Dutch vice-president "it is with the university that I have close professional relations. (...). In terms of activity, mine is more related to knowing what is happening in terms of research, and relate with the institutions that do research and to go to the conferences. Due to these relations we are members of 10 international projects and our partners are universities, governments and all that relate to this industry". The foundation of the Dutch subsidiary has been linked to the university as the owners come from there. Company's relation with the academic world was crucial in the beginning of the firm not only providing professional training of employees but also in the subsequent R&D activities developed by the company. Currently, the position of the company towards university is different as nowadays the company prefers to steer away from the connection with the academic world projecting a more "business world" image of itself.

Knowledge transfer: the predominance of informal mechanisms

The knowledge internal management is a complex question because of the context of a small MNC, where the majority of the subsidiaries are only dedicated to commercial activities or to local Development activities, sometimes so specific that its diffusion and transfer don't bring advantages to other multinational's units. Besides, this multinational network knowing the important role of the knowledge change mechanisms (even more because we are talking about activities that imply high technology activities and high levels of innovation, where the know-how transfer is always an added value) doesn't use, systematically, formal mechanisms of knowledge interchange. Observing the knowledge transfer mechanisms, we can say that the fundamental ones are the informal mechanisms. In fact, as the project manager from Norway says: "we don't have a structured program of learning and share of knowledge. People talk to each other, personally or by e-mail. The informal network functions very well because we aren't a very big company, and we don't have yet a formal way to share knowledge." The director of the portuguese subsidiary tries to systematize the formal and informal mechanisms of knowledge transfer. The informal are: "meetings and workshops, which are a mean to change information"; the "learning actions" which are developed in the headquarters for the technicians, "who are there a couple of months absorbing know how and how to work"; the "learn by doing" in which "people learn while they work, for example, in a system or a programme". The formal mechanisms are "the new software tools, available only about 8 months ago, the new internal portal, the intranet, where we introduce experiences, ask questions, see the historical of the product. And when we do specific developments, new software, the technical information is essential. It is a borrower task but is crucial so that the knowledge doesn't stay only in people heads". The CEO of Norway emphasises other mechanisms related to the mobility and interchange of human resources and competencies. He states: "we try to use good people in other projects when they have time for that, so we try to map the competencies of people, to assure that people who gained experience locally can be used in other projects. (...) Nowadays, two engineers from Portugal are participating in the development of a central system, because they have the competencies". However, the CEO adds: "we don't transfer knowledge in a systematic way, at least not enough. We are trying but it is still everything very informal." And as the director of the portuguese subsidiary says, it is always difficult to make documentation, software specifications, and other kind of formalizations, when they are not currently done in the company. Nevertheless, the company is trying to grow on the knowledge transfer knowledge, because, as state several authors (Sölvell e Birkinshaw, 2000; Lundan, 2002; Pedersen, et al, 2003), an effective knowledge transfer can be an important competitive advantage on a MNC and, consequently, the correct use of facilitating mechanisms is very important. However, the Dutch subsidiary is a peculiar example of knowledge management. Actually, we can't forget that this subsidiary is more than an unit from a MNC. It is an R&D company with a clear strategy in what concerns its management and its goals, which was acquired by the MNC A. Consequently, the knowledge transfer process is different from the one of the rest of the MNC. In the Dutch company, there is, not only, a clear concern in formalizing knowledge, but also objective mechanisms for it, which allow keeping the knowledge in the company. The CEO of the company says: "in what concerns the knowledge management, what we do is to be sure that we keep all the knowledge inside the company. Every time someone discovers a new way of knowledge or a new method, we develop software capable to catch that new knowledge and keep it in the company". In this manner, there is a clear concern on keeping the knowledge in the company, because the strongest value of this company is its knowledge and its innovation's activities. This "knowledge keeping" is achieved by formal mechanisms of tacit knowledge explicitation. Concluding: with the exception of the Dutch subsidiary, the predominance of informal transfer mechanisms could be a result of the recent rearrangement of the management logics of the MNC by the actual CEO, which doesn't allow yet a systematic utilization of the formal mechanisms, which, by its turn, only recently began to be implemented.

The limitations of tacit and local knowledge diffusion

In MNC A the Dutch subsidiary has a big concern in formalize knowledge in order to keep it inside the company. Nevertheless, the tacit knowledge explicitation is a complex process, as the Dutch CEO states: "the knowledge issue is always complicated, because it is in the researchers' head, it is always difficult to become explicit the tacit knowledge. When we loose a researcher we always loose knowledge." As the majority of the authors state, the tacit knowledge can be converted in explicit knowledge, however this process implies inevitably the information lost, due to the fact that part of the knowledge always stays in the head of the individuals that know, and also implies high costs (Oliveira, 2008: 54, Oliveira, 2007: 278 e Lança, 2004: 39).Another problem in the knowledge transfer process is associated with the transfer of local, contextualized and specific knowledge. The relations with costumers and the local market are crucial for the local Development of products. As the director of the Portuguese subsidiary says: "the relations with local the costumer and allied are very important to figure out the local specifications which a product needs". Nevertheless, the local Development and the associated knowledge are hardly transferable to other units of the network, due to the big specificity of those Developments. Actually, and as Foss and Pedersen (2002) and Andersson et al. (2002) argue, because the more specific the knowledge is, the more difficult it is to transfer, since it becomes harder for other units to learn it and less useful for them.This barrier is related with the sociocultural and institutional context, emphasized by Pedersen et al. (2003). The appropriated knowledge in one country cannot serve the needs of the companies in other countries. This is the case of the Center of Excellence of Malaysia where are being done Developments for manual tolls, which are common in Asia, but the knowledge associated with this kind of activities won't be useful in other cultural contexts, due to the specificities, in this particular case, of the tolls, for example, in European countries.

3.3 Case Study B

The MNC B consists of a network of 40 companies from all over the world. Founded in 1949, the company has its headquarters in Barcelona (Spain) and relies on a team of 6900 people who work in 19 countries in Europe, North America, South America and Asia. MNC B is a multinational devoted to the research, development, production and commercialization of systems and parts for the automobile, as well as for both commercial and industrial vehicles. Portugal (Oporto) was MNC B's first international expansion abroad, in the beginning of the 70's. In Portugal the company has about 550 employees.

The local relations in the development of the portuguese subsidiary

MNCB has always developed relations with its surrounding environment, i.e., other companies, costumers and, mainly, suppliers. The close relations between the subsidiary and suppliers can be seen in the words of the process-engineering director as an extension of the company: "Our suppliers are an extension of this company. We help them to grow up, and we grow up with them as well. They are a key element for us, and our relations are very important." In point of fact, MNCB always tried to establish local contacts that could allow it to grow up and to obtain the autonomy that it has nowadays. Indeed, as stated Cantwell and Mudambi (2005), the relations established between the subsidiary and the local environment, seem to be a key factor in the trajectory of this R&D unit. In this sense, the history of MNCB is strongly linked with its privileged relations with local companies. This leads to a conclusion about local processes of innovation as sources of competitiveness for multinationals (Sölvell and Birkinshaw, 2000). Actually, the MNCB is an example of the importance of local costumers as sources of innovation. One can say that this subsidiary is an example of the innovation process development in local contexts. Innovation emerged from interactions between the subsidiary and local actors. MNCB is also an example of the Sölvell and Birkinshaw (2000) concept of "good practices" that are diffused in the multinational network, despite the specificity of competences of the different subsidiaries. As the director of product engineering says: "we have here good practices that were adopted by the group". As a matter of fact, and as we have seen above, the knowledge transfer in this firm seems to have just one direction, which is from the portuguese subsidiary to the others subsidiaries of the MNC. As the director of processes engineering points out: "the other subsidiaries come here more frequently to look for the information they need. There is a tendency to come here and search for knowledge and competencies and put them in practice in others subsidiaries of the group." Summing up, MNCB is an example of a subsidiary that took advantage from the existing resources, developed strategic relations with local agents and gained influence within the headquarters.

Knowledge and "good practices" dissemination

In MNC B there is a concern in developing knowledge management tools, which can help the diffusion of the knowledge between all the units of the network. One can see this concern by the creation of common databases, which goal is standardization of information so that any subsidiary can take advantage of other subsidiaries' knowledge. Nevertheless, this data base project is very recent and is starting to be diffused in the network and in the portuguese subsidiary. As the director of processes engineering says: "in these bases we can find factory problems, processes, standardizations, i.e. all the information that can be useful for MNC network B. And these bases have a lot of advantages, for example, if we are talking about common processes to all subsidiaries, the interest of the database will be enormous. They have a great potential." Actually, these databases facilitate knowledge transfer because they transform tacit knowledge, which is very "context specific" and hard to transfer, in explicit knowledge, which is easier to transfer and be used by other units (Pedersen et al., 2003). In this manner, MNC B through the databases, try to decontextualize and standardize knowledge in order to easily diffuse it in the multinational network. As the industrial process manager says: "we should warrant that there is a standard procedure in all the subsidiaries, so that everyone could follow the same procedures. Indeed, the Portuguese subsidiary can be considered also an example of the Sölvell and Birkinshaw (2000) concept of "good practices" that are diffused in the multinational network, through a geocentric attitude, in which good practices come from the success of a subsidiary and their dissemination is implemented in other contexts. As the director of product engineering says: "we have here good practices that were adopted by the group". We can conclude that the use of transfer mechanisms, which can facilitate knowledge transfer, is a concern in both companies. They are different multinational companies, which are in different stages of development and consequently some concerns, like the use of formal mechanisms, are more developed in one of them. However, both are tying to create formal mechanisms, essentially data bases, in order to formalize knowledge and not to keep it only in researcher's heads but inside the company.

The problem of local and specific knowledge transfer

Considering the barriers to knowledge transfer, one can observed that subsidiary B has the predominant characteristics of business area division of subsidiaries, which means that the units are divided in business areas and each units develop a certain product. The MNCB's subsidiaries have very specific roles in the network, resulting in specialized knowledge and competences that there are difficult to transfer. As stated by Foss and Pedersen (2002), the context and specificity of the knowledge influence the extent of its sharing interest. This is because the more specific and contextualized the knowledge is, the harder will be for the units to absorb it and the less useful the knowledge will be to them. This is an important barrier to transfer competences in multinationals. As a product engineer underlined: "this company is composed of business units each one has its own competencies", and in this way the knowledge of one unit will be less useful to another unit that has different activities and practices and that require different competencies. Although, knowledge transfer happens, as the same engineer point out: "there are knowledge and information transfer when there's a problem that can be common to all units (because there are common problems even when we talk about different processes and products). In this case it is very useful to share information about the solutions for the problem." Another barrier emphasized by Andersson, Björkman and Furu (2002) is internal competition between subsidiaries. In MNC B, interviewees do not recognize that competition. What they emphasize is that MNC B is almost always the sender and rarely the receiver of knowledge and information. As the director of processes engineering says: "I don't think we can talk about competition here, because what happens is that the others subsidiaries come here to obtain information and knowledge." In this manner, we believe that competition in this case, even if it exists, is not a barrier to knowledge transfer, for the reason our interviewee pointed out and for two more reasons. First, because subsidiary B has already a privileged position in the multinational group and by diffusing knowledge to other units will not loose bargaining power within the group. Second, because the multinational is divided in business units, each unit has its own competences that are very specific and hard to transfer.

4 Conclusion

This paper aimed at understanding the knowledge creation and diffusion processes of two MNC, one based on the general perspective of the multinational network (A) and the other based on the local perspective of a portuguese subsidiary of a MNC (B). We reach some common conclusions. In both MNC's, in different ways, the competences of local agents are crucial. There are also some common barriers to knowledge transfer, like the difficulty of transfer specific and contextualize knowledge, which need to be passed.

Nevertheless we should emphasize, in what concerns the directionality of knowledge flows, the role of the portuguese subsidiary of MNC B as a source of knowledge to the entire network. This subsidiary exports a lot of knowledge (especially in the processes area), being strong subsidiary in terms of developing innovations to diffuse to the multinational network. In MNC A, despite some exceptions, the main knowledge become from the headquarters, being then transferred to the network. In general, we can say that the effective dissemination throughout the MNC organization of valuable knowledge is seen as an important source of competitive advantage. For this reasons, multinational companies try to develop mechanisms in order to facilitate the effective dissemination of knowledge inside the networks. These mechanisms consist basically, in both examples, in common databases and internal communication networks, which, in turn, allow every unit of the multinational network to accede to the same information and knowledge. The cases presented here illustrate that concern, despite being in different stages of this process of creating mechanisms to formalize knowledge.

Acknowledgments. This paper references research work developed under the R&D.COM – Local R&D Competences in Global Value Chains - project with contributions from Maria João Manatos.

References

1. Andersson, U., et al.: Subsidiary Absorptive Capacity, MNC Headquarters' Control Strategies and Transfer of Subsidiaries Competencies. In: Lundan, S. (ed.) Network Knowledge International Business. Edward Elgar Publishing, Cheltenham (2002)
2. Cantwell, J., Mudambi, R.: MNE Competence-Creating Subsidiary Mandates. Strategic Management Journal 26 (2005)
3. Dunning, J.H.: The Eclectic Paradigm as an Envelope for Economic and Business Theories of MNE Activity. International Business Review 9 (2000)
4. Foss, N., Pedersen, T.: Sources of Subsidiary Knowledge and Knowledge Transfer in MNCs. In: Lundan, S. (ed.) Network Knowledge International Business. Edward Elgar Publishing, Cheltenham (2002)
5. Lança, I.S.: Conhecimento, economia e sociedade. In: Lança, I.S., Suleman, F., de Fátima Ferreiro, M. (eds.) Portugal e a sociedade do conhecimento – dinâmicas mundiais, competitividade e emprego, Oeiras, Celta (2004)
6. Lundan, S.: Introduction. In: Lundan, S. (ed.) Network Knowledge International Business. Edward Elgar Publishing, Cheltenham (2002)
7. Pedersen, T., et al.: Knowledge Transfer Performance of Multinational Companies. Management International Review 43 (2003)
8. Schmidt, S., et al.: The MNC as a Network: a Closer Look at Intra-Organizational Flows. In: Lundan, S. (ed.) Network Knowledge International Business. Edward Elgar Publishing, Cheltenham (2002)
9. Simões, V.C., et al.: Subsidiary Decision-Making Autonomy: Competences, Integration and Local Responsiveness. In: Lundan, S. (ed.) Network Knowledge International Business. Edward Elgar Publishing, Cheltenham (2002)
10. Soete, L.: The challenges and the potential of the knowledge-based economy in a globalised world. In: Rodrigues, M.J. (ed.) New Knowledge Economy in Europe: a Strategy for International Competitiveness and Social Cohesion, pp. 28–53. Edward Elgar Publishing, Massachusetts (2002)
11. Sölvell, Ö., et al.: Multinational Enterprises and the Knowledge Economy: Leveraging Global Practices. In: Dunning, J.H. (ed.) Regions, Globalization, and the Knowledge-Based Economy. Oxford University Press, New York (2002)

Knowledge Creation and Diffusion in Regional Collaborative Networks

Rafael H.P. Lima and Luiz C.R. Carpinetti

School of Engineering of Sao Carlos, University of Sao Paulo, Brazil
400 Trabalhador Sao Carlense Ave, Sao Carlos-SP 13566-590
{rhlima,carpinet}@sc.usp.br

Abstract. Industrial clusters can be seen as a type of collaborative networks with a geographically limited scope, since they are environments where firms can collaborate to improve collective efficiency and form networks for knowledge creation and sharing. This paper reviews some contributions found in the literature concerning knowledge management in industrial clusters and proposes a new knowledge management framework to assist local governance in conducting initiatives aiming at creating and sharing knowledge among firms. The framework is still theoretical and future research is necessary for improvement and validation of its phases.

Keywords: Collaborative networks, industrial clusters, knowledge management.

1 Introduction

Networks have been a central topic in the operations management field and may emerge in several forms, such as partnerships, strategic alliances, inter-organizational relationships or collaborative arrangements [1]. More specifically, a collaborative network (CN) is a type of network constituted by a variety of entities that collaborate to better achieve common or compatible goals [2]. Following this concept, there is a considerable amount of literature that deals with the formation of collaborative networks in regional clusters. The term industrial cluster is probably the most commonly used to refer to geographic concentrations of firms from a specific economic sector, as well as other entities such as supporting institutions, specialized suppliers and universities [3]. In this sense, regional concentrations of firms can also be seen as environments where collaborative networks are likely to emerge [2]. Recent research on clusters has emphasized the linkages between firms both for material and knowledge exchange, thus viewing the clusters as a multitude of network relationships [4]. Additionally, the topic has drawn special interest from both academia and regional governments, who have proposed and set out policies for regional development [5].

Given the importance of knowledge linkages between networked firms, this paper addresses the issue of knowledge creation and diffusion in collaborative networks that involve firms located in industrial clusters. These are referred to in this paper as regional collaborative networks due to the geographic proximity of the parts involved. The purpose of this paper is to propose a knowledge management (KM) framework to

L.M. Camarinha-Matos et al. (Eds.): PRO-VE 2011, IFIP AICT 362, pp. 225–232, 2011.

assist local governance and CNs in the promotion of initiatives aimed at creating and disseminating knowledge, which may impact positively on the overall network performance and reduce the cognitive distance between the entities taking part in the network.

This paper is organized as follows. Section 2 draws from the literature about knowledge management in industrial clusters to build the theoretical background for the framework proposed in this paper. Section 3 consists of this paper's theoretical contribution by describing the knowledge management framework for CNs formed in industrial clusters and proposing an information and communication (ICT) infrastructure to facilitate the framework operation. Finally, Section 4 discusses the theoretical contribution, its limitations and future research opportunities.

2 Theoretical Background

Industrial clusters have drawn interest from several researchers, policy makers and practitioners due to their focus on regional development, which give way to several initiatives and policy interventions aiming at upgrading firms and integrating institutions [6]. Studies on geographical concentrations of firms began in the 19th century with economist Alfred Marshall, who emphasized the external economies obtained by businesses such as skilled workforce, specialized suppliers and training services, and so forth. These benefits tended to emerge naturally due to the concentration of firms from the same industry and required little or none inter-organizational collaboration to occur [7].

More recently, the focus has shifted from mere external economies to more complex forms of gaining competitive advantage in clusters. Schmitz and Nadvi [8] argue that companies located in clusters should cooperate through joint actions, which are planned initiatives that enable further benefits and may boost competitive advantages of the firms involved. This goes beyond external economies and may increase the collective efficiency of firms. In light of organizational network literature, joint actions can be viewed as a type of CN that may emerge in industrial clusters, since they seek to combine common objectives and articulate activities among several entities so that these objectives can be achieved.

In this regard, governance becomes a relevant issue so that joint actions can be coordinated and yield positive outcomes. Gilsing [9] claims that governance in clusters refer to the planning and conduction of joint actions that involve local actors and seek to upgrade the cluster as a whole. In this sense, local governance in regional collaborative networks become crucial in determining the strategic issues that need to be addressed by improvement and upgrading processes.

Some researchers have studied the processes by which governance can upgrade the cluster building on the existing literature on organizational performance management. For example, Sölvell et al. [6] developed the Cluster Initiative Performance Model to assist local governance in determining common objectives and devising management processes for areas such as innovation, training, research and cooperation. Other attempts to put forward frameworks for clusters management have been made by authors as Carpinetti et al. [10] and Meyer-Stamer and Harmes-Liedtke [11]. Nevertheless, these contributions lay focus mainly on management processes and address superficially knowledge creation and diffusion processes.

In recent years, knowledge management at the cluster level has gained significant attention from researchers by drawing from the literature on organizational knowledge management. One such case is the adoption of Nonaka's [12] knowledge spiral by clusters to devise knowledge management initiatives. According to Nonaka's theory, knowledge is created through conversions between tacit and explicit knowledge, which occur by means of interactions between individuals. The processes of socialization, combination, internalization and externalization are used to explain how knowledge can be converted between its explicit and tacit forms, thus enhancing the organizational knowledge base. Following this theory, Evers et al. [13] argues that clusters may gain competitive advantage primarily through the direct transfer of tacit knowledge between firms.

There seems to be a consensus that knowledge is a fundamental resource in industrial clusters, since they enable innovation and upgrading in local firms. For example, Iammarino and McCann [14] claim that regional clusters that wish to efficiently access and use knowledge should develop processes in three dimensions:

(i) Absorption of new knowledge, technologies and innovations and their adaptation to local needs;
(ii) Diffusion of innovations to strengthen the existing knowledge base;
(iii) Creation of new knowledge, technologies and information.

Moreover, some authors believe that successful innovative companies tend to join innovation networks that allow them to combine knowledge and competencies to offer not only products, but more complete solutions. Bullinger et al. [15] argue that innovation networks require strong links between firms, research labs, suppliers and customers, thus forming a dense network of knowledge sharing. Proximity of all actors in the network becomes fundamental, especially because of the tacit nature of most of the knowledge shared among them.

There are some authors who believe that local governance should play an active role in implementing knowledge management practices. Bocquet and Mothe [16] defined three phases for external knowledge integration in clusters and discuss how local governance should act upon them:

(i) *Knowledge identification:* local governance should identify sources of knowledge that are relevant for companies in the cluster;
(ii) *Knowledge acquisition:* the knowledge identified needs to be acquired and made available for local firms;
(iii) *Knowledge use:* local governance should promote initiatives to stimulate firms towards using and making available the new knowledge acquired.

Finally, the authors argue that these three phases are especially suitable for smaller firms in the cluster, since they may not have the amount of resources and capabilities required to identify relevant sources of knowledge. Thus, initiatives carried out by local governance in any of these three phases may increase the overall level of knowledge in the cluster.

3 Theoretical Contribution

As discussed in the previous section, knowledge management in industrial clusters is a topic that still needs to be studied further, though some attempts have already been made in the literature. Hence, this paper seeks to build on previous contributions and give a step forward by introducing a more detailed framework to assist local governance in conducting knowledge management initiatives. Section 3.1 describes the knowledge management framework for industrial clusters and Section 3.2 proposes a supporting ICT architecture to facilitate the framework operation.

3.1 Knowledge Management Framework

The knowledge management framework for industrial clusters is shown in Figure 1. It tries to build on previous efforts reported in the literature by combining the three phases described by Bocquet and Mothe [16] with the four knowledge creation processes proposed by Nonaka [12]. The contribution phase complements the model by outlining activities through which companies can contribute to the enhancement of the cluster's knowledge base.

Identification	Acquisition	Use	Contribution
Explicit knowledge			
- *Internal sources:* firms, governance, supporting institutions, internal consultants - *External sources:* suppliers, gorvernment, regulators, external consultants, specialized publications	- Specialized libraries - Digital distribution - Publication of reports (performance, joint actions, market trends, etc)	**Combination** - Working groups (preparation of manuals, tutorials, procedures, etc) **Internalization** - Working groups (on-the-job learning, problem solving)	- Repors on good practices - Publication of tutorials and manuals - Participation in Web 2.0 applications as Wikis and discussion forums
Tacit knowledge			
- Internal sources: firms, consultants, education and training centers, workshops, meetings - External sources: trade fairs, consultants, suppliers, customers	- Joint training - Workshops with local companies - Distance education - Technical visits - Participation in trade fairs - Benchmarking (best practices)	**Socialization** - Working groups (on-the-job learning, problem solving) - Social networks **Externalization** - Working groups (preparation of manuals, tutorials, procedures, etc) - Discussion forums	- Social networks and interpersonal relationships - On-the-job training - Technical visits

Fig. 1. Phases of the knowledge management framework and the proposed practices for both explicit and tacit knowledge

The framework suggests a set of knowledge sources and practices that can be adopted by local governance in the promotion of knowledge management initiatives. Thus they should be seen more as suggestions than requirements for the framework to function, since each industrial cluster has its own particularities and may tailor the knowledge sources and practices according to its needs. In summary, each of the four phases seeks to answer one specific question:

(i) *Identification:* what are the relevant internal and external knowledge sources from which local governance can find knowledge of interest to local firms?

(ii) *Acquisition:* how should local governance acquire and make available the knowledge identified in the previous phase?

(iii) *Use:* how should local governance stimulate the use of the knowledge available by local firms in the innovation and improvement of products and processes?

(iv) *Contribution:* how should local governance and firms share the knowledge they acquired and used, thus contributing to the enhancement of the cluster's knowledge base?

The *identification* phase seeks to find knowledge sources from which local governance can extract tacit and explicit knowledge. These sources may be available both internally and externally. Many companies, specially the smaller ones, have little ability in finding knowledge sources and determining which of them are relevant [16]. During the *acquisition* phase, local governance needs to determine how the knowledge sources are to be made available to firms taking part in its initiatives. This can be achieved by means of social channels and the use of ICT.

The use phase refers to the processes by which local governance and firms will use the knowledge acquired to their own needs and consequently create new knowledge. This can be done by applying Nonaka's theory of knowledge creation. The sources made available by local governance may be either tacit or explicit. Moreover they can be used to generate new tacit or explicit knowledge, which is represented by the socialization, internalization, externalization and combination processes. After acquiring and using knowledge, companies and local governance can contribute to the enhancement of the overall cluster knowledge base by sharing the new knowledge they created. This needs not occur with all companies at the same time. Instead, new knowledge may be made available first for partners, suppliers and customers. It is then likely that this knowledge will flow throughout the cluster by other collaboration links, thus eventually covering most of the companies taking part in the governance knowledge management initiatives.

3.2 ICT Architecture

Information and communication technologies are reported in the literature as enablers of competitive advantage in collaborative networks, which can be achieved through information sharing and flow among CN participants [17]. As for CNs formed in industrial clusters, some authors have reported on the use of Web 2.0 applications for knowledge creation and sharing [18]. Hence, an ICT architecture constituted by a set of ICT applications can facilitate the operation of the knowledge management framework described in Section 3.1. The use of these technologies should not be seen as a requirement for the framework to function, but instead as a complement or facilitator that will enable local governance to create and diffuse knowledge more efficiently and effectively. Figure 2 shows the proposed ICT architecture, as well as some examples of Web 2.0 applications that can be used to support the operation of the knowledge management framework. The ICT architecture is organized as a knowledge portal in which tacit and explicit knowledge can be stored and shared [19]. It will thus be referred to as the cluster's knowledge portal (CKP).

The CKP is a theoretical ICT architecture that makes use of web technologies to enhance knowledge sharing and interactions between firms in the cluster. The applications and databases should be located in a web server at the local governance

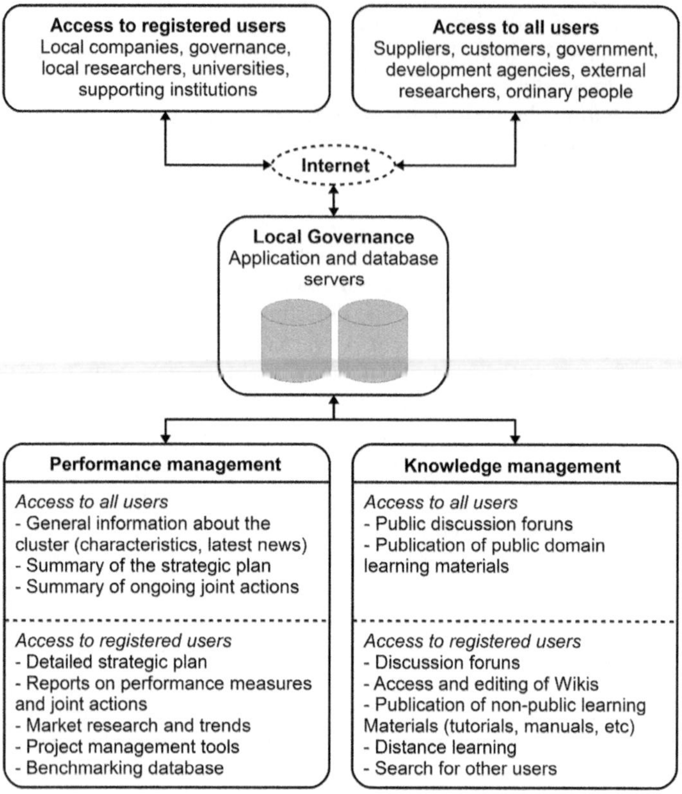

Fig. 2. Set of applications that can be incorporated into the ICT solution to support the implementation of the knowledge management framework for industrial clusters

agency's facilities, in order to avoid conflicts of interest concerning the property of data. The governance agency may manifest as local associations of firms, which implies some level of collaboration and trust among them. Therefore, using the governance agency as the CKP host may increase the likeliness of the applications being effectively used by local firms.

Because the CKP is designed as a web portal and made available using the internet, it becomes necessary to define two levels of access, as depicted in the upper part of Figure 2. Some features should be accessible only to registered users, which are the firms that formally participate in the initiatives promoted by local governance. This requires user account control to restrain access to the applications implemented in the CKP. Users who are not registered to use the CKP applications will only have access to public content that are published as an informative web portal.

As shown in the lower part of Figure 2, the CKP features are divided in two groups. The first group includes a set of performance management features that can be made available for companies to keep track of the cluster's overall objectives, performance measures and ongoing joint actions. The contents of this group are further divided according to their level of access. Hence, general information about the cluster is publically available in the CKP, whilst benchmarking and project management tools are accessible only to registered users.

The features included in the second group aim at increasing interactions and knowledge exchange between firms. By means of Web 2.0 technologies, firms can communicate and generate tacit and explicit knowledge, thus increasing the cluster's overall knowledge base. Some features are accessible to all portal visitors, such as public discussion forums and public-domain learning materials. However, most of the features are targeted to firms and other actors from within the cluster. Companies, universities and local governance can work together in the publication of materials and in the stimulation of local actors towards the adoption of these technologies.

4 Conclusions

This paper contributes to the field of collaborative networks by proposing a theoretical framework that guides companies and local governance located in regional clusters to implement joint actions aiming at creating and disseminating knowledge. Though the contribution is still theoretical, it builds on previous research reported in the literature and creates a more comprehensive framework that integrates KM practices and information and communication technologies.

Implementing the activities outlined in the KM framework requires a certain degree of commitment and trust from all the parties involved. Local governance should be an unbiased and independent agent that promotes initiatives that benefit all the firms willing to support such initiatives. Although the framework gives local governance a central role, it is also possible that joint initiatives concerning KM be initiated by other types of actors as local lead-firms or universities.

Following this idea, installing the CKP applications and databases in the governance agency is suitable for clusters in which collaboration is still incipient, which requires interventions from external actors to occur. In an alternate scenario, where a collaborative network and its participants are mature with respect to collaboration and social capital, the CKP and the KM framework could be operated by one of the firms from the network, instead of leaving this role for local governance.

Future research should aim at testing both the KM framework and the CKP empirically to determine their appropriateness and identify areas for improvement. Based on the theoretical contribution herein presented, the authors will carry out a series of case studies in clusters to determine the levels of importance and adoption of each of the activities and technologies outlined in the KM framework and ICT architecture.

References

1. Provan, K., Fish, A., Sydow, J.: Interorganizational Networks at the Network Level: A Review of the Empirical Literature on Whole Networks. Journal of Management 33, 479–516 (2007)
2. Camarinha-Matos, L.M., Afsarmanesh, H.: Collaborative networks: a new scientific discipline. Journal of Intelligent Manufacturing 16, 439–452 (2005)

3. Porter, M.: Clusters and the new economics of competition. Harvard Business Review, 77–90 (November-December 1998)
4. Steiner, M., Ploder, M.: Structure and Strategy within Heterogeneity: Multiple Dimensions of Regional Networking. Regional Studies 42, 793–815 (2008)
5. Enright, M.J.: Regional clusters: what we know and what we should know. In: Bröcker, J., Dohse, D., Soltwedel, R. (eds.) Innovation Clusters and Interregional Competition. Springer, Berlin (2001)
6. Sölvell, O., Lindqvist, G., Ketels, C.: The cluster initiative greenbook. Ivory Tower, Bromma Tryck AB (2003)
7. Marshall, A.: Principles of economics. MacMillan and Co., London (1920)
8. Schmitz, H., Nadvi, K.: Clustering and industrialization: introduction. World Development 27, 1503–1514 (1999)
9. Gilsing, V.: Cluster governance: how clusters can adapt and renew over time. Paper prepared for the DRUID PhD Conference. Erasmus University, Copenhagen (2000)
10. Carpinetti, L., Cardoza, E., Gerolamo, M.: A measurement system for managing performance of industrial clusters: a conceptual model and research cases. International Journal of Productivity and Performance Management 57, 405–419 (2008)
11. Meyer-Stamer, J., Harmes-Liedtke, U.: How to promote clusters. Inter-American Development Bank (2005)
12. Nonaka, I.: A dynamic theory of organizational knowledge creation. Organization Science 5, 14–37 (1994)
13. Evers, H., Gerke, S., Menkhoff, T.: Knowledge clusters and knowledge hubs: designing epistemic landscapes for development. Journal of Knowledge Management 14, 678–689 (2010)
14. Iammarino, S., McCann, P.: The structure and evolution of industrial clusters: transactions, technologies and knowledge spillovers. Research Policy 35, 1018–1036 (2006)
15. Bullinger, H., Auernhammer, K., Gomeringer, A.: Managing innovation networks in the knowledge-driven economy. International Journal of Production Research 42, 3337–3353 (2004)
16. Bocquet, R., Mothe, C.: Knowledge governance within clusters: the case of small firms. Knowledge Management Research & Practice 8, 229–239 (2010)
17. Chituc, C., Toscano, C., Azevedo, A.: Interoperability in Collaborative Networks: Independent and industry-specific initiatives – The case of the footwear industry. Computers in Industry 59, 741–757 (2008)
18. Adebanjo, D., Michaelides, R.: Analysis of Web 2.0 enabled e-clusters: a case study. Technovation 30, 238–248 (2010)
19. Fernandes, K., Raja, V., Austin, S.: Portals as a knowledge repository and transfer tool—VIZCon case study. Technovation 25, 1281–1289 (2005)

Part IX

Advanced Logistics Networks

From Private Supply Networks and Shared Supply Webs to Physical Internet Enabled Open Supply Webs

Helia Sohrabi[1,2] and Benoit Montreuil[1,2,3]

[1] CIRRELT Interuniversity Research Center on Enterprise Networks, Logistics and Supply Chains
[2] Laval University, Québec, Canada
[3] Canada Research Chair in Enterprise Engineering
{Helia.Sohrabi,Benoit.Montreuil}@cirrelt.ulaval.ca

1 Introduction

The way supply networks are designed has evolved through the years in order to address changes in the business environment, such as increasing customer service requirements, shortening of product life cycles and never ending pressures for inventory reduction. It is thus not surprising that hundreds of supply chain and supply network researches have been reported since the introduction of the concepts, focused on designing supply chains and networks so as to concurrently minimize logistics costs and maximize customer service in a turbulent and competitive environment.

Yet there are still evidences of supply network malfunctions in terms of stock excess, lost orders and unused facility space as the whole supply network is designed and planned at a strategic level long before operation time while the current business environment is fast changing. This urges the redesign of supply networks and their adaptation to real time business.

The Physical Internet (PI or π) recently introduced by Montreuil [1] offers a vision that can potentially enable a fundamental rethinking of supply network design. As one of its thirteen key characteristics, the Physical Internet empowers a global Open Supply Web (OSW) enabling producers, distributors, retailers and users to realize, move and store their products for fast, efficient and reliable response to quickly evolving demand. In such an Open Supply Web, products embedded in standardized modular containers can be dynamically deployed through an open geographically dispersed web of product realization centers, distribution centers, warehouses, hubs and transit centers. In an open supply web, the design of a supply network shifts from being in a strategic long-term decision territory to an operational and tactical decision making territory. It can be finely attuned to market conditions, efficient through better facility utilization and more reliable service to customers, and robust in responding to distributed stochastic demand.

This paper presents an exploratory research study aiming to assess the potential gains associated with moving away from the current ways of supply network design, expressed as Private Supply Networks and Shared Supply Webs, to the envisioned Physical Internet enabled Open Supply Web way. Section two proceeds with defining existing supply network designs and introducing further the concept of Open Supply Web. Section three presents the exploratory investigation, including numerical case

L.M. Camarinha-Matos et al. (Eds.): PRO-VE 2011, IFIP AICT 362, pp. 235–244, 2011.

generation and design optimization. Section four analyzes the experimental results. Section five concludes and synthesizes the value contribution of the paper, discusses its limitations, and provides future research avenues.

2 On the Evolution of Supply Network Design

Here we divide supply network designs introduced in the literature into two major groups; Private Supply Networks (PSN) and Shared Supply Webs (SSW). PSN are single-company focused. The design decisions are made in order to provide the company's products, from sourcing the required materials and components to producing and delivering final products to its clients in its targeted markets. When designing its supply network, the company is bound by a compromise between on one side providing better service and potentially gaining market revenues and on the other side requiring higher investments and incurring higher costs. This impacts its choices in terms of number, location and capacity of facilities in the network, and the service level that they are capable of offering and delivering to their clients in terms of speed and reliability. Illustrations of private supply network designs can be found in [2]-[6].

The compromise expressed above is a strong incentive for companies to engage in partnerships with each other, so as to share their production and logistic facilities as well as transportation means. Partnering companies aim to reduce both investments and operating costs associated with achieving their target service level. The synergistic coupling of their respective supply networks forms a shared network of supply networks, here called a shared supply web. Illustrations of shared supply web designs are discussed in [7,8].

In the private supply network of a company, resources such as facilities are available only to that company. In shared supply webs, resources are available for exploitation in each partnering company's supply network. In a Physical Internet enabled open supply web, companies can exploit any openly available resource and deploy their products dynamically within this open web.

Open supply webs are characterized by (1) their nodes being openly accessible to any actor, be they producers, distributors, logistics providers, retailers or users; (2) the service capacity of their nodes available for contract on demand, on a per-use basis, be it for processing, storage or moving activities; and (3) by dynamic and interlaced virtual private networks created by actors to realize and deploy the products, services and solutions in anticipation of and response to real time business characteristics [1]. Table 1 contrasts the characteristics of existing private supply networks and shared supply webs with those of the proposed Open Supply Webs.

Except in special contexts, strategically designed private supply networks are hard to efficiently adapt to the real time demand and business environment. Shared supply webs allow a higher adaptability, yet are still constrained to the set of partnering companies and their strategic configuration of their shared supply web. When exploiting an open supply web, companies can readily adapt their supply network to the real time characteristics of demand and business environment. They can dynamically realize and deploy their products through a globally extended open web of available facilities.

Table 1. Contrasting characteristics of existing private supply networks and shared supply webs with the proposed open supply webs

Supply Network design	Decision making level	Facility utilization	Geographical extension	Customer service level
PSN	Strategic	Poor as facilities are utilized by a single company through long-term contracts	Constrained to the single company's network	Compromised by location and capacity of single company's facilities
SSW	Strategic	Improved relative to PSN but still constrained to partnering companies and long-term commitments	Constrained to the shared web of partnering companies	Compromised by location and capacity of partnering companies' facilities
OSW	Tactical, Operational	Improved by opening available space to other companies within short-term contracts	Globally extended	Fast and reliable by exploiting globally dispersed open facilities

Open supply webs are currently a vision. Some parts of this vision are dependent on the implementation of the Physical Internet. Some parts can be readily achievable by actors changing their worldview, their mental model of the best way to design supply networks, logistics and facilities.

3 Exploratory Investigation

An exploratory investigation of the potential of open supply webs relative to private supply networks and shared supply webs is introduced in this section. The studied context involves a set of companies, each having to design its supply network so as to best serve its targeted markets. The supply networks here embed factories to make products, distribution centers to serve clients, factory-DC flow links and DC-client flow links. Transportation is limited to truck travel. Here we have simplified the supply network design model to a location-allocation model and assumed that business characteristics such as demand and cost functions are deterministic. In forthcoming research, we plan to extend our investigation to uncertain environments requiring to model adaptability and robustness in a rigorous way, such as proposed in [9]. In the following subsections, the numerical case generation method and the optimization models are described.

3.1 Case Generation: Business, Territory, Demand and Potential Sites

The investigation has been bounded to a maximum of fifteen businesses, each producing a single product in a single factory and serving its targeted markets across the USA and Canada. This geographical area has been divided into 13 regions, four for Canada (northern territories are not considered due to their low population) and nine for the USA (based on US census regions).

Generating a case first involves generating for each company the locations of its customers, its overall demand and the demand from each customer, and the location of its factory. Second, generating a case requires generating the set of potential locations for opening distribution centers. The set of potential customer locations includes the 283 cities in Canada and the USA having a population larger than 100,000 inhabitants. Each company sells a distinct product whose price is randomly chosen between 200 and 400 \$. Annual sales of a company are randomly generated between 10^7 and 10^9 \$. The number of served regions by a company is randomly generated. In each served region, a company has demand in a randomized number of cities, including those with higher population. In each served city, a randomized percentage of citizens are clients of a company. The annual demand in each city for the product of a company is computed from the company's overall demand by applying the ratio of the city's served population over the total number of clients served by the company. Each company's factory is randomly located in one of its served cities. Potential sites for distribution centers include 273 locations at the intersections of intercity highways. Distances between every potential site and every client city as well as every factory are calculated using their road distance from Google Map.

3.2 Design and Assess: PSNs, SSWs and OSW

In this section, the location-allocation models used to respectively optimize the design of each company-specific private supply network, the design of the shared supply webs and the design of the open supply web are described. The models use well known network modeling and integer programming techniques to support the goal of this research to compare performance of different companies designed in three different design modes and investigate the improvement achieved by exploiting an open supply web.

Here are the decision variables and parameters used across the three models.

I_s : Binary variable for the implementation of a distribution center in site s

A_{scp} : Binary variable for the assignment of site s for servicing city c with company p product

F_s : Non-negative continuous variable for the product flow through the distribution site s (one distribution center in PSN and SSW, a potential combination of open distribution centers in OSW)

F_{ps} : Non-negative continuous variable for the flow of company's p product through the distribution site s

F_{scp} : Non-negative continuous variable for the product flow from distribution site s to client city c for company p product

c_s : Throughput capacity of the distribution site s

d_{cp} : Client demand in city c for the product of company p

f_{ps} : Present value of unitary factory-to-site transport cost for site s served from the factory of company p

f_{scp} : Present value of unitary transport cost of products of company p flowing from site s to client city c

i_s : Present value of distribution center implementation at site s

M : A large number

n : Intended number of distribution centers to exploit

t_{scp} : Present value of site-to-city transport cost for serving from site s the entire demand for company's p product by clients in city c

First is the private supply network design model for a company with product *p*.

$$\text{Minimize} \quad \sum_s (i_s I_s + f_{ps} F_{ps}) + \sum_{s,c} t_{scp} A_{scp} \tag{1}$$

$$\text{Subject to} \quad \sum_s A_{scp} = 1 \qquad \forall c \tag{2}$$

$$\sum_c d_{cp} A_{scp} = F_{ps} \leq M * I_s \quad \forall s \tag{3}$$

$$\sum_s I_s = n \tag{4}$$

In this mixed integer programming model, the objective function (1) is minimizing the total cost of opening new distribution centers, transporting products to client cities from their assigned distribution center, and transporting products from the factory to the distribution centers. Through constraint (2), each client city has to be served by a single distribution center. Constraint (3) insures that the flow through a distribution center equals the sum of the demands of all client cities assigned to it, and that no flow can go through it if it is not implemented. This flow is unconstrained, so that the distribution centers are capacitated as needed. Through constraint (4), the total number of implemented distribution centers is constrained to a specified number for experimental reasons.

Second is the shared supply web design model given previously existing private supply networks.

$$\text{Minimize} \quad \sum_{s,p} f_{ps} F_{ps} + \sum_{s,c,p} t_{scp} A_{scp} \tag{5}$$

$$\text{Subject to} \quad \sum_s A_{scp} = 1 \qquad \forall c, p \tag{6}$$

$$\sum_c d_{cp} A_{scp} = F_{ps} \qquad \forall s, p \tag{7}$$

$$\sum_p F_{ps} = F_s \leq c_s \qquad \forall s \tag{8}$$

The objective function (5) of the SSW is similar to that of PSN, except that it is summed over all companies' products and that there are no installation costs, reflecting the fact that in the experiment the partnering companies share the distribution centers that they installed when designing their private supply networks. Assignment constraints (6) are company specified, as contrasted to constraints (2) of the PSN. Constraints (7) compute the flow of company p product incoming each open distribution site s. Constraints (8) sum up the product flow of each company p in each open site s and insure that the open site capacity is not exceeded. In the experiment, the capacity of each site is set equal to the total demand of the cities assigned to it in the PSN, plus an additional percentage experimented with three values 20%, 50% and 70%. The site capacity is expressed in terms of product flow, assuming unit load equivalence among the products.

Third is the Supply Network Exploiting an Open Supply Web design model.

$$\text{Minimize} \quad \sum_{s,p} f_{ps} F_{ps} + \sum_{s,c,p} f_{scp} F_{scp} \tag{9}$$

Subject to constraints (8) and

$$\sum_c F_{scp} = F_{ps} \qquad \forall s,p \tag{10}$$

$$\sum_s F_{scp} = d_{cp} \qquad \forall c,p \tag{11}$$

The objective function of OSW minimizes both distribution center feeding costs and client city serving costs, directly computing the flows instead of relying on assignment variables as in PSN and SSW since clients of each company p may be fed from multiple open distribution sites. Constraints (10) compute the flow of products form the factory of company p to each open distribution site s. Constraints (8) are used to insure site capacity respect. Constraints (11) ensure that the demand of each client for the product of each company p is satisfied form the combination of open distribution sites.

In the OSW model, it is assumed that there is distribution center capacity openly available in each city. The capacity available in a city is considered to be a random number normally distributed with an average set as the total demand of all companies at that city plus an additional percentage (with four values 0, 10, 20 and 50%). The capacity available at intersecting highway locations has been purposefully omitted. Companies exploit available spaces in the currently open distribution centers. To determine the open available capacity in the open supply web, first for each city the total demand over all companies is calculated. Then the closest distance between each site and all cities is calculated. Finally for each site a weighted summation of the closest cities' demand is calculated while the larger weights are assigned to the closer cities. In the experiment, to fix the site capacity, this value has been enlarged by 0, 10, 20 and 50 % and the available capacity is set equal to a normal random number with average equal to any of these four values boosted 10, 20 and 50 %, resulting in twelve capacity scenarios.

4 Analysis of Experimental Results

The private supply network model described above has been solved for each of the fifteen generated companies for four variants each, respectively with one, three, five and ten distribution centers to be implemented. Fig. 1(a) presents as an illustration the optimized private supply network of a company having three distribution centers.

The shared supply web model has been solved for three groups of companies, respectively with five, ten and fifteen partners. Again each of these has been optimized for four variants, respectively assuming that each partner company contributes one, three, five and ten distribution centers. Fig. 1(b) presents the optimized shared supply web for five partnering companies, each contributing three DCs.

The open supply web model has been solved assuming that all fifteen companies are to concurrently exploit it, under twelve distinct randomized capacity scenarios for open distribution centers. Fig. 1(c) displays the resulting massively meshed web, taking a collective perspective displaying the interplay of all flows from all companies, for a given capacity scenario. From an individual perspective, Fig. 1(d) displays the optimized flows associated with one company in the open supply web. Even in this simpler view, it is clear that the individual companies exploit widely more distribution centers than in the other settings, adapting their supply network much more finely to the distributed client demand.

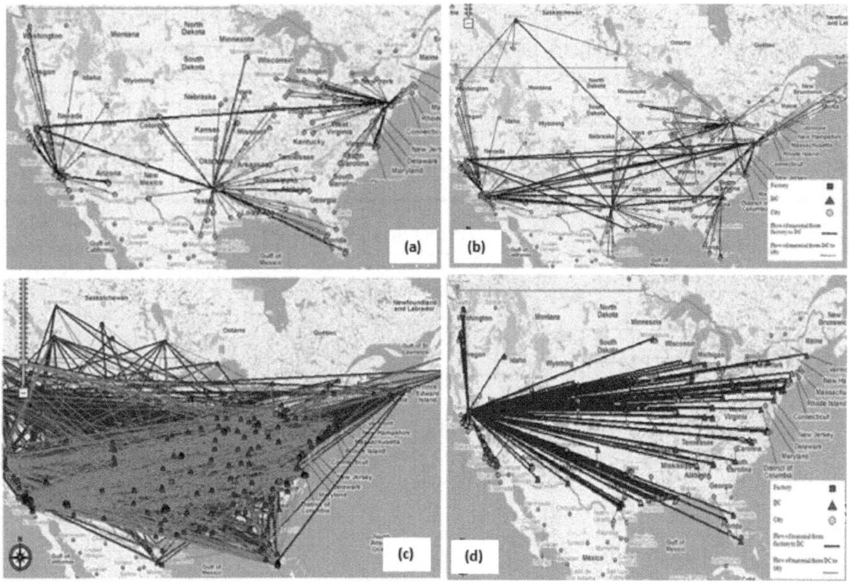

Fig 1. Map of a single company 's private supply network having three DCs (a), shared supply web of five partnering companies having three DCs each (b), Open Supply Web from collective perspective (c) and Open Supply Web from individual company perspective (d)

Table 2 provides a summary of the experimental results, based on model resolutions using the ILOG OPL 5.0 solver. As the three models have distinct objective functions, in line with the experimentation, instead of displaying them, for each set of designs Table 2 provides key comparable surrogate indicators extracted from analyzing the solutions: the scenario-based number of distribution centers available for exploitation as well as the number of distribution centers exploited in the optimal solution, the number of served cities and average delivery time offered to the customers.

The delivery time results assume that each 500 km distance shipment by truck corresponds to a one-day delivery time, considering loading-unloading times and truck speed limits. By increasing the number of companies partnering in a shared supply web, the service coverage attained by private supply networks can be achieved by exploiting a significantly lower number of DCs. For example, when companies each contribute five DCs, the average service coverage is 16 hours exploiting their private supply network while it is 13 hours, 11 and 10 hours respectively when they collaborate in a shared supply web of five, ten and fifteen partners.

In the open supply web, all open distribution sites were available for usage. Out of these 273, 191 were indeed exploited, which is more than available in the biggest sharing strategic partnership in SSW scenarios. Without explicit strategic partnerships with other companies or significant investment, the achieved mean delivery time is 6 hours, which was achieved in the shared supply web only when at least 10 companies entered in a sharing strategic partnership, each contributing 10 distribution centers, engaging at least 100 facilities in which the partners had invested in. is 6 hours, achieved when 10 or15 companies each contributed ten DCs. In the two SSW scenarios where the 6-hour mean delivery time was achieved, the partners did not even exploit all their engaged facilities, 77 out of 100 in one scenario and 114 out of 150 in the other, thus leaving significant unused wasted space.

Table 2. Performance of each supply network design in terms of number of required DCs, mean and maximum delivery time served in the network

Supply network design	Available DCs	Exploited DCs	Mean Delivery time [hr]	Number of served clients
Private supply network (Total over 15 companies)	15	15	90	110
	45	45	25	
	75	75	16	
	150	150	9	
SSW-5 companies- 1 DC each	5	5	57	573
SSW-5 companies- 3 DC each	15	12	19	
SSW-5 companies- 5 DC each	25	22	13	
SSW-5 companies- 10 DC each	50	41	7	
SSW-10 companies- 1 DC each	10	9	54	1087
SSW-10 companies- 3 DC each	30	24	17	
SSW-10 companies- 5 DC each	50	40	11	
SSW-10 companies- 10 DC each	100	77	6	
SSW-15 companies- 1 DC each	15	12	51	1645
SSW-15 companies- 3 DC each	45	37	16	
SSW-15 companies- 5 DC each	75	63	10	
SSW-15 companies- 10 DC each	150	114	6	
Open supply web	**273**	**191**	**6**	**1645**

5 Conclusion and Research Perspectives

This paper has contrasted the concepts of private supply networks, shared supply webs and open supply webs. It then investigated the potential of switching from the formers to an open supply web. The companies exploiting an open web have access to a wide number of open distributed facilities that they can use through short-term contracts without requirement to engage in large investments, long-term leasing or strategic partnerships. Therefore their supply networks can be redesigned in accordance to changes in the business environment of the operation time in an easy, cheap and quick way compare to the conventional supply network designs.

In order to explore the performance potential at stake, a case including 15 businesses serving clients in US and Canada were generated and optimized according to the three studied design alternatives. The results were highly conclusive.

Even though the added synergy potential made it clear that performance improvements were to be incurred when switching from the more restrictive to the more open alternatives, the amplitude of that gain has been highly significant and revealing. Open supply webs allowed companies to achieve the best service coverage by exploiting a large number of open DCs distributed throughout the territory while avoiding large investments, long-term leasing or long-term partnership commitments.

This exploratory investigation has clear limitations, with a case simplified to single-factory single-product companies, a low number of companies and potential sites, no dynamism consideration, known deterministic demand, no inter-company competition, only truck-based transportation, a geographical area limited to Canada and the USA, and performance measures limited to flow costs, investments, delivery time and number of sites available and exploited. Yet the obtained results confirmed the objectives of research, motivating further research toward investigating the potential of open supply webs under more comprehensive and realistic scenarios.

References

1. Montreuil, B.: Towards a physical internet: meeting the global logistics sustainability grand challenge. Logistics Research 3, 17 (2011)
2. Miranda, P.A., Garrido, R.A.: Incorporating inventory control decisions into a strategic distribution network design model with stochastic demand. Transportation Research Part E 40, 183–207 (2004)
3. Sabri, E.H., Beamon, B.M.: A multi-objective approach to simultaneous strategic and operational planning in supply chain design. Omega : The International Journal of Management Science 28, 581–598 (2000)
4. Vidyarthi, N., Elhedhli, S., Jewkes, E.: Response time reduction in make-to-order and assemble-to-order supply chain design. IIE Transactions 41, 448–465 (2009)
5. Goetschalckx, M., Vidal, C.J., Dogan, K.: Modeling and design of global logistics systems: A review of integrated strategic and tactical models and design algorithms. European Journal of Operational Research 143, 1–18 (2002)
6. Martel, A.: The design of production-distribution networks: a mathematical programming approach. In: Geunes, J., Pardalos, P. (eds.) Supply Chain Optimization. Kluwer Academic Publishers, Dordrecht (2005)

7. Pan, S., Ballot, E., Fontane, F.: The reduction of green-house gas emissions from freight transport by pooling supply chains. International Journal of Production Economics, 9 (2010) (manuscript accepted, online access)
8. Nagurney, A.: A system-optimization perspective for supply chain network integration: the horizontal merger case. Transportation Research Part E 45, 1–15 (2009)
9. Klibi, W., Martel, A.: The design of effective and robust supply chain networks, research document CIRRELT. Laval University, 35 (2009)

Remarks on Collaborative Maritime Transportation's Problem Using System Dynamics and Agent Based Modeling and Simulation Approaches

Vanina Macowski Durski Silva[1], Antonio Sérgio Coelho[1], Antonio Galvão Novaes[1], and Orlando Fontes Lima Jr[2]

[1] Federal University of Santa Catarina, Department of Production and Systems Engineering Trindade, Florianópolis, Brazil, 88040-970
vaninadurski@gmail.com
[2] State University of Campinas, Department of Civil Engineering, Campinas, Brazil

Abstract. This paper deals with the collaborative maritime transportation problem which can be modeled with two different approaches: System Dynamics (SD) and Agent Based Modeling and Simulation (ABMS). In the literature concerning this topic they are indicated to model systems containing large numbers of active objects (industries, people, vehicles, warehouses, products) and their applications vary according to the required level of abstraction, which can consider more or less involved details. In order to contribute with the decision-making, one important logistic problem is adopted as example; and in the sequence, a comparative analysis between these two possible techniques to examine such problem is presented. Finally, this study describes how to model this problem using these techniques which improve the analysis of the global behavior of the supply chain. For further implementation, some recommendations are given.

Keywords: Manufacturing industries, System Dynamics, Maritime transportation, Decision taking, Collaboration.

1 Introduction

The understanding of logistics as the integrated planning, control, realization and monitoring of all information and products is becoming more and more dependent on technological innovations. One reason for this is the increasing complexity in combination with a high incidence of factors. Besides, most of people think of complexity in terms of number components in a system or the number of combinations one must consider on making decision, dynamics complexity, in contrast, can arise even in simple systems with low combinatorial complexity. The Beer Distribution Game provides an example: complex and dysfunctional behavior arises from a very simple system whose rules can be explained in 15 minutes [1]. Dynamics complexity arises from the interactions among the agents over time.

In order to support these requirements the integration of new technologies and analysis tools has become necessary. The recently trend is the developments within

L.M. Camarinha-Matos et al. (Eds.): PRO-VE 2011, IFIP AICT 362, pp. 245–252, 2011.

Simulation techniques which are moving beyond the classical methods, propitiating a better overview of the systems, such as logistic and supply chains systems.

In these particular systems, there are numerous elements and actions involved like suppliers, warehouses, trucks, ships, industries, routes and customers, not to mention all. They have been influenced by the changes generated with the globalization which highlight the companies' inability to aggregate internally all the required skills to their survival. Consequently, relationships among companies have become a forceful differential in companies' facilities, which can contribute to their success in the market.

Since taking decisions involves a complex system, companies need to create different scenarios to better analyze the behavior of the global supply chain. Thus, modeling logistic and supply chains scenarios are a challenging work, but it can be done with the use of good tools. The aim of this paper is to discuss a possible way to do it; thus, it contains five main topics including this brief introduction. The second topic exposes one real logistical problem which is difficult to optimize but with the aid of some Simulation techniques can be better analyzed. The third topic presents a comparative analysis between the two possible techniques, System Dynamics and Agent Based Modeling and Simulation, to examine such problem and, the fourth topic comments about how to interpret the mentioned logistical problem using the concept of these techniques. Finally, recommendations for further studies are given at the end of the work.

2 Collaborative Maritime Transportation's Problem

When studying logistic problems the initial step to better understand it is recognizing the main system's elements (industries, warehouses, suppliers and products) and their interdependences. In this topic the collaborative maritime transportation problem will be presented, which can be modeled based on SD and ABMS.

2.1 Maritime Transportation in Case of Exportation

When deciding to export, industries should observe the stages of the process, aiming at knowing its client market, its demands, habits and characteristics. According to [2] it should also define other factors like: transportation mode, specific packing for its product in order to maintain its integrity, freight form to be adopted in the negotiation, as well as the carrier to perform the transportation, besides considering the insertion of an intermediate agent (freight forwarder) or NVOCC (non vessel operator common carrier) in the negotiation.

Since most of the exportations are performed through maritime transportation, the focus in this example should only discuss maritime exportation. Figure 1 shows the main stages of the exportation mechanism.

In maritime transportation the most important active agents are the industries, land carriers maritime carriers, maritime agency, NVOCC, load freight contractor, multimodal transport operator and cargo broker. Upon the performance of a sale or purchase, a delivery destination of the products should be established, where the liabilities should be shared between the vendor and the purchaser. Such liabilities comprise costs and risks on the transaction as well as accordance in the definition of deadline and volume to be transported.

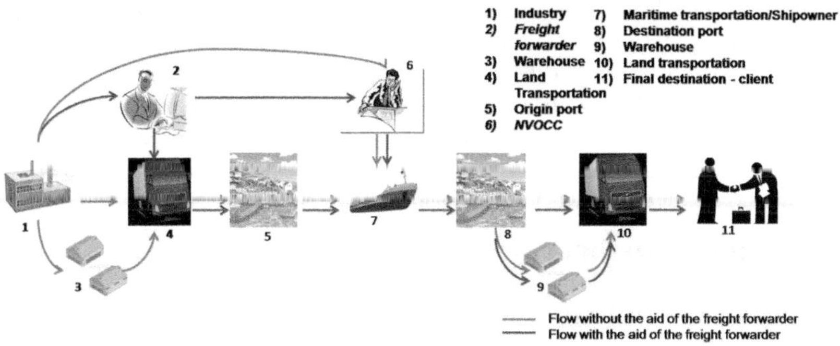

Fig. 1. Stages of exportation mechanism Source: [2]

2.1.1 Transport Negotiation

Normally, in case of transporting general cargo or even pallets, the export industries or the freight forwarder should be able to perform booking of a conventional ship in a regular line (trough a NVOCC or not).

The next step is the decision of a port, as well as the terminal and shipowner/maritime carrier to be used. In the same time, should be evaluated transportation costs, traffic time and deadline for delivering the products. One possibility to be considered is the convenience to have a safety warehouse in another city, which means, to maintain an inventory in any region to solve quickly delivery problems. As a consequence of the planned logistics it is possible to reduce the costs of transportation, inventory level in industries, loss of time on traveling and, finally, problems in the delivery and compliance with sales contract.

It is important to mention the real situation where frequently the maritime carriers decide in a *Freight Conference* the prices to be practiced in the maritime market. In these situations, industries acting alone do not have enough power to better negotiate with them. In situations like this, the concept of collaboration can be applied in order to create groups of industries with the same goal, negotiating with the maritime carriers in order to stop the oligopoly created by them. To a better comprehension about Collaborative Transportation, see [3].

2.1.2 How to Operate in Exportation? Individually or in Collaboration?

After defining the general maritime exportation mechanism, it is observed that it is very ample, comprising several variables and requiring updates regarding volumes, capacity of the ships, prices, maritime fees, extras fees and law among others. One point to be discussed is how the export industries involved in this mechanism should act: individually or in collaboration? If isolated, each exporter industry should analyze the manner to perform the transportation of its products, considering all the stages showed in Figure 1.

Adopting the collaboration concept, another possibility is searching for help from a freight forwarder who arranges such stages. If possible, this professional can join cargoes from several industries in order to achieve economies of scale in the transportation. It can be also performed directly through partnerships among export industries, without the addition of the freight forwarder.

Through this collaboration in the transport activity it is observed the formation of global logistics networks articulating productive areas, not only expanding service coverage but also frequency, efficiency and circulation rate of the products [4].

In this example, the number of involved agents and their transactions can be a limiting factor for optimization techniques. In such case, this problem can be modeled with the use of the proposed tools: SD and ABMS.

3 Simulations Methods

3.1 Comparative Analysis

According to [5] problems can be generally arranged on the scale with respect to the level of abstraction. Normally, supply chains can be modeled in middle to high abstraction range. SD is a traditional approach while ABMS is relatively new. SD deals with continuous processes whereas ABMS deals with discrete time. Each approach corresponds to an abstraction level: SD has the highest abstraction level and ABMS can be used in all of abstraction levels, varying the nature and scale of the elements. Since logistic and supply chain problems involve several elements which cannot be modeled with such detail (varying from medium to high level of abstraction), the ABMS and SD approaches fit better in their analysis. Thus, in the next topics both will be better presented.

3.2 System Dynamics

SD is a continuous modeling and simulation method. However, the method main differential lies in its ability to represent capacity non-linear relationships between the several system variables [1]. This characteristic is extremely useful to understand systems behavioral patterns and its long-term behavior, front the adoption of different management polices and scenarios [6]; [7].

As consequence, SD models are aggregated and have high abstraction level [5]. Thus, some of the methods' limitations are: the difficulty on representing detailed processes as in discrete event processes; the difficulty on modeling activities with fixed duration time and the inability to model complex entities which possess characteristics of decision and heterogeny [7].

3.3 Agent-Based Modeling

Agent-based Modeling and Simulation (ABMS) is a computational method widely used to understand and analyze systems composed of many interacting individuals [7]; [8].

According to [7] the basic principle of the ABMS is: systems are larger than the simple sum of its components and the behavior of the system emerges from the interrelations between these several components. Each one these components has its own set of rules and behaviors, which provides them the ability to affect in greater or lesser degree the system's global behavior.

Unlike other paradigms or modeling methods discussed, there is lack of a universal definition for the key-concept of ABMS [9]. For the authors this deficiency occurs in function of the diversity of science areas that use the concept of agent. One consequence of this limitation is reflected in the ABMS tools. Many of them are not user-friendly. This feature was very important for the popularization of SD method.

Other important method's drawback is the high computational requirements of ABMS when it comes to modeling large systems. ABMS looks at a system not at the aggregate level but at the level of its constituent units. In this case, simulating the behavior of all units can be a extremely intensive computation and therefore time consuming [10].

4 Practical Application and Outlooks

4.1 Application of System Dynamics

When using this technique the first step is to define the system's boundary. For this problem it was decided to consider the actions of the manufactured industries and the maritime carriers. Such consideration represents a simplification of the system showed in Figure 1.

In the second step were defined the agents' objectives and the main variables which influence these objectives. The exports industries' objectives contemplate increase its competitiveness in the market and reduce logistics costs, while the maritime carriers' objectives are the reduction of offer-demand gap and the increase of its profit. These objectives can be reached based on the agents' actions like: increasing collaboration among the export industries and changes in the maritime transportation offer.

The decisions taken by the agents in the way to reach their objectives cause actions and reactions as showed in Figure 2 through the Causal Loop Diagrams. The necessity to reduce logistics costs leads the exporter industries to increase the collaboration with others. As a reaction, the increase of the bargaining power occurs which leads to the freight price decreases and consequently, logistics costs reduction. This reaction is showed in the reinforcing *R1* looping.

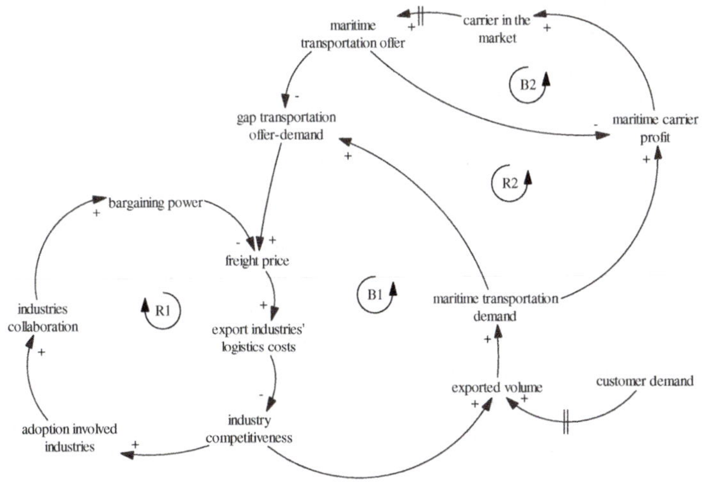

Fig. 2. Reinforcing and balancing loopings between exporters and maritime carriers' negotiation

With the export industries' logistics costs reduction, the export industries increase their competitiveness in the market impacting on the exported volume. Consequently the maritime transportation demand is affected which changes the gap transportation offer-demand. This influences the freight price and also the logistics costs, according to the balancing *B1* looping. The changes in the maritime transportation demand affects the maritime carrier profit, impacting the number of carriers in the market, which changes the maritime transportation offer and consequently, the gap transportation offer-demand. This is showed in the reinforcing *R2* looping. Finally, in the balancing *B2* looping is showed the impact in the maritime transportation offer over the maritime carrier profit.

4.2 Application of Agent Based Modeling and Simulation

As previously mentioned, agent-based modeling does not have a set of standard for the model development and agent representation such as happen on SD method. According to [7] the general steps in building an agent model are the following:

1. Agents: Identify the agent types and other objects (classes) along with their attributes.
2. Environment: Define the environment where the agents will live in and interact with.
3. Agent Methods: Specify the methods by which agent's attributes are updated in response to either agent-to-agent interactions or agent's interactions with the environment.
4. Agent Interactions: Add the methods that control which agents interact, when they interact and how they interact during the simulation.
5. Implementation: Implement the agent model in computational software.

In the maritime transportation problem, the main agents consist of industry, NVOCC, 3PL, maritime carrier, land carrier and customer. A convenient way of representing these agents is through a UML (Unified Modeling Language) class diagram. For example: the industry agent is represented by the following attributes: the agent's name, shipment, deadline, costs, cargo and cargo destination.

In the maritime model, the environment consists of the market where the agents negotiate the transportation. For example: an environment variable could be the offered routes and their related prices. The next step is to specify how the agent attributes are updated during the simulation in response to the agents' interactions both with the environment and/or other agents. As example, an interaction can be the choice of a maritime carrier or the choice of the route.

In the fourth step occurs the definition of the methods that control how the agents will interact. In this model, in every time period the following sequence must be solved: search a partner; choose a NVOCC and/or a carrier and finally, send the shipment. The representation of the agents (their attributes and rules) can be seen in the UML class diagram in Figure 3.

Finally, the last step contemplates the implementation of the model in an appropriated tool. There are several available modeling tools and the selection step must be done in the step ahead which was not performed in this work.

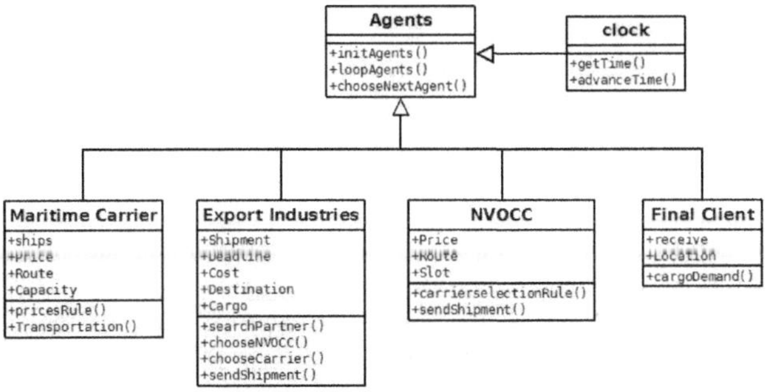

Fig. 3. Agent UML class diagram

5 Conclusions and Further Studies

In this work the collaborative maritime transportation's problem was briefly presented, showing how the interactions among the involved agents occur. After it, two simulation techniques were selected and a comparative analysis between two of them (SD and ABMS) were done. This analysis presents the main differences, drawbacks and technical limitations.

Considering each technique has a different approach for the problem, in section 4 was presented in a summarized way two proposals for modeling the problem in study. As expected, the SD model showed an aggregate view of the problem where the borders among the different agents of the system were blurred. In this case the analysis' point of view is in the policies development, which can support the collaboration improvement and consequently, cause a change in the agents' forces and the system long-term behavior.

On the other hand, the ABMS model permits a better definition of the agents' behaviors and rules. This characteristic allows visualizing how the collaborative behavior will emerge from the interactions between the agents and between the agents and the environment.

For future studies these models will be implemented through the appropriated computational tools which will be selected after a comparative analysis between the several available tools.

Acknowledgments. CNPq/Fapesc Project n° 1.0810-00684 (Pronex), Capes/DFG Bragecrim Project n° 2 and CNPq Project n° 402410/2009-2.

References

1. Sterman, J.: Business dynamics: systems thinking and modeling for a complex world. Irwin/McGraw-Hill, Boston (2000)
2. Silva, V.M.D., Loureiro, S.A., Novaes, A.G.N., Scholz-Reiter, B.: Kollaborativer Seetransport: Beziehungspolitik der brasilianischen Exportkette für Fertigungsprodukte. Industrie Management 27, 23–26 (2011)

3. Silva, V.M.D., Coelho, A.S., Zago, C.A.: Collaborative Transportation Management (CTM): uma nova ferramenta de apoio à cadeia de suprimentos. Revista Tecnologia 30(2), 265–272 (2009)
4. Souza, E.A.: América Latina e sistema marítimo portuário mundial. Anais do 120 Encuentro de geografos de America Latina, 3-7 de abril, Montevideo, Uruguay (2009)
5. Borshchev, A., Filippov, A.: From System Dynamics and Discrete Event to Practical Agent Based Modeling: Reasons, Techniques, Tools. In: The 22nd International Conference of the System Dynamics Society, Oxford (2004)
6. Sanches, L.M.: Análise do acúmulo da demanda logística no final do periodo de comercialização: um modelo de dinamicas de sistema para o setor de bens de consumo brasileiro. Tese (Doutorado) - Departamento de Geotecnia e Transportes, Universidade Estadual de Campinas, Faculdade de Engenharia Civil, Arquitetura e Urbanismo, Campinas (2009)
7. North, M.J., Macal, C.M.: Managing business complexity: discovering strategic solutions with agent-based modeling and simulation. Oxford University Press, New York (2007)
8. Gilbert, N.: Agent-based models. Sage Publications, Los Angeles (2008); Quantitative applications in the social sciences, 153
9. Macal, C.M., North, M.J.: Tutorial on Agent-Based Modelling and Simulation. In: Euhl, M.E., Steiger, N.M., Armstrong, F.B., Joines, J.A. (eds.) Proceedings of the 2005 Winter Simulation Conference (2005)
10. Bonabeau, E.: Agent-based modeling: methods and techniques for simulating human systems. Proc. Natl. Acad. Sci. U.S.A. 99(suppl. 3), 7280-7 (2002)

An Innovation and Engineering Maturity Model for Marine Industry Networks

Kim Jansson

VTT, Technical Research Centre of Finland,
Tekniikantie 2, Espoo, P.O.Box 1000, FI-2044 Finland
kim.jansson@vtt.fi

Abstract. There is only one way for the maritime cluster in Finland to survive. It has to be ready to respond rapidly to changes from the outside world. In order to prepare for the future, design companies and engineering consultants in the marine sector have to assess their current collaboration competence and continuously invest in increasing their engineering capability. It is becoming increasingly important to manage and develop competences for future new business environments. This paper presents a new approach to expanding the use of maturity models with the assessment of innovation and engineering capability. The paper reports on the development work of the new Innovation and Engineering Maturity Model and experience of using the model to identify fundamental and urgent competence development needs.

Keywords: Innovation and Engineering Maturity Model, marine industries, competence development, future business environment.

1 Introduction

The Finnish marine industry has experienced tremendous metamorphosis during the last two or three decades. Outsourcing of activities at all yards has resulted in permanent restructuring of the industry. Thirty years ago, the shipyards produced almost everything themselves. Today, a whole network is needed. The yards have outsourced much of their activities. Today, the yards' main tasks are to manage customer relations from the network to the outside world. Project management and coordination of project operations are other important roles at the yards. The yards also offer facilities for turnkey partners to build large assemblies to their own internal design and planning. These partners have their own sub-networks of specialised partners. The restructuring has imposed new requirements on the partner network but also created new opportunities. Fig. 1

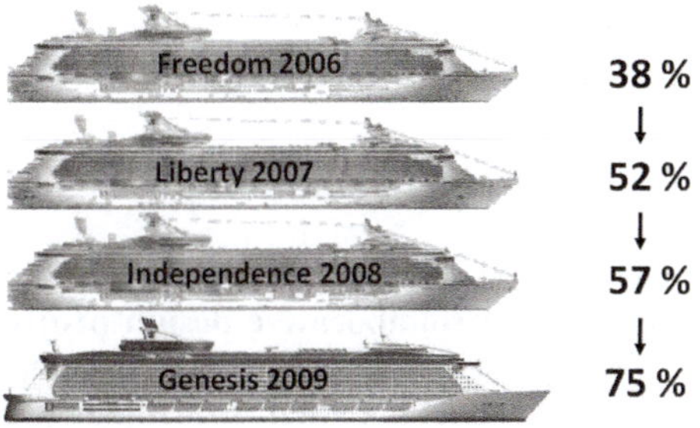

Fig. 1. Development of outsourcing in large ship projects

L.M. Camarinha-Matos et al. (Eds.): PRO-VE 2011, IFIP AICT 362, pp. 253–260, 2011.

illustrates the development of the degree of outsourcing in outfitting work for large ship projects [1]. Using established terminology from the Collaborative Networked Organisation (CNO) research community, the Finnish marine industry can be said to be a Virtual Organisations Breeding Environment (VBE) or Source Network [2], [3].

1.1 From Boom to Recession

The past two decades saw an immense boom in the production of cruise liners in Europe. The project Genesis 2009, illustrated in Fig. 1, materialised in the ship *MS Oasis of the Seas*, which surpasses the biggest cruise ships in size and is now the world's largest passenger vessel. Her sister ship was successfully delivered in November 2010. The past period was characterised by a shortage of labour, the use of foreign workers, engineering work overload, etc. Every company in the industry cluster was operating at full capacity.

The recent economic downturn hit the shipbuilding industry with its full strength. Newbuilding orders dropped to almost zero and the yards and the industry now face major restructuring. There is some light at the end of the tunnel, however, as shipowners placed some new cruise ship orders with European yards in 2011.

1.2 Research Programme

The maritime cluster in Finland has to be agile and ready to respond rapidly to changes from the outside world. Engineering and design companies will operate globally, to an even greater extent, with international customers. To respond to the changed industrial and business requirements, FIMECC Ltd. [4] is working to boost strategic research in metals and engineering industries. The aim of FIMECC Ltd. is to increase and deepen cooperation between companies, universities and research institutes in the area of top-quality research. The FIMECC Innovations and Network research programme was launched in the beginning of 2009 with special focus on marine industries. Its main objectives are to develop new innovations, methods, business models and processes through basic research and industrial innovations to be applied to future generations of prototypes and platforms. The goal is to create a business environment in which product design is based on concurrent engineering, open innovation and the use of global development and production networks. In this changing business environment, competence management is becoming crucial. VTT is contributing to the programme by developing an Innovation and Engineering Maturity Model that will be used to identify urgent innovation and engineering capability development demands.

2 Research Methodology

The overall long-term objective is to develop approaches to support efficient operation in **collaborative design project environments** for marine industries. The objective of the research and development of the Innovation and Engineering Maturity Model is to deliver methods to measure and improve networked design and innovation competence. The scope of the work is limited to engineering design projects, product development and innovation activities, and collaborative and networked engineering activities for marine products and services, including:

- Physical products, possibly extended with services
- Marine and offshore structures, subassemblies and components
- Ship modifications, re-buildings, retrofits and modernizations

The research methodology advances through the following steps:

- Scoped definition
- Review of existing maturity models
- Definitions of requirement for the Innovation and Engineering Maturity Model
- Collecting input for the first model based on company interviews
- Defining the first set of process areas
- Prototype tool development
- Defining the marine industry domain's first reference model
- Positioning interviewed companies in the first model
- Verifying the model through a web questionnaire or web testing
- Improving the model
- Dissemination (continuous)

3 About Maturity Models

A maturity model is a framework that describes a number of levels of sophistication at which activities can be carried out for a specific area of interest. Maturity models focus on different disciplines that an organization can address to improve its business [5]. A maturity model defines a structured collection of elements that describes the characteristics of effective processes. A model can show what is to be done but it does not specify how it is to be done. It is often used to achieve two objectives:

- Help set process improvement objectives and priorities
- Appraise organizations for the sake of improvement

3.1 Previous Work on Maturity Models

Due to the limited space available, this section only references a limited number of previous works in the large domain of maturity models. There are many software-tool-supported maturity models. These models differ from each other in terms of their factors and characteristics: there is no standard related to these models [1].

Pikka describes a five-level maturity model as a framework for the development and assessment of regional business networks. The maturity levels of a business-enabling network are *Initial, Existing, Established, Managed* and *Optimizing* [7]. Essmann et al. describe an innovation capability maturity model. Now more than ever, organizations are required to grow and mature their innovation capability – rending consistent innovative outputs. The process of developing an innovation capability maturity model is presented in [8] and [9]. Narasimhalu also describes a research capability maturity model for managing technological innovations. The suggested maturity model has five layers: *Ad-Hoc, Directed, Managed, Optimized* and *Outsourced.* All research organizations are likely to operate at one of these five levels [10]. Turner et al. describe experimental learning practices adopted by project-based organizations and consider whether they deliver improved project management maturity [11]. Williams states that innovation as a management practice is more diversified than other management methods. Innovation practices can be viewed within the framework of a maturity model. The dimensions and contexts of innovation are very wide and hard to synthesize into a single model however [12]. Stark also suggests a maturity model for PDM implementation with four stages of evolution: *Traditional, Awakening, Adapting* and *Modern* [13]. Tapia presents a two-dimensional, five-level maturity model. It addresses five levels of maturity and four domains to which these levels apply to assess and improve the maturity of business IT alignment in collaborative networked organizations [14].

The COIN project is currently developing an Enterprise Collaboration Maturity Model (ECMM). The ECMM is a process-improvement maturity model that focuses on **Collaboration and Interoperability** capabilities. It consists of a set of best practices that enables the improvement of the collaboration and interoperability capabilities of organizations and networks [15].

3.2 Conclusions of Analysing the Existing Maturity Models

Levels are often used in maturity models to describe an evolutionary path recommended for an organization that wants to improve the processes it uses. In maturity models, process areas can be organized into one of two 'representations': a *continuous* representation or a *staged* representation.

The staged representation offers a systematic, structured way to approach process improvement at company level, one stage at a time. Achieving each stage ensures that an adequate process infrastructure is laid as a foundation for the next stage. The continuous representation offers greater flexibility. An organization may choose to improve the performance of a single process-related trouble spot or to work on several areas that are closely aligned to the organization's business objectives. The continuous representation also allows an organization to improve different processes at different rates.

Many of the models use a five-level approach. The optimum level of maturity is recognised as being the level that delivers the organization's strategic objectives most effectively and efficiently, which does not necessarily mean level five. Most of the software on the market is subject to a usage fee and is not open source. A continuous representation involving five levels was selected as the basis for the new Innovation and Engineering Maturity Model.

4 Requirements of the Innovation and Engineering Maturity Model

Based on the review of existing models and interaction with marine industrial companies, the requirements for an Innovation and Engineering Maturity Model can be summarized as:

- supporting development of competences according to the needs of the future business environment
- accepted by marine industrial companies

- flexible and configurable
- easy to use, intuitive and self-explaining
- web-based benchmarking
- allowing international benchmarking
- free of charge for the marine sector

4.1 What is the Future Business Environment?

The question 'what is the future business environment?' has been addressed in two different endeavours at VTT. The first was conducted with the objective of assessing whether a national development programme was needed to strengthen *project management* capabilities in different industrial sectors. VTT conducted a large number of interviews (>25) on development needs within marine industries. It must be noted that the research was carried out during the boom period, as described above. The main findings were that clustering has made it possible to build, e.g., the two largest passenger ships in the world. Taking care of and further developing the networked organization and collaboration is vital to existence in the future. Based on the research, three general themes emerged that require development effort: 1) technological competence in international and global operations, 2) networking, collaboration and sharing, (re) organising work in large units and 3) sustainable development, green values and security. These themes are by no means new or surprising, but they still require attention.

A second series of company interviews was carried out with the FIMECC programme. The interviews conducted in the recession period also revealed development needs. The results of the interviews gave the first view of industrial companies on the drivers for change in current business operations. A common opinion emphasizes the importance of continuous development of innovative offerings to customers and their customers. Only the forerunners are capable of offering something new each time, and this calls for both technical and conceptual innovations.

5 First Model Defined

The first version of an Innovation and Engineering Maturity Model for Marine Industry Networks (IEMM) was defined based on the stat-of-the-art review and company interviews. A comparison of the interview findings from two different market situations does not show any significant change in the views on the future business environment. The success factors of tomorrow can be summarised and grouped into:

1. Capability to offer solutions to new markets outside shipbuilding (Innovation dimension)
2. Having the courage to act globally, being present in the market close to the customer (in practice, going to Asia) (Internationalisation dimension)

3. Networking and collaboration in efficient supplier relations (Collaboration dimension)
4. Improving the designers' project management skills and capabilities in supervision of work, and awareness of costs and consequences (Project Management dimension)
5. Superior technical knowledge and quality of engineering, and taking environmental issues into consideration (Technology dimension)
6. Knowledge management (PDM dimension)

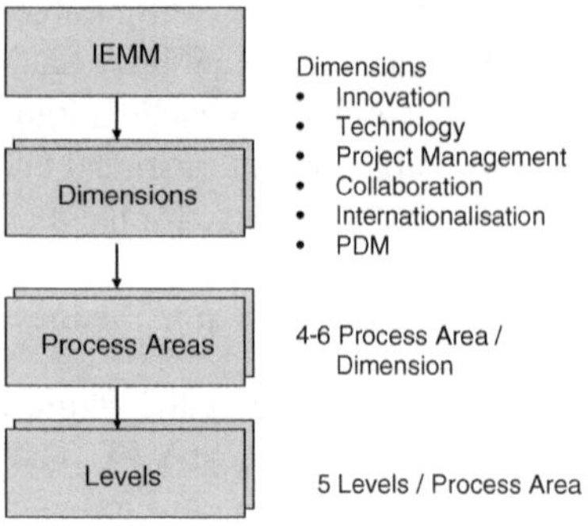

Fig. 2. First maturity model

The six dimensions were then further divided into four to six process areas per dimension; see Fig. 2. For each dimension and process area, five levels of maturity have been defined. Fig. 3 is a partial extract from the model.

Internationalisation dimension			
Process Area:			
Customers	**Staff & Personnel**	**Experience**	**Organisation Nationality**
1 Local customers only.	1 The staff & personnel have no international interaction.	1 Has no international business experience.	1 Has only one office or facility.
2 National customers only.	2 Language skill limit internationalization.	2 Has recognized the need for internationalization.	2 Has more the one nationally located office or facility.
3 Customers within one industry segment only.	3 The staff & personnel have project based interaction with customers abroad.	3 Has project-based international experience.	3 Also has offices or facilities abroad.
4 Customers world wide.	4 The staff & personnel have an open attitude towards international contacts.	4 Capable to manage independently global projects.	4 Has an international presence
5 Business units established near the main customers' base.	5 The staff & personnel are multicultural.	5 Conducts only international business.	5 Also has offices or facilities co-located with customers abroad.

Fig. 3. An extract from the IEMM model

With this model structure, a web questionnaire consisting of 59 questions was established. In the questionnaire, companies were asked to position themselves for each process area **'Today'** and **'Where you want to be in two years from now'**. In addition, they were asked the relative importance of each dimension. All FIMECC partners were invited to participate in the questionnaire, and 23 answers were collected.

5.1 Results of the Model Evaluation

The graph in Fig. 4 gives a summary of the average maturity of the responders. The preliminary analysis reveals that most development is needed in the dimensions: Innovation, Technology and Project Management.

Figs. 5 and 6 serve as examples of results from work the 'Product and services' process area in the Innovation dimension.

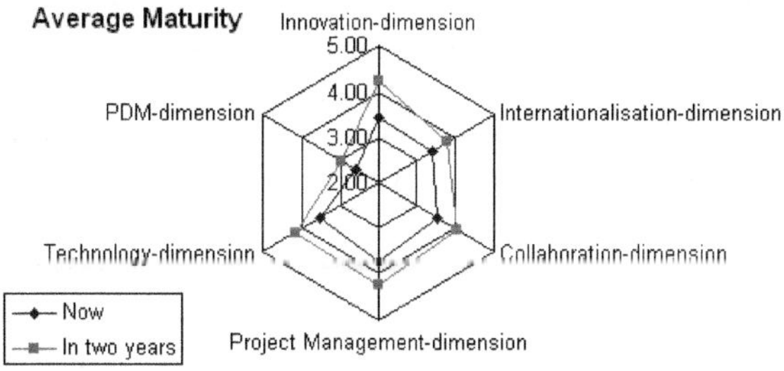

Fig. 4. Average maturity levels

Fig. 5. Current products and services

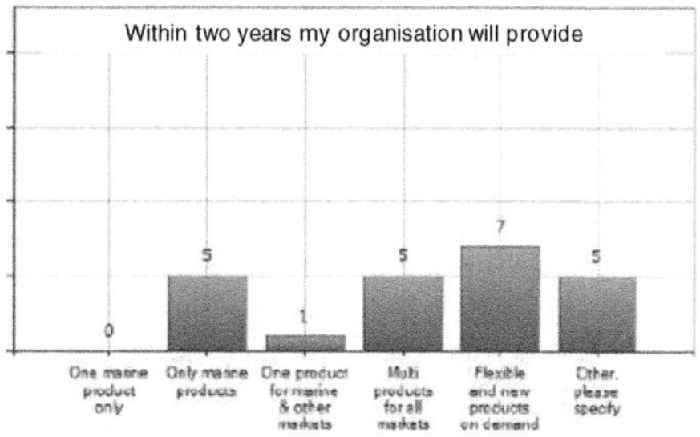

Fig. 6. Products and services within two years

6 Conclusions and Future Work

VTT, together with a number of industrial organizations in the marine sector, has defined and developed an Innovation and Engineering Maturity Model for Marine Industry Networks. The model has been evaluated through an online questionnaire. The preliminary analysis and feedback on use from the questionnaire confirm the usefulness of the model. In the future, effort will be put into enhancing the IEMM and possibly extending it with more process areas. The IEMM must be seen just as a tool, however, keeping in mind that the use of the tool must result in real implementation of competence development actions.

Much valuable and irreplaceable experience and knowledge are already available in the cluster. One question that needs attention is that of how to capitalize also in the future and how to support young people entering the industry branch. The next steps will be to review engineering knowledge transfer methodologies, map them to the Innovation and Engineering Maturity Model and find appropriate suitable knowledge transfer methodologies.

Acknowledgement. This work has been partly funded by Tekes (the Finnish Funding Agency for Technology and Innovation, Finland) through the FIMECC Ltd (Finnish Metals and Engineering Competence Cluster) I&N Programme. We would also like to acknowledge our gratitude and appreciation to all the companies for their contributions to the interviews during the development of the concepts presented in this paper.

References

1. Degerman, T.: Aker Yards, Presentation at the Merike Programme seminar at the Manuo Koivisto Center, Turku Finland (2006)
2. Camarinha-Matos, L.M., Afsarmanesh, H. (eds.): Collaborative Networks: Reference Modeling. Springer, New York (2008) ISBN 13: 978 0 387 79425 9
3. ECOLEAD. IST FP6 IP Project 506958 ECOLEAD, European Collaborative Organizations Leadership Initiative, `http://virtual.vtt.fi/virtual/ecolead/`
4. FIMECC: Finnish Metals and Engineering Competence Cluster, `http://www.fimecc.com/fi/index.php/Etusivu`
5. CMMI. The Carnegie Mellon Software Engineering Institute, Pittsburgh, the United States. CMMI® for Development, CMU/SEI-2006-TR-008, ESC-TR-2006-008, Improving processes for better products
6. Khoshgoftar, M., Osman, O.: Comparison of maturity models. In: 2nd IEEE International Conference on Computer Science and Information Technology, ICCSIT 2009, pp. 297–301 (2009)
7. Pikka, V.: A Business Enabling Network, A Case Study Of A High-Tech Network; Its Concepts, Elements And Actors. Oulu University Press, Oulu (2007) ISBN 978-951-42-8391-8
8. Essmann, H., Preez, H.: An Innovation Capability Maturity Model – Development and Initial Application. World Academy of Science, Engineering and Technology 53, 435–446 (2009)
9. Essmann, H., Preez, H.: Practical Cases Of Assessing Innovation Capability With A Theoretical Model: The Process And Findings. In: 23rd Annual SAIIE Conference, Conference Proceedings, October 28-30, pp. 42–56 (2009) ISBN: 978-0-86970-667-1
10. Narasimhalu, A.D.A.: Research Capability Maturity Model For Managing Technological Innovations. In: Proceedings of PICMET 2006, Istanbul, Turkey, July 9-13, pp. 761–766 (2006)
11. Turner, J.R., Keegan, A.E., Crawford, L.: Delivering Improved Project Management Maturity Through Experimental Learning. Project Management 8(1), 72–81 (2002)
12. Williams, R.: Innovation Maturity. In: Boeing Phantom Works, March 10. ILN Network, Baltimore (2009)
13. Stark, J.: Maturity Model for PDM. In: Product Lifecycle Management: 21st Century Paradigm for Product Realisation. Springer, New York (2004)
14. Tapia, R.S.: ICoNOs MM: The It-Enabled Collaborative Networked Organizations Maturity Model. In: Camarinha-Matos, L.M., Paraskakis, I., Afsarmanesh, H. (eds.) PRO-VE 2009. IFIP AICT, vol. 307, pp. 591–599. Springer, Heidelberg (2009)
15. COIN. IST FP7 IP Project 216256 COIN, Collaboration and Interoperability for Networked Enterprises, `http://www.coin-ip.eu`

Part X

Behavioral Aspects

Addressing Behavior in Collaborative Networks

Mahdieh Shadi and Hamideh Afsarmanesh

Federated Collaborative Networks Group, Informatics Institute,
Computer Science Department, University of Amsterdam
{m.shadi,h.afsarmanesh}@uva.nl

Abstract. Many factors such as weak partner commitment, lack of proper partners' alignment on interest and values, individualism, lack of flexibility, and loss of autonomy may cause partnership's failures in collaborative networks. Most of these serious causes for conflicts in collaborative networks are rooted in partner's behavior, therefore analyzing and modeling the behavioral aspects of collaborative networks are important to enforce their success. This paper first addresses two kinds of behavior related to collaborative networks including *Individual Collaborative Behavior* and *Network Collective Behavior*, and then introduces an approach to measure the comparative individual collaborative behavior of partners in networks.

Keywords: Collaborative Networks, Individual Collaborative Behavior, Collective Behavior, Causal Reasoning.

1 Introduction

With advances in communication and information technology, today organizations can interact and communicate with each other and exchange sensitive information without the traditional limitations of time and location. Collaborative networks, such as global supply chains, support industries to manufacture and deliver products to markets with the required speed and efficiency. A CN (collaborative Network) is an alliance constituting a variety of entities (e.g. organizations and people) that are largely autonomous, geographically distributed, and heterogeneous in terms of their operating environment, culture, social capital, and goals, and that cooperate and collaborate to better achieve common or compatible goals, and whose interactions are supported by the computer network [1],[2].

In general, each organization (or person) involved in a collaborative partnership works and interacts with other members to achieve common or compatible goals. During this interaction partners expose various behaviors, according to the situations in which they are involved. This kind of behavior is called *Individual Collaborative Behavior*, regarding to how one behaves within a CN. If it were possible to analyze, model and predict the organizations' behaviors, many conflicts and difficulties in CNs could have been resolved and ultimate productivity of individuals at the CNs would have been drastically improved [3]. Another kind of behavior related to CNs is the *Network Collective Behavior* which shows the behavior of a group of partners, as a whole. Effective Network Collective Behavior leads to improved CN productivity and

L.M. Camarinha-Matos et al. (Eds.): PRO-VE 2011, IFIP AICT 362, pp. 263–270, 2011.

higher quality, thus more customer satisfaction, as well as more profit and more power for the CNs.

Inspired by the modeling frameworks introduced earlier in the literature related to collaborations and network aspects [4] and considering the complexity of CNs, the ARCON (A Reference model for Collaborative Networks) modeling framework is developed. This framework divides the CNs complexity into a number of perspectives. Its environment characteristics perspective includes two subspaces that cover the internal elements characteristics of CNs, labeled as "Endogenous Elements (Endo-E)", as well as the external interactions characteristics, labeled as "Exogenous Interaction (Exo-I)", that address the logical surrounding of the CNs. The Endo-E subspace consists of four perspectives, as follows: Structural dimension, Componential dimension, Functional dimension and Behavioral dimension [5],[6]. Among these four, the behavioral dimension is the least studied in the research on CNs. However, there are some base applicable research related to human behavior and agent behavior. In [7], the authors show the feasibility of soft control on collaborative behavior of a group by a case study. In [8], a new attempt for modeling and simulation of group behavior in e-government organizations is provided and also [9] presents a qualitative simulation method for analyzing employee group behavior by integrating QSIM (Qualitative SIMulation) with basic causal reasoning. Moreover, some issues such as the small world phenomenon, clustering and power relationships from the area of Social Networks Analysis (SNA) may contribute to this topic. For example, in [10], some indicators related to promote the fairness and transparency are proposed. Some Other indicators, such as reliability, responsiveness, flexibility, etc. are defined in the SCORE model [11] known throughout industrial branches. Standardizing processes within a supply chain because of making the process comparable and compatible is the goal of this model and these indicators are used to measure the performance of organization in supply chains.

This paper is organized as follows: in section 2, the individual collaborative behavior and a new approach to measure the comparative individual collaborative behavior are addressed. In section 3 the Network Collective Behavior is discussed, and finally in section 4 some conclusive remarks are drawn.

2 Individual Collaborative Behavior

The principles, policies, and governance rules that either drive or constrain the behavior of the CN and its member over time, are addressed in behavioral dimension of the ARCON reference model [5]. This may include elements such as honesty and integrity, trust, openness, well performance, professionalism, mutual respect, commitment to network, code of ethics and IPR policy. Considering these governance rules and some other related factors, it is possible to introduce an approach for measurement of comparative individual behavior. Below, we first discuss the importance of the individual collaborative behavior (in section 2.1) and then we explain our approach to model it (in section 2.2).

2.1 The Role of Individual Collaborative Behavior in CNs

Due to the impressive number of both human and organizational behavioral factors found in the analyzed reports, an assumption can be made that probably most partnership failures and successes are strongly related to, if not caused by, the behavioral factors of the involved partners [3]. Good communication, decision by consensus, creativity, fairness, flexibility, best use of interests, knowledge sharing, joy in working together, visible leadership, readiness, open and honest participation, willingness to commit resources and capabilities, development of social skills, transparency in provision of information are behavioral factors leading partnership's success.

Moreover, partners' behavioral factors have a vital influence on their collaboration readiness and establishing trust relationship with other partners, while individual collaborative behavior can be motivated through creation of incentives and rewarding models and mechanisms as a part of CN's governance model.

Analyzing the behavior of a CN's members is therefore necessary. Obviously, the purpose of modeling and analyzing the individual behavior may target specific objectives. These objectives may include identification or prediction of conflicts, selecting the best-fit members to create a new VO, better role and right assignment in CNs, effective membership structure management, and general measuring of individual collaborative behavior in networks.

2.2 Measuring the Comparative Individual Behavior

Modeling and analyzing behavior of CN partners involve different sets of characteristics, and depends on the perspective for which the behavior is considered. Therefore, it is better to consider some perspectives for each of above mentioned objectives.

As such, behavior for a CN partner cannot be represented by an absolute value; rather it can be measured for instance regarding a specific purpose against the behavior of other CN partners. Mechanisms can be defined to assess the individual behavior of a CN partner in comparison to others. For this purpose, every perspective can be characterized by a set of traits / actions. Also, specific metrics (variables that can be measured) and constraints shall be specified for each trait/action.

For example, when a VO planner wants to select a VBE member as a partner for a VO, different aspects of the past individual behavior of that member can be compared with others, according to different perspectives as exemplified by three perspectives presented in table1.

Furthermore, in order to assess the individual behavior, inter-relation among different traits/actions should be studied and well understood. In this work, causal relationships among different traits/actions are used to represent how they influence each other. To present this approach, consider the first perspective in Table1, conforming to past VO regulations. A causal diagram for this example is shown in Figure 1. In this causal diagram, the plus sign (+) indicates that the increase or decrease of the first factor causes the increase or decrease of the second factor, while the minus sign (-) indicates that the increase or decrease of the first factor causes the decrease or increase of the second factor [12].

Table 1. Perspectives, traits and metrics *for partner selection objective*

Perspectives	Traits/Actions		Metrics
Conforming to past VO Regulations (CR)	Punctuality		e.g. average hours/days of delay in product delivery
	Pro-activity		e.g. number of articles published in the press, number of new recommended members, and number of awards won
	Flexibility		e.g. average period of time (in hours or days) to develop or change a new logistic process and percentage of time without process faults
	Responsiveness		e.g. average response time to emails (in hours or days)
	Responsibility		e.g. number of successful collaboration involved, number of responsibilities or roles accepted in past experiences
	Innovation		e.g. average number of industrial patents per year in last five years
	Keeping commitment	Problem/conflict resolution	e.g. number of problems that escalated to VO management
		Willingness to adapt	e.g. percentage of accepted adaptations to new required plans
		Willingness to compensate	e.g. difference between delay in input and delay in output
		providing impulses	e.g. number of suggestions realized for improvements
		Problem avoidance	e.g. provided reaction time (in hours or days) when critical status is reported
		Cooperation	e.g. number of contacts with other VO members
	Trustworthiness		e.g. number of tasks successfully completed
Value Adding to past VOs (VA)	Sharing assets		e.g. number of different assets which a member shares in a VO
	Reputation		e.g. number of Years in business, number of customers, size of market
Special collaborative business Traits (ST)	Being Fair		e.g. number of disagreement on benefits distribution, either against the original contract, or against the consortion majority
	Reuse of existing results		e.g. number of use and provision of references to other member's articles/results
	Tolerance to stress		e.g. number of times pulling out of commitment
	Being courageous		e.g. number of administration roles accepted, number of risks taken
	Information sharing		e.g. frequency of information provision to other collaborators

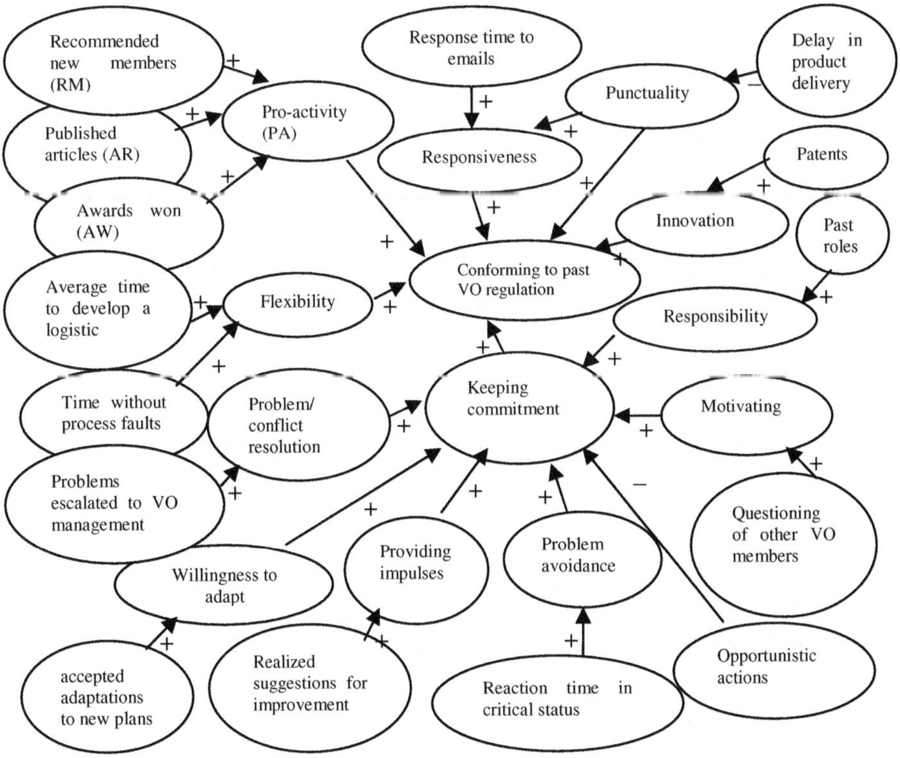

Fig. 1. Quantitative analysis of relations among trait/actions using causal diagram

Causal effects in Figure 1 represent the relations among different traits/actions in form of mathematical equations. By reasoning on the base of these causal relationships, some mathematical formulas can be derived to calculate values for comparative individual behavior of CN members. The plus sign (+) in the causal diagram represents either addition or multiplication, and the minus sign (-) represents subtraction or division depending on the metrics that are related to the traits/actions. The selection of the correct arithmetic operator depends on the metrics that scales it and the balance of dimensions [13], [14]. For example, for measuring the rate of pro-activity (PA), it is needed to add the number of recommended new members (RM), number of articles in press (AR) and number of awards won (AW) as equation 1 shows:

$$PA = RM + AR + AW. \tag{1}$$

The derivative of equation (1) represents the rate of change of each of the factor with respect to time and the relations among the changes, as illustrated in equation 2. The integration of equation 2 provides the accumulation of PA, which represents the total rate of pro-activity for a period of time t_1 to t_2 (equation 3).

$$\frac{d}{dt}PA = \frac{d}{dt}RM + \frac{d}{dt}AR + \frac{d}{dt}AW. \tag{2}$$

$$\int_{t_1}^{t_2} \frac{d}{dt}PA = \int_{t_1}^{t_2} \frac{d}{dt}RM \int_{t_1}^{t_2} \frac{d}{dt}AR + \int_{t_1}^{t_2} \frac{d}{dt}AW. \tag{3}$$

The rates of change as well as the accumulations equation for all factors in Figure 1 can be considered in the same way (according to their relationships). After that, there is a formula for measuring the rate of Conforming to past VO Regulations (CR). Also, it can be done for the other two mentioned perspectives in Table1 (VA and ST). Consequently, to calculate the final comparative behavior score for suitable partner selection objective, we should compute an average of weighted scores of all perspectives, as equation 4 illustrates:

$$Score = average\ (W_1 \times CR\ + W_2 \times VA\ + W_3 \times ST). \tag{4}$$

The weights (W_1, W_2, W_3) shall be defined by experts in the field, depending on the specific type of VO to be established. These weights should belong to the [0,1] interval and the sum of all these weights should be equal to 1. Finally, since we calculate the score for each member in the VBE, when a VO planner decides to select a most suitable member, she/he can compare how they rate against each other.

3 Network Collective Behavior

Analyzing and modeling the Network Collective Behavior which refers to how a group behaves as a whole and the factors which influence it, is more complex than individual behavior. In fact, modeling collective behavior involves contributions from multiple disciplines.

Mechanisms, such as incentives and rewards, assessing of alignment of values and approach applied to the governance of a CN are factors affecting Network Collective Behavior of the CN. These factors are discussed respectively in the following paragraphs.

Incentives and rewards mechanisms may result in changes in the behavior of a CN. Networking sustainability through fair and transparent distribution of benefits, and addressing contributors' expectations are objectives of theses mechanisms. The basis of the incentive system is on the motivation that a CN convinces its participants to be pro-active in relation to business opportunities.

The individual and Network Collective Behavior in a CN are influenced by the *value system* of network members. Therefore, it is important to identify the value system of the networks and their individual members to have an improved collaborative process. A CN consists of independent and autonomous entities which each of them has its own value system. Many conflicts among partners might come up because of misalignment of values. In the absence of identical value systems, the members' perceptions of the results of the collaboration processes may be different and consequently, they may show some non-collaborative behaviors, such as unwillingness to share knowledge and other inter-organizational disagreements [15].

CN Governance includes some structures, principles and rules for resources allocation and rights assignment. Moreover, it supervises the entities and activities within a CN. Governance and the behavioral aspects influence each other, mutually. The constraining rules of CN governance may lead changes in collective and individual behavior of network members, and also behavioral aspects such as character of a CN member influence the CN's governance.

For modeling the Network Collective Behavior, it is needed to identify the objectives, perspectives, traits/actions and metrics such as presented for modeling the individual collaborative behavior in the previous section. In this case, objectives may include improving: customer satisfaction, benefits to CN, CN achieving more power in the market/society. These objectives can be considered according to the two perspectives: financial and social perspectives.

4 Conclusion

Quantitative causal modeling is a powerful aid to understand and enable practical decisions about what might be the best action to take in a certain circumstance. Therefore, in our approach we measure the comparative individual collaborative behavior by using quantitative causal modeling. This approach could lead to identify or predict conflicts, select the best-fit VO members, assign the roles and rights in CNs more effectively, and measure the individual collaborative behavior in networks. Analyzing and improving the individual collaborative behavior of CN members will influence the Collective Behavior of the CN. According to our approach, partners' behavior could be compared with each other, and partners will be informed that enhancing their individual behavior will result in more success in their collaboration. As such, improving the individual behavior through factors such as incentives and rewards as well as alignment of values and fairness in governance rules are proposed to influence the network's collective behavior.

References

1. Camarinha-Matos, L.M., Afsarmanesh, H.: Collaborative networks: Value creation in a knowledge society. In: Knowledge Enterprise: Intelligent Strategies in Product Design, Manufacturing and Management, pp. 26–40. Springer, Heidelberg (2006)
2. Afsarmanesh, H., Ermilova, E., Msanjila, S.S., Camarinha-Matos, L.M.: Modeling and Management of Information Supporting Functional Dimension of Collaborative Networks. In: Hameurlain, A., Küng, J., Wagner, R. (eds.) Transactions on Large-Scale Data- and Knowledge-Centered Systems I. LNCS, vol. 5740, pp. 1–37. Springer, Heidelberg (2009)
3. Rosas, J.: Assessing organizations collaboration readiness, a behavioral approach. PhD thesis (2009)
4. Camarinha-Matos, L.M., Afsarmanesh, H.: A comprehensive modeling framework for collaborative networked organizations. The Journal of Intelligent Manufacturing 18(5), 527–615 (2007)
5. Camarinha-Matos, L., Afsarmanesh, H.: On reference models for collaborative networked organizations. International Journal of Production Research 46(9), 2453–2469 (2008)

6. Afsarmanesh, H., Camarinha-Matos, L.M.: The ARCON modeling framework. In: Collaborative Networks Reference Modeling, pp. 67–82. Springer, Heidelberg (2008)
7. Han, J., Li, M., Guo, L.: Soft control on Network Collective Behavior of a group of autonomous agents by a shill agent. Jrl. Syst. Sci. & Complexity, 54–62 (2006)
8. Wu, J., Hu, B.: Modeling and simulation of group behavior in e-government implementation. In: Proceeding of the 2007 Winter Simulation Conference, pp. 1284–1291 (2007)
9. Hu, B., Gongcheng, X.: Integrated Description and qualitative simulation method for group behavior. Journal of Artificial Societies and Social Simulation 8(2) (2005)
10. Abreu, A.: A contribution to the development of a theory for collaborative networks. PhD Thesis, New University of Lisbon (2007)
11. Beamon, B.M.: Measuring supply chain performance. International Journal of Operations and Production Management 19(3), 275–292 (1999)
12. Pearl, J.: Causality Models Reasoning, and Inference. Cambridge University Press, Cambridge (2000)
13. Krikwood, C.W.: System Dynamics Method. Ventana System Inc. (1998)
14. Ge, Y., Yang, J.B., Proudlove, N., Spring, M.: System dynamics modeling for supply-chain management. The International Transactions in Operational Research 11, 495–509 (2004)
15. Camarinha-Matos, L.M., Macedo, P.: Towards A Conceptual Model Of Value Systems In Collaborative Networks. Virtual Enterprises and Collaborative Networks, 53–64 (2007)

Issues on Conflict Resolution in Collaborative Networks

Davide Carneiro[1], Paulo Novais[1], Flávio Lemos[1],
Francisco Andrade[2], and José Neves[1]

[1] Department of Informatics,
University of Minho, Braga, Portugal
{dcarneiro,pjon,jneves}@di.uminho.pt, pg15990@uminho.pt
[2] Law School, University of Minho, Braga, Portugal
fandrade@direito.uminho.pt

Abstract. Conflicts are frequent in virtually every scenario involving complex interactions. Collaborative Networks, in which there is a compromise between skills, competencies and resources, are not an exception. Moreover, these conflicts can be different in nature, ranging from cultural or relational conflicts to conflicts of interests. Although conflicts are common in these virtual settings, very few tools exist to settle them. Therefore, parties involved in conflict resolution generally have to resort to traditional approaches, which delay the process and waste the advantages of these Virtual Organizations. In this paper we present a structured model of a contract for a Collaborative Network. Based on this model, we developed an information system which is able to build conflict scenarios and determine the possible and probable outcomes. We combine this development with the UMCourt platform, which comprises a rich negotiation and mediation tool, to build a conflict resolution framework in the context of Collaborative Networks.

Keywords: Virtual Organization, Conflict Resolution, Decision Support System.

1 Introduction

Conflicts are natural and emerge as a consequence of our complex society, in which each individual focuses on the maximization of the own gain. A conflict can be seen as an opposition of interests or values which, in a certain way, disturbs or blocks an action or a decision making process. In order for the action to be carried out, the conflict has to be solved [1]. The concept of conflict and its resolution is usually addressed by two main scientific fields: Social and Information Science. The intersection of these two fields is of great interest, particularly from the point of view of a Virtual Organization (VO).

In fact, conflicts in VOs are frequent given the unstable balance between skills, competencies and resources. These conflicts are generated in virtual settings, most of the times supported by an electronic contract. However, very few tools exist to settle conflicts inside their context. As a consequence, conflicting members have to resort to traditional conflict resolution methods, throwing away significant advantages of VOs,

L.M. Camarinha-Matos et al. (Eds.): PRO-VE 2011, IFIP AICT 362, pp. 271–278, 2011.

rendering them inefficient. The use of technology to develop tools that can support the conflict resolution process, together with the creation of virtual environments for that purpose is thus of interest. Moreover, Pitt et al. address the issue of the costs of conflicts in the context of VO and the need for alternatives to litigation [2]. In particular, the authors argue that litigation is a slow and costly process which may have a significant impact on the business of companies and governments. The potential for appeals also adds to the amount of delay and cost.

In this paper we present a model for an electronic contract that defines the rules that govern the lifecycle of the VO, focusing on solving Operational Conflicts. Given its structured nature, this model can be handled by a software agent. Specifically, we are interested in developing software agents able to point out the consequences of violating specific rules. The integration with the UMCourt conflict resolution platform [9], specialized in negotiation and mediation algorithms, allows the development of a framework for conflict resolution in line with the recent trend of Online Dispute Resolution (ODR) [3]. In this work we take into consideration the work of prof. Lewiki et al. [6] and Goldberg et al. [8] on the dynamics and processes of conflict resolution, and the work of Raiffa [7] on decision theory and negotiation analysis. During its development, an agent-based approach was followed [10, 11].

2 Conflicts in Virtual Organizations

Conflicts are part of the lifecycle of the VO and should be regarded as natural. Moreover, depending on how well they are managed, conflicts can even be seen as a catalyst for the success of the VO. When it comes to conflicts, solving them in VOs may, at first sight, appear to have an added challenge, when compared to traditional conflicts: the environment of the conflict is a virtual one (e.g. no physical interaction, no social contact, geographical dispersion of members). As a way to overcome these challenges, Online Dispute Resolution tools can be used that support distributed and asynchronous conflict resolution. Such tools aim conflict resolution methods processes that are agile and flexible, in line with the requirements of the VO.

The nature of the conflict in a VO can be quite diversified. Taking ARCON [11] as a reference model, several types of conflicts can be identified. Considering the intrinsic nature of the VO, four dimensions can be pointed out in which conflicts are likely to emerge:

- *Structural dimension*: this dimension includes features related to the structure and composition of the VO, including the members, their relation and roles;
- *Component dimension*: includes hardware/software/human resources as well as knowledge or information;
- *Functional dimension*: includes all the tasks and functionalities supported by the VO as well as methodologies and process models;
- *Behavioral dimension*: includes guidelines for cooperation or conflict resolution, contracts, policies and governance rules applicable to all the members.

On the other hand, considering the environment around the VO, another four dimensions in which conflicts may raise can be identified:

- *Market dimension*: includes the issues related to the interaction of the VO with external entities *such* as clients and competitors;
- *Support dimension*: this *dimension* refers to external support services, including certification, financial or insurance;
- *Social dimension*: *includes* the impact of the VO on the society, including in issues like employability, legal, or educational.
- *Constituent dimension*: models the impact and consequences of the integration of potential *new* members, including issues like sustainability or membership rules.

After performing an analysis of these eight dimensions, it is possible to identify the main types of conflict that can arise in the context of a VO:

- *Operational Conflicts*: operational conflicts emerge from situations in which the norms established in the creation (or modified during the operation) of the VO are being *violated*. Conflicts may emerge from a member not providing a given service as contracted, lack of communication, refusal to share some resource or general infringement of the governance rules;
- *Relational conflicts*: although the members of the VO are independent, they are inter-dependent in terms of *resources*. Trust is thus an important factor. Incompatibilities in the interactions between the members can be seen as relational conflicts. These conflicts can be originated by past negative experiences that influence the level of trust;
- *Conflicts of interests*: the correct availability and use of resources is fundamental for the correct operation *of* a VO. This kind of conflicts is generally related with the misuse of resources, namely the scenarios in which members use resources of the VO outside of its scope;
- *Business strategy conflicts*: members of VO are generally attracted by the eventual access to new technologies, *markets* or information. However, this can be seen as a threat by the members sharing these resources. These conflicts are more evident in the initial phase of the VO, when the members are defining the availability and access to resources and tend to diminish with the time;

3 Monitoring Conflicts in Virtual Organizations

The contracting process in a VO is an important aspect in which the activities of the members of the organization are depicted. The result of this process is a contract in which the VO is described in all its dimensions. Contracts define the role of each member as well as the rules and operating principles of the organization. In that sense, the monitoring of a contract throughout the lifecycle of the VO, mainly during the operational phase, is of utmost importance. In this section we describe the structure of the contract and the monitoring mechanism, developed to deal with Operational Conflicts.

3.1 The Contract

Given that contracts are essential for the detection of Operational Conflicts, there is the need for a contract model that allows representing all the endogenous elements of the VO, with a special focus on the behavioral and structural dimensions. Based on several works on the field [12 - 14], it is possible to define a contract model from a logical point of view, with four central components:

- ***Actions*** – are seen as atoms and describe what each member can do. An action is defined as a 4-tuple: $a = (name, sender, receiver, t)$, where *name* is the unique identifier of the action, to be executed by the *sender*, whose recipient is *receiver*, in time *t*. The set of all possible actions within the scope of a contract is defined as: $A = \cup\, a_i$
- ***Events*** – identify the events that take place within the environment of the organization. Events are defined as: $e = \left(a(n, s, r, t), event_{type}\right)$, where $a \in A$ and $event\_type \in \{fact, fulfill, violated\}$ describes the type of event. In this description, *fact* denotes that an action *a* occurred in a given time, *fulfill* denotes that an action *a* was fulfilled in a given time and *violated* denotes that there has been a violation of a norm in a given instant;
- ***Obligation*** – identify all the obligations that can be subscribed by the members of the organization. An obligation is defined as: $o = (a(n, s, r, t), liveline, deadline)$, where $a \in A$ denotes an action that must be executed within a timeframe defined as $[liveline, deadline]$;
- ***Norms*** – establish the rules that will guide the behaviour of the members of the *organization*. A norm is defined as: $n = (name, antecedent, consequent)$, where *name* is the unique identifier of the norm and *consequent* describes obligations that must be implemented when a given *antecedent* (an event) is true.

Based on this, a model for a contract has been defined using XML Schema, a rich data typing system that allows defining the structure of XML documents with detailed constraints on its logical structure. Instances of contracts are thus XML files.

3.2 Monitoring Conflicts

In order to monitor the emergence of conflicts during the operation of the VO, a software agent was developed that is able to interpret the contract defined. This model works under the assumption that members of the VO advertise their actions in the form of events, i.e., the model will fail if a member hides his actions from the rest. Thus, during the operational phase, the members of the VO use a framework for advertising actions. The approach followed consisted in developing a software agent that constantly monitors these actions in search for violations of contract. On initialization, it interprets the contract and creates a temporal knowledge base describing the norms, the state of the VO, among other issues. This agent is built by two main modules: *Inference* and *Communication*. The *Communication* module is responsible for establishing a bridge between the framework and the inference mechanism. In that sense, it receives the events and forwards them to the *Inference* module, receiving back messages that it will forward to the framework, in order to inform the members. The *Inference* module is implemented in Prolog, a general purpose logic programming language. In that sense, the rules and facts retrieved from the contract and forwarded by the *Communication* module are represented in the form of Horn clauses.

Whenever a new event arrives in the *Inference* module, it is added to the knowledge base. The inference mechanism will then check if there is a norm $n = (name, event, obligation)$ whose antecedent $(event)$ is true. If that is the case, the inference mechanism will point out the resulting obligation. This obligation will be added to a set *M* of obligations under monitoring. *M* is defined as: $M = \cup \{(o, s)\}$, where *o* represents an obligation and $s \in \{fullfilled, pending, violated, pre\_violated\}$ its state.

Definition 1. Given an event $\mathbf{e} = (\mathbf{action_a}(\mathbf{n_a}, \mathbf{s_a}, \mathbf{r_a}, \mathbf{t_a}), \mathbf{event\_type})$ and an obligation $\mathbf{o} = (\mathbf{action_b}(\mathbf{n_b}, \mathbf{s_b}, \mathbf{r_b}, \mathbf{t_b}), \mathbf{liveline}, \mathbf{deadline})$, *o* is considered to be fulfilled when $\mathbf{action_a} = \mathbf{action_b}$ and $\mathbf{t} \in [\mathbf{liveline}, \mathbf{deadline}]$. Otherwise, the event *e* does not satisfy obligation *o*.

In order to monitor all the obligations in *M*, the software agent goes through all of its members at regular intervals, with the objective of updating the state of each obligation. As stated above, in a given time instant *t*, the state of an obligation *o* can be one of four:

- ***Fulfilled*** – when there is an event *e* such that *o* is fulfilled;
- ***Pending*** – when there is no event *e* such that *o* is fulfilled and $t < liveline$;
- ***Violated*** – when there is no event *e* such that *o* is fulfilled and $t > deadline$;
- ***Pre_Violated*** – when there is no event *e* such that *o* is fulfilled and $t \in [\text{liveline}, \text{deadline}]$.

Whenever there is a pair $(o, e) \in M$ such that $e = \text{violated}$, the inference builds and sends a message to the *Interface* module describing the occurrence. The interface will then identify all the members directly and indirectly involved in the action associated with obligation *o*. The members will then decide the course of action. To do it, they may make use of a negotiation platform being developed under the scope of the TIARAC project, presented in the following section.

4 Reaching an Outcome

Members of the VO can use the previously depicted method as a decision support system, to detect violations of contract and possible solutions, in the form of actions. However, the members may not agree on the solution. In that sense, this work was integrated with a negotiation support tool developed in the context of the TIARAC project – *Telematics and Artificial Intelligent in Alternative Conflict Resolution*. The negotiation tool is based on the Case-based Reasoning paradigm. In that sense, it implements an algorithm that looks into past similar conflicts and their respective solutions [15, 16] (Figure 1). It is a dynamic method in the sense that it is able to adapt strategies according to how the process evolves. In that sense, it considers parameters like trust, the attitudes of each member or the historic of actions.

It is now possible to provide a general view on how the whole process develops (Figure 2). At the beginning, the VO is created and a contract is defined according to the model. In the Monitorization module, a logical representation of the norms is created and stored in the knowledge base. When the VO reaches the operational phase, the process develops around the interactions between the members. Whenever a new event is published by a member, it is forwarded to the Monitorization module, which in turn will check if there is any norm whose antecedent matches the event. If it is true, it will check if the antecedent is violated, in which case a notification is sent to the members of the VO and a conflict resolution process starts.

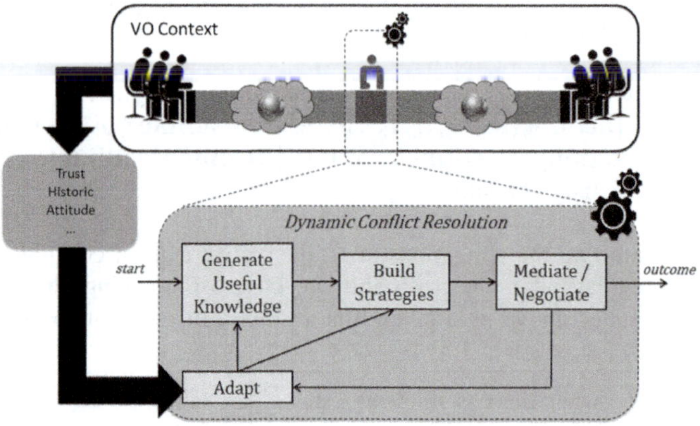

Fig. 1. High level view of the conflict resolution process in the context of a VO

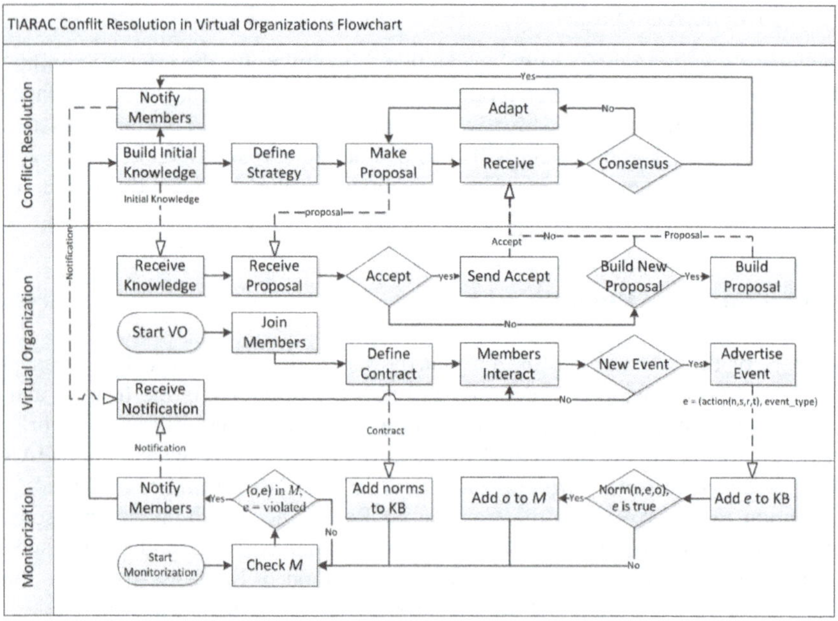

Fig. 2. The flowchart of the Conflict Resolution process in Virtual Organizations

The process starts by building initial knowledge that is made available for the members. To select this knowledge, the algorithm analyzes past known conflicts and assesses their similarity in terms of the contracts and the nature of the norms addressed and violated. Based on this, it selects a list of relevant cases (i.e. cases above a given threshold of similarity) and sorts them according to that value of similarity. From this point on, the conflict resolution process develops in repetitive rounds. In each round the Conflict Resolution module proposes a solution (retrieved from the similar cases). Each member of the VO may accept it, reject it or build new proposals for solution (Figure 3). If there is a consensus on the proposals sent by the members, the process ends successfully and the VO may resume its activity. If there is no consensus, the system will adapt its strategy and propose a new solution. This process goes on until all members agree on a solution or at least one member leaves the process.

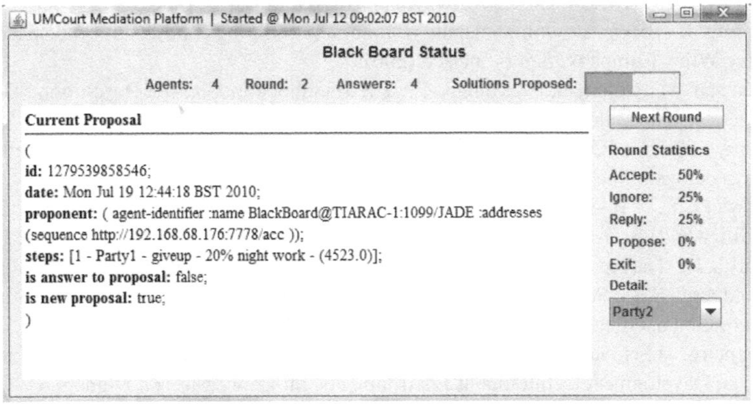

Fig. 3. The interface for the *blackboard* agent, responsible for the control of the lifecycle of the negotiation

5 Conclusions

In a broad sense, conflicts configure an obstacle in a decision making or action taking process. In that sense, for the action to be carried out, the conflict must be solved first. Inefficient conflict resolution mechanisms may delay these processes. This is particularly disturbing in the context of VOs, especially when no technology-based tools exist to support the process, throwing away significant advantages of this organization paradigm. Particularly negative are the costs and time spent litigating in court, which has a significantly negative impact on the performance of governments and companies. In this paper we presented a tool for conflict resolution, based on the paradigm of Online Dispute Resolution. This tool consists of two main components. The first one constantly monitors the actions of the members of the VO and, with a representation of the contract, determines when a violation occurs, pointing out the obligations of the parties involved. The second component comprises a negotiation tool which allows the members to work out a satisfactory solution. This tool considers past similar problems to more efficiently propose solutions that can rapidly lead to the resolution of the conflict. With this approach we expect to achieve conflict resolution mechanisms fit for the context of Virtual Organizations.

Acknowledgments. The work described in this paper was developed under the TIARAC - Telematics and Artificial Intelligence in Alternative Conflict Resolution Project (PTDC/JUR/71354/2006), a research project supported by FCT (Science & Technology Foundation), Portugal. The work of Davide Carneiro is supported by a doctoral grant by FCT (SFRH/BD/64890/2009).

References

1. Lewin, K.: Resolving social conflicts: Field theory in social science. American Psychological Association (1997) ISBN 1557984158
2. Pitt, J., Ramirez-Cano, D., Kamara, L., Neville, B.: Alternative Dispute Resolution in Virtual Organizations. In: Artikis, A., O'Hare, G.M.P., Stathis, K., Vouros, G.A. (eds.) ESAW 2007. LNCS (LNAI), vol. 4995, pp. 72–89. Springer, Heidelberg (2008)
3. Katsch, E., Rifkin, J.: Online dispute resolution – resolving conflicts in cyberspace. Jossey-Bass Wiley Company, San Francisco (2001)
4. Deutsch, M., Coleman, P., Marcus, E.: The Handbook of Conflict Resolution: Theory and Practice. John Wiley and Sons, Chichester (2006)
5. Peruginelli, G., Chiti, G.: Artificial Intelligence in alternative dispute resolution. In: Proceedings of the Workshop on the law of electronic agents – LEA (2002)
6. Lewicki, R.J., Barry, B., Saunders, D.M., Minton, J.W.: Negotiation, 4th edn. McGraw-Hill/Irwin, Boston (2003)
7. Raiffa, H.: The Art and Science of Negotiation. Harvard University Press, Cambridge (2002)
8. Goldberg, S.B., Sander, F.E., Rogers, N., Cole, S.R.: Dispute Resolution: Negotiation, Mediation and Other Processes. Aspen Publishers, New York (2003)
9. Carneiro, D., Novais, P., Costa, R., Neves, J.: Enhancing the Role of Multi-agent Systems in the Development of Intelligent Environments. In: Demazeau, Y., Dignum, F., Corchado, J.M., Bajo, J., Corchuelo, R., Corchado, E., Fernández-Riverola, F., Julián, V.J., Pawlewski, P., Campbell, A. (eds.) Trends in PAAMS. AISC, vol. 71, pp. 123–130. Springer, Heidelberg (2010) ISBN 978-3-642-12432-7
10. Wooldrige, M.: An Introduction to Multiagent Systems. John Wiley & Sons, Chichester (2002)
11. Camarinha-Matos, L.M., Afsarmanesh, H.: Towards a Reference Model for Collaborative Networked Organizations. In: Information Technology for Balanced Manufacturing Systems. IFIP, vol. 220, pp. 193–202 (2006), doi:10.1007/978-0-387-36594-7_21
12. Boella, G., van der Torre, L.: Contracts as Legal Institutions in Organizations of Autonomous Agents. In: Jennings, N.R., Sierra, C., Sonenberg, L., Tambe, M. (eds.) Third International Joint Conference on Autonomous Agents & Multi Agent Systems, pp. 948–955. ACM Press, New York (2004)
13. Xu, L.: A multi-party contract model. ACM SIGecom Exchanges 5(1), 13–23 (2004)
14. Cardoso, L., Oliveira, E.: A contract model for electronic institutions. In: Sichman, J., Padget, J., Ossowski, S., Noriega, P. (eds.) COIN 2007. LNCS (LNAI), vol. 4870, pp. 27–40. Springer, Heidelberg (2008)
15. Carneiro, D., Novais, P., Andrade, F., Neves, J.: Using Mediation to Solve Disputes with Avoiding Parties. In: Proceedings of the JURISIN 2010 – Fourth International Workshop on Juris-informatics, Tokyo, Japan, pp. 17–28 (2010) ISBN 978-4-915905-42-1
16. Carneiro, D., Costa, A., Novais, P., Andrade, F., Neves, J.: Providing Relevant Knowledge in Disputes. In: Proceedings of the 6th International Workshop on Online Dispute Resolution, JURIX 2010, pp. 63–78 (2010)

A Product-Oriented Power Taxonomy Framework

Yan Liu and Marc Zolghadri

IMS, UMR CNRS 5218, University of Bordeaux 1, 351 Cours de la Liberation, 33405 Talence, France
firstname.familyname@ims-bordeaux.fr

Abstract. Power of partners in supply chain is an essential concept in collaboration, which can influence the decisions and behaviours of the focal company. Therefore, any company has to have a good understanding on the power of partners in order to determine the possible opportunities or threats in a potential collaboration. In this paper we present a product-oriented power taxonomy obtained from the analyses on two classes of power factors: the partner-independent power factors and the partner-dependent power ones. The former are related to the product and market while the latter are intrinsic ability factors of partner such as reputation, knowledge and performance. Then we analyse the different aspects of each type of power and corresponding determinants. Furthermore, we propose a method to assess those determinants.

Keywords: power, power taxonomy, power determinants.

1 Introduction

Supply chain brings more profits but not all the members can benefits evenly, because sometimes members are in asymmetry positions [1][2]. The stronger parties may use their power to gain their own goals and outcomes by coercing others to do what they would be reluctant to do [3]. This paper reflects a consideration as perceived from focal company's point to analyse the power of its partners/potential partners, regarding the factors arising from the focal company itself and intrinsic factors of partners such as reputation, knowledge and performance. Here the focal company is a company on which the study is focused. As said by Sun Tzu, an ancient Chinese philosopher, "knowing the enemy and knowing yourself, you can fight a hundred battles without danger of defeat". Based on the analyses, the focal company can make its "pre-activation" evaluation on its potential partners before collaboration, i.e. a power-based partner selection strategy. On the other hand, the focal company can also conduct a "post-activation" estimation, i.e. to estimate the existing relationship between partners and to anticipate potential threat from other partners.

However, the sources of power come from various aspects [2][4][5], which results in a variety of power factors. In order to achieve a clear understanding, it is necessary to classify those factors. Most of the research considers the classification and analyses power from the perspectives of social science [2][6]. In this paper, we establish a power taxonomy from the engineering view so that it can help not only to understand the sources and drivers of the power of partners but also to deploy a method to assess the power.

L.M. Camarinha-Matos et al. (Eds.): PRO-VE 2011, IFIP AICT 362, pp. 279–286, 2011.

Section 2 reports on existing research works on power from its concepts to impact. In section 3, we introduce a systematic framework to elaborate power taxonomy and discuss about how to calculate the power value regarding the involvement of partners in the product development. In section 4 we provide an illustrative case and after some discussions we conclude in section 5.

2 Related Work

The general agreement on the definition of power is "the ability to evoke a change in another's behavior" [7][8]. When it is extended to apply in market fields, there are more precise definitions. Emerson defines power as "the ability of one firm (the source) to influence the intentions and actions of another firm (the target)" [9]. Yeung et al. provide a similar definition, i.e. "Power is one channel member's ability to influence the behaviour and decision of other members" [10]. Other researchers also mention several derivative concepts such as "relative power", "bargaining power", "customer power", "retailer power" and "organizational power" [11-16]. In essence, all these concepts focus on the ability of one party to influence the others.

Power sources from various aspects such as reputation, resource, knowledge and so on. French and Ravens [4], largely cited in scientific literature, classify power into five bases, i.e. reward power, referent power, legitimate power, coercive power and expert power. Based on this classification, Tedeschi et al. [17] summarize them into mediated power and non-mediated power. The mediated power including reward, coercive, and legal legitimate represents the strategies that the source will take to influence the target. On the contrary, the non-mediated power is more relational and positive [18] in orientation that includes referent power, expert power and legitimate power.

The theory of power applies in various aspects of supply chain such as supplier integration, partner selection, decision-making and so on. In [10], they argue that coercive power could lead to worse cooperation in western cultures but improve the supplier integration in China. Generally, company can use coercive power to enhance buyers' internal integration that may lead to supplier integration under a trust-based relationship. Zolghadri et al [19] introduce a method to select partners by comparing the power between the focal company and its potential partners in the mutual relationship. In [11] and [18], the authors conclude that the mediate power could throw negative influence on buyer-supplier relationship while the non-mediate power could retain positive effect on partnership. Zhao et al [20] present a more detailed discussion on the influence of each of the five bases power on the partnership in supply chain.

3 Power Taxonomy and Determinants

3.1 Power Taxonomy Framework

When considering the power of partner, it can be derived from two dimensions. One dimension is the power arising from the focal company instead of individual partner, which we called "partner-independent power". Take automobile manufacturing for example. There may be several candidates to supply engines. Though their promised price, quality and experience are different, the power of those candidates is on the same level in terms of the activity of supplying the module of engine. However when compared with the activity of supplying window glass to the automobile, to supply the module of engine could be considered more critical because engines play a more essential role to the end product. On the other hand, the marketing factors such as the available number of suppliers could also influence the decision or strategy of the focal company. Suppose there are three alternative suppliers in one solution and only one in another. Undoubtedly, the supplier in the latter will affect the focal company more than any supplier in the former situation regardless of the products provided. Therefore we examine partner-independent power from two dimensions: the demand of focal company to the final product (function-oriented power) and the market situation (market-oriented power).

The other dimensions is the power emerging from the partner, which is the ability closely related to a particular partner. We call it "partner-dependent power". We also subdivide this type of power into two dimensions regarding the partners' capability and performance on the product. One is product-independent power, a kind of power concerning the aspects of a partner itself like expertise, reputation and such capability issues except the concrete product related issues; the other is product-dependent power, which is the performance factors of a partner with regards to the demanded product.

In light of the above discussion, we propose a product-oriented power taxonomy framework, illustrated in figure 1.

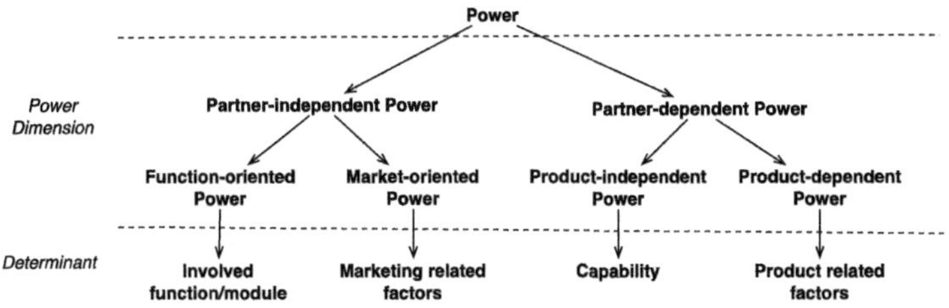

Fig. 1. Power Taxonomy Framework

We adopt a two-level-criteria method to finalize the framework: the first level criteria is "partner dependent or not" that indicates the first two dimensions of power, i.e. partner-independent power and partner-dependent power; the second level criteria is "product dependent or not" that is used to apply on the first two dimensions. When considering the sub-dimensions of partner-independent power, the dependence on product indicates the function-oriented power and correspondingly no dependence indicates market-oriented power. It is the same for the partner-dependent power. The following section introduces some determinants of each dimension.

3.2 Power Determinants

3.1.1 Determinants of Function-Oriented Power

Function-oriented power comes from the importance of modules. We evaluate the importance based on the functions the modules perform. In this way, it is possible to establish a mapping between functions and modules and rank the importance of modules by ranking the importance of function. To evaluate function-oriented power, the first step is to mapping modules into functions. There are several methods that can be used for this purpose. Take F.A.S.T. (Functional Analysis Systems Technique) methodology [21] for example, which is a method of developing and decomposing the system functions. We establish a matrix to illustrate this mapping (see figure 2).

The second step is to calculate the importance of the function. We adopt AHP technique [22] to rank the functions. To compare the two functions, the values v = {1, 2, …, 9} representing the preferences are assigned (see table 1) and the matrix of these pairwise preferences are deduced as illustrated in figure 3. High-level functions are compared first and then are the sub-functions inside. The weight of a high level function is the sum of all the weights of its sub-functions. To be noticed, for the case that function (like F4) contains its sub-functions (F4_1, …, F4_M) but finally is implemented by one module (M4), there is no necessity to compare the sub-functions inside.

The last step is to transform the weights of functions to the weight of modules based on the mapping matrix (see figure 4a). Therefore, the importance of supplying certain modules is deduced. When it comes to calculating the power of particular partners, we can relate the partners with modules and aggregate the weight values (see figure 4b and 4c).

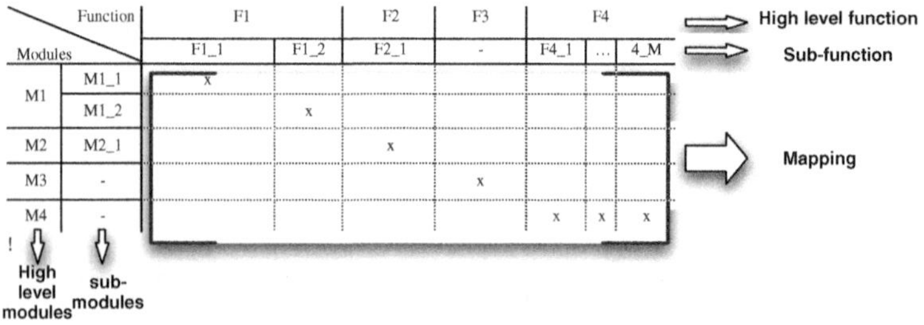

Fig. 2. Mapping modules into functions

	F1	F2	F3	F4	Weight
F1	1	x_{12}	x_{13}	x_{14}	x_1
F2	$1/x_{12}$	1	x_{23}	x_{24}	x_2
F3	$1/x_{13}$	$1/x_2$	1	x_{34}	x_3
F4	$1/x_{14}$	$1/x_{24}$	$1/x_{34}$	1	x_4

a. High level comparison

	F1_1	F1_2	Weight inside	Overall weight
F1_1	1	x_{12}'	x_{1-1}'	x_{1-1}
F1_2	$1/x_{12}'$	1	x_{1-2}'	x_{1-2}

b. Inside functions comparison

Fig. 3. Modules preference matrix

Table 1. Fundamental scale of relative importance

Intensity of Importance	Numerical assessment
Extreme importance	9
Very strong or demonstrated importance	7
Strong importance	5
Moderate importance	3
Equal importance	1
Intermediate values	2, 4, 6 and 8

Modules		Weight
M1	M1_1	x_{1-1}
	M1_2	x_{1-2}
M2	M2_1	x_2
M3	-	x_3
M4	-	x_4

a. Weights of modules

Modules / Suppliers	M1_1	M1_2	M2_1	M3	M4
S1	x		x		
S2		x		x	
S3					x

b. Mapping between partners into modules

Suppliers	S1	S2	S3
Power value	$x_{1-1}+x_2$	$x_{1-2}+x_3$	x_4

c. Weights of partners

Fig. 4. Retrieving modules weight and weights of partners

3.1.2 Determinants of Market-Oriented Power, Product-Independent Power and Product-Dependent Power

Market-oriented power is determined by the factors related to market situation, i.e. availability of alternative partners and criticality of product. It is easy to understand that the more alternative partners exist, the more powerful the focal company is whereas the less power the partners own and vice versa. If the final product is critical to the focal company's business or its future performance in its trading area, the partners' power will be increased, whereas the focal company's power will be decreased. As we mentioned before, product-independent power is a kind of power related to partners' capability. The capability can be leveraged to the focal company's advantages in the long term [23]. In order to assess this power, the factors of capability need to be determined in the first place such as volume of sales, switching cost and expertise knowledge. While product-dependent power is tightly associated with concrete product, including price, quality, deliver cycle time, technical support and fill rate.

All the factors mentioned above can be catalogued to two types according to their nature: quantitative factors (e.g. availability of alternative partners, volume of sales, price) and qualitative factors (e.g. criticality of product, expertise knowledge, quality). We propose a method to calculate the power value of each sub-dimension. The first step is to determine the weight of each factor by comparing every two factors, which stands for the criticality of every factor to the focal company. The second step is to determine the level of each (potential) partner's activity upon each factor. We adopt a similar table as table 2, in which the numbers {1, 2, …, 9} represent the level of activity, i.e. 1 indicates lowest level and 9 indicates the highest. Finally, we obtain the power value by aggregating the factors values:

$$V(P)=\sum_{i=1}^{t}\alpha_i\cdot x_i\,,\qquad \sum_{i=1}^{t}\alpha_i=1\,. \tag{1}$$

In the formula, t is the number of factors in one sub-dimension while α_i is the weight. Table 2 shows an example completing the above calculation procedure.

Table 2. Calculation of power factors

Weights / Partners	Factor 1 0.35 (α_1)	Factor 2 0.2 (α_2)	Factor 3 0.3 (α_3)	Factor 4 0.15 (α_4)	Total (V(p))
P1	3	7	5	4	4.55
P2	6	4	2	4	4.1

4 Illustration and Analysis

In this section, our method is applied to a case study. Various initiatives exist all over the European territory to promote bicycle by public authorities in highly jammed traffic cities like Paris or Berlin. However, the use of bicycle remains difficult. A possible solution to extend the use of bicycle is to transform basic bicycles into electrical power-aided ones by assembling electrical power-assist kits. To simplify the case, suppose the electrical power-aided bicycle consists three modules fulfilling one function respectively: basic bicycle, electrical motor and high-charge batteries, and the bicycle manufacture intends to purchase electrical motors from other suppliers. By estimating the function importance, the module weight is deduced and further the power values of providing modules are achieved (see figure 5).

	F(bicycle)	F(motor)	F(battery)	Weight
F(bicycle)	1	2	6	0.577
F(motor)	1/2	1	5	0.342
F(battery)	1/6	1/5	1	0.081

a. Function comparison

Modules	Weight
M(bicycle)	0.577
M(motor)	0.342
M(battery)	0.081

b. Module weight

Fig. 5. Deducing value of function-oriented power

Considering the factors of market-oriented power, suppose there are three potential suppliers (P1, P2 and P3) and the weights of each factor (availability and criticality) are 0.4 and 0.6 respectively. Because there are only three alternatives, we can consider this will highly increase the power of those potential partners. Moreover, this product could be the future trend, so it is important to the manufacture. Therefore the numbers representing the level of importance of the two factors are 5 and 3 respectively. The power value is calculated (see figure 6a). The calculation processes of the product-independent power value and the product-dependent value of each potential partner are similar to that of the market-oriented power value. The first is to decide the weights of each factor under the two dimensions. The second is to assign numbers representing the level of activity and finally all the values will be aggregated. Based on those calculations, we can get a result like figure 6b.

	Availability	Criticality	Power value
Weights	0.4	0.6	
Levels	5	3	3.8

a. Value of market-oriented power

	F-O	M-O	P-I	P-D
P1	0.342	3.8	4.5	7.3
P2	0.342	3.8	3.1	6.9
P3	0.342	3.8	3.45	2.6

b. Final result with power values

F-O: function-oriented Power
M-O: market-oriented Power
P-I: prodcut-independent Power
P-D: prodcut-dependent Power

Fig. 6. Power values

In this case, partner 2 (P2) is the best choice. Dealing with P1 could be too risky because it is with a high value of partner-dependent power (11.8) that means P1 could restrain the manufacture, though this value could also indicate good performance and capability. Dealing with P3 could suffer least risk, however, the lower value of power could also means lower ability. Dealing with P2 could be less risky, and looking inside the partner-dependent power, it is not hard to find out the product-dependent power is close to that of P1. In general, on the premise of same value in partner-independent power, the focal company should choose partner with lower (not lowest) partner-dependent power value. If there are several candidates with close values, look inside the partner-dependent power and analyse its two sub-dimensions. This method can also assist the focal company to choose between two solutions in terms of partners. In this case, the values in the partner-independent power will be different. It is better to the solution with lower values of function-oriented power and market oriented power but middle level value of partner-depended power.

5 Conclusion

This paper proposed a product-oriented power taxonomy with analyses of power determinants. When analyzing the power of partner, the focal company can first follow a top-down method to list all the determinants it concerns and then follow a bottom-up method to aggregate the power value of each dimension based on the weights of its determinants. This taxonomy can be applied not only to the companies in supply chain but also other types of alliances such as virtual enterprise. On one hand, this taxonomy can be used to assess the (potential) partners or solutions in terms of partners; on the other hand, it can also be used to analyses the focal company itself if it is a subcontractor. In the future, we will focus on refining the assessment method of power value and a further study on the analyses of the assessment results.

References

1. Harland, C.M.: Supply chain management- relationships, chains and networks. British Journal of Management 7(S63-S80) (1996)
2. Crook, T., Combs, J.: Sources and consequences of bargaining power in supply chains. Journal of Operations Management 25(2), 546–555 (2007)
3. Charles, L., Munson, M.J.R.: Zehava Rosenblatt, The Use and Abuse of Power in Supply Chains. Business Horizons 42(1), 55–65 (1999)
4. French, J.R., Raven, B.: The basis of social power. In: Cartwright, D. (ed.) Studies in Social Power 1959, University of Michigan Press, Ann Arbor (1959)
5. Dong-Sung Cho, W.C.: Determinants of bargaining power in oem negotiations. Industrial Marketing Management 23, 343–355 (1994)
6. Maloni, M., Benton, W.C.: Power Influences in supply chain. Journal of Business Logistics 21 (2000)
7. Simon, H.A.: Notes on the Observation and Measurement of Political Power. Journal of Politics 15, 500–516 (1953)
8. Gaski, J.F.: The Theory of Power and Conflict in Channels of Distribution. Journal of Marketing 48, 9–29 (1984)
9. Emerson, R.M.: Power-Dependence Relations. American Sociological Review 27, 31–41 (1962)
10. Yeung, J.H.Y., et al.: The effects of trust and coercive power on supplier integration. International Journal of Production Economics 120(1), 66–78 (2009)
11. Brown, J.R., Lusch, R.F., Nicholson, C.Y.: Power and relationship commitment: their impact on marketing channel member performance. Journal of Retailing 71(4), 363–392 (1995)

12. Ganesan, S.: Determinants of long-term orientation in buyer–seller relationships. Journal of Marketing 58(1), 1–19 (1994)
13. Song, M., Dibenedetto, C.: Supplier's involvement and success of radical new product development in new ventures. Journal of Operations Management 26(1), 1–22 (2008)
14. Marjolein, C.J., Caniëls, A.R.: Power and dependence perspectives on outsourcing decisions. European Management Journal 27(6), 402–417 (2009)
15. Consumer, M.P.: behaviour, retailer power and market performance in consumer goods industries. Review of Economics and Statistics 56(4), 419–436 (1974)
16. Hua, Z., Li, S.: Impacts of demand uncertainty on retailer's dominance and manufacturer-retailer supply chain cooperation. Omega 36(5), 697–714 (2008)
17. Tedeschi, J.T., Schlenker, B.R., Lindskold, S.: The Exercise of Power and Influence: The Source of Influence. The Social Influence Process, 287–345 (1972)
18. Benton, W., Maloni, M.: The influence of power driven buyer/seller relationships on supply chain satisfaction. Journal of Operations Management 23(1), 1–22 (2005)
19. Zolghadri, M., Amrani, A., Zouggar, S., Girard, P.: Power assessment as a high-level partner selection criterion for new product development projects. International Journal of Computer Integrated Manufacturing (2011) (accepted, in print)
20. Zhao, X., et al.: The impact of power and relationship commitment on the integration between manufacturers and customers in a supply chain. Journal of Operations Management 26(3), 368–388 (2008)
21. Bytheway, C.: FAST Creativity & Innovation. In: Rapidly Improving Processes, Product Development and Solving Complex Problems, J. Ross Publishing (2007)
22. Saaty, T.L.: Relative Measurement and Its Generalization in Decision Making Why Pairwise Comparisons are Central in Mathematics for the Measurement of Intangible Factors The Analytic Hierarchy/Network Process. Revista de la Real Academia de Ciencias Exactas, Físicas y Naturales. Serie A, Matemáticas 102(2), 251–318 (2008)
23. Sarkar, A., Mohapatra, P.: Evaluation of supplier capability and performance: A method for supply base reduction. Journal of Purchasing and Supply Management 12(3), 148–163 (2006)

Modelling Dynamics in Collaboration: An Extension to the Collaborative Network Relationship Analysis

Heiko Duin, Jens Eschenbächer, and Klaus-Dieter Thoben

BIBA – Bremer Institut für Produktion und Logistik GmbH,
Hochschulring 20, D-28359 Bremen, Germany
{du,esc,tho}@biba.uni-bremen.de

Abstract. This is a concept paper which introduces a dynamic extension to a collaborative network relationship analysis approach. The extension is based on the MetaMatrix approach known from the Dynamic Network Analysis field. Several entity classes representing agents, tasks, resources and knowledge are introduced and possible relations between entities of the different classes are analysed. All entity classes and relation classes are attributed with time related data which allows dynamic changes the system. Finally, some illustrative examples of typical collaborative interactions are introduced and explained.

Keywords: Dynamic Collaborative Network Relationship Analysis (DCNRA), MetaMatrix, Modelling and Simulation.

1 Introduction

The Social Network Analysis (SNA) is an appropriate method to capture and analyze relations between individuals or organizations for a given point in time (Wasserman & Faust, 2007). The Collaborative Network Relationship Analysis (CNRA) is based on the SNA and focuses on the relations between independent organizations collaborating in networks (Jagdev & Thoben, 2001) and forming a Collaborative Networked Organization (CNO) (Camarinha-Matos et al, 2009). It analyzes the type and intensity of interactions between those organizations (Eschenbächer & Thoben, 2009; Eschenbächer et al, 2009). The CNRA still lacks the inclusion of dynamic changes in such relationships caused by continuous changes in network constellations over time.

Dynamic Network Analysis (DNA) has been developed to overcome the limitation of considering static network models and includes a dynamic component (Carley et al, 2007). The heart of this approach is the so-called meta-matrix which allows defining multi-modal, multi-plex dynamic networks supporting various properties and measures connected to nodes, edges and graphs.

This paper presents an extension to the CNRA approach based on DNA to include mechanisms allowing the modelling of dynamic aspects of Collaborative Networked Organizations. The focus of the modelling is still on different types of interactions between organisations in a network but includes their evolution. This allows a more

L.M. Camarinha-Matos et al. (Eds.): PRO-VE 2011, IFIP AICT 362, pp. 287–294, 2011.

comprehensive and prospective evaluation of the performance and the design of the network. The dynamic extension of CNRA is called the DCNRA. A short example explains the application of the DCNRA.

As the traditional SNA approaches often use graph theory terminology and notation (Wasserman & Faust, 2007), this style is also used within this paper.

2 Current State-of-the-Art

This section provides a short overview on what has been done in Collaborative Network Relationship Analysis and introduces the MetaMatrix approach which is the basis for Dynamic Network Analysis.

2.1 Summary of the CNRA

The Collaborative Network Relationship Analysis (CNRA) has first been introduced by Eschenbächer (Eschenbächer et al, 2009). The general idea behind this approach is the quantification of relations between organizations engaged in a Collaborative Networked Organisation as defined by the ECOLEAD project (Camarinha-Matos et al, 2008). The quantification of inter-organizational relations allows the calculation of specific indicators measuring among others the collaboration intensity in the network.

The CNRA knows just one entity class (node type) representing organizations, but introduces several relation (edge) types representing different categories of interactions (see Fig. 1). For each existing edge an intensity is calculated based on estimations for a set of variables connected to that category. By simply summing all intensities of all categories between two given nodes, the collaboration intensity between those organisations is calculated.

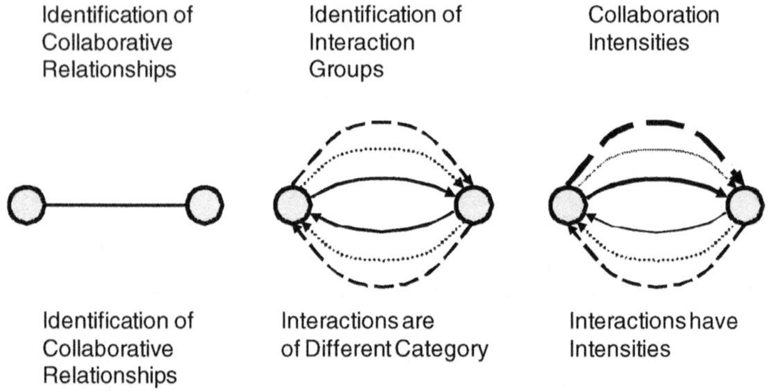

Fig. 1. Concept of Collaborative Network Relationship Analysis

The first application area of the CNRA were innovation related projects executed in a consortium (Eschenbächer et al, 2009). The first approach to dynamics with a project management example was introduced by Eschenbächer, Duin and Thoben (2009) by introducing a start and end point in time to collaborative interactions. This allows the calculation of how strongly specific partners are involved in the execution of tasks, but still lacks the differentiation of interaction types and only has one visualisation of the Collaborative Network covering the time span from beginning to end. There is no dynamic change of the underlying graph representing the Collaborative Network.

2.2 The MetaMatrix Approach

The MetaMatrix emerged from the work of the Center for Computational Analysis of Social and Organizational Systems (CASOS) located at the Carnegie Mellon University of Pittsburgh (USA). The objective behind the MetaMatrix is to introduce dynamics to Social Network Analysis (SNA) approaches (Carley at al, 2007).

The MetaMatrix is a multi-mode, multi-plex approach to organizational design and serves as ontology. The main entities classes are agents, knowledge, resource, task, organization and location. Nodes belonging to any two entity classes and their relations (edges) form a network like a social network or a knowledge network (knowledge by agents). Furthermore, there can exist several types of relations between nodes of two given entity classes, e.g. "is related to" or "receives instructions from" for nodes belonging to the agent entity class.

This approach seems to be perfectly suited to extend the CNRA with dynamic capabilities.

3 Extending the CNRA to the DCNRA

The basic ideas of the MetaMatrix approach are taken to extend the current CNRA approach. This includes an extension of the type of nodes, an analysis of the type of edges and the addition of properties allowing dynamic changes in the models. As this paper introduces the basic conceptual ideas behind DCNRA no formal notation is introduced which has to be done in future work.

3.1 Extending Node Types

Nodes which do only represent organizations in the CNRA approach are extended to represent other entity classes necessary to model the involvement of organizations in tasks providing necessary knowledge and/or resources. This leads to the definition of the following entity classes (Carley at al, 2007):

- Class 1 – **Agent**: A node of this type represents a business organisation (enterprise or company), a research organisation, a public authority or a natural person. For diagramming collaborative networks we use a circle to represent nodes of this type.
- Class 2 – **Task**: A task is another type of a node representing an operational job where one or more agents are involved to complete the task. A task is a time consuming operation which normally provides some kind of result at its completion time. For diagramming purposes we use a parallelogram representing a task node.

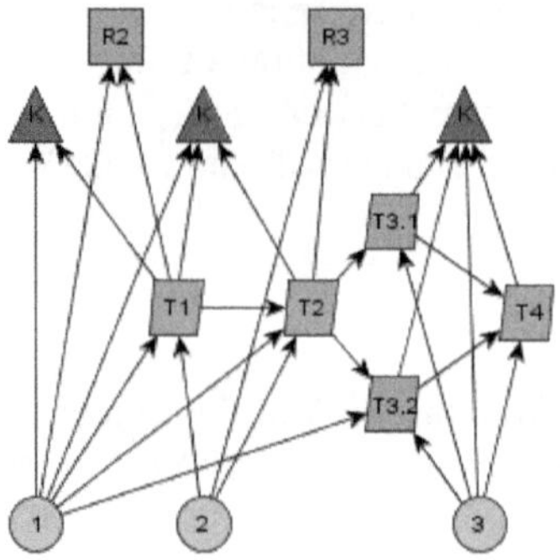

Fig. 2. Modelling example with this approach

- Class 3 – **Resource**: A resource is any kind of machine, supporting material, working power, or other resource like energy and water. In diagrams a square is used to represent a resource node.
- Class 4 – **Knowledge**: Knowledge can be any information stored in the brains of employees or in computers as well as competences of staff. For diagramming collaborative networks we use a triangle to represent nodes of this type.

Note: in difference to the MetaMatrix there is no differentiation between agents and organizations. These two classes are represented here by just one class: the agent. Another class – the location – is also missing, but can easily be included if necessary.

It makes no sense to allow edges between all of the entity classes (node types). On the other hand there may be more than one relational type between two given entity classes. A first approach to the modelling of relations is provided in Table 1. Most of

Table 1. Possible sets of relations and their interpretation

	Agent	Task	Resource	Knowledge
Agent	hierarchical relation (belongs to)	is involved in task	has the resource	has the knowledge
Task	∅	order relation (follows); hierarchical relation (belongs to)	needs the resource	needs the knowledge
Resource	∅	∅	hierarchical relation (belongs to)	∅
Knowledge	∅	∅	∅	hierarchical relation (belongs to)

the possible relations are intuitive and do not need further explanation. The reverse relations (e.g. Task → Agent, meaning that a task is performed by one or more agents) might be included for better graph traversal support, but is not necessarily needed as this information can also be retrieved by generating the set of all agents executing this task.

A set of interconnected tasks with relations of class "is followed by" can be considered as a project. The corresponding consortium (forming a Virtual Organisation) is the set of agents which have a "is involved in" relation to the tasks setting up the project. Fig. 2 shows an example of a CNO modelled with this approach. There are three organisations involved in the collaborative execution of a couple of tasks. For task execution some kind of resources and knowledge is needed and provided by the involved organisations.

All entities and relations can have additional attributes. Especially the relation Agent → Task should have an entity story the intensity of involvement of the agent in that task. A first approach could be store the percentage of the total working power of that agent put at the corresponding task.

3.2 Adding Dynamic Properties

Each of the entity classes and their corresponding relations can have dynamical properties as shown in Table 2.

The relation class Task → Task can be twofold, i.e. describing that one task follows another one or that the task is a sub-task of another one. Both relation classes don't have direct time related attributes, but can be used for consistency checks, e.g. whether a follow-up task really starts after the predecessor finishes.

Table 2. Time related properties of relations

Entity Class	**Time Related Properties**
Agent	begin (birth), end (dead)
Task	planned start and end, real start and end
Resource	begin (e.g. date of acquisition), end (end-of-life or selling), availability, usage
Knowledge	creation date, (outdating date)

Relation Type	**Time Related Properties**
Agent → Agent	begin, end
Agent → Task	beginning and end of involvement (planned and real)
Agent → Resource	begin, end
Agent → Knowledge	begin, end
Task → Task	-
Task → Resource	begin, end
Task → Knowledge	begin, end
Resource → Resource	-
Knowledge→ Knowledge	-

Table 2 summarises time related attributes given to entity and relational classes. All of them have some kind of a beginning (start or birth) and an end-date of their existence. With the help of the definition of these times related attributes a kind of dynamics can be introduced. For a given point in time *t* only those entities are existent where *t* is between the beginning and the end of the existence. Formally, all the other entities do exist as well but only virtually. They are not visible for that moment *t*. When moving the along a timeline the shape of the considered graph is changing depending on the life spans of the single nodes and edges. A few examples are shown in the following chapter.

Several time dependent indicators can be calculated, stored and dynamically updated. Examples are:

- Collaboration intensity of an agent for a given time span.
- Cumulative collaboration intensity for a set of tasks.
- Needed collaboration intensity for the execution of a set of coherent tasks.
- Total planned collaboration intensity for a Virtual Organisation
- Total real collaboration intensity for a Virtual Organisation
- etc.

Time related attributes for nodes of the task class are differentiated in planned and real beginning and end. This allows executing a simulation of the task models by making assumptions on the real start and end for the considered tasks. One option could be to define a probability distribution function which could be used by a simulation algorithm to determine the "real" start and end by a random generator.

The corresponding changes in the graph over time can be performed by graph grammars or graph transformation systems.

4 Illustrative Example

This chapter introduces and explains some illustrative examples covering basic collaborative interactions such as information exchange, cooperative planning, and collaborative execution of tasks. Similar situations are found e.g. in the execution in European research projects. Concerning the modelling of the research information there is the Common European Research Information Format (CERIF) (Jörg, 2008) which might be used in conjunction with the DCNRA approach.

4.1 Information Exchanges

Information exchange between two partners in the network is modelled using a task which changes the relation of another partner to a specific knowledge entity.

The situation is described by Fig. 3. At a given point in time t_0 there are two partners, one of them (partner 1) having specific knowledge. Both of them are involved in a knowledge transfer task at a later point in time, t_1. During this task another relation to the same knowledge item is established originating at the other partner (partner 2). Later at t_2 the task has finished, and the "birth date" for partner 2 having specific knowledge is during the execution time span (or latest at the real end of that time span) of the corresponding knowledge transfer task.

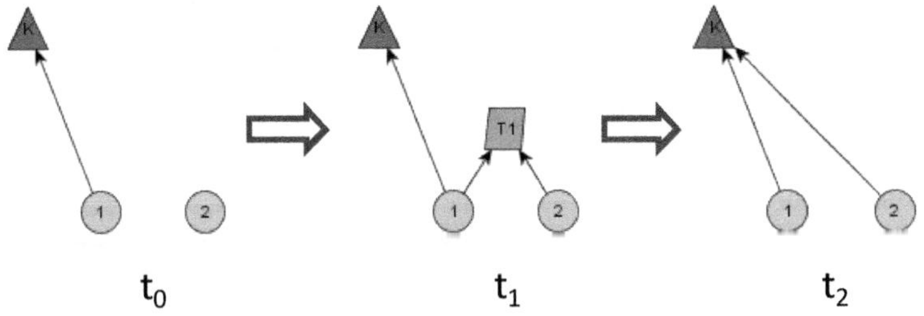

Fig. 3. Example: Knowledge transfer between two organisations

4.2 Collaborative Execution

The collaborative execution of the modelled project example shown in Fig. 2 is presented in Fig. 4. Time t_0 only task T1 is active. The other tasks and their relations are not visible. At time t_1 task T1 has been finished and disappeared. Task T2 is now active and visible. In the next considered time step t_2 task T2 is also finished and tasks T3.1 and T3.2 are executed in parallel. During the first two tasks partners 1 and 2 are involved while in executing T3.1 and T3.2 partners 1 and 3 are involved.

5 Conclusions

The presented concept has the potential to enhance the Collaborative Network Relationship Analysis with a dynamic component. This approach allows the visualisation and simulation of dynamic changes while a Collaborative Network is operating and developing. Additionally, it supports some kind of consistency checks, e.g. whether the involved agents do have the necessary capacities in terms of knowledge and resources. The definition of indicators allows the dynamic calculation of performance and collaboration intensities of involved partners.

Planners of Collaborative Networked Organisations are supported with a tool allowing the beforehand simulation and validation of that CNO. Several scenarios having changed or balanced collaboration intensities can be generated and compared. This allows also an assessment of the risks associated to each of the scenarios.

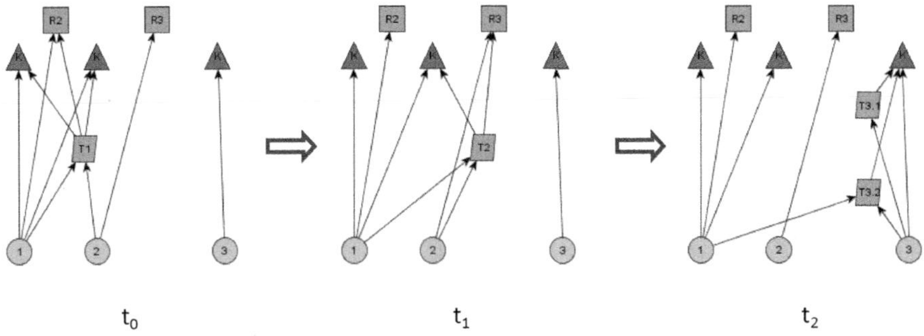

Fig. 4. Example: Collaborative execution of tasks

However, this approach is still in its conceptual phase. First ideas are presented here and further development of the formalism (including indicators and their formulas) is still needed. An example case study needs to be executed in a master project to show that static SNA results are not helpful in a complex and dynamic world. Also an application in real world contexts is still missing but necessary to prove its usefulness.

Acknowledgements. This work has been partly funded by the European Commission through ICT Project COIN: Collaboration and Interoperability for networked enterprises (No. ICT-2008-216256). The authors wish to acknowledge the Commission for their support. We also wish to acknowledge our gratitude to all COIN project partners for their contribution.

References

1. Camarinha-Matos, L.M., Afsarmanesh, H., Galeano, N., Molina, A.: Collaborative Networked Organizations - Concepts and Practice in Manufacturing Enterprises. Computers and Industrial Engineering 57, 46–60 (2009)
2. Camarinha-Matos, L.M., Afsarmanesh, H., Ollus, M.: Methods and Tools for Collaborative Networked Organizations. Springer, New York (2008)
3. Carley, K.M., Diesner, J., Reminga, J., Tsvetovat, M.: Toward an Interoperable Dynamic Network Analysis Toolkit. Decision Support Systems 43, 1324–1347 (2007)
4. Jagdev, H.S., Thoben, K.-D.: Anatomy of Enterprise Collaborations. Production Planning and Control 12, 437–451 (2001)
5. Jörg, B.: CERIF: The Common European Information Format Model. Insight into the CERIF 2008 Release. In: 9th International Conference on Current Research Information Systems (CRIS 2008), Maribor, Slovenia, June 5-7, pp. 5–7 (2008)
6. Eschenbächer, J., Duin, H., Thoben, K.-D.: Planning Distributed Innovation Processes in Virtual Organisations by Applying the Collaborative Network Relationship Analysis. In: Thoben, K.-D., Pawar, K.S., Katzy, B., Bierwolf, R. (eds.) ICE 2009 - Proceedings of the 15th International Conference on Concurrent Enterprising: ICE 2009 - Collaborative Innovation: Emerging Technologies, Environments and Communities, Leiden, The Netherlands, June 22-24 (2009)
7. Eschenbächer, J., Seifert, M., Thoben, K.-D.: Managing Distributed Innovation Processes in Virtual Organizations by Applying the Collaborative Network Relationship Analysis. In: Camarinha-Matos, L.M., Paraskakis, I., Afsarmanesh, H. (eds.) Leveraging Knowledge for Innovation in Collaborative Networks, pp. 13–21. Springer, New York (2009)
8. Wasserman, S., Faust, K.: Social Network Analysis. Methods and Applications. Cambridge University Press, New York (2007)

Part XI

Collaborative Networks Modeling and Theory

Modelling Virtual Organisations: Structure and Reconfigurations

Stephan Reiff-Marganiec and Noor J. Rajper

Department of Computer Science, University of Leicester, Leicester, UK
{srm13,nr76}@le.ac.uk

Abstract. Organisations have to adapt rapidly to survive in today's diverse and rapidly changing environments. The idea of virtual organisations emerged as an answer. There is a strong need to understand virtual organisations (VOs) in a formal way: changes can have side effects and hence one might wish to understand precisely what consequences a change might have. The Virtual Organisation Modelling Language (VOML) consists of sub-languages to model different aspects of VOs such as their structure or operational models: VO-S deals with structural aspects while VO-R addresses reconfigurations. The concepts are exemplified through a travel booking VO that needs to cope with extra demands imposed by a large event such as the Olympic games.

Keywords: Virtual Organisations, Structural Model, Reconfigurations.

1 Introduction

Changing business environments and a diversity of emerging requirements make entities' (organizations, individuals, etc.) survival and success dependant on their ability to adapt dynamically to changing operating conditions [4, 6, 8]. VOs provide a solution when it is impossible for any single organization (particularly small or medium size enterprises; SMEs) to keep up with the speed of change in the environment and the diversity of demands prevailing in the market. Adaptability and diversity are some of the main defining characteristics of VOs – adaptability allows to cope with changing demands while diversity is multidimensional (e.g. the range of involved stakeholders, the offerings made, cultural and geographic positioning, etc.).

A VO is a loosely bound consortium of organisations that together address a specific demand that none of them can (at the given time) address alone – once the demand has been satisfied the VO might disband. A VO is created in the context of a VO Breeding Environment (VBE), which is a more stable grouping of business partners, but without a specific current goal [4]. Some VOs persist over longer time, but adapt to realign themselves to address changes in demand.

A VO has a structure that defines the tasks it is conducting to achieve its goals as well as defining which partners are involved. There is a need to rigorously define this structure, as it is the foundation to describing and analysing the reconfigurations of the VO [3], which are the way in which a VO adapts to changing demands.

L.M. Camarinha-Matos et al. (Eds.): PRO-VE 2011, IFIP AICT 362, pp. 297–305, 2011.

In this paper we present VOML (the VO Modelling Language) focusing on two aspects: the modelling of the structure of a VBE/VO and the description of reconfigurations. For the former we present a new language that captures the key aspects of the VO at a level of abstraction meaningful to business users by making key concepts first class citizens of the language but still concrete enough to be mapped into more rigorous languages for operational models and rigorous reasoning and analysis. For the latter we introduce VO-R, the VO reconfiguration language. VOs can adapt in two fundamental ways: The ultimate goal of the VO might change, i.e. the VO should address a demand unrelated to its original purpose, in which case a new VO should be formed, possibly including current members. However, often the VO needs to adapt in more subtle ways to deal with fluctuations in capacity demands or alternative ways of achieving a task – it is this aspect which is addressed by VO-R.

The paper is organized as follows: Section 2 presents an overview of the VOML approach for modelling VOs, sections 3 and 4 introduce the structural and reconfiguration languages. The paper is rounded off with a discussion, related work and some concluding remarks and future directions in the final sections.

2 Overview of Approach

The Virtual Organization Modelling Language (VOML) is dedicated to VO development. VOML operates in the context of a VO Breeding Environment; VOs are formed dynamically to provide high-level functionalities by sharing a number of resources in a distributed way. The VOML approach [2] supports the definition of a structural and behavioural model of a fixed VBE based on three different levels of representation: (1) the definition of the persistent functionalities of the VBE; (2) the definition of the transient functionalities of the VOs that are offered by the VBE at a specific moment in time (a business configuration of the VBE) and (3) the ensemble of components (instances) and connectors that, at that time, deliver the services offered by the VOs present in the business configuration (a state configuration).

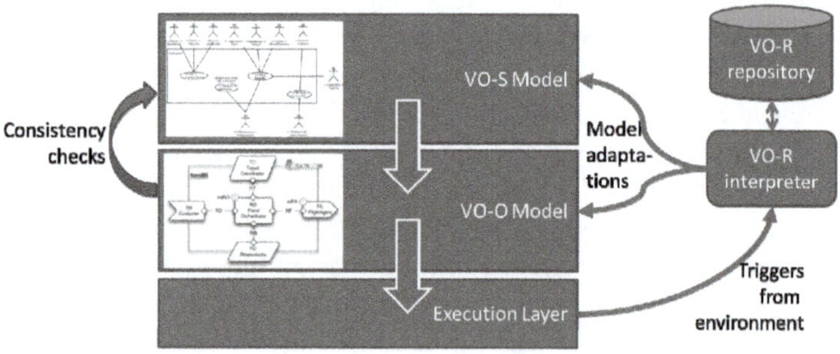

Fig. 1. Overview of Framework

Very briefly, structural models present the general structure of the VO (or VBE); these are mapped semi-automatically (semi as some refinement is required) into operational models. The operational models are quite close to respective execution frameworks (such as agent based systems or service oriented systems) and can be mapped to these. The execution framework is monitored and any changes are reported back to the model levels where policies are activated to refine the VOs and ensure that they remain competitive. Reconfiguration rules are checked for consistency and furthermore any VO-model should be correct by construction (that is it should be a true refinement of the respective structural model) – however this is further ensured by consistency checks. Figure 1 depicts this overview in a graphical manner.

3 Structural Models: VO-S

The VO Structural Modelling Language (VO-S) defines the basic structure of the VO, its constituent elements, abstract process, and other details which define the essential structure of the VO and provide the basis for its operational models. The VO structural model consists of five basic elements: (1) Members, (2) Process, (3) Tasks, (4) VBEResource and (5) Data-Flow. Of these, Members, Tasks and VBEResources are elements that can occur in VBE specifications, too.

Members can be of one of three types: *Partners* are permanent members of the VBE, *Associates* are transient members of the VBE who have joined temporarily based on demands of some VO which requires some capability for which there is currently no member available in the VBE and finally *extEntity* which are transient members of a VO and are discovered for each VO instance and leave the VO when the instance finishes its life. For the travel booking VO, the hotel provider is a partner, while FlightBooking is an extEntity.

Process describes the workflow which leads to meeting the requirements of the customer of a VO at the highest level of abstraction. It lists only those tasks that contribute directly towards achieving the goals of the VO.

Task specifications define the competencies required by the VO from its members. They help in deciding the kind of restructuring that a task and hence a VO can undergo, having effects ranging from VO topology to member relationships. Tasks are complex and we will here only show some key features. Attributes exist in the *TaskScope* (where they provide a domain of discourse for configurations) and in the *ConfScope* (where they describe the current configuration). E.g. the `performedBy` attribute in the *TaskScope* might specify that the task can be performed by Associates and Members, the *ConfScope* would make precise who is performing the task in the current configuration. Also, each tasks specifies the competencies required for performing it: which *capability* does a performing partner need and what *capacity* is needed (e.g. a partner needs to provide accommodation, and 50 rooms are needed).

Reasons for forming virtual organizations are (a) an entity (organization) lacks some capabilities to take on a job; and (b) an entity has all the capabilities required but lacks the required capacity (often the case with Small and Medium organizations (SMEs) competing for large jobs). VO-S addresses this by offering three types of tasks: *AtomicTask* (tasks to be performed by only one member), *ReplicableTask* (tasks that can be shared to gain extra capacity) and *ComposableTask* (tasks that can be shared to address capability issues). Members can compete or cooperate *ReplicableTasks*.

VBEResource are resources that are owned by the VBE and made available to all VOs that stem out of the respective VBE. The VBE will have rules on their usage.

Data-Flow specifies the relationship between data items to assist with realizing concrete orchestrations, transitions and wires in operational model. It expresses which data items are expected from the customer and partners and their flow between tasks.

```
VO-Smodel TravelBK
      ...
AtomicTask TransportProvision

STRUCTUURE
TaskScope
        {
        performedBy : ExtEntity
        supportedBy : PayAgent
        }
ConfScope
        {   ... }
Competency
{
  Capability byAir
     {
      resource : plane
      capacity {flightsPerDay : 30}
     }
}

STRUCTURE
Request:
        from, to: location;  out,in: date; traveller: usrdata
Reply:
       flightBooking.fcong: fcode; amount : money; bank-id

AtomicTask HotelBooking

STRUCTURE
TaskScope
{
performedBy: Partner
}
ConfScope
        {
        }
Competency
          {
           capability roomReservation
                  {
                   resource rooms
                   capacity
                          {totalRooms : 500}
                  }
          }

BUSINESS FUNCTIONALITY
Request:
         from, to   : location
         out, in : date
         name     : usrdata
Reply :
        roomReservation.hconf : hcode
        amount : moneyValue
```

```
AtomicTask GuideProvision

STRUCTURE
TaskScope
        {
          performedBy: VBEParticipant
        }
ConfScope
        { ... }

Competecy
{
   capability guidingTour
             {
              resource guide
              capacity
                      {totalGuides : 250}
             }
  }

BUSINESS FUNCTIONALITY
 {
   Request :
                   start, end: date
                   name : usrdata
   Reply :
                 amonut: moneyValue
                 guidingTour.gInfo : guideInfo
  }

DATA FLOW
Customer.from ==⇉ TransportProvision.from
Customer.out ==⇉ HotelBooking.checkin, TransportProvision.out, GuideProvision.start
Customer.amount ⇇== HotelBooking.amount, TransportProvision.amount, GuideProvision
VO.amount
Customer.hconf ⇇== HotelBooking.hcong
Customer.fconf ⇇== TransportProvision.fconf
Customer.gInfo ⇇== GuideProvision.gInfo
        ...

Members

Partners

Partner AccomProvider1
   {
 performsTask : {HotelBooking}
 competency {roomReservation.room.totalRooms : 500}
   }
Associates

Associate TourAg
{
 performsTask : {GuideProvision}
 competency
        { guidingTour.guide.totalGuides : 250          }
}
```

Fig. 2. VO-S Structural Model of the TravelBK VO

The TravelBK VO (Fig. 2) specifies a VO that is concerned with offering trip itineraries that include transport via air, accommodation and local excursions. There are two members in the VO (the AccomProvider1 is a VBE member, the TourAg is an associate). Air transport is provided by suitable external entities. All three tasks are atomic meaning each is performed by a single member.

4 Reconfigurations: VO-R

Policy languages have been successfully used for dynamically adapting systems. In this work we are particularly interested in policies which allow to reconfigure (adapt) a VO to cope with the changes that it is subjected to. We require and wish to model replication of tasks so that a number of members can combine capacity (either jointly or in competition) and decomposing complex tasks into smaller ones, so that several members can combine their skills. Additionally we like to be able to change the membership of the VO by adding or removing members.

While policies provide a feasible approach towards reconfiguration, a special policy language is required which provides explicit constructs suitable for the domain of VO reconfigurations. Typically a policy language can be completely domain specific or a more generic ECA (event-condition-action) language can be adapted to new domains by providing appropriate actions, triggers and conditions. We adapt the APPEL [1] language – APPEL had been developed with a clear separation of domain and core language. APPEL has a style closer to natural language as it was aimed at non-technical end users, rather than developers or system administrators, something clearly of benefit the users of VO modelling languages. APPEL was originally aimed at call control, but has since been specialised for e.g. sensor networks or elderly care.

Policy rules are the basic building block of APPEL. Each rule consists of an optional trigger, optional condition and an action. A rule is applicable when its trigger has occurred (if one is defined) and its conditions (on the state and possibly trigger parameters) are satisfied (with the empty condition being trivially satisfied). Actions have an effect on the system to which the policies are applied. Policy rules can be grouped into larger policies. A typical APPEL policy looks as follows:

```
policy policy-name appliesTo task-id/member-id/VO-id
when [trigger(s)]
if [condition(s)]
do action(s)
```

For VO-R we have to add a number of triggers, conditions and actions. We also need to consider the meaning of the localisation: **appliesTo** allows to 'locate' a policy. In distributed settings this would allow to specify the location of a policy, for VOs this allows to express which task(s), member(s) or VO(s) a policy applies to. The specialization of APPEL to Virtual organizations forms the Virtual Organisations Reconfiguration language VO-R. There are several triggers (Table 1) and actions (Table 2) specific to the domain, some of which are shown below – we do at this stage not claim that this list is complete and ongoing investigation studies this aspect.

Table 1. Sample triggers for VO Reconfigurations.

Trigger	Description
`NoMemberWithRequiredCapacityFound`	Arises when no existing VBE member is found to provide suitable capacity (either because they are not willing to provide more resources to the VO or because they cannot).
`CapacityDeficit`	The VO has all required capabilities, but is lacking capacity to satisfy current demand by a task. The task could be conducted, but with limitations.
`CapabilityDeficit`	The VO lacks a required capability. A capability deficit means that certain tasks cannot be conducted.

Table 2. Sample actions for VO Reconfigurations

Action	Description
`MakeTaskReplicable (task-id, allowedMembers, relationship)`	Changes the type of a task so that it can be shared between members. The resulting type will be a ReplicableTask that can be shared between at most `allowedMembers` members who compete or cooperate (depending on `relationship`).
`AssignTask(member-id, task-id)`	Assigns a member to a task. If the task is atomic or was unassigned this member will be the one conducting the task; if the task is replicable or composable this member will perform some part of the task.
`AddNewMember(member-id)`	Adds a new members to the VO.

Let us now consider two examples based on the TravelBK VO, which was presented earlier in detail. Specifically the VBE management has decided that TravelBK has a big role to play during a big upcoming event, such as the Olympic games, but needs to adapt to cope with the demands.

Scenario 1: *More hotel beds are needed than the current provider can provide.* The Olympic games will bring an influx of people who require accommodation. The current member responsible for the HotelProvision task has limited capacity and no other member can individually meet the expected demand, but each provider could contribute to the demand. The following reconfiguration policy makes the HotelProvision task shareable between up to 3 members; the allocation will be given to the cheapest one.

```
policy MoreBeds appliesTo HotelProvision
when NoMemberWithRequiredCapacityFound
do MakeTaskReplicable(HotelProvision,3,[competition,cheapest])
```

Scenario 2: *One of the hotel partners has had a fire and had to withdraw their commitment.* Sadly one of the hotels had a fire and cannot provide the promised accommodation. This is a kind of contract violation in the eyes of the VBE – clearly in business cases this happens and the VO is prepared to react to it as it has the following rule (this rule assumes that memberX is only involved in TaskY). Before a member can be removed the tasks assigned to that member need to be removed. The application of the rule might lead to a follow-on problem of a capacity or capability deficit (a capacity deficit was shown in Scenario 1 and capability deficits are similar).

```
policy MemberQuits appliesTo memberX
do UnAssignTask(memberX, TaskY)
  andthen RemoveMember(memberX)
```

5 Related Work

VO's have been modelled using a number of generic modelling frameworks, such as UML, ERP or PetriNets. For example, in [3] a VO is modelled using the Vienna Development Method in five dimensions: membership, information representation, provenance, time and trust. The formal model allows for analysis and verification. Our modelling language raises the level of abstraction to a point where it is possible to directly support notions and concepts that are paramount in the domain of VO such as members and resources. The use of UML stereotypes to achieve the same could be investigated, and indeed would be interesting to enhance our work with a graphical syntax – VO-R could then be expressed through graph transformation rules.

Like our proposal, [12] allows tasks to be shared, however they only allow sharing of a task based on capacity whereas we allow sharing based on capabilities as well. Additionally we cover the effects of such sharing on the members and on the process model. Besides, [12] is based on Agent Technology whereas our work is at a higher level of abstraction than a platform or technology specific solution.

The field of dynamic adaptability in general [7] is relevant. ASSL [13] in particular focuses on flexibility by providing a modelling language for autonomous systems. ASSL abstracts away from business level requirements of the system, however these are at the heart of VO modelling. More in the domain of VOs, the Arcon framework provides a reference model at an abstract level, while we attempt to make precise more of the structural and operational aspects of the VO and its reconfigurations.

In many areas of computing policy languages have become widely accepted as a way of reconfiguring systems to cope with changes in the environment [13]. Often policy languages describe security or low level system management aspects [10]; at higher levels of abstraction the APPEL [1] policy language has been adapted for workflows, where it allows to insert and delete tasks [9]. For VO's no such language currently exists but the presented reconfiguration language is a variant of APPEL.

6 Conclusions and Future Work

VOs capture organizations that are formed as relatively short lived consortia from other organizations. The ability to dynamically adapt to diversity in demands extends the lifespan and profit of VOs. In this paper we put forward a novel language to allow for modelling the structure and reconfigurations of VOs. VO-S allows to describe the structure of a VBE or a VO in terms of the key elements such as tasks or partners, while VO-R allows to specify rules that describe how a VO should adapt if asked to do by the VBE or if events occur from the VO's environment that need to be addressed. The VBE might stipulate changes when it sees them as beneficial to the business; the environment might raise triggers e.g. a capability or capacity shortage.

As reconfigurations are a core aspect of VOs, other approaches provide attempts at dealing with similar issues. Our approach is quite close to how real organisations behave in that we are providing a flexibility by allowing reconfiguration of tasks into a different task type by *replication* or *decomposition*. It is crucial to understand the changes as they can range from the VO architecture (its structure) to relationship between members and further more to changes in control and data flow. Existing work often focuses on replication of resources rather than on the members, however it is usual that new capacity or capability comes from new partners.

Our modelling and reconfiguration is close to the business requirements as shown in the reconfiguration scenarios and the respective policies – the policy language is intuitive and staff with business knowledge can write the required policies (actually the previous uses of APPEL in telecommunications were targeted at lay end-users).

Finally, we have clearly separated changes that change the tasks and hence can have an affect on the goal of the VO from those that make it more competitive in its environment. Changes to goals are achieved by new VOs being created from the VBE, while the presented reconfigurations allow for adaptations that maintain the overall goal. This distinction is critical, as it allows specification of properties that the VO needs to achieve or preserve and ensure that these are indeed adhered to.

In future work we will analyse whether VO-R can be lifted to the VBE level, to see if 'changes' to the structure that occur during the creation of new VOs can described in the same way (e.g. rules on selection of VO partners). Initial analysis shows that this is feasible, but will require further domain specific actions and triggers in VO-R. We will also consider performance modelling based on variants of VO-S models to understand the affect of VO-R rules on adaptability of the VO and more formal detection of conflicting rules, based on the formal semantics of APPEL [11]. These types of analysis will lead to an understanding that is useful for any VO.

References

1. Blair, L., Reiff-Marganiec, S., Turner, K.: APPEL: The ACCENT Policy Environment/Language. Technical report CSM-164. Department of Mathematics and Computer Science. University of Stirling (2005)
2. Bocchi, L., Fiadeiro, J.L., Rajper, N., Reiff-Marganiec, S.: Structure and behaviour of virtual organisation breeding environments. In: Bryans, J., Fitzgerald, J.S. (eds.) FAVO. EPTCS, vol. 16, pp. 26–40 (2009)
3. Bryans, J., Fitzgerald, J., Jones, C., Mozolevsky, I.: Formal modelling of dynamic coalitions, with an application in chemical engineering. In: Second International Symposium on Leveraging Applications of Formal Methods, Verification and Validation, pp. 91–98 (2006)
4. Camarinha-Matos, L.M., Silveri, I., Afsarmanesh, H., Oliveira, A.I.: Towards a framework for creation of dynamic virtual organisations. In: Camarinha-Matos, L.M., et al. (eds.) 6th IFIP Working Conference on Virtual Enterprises PRO-VE 2005, pp. 26–28. Springer, Boston (2005)
5. Camarinha-Matos, L.M., Afsarmanesh, H.: Collaborative Networks: Reference Modeling. Springer, US (2008)
6. Cummings, J., Finholt, T., Foster, I., Kesselman, C.: Beyond being there: A blueprint for advancing the design, development, and evaluation of virtual organizations. Final Report from Workshops on Building Effective Virtual Organizaions (2008)
7. Di Marzo Serugendo, G., Fitzgerald, J., Romanovsky, A., Guelfi, N.: A metadatabased architectural model for dynamically resilient systems. In: SAC 2007 (ACM Symposium on Applied Computing), pp. 566–572. ACM, New York (2007)
8. Foster, I.: The anatomy of the grid: Enabling scalable virtual organizations. International Journal of Supercomputer Applications 15 (2001)
9. Gorton, S., Montangero, C., Reiff-Marganiec, S., Semini, L.: StPowla: SOA, policies and workflows. In: Nitto, E.D., Ripeanu, M. (eds.) ICSOC 2007. LNCS, vol. 4907, pp. 351–362. Springer, Heidelberg (2009)

10. Lupu, E., Sloman, M.: Conflicts in policy-based distributed systems management. IEEE Transactions on Software Engineering 25(6), 852–869 (1999)
11. Montangero, C., Reiff-Marganiec, S., Semini, L.: Logic-based conflict detection for distributed policies. Fundamenta Informaticae 89(4), 511–538 (2008)
12. Norman, T.J., Preece, A., Jennings, N.R., Luck, M., Dang, V.D., Nguyen, T.D., Deora, V., Shao, J., Gray, W.A., Fiddian, N.J.: Agent-based formation of virtual organisations. Knowledge Based Systems 17 (2004)
13. Vassev, E., Hinchey, M.: ASSL: A software engineering approach to autonomic computing. IEEE Computer 42(6), 90–93 (2009)

Towards a Theory of Collaborative Systems

Donald Neumann[1,*], Luis Antonio de Santa-Eulalia[2], and Erich Zahn[1]

[1] Graduate School of Excellence for Advanced Manufacturing Engineering, University of Stuttgart, Keplerstr. 17, R10.027, 70174, Stuttgart, Germany
{donald.neumann,erich.zahn}@gsame.uni-stuttgart.de
[2] UER Travail, Économie et Gestion, Télé-université, Université du Québec à Montréal, 455 rue du Parvis, Québec, G1K 9H5, Canada
leulalia@teluq.uqam.ca

Abstract. High failure rates often observed in practice suggest that collaborative relationships are still not well understood. In this paper we investigate the nature of these relationships from second-order Cybernetics and Social Systems Theory perspectives. Thereby we develop a novel theoretical framework, the Collaborative System, which explains: 1. the organizational function of collaboration; 2. the system's elementary operation; 3. its coupling mechanism; 4. the system autonomy and; 5. its 'value' creation mechanism. The proposed framework is innovative and has far reaching consequences for the understanding of different forms of collaborative relationships. Nevertheless, it raises a whole new set of questions yet to be explored.

Keywords: Collaborative System, Interorganizational Relationships, Collaborative Networks, Cybernetics, Social Systems.

1 Introduction

In different forms, Collaborative Networks have been recognized as 'the societal structure of the 21st century' [16]. At the heart of these networks is the interaction among organizations, the collaborative relationship, which we broadly define as *a voluntary interaction among autonomous organizations that is not strictly based on economic transactions*.

Collaborative relationships are not a new phenomenon. They have been studied for almost 50 years, mainly under the labels 'Hybrid Governance Forms', 'Supply Chain Management', 'Strategic Alliances' and 'Networks', culminating with the recently proposed discipline 'Collaborative Networks' [4]. Although different benefits have been associated with interorganizational collaboration, high failure rates are

* We would like to thank CAPES in Brazil, the DFG in Germany and FQRNT in Canada for supporting this research. Also, we would like to acknowledge Dr. André Reichel, M.A. Lukas Scheiber and Prof. Sophie D'Amours for the interesting and very important discussions. Finally, we thank four anonymous reviewers, which contributed greatly to the better exposition of our ideas.

L.M. Camarinha-Matos et al. (Eds.): PRO-VE 2011, IFIP AICT 362, pp. 306–313, 2011.

commonly recognized in practice[1]. This suggests that our understanding of collaborative relationships is still incomplete.

Abstracting from specific forms of relationships, we set ourselves to investigate their nature. Therefore, we propose a novel explanatory theory: the Collaborative System. Our theory is mainly derived from the work of the great German sociologist Niklas Luhmann[2] and is innovative in different ways. First, it is a new theory about interorganizational relationships. Second, it extends Social Systems Theory by suggesting that another type of system emerges from the relationship among organizations. Third, it constitutes a new *unit of study*, the Collaborative System, which is capable of observing and distinguishing itself from everything else. Fourth, it enables a completely new understanding of collaborative relationships, from which emerges great explanatory potential but also many questions.

In section 2 we briefly present the main concepts of Social Systems Theory and Organizations. The Collaborative System is discussed in section 3. Two implications of our work, namely autonomy and value creation in Collaborative Systems, are discussed in section 4. Finally, section 5 concludes with some important questions that our theory raises.

2 Social Systems and Organizations

Recognizing communication at the heart of everything social, the theory of Social Systems addresses: i) how communication comes about and; ii) how complex societal structures emerge from different forms of communication. Composed of three selections: information, utterance and understanding [9, pp. 137-175], communication is an instantaneous event that refers itself to past communications and generates further communications: they are autopoietic[3]. Furthermore, a nexus of communications can only be maintained through selective relations among its elements. These selective relations are structured by *expectations* that constrain further operations. Such an *'organized complexity' can come about only through the system formation* [9, p. 24]. Thus, social systems are boundary reproducing, operationally closed, self-referential and autopoietic systems, whose basal operation is communication [9]. Everything else besides communication belongs to the environment of these systems, for cells, people, thoughts and stones do not take part in the autopoietic (re-)production of communication. As Luhmann puts it: *'only communication communicates'*, (re-)producing the system's boundaries, i.e. the difference between system and environment [9, p. 137-175]. Thereby social systems are autonomous and construct their own reality through internally developed structures.

[1] For interesting remarks about benefits and problems of collaboration in different forms, please see [7, 8, 6, 15] and the references therein.

[2] In a life of work, Niklas Luhmann elaborated a coherent but intricate theory of society based on Parsons' Social Systems, Second-Order Cybernetics, the concept of autopoietic Systems and evolutionary theory. For details see [9, 10].

[3] As proposed by Varela, Maturana and Uribe in [18, p. 188], *'the autopoietic organization is defined as a unity by a network of productions of components which (i) participate recursively in the same network of productions of components which produced these components, and (ii) realize the network of productions as a unity in the space in which the components exist'*.

Interactions among people constitute the simplest social system [14, p. 93]. However, society also comprises other social systems, each one of them fulfilling one of society's major functions, e.g. religion, science, politics, economy, arts, etc. [10]. These function systems developed their own operations and structures, but they are not capable of acting[4]. Another type of social system is therefore necessary: organizations.

Organizations are social systems (re-)produced by the communication of decisions [11, pp. 45-56]. In a decision, a selection is communicated *as a selection* [1, p. 139]. Thus, decisions involve two selections: the (mostly implicitly communicated) set of alternatives and the selected one. By communicating these two selections, a decision absorbs uncertainty by: i) functioning as a unity, an instantaneous event that divides present time in past and future; ii) fixing the future, at least until further decisions change it, and; iii) enabling other decisions to refer to it as a decision premise [12, p. 396].

Because both the set of alternatives *and* the chosen one are contingent (i.e. they are neither necessary nor impossible), decisions are doubly improbable to become accepted [1, pp. 139-142], [11, pp. 123-151]. In order to overcome this problem, improving the probability of further (re-)production of decisions, organizations developed specific expectation structures called decision premises [11, pp. 222]. These premises are special types of decisions that, by constraining the set of possible decisions, reduce complexity [11, pp. 237]. There are nine types of decision premises: membership, communication pathways, decision programs, personnel, position, planning, culture, self-descriptions and cognitive routines[5]. Decision premises grant organizations the ability to observe and construct an individual reality, making sense of and giving sense to their environment [20]. Only thus they can recognize themselves as a dynamic boundary reproducing unity incapable of being divided, even though decisions are constantly being made and premises are constantly being changed. It is precisely the operational closure and its constructed reality that allow organizations to observe themselves as a 'self' in an environment [11]; only thus are organizations able to make sense of the environment and structure internal complexity to absorb uncertainty in very improbable ways.

3 Collaborative Systems

As a specific type of social system, organizations can communicate under their own identity. Therefore, organizations (alter[6]) situated in the organizational environment of ego are recognized as systems of the same type, as organizations, or alter-egos. Just

[4] As in a conversation, the conversation *per se* cannot act, only participants can.

[5] For example, by deciding about membership organizations are capable of recognizing which decisions belong to them. Moreover, membership improves decisions' acceptance, since contesting them might risk membership itself. A complete description of these premises can be found in [1, pp. 145-152] and [11].

[6] Coherently with the social systems theory, we consciously abuse from the terms 'ego' to denote the focal organization, 'alter' to denote other organizations in ego's environment and 'alter-ego' to express that ego recognizes other organizations (alter) as systems of the same type as ego is. Nonetheless we do *not* restrict ourselves to the dyad. Alter is understood as any number of organizations in ego's environment.

like ego himself, alter's decisions are neither impossible nor necessary [12]. Thus, as an alter-ego, alter is identified by ego as a special source of contingency.

This contingency is experienced by ego in two different ways. First, when organizations perceive external relations as resources, contingency is experienced as dependency. Second, if external relations are perceived as information, contingency is perceived as uncertainty [9, p. 184]. By deciding to interact with other organizations, ego interprets uncertainty and dependency as risks that derive from ego's own decisions and affect its capacity to secure future necessities [13]. These risks offer guidance to internal goal oriented decision making. Organizations can deal with such risks in three different ways.

First, they can improve the degree of internal ordered complexity deciding upon further decision premises. Such decisions create internal redundancies in the effort to reduce risks from environmental uncertainty and dependency[7] [9, p.184].

Second, if environmental conditions apply, organizations can decide to improve internal complexity through the integration of external ordered complexity. By acquiring other organizations, they 'internalize' sources of contingency, turning them into hostages of their own decision premises. However, by increasing quantity and variety of decision premises, either internally or through acquisition, organizational size and complexity also increase [11, pp. 307-311].

Third, recognizing alter-egos in their environments, organizations can decide to interact with them trying to influence them in such a way that ego's complexity and uncertainty are reduced. Thus, we propose:

Proposition 1: A collaborative relationship has the organizational function of absorbing uncertainty and reducing complexity.

Nevertheless only further decision premises can alleviate the pressure to select [1, pp. 143]. Hence, ego can only reduce its uncertainty, complexity and risks by adopting alter's decision premises as ego's own decision premises. This requires that alter communicates to ego about it's decision premises. In this context, we define:

Definition 1: Commitment: a decision to communicate a decision premise.

When alter commits to ego, alter communicates a decision (as a decision) to communicate about its decision premises to ego. If this commitment improves the probability of ego choosing some decisions among others, it reduces ego's necessity to select, thus structuring ego's decisions and reducing complexity. It is interesting to highlight that alter's commitment hence reduces *ego's* complexity. Three different forms of committing exist: a. *communicating the commitment* - e.g. the communication of the decision to disclose an internal process; b. *communicating the decision premise itself* - e.g., the partner's actual communication of an internal process (a decision premise), and; c. *acting* - e.g. the partner's investment in a relationship specific asset (e.g. buying a machine) for a collaborative process. This

[7] Examples of these decisions are building up stock, redundant suppliers, diversification and phantom orders. But by trying to reduce uncertainty through internal decision premises, the environment might also be affected, originating undesired 'side-effects', e.g. the Bullwhip Effect.

action communicates both the premise (the asset) and the commitment (the decision to communicate it).

Differently from creating redundancies through further internal decision premises or acquisitions, commitments allow ego's reduction of complexity through alter's premises. Consequently, we propose:

Proposition 2: In a collaborative relationship, partners' commitments are necessary and sufficient to reduce organizational complexity.

Less abstractly, this proposition implies, for example, that what is commonly known as 'collaborative synergy' (e.g. performance improvement) is only possible if (or, it is necessary that) each organization uses its partner's decisions (premises) to guide their own decisions (i.e. to make them 'better'). On the other hand, structuring internal decisions through partner's premises also comprises risks. As future remains unknown, further structuring decisions can become a hindrance (commonly known as lock-in effect or path dependence) if environmental and systemic conditions change; that is why proposition 2 states that commitments are necessary and sufficient *only* to reduce *complexity* (the pressure to select). Nonetheless, complexity reduction does *not* necessarily improve performance.

Being decisions, commitments always communicate along their parasite contingency. Differently stated, alter's commitment grants ego the possibility of reducing complexity, *even though alter could have decided otherwise*. Thus, a single commitment can be interpreted as an act of altruism. Yet, by committing to ego, alter also expresses an interest about ego's own commitment, since this is the only way in which ego can benefit from the interaction. Hence, each commitment generates an expectation about further commitments. Moreover, when ego commits himself too, past commitments constrain the set of possible further commitments, i.e. commitments always refer back to past ones. Ego commits back based on its expectations about alter's expectations for further commitments. In simple words: 'you gave me your forecasting plans, so I assume thereby you expect higher service levels!' Hence commitments structure themselves, self-referentially restricting the set of further possible commitments. Joining proposition 2, self-reference and expectation structures, commitments (re-)produce themselves in an operationally closed nexus: they are autopoietic operations and constitute a social system. This leads us to our third proposition:

Proposition 3: A collaborative system is a (self-referential, operationally closed and autopoietic) social system composed of commitments.

Commitments are the medium of communication by which collaborative systems couple organizations in a specific way: they become decision premises for the organizations involved. Thereby, collaborative systems are necessary and sufficient for collaborative relationships to fulfill their function. Furthermore, operational closure grants collaborative systems the possibility of constructing their own reality and identity, which can be interpreted as the semantic differentiation of *'us'* and *'our relationship'* from *'you'* and *'me'*. It also explains how and why different semantics and identities emerge among different collaborative relationships, even when the organizations involved are the same.

4 Implications

Different implications can be derived from collaborative systems, from which we briefly discuss 1. autonomy and 2. value creation[8].

1. *Autonomy.* Operationally closed systems are autonomous [19]. In such systems, internal order emerges without centralized control. Consequently collaborative systems *cannot* be controlled; as neither alter, nor ego can control a conversation [9, pp. 404-436], organizations cannot control a collaborative system. They can only irritate, stimulate or destroy it. Furthermore, collaborative systems cannot be engineered, deployed, installed or achieved, since they are part of the organization's social dimension. This is a much more modest view of collaborative relationships than often encountered in literature. Moreover, it suggests that high failure rates can be the result of the misunderstanding of collaborative relationships as a sort of single-sided controllable input-output system.

Operational closure implies that collaboration can only come about through commitments. This apparently tautological expression hides the profound implication that social and network capitals are only 'useful' in a collaborative setting when they are translated into commitments embedded within a system. Organizations can only try to influence collaborative systems through further commitments and nothing more; everything else is external to the system, which autonomously observes and interprets through its own constructed reality or 'logic'. This closure explains why self-enforcing safe-guards contribute to relationships, while contracts and the extensive use of power do not [5]. While self-enforcing safe-guards are 'commitments par excellence', by using power ego communicates the unwillingness to commit himself, even though it is forcing alter to commit. The extensive use of power frustrates expectation structures and results in commonly related disadvantages for relationships.

2. *Value Creation.* Value is a common buzz word that draws, by itself, no clear distinction (see, for example, the definition offered in [3]). Examples of its possible meanings are utility, share holder value, societal values, etc. In spite of the lack of consensus about the its definition, 'value' always denotes a *form of observation.* By marking something as valuable, a system indicates something capable of improving the probability of continuation of a system. This probability of continuation can only be achieved through uncertainty absorption and the emergence of boundary setting structures [9, Chap. 3 and 5].

In a collaborative relationship, commitments are the *only* mechanism capable of absorbing uncertainty. Thereby commitments have the *potential* for improving viability (or creating 'value'), independently of the specific definition of value. By assuming partner's commitments as premises, organizations *can* improve decision making, because 1. only specific alternatives must be evaluated; 2. partner's behavior can be better predicted, and; 3. decisions can be adapted to partner's decisions. Nevertheless, even though this potential might be realized, such that resulting

---

[8] Unfortunately, space requirements restrict the exploration of the full potential of this theory. Nonetheless, it is important to highlight that it opens the possibility of applying established social systems techniques, as the ones described in [2], to the analysis of collaborative relationships, significantly augmenting the potential of knowledge generation.

decisions improve system's continuity (they are 'more valuable'), uncertainty and complexity reduction does not imply the creation of 'value' in a specific sense. For faster and to the partner better adapted decisions can still became worse decisions if environmental conditions change. Thus, the collaborative system is a *necessary but not sufficient* mechanism for value creation in the collaborative relationship. For sufficiency is a much more complex matter, which also depends on content and, therefore, belongs to a future discussion.

5 Conclusions and Future Work

Based on Systems Theory we developed the theoretical background of Collaborative Systems, whose main contributions are: 1. by recognizing collaborative relationships as boundary setting autopoietic systems, it is a new theory about interorganizational relationships; 2. it extends Social Systems Theory; 3. it explains the coupling mechanism between organizations; 4. it is not restricted to interfirm relationships, but it is equally valid to interorganizational ones; 5. it offers support to change the common view of collaboration as a strategy or an input-output system to a more realistic, social founded, but modest, view; 6. it opens a wide horizon for application of established social system techniques to collaborative relationships; 7. it suggests a new clear-cut unit of study: the collaborative system, and; 8. it offers a strong social systemic foundation that can support and inspire further developments of reference models, such as the 'value systems' described in [17, 3]. Together, these contributions can account to a whole new set of theoretical and practical insights about collaborative networks. For example, by analyzing how the flow of different types of commitments on time constitute the identity, expectations, past, present, future and 'success' of the system, new knowledge about the role of contracts, trust, governance, coordination processes, 'value' creation and organizational culture might be developed. Nonetheless, this work is only the first theoretical sketch that opens up a wide horizon of possibilities for further examination. Much research effort must still be invested in detailing it and in understanding how this theory relates to other commonly cited theories of collaborative relationships (e.g. Institutional Economics, Resource-Based View, Game Theory, etc.).

References

1. Achterbergh, J., Vriens, D.: Organizations: social systems conductiong expderiments. Springer, Heidelberg (2009)
2. Besio, C., Pronzini, A.: Inside organizations and out. methodological tenets for empirical research inspired by systems theory. Forum: Qualitative Social Research 11(3), Art. 16 (2010)
3. Camarinha-Matos, L., Macedo, P.: A conceptual model of value systems in collaborative networks. Journal of Intelligent Manufacturing 21, 287–299 (2010)
4. Camarinha-Matos, L.M., Afsarmanesh, H.: Collaborative networks: a new scientific discipline. Journal of Intelligent Manufacturing 16(4-5), 439–452 (2005)

5. Dyer, J.H., Singh, H.: The relational view: Cooperative strategy and sources of interorganizational competitive advantage. The Academy of Management Review 23(4), 660–679 (1998)
6. Gulati, R.: Managing Network Resources. Oxford University Press, Inc., New York (2007)
7. Kale, P., Singh, H.: Managing strategic alliances: what do we know now, and where do we go from here? The Academy of Management Perspectives 23(3), 45–62 (2009)
8. Kampstra, R., Ashayeri, J., Gattorna, J.: Realities of supply chain collaboration. The International Journal of Logistics Management 17(17), 312–330 (2006)
9. Luhmann, N.: Social Systems. Stanford University Press, Stanford (1995)
10. Luhmann, N.: Die Gesellschaft der Gesellschaft. Suhrkamp (1998)
11. Luhmann, N.: Organisation und Entscheidung, 2nd edn. VS Verlag (2006)
12. Luhmann, N.: Organisation und Entscheidung. In: Soziologische Aufklärung 3: Soziales System, Gesellschaft, Organisation, 4th edn., pp. 389–450. VS Verlag (2009)
13. Luhmann, N.: Risiko und Gefahr. In: Soziologische Aufklärung 5 - Konstruktivistische Perspektiven, 4th edn., pp. 126–162. VS Verlag (2009)
14. Luhmann, N.: Schematismen der Interaktion. In: Soziologische Aufklärung 3: Soziales System, Gesellschaft, Organisation, 4th edn., pp. 93–114. VS Verlag (2009)
15. Ménard, C.: The economics of hybrid organizations. Journal of Institutional and Theoretical Economics JITE 160(3), 345–376 (2004)
16. Raab, J., Kenis, P.: Heading toward a society of networks: Empirical developments and theoretical challenges. Journal of Management Inquiry 18(3), 198–210 (2009)
17. Romero, D., Galeano, N., Molina, A.: Virtual organisation breeding environments value system and its elements. Journal of Intelligent Manufacturing 21, 267–286 (2010)
18. Varela, F., Maturana, H., Uribe, R.: Autopoiesis: The organization of living systems, its characterization and a model. Biosystems 5(4), 187–196 (1974)
19. Varela, F.J.: Autonomy and autopoiesis. In: Roth, G., Schwegler, H. (eds.) Self-Organizing Systems: an interdisciplinary approach, pp. 14–23. Campus, Frankfurt a.M, New York (1981)
20. Weick, K.E., Sutcliffe, K.M., Obstfeld, D.: Organizing and the process of sensemaking. Organization Science 16(4), 409–421 (2005)

Refinement-Based Techniques in the Analysis of Information Flow Policies for Dynamic Virtual Organisations

Jeremy W. Bryans[1], John S. Fitzgerald[1], and Tom McCutcheon[2]

[1] Newcastle University, UK
[2] DSTL, UK

Abstract. Dynamic virtual organisations (VOs) can arise in situations in which it is critical that they continue to operate, even in sub-optimal environments. Models of information flow in dynamic VOs are therefore needed in order to permit the rigorous verification of resilience properties before commitments are made to implementation. This paper proposes a refinement-based modelling approach for the design and analysis of VO policy resilience. The approach is demonstrated by using the refinement-based formalism Event-B to model a VO structure, commonly referred to as the Bronze/Silver/Gold structure that frequently arises in multi-agency response to emergencies. Machine-assisted proof is used to compare the validity of alternative information flow policies in Bronze/Silver/Gold when a fault is induced in the VO structure.

Keywords: Information Flow Policies, Refinement-based Modelling, Event-B, Emergency Response, Verification.

1 Introduction

Advances in networking technology have made it possible to establish virtual organisations (VOs) of collaborating entities that together enable new capabilities and services that cannot be achieved by the constituent systems alone [1]. In our work, we are particularly concerned with *dynamic* VOs whose membership, structure and goals may change during the life cycle [2] in response to changing circumstances, and particularly faults or malicious attacks. Dynamic VOs bring significant societal and business opportunities by offering, for example, more agile multi-agency emergency response, or coordinated management of resources such as energy.

In order to take advantage of the opportunities presented by dynamic VOs, it is necessary to address the challenges that stem from their complexity and heterogeneity. These include managing the complexity of the behaviours and interactions between participants, managing access to resources, and communicating effectively between diverse stakeholders. Furthermore, as VOs become established and reliance is placed on them, it becomes vital to have methods and tools that support the validation of properties such as safety or security, and the resilience of the VO in maintaining these properties in the face of failures or malicious attack.

To gain confidence in a VO's resilience, it is paramount to have a precise model of its architecture, the resources, functionality and behaviour of the participant systems,

L.M. Camarinha-Matos et al. (Eds.): PRO-VE 2011, IFIP AICT 362, pp. 314–321, 2011.

infrastructure, and environment [3]. Models support "trade-off" analysis of alternative designs at early development stages, and the precise determination of the contract (rights and responsibilities) that exists between each participant and the VO. Further, the models themselves can assist communication between the diverse stakeholders.

The goal of our research is to provide models and analysis techniques that can be used to support the comparative analysis of alternative VO models, architectures and policies. We use formal modelling notations in order to take advantage of the analytic techniques underpinning these notations, including proof and model-checking. Rather than attempt to prove the properties of a complex VO in a single attempt, there is a strong case for managing the verification as a series of refinement steps starting with a highly abstract description embodying the desired properties of the VO. From this abstract model, detail can be added step by step, with each incremental refinement being verified.

The contribution of this paper is to demonstrate the viability of a refinement-based approach to the modelling and verification of information flow within VOs and to the analysis of alternative VO policy models with respect to resilience. We describe the relevant state of the art in formal modelling of VOs (Section 2) and introduce our proof-of-concept study based on real major incident response procedures in the London area (Section 3). We present a refinement-based model of this VO in Section 4, focussing on response to serious communications failure. Finally we draw conclusions from the modelling approach and discuss further work (Section 5).

2 Formal Modelling of Virtual Organisations

Although there is a perception that formal engineering methods are "very hard to apply" [3], improvements in tools and automation are leading to their increased successful deployment on an industrial scale [4]. Their major benefit is in reducing risk in the development of complex systems such as VOs by allowing early detection and elimination of defects and bottlenecks through the analysis of formal, abstract models using static analysis techniques such as proof and model-checking.

Several characteristics of dynamic VOs – operational and managerial independence of participants, heterogeneity and dynamic change – make the formal modelling of VOs a challenge. A truly comprehensive framework would require abstractions to describe functionality, concurrency, distribution and mobility but few, if any, formal methods currently handle all these features successfully.

Although the formal modelling of VOs is in its infancy, useful models of specific aspects of VOs are being constructed. Recent examples include: the use of the model-oriented formalism Z combined with the CSP process calculus to describe identity management problems [5]; a formal operational model for VO creation [6]; and 'infrastructure-agnostic' formal models of business VOs and Virtual Breeding Environments [7]. The Vienna Development Method (VDM) has been used to model dimensions of VOs with respect to information flow, including structure, membership, responsibility and provenance [8], consistent with (sub-)dimensions identified by [3]. However, the VDM models are only analysed by means of simulation [9], since proof support for VDM is not yet well supported by tools. The Event-B formalism manages the complexity of proof by structuring models as chains of machines linked by refinement relations, and is well supported by proof tools.

Further, Event-B has been demonstrated as a viable basis for modelling conflicts of interest within VOs [10], as well as QoS parameter negotiation [11].

Most work on formal modelling of VOs has concentrated on the description of normal behaviour, and not faults, accidental or malicious. Error detection and recovery can complicate VOs considerably, increasing the risk of design errors, and we expect that formal models could assist the developer of VO policies to assess the impact of faults and the suitability of resilience mechanisms.

The study in this paper aims to investigate the feasibility of using a refinement-based formal method to analyse the resilience of VO structures in advance of deployment. We use Event-B because of its tool support for proof, and its ability to represent the information flow characteristics of a VO. We model a VO that provides opportunities to explore abnormal behaviour because it exists in a volatile environment that may disrupt its operation. We describe the case study in Section 3 and its refinement-based model, including disruption and recovery, in Section 4.

3 Bronze-Silver-Gold: The London Major Incident Procedures

Our case study is based on the London Emergency Service Liaison Panel (LESLP) manual [12], which summarises procedures and responsibilities of the emergency services (e.g., police, fire, or ambulance) in response to a major incident. Activities governed by the manual include rescue and transport of casualties, coordination of resources, and handling release of information to the media. Once a major incident is declared, a VO (which we term a *coalition*) is formed by the services.

The LESLP manual covers many aspects of the coalition life cycle, but we focus on the structural and information flow aspects. These are vital to the successful functioning of the coalition, particularly in managing the release of accurate information, for example regarding the number and location of casualties.

A typical response coalition contains several levels of command: referred to as *bronze, silver,* and *gold* (B/S/G). Each service has members working at each level, so we may refer to "Bronze Police" or "Silver Medic". Silver and Gold commands work in inter-agency coordinating groups. Bronze implements tactics defined by silver. Silver formulates tactics to be adopted by each service following strategy determined by Gold. Gold command, geographically distant, contains the service commanders.

Agents at a common level may communicate freely, but between adjacent levels communication is only between agents of the same service. Information flow out of the coalition is subject to several alternative policies. Certain information may be independently released to the media by an individual service, but casualty figures must be cleared by Gold Police. In our case study, we model an alternative information clearing policy in which all members of the Gold co-ordinating group must clear information for release.

4 Refinement-Based Event-B Modelling of Information Flow

An Event-B model [13] is a series of *machines*, each (apart from the first) linked to its predecessor by a refinement relation. A machine contains *variables* modelling state information, *invariants* (labelled *inv*) which constrain the variables, and *events* which change the state. An event has *guards* (labelled *grd*) which must be true for the event to occur, and *actions* (labelled *act*) which change the values of state variables. Each machine may have associated *carrier sets* held in a *context* visible to the machine.

For each step in the refinement chain, a *refinement relation* links the variables in the abstract model with those in the concrete model, and is defined by *gluing invariants*. Adding a machine or a refinement step generates *proof obligations* to ensure the consistency of the machine and the validity of the refinement. For example, the *invariant preservation* obligation ensures that invariants hold after an event occurs. An event in the concrete model refines an event in the abstract model if the concrete guards imply the abstract guards, and the variable states reached after the occurrence of the concrete and abstract events are linked by the gluing invariants.

Proof obligations are generated and in some cases proved automatically by the Rodin tools [14]. Those that are not proved automatically may be discharged by the developer with the help of the theorem proving interface. Proof obligations may be impossible to prove, in which case the model is inconsistent and should be corrected. Models which are proven consistent are said to be *machine-checked.*

Section 4.1 outlines a normative model of the B/S/G coalition[1], including a policy governing the flow of information into, through, and out of the coalition. An additional step refines this policy by distributing responsibility for executing it across several coalition agents. Both policies are machine-checked. The model is then extended with an event modelling the loss of a coalition level, and the policies are re-examined with respect to this enhanced model in Section 4.2.

4.1 Normative Coalition Model and Information Clearing Policies

The model has four levels of abstraction. The most abstract machine treats the coalition as a single entity. The second machine introduces the B/S/G architecture, and the third machine realises this architecture in terms of individual agents. These model a centralised information clearing policy, in which all Gold members simultaneously clear information for release, for example at a joint meeting. Information is learned, cleared for release, and released in separate, atomic events. In the fourth machine, this policy is refined into a set of actions distributed across members of Gold to give a distributed information clearing policy in which information is ready for release when it has been cleared by all members.

inv1: known, cleared, released $\subseteq$ *INFO*
inv2: released $\subseteq$ *cleared*

LearnNewInfo(i) $\equiv$
 grd: i $\in$ *INFO*
 act: known := known $\cup$ *{i}*

ClearInfo(i) $\equiv$
 grd: i $\in$ *known*
 act: cleared :=cleared $\cup$ *{i}*

ReleaseInfo(i) $\equiv$
 grd: i $\in$ *cleared*
 act: released := released $\cup$ *{i}*

Fig. 1. Learning, clearing and releasing information at the coalition level

[1] The models used in this paper are available at
http://deploy-eprints.ecs.soton.ac.uk/

Let *INFO* be the set of all information. At the initial level, sets of the *known*, *cleared* for release and *released* information are given as global variables. *Learning*, *clearing* and *releasing* of information are represented by events. Here, the Event-B model is shown in abbreviated form. *inv2* in Fig. 1 is a key security property of the information flow policy: only cleared information may be released.

The B/S/G structure is given by the intermediate machine, part of which is shown in Fig. 2. *Bronze*, *Silver* and *Gold* are defined as members of a carrier set *ELEMENT*. The *coalition* variable records the levels currently in the coalition, and *coal_known* records the information known at each level (*inv2*). Separate events describe the creation of a coalition at *Bronze* level and addition of *Silver* and *Gold* in ascending order, as envisaged in [12]. Communication takes place only between adjacent levels. For this study, we consider a policy whereby only *Gold* can clear information for release (*ClearInfoGold*). The information must be known by *Gold* (*grd1*) and not previously cleared (*grd2*). In *ReleaseInfoGold*, *grd3* ensures that information may be released only after it is cleared.

The next level introduces agents. An agent's service (*Police*, *Fire* or *Ambulance*) and level are given by the functions *service* and *element* respectively. The relation *info* gives the information known by individual agents (*inv1* in Fig. 3). *inv2* and *inv3* are the gluing invariants between *info* and *coal_known*. They ensure that information known by an agent in *info* must be known at the level of the agent in *coal_known* and vice versa. *ClearInfoGoldAllElements* is the atomic clearing event in this machine.

inv1: $coalition \subseteq \{Bronze, Silver, Gold\}$

inv2: $coal\_known \in coalition \leftrightarrow INFO$

ClearInfoGold(i) $\equiv$
 grd1: $i \in coal\_known[\{Gold\}]$
 grd2: $i \notin cleared$
 act1: $cleared := cleared \cup \{i\}$

ReleaseInfoGold(i) $\equiv$
 grd1: $i \in coal\_known[\{Gold\}]$
 grd2: $Gold \in coalition$
 grd3: $i \in cleared$
 act1: $released := released \cup \{i\}$

Fig. 2. The architectural-level machine

inv1: $info \in AGENT \leftrightarrow INFO$
inv2: $\forall i, ag \bullet ag \in dom(service) \wedge i \in info[\{ag\}] \Rightarrow element(ag) \mapsto i \in coal\_known$
inv3: $\forall lvl, i \bullet lvl \in dom(coal\_known) \wedge lvl \mapsto i \in coal\_known \Rightarrow$
 $(\exists ag \bullet ag \in dom(element) \wedge element(ag) = lvl \wedge ag \mapsto i \in info)$

ClearInfoGoldAllElements(i) $\equiv$
 grd1: $element\sim[\{Gold\}] \neq \{\}$
 grd2: $\forall a \bullet (a \in dom(element) \wedge element(a) = Gold) \Rightarrow i \in info[\{a\}]$
 grd3: $i \notin cleared$
 act1: $cleared = cleared \cup \{i\}$

Fig. 3. The agent-level machine

The fourth machine refines the centralised clearing policy into a distributed one (Fig. 4). Any services represented at *Gold* individually clear information for release (event *ClearInfoService*), and when all services represented at *Gold* have cleared information, it can be cleared by the coalition (event *ClearInfoGoldDistrib*). We also include the consistency invariant (*inv1*) between the information cleared by the coalition as a whole (variable *cleared*) and the information cleared by each service (variable *serviceCleared*). This records the intuition that all information cleared by the coalition must have been cleared by all members of *Gold*. This requires a change to the event which adds an agent to the coalition: if an agent joins *Gold* it must agree with the information clearing decisions already made by the coalition.

inv1: $\forall ag \bullet ag \in dom(service) \Rightarrow$
  $(element(ag)=Gold \Rightarrow cleared \subseteq serviceCleared[\{service(ag)\}])$

ClearInfoService(ag,i) ≡
 grd1: $ag \in dom(element)$
 grd2: $element(ag) \in Gold$
 grd3: $i \notin serviceCleared[\{service(ag)\}]$
 act1: $serviceCleared := serviceCleared \cup \{service(ag) \mapsto i\}$

ClearInfoGoldDistrib(i) ≡
 grd1: $element\sim[\{Gold\}] \neq \{\}$
 grd2: $\forall a \bullet (a \in dom(element) \wedge element(a)=Gold) \Rightarrow i \in info[\{a\}]$
 grd3: $\forall a \bullet (a \in dom(element) \wedge element(a)=Gold) \Rightarrow i \in serviceCleared[\{service(a)\}]$
 grd4: $i \notin cleared$
 act1: $cleared = cleared \cup \{i\}$

Fig. 4. The distributed clearing policy

4.2 Analysis of Policy Resilience

A significant risk to the coalition is the loss of a command layer, for example through communications failure. We consider the case where *Gold* is lost and must be replaced by a new set of agents, and the effect this has on the centralised and distributed information clearing policies. Since it is possible that the level lost was the sole holder of certain information, possible information loss must be included at each abstraction level in the model. In the first machine, this is modelled by the event *LoseInfo* (Fig. 5). We do not give the event in the intermediate machine. The event which models the loss of an entire level of command in the third machine is *RemoveLevelTotal.*

All obligations resulting from the addition of these events can be proved, although three extra invariants are required in the third machine. However, the distributed clearing policy causes a problem: it is now impossible to prove *inv1* in Fig. 4. The offending event is *CreateGold*. If Gold has been lost and is being recreated, we cannot show that the agent re-forming Gold belongs to a service that is prepared to clear all information that has been cleared by the previous instantiation of Gold.

LoseInfo(inf) ≡
  grd: inf $\subseteq$ *INFO*
  act: known := known \ inf

RemoveLevelTotal(lvl) ≡
  grd1: lvl $\in$ *ran(element)*
  act1: coalition := coalition \ {lvl}
  act2: service := element~[{lvl}] $\lhd$ *service*
  act3: element := element~[{lvl}] $\lhd$ *element*
  act4: info := element~[{lvl}] $\lhd$ *info*

Fig. 5. Removing a level of command

Investigation of the failed proof, offending event and consistency invariant suggests several ways forward. The policy could be extended to require that an agent re-forming Gold agrees with all previous clearing decisions. This would entail altering the event *CreateGold*. Alternatively, the consistency requirement between the two policies could require that any released information was once cleared by all services that made up *Gold*. This would entail maintaining a record of the membership of *Gold* at all times, and the information cleared by each *Gold* grouping. A further alternative is to treat the creation of Gold as different from its recreation, and the set of information cleared by the coalition could be reset to empty. The choice between these alternatives would rest with the policy developer and stakeholders. The advantage of the formal model is that the precise cause of the inconsistency is quickly identified and can be communicated to stakeholders, along with the avenues for re-design.

5 Discussion

This paper has shown how a formal model of a virtual organisation can provide a good basis for an analysis of the information flow policy of the organisation. When potential defects came to light, several options for alternative designs were readily identified.

Many topics are open for further research. Extensions to the model are possible, such as considering the response to multiple intersecting crises. The information model could be refined to include, for example, policies for handling classified information. Modelling the roles and the associated responsibilities of the agents would also lead to richer possibilities for policy analysis, including policies other than information flow. Many emergency response coalitions are much more ad-hoc than B/S/G, and looking at ways to model these less structured ways of dealing with complex crises is also of interest, including ways to integrate formal and semi-formal approaches [3,15].

Acknowledgements. The authors' work is supported by the EU FP7 Integrated Project DEPLOY (www.deploy-project.eu) and the EPSRC Platform Grant TrAmS.

References

1. Camarinha-Matos, L.M., Afsarmanesh, H., Garita, C., Lima, C.: Towards an architecture for virtual enterprises. Journal of Intelligent Manufacturing 9, 189–199 (1998)

2. Dimitrakos, T., Golby, D., Kearney, P.: Towards a Trust and Contract Management Framework for Dynamic Virtual Organisations. In: eAdoption and the Knowledge Economy: eChallenges 2004, pp. 27–29. Kluwer Academic, Dordrecht (2004)
3. Camarinha-Matos, L.M., Afsarmanesh, H.: A comprehensive modeling framework for collaborative networked organizations. Journal of Intelligent Manufacturing 18, 529–542 (2007)
4. Woodcock, J.C.P., Larsen, P.G., Bicarregui, J., Fitzgerald, J.S.: Formal methods: Practice and experience. Computing Surveys 41(4), 1–36 (2009)
5. Haidar, A.N., Coveney, P.V., Abdallah, A.E., et al.: Formal Modelling of a Usable Identity Management Solution for Virtual Organisations. In: Bryans, J.W., Fitzgerald, J.S. (eds.) Proc. 2nd Workshop on Formal Aspects of Virtual Organisations, Eindhoven (November 2009); Electronic Proceedings in Theoretical Computer Science 16, 41–50 (2010)
6. McGinnis, J., Stathis, K., Toni, F.: A Formal Framework of Virtual Organisations as Agent Societies. In: Bryans, J.W., Fitzgerald, J.S. (eds.) Proc. 2nd Workshop on Formal Aspects of Virtual Organisations, Eindhoven (November 2009); Electronic Proceedings in Theoretical Computer Science 16, 1–14 (2010)
7. Bocchi, L., Fiadeiro, J., Rajper, N., Reiff-Marganeic, S.: Structure and Behaviour of Virtual Organisation Breeding Environments. In: Bryans, J.W., Fitzgerald, J.S. (eds.) Proc. 2nd Workshop on Formal Aspects of Virtual Organisations, Eindhoven (November 2009); Electronic Proceedings in Theoretical Computer Science 16, 26–40 (2010)
8. Bryans, J.W., Fitzgerald, J.S., Jones, C.B., Mozolevsky, I.: Formal Modelling of Dynamic Coalitions, with an Application in Chemical Engineering. In: Proc. IEEE Intl. Symp. on Leveraging Applications for Formal Methods, Cyprus, pp. 91–98. IEEE, Los Alamitos (2007)
9. Fitzgerald, J.S., Bryans, J.W., Greathead, D., Jones, C.B.: Animation-based Validation of a Formal Model of Dynamic Virtual Organisations. In: Boca, P., Bowen, J.P., Larsen, P.G. (eds.) Proc. BCS-FACS Workshop on Formal Methods in Industry, Electronic Workshops in Computing. British Computer Society (2008)
10. Arenas, A., Aziz, B., Bicarregui, J.C., Matthews, B.: Managing Conflicts of Interest in Virtual Organisations. Electronic Notes in Theoretical Computer Science 197(2), 45–56 (2008); Proc. 3rd Intl. Workshop on Security and Trust Management (STM 2007)
11. Belhay, H., Balouki, Y., Boudadi, M., El Hajji, S.: Using Event B to Specify QoS in ODP Enterprise Language. In: Camarinha-Matos, L.M., Boucher, X., Afsarmanesh, H. (eds.) PRO-VE 2010. IFIP AICT, vol. 336, pp. 478–485. Springer, Heidelberg (2010)
12. London Emergency Services Liaison Panel: Major Incident Procedure Manual. Seventh Edition (2007), `http://www.met.police.uk/leslp`
13. Abrial, J.-R.: Modelling in Event-B: System and Software Engineering. Cambridge University Press, Cambridge (2010)
14. Abrial, J.-R., Butler, M., Hallerstede, S., Voisin, L.: An Open Extensible Tool Environment for Event-B. In: Liu, Z., Kleinberg, R.D. (eds.) ICFEM 2006. LNCS, vol. 4260, pp. 588–605. Springer, Heidelberg (2006)
15. Fitzgerald, J.S., Bryans, J.W.: The Verifiable Virtual Organisation: a Position Paper. In: Proc. Formal Aspects of Virtual Organisations 2008, Technical Report CS-TR-1098, School of Computing Science, Newcastle University (2008)

Part XII

Business Processes Modeling

Process Modeling for Internet Scale Virtual Enterprise Collaborations

Chong Wang[1], Lai Xu[2], Paul de Vrieze[2], and Peng Liang[1]

[1] State Key Lab. of Software Engineering, Wuhan University, China
{cwang,liangp}@sklse.org
[2] Software Systems Research Centre, Bournemouth University, UK
{lxu,pdvrieze}@bournemouth.ac.uk

Abstract. The ever-increasing need for flexibility of business collaborations that ultimately involve a large number of virtual enterprises puts demands on their design. Competitive markets require the collaborations to be highly agile, effective, and efficient. This paper defines Internet scale virtual enterprise collaborations (ISVECs) as well as their characteristics. We further present a process modeling method for Internet-based virtual enterprise collaborations. An end user process modeling language of ISVECs and a meta-model of the language are provided. Finally, we demonstrate how the method and language are used.

Keywords: Internet scale business process, Business process modeling, Virtual enterprise process collaboration, Web-scale workflow.

1 Introduction

In recent years, the service-oriented architecture paradigm has provided an easy approach to software development. Virtual enterprise systems are increasingly depending on and functioning as driver for the development of large scale distributed applications by reusing services [5].

Internet scale virtual enterprise collaborations (ISVECs) are business collaborations among virtual enterprises. This normally involves great numbers of services available through the Internet. These services should be annotated with semantic descriptions enabling dynamic selection, resource binding, and verification. As the services are provided by different providers, there is a strong likelihood that some of these services are modified, substituted, or disappear. Different versions of the services may include different features or have incompatible semantics. The services can be invoked from outside their own infrastructure, i.e. from a business partner's site. The semantic annotations can help detecting these changes and provide an early warning when the changes are incompatible.

Internet scale virtual enterprise collaborations are possible due to service that exist both inside and outside a virtual enterprise. Any ISVEC architecture should be a service-based development approach with a range of services that represent capabilities across a wide variety of domains.

L.M. Camarinha-Matos et al. (Eds.): PRO-VE 2011, IFIP AICT 362, pp. 325–332, 2011.

As a business environment changes rapidly, the ability to set up a collaborative business process in a virtual enterprise is desirable [8]. Collaborative business processes are increasingly driven by business agility, adaptability, and flexibility, particularly in a virtual enterprise environment. There is increased pressure to build enterprise applications quickly in order to respond to situational needs of the business.

In this paper, we deal with lightweight business process modeling issues. We start with a motivating example. We define a lightweight business process modeling language and provide its meta-model. The paper also uses the lightweight business process modeling language to model a motivating example. Finally, conclusions and future research are presented.

2 Motivating Example: Internet Moving Services (IMS)

As a motivating example we introduce a hypothetical international moving service. An international moving service aims to facilitate international relocations in various ways. These services go beyond moving items and can include things such as visa applications and assistance in finding a new residence. In brief, the goal of international moving services starts with helping customers to find moving companies and request quotes, but extends to many aspect of managing an international relocation. A very brief, incomplete and abstract description of the various services offered by an international moving service includes:

- Find moving companies: compare the services of international movers by requesting free quotes for the customer; provide moving tips, and information documents needed for international moving such as official government customs, visa and immigration, health, weather, etc.
- Travel arrangements: find cheapest tickets and/or car renting in both places of departure and destination if needed.
- Temporary stay arrangement: find hotels or holiday/serviced apartments in both the departure location and the destination if needed.
- Home search: pre-select properties according to client requirements such as proximity to a childcare centre and provide neighborhood guide which contains information on doctors, shopping, schools, leisure activities etc.
- School/childcare search: provide explanation of the local education system, options including public, private and international schools, provide information on pre-school options including nurseries, toddler groups and other childcare facilities, provide list of possible schools, childcare or other facilities relating to the home search area.
- Settling-in services: advice on banking systems, provide information on insurance of health, home, car etc., and advise on importing a car into the destination if applicable.
- Leaving assistance: arrange property hand-back or sale, close utility accounts and arrange final bills, and manage property if client leaves before end of tenancy.

We have found the following available Web services, feeds, widgets, and mashups from websites like *syndic8.com* and *programmableweb.com*. A list of available feeds,

Web services, widgets, gadgets, mashups that can be used as components in implementing the example:

1. Moving company feeds from 123movers.
2. Moving tip feeds from 123movers.

Both Feeds 1 and 2 can support the service of "find moving companies"

3. SmartTravelDeals: publishes the best travel deals on the web. It publishes current travel offers to worldwide destinations and connects users to the direct booking path.
4. Hotwire Travel-Ticker Deals: connect with more than 10,000 travel companies. The deals can be sceached by destination, theme, dates, or price.

Both API 3 and 4 sustain the service of "travel arrangements"

5. Cleartrip Hotel API: provides booking for flights, hotels and trains, as well as other travel services across the world.
6. Active.com Camping API: provides access to campground data for 97% of the US and Canada's national and state/provincial parks.
7. HomeFinder.com connects home buyers, sellers and real estate professionals through local newspapers' online real estate section.
8. ImmobilienScout24 API provides rental listings, house listings, and building construction information from Germany.
9. PeekaCity API: using google street view for neighborhood amenities which is used primarily by real estate agents as a service to their customers (currently in Chicago and Dallas/Fort Worth).
10. Easy one loan and home values: mashup of zillow and yahoo maps as supplement to on-line mortgage service.

Above five APIs can be included to implement the service of "temporary stay arrangement"; API 5,7,8, 9 and 10 can be used for the service of "home search".

11. Child care finder mashup: find babysitters, nannies, and other care options visually with google maps
12. California school finder mashup provides information such as, the school rankings, course offerings, and other details.
13. Feed Childcare position offered in France.
14. Feed Childcare position wanted in France

Above API 9, Mashup 11 and 12, and Feed 13 and 14 can be applied to implement the services of "school/childcare search".

15. NHS Choices has created a set of web services to allow approved partners to interact with the service, free of charge.
16. Patient Opinion is a UK organization that collects patients' opinions about heath care and treatments they have recently received.
17. Hospital Compare API allows developers to get various hospital information like addresses, mortality rates, prices for operations and other hospital-related data.
18. Monster Web Services Toolkit API allows users to publish job ads to the Monster.com job search and placement service. Monster service includes job seeking, career management, recruitment and talent management products and services.

Above APIs and Mashups are useful for the "settling in service".

19. Home value calculator: uses zillow data to calculate the value of single family homes in the U.S. Small widget suitable for placing on your google home page. It is a useful mashup for the service of "leaving assistance"

In this example case, it will be expensive and difficult to build a traditional workflow system to support the business process. Doing so would mean that either all information would have to be known in advance or an interface would need to be provided to add information to the traditional workflow solution. Few relocations would be exactly alike even though aspects could be shared. The dependences are various, such as finding a home close to the best school or the available childcare, find the good schools close to the home address. It would however be handy for a business process mashup solution, specially, if automatically invocation of needed feeds, Web services, etc. and execution processes are supported. The different processes of IMS can be implemented by different process instances. Users (i.e. owner of IMS) may only need to edit the certain processes to be able to meet all requirements from new customers.

3 Meta-Model of the ISVECs Language

In this section, we introduce the meta-model of the ISVEC language which the end users can use it to establish the business processes mentioned in Section 2. The notations of the ISVEC language are presented in Figure 1. Eight symbols are adopted from BPMN [1]. The choice of BPMN as basis is motivated by its wide acceptance within the business world. Other alternatives may offer different advantages for different user groups. The ISVEC language is based on workflow patterns [8]. Adoption of different notations should not change the semantic of the languages.

Since the process model is finally mapped into concrete services, we introduce new notations in the form of goals, which will allow business users to define abstract and user-friendly processes. Goals are the representation of an objective in which fulfillment is sought through the execution of a possibly complex service. The goals are always associated with an activity or process. We define two types of goals: atomic goals and composite goals. Atomic goals are associated with a single concrete Web service or computing resource, involving just one step of computation. Composite goals involve other simpler subgoals for fulfillment. In practice, if a process or activity is a process associated with a complex goal then the process or activity is fulfilled by achieving other goals, or invoking composite concrete Web services or computing resources. Hence, there are, in total, ten notational symbols within our lightweight process modeling language. This minimal subset of notation means a user will have reduced learning, whilst, we contend, still providing sufficient expressive power.

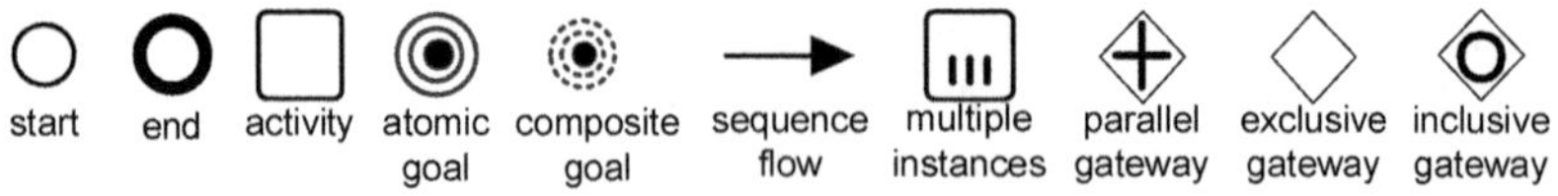

Fig. 1. Notations of Lightweight Process Modeling Language

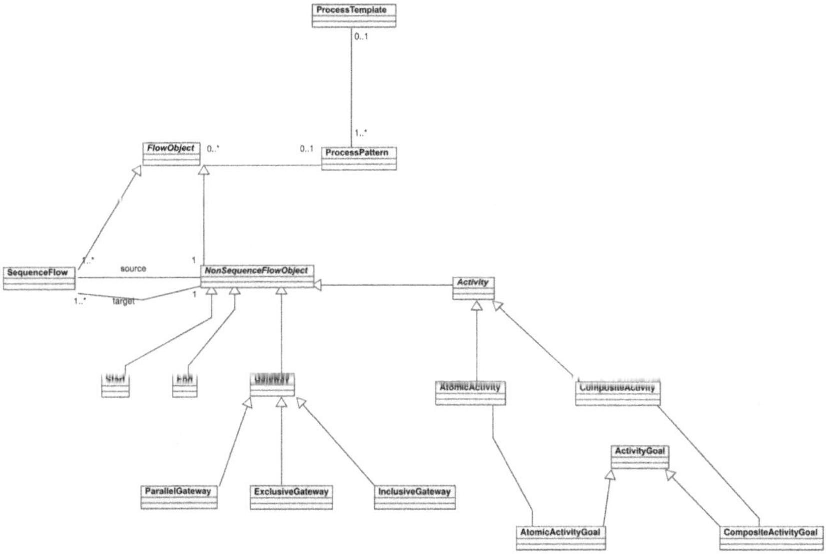

Fig. 2. Meta-model of Lightweight Process Modeling Language

Figure 2 provides a meta-model for the control flow of the lightweight process modeling language. The meta-model describes the relationships among all elements within the process model, namely ‘start’, ‘end’, ‘activity’, ‘sequence flow’, ‘exclusive gateway’, ‘parallel gateway’, ‘inclusive gateway’, ‘atomic goal’, and ‘composite goal’. An abstract concept ‘gateway’ is used as a super set of three gateways. An ‘atomic activity’ is the smallest unit of activity, e.g., a concrete Web service or a computing resource. A ‘composite activity’ consists of several other activities, either atomic or composite. An ‘activity’ is either an ‘atomic activity’ or ‘composite activity’. The terms ‘process pattern’ and ‘process template’ are explained [8], and ‘flow object’ in the figure represents a process model. We separate ‘non sequence flow object’ from ‘sequence flow’, to ensure the alternating ordering of ‘sequence flow,’ i.e., arrows and other objects, and thus avoid the situation where two ‘sequence flow’ elements link directly to each other.

4 Model of the Motivating Example

An overview of the services for Virtual Enterprise-Internet Moving Services (VE-IMS) can be found from Figure 3. Being a VE-IMS, the payment, CRM, and bookkeeping functions that should be included for being a normal business are sourced from third parties. However, we only concentrate here on the VE's core business processes. General business related processes are not discussed here.

Because of the various requirements from its customers, the services provided by a VE-IMS are dependent on the particular situation of its customers. Different customers require a different process. This process is supported by a special-purpose piece of software, which we call an business process mashup, with particular services, processes or activities. In addition to the added capability, new business process mashup can

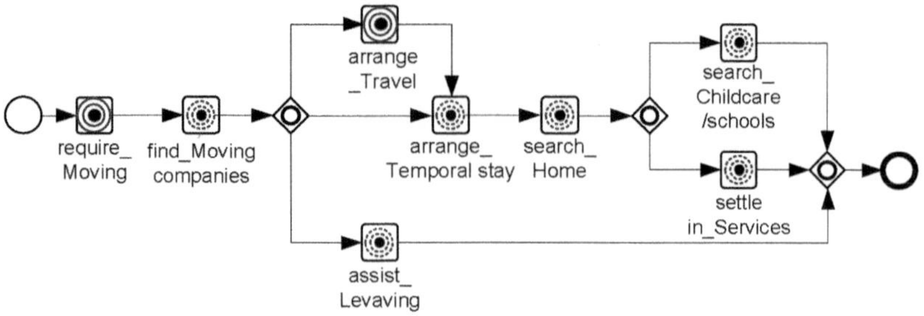

Fig. 3. Meta level services of the VE-IMS

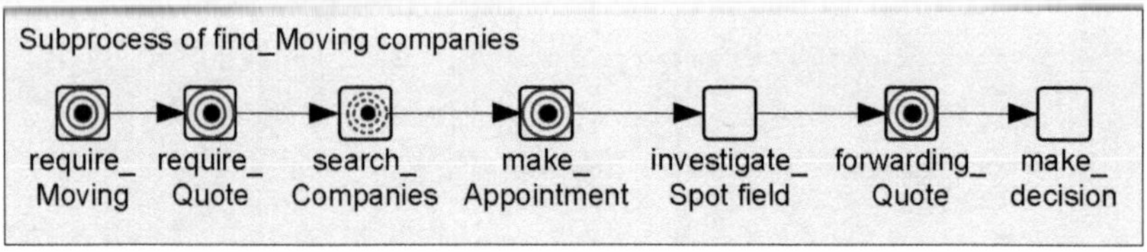

Fig. 4. Subprocess of finding a moving company

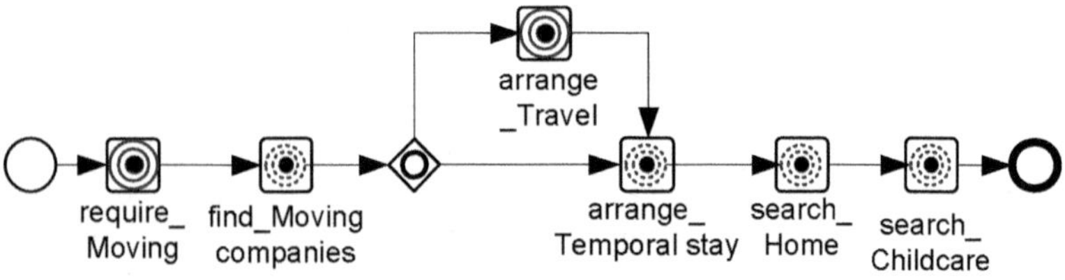

Fig. 5. Processes for the extended VE-IMS

modify, enhance, customize or extend an existing service mashup, or include and combine parts or components (or both) from multiple existing service mashups.

A preliminary service of the VE-IMS is to help customers to find a moving company for shipping their household effects to the new place of residence. Figure 4 shows the process of the finding a moving company. First, the VE-IMS will request free quotes from moving companies according to the customer's place of departure and destination, and if needed, arrange for visits, and provide a list of competent movers with their quotes.

Another, extended, service the VE-IMS may provide is finding an international mover and arranging temporary places of residence at both the locations of departure and destination, based on the dates of moving, travel, and the arrival of the household effects. The temporary place of residence at the destination should be close to a certain address such as the customer's working place. Customer can also ask for travel arrangements to be made. The time to fly and time of staying at the temporary address should be worked out to minimize the total costs. Further, the customer may want the VE-IMS to find an available childcare place for the children of the customer as soon as possible, then find a rental home close by around the time that the household effects arrive. The second extended international moving service is shown in Figure 5.

5 Related Work

The concept of Internet scale workflows is sometimes used interchangeably with that of Web-scale workflows. Both Internet and Web scale workflows involve great number of internet based services and adopt a service-oriented paradigm [2, 4]. However, not all service-based workflows are Internet scale workflows or Web scale workflows. Internet or Web scale workflows involve services distributed though the Internet. There are many open issues related to Internet or Web scale workflows. Lightweight and user friendly process modeling is one of information issues at a design stage. Process modeling further effect to service description and process execution.

Lightweight process modeling language is designed for process oriented business [3]. The language is designed for business users who do not have deep business process design knowledge. It requires the process mashup engineer who could map the abstract activities into the concrete services. Our modeling language for ISVECs is based on the lightweight business process modeling language [3] and lightweight process modeling for virtual enterprise process collaboration language [8]. It provides strong end user aspects on business flexibility, adapbility and agility. The Internet-scale virtual enterprise collaboration is therefore different with an approach mentioned in Internet-scale workflow [2]. The process mashup engineer will discover services and map abstract process activities into concrete services [7].

Similarly, the concept of instant virtual enterprises (IVEs) is introduced in [6] to dynamically select collaborating partners and weave the interorganisational links between their local processes. Moreover, CrossWork system is developed to create and operate IVEs by decomposing high-level goal into a set of operational business goals, identifying collaboration partners that can fulfill the goals, retrieving the external specifications of selected local process, and finally mapping the composed global business process onto the IVE's distributed infrastructure and executes it there. Different from creating IVEs, our approach concentrates on the business collaborations among virtual enterprises. Particularly, it proposes a lightweight process modeling language and the corresponding metamodel to create the Internet scale virtual enterprises collaborations, and introduces goals to help business users define abstract processes and finally map them into concrete services available on the Internet.

6 Conclusions

Internet scale workflows put more demands on process modeling. Multiple service providers are generally involved, and their actions are largely independent and outside control of the process owner, services can suddenly change because of new versions. Networking issues can make services temporarily unavailable or have unacceptable latencies.

Virtual enterprises have a strong advantage in business agility. Their small size and loose ties with partners make that they are not held back by large bureaucracies. They depend on tight integration with suppliers of various services. Internet and automation enable this integration. Automation of business processes is generally provided by business process management systems. For virtual enterprises to be able to quickly respond to changing business environments they therefore need agile business process support.

Agile business process support has two parts. The first part is run-time support for change on-the-fly, a topic not discussed in this paper. The second part is to make it easy to change business processes. To enable business process agility modification of processes should be possible by a broad set of stakeholders, not only by business process specialists as an extra link in the chain.

Business process mashups [7] are designed to provide agility, resilience and end user modifiability. Therefore, they are a good candidate to support internet scale virtual enterprise collaborations.

Acknowledgement. This research project is supported by the National Basic Research Program of China (973) under Grant 2007CB310801, the National Natural Science Foundation of China under Grant No. 60970017, and the Fundamental Research Funds for the Central Universities under Grant No. 3101032.

The authors would like to thank the EU SOA4All and FAST projects. Part of work by Dr. Lai Xu and Dr. Paul de Vrieze was performed at the SAP Research, Switzerland.

References

1. BPMN, `http://www.bpmn.org/`
2. Tretola, G., Zimeo, E.: Autonomic internet-scale workflows. In: Proceedings of the 3rd International Workshop on Monitoring, Adaptation and Beyond (MONA 2010), pp. 48–56. ACM, New York (2010)
3. Xie, L., Xu, L., de Vrieze, P.: Lightweight Business Process Modelling. In: 2010 International Conference on E-Business and E-Government (ICEE 2010), Guangzhou, China, May 7-9 (2010)
4. Blake, M.B., Huhns, M.N.: Web-Scale Workflow: Integrating Distributed Services. IEEE Internet Computing 12(1), 55–59 (2008)
5. Papazoglou, M.P., Georgakopoulos, D.: Service-oriented Computing. Communications of the ACM 46(10), 24–28 (2003)
6. Grefen, P., Eshuis, R., Mehandjiev, N., Kouvas, G., Weichhart, G.: IEEE Internet Computing 13(6), 65–73 (2009)
7. de Vrieze, P.T., Xu, L., Bouguettaya, A., Yang, J., Chen, J.: Building enterprise mashups. Future Generation Computer Systems 27(5), 637–642 (2011)
8. Xu, L., de Vrieze, P.T., Phalp, K.T., Jeary, S., Liang, P.: Lightweight Process Modelling for Virtual Enterprise Process Collaboration. In: Camarinha-Matos, L.M., Boucher, X., Afsarmanesh, H. (eds.) PRO-VE 2010. IFIP AICT, vol. 336, pp. 501–508. Springer, Heidelberg (2010)

E^3value to BPMN Model Transformation

Hassan Fatemi, Marten van Sinderen, and Roel Wieringa

Information Systems (IS) Research Group, EEMCS Department,
University of Twente, Enschede, The Netherlands
{h.fatemi,m.j.vansinderen,r.j.wieringa}@utwente.nl

Abstract. Business value and coordination process perspectives need to be taken into consideration while modeling business collaborations. The need for these two models stems from the importance of separating the how from the what concerns. A business value model shows what is offered by whom to whom while a coordination process model shows how these offerings are fulfilled operationally. This case study addresses the model transformation between e3value and BPMN, commonly used for modeling business collaborations from value and coordination perspectives respectively.

Keywords: Value model, coordination process model, model transformation.

1 Introduction

Value models support business design decisions, while coordination models support IT design decisions. The motivations for business decisions are commercial and strategic, while the motivations for IT decisions are technical. The business decisions must be made by business managers and the IT decisions by IT managers. Value and coordination models represent different aspects of an e-business network but they have obvious consistency relations that enable partial automated support for designing one of these models based on the other. This is not only useful for e-business design, but it also helps us to understand the similarities and differences between value and coordination models and improves our insight into the logic of the decisions that must be made in e-business network design. These insights are independent from notation.

The purpose of this case study is to define a model transformation between two languages commonly used for modeling business collaborations: the e^3value methodology [1] and the Business Process Modeling Notation (BPMN) [2].

A business web is a collection of enterprises designed to jointly satisfy a consumer need [3]. E^3value is a notation to model a business web from a value point of view. It shows the creation, distribution, and consumption of goods or services of economic value in a business web. The main goal of value modeling is to reach agreement amongst profit-and-loss responsible stakeholders regarding the question "Who is offering what of value to whom and expects what of value in return?" It also enables the stakeholders to assess their potential profitability in the business web and therefore develop an insight into the economical viability and sustainability of the whole business web. The target users of this notation are business stakeholders.

BPMN, on the other hand, is a standard notation for modeling business processes for the purposes of business analysis and its target users are business analysts.

L.M. Camarinha-Matos et al. (Eds.): PRO-VE 2011, IFIP AICT 362, pp. 333–340, 2011.

Business value models have different goals and concepts compared to process models [4]. Nevertheless they should be consistent with each other because they both refer to the same system. A lot of researches have been done regarding generating one of the models based on the other [5-9] and checking their consistency [10-12].

In [9] we have proposed a stepwise and pattern-based method for generating a coordination model from a value model. In our transformation method, we start by finding value patterns in the value model and add their counterpart coordination patterns to the coordination model. This paper discusses the automation of this transformation process by modeling the value model in a graph and applying transformation rules on it using a graph transformation tool (Groove) [13].

2 (Business) Value Models

An e^3value model consists of a graphic part and a computational part. The graphic part is a diagram and the computational part is a spreadsheet with algorithms that can do Net Present Value (NPV) estimations for the stakeholders involved in the diagram. In e^3value we model a business web as a graph in which the nodes represent economic actors and the edges represent economic transactions. An e^3value model also shows how a consumer need is met by a set of economic transactions between actors[1].

Consider the e^3value model (Fig. 1) in which Buyer gives Money to Seller and receives Good in return and the Seller gives Money to the Transporter and receives Transport. This simple model illustrates the following modeling constructs of e^3value:

- **Contract Period.** A value model describes economic transactions during a specific period of time. It should be specified in supporting documentation.
- **Actor.** An actor is an independent economic (and often also legal) entity with a specific interest in the collaboration (making profit, increasing utility, earning experience ...). Actors in Fig. 1 are Buyer, Seller and Transporter. The actor for whom the business web is made to satisfy his needs is called the consumer. We represent the consumer need by a bullet placed inside this actor (Buyer in Fig. 1).
- **Market Segment.** A market segment is a set of actors that assign economic value to objects equally. They are shown as overlapping rectangles.
- **Value Object.** A value object is a service, good, money, or experience, that is of economic value to at least one actor and that is exchanged between actors. In our example value objects are Money, Good, Money and Transport.
- **Value Port.** An actor uses a value port to provide/request value objects to/from other actors. A value port is a conceptual construct indicating that during the contract period, an actor is capable of giving or receiving a value object. Value ports are represented by tiny triangles on the edge of the shapes depicting actors.

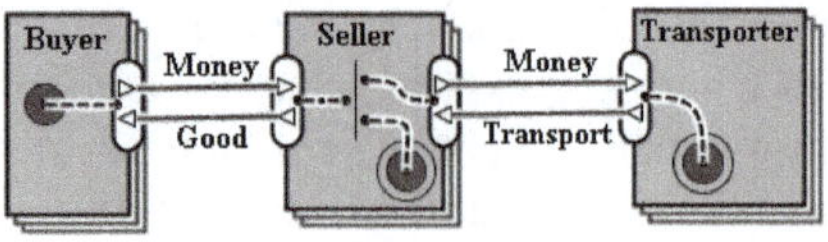

Fig. 1. A simple value model

- **Value Interface.** Value interfaces group value ports and indicate atomicity: if one value port in the interface is triggered in the contract period, all of them are triggered in that period (however the model makes no statement about when this will happen: this has to be specified in a corresponding coordination model). Value interfaces are represented by oval shapes surrounding the value ports.
- **Value Transfer.** Value transfers link value ports of different actors, implying that the actors are willing to transfer value objects in the indicated direction.
- **Value Transaction.** Value transfers should come in economic reciprocal pairs, which are called value transactions.
- **Dependency Path.** A dependency path connects value interfaces of the same actor together, meaning that if one of the value interfaces is triggered the connected value interfaces also must be triggered [1]. It consists of dependency nodes and connections. A dependency node is a consumer need, an AND-fork (the sign in the actor Seller) or AND-join, an OR-fork or OR-join, or a boundary element (Bull's eye sign). A consumer need is the trigger for the transfer of value objects. A boundary element indicates that no more value transfers can be triggered. A dependency is represented by a dashed line. After estimating the frequencies and values of the transactions in the computational part of the value model profitability estimations can be done by tracing the dependency path of transactions that are triggered by each occurrence of the consumer need.

2.1 Value Model Example

We take an example that handles clearing Intellectual Property Rights (IPR). It has two steps: 1) collecting fees from IPR users (owners of radio stations, bars, discotheque, etc.) who play music in public spaces to get money from it, and 2) repartitioning the collected fees to Right Owners (artists, producers, publishers, etc.). IPR fee collection is currently done based on statistical evidence, but SENA (http://www.sena.nl/), one of the main IPR societies in the Netherlands, is interested in a business model in which fees are collected on a pay-per-play basis, where for each music track, a track-specific business web of clearing organizations is composed.

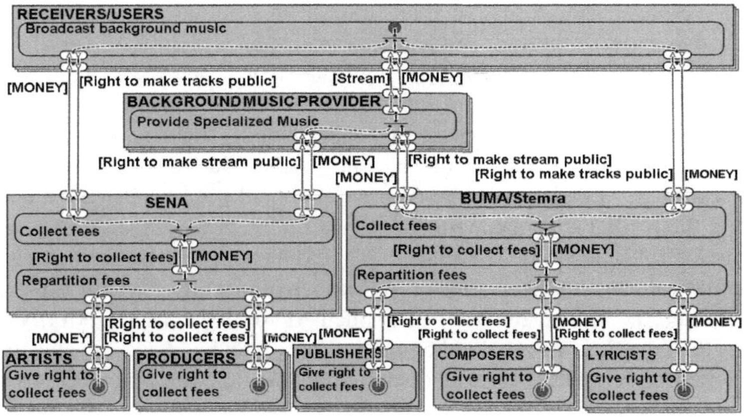

Fig. 2. Value model of providing music by Streaming

The diagram (Fig. 2) shows a number of actors that are engaged in commercial transactions. Receivers of music (bars, restaurants, supermarkets, etc.) receive music from specialized companies that provide background music. The receivers as well as the background music providers have to pay for the rights of those involved in creating this music. In the Netherlands these rights are collected by two organizations, SENA and BUMA/Stemra each responsible for collecting rights on behalf of some specific right owners. All transactions, including music distribution, are done on-line.

3 From Value Model to Coordination Model

While there are satisfactory solutions for transforming models to text, this is not the case for transforming models to models. Graph-based-transformation approaches are inspired by theoretical work in graph rewriting. These approaches are powerful and declarative, but also complex. The complexity stems from the non-determinism in scheduling and application strategy, which requires careful consideration of termination of the transformation process and the rule application ordering.

We model the value model shown in Fig. 2 as a graph in Groove (Fig. 3). The AND/OR nodes connected to stakeholder's node by an edge labeled with 'r' indicate the logical relation (AND/OR) of the incoming/outgoing edges to/from a node. Each stakeholder node and the AND and OR nodes connected to it by an edge labeled with ‘r’ represent one integrated conceptual node. In this way, the model indicates that Receiver has three value exchanges with SENA, BMP and BUMA with an AND relation between them i.e. they make a unit of exchange which means either all of them occur or none. SENA has two value exchanges with Receiver and BMP with an OR relation between them. Upon receiving money either from Receiver or BMP, SENA should distribute it to the appropriate right owners. This graph is the starting graph in the model transformation process.

Two transformation rules are shown in Fig. 4. The rule in Fig. 4(a) indicates that if there is a pair of edges (value transfers), namely 'x' and 'y', between two distinct nodes (stakeholders), delete those two edges and add four nodes labeled with 'Send' and 'Request' connected to those two nodes by edges labeled with 'x' and 'y' as shown in Fig. 4(a). To prevent the recursive application of this rule on the newly added nodes, we need to specify in the rule that the two main nodes should be neither Send nor Request. Similarly, the rule in Fig. 4(b) indicates that if there is a single edge (value transfer), namely 'x', between two distinct nodes, delete that edge and add a node labeled with 'Send' connected to those two nodes by edges labeled with 'x' as shown in Fig. 4(b). To prevent application of this rule on the fake edges labeled with 'r' it is stipulated that the edge between the two nodes should not be labeled with 'r'. Again, to prevent the recursive application of this rule on the newly added node, we need to specify in the rule that the two main nodes should be neither Send nor Request.

The first rule has a higher priority, so Groove applies it first until it has no more matches. Then the second rule will be applied. If we don't specify priority for these two rules they conflict with each other and in case of having a pair of value exchanges between two stakeholders, instead of applying the first rule, the second rule may apply twice.

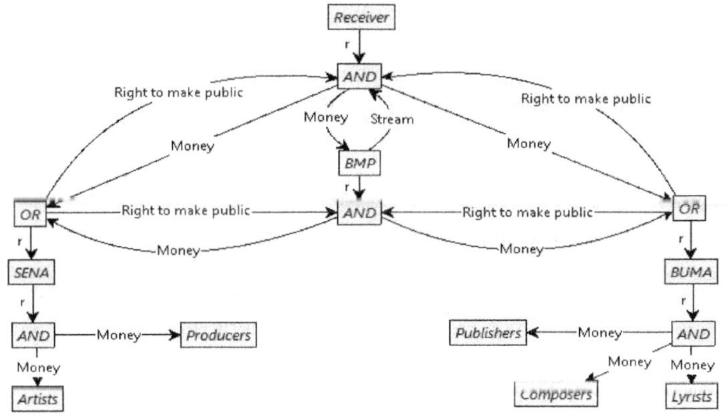

Fig. 3. Start graph for value model of providing music by streaming (Fig. 2)

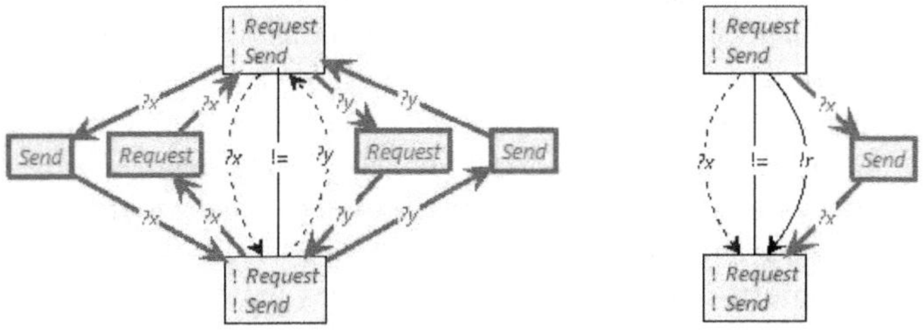

(a) A pair of related value transfers (x,y) **(b) A single value transfer (x)**

Fig. 4. Two transformation rules modeled in Groove

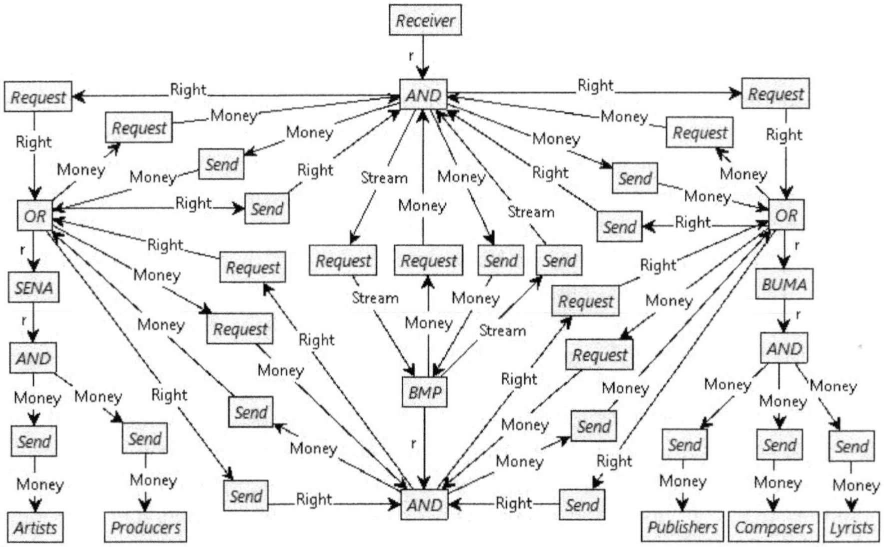

Fig. 5. Final graph after applying the above two transformation rules

Fig. 5 shows the final graph resulting from applying the transformation rules shown in Fig. 4 on the start graph. It shows all the necessary message exchanges between the stakeholders and the logical relation between the incoming/outgoing messages to/from a stakeholder's node. Note that there is no temporal ordering between the messages in this graph. Hence, the resulting graph is an interaction/communication model rather than a coordination model.

3.1 Making the Coordination Model

As we mentioned above, the result of the transformation process (Fig. 3) is not a coordination model but rather an interaction/communication model which shows all the necessary message interactions between the stakeholders and the logical relation between the incoming/outgoing messages to/from a stakeholder's node. To make a coordination model we need to add temporal ordering to the model, i.e. indicating the order in which the messages are exchanged between the actors.

The temporal meaning of the dependency path is merely that if the consumer need is triggered in the contract period, then the connected transactions are also triggered in the contract period. The dependency path actually represents the structure of the profitability computations not a process that coordinates the transactions. Many different coordination processes are compatible with a single value model.

Putting messages in a correct and meaningful order needs expert intervention and cannot be automated using the value model only. We need to supplement the value model with more information. Some of the messages indicate the transfer of value from one actor to the other, for example the Send message labeled with 'Money' from Receiver to SENA and the Send message labeled with 'Right' from SENA to Receiver imply the transfer of money and right respectively. The order in which these value objects are exchanged between stakeholders depends among others on the trust relations between the stakeholders. If, initially, Receiver sends the money to SENA in the hope that SENA acts reciprocally by returning the requested rights, it means that Receiver trusts SENA. Otherwise, if SENA, before receiving the money, sends the requested right to Receiver in the hope that Receiver will pay later, it means that SENA trusts Receiver. The third scenario, in which both SENA and Receiver need to trust each other at some point in time, is the case in which, initially, Receiver pays not all the money but part of it to SENA and then SENA sends the requested right to Receiver and finally Receiver sends SENA the remaining of the payment.

If we had the trust relations between the stakeholders or the way in which they want to transfer the value objects, then we could accordingly determine the temporal ordering of messages in the coordination model. For further discussions on the issue of message ordering using trust relations, we refer the reader to our recent work in [14].

We derived a coordination model from the model produced by the tool, but there is no space to show the resulting coordination model (which also is not of interest for this paper anyway). Ways to support this last part of transformation with automated solutions (e.g., providing the expert with decision support, or applying constraints implied by trust relations automatically) are for further study.

4 Discussion

According to [4], business value models and coordination process models can have different actors. This happens only when the two models have different granularities. By abstracting from the sub-actors and the internal activities inside the actors, both models can always be designed using the same actors. In what follows we assume that this has been done.

One of the main remaining differences between business value models and coordination process models is type of objects exchanged by actors [4, 9]. In a value model every object should be of value to at least one partner, but in a coordination model objects are not included necessarily because they are of economic value to a partner. They can also be included because they help coordinating the activities of the partners. The application of the transformation rules covers this difference by adding all the necessary interaction messages to the model regardless of whether they are of economic value to a partner. In this paper we use a pattern with minimal interaction messages (a pair of 'Request', 'Send' messages) to realize a value transfer. In general, patterns which include more detailed pre and post interaction messages can be used. As a difference between business value models and coordination process models, [4] mentions a special case in which there is a value exchange (e.g. experience, entertainment, pleasure …) that has no associated direct physical or information flow in the coordination model. We think all value transfers, and all objects in a coordination model, are physical. In a coordination model, we abstract from the physical world and represent the manipulation and transfer of information, but the information is of course implemented physically. But this physical implementation (on paper, as electric signals, dots on a screen etc.) is not relevant and not insightful, so we abstract from it. In a value model, all transfers are physical too: on paper (money, books, pictures etc.), as sound (music, spoken information), etc. therefore we think this special kind of value exchanges are not real value exchanges. Instead they are the cause or effect of another value exchange. For example, assume that there is an online radio station that charges you if you want to listen to its music. In this case there is one obvious value transfer from the user/listener to the radio station which is 'Money'. However the reciprocal value object may be modeled as 'entertainment' in the value model. If so, applying our pattern does not yield an appropriate result. Nevertheless we think 'entertainment' is not a value transfer but it is the effect of a value transfer, namely 'Broadcasting Music'. Therefore, in this case 'Request'and 'Send' messages are indicating asking and giving permission.

The other main difference between business value models and coordination process models mentioned by [4, 9] is the notion of temporal ordering. In an e^{3}value model there intentionally is no notion of time ordering at all [1]. Behavior and temporal order are beyond the value perspective and are part of the coordination perspective.

E^{3}value models have a value reciprocity concept which basically means every value transfer should have an associated value transfer in reverse direction. This concept has no associated counterpart in the coordination process model. E^{3}value also includes a computational part which enables the stakeholders to do profitability analysis which also has no associated counterpart in the coordination process model.

5 Conclusion

In this paper we address the automation of our business value model to coordination process model transformation method [9] using Groove. It turns out that we can automatically cover all the gaps caused by different factors except the one caused by the notion of time/temporal ordering, which is not present in business value models while it is a fundamental concept in coordination process models. The resulting model form the automated transformation of value model is an interaction/communication model rather than a coordination model. It needs expert intervention to add time/temporal ordering to the exchanges messages and make the final coordination process model.

References

1. Gordijn, J., Akkermans, H.: Value based requirements engineering: Exploring innovative e-commerce ideas. Requirements Engineering Journal 8, 114–134 (2002)
2. OMG: Business Process Modeling Notation (BPMN) Version 1.0. OMG Final Adopted Specification. OMG (2006), `http://www.bpmn.org/`
3. Tapscott, D., Ticoll, D., Lowy, A.: Digital Capital: Harnessing the Power of Business Webs. Harvard Business School Press, Boston (2000)
4. Gordijn, J., Akkermans, H., van Vliet, H.: Business modelling is not process modelling. In: ER Workshops, pp. 40–51 (2000)
5. Andersson, B., et al.: From business to process models - a chaining methodology. In: 8th Int. Conference on the Advanced Information Systems and Engineering, CAiSE 2006 (2006)
6. Wieringa, R., Pijpers, V., Bodenstaff, L., Gordijn, J.: Value-driven coordination process design using physical delivery models. In: Li, Q., Spaccapietra, S., Yu, E., Olivé, A. (eds.) ER 2008. LNCS, vol. 5231, pp. 216–231. Springer, Heidelberg (2008)
7. Weigand, H., et al.: Value object analysis and the transformation from value model to process model. In: Enterprise Interoperability, pp. 55–65. Springer, London (2007)
8. Fatemi, H., van Sinderen, M.J., Wieringa, R.J.: From business value model to coordination process model. In: Poler, R., van Sinderen, M., Sanchis, R. (eds.) IWEI 2009. LNBIP, vol. 38, pp. 94–106. Springer, Heidelberg (2009)
9. Fatemi, H., van Sinderen, M.J., Wieringa, R.J.: Value-oriented coordination process modeling. In: Hull, R., Mendling, J., Tai, S. (eds.) BPM 2010. LNCS, vol. 6336, pp. 162–177. Springer, Heidelberg (2010)
10. Zlatev, Z., Wombacher, A.: Consistency between e3-value models and activity diagrams in a multi-perspective development method. In: Chung, S. (ed.) OTM 2005. LNCS, vol. 3760, pp. 520–538. Springer, Heidelberg (2005)
11. Bodenstaff, L., Wombacher, A., Reichert, M.U.: On formal consistency between value and coordination models. Technical Report TR-CTIT-07-91, Enschede (2007)
12. Zarvi¢, N., Wieringa, R., van Eck, P.: Checking the alignment of value-based business models and it functionality. In: SAC 2008: ACM Symposium on Applied Computing, NY, USA, pp. 607–613 (2008)
13. Ghamarian, A.H., et al.: Modelling and analysis using GROOVE. International Journal on Software Tools for Technology Transfer (STTT), 1–26 (2011)
14. Fatemi, H., van Sinderen, M.J., Wieringa, R.J.: Trust and Business Webs. In: The Fifteenth IEEE International EDOC Conference, 29 August-2 September. IEEE Computer Society, Helsinki (in press, 2011)

Process Risk Management Using Configurable Process Models

Raimar Scherer and Wael Sharmak

Institute for Construction Informatics, TU Dresden, Germany
{Raimar.Scherer,Wael.Sharmak}@tu-dresden.de

Abstract. Almost no construction project performs totally as planned as dynamic changes are frequently needed. These changes can be ascribed to the high uncertainty, which is evaluated as potential causes of risks and risks is in turn are evaluated as potential causes of plan changes. Several concepts from the Business Process Modeling domain are adopted to build an explicit process-oriented knowledge documentation of the construction processes. A standardized process description is suggested that offers flexibility in its content to be usable in different contexts. Configurable fragments in the course of the process models express the uncertain parts of the process. A general structure of a Configurable Reference Process Model (CRPM) is developed as an ontology model to document the construction processes in a Process-oriented Knowledge base. By using this knowledge base a considerable planning effort will be saved. Moreover, the quality of the process schedules, since they will be derived from the reference process models, will be enhanced and the expenditure of time will be reduced.

Keywords: Uncertainty, Risk, Change, Configuration, Business Process Modeling, Reference Process Model.

1 Introduction

The construction industry is a project-based business sector. Each project can be considered as a temporary alliance among diverse partners that will execute, in a private or in a cooperative way, several processes. This results in achieving the planned project objectives.

In this industry, the experience showed that mostly no construction project goes totally as planned because of the needed dynamic changes to different management plans. These changes can be ascribed to the relatively high uncertainty in the planning phase of a construction project. Several factors play a role to increase the total project uncertainty, such as the lack of experience with a certain type of construction processes or the changeable environment that surrounds and affects a construction process. In view of that, the risk of changing the already planned course of work as a need to adjust to current situation is really high. Such adjustments could be carried out, as a proactive or reactive risk treatment, even several times within the execution phase of the targeted process, if different risks in different points in time will arise.

L.M. Camarinha-Matos et al. (Eds.): PRO-VE 2011, IFIP AICT 362, pp. 341–348, 2011.

The process knowledge collected from different resources is valuable for the effective process management, as it can reduce the uncertainty and, consequently, the error rate in the process planning will be lower. Hence, this knowledge should be documented in an explicit way to enable all the interested people to share and use their experiences properly. In a view of that, the standardization of construction processes that will include the best process practice can be a possible solution to reduce the accompanied uncertainty. Nevertheless, it is mostly impossible to apply the exact construction process as explicit work route in different projects. Accordingly, a degree of individuality is required within each process use. For that reason, a standardized process description should offer a certain degree of flexibility in its content to be usable in different project contexts.

In other business sectors, like insurance, banking and government, different Business Process Modeling techniques were successfully used to standardize and optimize business process knowledge. Moreover, they were used to communicate process contents between different disciplines or else to automate, partially or completely, process execution. Instead of that, for the modeling of construction processes, the traditional critical path method is still widely used. However, this method has no ICT support in its background.

The paper introduces a novel, process-centered view on process standardization that focuses on the risk management using some configuration aspects from the Business Process Modeling domain. Accordingly, a structure of a configurable reference process model (CRPM) that includes configurable fragments is suggested. These configurable fragments are based on the configuration templates mentioned in chapter 3. For a better management of the CRPMs, a knowledge base is introduced in chapter 5 that reflects the structure of the CRPM and enables the maintenance of the process-oriented knowledge.

2 Dependencies between Uncertainty, Risk, and Change Terms

Generally, the uncertainty in construction is a result of the lack of needed reliable information, which can be attributed to different environmental, organizational, or technical factors. The role and importance of each factor differs from project to project according to the specific project characteristics and to its surrounding environment. This uncertain nature may lead to a big variance between the results of deterministic methods used for project management planning and real practice. Usually, the deviation of the project management baselines can be reduced when the degree of uncertainty in the project can be decreased. This can be done as soon as a comprehensive knowledge about the project is available. As the practice in construction is project-based, better knowledge can be acquired from lessons learned and experiences gained from the past projects. This knowledge will help to make better planning decisions as well as to reduce mistakes on past projects to be repeated. When the project progresses, the accuracy of the made decisions becomes more clear and the ambiguity disappears gradually. However, it is generally impossible to acquire a comprehensive knowledge about the project in advance. Therefore, a systematic risk analysis should be undertaken to evaluate the project's risks and opportunities and, consequently, to reduce the negative effect of uncertainty on the project objectives.

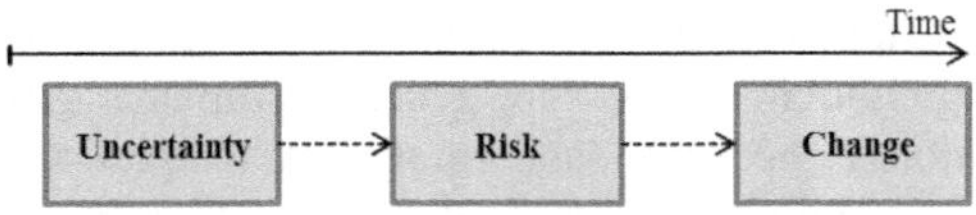

	Uncertainty	Risk	Change
Consequences	Unpredictable	Predictable	Mostly known
Occurrence probability	Unpredictable	predictable	Known (1 or 0)
Timing	Unknown	Unknown	Known

Fig. 1. The possible causality between uncertainty, risk and later change

Nevertheless, changes in construction projects are likely to occur at any stage and can affect different project management plans. In the literature on change management [1], [2], [3] it is emphasized that changes are inevitable in construction projects even if comprehensive studies have been made. The uncertainty in the project should be evaluated as potential causes of risks in the project [4]. In turn, in this work it is assumed that risks should be evaluated as potential causes of changes in the project management plan (Fig. 1). Based on this, a risk as an uncertain event may invoke one or more changes in the one or more project plans.

3 Configuration Templates

A main hypothesis of this work is that all possible ways of changes in the structure of process models, as a treatment to probable or even actual risks, can be standardized by generalized templates. For this purpose, several templates are suggested as types of configurable fragments within process models [5]. Those are assumed to cover all kinds of process model related structure changes and consequently they will offer the needed flexibility in the process model. These templates are based on the concepts suggested by [6] as an extension to the event-driven process chains (EPC) elements. In view of that, a configuration template can be defined as a basic type of configurable fragments in the process model that describes one possible way of model structure change as a response to a certain event. As a result, a configured and specified template can be used to represent the structural change in a process model caused by the treatment of a specific risk event. Nevertheless, more than one configuration template may be used to represent a complex effect of one risk when it will cause changes in more than one location in the process model. In this sense, dealing with complex issues does not require complex templates as the basic suggested templates can be used together to cover a complex change case.

Building upon the classifications of risks and changes in the literature of construction management two major aspects were considered important from the process-oriented perspective. These aspects are (1) the timing of response to the risk (proactive or reactive response) and (2) the effect of the risk on the progress of the process, i.e. will it cause progress interruption or not. In view of that, the templates are classified into three main groups. These groups are:

- General Templates; these templates can be implemented in either proactive or reactive treatment cases. The general templates group contains the Insertion, Substitution, Cancelation, and Parallelism templates.
- Interruptive Templates; used to describe a disturbance risk that affects and stops a process during its execution. The interruptive templates group contains the Stop and Action templates.
- Reactive Templates; used only as response to events which have affected tasks or products considered to be completed. The reactive templates group contains the Repetition and Demolition templates.

4 Using Configurable Fragments in Process Models

A configurable fragment is an implemented instance of one of the configuration templates in a process model. In this work, a configurable process model is defined as a process model that contains one or more configurable fragments. Fig. 2 shows a configurable process model that contains three configurable fragments, namely (I) insertion of T(r) after T(i), (II) T(y) parallelism to T(k) as well as (III) T(m) and T(n) substitution by T(s). The configuration requirement R(1) links the configurable fragments (I) and (II) together. So according to the Risk 1 status (ON, OFF) these two configurable fragments will be configured. The link of configurable fragments (I) and (II) through the requirement R(1) builds a way to reflect the case when a risk may cause changes in different positions in the process model.

The configurable fragment (III) in Fig. 2 is configured according to the (ON, OFF) status of Risk 2. Accordingly four Configured Cases (CCs) can be derived from the configurable process model in Fig. 2.

5 Knowledge-Base for the Specification of Configurable Reference Process Models

The configuration templates offer an approach to represent the flexibility, needed in construction processes, in the shape of configurable fragments within the process models. The configurable fragments represent risk treatments that may be adopted or skipped according to the risk status. Generally, a process model that contains, amongst others, all the exceptional cases, in the shape of configurable fragments, of the process is a candidate to be a CRPM for this particular process. Nevertheless, if the process may have several interrelated exceptional cases the corresponding model can be complex and, consequently, difficult to illustrate graphically, use or to update. Therefore, a knowledge-base (KB) is suggested to manage these reference models. The KB structure is designed as an ontology model that consists of several process-oriented concepts related to each other via proper properties [7]. The configuration templates represent a fundamental part of the KB structure, see Table 1. In view of that, every risk treatment fragment within the CRPM should be associated to a suitable configuration template that describes how to integrate it later within the process model.

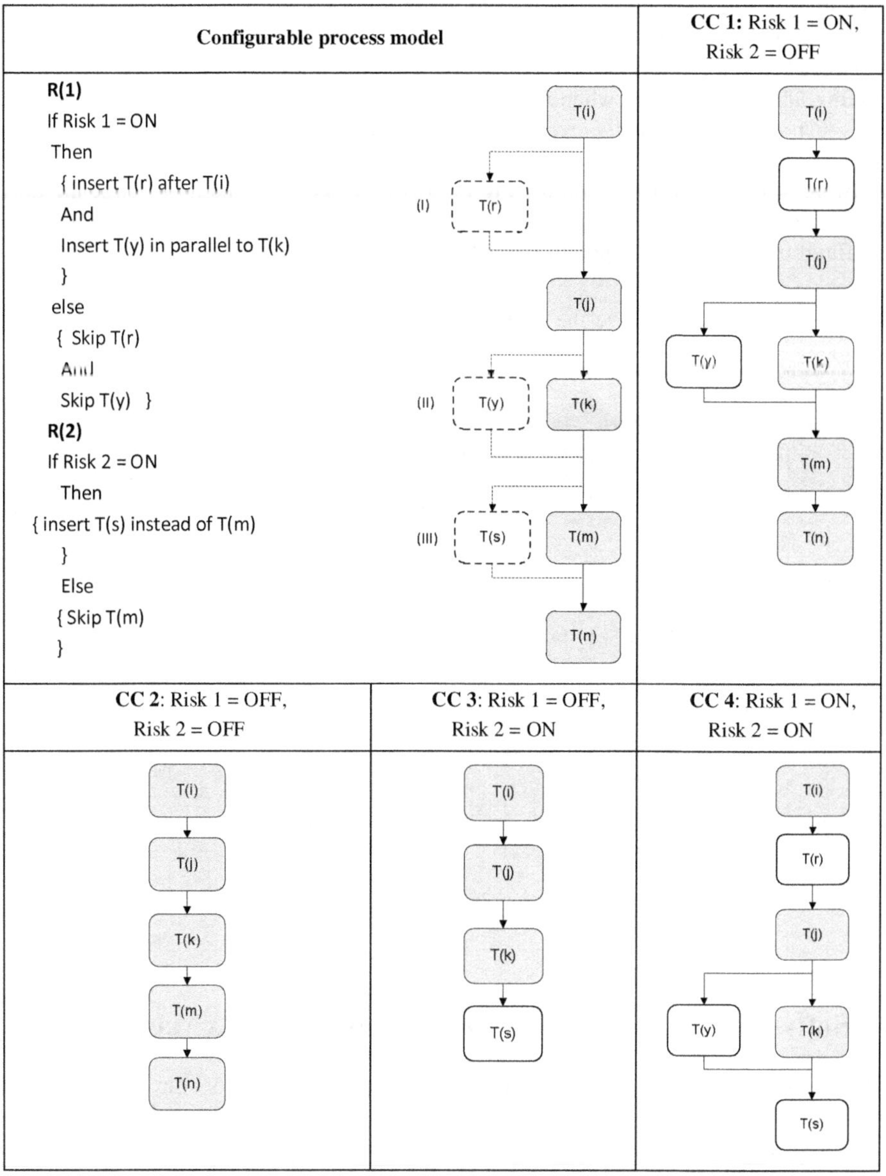

Fig. 2. A configurable process model and the four possible configured process models derived from it

Using such a KB within a construction company will enable the description of its process knowledge in a project neutral context. As a result, this could support decision-making and increase the intelligence of the construction processes. Consequently, the expenditure of time and money in the process design will be reduced. Also, A clearly defined semantics for the process models can be achieved by instantiating the elements of a CRPM from the concepts of an ontological KB. Accordingly, the ambiguity and the shortage in formality in process models can be avoided. Moreover, storing the construction CRPMs in an ontological KB will enable making advanced queries when retrieving information. These queries may even infer facts that were not explicitly created by the modeler of the CRPM. As a KB is passive data source, it is here considered as a commodity to develop a process management software tool. Therefore, it is needed to improve the access to the knowledge included in the CRPMs by developing methods, which can support the choice, the configuration, and the composition of the relevant CRPMs.

Table 1. The properties relate the configuration fragments to the Task concept through the Configuration Template concept in the ontology model

Concept	Property ⇔	Concept (Abstract)	Property ⇔	C-template groups	Property ⇔	C-template	Property ⇔	Concept
One Action Risk Treatment	Integrates/ integrated according to	Configuration Template	Is a	General Template	is a	Insertion	Before/ after/ between	Task
						Parallelism	Start - End	
						Substitution	Start - End	
						Cancelation	Target	
				Reactive Template	is a	Demolition	Target	
						Repetition	Target	
				Interruptive Template	is a	Action	Target	
						Stop	Target	

6 Software Architecture for CRPM-Based Process Management

The architecture of the suggested software tool consists of three tiers (Data, Application, and Graphical User Interface (GUI)). The data tier includes the Process-DB and the CRPM-KB. Within this tier, different types of information, CRPMs and versions of instantiated process models (IPMs), can be stored and retrieved. The retrieved information will be then passed through to the application tier for processing, and then, eventually, to the user. The data tier keeps the comprised information neutral and independent from the application tier, which improves the scalability and performance of the intended software tool. The Application tier moves the process data between the two surrounding layers. Moreover, it performs the needed procedures, e.g., configuration tasks, and makes the required procedures on the retrieved process data. Amongst others, the Application tier has to do the following:

- Query the CRPM-KB to get the relevant CRPMs.
- Configure the selected CRPM according to the preferences of the user.
- Instantiate the configured CRPM and to store it after that to the Process-DB.
- Establish a new CRPM.
- Compare different versions of the same IPM.

The GUI tier displays the processed and original information related to the process and, accordingly, allows the users to interact with the software application.

An example of the software implementation is shown in Fig. 3. During the implementation time of an IPM an exceptional event, i.e. risk, may arise and, accordingly, changes will be needed in the already planned IPM. The KB can be queried in order to find out if there is any relevant solution for the new condition. In the case that a solution is chosen from the KB, it needs to be configured, instantiated and integrated in the already planned IPM. Otherwise, an external solution will be sought after. An external solution can be used for the specific IPM and can be as well integrated in the CRPM to enhance the process knowledge included in the KB.

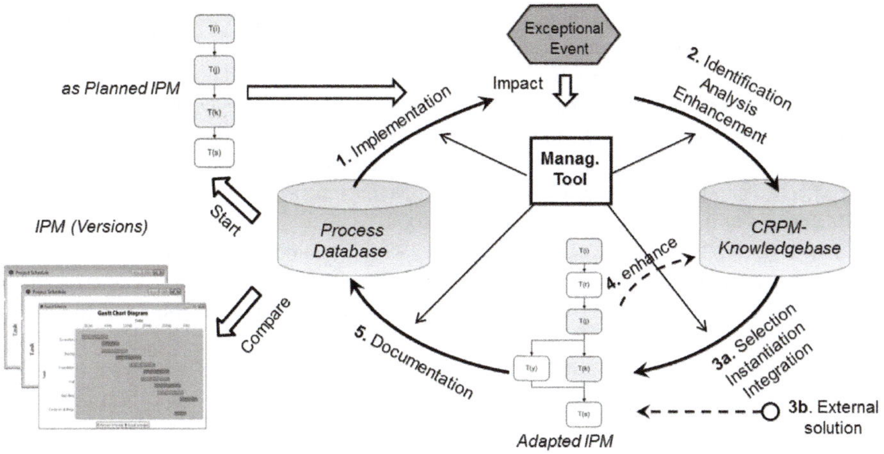

Fig. 3. The iterative adaptation cycle of an IPM

7 Conclusion

The presented approach can be used in the planning phase as well as in the execution phase of the project. In the planning phase this can help to speed up the planning and to ensure getting more reliable process schedule plans. In the execution phase it can help to accelerate the adaptability of the changed schedule plans by offering ready integrable solutions for recurring problems.

The exceptional events included in each CRPM can be used, in the planning phase of the project as a part of the checklist for risk management. Accordingly, risks can be identified based on the project relevant CRPMs and, subsequently, risk assessment can be carried out. Hence, the risks with probability/impact values above the agreed thresholds should be considered in the planning phase of the project in a proactive way. This means that the configurable fragments, which represents the risk treatment, should be adopted (included) as a part of the configured CRPM. Anyway, to realize these CRPMs in the construction practice it is still required from the construction companies to structure their knowledge in a process-oriented way and to classify the process model parts to essential and configurable fragments. Subsequently, the configurable fragments will be connected to their potential trigger-risks using the configuration templates. For this purpose, only qualified personnel should carry out the modeling of the needed CRPMs. Qualification means here that the modelers should possess enough knowledge concerning the construction process technical issues and the process modeling issues.

References

1. Lee, S., Peña-Mora, F., Park, M.: Web-enabled System Dynamics Model for Error and Change Management on Concurrent Design and Construction Projects. ASCE, Journal of Computing in Civil Engineering 20(4), 290–300 (2006)
2. Sun, M., Senaratne, S., Fleming, A., Motowa, I., Lin Yeoh, M.: A change management toolkit for construction projects. In: Architectural Engineering and Design Management. University of the West of England, University Press/Springer-Verlag, UK (2006)
3. Hao, Q., Shen, W., Neelamkavil, J., Thomas, R.: Change Management in Construction Projects. In: Rischmoller, L. (ed.) Proc. 25th W78 Conf., Improving the Management of Construction projects Through IT Adoption, Santiago, Chile (2008)
4. PMBOK Guide: A Guide to the Project Management Body of Knowledge. Project Management Institute, Pennsylvania, USA (2004)
5. Sharmak, W., Schapke, S.-E., Scherer, R.J.: Risk Treatment Templates for Configurable Reference Modeling in the Construction Industry. In: Camarinha-Matos, L.M., Picard, W. (eds.) Pervasive Collaborative Networks. IFIP International Federation for Information Processing, vol. 283, pp. 233–240. Springer, Boston (2008)
6. Mendling, J., Recker, J., Rosemann, M., van der Aalst, W.: Generating Correct EPCs from Configured C-EPCs. In: Proceedings of the 21st Annual ACM Symposium on Applied Computing, France (2006)
7. Gomez-Perez, A., Fernandez-Lopez, M., Corcho-Garcia, O.: Ontological Engineering: With examples from the areas of Knowledge Management, e-Commerce and the Semantic Web. Springer Publishing, Berlin (2004)

Part XIII

Mining Approaches in Collaborative Networks

Competence Mining for Collaborative Virtual Enterprise

Ali Harb[1], Kafil Hajlaoui[2], and Xavier Boucher[1]

[1] Ecole des Mines de Saint Etienne,
158 cours Fauriel, centre G2I, 42023 Saint Etienne, France
{harb,boucher}@emse.fr
[2] INIST – CNRS,
2 allée du Parc de Brabois CS 10310,
54519 Vandoeuvre les Nancy, France
Kafil.hajlaoui@inist.fr

Abstract. In a context of decision-aid to support the identification of collaborative networks, this paper focuses on extracting essential facets of firm competencies. We present an approach for enrichment of competence ontology, based on two steps where a novel effective filtering step is utilized. First we extract the correlation between terms of a learning dataset using the generation of association rules. Second we retain the relevant new concepts using an extracted semantic information. The suggested approach was tested on an ontology of mechanical industry competencies. Experiments were performed on real data, which show the usefulness of our approach.

Keywords: Enterprise networks, Ontology, Data mining, Association rules, Mutual Information.

1 Introduction

Several research work deal with the formalization of characteristic data concerning potential partners for networked organizations (Camarinha-Matos and Afsarmanesh 2003, Plisson.J et al. 2007, Ermilova & Afsarmanesh 2007). Most of these approaches are adapted to a semi-closed environment defined by a Virtual Breeding Environment (VBE). The VBE provides a pre-selection of potential partners, which facilitates the share of the information required.

This paper focuses on a complementary step, which consists in providing a decision aid support for identifying potential VBE when they do not exists. This research is based on the hypothesis of an open environment of potential partners to build VBEs. Typically, this issue appears when you have to analyse a regional business area so as to identify potential collaborative networks among firms. As a consequence of the initial hypothesis, the identification of potential collaborative partners will be based on the use of public information, available through the public web sites of the companies. This assumption induces specific information extraction mechanisms.

In reference to an economic approach of firm coordination (Richardson, 1987), this research focuses the information extraction procedure on two key coordination

L.M. Camarinha-Matos et al. (Eds.): PRO-VE 2011, IFIP AICT 362, pp. 351–358, 2011.

factors: the activity fields of the companies and their internal competencies (see justification in (Hajlaoui & al, 2008a)). The information on company activities and competencies will be further used, at a second stage, in order to generate new knowledge on the potential settlement of VBEs. The overall approach of decision aid has been already described in (Hajlaoui & al, 2008b).

In the current paper, we only focus on extracting key information concerning company competencies, from public and non-structured data (company web sites). Due to the complexity of the concept of competence, a semantic oriented approach is required for the extraction. In this objective, we describe in this paper the procedure of automated enrichment of an existing competency ontology, which will be used later on for an information extraction procedure based on the use of syntaxic and semantic patterns. The use of such patterns will make possible a semantic and pragmatic treatment of available data. To reduce the complexity of ontology creation, we focus our research on enhanced semantic automatic ontology enrichment specific.

This extraction approach follows the three layer model of (fig.1, Ehrig and al, 2005):

In this model the data layer structures the data source. In our procedure, data are extracted from company web sites. The html pages are cleaned and standardized with a lemmatization process. At this stage, data are considered as lexical entities. The ontology layer handles the semantic concepts to be extracted from the data sources. The concepts and their relations can be represented through an ontology which helps sharing information among distinct companies thanks to its genericity, and which make possible various semantic treatments. The third context layer is oriented towards a finer pragmatic analysis of the information to be extracted. In our approach, this layer will be developed by the formalisation and use of patterns.

It is important to note that, in this decision aid approach, there is no need to extract a precise map of company competencies. The final information expected is a similarity measure among the competency fields of distinct companies. In that objective, the ontology based extraction mechanism we will use intends to extract a set "traces" concerning the competencies of a given company.

The objective of the paper is to present a method used for automatic enrichment of competency oriented ontology. In section 2, we provide some key characteristic of the initial competency ontology that ahs been formalized and some insights on ontology building methodologies. In section 3 we describe the methodology for discovering potential conceptual term to be integrated within the ontology. In section 4, we briefly introduce some learning concepts of this approach.

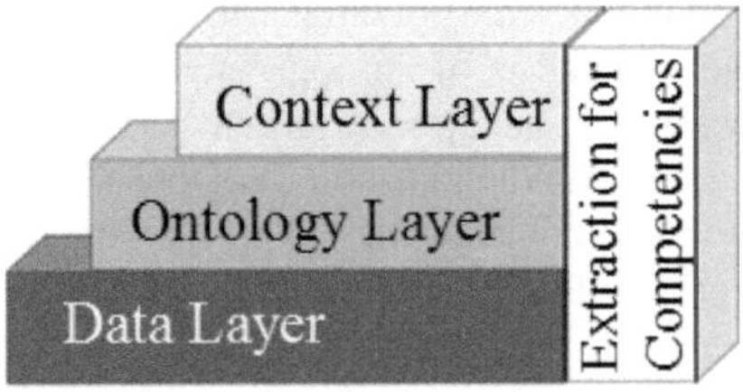

Fig. 1. Three layer model for extraction

2 Ontology for Competence Mining

The identification of company competencies is a key factor for a decision support to build collaborative networks. The ontology requires rigorous conceptualization of the notions related to firm competencies. ARCHONTE ontology building methodology (Bachimont & al., 2002) was chosen, because it defines precise cognitive principles and mechanisms for each step of ontology formalization. This method makes possible a good semantic representation of the conceptual network of the ontology through a « semantic normalisation » mechanism.

From a company website, it is often impossible to extract a relevant structured and exhaustive identification of firm competencies. However it remains possible to extract a sufficient set of competence "traces", which makes possible to assess with a good degree of precision an indicia of competence similarity among firms. To implement the extraction mechanism, an ontology of "competence traces" has been formalized. This ontology is composed of two sub-ontologies: a *generic ontology* and a *domain ontology*. The former provides a very generic conceptual model of "competence traces", which is independent of any business sector. However because of this high generality level, the generic ontology is not directly applicable for information extraction. Then, it is complemented by a *domain ontology,* which constitutes an extension of the generic ontology, specific to some selected business sector (mechanical industry in our case). The "competence traces" concepts of this domain ontology are directly linked to the applied field of the mechanical industry. Furthermore, at the lower level of the domain ontology, each ontological concept is associated to specific terms of the domain, further used in the extraction mechanism as "competence trace *identifiers*". The *identifiers* will be used to detect the presence of a competence trace concept within document corpora (extracted from company websites). This detection of "competence traces" is called the activation process applied to the ontology conceptual classes.

To fulfill the objective of extraction information, the direct detection of terms in a corpus is not a sufficient condition. To confirm the presence of an ontology concept (associated to one or several *identifiers*) in the corpus, we have to cope with context-dependent linguistic phenomena which can change the semantic of the *identifiers*: synonyms, antonyms and, more generally, semantic similarity among terms make necessary to use specific semantic techniques. To deal with such ambiguity phenomena we propose the use of linguistic patterns.

UNICOMP system is the implementation of our approach which aims at extracting company competence traces, using public information available on websites.. The coupling between ontology and patterns present a real added-value for the richness of information extraction. This research has already been further developed to integrate these results in a Decision Support System for collaboration Network Building using competence similarities measures (Hajlaoui, 2009). In the next section, an automatic or semi-automatic enrichment of the ontology and the pattern base, using case-learning techniques would be able to increase the semantic representation of competence and the overall performance of the system.

3 Discovering Potential Conceptual Term

We distinguish two types of methods for the discovery candidate's concepts: the first is based on statistical calculations using several measurements to select potential terms according to their distribution in corpora (Agirre & al., 2002), (Steinmetz & al., 2006),(Parekh & al., 2004), such as complex measurements such as mutual information, tf-idf, etc, or the use of statistical laws of term distributions (Neshatian & al., 2004). These various proposals enable identifying new candidate of enrichment terms, but do not allow placing them in ontology, without a tiresome human intervention (Jorio & al., 2007). The second type refers to syntactic methods which determine the grammatical function of a word or a word group within a sentence. It is based on the following assumption: the grammatical structure reflect semantic dependences (Bendaoud , 2006). It uses the grammatical functions of a word or a word group to present new concepts. Such methods present the drawbacks of identifying only the relations labelled by verbs. Other approaches also use syntactic patterns (Pekar & al., 2002). The extracted terms illustrate the new potential enrichment concepts.

To insert the provisional terms within an existing ontology, it is essential to detect the relations among these new terms and initial ontology concepts.), (Steinmetz & al., 2006) proposes a statistical approach based on the frequent co-occurrence of candidates terms with the concepts of initial ontology. A lack of precision is noticed among the new concepts and the ontological structure. Other approaches are based on data mining techniques (Hernandez & al., 2007). Several approaches suggest using frequent correlations among the corpora terms while using extracted association rules (Srikant & al., 1997) among potential concepts (Bendaoud , 2006). Each rule expresses the relation between two or more concepts of the field. This enrichment process requires filtering considering the large number of rules generated. Consequently human intervention is necessary to define the semantic relations discovered. Other work (Han & al., 2000), (Neshatian & al., 2004) is based on the classification methods in order to bring closer the candidates terms contained in the texts to the concepts present in ontology. The principle consists in gathering terms according to their number of occurrences within corpora (Parekh & al., 2004), using a clustering method. The disadvantage of these approaches is that they do not detect the relations among the candidates terms, i.e., unfortunately they require a human intervention for the addition of these new terms.

3.1 Approach for Discovering Concept

The purpose of this section is to present our approach. The overall process is described in figure 2. It consists of three phases. In the following sub-sections these three phases are presented in detail.

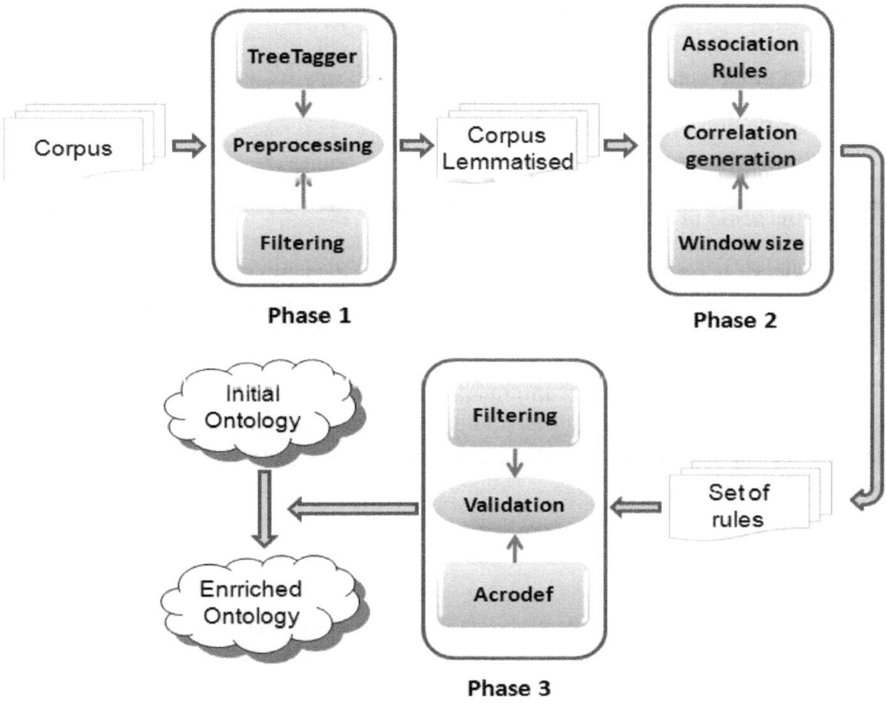

Fig. 2. Approach of ontology enrichment for competence extraction

3.2 Corpora Preprocessing

To extract and to preserve the context of sentences contained in the corpora (Hajlaoui, 2009) initially obtained from web sites, we manually built a list of stop words to be filtered (e.g. , mailto, next, previous, GIF, jpg . . .). These words are always frequent in the corpus in spite of the extraction text phase (passage of the format HTML with the textual format. This list is used to filter and clean the corpora. According to the expert analysis of the field for the initial ontology concepts and the texts of the companies describing the field of ontology, the choice of the words to be kept is according to three grammatical categories (Verb, Noun and Adjectif). In order to do that, we treated morpho-syntactically the corpora using TreeTagger (Schmid, 1994). This application enables us to obtain the category and lemma of each word. A filtering step according to these three categories was made to build a new corpora based on words considered grammatically relevant.

3.3 Window Size Creation and Concept Extraction

The objective is to search within the corpora the words which are correlated to the concepts of the ontology. Perhaps, a brief explanation of our use of the term *windowsize* is in order. A window size is a set of words that surround a given concept. For this, from the processed corpora, we seek correlations between ontological concepts and words of documents so as to enrich the ontology with more relevant and useful words. The question that arises at this point is: How to search for words correlated to the ontological concepts? The answer consists in two steps:

1) construction of Window size;
2) generation of association rules;

3.4 Generation of Association Rules

Nevertheless, in order to obtain more relevant concepts, consider the following hypothesis: the more a word is close to an initial concept, the more likely this word has strong semantic correlation. Thus, sentences are defined by considering window sizes (WS). A window size is a set of words that include one or more initial concept of ontology. In other words, as aforementioned a set of words that surround concepts. Our goal is to identify in sentences how to represent these WS. For instance, if WS is set to 1 that means that a sentence is composed by one word before and one after the pivot concept.

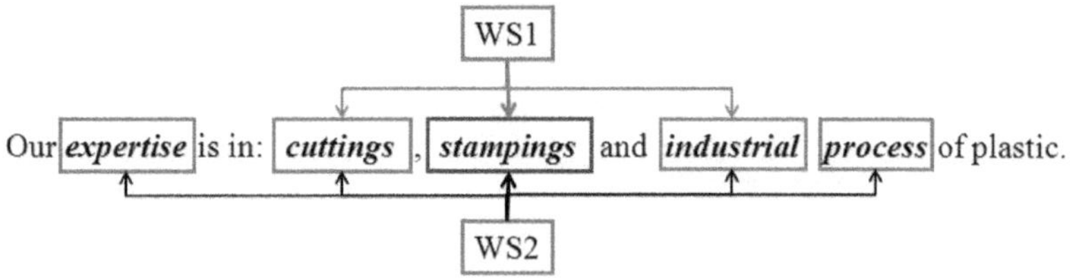

Fig. 3. Contextual localisation of competence concept

In figure 3 the pivot is stampings. Using WS whose size 1, we get the following transaction "stampings, cuttings and industrial", and by specifying a WS= 2 : "stampings, cuttings, expertise, industrial and process. These windows are the transactions for the next step. The second step is the generation of the association rules. In order to detect the semantic correlation between the terms in documents and the ontology's concepts, an association rule algorithm has been adapted (Agrawal & al., 1994) to our concern. More formally, let $I = \{i_1, ..., i_n\}$a set of terms, and D a set of sentences, where each sentence corresponds to a subset of elements of I. An association rule is thus defined as $X \rightarrow Y$, where $X \subset I$, $Y \subset I$, and $X \cap Y = \phi$. The support of a rule corresponds to the percentage of sentences in D containing $X \cup Y$. The rule $X \rightarrow Y$ has a confidence ratio c, if c% of sentences from D containing X also contain Y.

4 Experimentation

The initial domain ontology contains a large number of concepts, and the enrichment is a tedious task that requires a lot of time. Consequently, in a first time we chose to test on a single conceptual domain of the initial ontology to measure the performance of our approach. The initial list of concepts described in Table 1.

Table 1. Result of learning concepts

Initial Concepts	Generated Association Rules	Learned Concepts
Assembly, Production	Assembly !- injection(3.2, 100.0)	Adjusting, Injection
Boiler, Grinding	Stampings !- cutting (4.0, 90)	Metal, Welding
Turning, Surface	Forging !- Threading (1.7, 100.0)	Metrology, Simulation
Stamping, Treatment	Area !- metrology (2.1, 100.0)	Tools, Threading
Manufacturing, Usage	Area!- welding (1.6, 100.0)	expertise
Forging, Thermal	Machining !- expertise (2.3, 100.0)	Molding
Milling, Machining	Machining !- accuracy (1.8, 100.0)	Turning
Laser, Carry	Machining !- installation (2.9, 100.0)	Cutting

As seen from, the fact of using windows where the pivots words are the initial concepts of the ontology, and the using nouns, verbs and adjectives enables to improve considerably the detection of correlation in texts. In the same way, the use of filters significantly retained correlated relevant concepts. It should be noted that our approach was sufficiently automatic to be applied in various fields and thus extract the significant concepts elsewhere. The first results obtained are promising: we discovered and placed suitably new concepts. The analysis of the ontology obtained showed that the whole of the concepts discovered is coherent since most of them could be attached to ontology via the rules obtained. These results were also validated by the expert of the field.

5 Conclusion

In this paper, we present a new approach of ontology enrichment based on data mining techniques specifically the association rules and the use of extracted semantic information to retain relevant new concepts. Our approach is based on three steps:

1) Preprocessing of a textual corpora (cleaning and lemmatising: treetagger).

2) Creating window size to promote the correlation between corpora words and concepts of the ontology, then the application of the APRIORI algorithm to extract association rules according to validated parameters (support, confidence).

3) Automatic Analysing and filtering of generated rules to keep those that are relevant to the initial domain ontology.

The obtained enrichment results seem auspicious for the chosen domain ontology. This approach is sensitive to the domain studied: it is important to have a corpora that describes the subject domain accurately, so there is a very rich language with nouns and adjectives available. Although the company websites do not represent the ideal source for building such a corpora for the domain studied (companies competency in the mechanical industry), but we have had promising results.

References

1. Camarinha-Matos, L.M., Afsarmanesh, H.: Elements of a base VE infrastructure. Computers in Industry 51, 139–163 (2003)
2. Ermilova, E., Afsarmanesh, H.: Modeling and management of profiles and competencies in VBEs. Journal of Intelligent Manufacturing 18, 561–586 (2007)

3. Ehrig, M., Haase, P., Stojanovic, N., Hefke, M.: Similarity for Ontologies – a Comprehensive Framework. In: Proceedings of the 13th European Conference on Information Systems, Regensburg, Germany (2005)
4. Hajlaoui, K., Boucher, X., Mathieu, M.: Information Extraction procedure to support the constitution of Virtual Organisations. In: Research Challenges in Information Science, RCIS 2008, Marrakech (2008a)
5. Hajlaoui, K., Boucher, X., Mathieu, M.: Data Mining To Discover Enterprise Networks. In: 9 th IFIP Working Conference on Virtual Entreprises (PRO-VE 2008) Poznan, Poland, September 8-10 (2008b)
6. Plisson, J., Ljubic, P., Mozetic, I., Lavrac, N.: An ontology for Virtual Organisation Breeding Environments. IEEE Trans. on Systems, Man, and Cybernetics (2007) (to appear)
7. Richardson, R.J.: Directorship interlocks and corporate profitability. Administrative Science Quarterly 32, 367–386 (1987)
8. Bachimont, B., Issac, A., Troncy, R.: Semantic commitment for designing ontologies. In: Gómez-Pérez, A., Benjamins, V.R. (eds.) EKAW 2002. LNCS (LNAI), vol. 2473, pp. 114–121. Springer, Heidelberg (2002)
9. Hajlaoui, K.: Thèse, Dispositifs de recherche et de traitement de l'information en vue d'une aide à la constitution de réseaux d'entreprises. EMSE Saint Etienne, France (December 2009)
10. Agirre, E., Ansa, O., Hovy, E., Martinez, D.: Enriching very large ontologies using the www. In: Proceedings of ECAI 2000 workshop on Ontology Learning (2002)
11. Faatz, A., Steinmetz, R.: Ontology enrichment with texts from the www. In: Proceedings of the 2nd Semantic Web Mining Workshop at ECMLI/PKDD, WS 2002 (2006)
12. Parekh, V., Finin, J.G.T.: Mining domain specific texts and glossaries to evaluate and enrich domain ontologies. In: Proceedings of the International Conference of Information and Knowledge Engineering (2004)
13. Neshatian, K., Hejazi: Text categorization and classification in terms of multi-attribute concepts for enriching existing ontologies. In: Proceedings of the 2nd Workshop on Information Technology and its Disciplines, pp. 43–48 (2004)
14. Jorio, L.D., Abrouk, L., Fiot, C., Hrin, D., Teisseire, M.: Enrichissement d'ontologie bas sur les motifs squentiels. In: de la Plateforme, A. (ed.) AFIA 2007, Atelier Ontologies et gestion de l'htrognit smantique (2007)
15. Bendaoud, R.: Construction et enrichissement d'une ontologie partir d'un corpus de textes. In: Actes des Rencontres des Jeunes Chercheurs en Recherche d'Information (RJCRI 2006), Lyon, pp. 353–358 (2006)
16. Pekar, A.M.V., Staab, S.: On discovering taxonomic relations from the web. Journal of Information Retrieval, Contextual Information Retrieval Systems, 301–322 (2002)
17. Hernandez, N., Chrisment, J., Egret, D.: Modeling context through domain ontologies. Journal of Information Retrieval, Contextual Information Retrieval Systems 10, 143–172 (2007)
18. Srikant, R., Agrawal, R.: Mining generalized association rules. Future Generation Computer Systems 13(23), 161–180 (1997)
19. Han, E., Karypis, G.: Centroid based document classification: Analysis and experimental results. In: Proceedings of The 4th European Conference of Principles of Data Mining and Knowledge Discovery, pp. 424–431 (2000)
20. Schmid, H.: Probabilistic part-of-speech tagging using decision trees. In: Conference on New Methods in Language Processing, Manchester, UK (1994)
21. Agrawal, R., Srikant, R.: Fast algorithms for mining association rules in large databases. In: VLDB 1994 (1994)

Mining Collaboration Opportunities to Support Joined-Up Government

Rilwan Basanya[1,2], Adegboyega Ojo[1], Tomasz Janowski[1], and Franco Turini[2]

[1] UNU-IIST Center for Electronic Governance,
P.O. Box 3058, Macao
[2] Department of Computer Science,
University of Pisa, Italy
{rilwan,ao,tj}@iist.unu.edu, turini@di.unipi.it

Abstract. Governments strive to achieve improvements in delivering public services, developing and implementing public policies, responding to crisis situations, and optimizing the use of public resources, among others. Achieving such goals requires collaboration across different levels and functions of government, and across public and private sectors in a Joined-Up Government. Establishing such collaboration requires information on prospective participants including their goals, resources, processes and services. Such information is rarely available in structured forms e.g. in databases, but instead scattered over government portals, publications and other textual sources. This paper proposes the use of semantic text mining for extracting collaboration-related information (focusing on government collaboration) from unstructured data sources. The proposed solution applies natural language processing techniques supported by the relevant domain and process ontologies. It consists of three steps: 1) extracting process-related information from textual sources, 2) creating process ontology instances from extracted information and 3) mining shared and integrated processes based on process instances and the service goal hierarchy in the domain ontology. The paper describes the rationale of and approach adopted in this research, the progress achieved in implementing step 1, the challenges encountered and how we intend to address them in pursuing subsequent steps.

Keywords: Joined-Up Government, Collaborative Networks, Goal Hierarchy, Data Mining, Text Mining, Process Mining.

1 Introduction

Governments face enormous pressures in coping with their regular responsibilities of delivering the required services to their stakeholders – citizens, businesses and governments, and developing effective policy interventions to societal issues in various national and international contexts characterized by financial and economic pressures, increasing terrorism-related threats to national security, and increasing incidents of health pandemics and natural disasters. A common element in various responses by governments to these challenges is the adoption of a holistic, whole-of-government

L.M. Camarinha-Matos et al. (Eds.): PRO-VE 2011, IFIP AICT 362, pp. 359–366, 2011.

approach. This approach aims at creating a single virtual organizational view [1] from various government and non-government entities, based on collaboration across different levels and functions of government as well as collaboration with non-state actors from the private and voluntary sectors [2].

Developing collaboration structures and relationships requires coordination and integration of services, processes and information-related assets like databases, applications, devices, hardware and networks, offered by collaborating parties. Specifically, establishing any collaboration requires information on the shared goals, prospective participants, their interests and resources [1][3]. However, such information is rarely available as structured data (e.g. in databases) or from a single source. The information is generally unstructured and found in disparate sources like agency portals and online publications related to the entities of interest. This makes the discovery, analysis and integration of information on prospective collaboration parties difficult. Even when such information is available, integrating this information to achieve the objectives of a joined-up government remains difficult due to various organization issues and in the absence of explicit domain ontologies.

Text mining, a data mining technique for unstructured or textual data, which also draws from various disciplines including information extraction, semantic web and computational linguistics, offers significant promise for automatic extraction of important terms, concepts and patterns. Presently, there are a number of tools for text mining which enable annotation of text with user information. When considering text mining in a specific context, like government-wide collaboration, specific domain structures (e.g. goals, services and processes) would be of interest. In this regard, process mining [4] offers concrete technique for mining process-related structures. However, workflow logs used in process mining are structured.

In this work, we are concerned with textual descriptions of such processes and the services they implement. We aim at investigating how text mining, and particularly semantic text mining (text mining supported by relevant ontologies) could be used in discovering various collaboration structures from their descriptions in various textual sources, provided by government agencies, private sector organizations and other entities within the joined-up government context. Our final goal is to enable semi-automatic discovery of shared and integrated processes to realize collaborations and joined-up government. We adopt ontology-based tagging of terms in collaboration descriptions, using service-oriented process ontology obtained from our analysis and augmentation of existing e-government service models. The tokenized terms are subsequently combined, guided by their meanings expressed in the ontology, into collaboration structures. This paper contributes to the final goal through the synthetic analysis and augmentation of existing e-government service description models.

The rest of this paper is structured as follows. Section 2 presents the background in semantic text mining, information extraction, collaboration networks and joined-up governments. Section 3 explains the problem to be addressed. Section 4 discusses the approach adopted to solve this problem, followed by solution steps in Section 5. Finally, Sections 6 and 7 present discussion and conclusions respectively.

2 Background

A number of foundational concepts are essential in explaining our motivation and research approach. These concepts, drawn from the domains of Text Mining, Collaborative Frameworks and Joint-Up Government are briefly introduced below.

Text Mining: Data mining [5] refers to the extraction of knowledge from large amounts of data. A key step in knowledge discovery, it is an iterative process aimed at identifying valid, novel, potentially useful, and ultimately understandable patterns in data. Text mining intersects with Natural Language Processing (NLP), machine learning, data mining, and information retrieval. Knowledge discovery in text, however, involves intelligent text data analysis aimed at uncovering previously unknown patterns in existing unstructured textual resources [6]. By appropriately integrating techniques from each of these disciplines, useful new methods of discovering knowledge from large textual sources can be developed. For our purpose, we explore such techniques in extracting useful patterns in describing e-government services provided by prospective collaborators. Information Extraction (IE) is a key component in text mining, as it enables the application of data mining to unstructured text corpora to discover predictive rules useful for improving the performance of text mining tasks [7]. Handling the representation of background knowledge in IE is a very important challenge [8] and ontologies are used to supply such knowledge and annotations, as they effectively enable the representation of domain schemas containing technical terms, domain concepts and the relationships between them.

Collaborative Frameworks: Collaboration involves exchanging information, altering activities, sharing resources, and enhancing the capacity of another for mutual benefit and a common purpose. Each participating organization aims to help others become the best that they can be at what they do [9]. Studies in network theory and its effect on inter-agency collaboration [10] have also shown enhanced cooperation among government agencies. For our purpose, we adopt the definition of collaboration as the act or process of "shared creation" or discovery [11] involving the creation of new value by doing something new or differently.

Joined-Up Government: Joined-Up government denotes public service agencies working across portfolio boundaries to achieve shared goals and an integrated government response to pressing issues [12]. The rationale for joined-up government is two-fold [13]: 1) avoiding duplication of efforts through improved information flow resulting in increased situational awareness and enhanced capacity for strategic planning and intelligent decision-making; and 2) harmonization of efforts among all stakeholders recognizing the co-dependent nature of their shared and individual goals, and the required compromise and understanding among collaborators in jointly achieving the goals towards attaining a more agile government enterprise. Achieving such goals must be based upon collaboration across different levels and functions of government, and across public and private sectors. However, the complexities of configuring all possible collaborations among agencies are enormous and require a systematic approach dealing with the various scenarios. We seek an environment where collaboration structures for all agencies – processes, capabilities and competencies – can be extracted and modeled along with the collaboration objective to be achieved, leading to the configuration of a collaborative initiative.

3 Problem

Our major goal is to investigate how data mining can be used to support the discovery of information to build collaborative government services towards joined-up government. Since government services are usually described in textual forms on government portals and in other sources, we employ semantic text mining to identify different parts of service descriptions and on this basis discover opportunities for developing shared and integrated services. Discovering such services will optimize the use of financial, human, data, organizational and technical resources. It will also enable improvements in the delivery of government services.

There are two inherent challenges to this problem. The first is addressing the contextual semantic issues posed by textual sources containing service descriptions. For example, a step such as "Issue license" extracted from two different service descriptions e.g. driving license or construction license, could be very different in terms of implementation complexity. The second is mining processes representing shared and integrated services from process ontology instances, as opposed to using structured event logs which is the standard practice in traditional process mining.

4 Methodology

Our approach is to first model Joined-up Government as a Collaborative Networked Organization (CNO) whose members are agencies involved in shared or integrated service arrangements. We then develop the required ontologies to guide the extraction of information from textual descriptions of services and to represent the extracted information as process models. Two ontologies are required for this purpose: 1) a domain ontology to define and relate e-governance concepts and provide a hierarchy of service delivery goals, and 2) a process ontology to represent extracted process models. Since our process models are service-oriented, the process ontology is developed by extending existing e-government service-related ontologies by additional elements discovered through our review of service descriptions available on six national government portals – South Africa, United States, United Kingdom, Canada, Korea, and Germany. Fig. 1 below shows three major steps of our approach to the problem, with steps 1 and 2 executed concurrently.

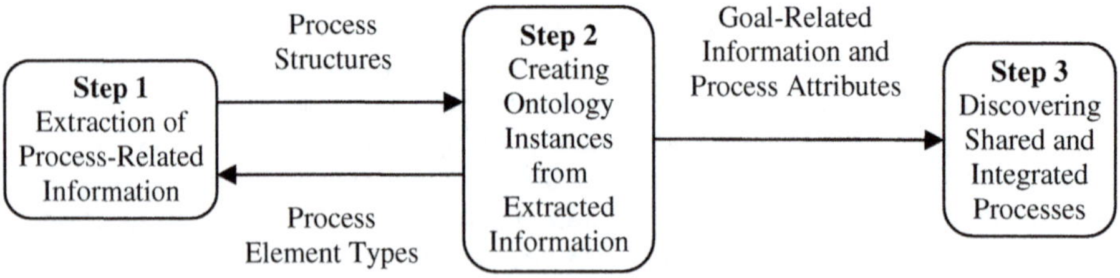

Fig. 1. Three-Step Research Methodology

Using these ontologies, models and recognizers will be developed to identify and tag different elements (e.g. goals, subjects or eligibility criteria) of a service from its descriptions. The extracted information will be stored in the process ontology as process instances. With such instances captured in the process ontology, the final task will be to: 1) discover common sub-processes across process models as a basis for building shared services and 2) suggest possible super-processes as a basis for seamless or integrated services using the service delivery goal hierarchy.

5 Solution

This section describes in some detail the three steps in Figure 1.

Step 1 - Extraction of Process-related Information: This step involves pre-processing process-related descriptions to conform to some standardized and structured process syntax. We gather service descriptions from various government websites and carry out rigorous analysis to extend existing public service description models. This task involves selection of sentences describing key service components and processes. It also involves decomposing the sentences into tokens for the recognizer to identify named entities and co-references. Next, the tokens will be combined into structures based on their meanings in the ontology. Figures 2 and 3 show the examples of two service descriptions on the South African Government's (www.gov.za) and Alberta Government's (www.alberta.ca) portals.

The resulting service-oriented process ontology consists of the following elements: 1) Service – a clear reference to the nature of the service, 2) Type – the type of service based on the authorization, certification, control, and production types [14], 3) Source – the government offering the service, 4) Subject – the actors involved in different roles in delivering the service including service requestor, provider and their collaborators, 5) Eligibility – the rules determining which requestor can receive the services, 6) Evidence – the confirmation of receipt of request to provide a service, 7) Location – the place where interactions in the service delivery process take place, 8) Duration – how long will it take to deliver the service, 9) Legal – the legal provision e.g. government decrees empowering the provider to provide the service and specifying which requestors can receive the service, 10) Payment – fees to be paid for receiving the service, 11) Outcome – the result of the service, 12) Review – what can be done if the requestor is not satisfied with the outcome, 13) Suspension – if a positive outcome can be suspended and for how long, 14) Validity – when a positive outcomes will expire, 15) Contact – who can be reached for enquiries on the service, and 16) Appeal – if and how to challenge the negative outcome of a service request.

Following the development of the process ontology, the next task is to develop recognizers for each element and tag extracted text with the appropriate element. In summary, this step involves: 1) preprocessing, 2) development of service description-based recognizers, and 3) extracting service elements from their textual descriptions.

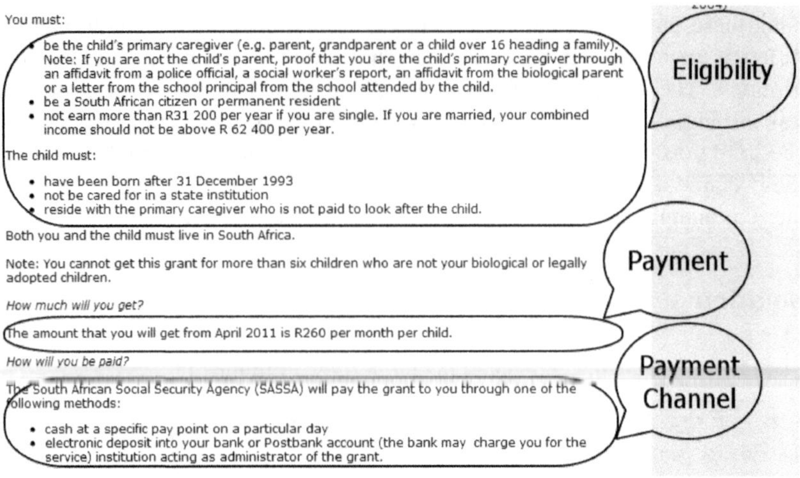

Fig. 2. Sample Service Description from www.gov.za

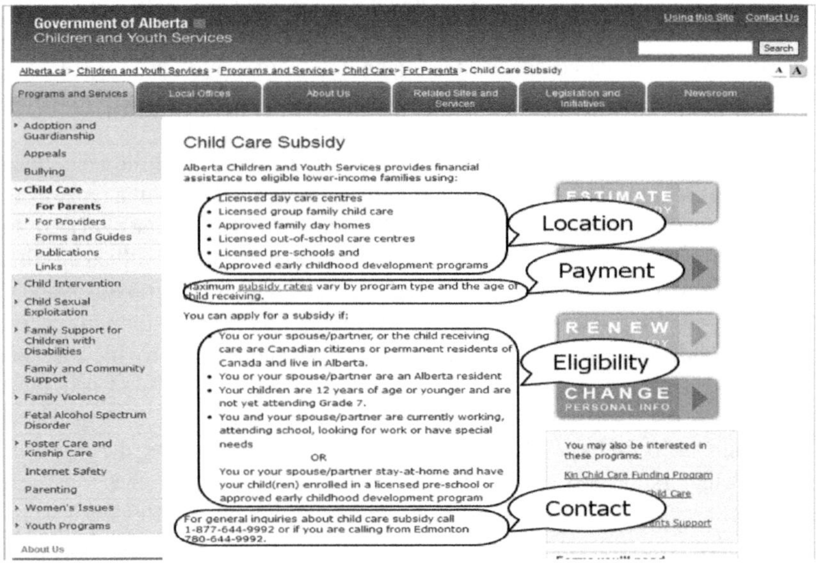

Fig. 3. Sample Service Description from www.alberta.ca

Step 2 - Creating Process-Ontology Instances: This step involves developing a formal process ontology based on the service description elements and the domain ontology. The extracted text is created as individuals or instances in the developed process ontology, where each instance represents a complete service description. This is followed by creating relationships between the instances based on the service goal hierarchy defined in the domain ontology. The goal hierarchy specifies how a higher level or conjugate goal is obtained by fulfilling simpler goals in addition to goal prioritization. For instance, the service goal related to Obtaining Licenses can be fulfilled by goals Successfully Filing an Application and Obtaining Decision on the Application. Therefore, a process that implements the submission of applications and another process implementing decision making on applications could be combined into a single process with the goal of license service delivery.

Step 3 - Discovering Shared and Integrated Services: Our target is to extract two main types of process information structures. The first is processes common to several agencies. For example, most agencies require authorization services to evaluate or decide on applications based on some criteria. The second is integrated processes that could be constructed from the processes of various entities towards fulfilling a higher-level goal. For instance, responding to a health pandemic may require that screening services (checking travelers) at all ports of entry are linked with ambulatory services (for transfer) and with emergency services (treatment) at hospitals.

6 Discussion

So far, our research has focused on the Step 1 – Extraction of Process-Related Information. To this end, we attempted to extract process-related information from the online sources provided by the national governments of United States, United Kingdom, Canada, Germany, Korea and South Africa. However, we were confronted with a number of challenges that further highlight that meaningful extraction, parsing and construction of processes and other higher-level structures from these descriptions require semantic support. Here we describe three specific challenges. The first challenge is non-standard form of service descriptions. We observed that there is no standard form, nor a controlled language, for describing available government services even within the same government. In general, the descriptions present across various government portals use free narrative forms. We also discovered that service descriptions and presentations vary according to the government's level of e-government maturity. For example, some portals like the US federal government's www.usa.gov tailored and personalized their service descriptions to individuals based on their interactions with the portal. The second challenge concerns the existence of huge variations in the details of service descriptions. Some descriptions, for instance, may not contain process-related information. The third challenge is inconsistent naming of services, with the same or related services referenced differently across different government portals. For example, Child Support Grant, Child Care and Development Fund, Child Care Subsidy, and Child Care Benefit all refers to essentially the same services. We are currently working to address these challenges through the techniques employed in resolving semantic conflicts in general.

7 Conclusions

The goal of this paper is to present the research approach and initial implementation of this approach in automating the identification of shared or integrated services to underpin Joined-up Government – one of the most important forms of Collaborative Network Organizations in the public sector domain targeting complex, cross-sector challenges. Unlike existing work on service development and composition that relies on structured repositories and service descriptions, we seek to identify opportunities for shared and integrated services from non-structured textual descriptions commonly found on government portals and in government publications using semantic text mining. Despite various semantic challenges encountered in the course of this work, we consider the discovery task feasible. In our view, once the implementation of step 1 in our research methodology (extraction of process-related information) is complete, creating ontology instances from extracted information (step 2) and discovering shared and integrated processes (step 3) through ontology-based reasoning will be more tractable. This is the direction of our future work.

References

1. Camarinha-Matos, L., Afsarmanesh, H.: On Reference Models for Collaborative Networked Organizations. International Journal of Production Research 46, 2453–2469 (2008)
2. Stanton, T.H.: Improving Collaboration by Federal Agencies: An Essential Priority for the Next Administration. Management (2008)
3. Reillly, T.: Collaboration in Action - An Uncertain Process. The Haworth Press (2001)
4. de Medeiros, A.K.A., van der Aalst, W., Pedrinaci, C.: Semantic Process Mining Tools: Core Building Blocks. In: 16th European Conference on Information Systems, pp. 1953–1964. Citeseer (2008)
5. Han, J., Kamber, M.: Data Mining: Concepts and Techniques. Morgan Kaufmann, San Francisco (2006)
6. Novak, P.K., Vavpetic, A., Trajkovski, I., Lavrac, N.: Towards Semantic Data Mining with g-SEGS. Business, 3–6 (1990)
7. Nahm, U.Y., Mooney, R.J.: Text Mining with Information Extraction. In: Proceedings of the 4th International MIDP Colloquium, Bloemfontein, South Africa, pp. 141–160 (2005)
8. Stavrianou, A., Andritsos, P., Nicoloyannis, N.: Overview and Semantic Issues of Text Mining. ACM SIGMOD Record 36, 23 (2007)
9. Himmelman, A.T.: Collaboration for a Change: Definitions, Decision-Making Models, Roles, and Collaboration Process Guide, Available through Partnering Intelligence at http://www.partneringintelligence.com/documents/5.0_Collaboration%20for%20a%20Change.doc
10. Bardach, E.: Can Network Theory Illuminate Interagency Collaboration. In: Workshop on Network Analysis and Innovations in Public Programs. LaFollette Institute of Public Affairs, University of Wisconsin-Madison (1994)
11. Thomson, A.M., Perry, J.L.: Collaboration Processes: Inside the Black Box. Public Administration Review (2006)
12. Christensen, T., Lægreid, P.: The Whole-of-Government Approach to Public Sector Reform. Public Administration Review 67, 1059–1066 (2007)
13. Baker, J.: Quick Impact Projects: Towards a Whole of Government Approach. Paterson Review 8, 1–21 (2007)
14. Ojo, A., Janowski, T., Estevez, E.: Domain Models and Enterprise Application Framework for Developing Electronic Public Services. In: Proceedings of the 6th International EGOV Conference, Regensburg, Germany, pp. 157–164 (2007)

The Player Manager: Collaboration and Involvement

Oihab Allal-Chérif

BEM Management School Bordeaux France,
680 cours de la Libération 33400 Talence France
oihab@bem.edu

Abstract. This paper has as its objective to put forward a profile for the 'manager of the future'. It draws on a review of the literature and on a series of unstructured interviews with 12 trainers, recruiters, directors and young graduates. Research carried out in large global companies in the fields of industry and multimedia confirms the under-exploitation of certain competences and the immergence of new forms of management and recruitment in modern companies. Generation Y is blossoming and, with its practices and its new demands, is jostling against traditional modes of management. This paper first highlights the tensions between individuals, the organization and its environment, plus the lack of recognition regarding these neo-managers' competences and valuable talents. An analogy between managers and video game players leads us to the analysis of three case studies and to interviews with 12 experts in their individual professional fields: three trainers, three purchasing directors, and three young purchasing graduates. Their contributions, combined with the conclusions drawn from the case studies permit the co-construction of the profile of tomorrow's manager, the "player manager".

Keywords: Manager, video games, Y generation, forecasting, collaboration.

1 Introduction

A part of the intellect of today's young managers is not welcome in those companies where it is considered as of little real business worth. Indeed, this intellect does not fit in with organizational constraints, and does not correspond to the working ways currently in place. It seems too playful and not professional. This intellect is developed though the use of video games. It is characterized by (1) the mastery of information and communication technology (ICT), (2) the ability to find one's way around virtual environments, (3) the capacity to combine talents, in order to collectively achieve objectives that would be impossible on one's own, (4) digital communication between different socio-cultural profiles and (5) the ability to undertake several tasks at once and to flit between these, without losing productivity.

Young graduates feel themselves to be picked on, constrained, excluded and maladjusted. There is often no measure put in place to value them and to capture the product of this new form of intellect they manifest. In traditional companies, where these young graduates are expected to occupy a very precise function, they do not find

L.M. Camarinha-Matos et al. (Eds.): PRO-VE 2011, IFIP AICT 362, pp. 367–374, 2011.

community spirit and have to subscribe to a stifling vertical structure. How can they best be integrated? How can adapter tools be created to allow these young graduates to express their creativity in an optimal way? After having considered the characteristics of generation Y, this article examines several case studies of video games. Here, it highlights the possible transpositions between the practices employed by players and those of managers. The methodology is built around three axes, namely career forecasting, the case study method, and the scenario method, with interviews with 12 experts in their individual professional fields to complete the study. The final section puts forward the profile of a "player manager", 'along with recommendations for the welcome and integration of this new profile of manager.

2 Anticipating and Reducing Tensions between Individuals, Organizations and their Environment

The Y generation is made up of people born between the beginning of the 1980s and the early years of the 21st century. Also called the "millennium generation", the "Internet generation", the "digital generation", the "Google generation" or "digital Natives", in five years this generation will represent 40% of all working people (Crampton and Hodge, 2009). Members of the Y generation are "born surfers", with a perfect knowledge of how to use and optimize their social networks and develop in virtual environments. They communicate thanks to a new language, and are capable of managing several tasks at the same time.

Recruiters find themselves therefore faced with numerous difficulties linked to the gap between the professional environment they offer to young graduates and the world in which these new recruits live and have grown up. How can this new generation be integrated into a system which is largely dominated by highly structured, hierarchical, even state-owned companies? How can we conserve and develop this sense of collaboration, the talent to search for information and the ability to generate community know-how, in a population that refuses to be bullied by a system that it judges outmoded? This new intellect must not be channeled or formatted, as is essentially the case in traditional regulated structures. It must be stimulated and capitalized on, in order to create a new form of value.

Peter Drucker explains that the reason for being of any organization is to allow ordinary people to do extraordinary things. The very essence of an organization is to permit people to achieve a greater level of performance than the one they seem capable of, to reveal the slightest talent among its members, and to use each others' talents to improve each others' performances (Drucker, 1973). However, modern organizations do not adopt this approach, and inhibit their managers' potential for initiative and creativity. Indeed, managers are constrained to focus on realizing their objectives in an environment where the performance race and internal competition are predominant (Shaw, 2008).

The Y generation's ill-ease seems almost inevitable, faced with the inertia of companies who persist with models which are more and more blatantly out of step with the radical development of modern society (Simard, 2007). Drucker has already observed: "the largest proportion of what we call management consists of making people's work more difficult" (Drucker, 1973). Based on a study of 17000 Canadian employees, the sociologist Jean-Pierre Brun demonstrates that people's well-being is closely linked to organizational performance, whilst organizations consider this to be a completely secondary factor. Indeed, "managers often concentrate on financial indicators and complicate life by putting in place ambitious action plans and complex processes" (Brun, 2008).

3 Research Methodology: Three Complementary Approaches

Research is at the heart career forecasting. It permits greater clarity regarding past changes in a profession, in order to be able to anticipate future transformations (Boyer, Scouarnec, 2009). The objective here is to protect oneself against the dangers inherent in the contradictions which develop between the profiles of new managers and methods of management and recruitment. It is necessary to act and innovate before it is too late. It is a question of building the future according to both desired and non-desired scenarios, and of acting on the present to point changes in a direction that is favorable for us (Thamain, 2009).

A sample of three online role plays was defined, in order to observe specific practices of the Y generation. 12 experts in their individual professional fields were also selected, in order to undertake semi-structured interviews, designed to reveal the different facets of the issue and to offer some recommendations. The pre-formalization stage permitted an initial analysis of the interviews' contents, and an initial structure underpinning the "player manager" phenomenon to be identified, along with to identify the distinction between strong hypotheses and more ambiguous suppositions. The construction stage consisted in confronting the different points of view of these experts to each other by presenting them with their differing visions. The validation stage offers jointly constructed recommendations in order to act positively on this phenomenon (Boyer, Scouarnec, 2009).

This piece of research offers answers to the following questions: Why is there a discrepancy between the Y generation and practices within organizations? Why does this discrepancy constitute both a significant threat and a significant opportunity for companies to make a new start? How can the Y population be integrated, and how can their qualities be put to the service of the organization? In order to obtain the most pertinent answers, the case study method must be validated by a triangulation between the information collected. In other words, data must be compared against itself, and against testimonies and theories, alongside the use of several sources (Yin, 1994). The combination of a literature review, three case studies and interviews with 12 managers from the Y generation therefore constitutes a topographical fieldwork research strategy, designed to compare the information sources.

The data collection proceeds in four phases. The first phase corresponds to an exploratory phase. This stage concerns the discovery of the research field, the identification of opportunities to use and of obstacles which could crop up. The second phase is much more analytical and less descriptive, with exclusively semi-structured interviews with participants, in order to conduct an in depth study of applications. The gathering of documents and the choice of more structured questions brings us closer to our objective. The third phase consists of structured interviews with questions of a much greater precision asked to a larger number of sources with a more critical view with regards to the way the platform works, and the desire to encourage participants to engage in self-criticism and suggest improvements. The fourth phase consists of presenting the research outcomes of the analysis of these key sources and combining the different opinions.

Interviews will allow us to complete the conclusions from these case studies. Participants will be encouraged to make sense of their practices, to stand back and describe events, actions, values, experiences and the problems they face in everyday life (Thiétart, 2007).

Code	Category	Function / Program	Firm / Sector
A1	Trainer	Expert in E-learning	FNEGE
A2	Trainer	Expert in CVs / Interviews	APEC
A3	Trainer	Lecturer in HRM	Grenoble EM
A4	Recruiter	HR Manager	Nestlé
A5	Recruiter	Profiler / Head hunter	Big Fish
A6	Recruiter	HR Manager	EDF
A7	Director	Departmental Director	HP
A8	Director	Director of a Subsidiary	Nestlé
A9	Director	Purchasing Manager	Total
A10	Young graduate	MAI BEM Bordeaux	Purchasing
A11	Young graduate	DESMA GEM Grenoble	Communication
A12	Young graduate	SKEMA Lille	Sales

Fig. 1. List of the experts in their individual professional fields

4 MMORPG Players as a Source of Inspiration for Companies

EverQuest (EQ), which is very popular in the United States, and federates hundreds and thousands of members, many of whom are permanently connected. Each server supports a specific and independent version of Norrath, the EQ world which is permanently evolving in real time. This constraint encourages the players to be very active or to abandon the game: they do not want to miss certain events or to see themselves outdistanced by others. The collaboration is facilitated by the interface and recompensed by the completion of tasks which require complementary capacities from different types of characters. Players have to cooperate to accomplish certain quests which they could not complete alone. Playing a MMORPG does not have an end: moreover, certain players have been playing for years and have a particularly good knowledge of the world in which they are still developing and progressing.

The time spent in the conception and development of characters, plus learning the very elaborate rules and in discovering a complex world which is constantly evolving, encourages players to pursue their adventures and therefore to pay each month to access the site. At the launch of EQ, the principal was that each player would try to make him or herself as different as possible from other players. He or she would consider other players as potential enemies, likely to be surpassed during quests or from whom he or she could take one of a number of objects for use in combat or magic. It was almost against the will of the designers of these online role play games that players formed themselves into communities which, from then on, even constituted the foundation of MMORPGs (Fuger, 2003).

In DAOC, as explained on this game's website (www.daoc-europe.com), the player can join three different kingdoms: Albion – the kingdom of the late King Arthur, which is suffering from the absence of his authority and is in prey to multiple offensives – Hibernia – a primitive western hemisphere island inhabited by Celts – or Midgard – icy lands peopled by Vikings. The three nations have a choice of races (Trolls, Elves, Kobolds, Dwarfs…) and of single classes (disciple, apprentice, druid, sentry…) as well as different capacities and forms of specific magic. Players can adopt very different behaviors, but always in a team: there can be clashes between kingdoms (player versus player), a player can try to take possession of his adversaries' relics by attacking their reliquary fortresses. He or she can conquer territories, and accomplish quests (the player versus his environment) for his or her personal account or that of his or her guild. A MMORPG player launches him or herself into a virtual world by means of his avatar, a performance which combines both illusion and reality, in other words elements which are the player's own and others which are unfamiliar to him or her.

"Players attach a great deal of importance to their status because they know, perhaps unconsciously, that this will influence the relationships that they will enter into with other members" (Fuger, 2003). Indeed, the interpersonal aspect is extremely significant in MMORPG. Players seek, therefore, to improve their characteristics in order to progress through the levels of development and to become a legendary figure in their kingdom. "Climbing up the rungs of the virtual social ladder is one of the most important objectives for the majority of participants" (Fuger, 2003). In DAOC, there are a multitude of objects which make it possible to associate a character to his status and his level. As a result, players have to behave in the same way as managers in companies and act on according to these gauges and variables, in order to improve and work in partnerships to complete project or achieve objectives. Certain advantages can be associated with a good reputation as much as a player in a MMORPG as in a company: "the notions of good and bad reputations exist and have an influence on the status accorded to members of the community to which they attach a great importance" (Fuger, 2003).

Second Life, the best-known virtual world in the world with 15 million fans, has had to deal with a serious financial crisis which perfectly reflects the real crisis and has provided us precisely with information on how to manage crises in general" (Kaplan, 2009). Indeed, this game has its own currency, with a floating interest rate of 270 lindens dollars ($L) for one American dollar and its own banks which offer to place money with interest rates which can go as high as 40%. Real banks, such as the French national banks Crédit Agricole and the Caisse d'Epargne, have opened agencies in this virtual world and certain brands carry out virtual marketing there, examples include Toyota, which surveys avatars regarding its prototypes, or L'Oréal which organizes fashion parades in Second Life. Ailin Graef has become the "Rockefeller of Second Life" (Sloan, 2009) thanks to her avatar Anshe Chung through whom in 2006 she earned her first real million dollars as a virtual estate agent. Today she employs one hundred programmers and designers and has invested in several multimedia companies.

5 Tomorrow's Manager's New Competences: To Be the Best Player So His Company Wins

A game is fully characterised by four elements: (1) a list of players, (2) a list of possible strategies or actions for each player, (3) a description of the rewards allotted to players according to their strategic profile and (4) the rules of the game (Fisher and Waschik, 2002). In a similar way, company managers, competitors, clients, suppliers and other partners, all evolve in an environment where they know each other, where they have to make choices which are contingent on the others, where each decision can have serious consequences and where a certain number of rules need to be respected. Consequently, managers chose their strategies according to their competitors' former strategies, based on an anticipation of their future actions, on shape of the market, and the potential financial repercussions taking into account the rules of the economic game. "Our backdrop has changed and we are now probably entering into a veritable tempest of changes without precedence (…).

The waves of changes are tighter and tighter and closer and closer together. From now on, they overlap and we scarcely have the time to come to terms with the wave that has just arrived, than another one starts to gather force" (Saussereau, 2007). This instability is already present, and in a way even more intense in MMORPGs. Players are completely used to this. For them, this is no anomaly: it is natural. They have adopted the necessary reflexes to know how to act according to shifting parameters, so as to optimise personal and collective development and performance. In management, "momentum is precisely the moment at which the decision to act must have an impact" (Saussereau, 2007). Managers need to have the capacity to recognise this moment to put into place the right actions, in order to maximise their effects. They also need to play collectively and take their internal and external partners into account when taking this decision. Indeed, the performances of an organisation depend on the capacity of its employees to work collaboratively with each other and with their external partners.

New information technologies give us the illusion of equality between managers who participate in a community: they no longer have an age, a skin colour, beauty, a gender, qualifications, accents etc. They can create a new identity, sheltered from prejudices behind their computer screen, using their mastery of tools as a way of asserting themselves. The balance of power no longer relies on the same criteria. The power of having spent a long time studying is less significant than that of the mastery of virtual worlds and new qualification and evaluation codes. Communication with a "geek" is very different from traditional communication. In fact, young people group themselves into communities, clubs and tribes. Indeed, young people who play online and spend large amounts of time on forums, communities and networks have an intelligence which is structured differently from that of the traditional manager.

The serious games, which are already used in medicine and aviation in the United States, make for new modes of recruitment, training, evaluation and management of organizations based on virtualization and a heightened reality. The languages are encoded, symbolic, based on grading grids, scores or levels. In and of itself, knowing how to read is no longer even essential: like a child of six years who manages to complete an extremely complicated video game more rapidly than an adult, it is no longer the graduate who is the best equipped to understand these languages and to find his way in the socio-economic environment, modeled here in order to bring in the best business for his company. Managers are connected in socio-professional networks to each other, to the company, to their knowledge base, to their artificial intelligence, to forums and messaging services, as well as to different tools with applications which are specific to their individual professions.

Google is a Y company. It was created by the Y generation. At Google, the average age is 29 years old. Employees have the possibility to work in different company offices all over the world: Google sends them to New York, Atlanta, San Francisco, Paris, Dublin, Brussels, Milan, Oslo, Moscow, Buenos Aires, Sao Paulo, Mexico or Dubai. Every week, employees have appraisals with their managers. 20% of work time is consecrated to personal projects, from which Gmail is a fruit. Work spaces are divided between three or four people. The equipment includes all the new information and communication technologies, but also video games, musical instruments, athletic fields, a swimming pool or a climbing wall. The creation of associations and clubs is welcomed. Brainstorming sessions take place around the coffee machine or in the canteen where everything is free. Management development is participative, ethical, sustainable, collaborative, and the virtual is on the march, as is illustrated by the account of our expert in his professional field A7. Before, it was a real war to become a manager. Now, most of those who have the right predisposition and who could become a manager, do not want to do so. They work at all hours, day and night, they are constantly connecting and disconnecting and without losing efficacy, as a result. They adapt spontaneously to colleagues' demands, and need to maintain an extremely high level of motivation. They expect fewer constraints and less monitoring, with more autonomy and a greater level of ease at work.

Companies need to manage the collision between generations. Indeed, the gap between the competences of the "new recruits" and those of "older" ones is widening, and it is becoming bigger between smaller and smaller age gaps. This observation holds true in almost all activity sectors in the race for innovation and the necessity to be agile which are omnipresent. In certain companies, the average age, for that matter, is significant of the "freshness" of human resources, which can pose a problem, as in the case of the company Google who had a lawsuit brought against them for discrimination against older generations. It is possible to ask oneself questions about the desire to keep the average age of employees under the age of 30 and the ways of doing so.

New technologies make information, resources and interlocutors accessible anywhere in the world and at any time of the day or night. A colleague or partner who is on the opposite side of the world communicates with you as if her were in the office next door: You see him, you speak to him, you share the same documents, and you work on the same media. Managers can therefore find themselves working at home, in public transport, or in the middle of the night, according to constraints, either alone or with other people elsewhere in the world. There is no longer a notion of "early" or of "late" in this globalised world where the place where you are is no longer really of importance: everything comes down to opportunity and pro-activity. Respecting deadlines and anticipation are absolute priorities, regardless of conditions. It is the presence or absence of need which governs interactions between individuals. As a result, the amount of time something will take has become more and more difficult to comprehend. It is the tasks, the missions and the projects which determine employees' performance and remuneration.

6 Conclusion

The tensions between organizations, their environment and individual behaviors have become more and more difficult to manage. The situation is progressively getting worse and risks becoming very quickly decisive for a significant number of companies. This paper has shown how play can be the source of a regained humanity for companies, if they accept to study it with all the potential that it contains. In order to integrate the Y generation, practices associated with play need to be transposed, and in particularly those associated with MMORPGs, which can also bring with them effective solutions. Play makes up an integral part of the profile, which still remains atypical, of the "player manager" which will spread progressively.

References

1. Boyer, L., Scouarnec, A.: La Prospective des métiers. EMS (2009)
2. Brun, J.-P.: Les 7 pièces manquantes du management. Transcontinental (2008)
3. Crampton, S.M., Hodge, J.W.: Generation Y: unchartered territory. Journal of Business & Economics Research 7(4) (April 2009)
4. Drucker, P.F.: Management Tasks, Responsabilities and Practices. Harper and Row, Harper Business, New York (1973)
5. Fisher, T.C.G., Waschik, R.G.: Managerial Economics: a Game Theoretic Approach. Routledge, Taylor and Francis, London (2002)
6. Fuger, Z.: Les Communautés virtuelles des jeux massivement multi joueurs. Maîtrise de Communication, October 17 (2003); Université Paris III Sorbonne Nouvelle
7. Kaplan, A.M.: Second Life: leçons pour le monde réel. L'Expansion Management Review (58) (June 2009)
8. Saussereau, L., Roussin, T., Zimmer, E.A.: Quand le cirque inspire l'entreprise: Circus Company, Eyrolles. d'Organisation, Paris (2007)
9. Simard, S.: Génération Y: Attirer, motiver et conserver les jeunes talents. Viséo Solutions, 203 (2007)
10. Sloan, P.: The Virtual Rockefeller: Anshe Chung is raking real money in an unreal online world. CNNMoney.com, December 1 (2005)
11. Scouarnec, A., Yanat, Z.: La prospective métier: un instrument au service d'une GRH innovante. Congrès de l'AGRH, Grenoble (2003)
12. Shaw, S.: Engaging a New Generation of Graduates. Education & Training 50(5), 366–378 (2008)
13. Thamain, J.-L.: Anticiper en GRH, prévision et prospective, un diagnostic des pratiques et des représentations. Management et Avenir 25 (June 2009)
14. Thiétart, R.-A.: Méthodes de recherche en management, Paris, Dunod (2007)
15. Yin, R.K.: Case study research: Design and methods, 2nd edn. Sage Publishing, Beverly Hills (1994)

Part XIV

Service Orientation

Pro-activity in Collaborative Service Ecosystems

Tiago Cardoso and Luis M. Camarinha-Matos

Faculty of Sciences and Technology,
Universidade Nova de Lisboa / Uninova, Portugal
{tomfc,cam}@uninova.pt

Abstract. Service Orientation has been an extensively used approach to model the services Collaborative Networks' (CN) members are willing to provide to customers. The evolution of this paradigm has followed an improvement path since its early forms. Nevertheless bottlenecks still exist, namely in what concerns: 1) a gap between the business and the information and communication technology perspectives; 2) an adequate Quality of Service (QoS) assessment mechanism for the CN context. As a contribution to these issues, this paper proposes: 1) the creation of a collaborative Service Ecosystem, introducing pro-activeness elements towards an auto-initiative representation of CN member's services; 2) the introduction of a QoS mechanism needed to facilitate the assessment of services in a CN context.

Keywords: Pro-Active Service Entity, Conspicuity, Service Ecosystem.

1 Introduction

Service Orientation is, perhaps, the *most commonly used* approach for Collaborative Network's (CN) support systems in the existing case studies and proof of concept prototypes. Nevertheless, although this approach had a considerable evolution in the last decade, there still exist bottlenecks that act as inhibitors for a larger scale adoption of Service Oriented Architectures (SOA) in the CN context [1, 2].

On one hand, business and Information and Communication Technology (ICT) perspectives still diverge on the notion of service. Under the business perspective, entities deal with resource management, quality of service or client satisfaction issues. From the ICT perspective, the focus is on the definition of standard communication protocols, namely in what concerns remote method invocation, or information exchange formats among distinct systems, towards solving interoperability issues [3].

As discussed in [4], "the myth of open web-services" within a market without rules, as expected at the beginning, turned out not to be a realistic "dream". The main reason pointed out is that instead of an open marketplace of competing products or services, "it's about branding and simplicity: people want simplicity and quality rather than choices". The authors refer to the appearance of "industrial Service Parks" as the foreseen realistic approach instead of open independent Services spread around the Internet. Such structures "will offer sets of web-services with their own sets of rules for combining and modifying" the services.

L.M. Camarinha-Matos et al. (Eds.): PRO-VE 2011, IFIP AICT 362, pp. 377–387, 2011.

On the other hand, from the industry perspective as presented in [5], for example, next-generation systems, applications and services will raise opportunities and challenges based on their intelligence.

Finally, the evolution of the Services paradigm and industry practices point out the growing importance of customer interaction, as presented in [6], other than just assuring low cost, product performance and high quality, for long-term success.

These three factors are the base inspiration for the proposal made in this paper: the Pro-Active Service Ecosystem Framework (PASEF):

- Appearance of Service Parks – PASEF is a form of a delimited service park;
- Services Intelligence – the introduction of pro-activeness fosters one aspect of the implementation of intelligence at the service level.
- Client / customer interaction – based on pro-activeness, it becomes possible to develop a new QoS assessment mechanism that provides accurate and up-to-date information. Based on this mechanism, a method for the systematic client satisfaction information retrieval within PASEF is also introduced.

2 Service Orientation Evolution

Service Orientation, as well as the particular case of Web-Services, have experienced considerable evolution in the last decade. In the early forms of Web-Services, during the late 90s, the keyword was "publish" and the technology and standards provided the means needed to put Web-Services available through the Internet, expecting a worldwide range of new potential clients. As time proved, these worldwide potential new clients' benefit did not happen. Only big companies took advantage of this new approach, based on their marketing machinery. The SME Web-Services did not benefit mainly because they were not known by such worldwide potential client set.

Around 2002, the Web-Services' registries, like the case of UDDI, were added in order to solve this problem. Nevertheless, in the SME context, although the technological capabilities brought by UDDI introduced the possibility of being found, there still was no big change, given the lack on guarantees or trust requested by clients, among other factors, like the lack of specialists for development purposes. Nevertheless, at that time, technologically speaking, many web-services became able to be "plugged in", called and invoked - ready for the next stage that was the composition of distinct Web-Services, provided by disperse entities. The Service Oriented Architectures (SOA) appeared around 2006, introducing tools and mechanisms to automate web-services' composition.

More recently, in 2008, Franco et al. [7] proposed the Service Entity concept, introducing a first notion of an aggregation mechanism for distinct Web-Services provided by the same entity. Franco's proposal groups information concerning a service provider plus the services provided, all within the same construct – the Service Entity.

Fig. 1 represents a summary of the main perspectives of the Web-Service evolution towards the actual situation. Although this evolution brought sound improvements, compared to the early forms of Web-Services, there still exist bottlenecks that act as inhibitors for a wider usage of services, which can also be seen as a challenge for the creation of new solutions. Some of these bottlenecks are:

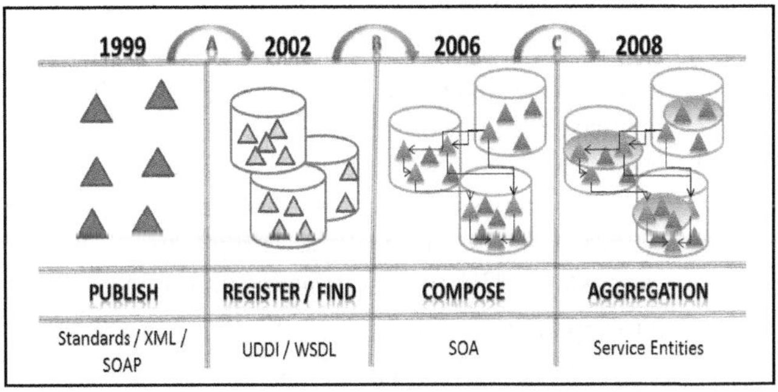

Fig. 1. Web-Service evolution

1. Passiveness – Web-Services are passive entities in the sense they stay still, waiting for a client side initiative. Although some pioneer initiatives connect SOA with some auto-initiative approaches, like the Multi-Agent Systems presented in the examples [8], [9] and [10] still there is no standard integrated approach yet, that could benefit from the strengths of both worlds: MAS & SOA.
2. Functional restriction – Web-Services do not directly cope with other non-functional elements, like the provision of a business process model or a touristic multimedia content, or even some intelligent content provided by an enterprise.
3. Aggregation – although Franco proposed a first approach for the aggregation of services provided by the same entity, all the Web-Service machinery is built on top of previous approaches, inspired in the remote procedure calling era, that is not an integrated approach considering the composition of distinct procedures forming a higher level one. In fact, although service registration in directories may already be made in an integrated manner, registering a set of services at once; the following queries made by clients to such repositories are made on the basis of one query for each service, resulting in independent replies. The fact that an entity may provide two services needed for a given business opportunity (BO) is not considered and thus no advantages may be taken from it.

3 Pro-Active Service Ecosystem Framework

The Pro-Active Service Ecosystem Framework (PASEF) proposed in this paper follows the service orientation paradigm evolution through the introduction of two novel aspects: 1) representatives of CN members' services, playing an "ambassador" role through the introduction of pro-activeness; 2) new Quality of Service mechanism, taking benefit from the pro-activeness, towards accurate and up-to-date data, concerning CN members QoS information.

PASEF comprises 4 groups of concepts (Fig. 2):

1. Service Ecosystem related concepts (SES) – the blocks for the construction of a service taxonomy built for the members of a Service Ecosystem to follow as a guide for interoperability purposes.
2. Membership Modeling related concepts (MM) - the blocks needed to model concrete entities and their services, within a collaborative Service Ecosystem.

3. Quality of Service related concepts (QoS) – the blocks needed to support QoS assessment, as well as clients' satisfaction that will serve as a base for service selection.
4. Business Process Modeling (BPM) – the blocks that model business processes associated with BOs within PASEF, as well as Proposals and / or suggestions CN members may submit in order to participate in such BOs.

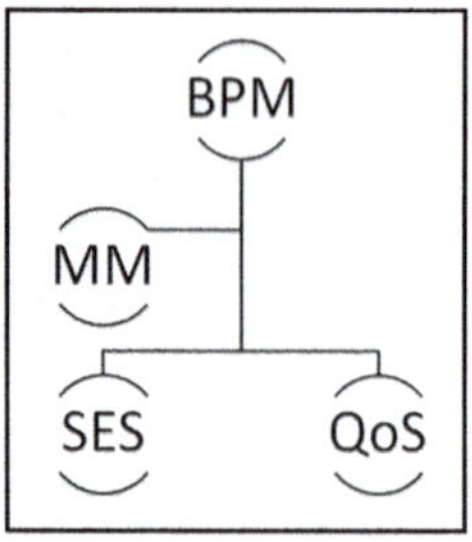

Fig. 2. PASEF Conceptual Groups

The Service Ecosystem related concepts are the first ones to be instantiated by the Service Ecosystem initiators, in order to define a common set of rules and mechanisms that will guide the CN members that join this structure. These definitions have to include not only a common terminology, but also standard skeletons for the services that may be provided within that Service Ecosystem. This group includes three concepts with the following definitions:

- D.1 - Meta-Service – the skeleton definition of a service, including details needed to specify service provision proposals or suggestions, both coping with functional services or intelligent-content provision services.
- D.2 - Service Category - a group of distinct Meta-Services.
- D.3 - Service Taxonomy - the concept that comprises distinct Service Categories and the corresponding Meta-Services.

The Membership Modeling related concepts group is composed of 5 concepts:

- D.4 - Service – the association of a specific CN member and a Meta-Service, including all particular service provision conditions. This concept also includes service connections, gathering the know-how from providers, identifying other Meta-services that usually are requested together with a specific Service.
- D.5 - Service Entity (SE) – the concept that aggregates distinct services provided by the same CN member, that is useful namely to create proposals and / or suggestions composed of more than one service. In such composed situations promotional conditions may be included for the cases where all the services from that proposal / suggestion become selected.
- D.6 - Pro-Active Service Entity (PSE) – a Service Entity element extended with the ability to behave in a pro-active manner, for example, towards finding new business opportunities or improving the chances that the represented services have to be selected among competitors in a given business opportunity.
- D.7 - Behavior Definition – concept for the configuration of PSE elements including a triggering mechanism; pre-conditions, post-conditions and the specification of a workflow of base actions that the PSE will perform towards the desired goals.
- D.8 - Service Ecosystem – the "space" that brings together all the CN members that are willing to collaborate in an environment created to support and foster the collaborative activity. This Ecosystem performs monitoring functionality, tracking all business opportunities from their early stages through their conclusion phase in order to provide accurate and up-to-date data for clients, concerning CN members' performance, helping them to make their choices whenever they have to select a particular provider for a service they need.

The Quality of Service mechanism proposed in this paper is based on three concepts:

- D.9 - QoS Characteristic – the atomic concept modeling data that may be measured, concerning some property of a service, the provider or the provision itself.
- D.10 - QoS Criteria – the combination of a relevant set of QoS characteristics and an evaluation schema for each.
- D.11 - Client Satisfaction – the classification of a given service provision under a specific QoS Criteria.

Through the usage of the first two concepts, it is possible to build up specific QoS assessment schemas within a Service Ecosystem. The client satisfaction should then be expressed in an automated manner every time a service provision takes place, in order to feed up PASEF in terms of accurate and up-to-date QoS data. In this way, high QoS from CN members is rewarded with a better selection probability.

Finally, the Business Process Modeling conceptual group is composed of 5 concepts:

- D.12 - Abstract Business Process Model (absBPM) – specification of a graph composed of Meta-Services, transitions and the data included in a process – a workflow model. It is abstract because it does not include service performers yet.
- D.13 - Call for Proposals (CfP) – including a list of needed services and provision conditions to which the proposals or suggestions should be posted.
- D.14 - Proposal / Bid – the reply to a CfP including the set of services that a CN member (proposer) intends to provide, as well as a set of provision conditions.
- D.15 - Additional Services Suggestion – based on the service connections included in the Service concept, from the Membership Modeling related concepts; providers may suggest the inclusion of additional services. If, for example, a Senior Professional (SP) provides a consultancy service (1) "evaluation of a BPM", it may be the case that SP also provides two other services: (2) "find similar case study BPMs", (3) "compare BPMs". In this situation, SP may connect these services if he or she thinks they make sense being together and, as a result, a suggestion is made by the PSE, for the inclusion of (2) and (3) whenever a call for proposals includes (1).
- D.16 - Executable Business Process Model (eBPM) – after an absBPM is created, CfP a is made. Based on the received proposals and / or suggestions the absBPM evolves and becomes an eBPM through the eventual inclusion of some suggestions in the workflow and the selection of the proposals that best fit the client's needs. An eBPM may be in one of two states: 1) complete, meaning that all services have a not-empty set of accepted service provision proposals, or 2) ready, meaning that all services that receive transitions from the start point of the workflow model have a not-empty set of accepted provision proposals, i.e., the start activities have at least one possible performer in order for the model execution to start. In this special case, the eBPM will eventually become complete afterwards, during its execution.

Table 1 shows the formal definitions of these 16 concepts:

Table 1. Summary of PASEF formal definitions

1.Meta-Service Skeleton service def. < N, R, D, SC > N – Service Name R – Reference to Implementation D – Description / service info. SC – Serv. Category	**2.Service Category** Meta-Services group < N, D, T > N – Category Name D – Category Description T – Services Taxonomy	**3.Service Taxonomy** Group of Service Categories. <N, D, V> N – Taxon. Name D – Taxonomy Description V – Version info.	**4.Service** Single service provided by a CN member < M, MS, SPC, SC > M – CN Member id MS – Meta-Service SPC –Prov. Conds. SC – Connection Set
5.Service Entity All services plus attributes from a CN member < M, ATS, SS > M – CN Member id ATS – CN member Attribute set SS – provided Service Set	**6.Behavior Def.** one configurable PSE behavior < ID, D, TM, BWD, PREC, POSC > ID –Behavior id D – Description TM – Trigger Mech. BWD – Workfl. Def. PREC – Pre-Cond. POSC – Post-Cond.	**7.PSE** CN member's service ambassador or representative < SE, BD > SE – Service Entity BD – Behavior Definition set	**8.Service Ecosystem** CN members' space < ST, PS, BO, PM, CR, BF > ST – Service Taxonomy PS – PSE set BO – BO set PM –Perform. info CR – Certif. Info
9.QoS Charact. Measurable property, from service, provider or provision < N, IM, MC > N – QoS id IM - Info to measure MC - Measurement Category	**10.QoS Criteria** Collection of QoS Charact. and evaluation schema < CS, ES, RC, RF > CS - QoS Ch. Set ES – Eval. Schema RC – Restrict Conds. RF – Overall Rating Formula.	**11.Clientnt Satisfaction** classification of service provision under QoS Criteria < QoS_Crit, {EV} > QoS_Crit. – Quality of Service Criteria EV – Evaluation of each QoS Ch.	**12.absBPM** Abstract Business Process Model < {(A, MS)}, RD, TS > {(A, MS)} Activity and Meta-Service set RD – Relevant Data Set TS - Transition set
13.CfP Call for Proposals < BPM, {S, SC, PC}, GPC > BPM - Business Process Model S – Serv. requested, SC – Serv. Category SPC - Service Provision Conditions GPC - General Provision Conditions	**14.Proposal / Bid** PSE provision intention proposal <{S, SC, PC}, GPC> S – Proposed Service, SC – Serv. Category PC – Serv. Provision Conditions, GPC - General Proposal Conditions	**15.Suggestion** PSE provision intention suggestion < {SS, SSC, BS, BSC, PC}, GSC > SS - Suggested Srv SSC – Sug.Srv.Cat. BS - Base Service BSC – Base Srv.Cat PC – Provision Conditions GSC - General Suggest. Conditions	**16.eBPM** Executable Business Process Model < {A, S, {SPP}}, RD, TS > A – Activity S – Service SPP – Provision Proposals RD – Relevant Data TS - Transition Set

In order to guarantee coherency and consistency in BPMs, a set of rules was defined for the creation of an absBPM (rules i to v) and the following eBPM (rule vi). These rules associate relevant data variables with all the information the services need and produce. The rules also guarantee that all activities are "reachable" and the workflow proceeds after their execution (Table 2).

Table 2. absBPM / eBPM specification rules

#	Rule	Description
i	$\forall\, A = \Pi_1(AS)$, $AS \in \Pi_1(absBPM)$ $\exists^1\, \mathrm{MS} \in \mathrm{T}$	for every activity A of the Activity and Service Set AS of an absBPM, there exists one and only one Meta-Service MS from the Service Ecosystem's Taxonomy T.
ii	$\forall\, A = \Pi_1(AS)$, $AS \in \Pi_1(absBPM)$ $\exists\, \mathrm{Tr(E,A)} \in \Pi_3\mathrm{absBPM}$	for every activity A of the Activity and Service Set AS of an absBPM there exists, at least, one transition Tr of absBPM from an element E to A – reach guarantee.
iii	$\forall\, A = \Pi_1(AS)$, $AS \in \Pi_1(absBPM)$ $\exists\, \mathrm{Tr(A,E)} \in \Pi_3(\mathrm{absBPM})$	for every activity A of the Activity and Service Set AS of an absBPM, there exists, at least, one transition Tr from A to some element E - proceed guarantee.
iv	$\forall\, MS(P) = \Pi_2(AS), AS \in \Pi_1(absBPM)$ $\exists\, \mathrm{RD} \in \Pi_2(absBPM)\ \vert\{p_i, \mathrm{i} \in \mathbb{N}\}$ $\{rd_j, j\ \in \mathbb{N}\}\ \forall\, p_i \in\ \mathrm{P}\ \exists\ \mathrm{rd}_j \in \mathrm{RD}$	for each Meta-Service MS with a parameter set P, there exists a relevant data variable set RD, associating a specific variable rd_j to each particular parameter p_i.
v	$\forall\, MS(OR) = \Pi_2(AS), AS \in \Pi_1(absBPM)$ $\exists\, \mathrm{RD} \in \Pi_2(absBPM)\ \vert$ $\exists\, \{or_i, \mathrm{i} \in \mathbb{N}\}, \{rd_j, j\ \in \mathbb{N}\}\ \vert$ $\forall or_i \in \mathrm{OR}\ \exists\ \mathrm{rd}_j \in \mathrm{RD}$	for each Meta-Service MS with an output result set OR, there exists a relevant data set RD, associating a specific variable rd_i, to each particular result or_i
vi	$\forall\, (A,S) \in \Pi_1(\mathrm{absBPM})$, $\mathrm{Tr(Start,A)} \in \Pi_3(absBPM)$ $\mathrm{SPP} \neq \emptyset$	for every Activity A associated with a service S, if there is a transition Tr from the Start point in the workflow to A, there is a not-empty set of provision proposals SPP identifying potential performer of S.

4 Application Area – Active Ageing

PASEF is being applied to a Professional Virtual Community (PVC) of Senior Professionals (SPs). The first article found foreseeing this challenge or need was [11] in 2004, based on the increase of life expectation, as well as the need for sustainable economies. The purpose of this application is to "support active ageing and facilitating better use of the talents and potential of retired or retiring senior professionals", as mentioned in [12]. In fact, three main perspectives can be identified concerning the current early retirement of people in many countries:

1. The retirement age is far from the age when elderly people's working capabilities start decreasing.
2. Many senior professionals prefer to continue working, although under a more flexible schema, instead of starting a process of a lonely experience.
3. The knowledge attained during a life-long experience is an asset that the economy thanks and elderly persons feel glad to share.

These facts pull the research community to find mechanisms and solutions in order to provide the base for these persons to be able to continue their active life after retirement. There are already many associations of SPs formed towards helping to find solutions. Actually, PASEF development was inspired on the needs identified in contact with two Portuguese associations of senior professionals.

As a result, an implementation of a prototype framework took place, following PASEF specification, composed of 6 modules:

1. PASEF Toolbox – The main objective of the PASEF Toolbox is to enable a fast scenario definition, as well as launch, test, and monitor all the modules form the Pro-Active Service Ecosystem Framework prototype. (Fig. 3)

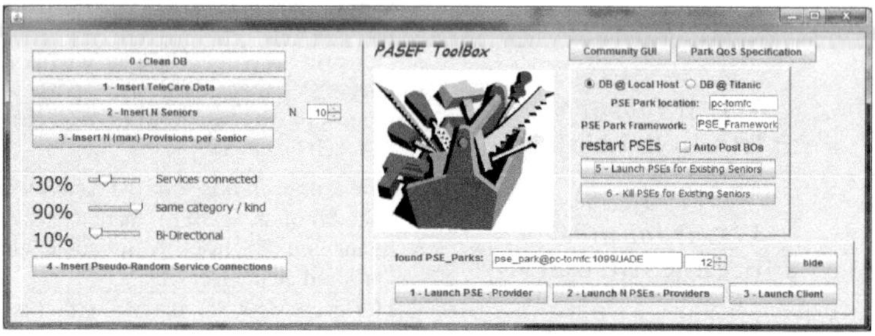

Fig. 3. PASEF Toolbox

2. Service Taxonomy Management – as identified in the Service Ecosystem related concepts group, a module was developed for the specification of a service Taxonomy to which the SPs should comply (Fig. 4 – lower side).
3. Seniors' Community Management – in this case, PASEF is intended to a PVC and a community management module was needed, in order to introduce the SPs that are willing to provide consultancy services where their life-time expertise can be used to keep them active. This module provides the functionality of service specification, as well as a service connections knowledge manifestation, towards the PSE launch, in order to represent the corresponding SP, in an "ambassador" like manner.

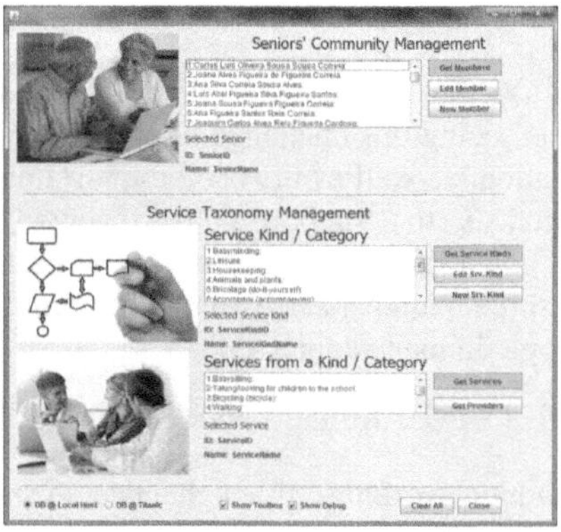

Fig. 4. Service Taxonomy Management & Service Community Management

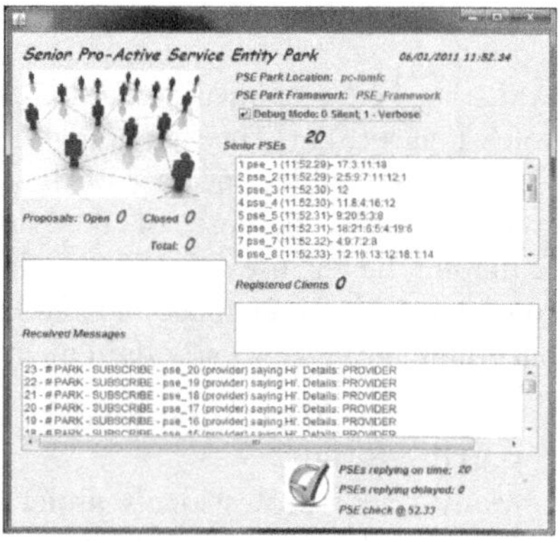

Fig. 5. Senior Pro-Active Service Entity Park

4. Senior Pro-Active Service Entity Park – the module that monitors the activity of the Ecosystem, showing active PSEs, open Business Opportunities and the messages exchanged among distinct actors of PASEF (Fig. 5).
5. Workflow Editor – The module for the specification of absBPMs and later for the selection of SP performers in order to achieve an eBPM. Fig. 6 represents an example absBPM, without performers, as explained above.
6. Workflow Engine – Finally, a workflow engine was needed, in order to launch the execution of the eBPMs. Fig. 7 represents an eBPM that is being executed.

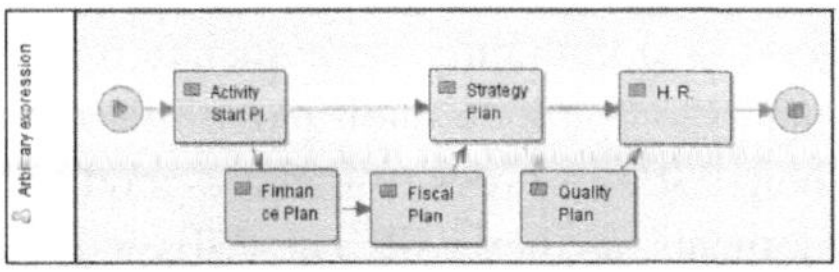

Fig. 6. Example absBPM

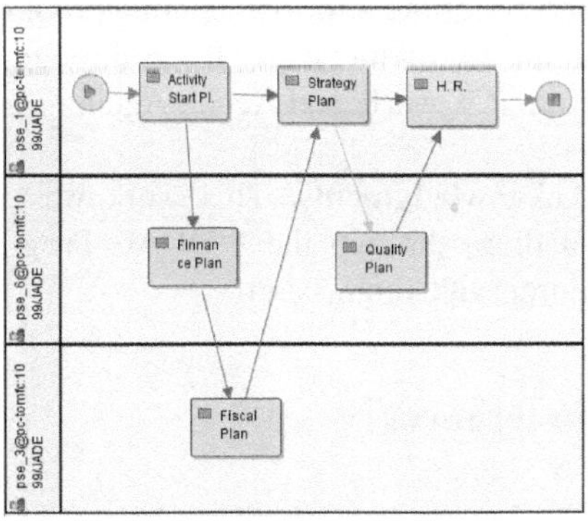

Fig. 7. Example eBPM being executed

The model of Fig. 7 corresponds to the absBPM of Fig. 6, to which 3 SPs were selected as performers of the consultancy services. The selection of the SPs for each service is supported by the QoS data stored at PASEF. It is interesting to notice that the lines in the model of Fig. 7 correspond to the PSEs representing the selected seniors, following the BPMN standard notation. In this particular example, two PSEs have made successful proposals composed of more than one service. These proposals are made by the PSEs themselves, following a configuration that the corresponding SP gave them, in terms of autonomy.

Besides supporting the professional life of seniors, collaborative networks can also play a relevant role in other life settings, namely independent living, healthy living, and recreation in life, as identified in the BRAID roadmap on ICT and Ageing. In all these areas there is a trend to evolve towards more integrated services, involving multiple stakeholders through well coordinated collaborative ecosystems. PASEF can be applied in such contexts.

5 Conclusions and Future Work

The main objective of this work was to define a set of base concepts that better match CN members' expectations concerning the mechanisms they have to model the services they are willing to provide to the network, following the service orientation paradigm evolution. This goal was achieved through the introduction of pro-activeness elements and a new QoS Mechanism that benefits from such elements.

The presented concepts allow CN members to model their services through PSEs, within a well-delimited Ecosystem, and configure them to better represent and promote the services they are willing to provide, under an auto-initiative basis, instead of the passiveness of current approaches. Furthermore, the QoS mechanism improves service selection processes towards rewarding the best providers.

Particularly for the case of senior professionals, the prototype developed intends to serve a community or association of elderly people in order to provide them the means to continue their active life after retirement. These people may then configure their PSEs in order to make a good balance of their working periods and the leisure moments, as they will. The PSEs will make all the "ambassador" work for them.

PASEF is the result of a research work that integrates distinct perspectives [1], [3], [13]. This paper presents the formal integrated framework definition of PASEF that served for the development of a proof of concept prototype system. The ongoing work is the validation stage, made through presentations of the prototype to stakeholders from ICT world and Active Ageing associations.

Acknowledgments. This work was supported in part by FCT (CTS multiannual funding) through the PIDDAC Program funds, and BRAID project funded by the European Commission.

References

1. Cardoso, T., Camarinha-Matos, L.: Pro-Active Asset Entities in Collaborative Networks. In: Camarinha-Matos, L., Pereira, P., Ribeiro, L. (eds.) Emerging Trends in Technological Innovation, pp. 93–102. Springer, Boston (2010)
2. Rabelo, R., et al.: The Ecolead ICT Infrastructure For Collaborative Networked Organizations. In: Network-Centric Collaboration and Supporting Frameworks, pp. 451–460. Springer, Boston (2006)
3. Cardoso, T., Camarinha-Matos, L.: Pro-Active Service Entity Framework for a Better Mapping between Business and Software. In: Camarinha-Matos, L., Boucher, X., Afsarmanesh, H. (eds.) Collaborative Networks for a Sustainable World, pp. 451–460. Springer, Boston (2010)
4. Charles, P., Christoph, B.: The Myth of Open Web Services: The Rise of the Service Parks. IEEE Internet Computing 12(3), 94–95 (2008)
5. Jammes, F., Smit, H.: Service-oriented paradigms in industrial automation. IEEE Transactions on Industrial Informatics 1(1), 62–70 (2005)
6. Burianek, F., Bonnemeier, S., Ihlenburg, D.: Solution Selling: The Need for Customer Interaction. In: Alt, R., Francyzk, B., Frahnrich, K.-P. (eds.) Proceedings of International Symposium of Services Science, pp. 127–137 (2009)
7. Franco, R., Ortiz Bas, A., Lario Esteban, F.: Modeling extended manufacturing processes with service-oriented entities. Service Business 3(1), 31–50 (2009)
8. Svirskas, A., et al.: Virtual Organization Management Using Web Service Choreography And Software Agents. In: Network-Centric Collaboration and Supporting Frameworks, pp. 535–542. Springer, Boston (2006)
9. Petersen, S.A., Rao, J., Matskin, M.: Virtual Enterprise Formation Supported by Agents and Web Services. In: Protogeros, N. (ed.) Agents and Web Service Technologies in Virtual Enterprises (2008)

10. Brazier, F.M.T., et al.: Agents and Service-Oriented Computing for Autonomic Computing: A Research Agenda. IEEE Internet Computing 13(3), 82–87 (2009)
11. Camarinha-Matos, L., et al.: Emerging Collaborative Forms. In: Collaborative Networked Organizations, pp. 41–64. Springer, Heidelberg (2004)
12. Camarinha-Matos, L., Afsarmanesh, H.: Active Ageing Roadmap – A Collaborative Networks Contribution to Demographic Sustainability. In: Camarinha-Matos, L., Boucher, X., Afsarmanesh, H. (eds.) Collaborative Networks for a Sustainable World, pp. 46–59. Springer, Boston (2010)
13. Cardoso, T., Camarinha-Matos, L.M.: Pro-Active Service Entities - Improving Selection Chances within large Senior Professional Virtual Community scenario (2011)

Services Discovery as a Mean to Enhance Software Resources Sharing in Collaborative Networks

Alexandre Perin-Souza and Ricardo J. Rabelo

Department of Automation and Systems, Federal University of Santa Catarina, Brazil
{perin,rabelo}@das.ufsc.br

Abstract. Collaborative Networks (CN) realization fundamentally relies on the need of collaboration, from diverse perspectives, among partners. From the software perspective, CN members who have SOA-based solutions keep the involved web-services at their local silos. This means that the collaboration potential of CNs might be enlarged and reinforced if such silos could be opened up and shared among their members, hence decreasing development and hosting costs. This is relevant as CN members are mostly composed of small and medium size companies with usual high limitations of ICT resources. This paper presents the result of an exploratory research that proposes a model for service discovery as a mechanism to leverage software services sharing among partners under the Software-as-a-Service (SaaS) access and business models. The developed model allows discovering the most suitable services for the required business processes, considering their contexts (using the UBL standard) and quality of services (QoS). A prototype has been developed to show the concepts. The assessment of the model is given in the end.

Keywords: Collaborative Networks, Web Service Discovery, Business Process, QoS, UBL, SaaS.

1 Introduction

Collaborative Networks (CN) paradigm has been considered one of the most promising strategies. Its ultimate goal is to enable networked organizations to agilely define and set up relations with organizations as well as to be adaptive according to business environment conditions and current organizations' autonomy levels [1]. This requires more effectiveness, flexibility and collaboration in businesses.

From the ICT perspective, new requirements have demanded more advanced infrastructures [2] and a number of ICT approaches have been proposed for that. Two of the most impacting ones are SOA (Service Oriented Architecture) and Utility paradigms [3], which jointly represent a scenario of a large scale of software services distributed over the Internet and accessed on demand, from everywhere, anytime.

The problem tackled in this work refers to the fact that CN members who have SOA-based solutions keep the involved web services stored in their local silos. This means that the SOA potential in terms of reuse could be extended and highly increased if such silos could be shared among CN members. Services could be then accessed by any member so enlarging and reinforcing collaboration while

L.M. Camarinha-Matos et al. (Eds.): PRO-VE 2011, IFIP AICT 362, pp. 388–399, 2011.

development and hosting costs are decreased. This is relevant as CN members are mostly composed of Micro, Small and Medium Enterprises, without conditions to maintain IT infrastructures and costly staff. In this sharing scenario, CN members could be both clients and service providers [2].

This is the underlying motivation of this work. CN members - VBE, VE, VO, PVC[1] members and other type of companies (e.g. logistics operators and software providers) have the potential to enlarge their collaboration via an interoperable and transparent collaboration "cloud". Several works have been developed in this direction, such as virtual machining [5], knowledge search and sharing over CN's information repositories [6], virtual shop-floor [7] and CN ICT infrastructures [2].

Supporting this higher collaboration requires, however, coping with many issues, of different levels of complexity. One of the issues refers to the access mode and business models that can be aligned to this collaborative scenario [8]. In the SOA context, SaaS (*Software-as-a-Service*) [9] has arisen as one of the most powerful models. Using SaaS, clients (i.e. CN members) can flexibly build and adapt their services portfolio according to their needs [10] instead of getting held to single vendors of monolithic software packages whose full set of functionalities are often few used/accessed. With SaaS, services are accessed remotely, upon request, paid-per-use, based on contractual rules specified in SLAs (*Service Level Agreement*) [11] for hosting, managing, providing access to them following QoS levels, no matter where the services providers are and how services have been deployed [12]. This seems suitable to CN members due to their intrinsic independence, autonomy, large geographic distribution and heterogeneity. A second issue refers to the discovery of services that are shareable, and this is what this paper is more about.

In this services discovery scenario, client and provider perspectives should be taken into account. From the CN clients' side this means how expressing the desired service as well as how finding, selecting and binding services to their composite SOA-based applications. From the CN providers' side, this means how publishing and making their services available. Besides that, CN clients must feel confident to access not only a given functionally-compliant service, but ideally to the most suitable service regarding the computing environment and business process' context [13].

The essential problem addressed in this paper is related to how to discover the most suitable software services dynamically over plenty ones that are made available at CN members' repositories. In this sense, this work presents a comprehensive, integrated, open and standard-based environment for dynamic services discovery and sharing, strongly based on processes and ICT standards, regarding CN particularities.

The paper is organized as follows. Section 1 has framed the problem and the tackled scenario of services discovery and sharing among CN members. Section 2 summarizes the main concepts and literature overview on services discovery. Section 3 presents the proposed model and section 4 presents a software prototype and section 5 discusses the results. Some conclusions are presented in section 6.

---

[1] VBE (Virtual Organization Breeding Environment), VE (Virtual Enterprises), VO (Virtual Organization), PVC (Professional Virtual Communities).

2 Basic Literature Overview

The problem of web services discovery involves many complex issues, such as: i) technological heterogeneity and low level of interoperability; ii) ambiguity of concepts due to differences of domain applications; and iii) limitations in the technologies used to design services [15]. There are plenty of works and visions on services discovery in the literature. The review here presented encompasses only the considered most relevant works for the purpose of this paper.

Two basic strategies resume the works on service discovery presented in the literature: static and dynamic discovery. There is a number of advantages and disadvantages in both. In the static way services are discovered at design time and they are immediately associated / bind to the given SOA application, but the previously chosen service may be not available when the service is invoked. The main advantage of the dynamic approach is the possibility of replacing services by others on-the-fly. However, this strategy usually presents higher discovery time (as all discovery actions should be done at execution time) and demands more sophisticated discovery algorithms. This sophistication can be in the form of criteria relaxation [16] or other techniques such as classification systems, providers' reputation, costs negotiation and quality of service development process [17].

Existing models and approaches for services discovery can be grouped into four dimensions: *information retrieval, architecture, QoS* and *standards* [15]. In general terms, in the information retrieval dimension the focus has been put on semantics in way to provide greater precision in the services selection [18]. In the architectural dimension, works have focused on aspects such scalability, security, availability, etc. [19]. In the QoS dimension there are three basic fields of research [20]. The first one refers to the definition of attributes and metrics for QoS. The second one involves the establishment of more comprehensive and robust frameworks to represent, select, verify and maintain QoS attributes. The third field involves the development of *ad hoc* strategies to solve specific cases involving QoS. In the standards dimension, the initiatives have focused on interoperability (in heterogeneous environments). ICT standards like UDDI [21], SOAP [22], WSDL [23] have been intensively used.

The problem is that the envisaged collaborative scenario requires a more holistic view about services discovery. Besides requiring a joint view of those four dimensions, other dimensions not tackled in any of the reviewed works are also necessary, namely the consideration of the business level. In spite of the very high complexity all this represents and challenges that have to be faced, this proposed model intends to contribute to this.

3 Proposed Model

Coping with all the requirements involved in the envisaged collaborative scenario of services discovery and sharing is extremely complex and also involves several challenges at business and IT levels [24].

In the developed model for services discovery within a CN scenario, there are five basic issues to be considered: *i) what to express; ii) how to express the desired service; iii) who expresses the desired service; iv) who evaluates and how discovery results are evaluated; and v) when expressing and searching.*

The first point refers to which information should be expressed to specify the desired service for the given BP. In the proposed model, this involves: i) functional aspects (service's name and operations); ii) inputs and outputs; iii) expected QoS values; and iv) BP's context.

The second point refers to services expression including the components and the relationship between them. Natural language, formal or dedicated languages are examples of how to do this. The proposed model adopts ontology. They create a uniform vocabulary to be used by the discovery mechanisms, besides improving discovery process accuracy and precision.

The third point refers to who informs the desired service. Traditionally, the SOA application designer is the one who explicitly specifies the details of the desired service. Considering the role of BPM systems in this work, four ways might be considered: Automatic (A), Strongly Based on Designer (SBD), Semi-Automatic (SA) and Assisted (As). In the 'A', the discovery task is left to the BPM environment. It automatically identifies needs, makes changes in the expression and determines which service will be selected and be bind to a given BP. This process occurs without designer intervention. In the 'SBD' way is somehow the opposite case, where the designer is the responsible for indicating the required service and for evaluating and deciding about the most adequate service to be selected. The designer interacts with the BPM environment intensively. 'SA' is a hybrid way. The BPM does the whole process but asks to the designer for some constraint relaxation in the case no expected service is found out. In the 'As' way, there is a closer interaction between BPM environment and designer. The designer specifies service's requirements whereas BPM informs BP's context. The discovery evaluation is jointly performed.

The fourth point involves determining who evaluates the discovery results and how this evaluation occurs (assisted, without designer participation, etc). Four situations are considered: i) more than one 'perfect' service (i.e. there is full compliance between desire and outcome), which means having the need for ranking and selecting the most appropriate service; ii) just one perfect service; iii) none service; iv) one partial service (any 'perfect' service); and v) more than one partial services.

The fifth point refers to at which moment the activities of identifying the BP, its requirements, the results evaluation, etc. will be made by of the discovery actions.

A key aspect in the proposed model is a change in the way the problem of dynamic services discovery have traditionally been seen. In this work, the problem is split into two phases: *design* phase and *running* phase (Fig. 1). The essential rationale of this separation is trying to prevent CN managers from handling IT issues as much as possible. In this sense, at BPM level, it is considered that they are familiarized with business rules and can specify how business processes should be executed. On the other hand, at the running time, users shouldn´t be worried about discovery itself as this should be essentially left to the SOA environment / discovery system to do it.

The design phase refers to the specification of the SOA application to be built, including capturing the given BP's context and indication of the required QoS, which are crucial elements for a more proper discovery (left side of Fig. 1). This is done off-line and CN managers are assisted by the composition environment (see third point above). Initially, they use a BPM environment for composing applications (step 1) which offers the access to a standard *BPs catalog* (step 2). This catalog, an additional element of the model, comprises all the business processes of UBL standard (the one chosen in this exploratory work), meaning that all composite applications will be compliant with a standard or with a specialization of it. Yet, it is possible to identify and to capture the BP's context. This speeds up the application design and provides greater semantic richness to the discovery since services (from the several CN providers) are published taking a UBL standard ontology into account.

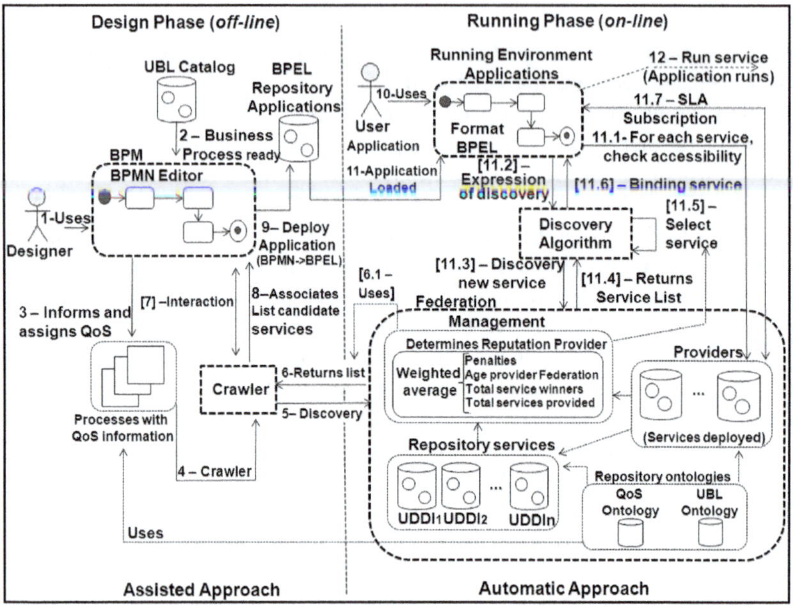

Fig. 1. Overview of the Model Operation

In step 3, CN managers, together with an IT technician, inform and assign QoS attributes for each BP's activity. A QoS ontology (see section 4) is used for this (Fig. 1 right / bottom), and it is also used by CN providers when publishing their services. The search expression is then assembled. The expression to find the web service *W* is structured as a 2-*tuple* $W = (F,Q)$, where *F* is the set of functional requirements identified via the BP's ontology, and Q the non-functional requirements (i.e. QoS).

An internal crawler service is activated (step 4) having the search expression as input. The crawler begins searching (step 5) for services in the CN members' services repositories with the aim of bringing a list of possible services that matches the subprocess requirements. It is also important to mention that the crawler acts in "background" (i.e. candidate services are retuned at design time and not at the running time). The underlying strategy is to decrease the whole discovery time, avoiding an exhaustive search when the composite SOA application would be in execution.

A list of services is returned (step 6) and further ranked according to CN providers' reputation (step 6.1 - historical, penalties, etc). As mentioned in the previous section, a 'perfect' matching may be not occur, and the crawler should handle this (step 7). If the list contains just one service, it is already settled. If the list is empty, the crawler asks for a requirements relaxation for a new search, or leaves the option (or risk) of keeping the same requirements and doing the search at running time. If the list has more than one service, they are stored as XML files for further treatment at run time. In step 8, still at the design phase, this list of candidate services is passed to the BPM environment. The SOA application is then composed, converted into BPEL [25] format and gets available to run (step 9).

It is important to clarify one aspect related to the used ontologies and the matching. The use of ontologies is a strategy to face semantics interoperability problems when consumers go for a discovery and providers publish their services. UBL and QoS ontologies act as a common and agreed set of terminologies and concepts used to express BPs and QoS. This allows a syntactic matching in the discovery, via a comparison of the same (semantic) terms used in the adopted ontologies.

The second phase of the model – the on-line phase – starts when the CN manager or collaborator wants to run a given application (that one previously composed). At this time, it is relatively transparent to him that it is a SOA-based application. He navigates through the process / BPEL repository and chooses which application he wants to run (steps 10 and 11, Fig. 1 right side). A runtime task checks if the pre-selected web services are actually available (step 12), invoking the selected ones in the case they are ok. Otherwise the second one from the list will be picked up, and so forth. In the case none of them are available then the whole discovery activity is triggered again, with a new possible list, etc. Once everything is settled for a given service, the respective SLA (Service Level Agreement) is dynamically generated (step 11.7) and integrated into the BPM environment, as proposed in [11]. Thus, and helped by a BPEL engine, the desired composite SOA application is ready to run, with the most appropriate services (step 12).

This proposed model has a set of assumptions. Two of them are important to be highlighted. The first assumption is what we call 1:1 relation. This means that the composition model is prepared to find and to compose *1* service for each *1* BP's activity. For instance, regarding UBL ontology, *Ordering* process is composed of a set of activities e.g. *AcceptOrder*. Therefore, the model will understand that a discovery action (considering functional, QoS and context requirements) will be carried out aiming at finding a sort of web services for *AcceptOrder* but only one web service will run it. This assumes that services providers would have implemented one (1) service per BP's activity (eventually they can have different versions, associated or not to different business models). The second assumption is that the so-called CN manager and IT technician are expected to be experienced on the company's processes and rules (and UBL ontology) as well as have the 'feeling' about suitable QoS metrics (and ontology) for the SOA application that is going to be built up.

4 Software Prototype

The architecture of the prototype is organized in five modules and one central internal repository of web services.

The *editor* module allows the definition of SOA-based applications (based on UBL standard). It uses the *IBM WebSphere Business Modeler* tool and supports BP management and BPMN modeling.

The *catalog* module implements a set of services and is itself a SOA application [26]. Fig. 2 shows the interface where the designer uses *WebSphere* tool and loads some process stored in the catalog. The designer knows the business rules, the context's semantics, the services' provider, the service's name and that the required SLA has been previously agreed. The SOA designer can either compose the application as presented by UBL (as a kind of default) or can compose it regarding companies' specificities. During this composition, the designer specifies QoS values and required composition's orchestration.

The *discovery* module has a crawling. It takes as input the required service (using UBL ontology), the QoS constraints (using QoS ontology), a variable related to the provider reputation and the list of available UDDIs in the Federation. The algorithm creates and triggers threads for doing the search and the services selection over each UDDI. A looping for a systematic search for services that satisfy the discovery expression is started. The algorithm tests each service comparing functional aspects (name and adherence with the UBL ontology) and checks QoS specifications against what has been required. If they satisfy the discovery expression then the service is added to the service candidates list. Once the search ends, the variable which considers providers' reputations is checked. If it is true, the list of candidate services is classified (using providers' reputation) and it is returned by crawler (Fig. 3).

The first column reports the list of names of services discovered (*AuthorizePayment, Notify of Payment, etc.),* the UBL's activity classification UBL is presented in the second column (according to the developed ontology), the number of QoS characteristics desired for a given activity is shown the third column (1, in this case). The total number of discovered services that satisfy the expression of discovery is showed in the fourth column (*Matching Services*).

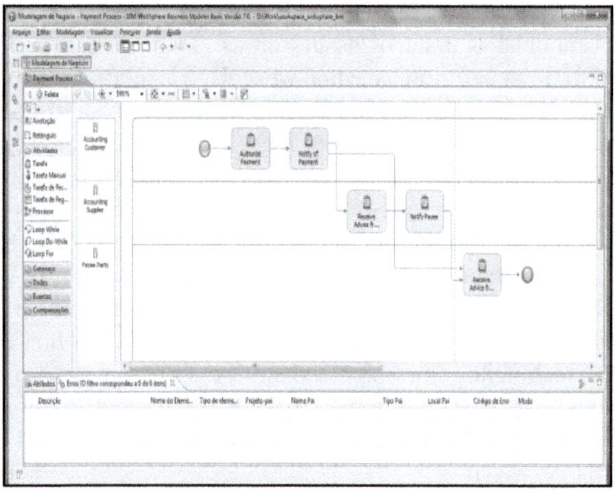

Fig. 2. Interface of an editing process accessing the catalog

Discover Services for Tasks

Task Name	Task Ontology	QoS Constraints	Matching Services
Authorize Payment	ubl/payment/paymentprocess/accounting...	1	9
Notify of Payment	ubl/payment/paymentprocess/accounting...	1	9
Notify Payee	ubl/payment/paymentprocess/accounting...	1	9
Receive Advice from Accounting Customer	ubl/payment/paymentprocess/accounting...	1	15
Receive Advice from Accounting Customer1	ubl/payment/paymentprocess/payeeParty...	1	12

Fig. 3. Sample of returned services after the crawling algortim

The forth module is used as an environment for running the composed SOA application. It was implemented using *Apache ODE* [27], integrated with *Intalio* BPMS tool. Intalio's web interface was used to visualize the status of running processes. This module uses the dynamic discovery algorithm (DDS) to test each candidate service in the list before invoking them; the DDS algorithm ends when it finds the first available service that meets the discovery expression. Similarly as in the crawling phase, this module also involves the generation and management of the SLA between the involved parts.

The fifth and last module refers to the implementation of the logical and virtual aggregation of providers (i.e. the CN members' services), which is called *federation*. It includes four elements: (1) Ontology repository (composed of UBL and QoS ontologies), both implemented using *Protégé* tool. QoS ontology was conceived based on a high-level ontology [28] and QoS definitions were based on [29]; (2) The set of repositories managed by the federation. The access to the repositories is made from a list of a XML file stored in a UDDI master (ubl-uddi). This was implemented using Apache jUDDI [30], which implements *UDDI 3.0*; (3) A general Management submodule, which determines the reputation of providers and; (4) UBL Providers, representing the UBL-compliant services providers that composes the federation.

5 Experiments and Evaluation

Four main experiments were performed to evaluate the developed model. The involved cases were deployed in a PC with 1.66GHz, 2GB RAM and Microsoft Windows XP. The first experiment aimed at checking the behavior of the prototype against the metrics of *precision* and *recall* (the two traditional metrics in the area of information retrieval [31]). The scenario was composed of 3 service repositories (uddi-ubl1, uddi-ubl2 and ubl-uddi3) and 10 providers registered in the federation (provider-ubl1 to provider-ubl10). A provider was chosen randomly and 10 services related to the UBL process *Ordering* were published. This process was repeated 20 times for each repository, applying the adopted UBL and QoS ontologies, giving a total of 600 services. These services are actually instances of the same process' activity, related to the *Ordering* process. Services' code was the same but with different QoS values assigned to each registered instance. These values were generated in a stochastic way, in the interval [0,100]).

The experiments 2 and 3 were performed using the same discovery expression but increasing the number of UDDIs to 5 and 7, all of them deployed in a local network. In the fourth experiment, 1 UDDI was locally deployed and 2 others were deployed remotely, simulating a more pervasive scenario. Table 1 shows the discovery time behavior and the total of services in the federation in the four experiments.

As imagined, the use of QoS has minimized the number of returned services while its usability (adequacy) for the current business and computing conditions is maximized. The use of UBL ontology mitigates interoperability / interpretation problems. This is also valid to QoS, where both clients and providers can share a common conceptual vocabulary.

Table 1. Results of experiments

Tests	Experiment 1		Experiment 2		Experiment 3		Experiment 4	
	Federation with 3 local UDDIs		Federation with 5 Local UDDIs		Federação com 7 local UDDIs		Federation with 3 UDDIs (1 local e 2 distributed)	
	Service (T/R)	**Time (s)**	**Service (T/R)**	**Time (s)**	**Service (T/R)**	**Time (s)**	**Service (T/R)**	**Time (s)**
1°	600/17	9	1000/27	6	1400/36	8	600/11	9
2°	750/19	6	1250/31	6	1750/45	7	750/13	10
3°	930/25	6	1550/36	6	2170/55	8	930/18	12
4°	1170/29	7	1950/41	7	2730/71	9	1170/23	14
5°	1470/34	7	2450/49	7	3430/90	9	1470/30	16
6°	1860/41	8	3100/65	11	4340/115	18	1860/41	22
7°	2340/52	11	3900/72	15	5460/152	28	2340/55	26
8°	2940/70	15	4900/112	23	6860/188	26	2940/72	32
9°	3690/92	17	6150/147	25	8610/226	51	3690/85	40
10°	4620/109	24	7700/191	46	10780/284	67	4620/105	51

Tests column identifies the set of discoveries carried out in the four experiments. For example, in the first test, 17 services were found out (i.e. attended the discovery expression) over 600 available in the federation, taking 9 seconds to perform this operation (in a local network). In the other extreme, in the tenth test, 105 services were discovered over 4620 available services, and this took almost 1 minute to be executed in a deployment scenario composed of 1 local and 2 distributed / remote UDDIs. Although part of this important increasing of time is caused by the intrinsic latency in the network, a good part of this is caused by the discovery algorithm itself, which grows almost exponentially as long as the number of nodes / providers increases.

Despite the complexity involved in a complete solution for services discovery, the proposed model presents some contributions. The experiments showed that the most suitable services for a given process can be found out. The crawler made possible filtering non adequate services, hence allowing a potential quicker decision about the final service. The quality of the selection is higher as the list brought up by the crawler only contains services that effectively cope with the indicated requirements, meaning a lower potential to have problems during the execution of the (SOA-based) application. The discovery can be considered more trustful as there is some computing assistance in the process. Once the company detects a need for a change in a given process, the designer can immediately redesign the business processes and a new SOA application can be "immediately" composed with suitable services.

Based on the literature overview and achieved results, it is believed that the model introduces some aspects of innovation. One of them concerns the integration and use of a catalog of business processes in the composition of applications, combing it with a flexible and ubiquitous CN scenario based on SaaS access mode. Furthermore, the model uses the semantics obtained from the ontology of UBL-based business processes to publish and discover services, allowing getting the process' context to better filter services. This somehow ensures that the results from the discovery action will only bring services semantically aligned with business processes expressed in UBL, i.e. with the BPM layer. The model uses of a logical entity (Federation), which highlights the importance of UDDI registries (or equivalent structure) in the discovery process as a way to provide some standardization in the publication process.

The presented results are very dependent of the adoption of BP standards and of the so-called 1:1 relation, two assumptions used in the model.

6 Conclusions

This paper has presented results of an exploratory work on dynamic services discovery as a mechanism to enhance collaboration among CN members at IT level with a sustainable business model (SaaS).

The proposed model creates a kind of cloud over CN members' services repositories and then a mean to access/share them. It is strongly based on standards, which mitigates interoperation problems and hence increases the potential of a larger acceptance of advanced concepts – BPM and SOA in the case – by CN members.

From the exploratory perspective of this research, it can be said that the proposed model is able to support the theoretical part of the problem (based on the chosen approach), which refers to how CN members can share their web services and enlarge their collaboration and trust building. This can give suitable conditions for a more agile adaptation in the members' business processes, in particular when they need to cope with specific business opportunities to create a virtual organization.

However, from the applied perspective of this research, a model like that cannot be seen as the solution for all issues involved in a full-fledged services discovery and services sharing model for CN. For example, SaaS in an emergent area and there is not solid theoretical foundations about it yet. Trust, adequate ICT infrastructures, security, cultural changes, BP (re)organization, integration with legacy systems & services, partners preparation to indeed offer their services under the SaaS base, the adoption of common ontologies (even though relied on standards), among many other aspects, are examples of additional and complex issues that should be dealt with.

From the SOA and composition points of view, it not believed that all enterprise applications should be transformed into services and accessed freely from any CN member. There are some applications that are naturally locally deployed and of private use besides the fact that some of them require very hard QoS metrics to be indeed useful, which happens in many cases. From the discovery algorithm itself, there is a need of a deeper analysis of its complexity to deal with potentially thousands of providers. This corresponds to one the main next steps of this work.

In spite of all this, it is believed that this model has a structure that can be used as a starting model and useful instrument to allow a wider collaboration among CN members, preserving their independence, autonomy and heterogeneity.

References

1. Camarinha-Matos, L.M., Afsarmanesh, H.: Collaborative Networked Organizations: a Research Agenda for Emerging Business Models. Kluwer Academic Publishers, Dordrecht (2004)
2. Rabelo, R.J.: Advanced Collaborative Business ICT Infrastructures. In: Methods and Tools for Collaborative Networked Organizations, pp. 337–370. Springer, Heidelberg (2008)

3. NESSI Strategic Research Agenda - Framing the future of the Service Oriented Economy, February 13 (2006), http://www.nessi-europe.com/documents/NESSI_SRA_VOL_1_20060213.pdf,
ICT for Enterprise Networking,
http://cordis.europa.eu/ist/directorate_d/en_intro.htm
4. Singh, M., Huhns, M.: Service Oriented Computing. Wiley, Chichester (2005)
5. de Souza Jr., J.L.N.J., et al.: An Internet-oriented Management and Control System in a Distributed Manufacturing Environment. International Journal of Manufacturing Research 5, 5–25 (2009)
6. Tramontin_Junior, R.J., Rabelo, R.J., Chirab, H.: Customizing Knowledge Search in CNOs through Context-based Query Expansion. Production Planning & Control 21(2), 229–246 (2010)
7. Ribeiro, L., Barata, J., Colombo, A.: Supporting agile supply chains using a service-oriented shop floor. Engineering Application Art. Intelligence (2009)
8. Borst, I., et al.: Technical Report (Deliverable) D62.2 ICT-I Business Models, http://www.ve-forum.org/default.asp?P=284
9. Cancian, M.H., Rabelo, R.J., Wangenheim, C.G.V.: An approach for the generation of SLAs for Software-as-a-Service. In: 8th I2TS Int. Conference, Florianopolis, Brasil (2009) (in Portuguese)
10. Tsai, W.T.: Service-oriented system engineering: a new paradigm. In: IEEE Inter. Workshop Service-Oriented System Engineering, SOSE, pp. 3–6 (2005)
11. Cancian, M.H., Rabelo, R.J., Wangenheim, C.G.V.: An approach for the generation of SLAs for Software-as-a-Service. In: 8th I2TS Int. Conference, Florianopolis, Brasil (2009) (in Portuguese)
12. Ma, D.: The Business Model of Software-As-A-Service. In: IEEE International Conference Services Computing, pp. 701–706 (2007)
13. Perin de Souza, A., Rabelo, R.J.: An Approach for a more Agile BPM-SOA Integration supported by Dynamic Services Discovery. In: Proc. of the EDOC 14th IEEE, Brasil (2010)
14. Perin de Souza, A., Rabelo, R.J.: Supporting Software Services Discovery and Sharing in Collaborative Networks. In: 11th IFIP Working Conference on Virtual Enterprises, Saint Etienne (2010)
15. Garofalakis, J.D., Panagis, Y., Sakkopoulos, E., Tsakalidis, A.K.: Contemporary Web Service Discovery Mechanisms. Journal of Web Eng., 265–290 (2006)
16. W3C. Web Services Architecture (WSA), http://www.w3.org/TR/2004/NOTE-ws-arch-20040211/
17. Mello, E.R., Fraga, J.S., Wangham, M.S.: Using a trust model for the composition of Web Services. In: Brazilian Symposium on Computer Networks (2009) (in Portuguese)
18. Kourtesis, D., Paraskakis, I., Friesen, A., Gouvas, P., Bouras, A.: Web Service Discovery in a Semantically Extended UDDI Registry: The Case of Fusion. In: The Foundation of Collaborative Networks. IFIP International Federation for Information Processing, vol. 243, pp. 547–554. Springer, Boston (2007)
19. Lamparter, S., Ankolekar, A., Studer, R., Grimm, S.: Preference-based Selection of Highly Configurable Web Services. In: Proceedings of the 16th International Conference on World Wide Web, WWW 2007, Alberta, Canada (2007)
20. Wang, X., Vitvar, T., Kerrigan, M., Toma, I.A.: QoS-aware Selection Model for Semantic Web Services. In: Service-Oriented Computing – ICSOC (2006)
21. OASIS. UDDI Specification V 3.0.2, http://docs.oasis-open.org/ubl/os-UBL-2.0/UBL-2.0.html

22. W3C. SOAP Specification V. 1.2, http://www.w3.org/TR/soap12-part1/
23. W3C. Web Services Description Language Specification V 2.0, http://www.w3.org/TR/wsdl20/
24. Dorn, J., Grün, C., Werthner, H., Zapletal, M.: From business to software: a B2B survey. Information Systems and E-Business Management 7, 123–142 (2009)
25. OASIS. Web Service Business Process Execution Language V 2.0, http://docs.oasis-open.org/wsbpel/2.0/OS/wsbpel-v2.0-OS.html
26. Bezerra, R.O.: Proposal for Electronic Catalog of Business Processes Based on UBL for Composition of SOA Applications. M.Sc. Thesis, Federal University of Santa Catarina (in Portuguese, 2011)
27. Apache Fundation. ODE, http://ode.apache.org
28. Tondello, G.F.: Semantic specification of QoS: The QoS-MO ontology. M.Sc. Thesis, Federal University of Santa Catarina (2008) (in Portuguese)
29. W3C. QoS for Web Services: Requirements and Possible Approaches, http://www.w3c.or.kr/kr-office/TR/2003/ws-qos/
30. Apache Fundation. jUDDI, http://juddi.apache.org/
31. van Rijsbergen, C.J.: Information Retrieval, http://www.dcs.gla.ac.uk/Keith/Preface.html

Cooperation Enabled Systems for Collaborative Networks

A. Luis Osório[1,3], Luis M. Camarinha-Matos[2], and Hamideh Afsarmanesh[3]

[1] Instituto Superior de Engenharia de Lisboa (ISEL), Portugal
aosorio@isel.pt
[2] Faculdade de Ciências e Tecnologia, Universidade Nova de Lisboa, Portugal
cam@uninova.pt
[3] University of Amsterdam (UvA), Netherlands
h.afsarmanesh@uva.nl

Abstract. A fast evolution to collaborative business models requires novel strategies for the development of collaboration-based information technology (IT) solutions. The complexity of building such solutions based on heterogeneous sub-systems requires a multidisciplinary approach, involving the perspectives of technology and business/management. In this direction, a novel approach is proposed, introducing the notion of Cooperation Enabled System as an autonomous and adaptive computational component as the base constructor to develop open (collaborative) IT solutions.

Keywords: Collaborative Networks Engineering, Cooperative Information Systems, Service Oriented Architectures.

1 Introduction

In a diversity of application domains we can notice that organizations are evolving towards becoming nodes of collaborative networks (CN) [1], [2] while participating in the offering of integrated business services. Ideally, these services are presented to clients in a way that makes transparent the participation of a diversity of organizations with their own information technology infrastructures.

The Brisa/Via-Verde tolling system and the national speed limit enforcement network are two examples of application domains that faced such challenge of adopting a collaborative networks strategy. The Brisa/Via-Verde case [4], [8] refers to the evolution of an existing tolling service to an integrated (multi-provider) business service, involving payments in parking lots and gas stations. One of the main problems faced in this case was the closeness of existing IT solutions; the electronic toll collection (ETC) subsystem was not prepared for the cooperation. An initial approach considered the development led by the ETC supplier as a unique possible integrator, but the adoption of proprietary processes and technology patterns resulted in an expensive "one-of-a-kind" solution. The national speed limit enforcement initiative, the SINCRO project from the Portuguese national road security authority had a quite different initial motivation. The objective of developing the network along different tendering phases suggested the adoption of a strategy aiming to guarantee

L.M. Camarinha-Matos et al. (Eds.): PRO-VE 2011, IFIP AICT 362, pp. 400–409, 2011.

the independence from the initial supplier(s). While the initial objective is to manage enforcement events directed to drivers, the adopted strategy is to establish a collaborative network involving public and private organizations.

In both Brisa/Via-Verde and SINCRO cases the aim is to offer ***integrated business services*** (IBS) implemented as collaborative processes which are supported by multiple stakeholders as nodes of a collaborative network (CN), Fig. 1. The adopted strategy in both cases features two key aspects:

i. The proposition of a *collaboration layer* (CL) [6] as a mechanism to isolate the processes and IT culture of each participating service provider;
ii. The proposition of a generic autonomous computational entity, the *collaboration enabled system* (CES) [6], aiming to handle the diversity at both organization's and collaborative network levels.

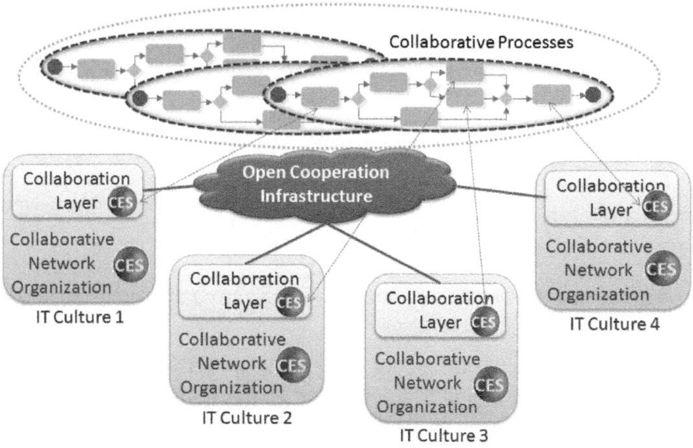

Fig. 1. Collaborative processes invoking CES services in CN nodes

A main research hypothesis is to consider the adaptive computational component CES [6] as a key strategy to promote the openness of complex integrated systems. The elements of the suggested approach are detailed and discussed in the following sections. The IBS are designed under a collaborative business model perspective and supported by a set of collaborative business processes (CBP) [13] deployed and executed in the context of a collaborative network [7]. The collaboration enabled system (CES), is then introduced as the base executive component of an open framework and infrastructure for collaborative networks.

2 The Need for Collaboration-Enabled Solutions

The challenge of developing open and integrated solutions for telematics domains such as the road tolling system, motivated the development of an open service bus, the ITSIBus [4], [9] as a first solution. In the beginning of the Brisa's project the road tolling systems were closed to competing suppliers besides the initial one. The independence from this unique supplier was then achieved through the development of an open service infrastructure involving a *service surrogate* as an adapter to make transparent the specificities of the different protocols from different road side equipments (RSE), as illustrated in Fig. 2.

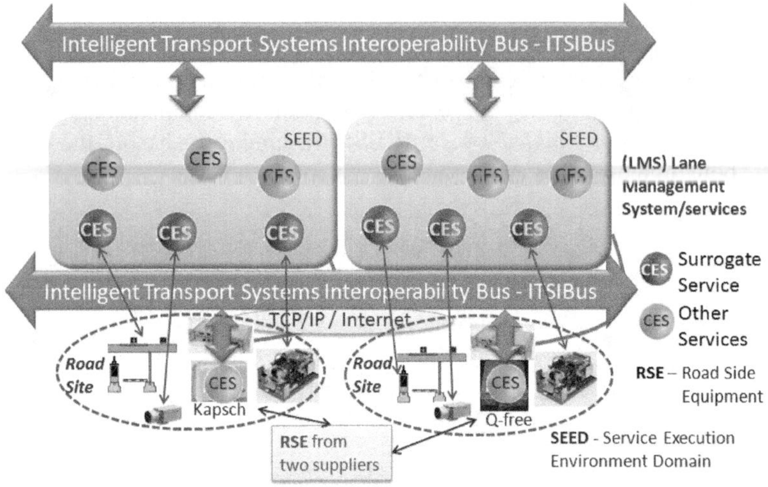

Fig. 2. Adapter-based integration of systems from different suppliers

This approach followed a quite usual integration pattern, which avoids the need for changes in legacy systems. Nevertheless, this exogenous integration effort has the drawback of implying extra costs and operational risks considering that there is an additional computational system, in some cases involving also hardware. Moreover, the complexity of the aimed integrated collaborative solutions suggests novel approaches regarding the lower levels components (e.g. sensor, actuators to user interacting channels). While the concept of adapter or surrogate might coexist for the cases where the inclusion of legacy systems might be an advantage, a more promising approach is to develop a collaboration enabled systems framework as a unifying bridge between business requirements and technology. The idea is to introduce an abstract component language able to process requirements against standard reusable components. Such generic and adaptive computational component aims to contribute to an endogenous integration paradigm. By endogenous integration we understand the approach that promotes that each subsystem is, from its inception, developed for operation in a collaboration context. In Fig. 2 this idea is illustrated by the embedding a CES element into the Kapch and Q-free (the current Brisa's RSE suppliers) subsystems, making them collaboration-enabled, without the need for exogenous adapters. The strategy here was to promote the technological change without the need for extra costs from the Brisa's side.

The SINCRO project considers a central operations management unit (CGO) that will be responsible for the quality control of each speed limit enforcement event (a multimedia object with a picture, a timestamp and the measured speed). This CGO subsystem, managed by the national authority, will cooperate with other subsystems to process and validate enforcement events. The interaction with a system managed by the authority responsible for the vehicle registration is an example of such required collaboration among public organizations. Although a simplified scenario, this is an interesting case to illustrate the complexity of the integrated collaborative solutions. An initial question was how to develop the national network in different phases starting with the most dangerous road points and gradually adding new control zones. Without a definition of an open architecture the national authority could only state WHAT is required and it would be up to the tender winner to decide about the HOWs. The next question is how to promote the development of an open solution towards the reduction, if not the elimination, of market dependencies regarding the development, life cycle management and evolution of the planned complex collaborative solutions. Taking this scenario as example (similar to the tolling case) the main problems are:

- The existing speed enforcement systems are based on an integrated kinemometer (Doppler Radar or Laser), a camera and a controller typically implementing a proprietary protocol to access enforcement events (through TCP connection);
- A cabinet system (or rack) has a specific design and development usually provided by the supplier of the radar or by an integrator;

  An equivalent CGO system is offered by the market, usually by suppliers of radar systems as an integrated solution to manage the national speed enforcement networks.

In this case it might be incorrect to talk about integrated business services, since is more an enforcement on citizens. Nevertheless it is possible to consider the national authority as an integrated service provider in the sense that the citizen has gets a single contact to solve the enforcement events independently of the number of involved collaborating organizations. Please note that this case includes the participation of municipalities with their own speed enforcement infrastructures, police authorities as unique persons authorized to move radar systems among enforcement points, etc. Recently, these organizations have been trying to evolve to higher levels of collaboration but their heterogeneous IT solutions are a drawback to this process. A more ambitious vision, already under discussion, is to evolve to a pan-European collaborative network to manage traffic safety and other security issues, as part of a global strategy to a safer mobility in Europe. We might foresee a Portuguese citizen travelling through Europe to be contacted by a subscribed integrated service warning her/him about enforcement events generated along her/his is trip. We can also foresee some form of warning regarding the entrance into a driving environment with different rules.

3 The Concept of Collaboration Enabled System

The collaboration enabled system (CES) concept aims to contribute to a separation between the realization and the modeling of requirements [11]. The idea is thus to contribute to the consolidation of the model-driven development (MDD) approach [10], [12] as an agile and adaptive mapping between requirements and execution components. The purpose is to promote a system's, rather than software development thinking. This proposed systems' thinking requires an effort to generalize the implementation perspective making subsystems adaptable to a diversity of requirements and able to support the derivation of new subsystems with the required capabilities. The CES concept aims to support such flexibility, making it possible for a components repository to support process development tools during technology bindings when executive resources are associated to process activities.

A Collaboration Enabled System (CES) addresses three main challenges:

i. Support a model-driven and process-oriented development of open complex collaborative solutions;
   - Mapping of functional and non functional requirements to CES capabilities;
   - Model based selection and evaluation of CES's compositions;
   - A CES generalization or specialization should precede unmatched requirements resolution. This is more a methodological assertion, suggesting the developing of a new CES only when the previous step is not a possible option.

ii. Leverage the reutilization of IT systems by promoting adaptive cooperation mechanisms;
   - A CES system embeds a number of mechanisms making it ready for collaboration in different scenarios, namely, different technology bindings for equivalent capabilities, associated metadata able to be interpreted by potential clients both at development and running time stages.

iii. A contribution to make the management of complex collaborative solutions more agile and autonomous (dynamic adaptability to a network and systems management application/service).
   - Given the growing diversity of systems, there is a need for a unified systems' management considering both monitoring and maintenance under a unique service level agreement. While this is not the main focus of this research, the adopted architecture establishes the basis for an adaptive and intelligent integrated monitoring and maintenance processes automation.

***Definition*:** A Cooperation Enabled System (CES) is an autonomous computational entity, made of interrelated components, defined as a tuple: CES = <SA, I, S, M, E, R, B>

where (Fig. 3):

- SA is a <u>Self-Awareness</u> subsystem embedding meta-data able to adapt the CES to a diversity of contexts; the SA subsystem manages CES capabilities;
- I is a set of <u>Interfaces</u>, considering an interface as a point of interaction or a cooperation point;

- S is the Security subsystem responsible for implementing the CES's security policies;
- M is the Monitoring subsystem aiming to implement the mechanisms making possible to plug the CES to an infrastructure management system (operational quality assurance);
- E is the Event management subsystem and it is responsible to support asynchronous interactions with CES clients;
- R represents the set of Resources necessary for the implementation behaviors. It might include configuration files, executable objects, user interface components among other resources to be used by the specialized behaviors;
- B embeds the business logic, implementing the modeled Behaviors that contribute to the declared capabilities.

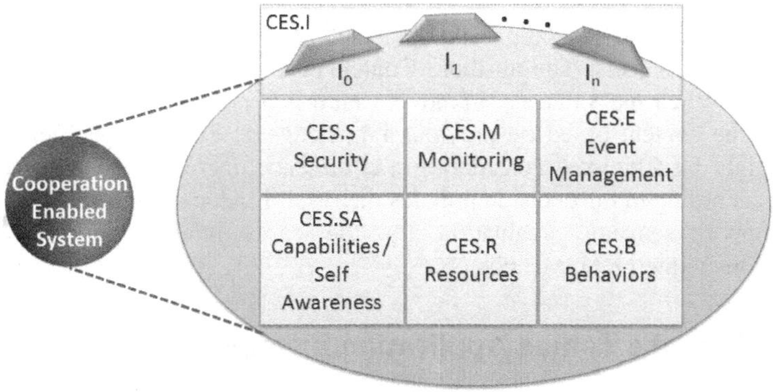

Fig. 3. The Collaboration Enabled System (CES) structure

One important aspect of the proposed concept is the generalization of the implemented interfaces making it possible for a CES to adapt to a diversity of execution environments. For instance, the road side equipment (RSE) has autonomy to store vehicle identification events; when reestablishing the connection to the lane management service (LMS), there is a need for a potential exchange of a huge amount of stored data. One option is to provide a specialized file transfer protocol for a reliable transfer of such data. However, other functionalities can be available through web services of other inter-systems communication mechanism (FTP, RMI, .NET, etc.). The need to cope with scenarios involving multiple technologies also motivates the need to increase CES adaptability.

According to the above definition, all the CES components can be organized as a collection of generic modeling entities (GME), Fig. 4. In the proposed framework a GME object aims to represent any kind of information from data, knowledge or behavior. In this way, both the run-time system and any CES can dynamically adapt for the cooperation with another CES.

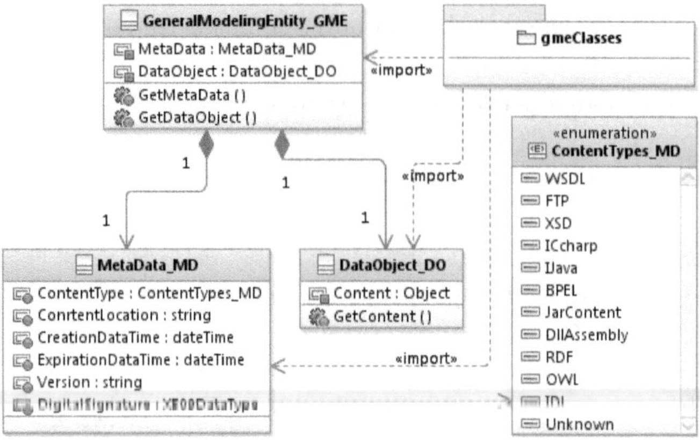

Fig. 4. The GME UML model

A GME instance is composed by exactly of one MetaData_MD and one DataObject_DO objects. The attribute ContentType identifies a known structure of the content. When the value is Unknown, there is a possibility to infer its type by analyzing the content based on previous knowledge of existing specifications. This feature might be addressed considering a confidence degree to the inferred content type and according to the decision policies the result is adopted or discarded. The idea is to support semantic evaluation for the cases information is lacking to unambiguously interpret GME objects.

4 Revisiting the Tolling Application Example

A road side equipment (RSE) reads vehicle electronic identification from an on-board unit (OBU). When plugged, the CES/RSE looks for a CES services directory (which might be also a CES) and registers its I_0 interface. A lane controller, also implemented as a CES, discovers the RSE and, through its I_0 interface, gets the necessary context information to retrieve vehicle identification events to be used in cooperation with other lane subsystems to generate electronic toll transactions. At the lane level, a typical electronic toll collection system has a lane controller that coordinates events generated by vehicle detection and classification and an enforcement subsystem. The lane controller logic is modeled by a process definition, Fig. 5. Some initialization process loads the LMS process definition to a CES space capable of interpreting process definition. The idea is to assume a CES as embedding a process virtual machine able to interpret declarative business logic definitions (e.g. a BPEL interpreter or execution engine).

The proposed framework considers specialized system CES offering communication and coordination mechanisms for the entire solution. The cooperation enabling Tuple Space system (CES Tuple Space), Fig. 5, is responsible for the communication among CES. In the implemented system, this communication follows the Linda [3], [5] shared space paradigm. By using a tuple space service each CES has only a single interlocutor. A LMS subscribes events with a specific signature

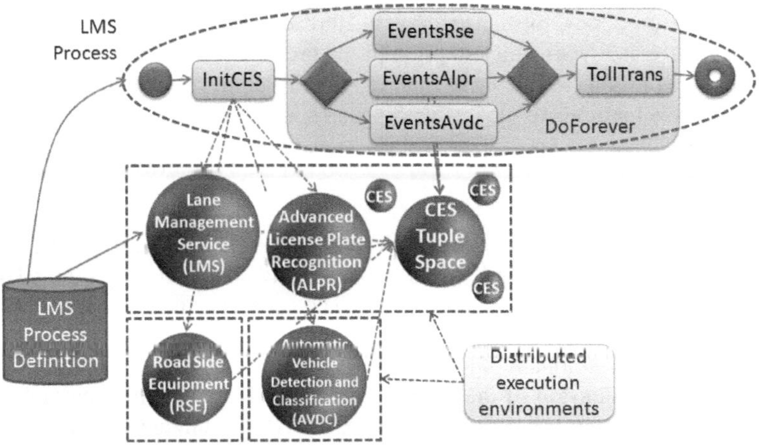

Fig. 5. The lane management service (LMS) architecture

on the Tuple Space CES to access events from the RSE, AVDC or ALPR subsystems. A strategy like this simplifies the implementation of a CES considering it does not need to be aware of the location of the other cooperating CES.

The CES proposal is grounded on the results from the adoption by Brisa of the ITSIBus service oriented (SOA) infrastructure [9]. The adoption of some of the features proposed in CES like the service monitoring, has contribute to a reduction of the total cost of ownership (TCO) of the deployed technology. It has also contributed to make simple and more competitive de evolution for new services as the case of the recent deployment of a new self-service tolling lane type (eTOLL).

5 Revisiting the Speed Limit Enforcement Example

The SINCRO project has established an initial functional granularity based on three autonomous subsystems being modeled as CES services:

i. The central operations management (CGO), which is modeled according to a business process modeling basis. The executive CES interprets the process representing the CGO responsibilities;
ii. The cabinet subsystem embeds a CES responsible for the management of the rack even when no radar subsystem is plugged in;
iii. The radar subsystem is modeled as a CES and is responsible to deliver speed enforcement events to the CGO.

In a first approach, single network management protocol (SNMP), file transfer protocol (FTP) and web services technology have been adopted to promote the open interfaces for the planned subsystems. A management information base (MIB) for the cabinet and radar subsystems were already defined to support the monitoring perspective of each the subsystems. A reference implementation to validate the proposed interface and models is under development. The strategy is to maintain a pragmatic development, close to the potential suppliers' innovation capabilities and, at the same time, develop a theoretical thread able to rupture processes and technology patterns towards the adoption of the proposed adaptive CES.

An eclipse plug-in is planned as a model drivel development (MDD) tool to manage the CES bindings to the business process activities.

6 Conclusions

The development of complex integrated collaborative IT solutions is an open and challenging task. Existing complex IT solutions are typically closed as they depend on a single responsibility (single provider). The ongoing development of a new generation of open electronic toll collection solution under a research project sponsored by Brisa company illustrates the existing problems. This research was motivated by the extension of the offered service to the payment in parking lots and gas stations and by the difficulties for the existence of a unique technology supplier (closed solution). The project is now evolving to the evaluation of the cooperation enabled system (CES) concept where an adaptive systems framework embedding service capabilities is being proposed.

The main objective of the proposed CES framework is to support the technology bindings for process definitions independently of considering intra-organizational processes or collaborative processes (or cross-organizational processes. The purpose is to offer a model-driven approach to the development of IT solutions (process oriented developments). This means that suppliers are invited to develop their systems able to plug into compositions of systems leading, in this way, to open integrated solutions. The openness of such complex IT solutions is not an easy issue. The responsibility constraint related to the possibility of any subsystem being replaced by a competing one, requires further research. For less critical systems, the interoperability certification is a mechanism being developed to guarantee the replaceability of a subsystem by an equivalent one (from a competing supplier).

The proposed CES structure is also being validated in a governmental authority application for the development of a national speed limit enforcement network, the SINCRO project, promoted by the Portuguese National Authority for Road Security (ANSR).

Acknowledgements. This work was partially supported by BRISA Innovation and Technology, and Galpgeste companies and National Authority for Road Security (ANSR) through a research and development grant.

References

1. Afsarmanesh, H., Msanjila, S.: EPAL vision 2020 for active ageing of senior professionals. In: Camarinha-Matos, L., Boucher, X., Afsarmanesh, H. (eds.) PRO-VE 2011. IFIP AICT, vol. 336, pp. 60–72. Springer, Heidelberg (2010)
2. Camarinha-Matos, L., Afsarmanesh, H.: Active ageing roadmap: a collaborative networks contribution to demographic sustainability. In: Camarinha-Matos, L., Boucher, X., Afsarmanesh, H. (eds.) PRO-VE 2010. IFIP AICT, vol. 336, pp. 46–59. Springer, Heidelberg (2010)

3. Ciancarini, P.: Coordination languages for open system design. In: International Conference on Computer Languages, pp. 252–260 (March 1990)
4. Gomes, J.S., Jacquet, G., Machado, M., Osório, A.L., Gonçalves, C., Barata, M.: An open integration bus for efc: The its-ibus. In: ASECAP Conference, ASECAP 2003, Portoroz, Slovenia, May 18-21 (2003)
5. Holvoet, T., Kielmann, T.: Behaviour specification of active objects in open generative communication environments. In: Proceedings of the Thirtieth Hawaii International Conference on System Sciences, vol. 1, pp. 349–358 (January 1997)
6. Osório, A.L., Afsarmanesh, H., Camarinha-Matos, L.: Open services ecosystem supporting collaborative networks. In: Ortiz, Á., Franco, R., Gasquet, P. (eds.) BASYS 2010. IFIP AICT, vol. 322, pp. 80–91. Springer, Heidelberg (2010)
7. Osório, A.L., Camarinha-Matos, L.: Towards a distributed process execution platform for collaborative networks. In: Shen, W., Camarinha-Matos, L. (eds.) Information Technology For Balanced Manufacturing Systems. IFIP, vol. 220, pp. 233–240. Springer, Boston (2006)
8. Osório, A.L., Camarinha-Matos, L., Gomes, J.S.: A collaborative network case study: The extended "viaverde" toll payment system. In: Camarinha-Matos, L., Afsarmanesh, H., Ortiz, A. (eds.) Collaborative Networks and Their Breeding Environments. IFIP, vol. 186, pp. 559–568. Springer, Boston (2005)
9. Osório, A.L., Gonçalves, C., Araújo, P., Barata, M., Gomes, J.S., Jacquet, G., Dias, R.: Open multi-technology service oriented architecture for its business models: The itsibus etoll services. In: Collaborative Networks and Their Breeding Environments. IFIP, vol. 186, pp. 439–446. Springer, Boston (2005)
10. Pastor, O., España, S., Panach, J.I., Aquino, N.: Model-driven development. Informatik-Spektrum 31, 394–407 (2008)
11. Scheer, A.W., Hoffmann, M.: From business process model to application system" developing an information system with the house of business engineering (hobe). In: Jarke, M., Oberweis, A. (eds.) CAiSE 1999. LNCS, vol. 1626, pp. 2–9. Springer, Heidelberg (1999)
12. Winkler, S., Pilgrim, J.: A survey of traceability in requirements engineering and model-driven development. Software and Systems Modeling 9, 529–565 (2010)
13. Zhao, X., Liu, C.: Tracking over collaborative business processes. In: Dustdar, S., Fiadeiro, J., Sheth, A. (eds.) BPM 2006. LNCS, vol. 4102, pp. 33–48. Springer, Heidelberg (2006)

Part XV

Collaborative Networks Planning

How to Move from Traditional to Innovative Models of Networked Organizations: A Methodology and a Case Study in the Metal-Mechanic Industry

Lorenzo Tiacci[1] and Andrea Cardoni[2]

[1] Università degli Studi di Perugia, Dipartimento di Ingegneria Industriale
Via Duranti, 67, 06125 Perugia, Italy
[2] Università degli Studi di Perugia, Dipartimento di Discipline Giuridiche e Aziendali
Via Pascoli, 20, 06123 Perugia, Italy
{lorenzo.tiacci,acardoni}@unipg.it

Abstract. Innovative forms of collaborations between companies have been proposed and modelled in literature in recent years. There is an increasing demand in the industrial world for concretely implement this new forms of collaborations. For example, demand often comes from pre-existent form of clusters or consortiums, which want to evolve to more efficient forms of collaboration. On the basis of a methodology whose guidelines have been proposed in a previous work by authors [1], the paper illustrates the steps and the tools utilized to analyze potential pool of partners in order to identify the type of long term Collaborative Networked Organizations (CNOs) alliance that would bring highest benefits to the partners. Three different forms of innovative CNOs are considered: the Virtual organizations Breeding Environment (VBE), the Virtual Development Office (VDO) and the T-Holding. The application of the proposed methodology is described in the case of a traditional industrial cluster of the metal-mechanic industry in Italy.

Keywords: Innovative Collaborative Networks, network creation, Virtual Breeding Environment, Virtual Development Office, T-Holding.

1 Introduction

The subject of the analysis and implementation of CNOs creation process is recently growing to the attention of academics and practitioners. Actually, there are several types of CNO manifestations. In many countries, as in Italy for example, several governmental and industry support institutions have promoted the formation of strategic alliances over the country, typically in the form of clusters or consortiums. But nowadays economy requirements, such as harder global competition, volatility, higher innovation needs, laid bare the limits of such traditional forms of collaboration [2][3]. The problem is to identify which kind of alliance evolution should they pursuit, if an alliance already exists, or, more generally, to analyse a potential pool of partner and to identify the most appropriate CNOs form that should be adopted.

This work is dedicated to the implementation of the framework elaborated by authors in a recent paper [1], in which a methodology to evaluate how a potential pool

L.M. Camarinha-Matos et al. (Eds.): PRO-VE 2011, IFIP AICT 362, pp. 413–420, 2011.

of partners can join together in different types of long-term Collaborative Networked Organizations (CNOs) has been proposed. In the framework, three possible types of final CNOs forms are considered: Virtual organization Breeding Environment (VBE) [2][4], Virtual Development Office (VDO) [1] and T-Hodling[1]. However, the methodology is generalizable and can be extended to include other forms of collaborative networks.

There are many interesting studies in literature related to partners selection and evaluation processes [5][6]. But most of these studies specifically address Virtual Organizations (VOs) creation process, i.e., they assume that a certain type of long-term CNOs has already been established and partners have to be selected to temporarily join in a VO, for example in order to respond to a specific business opportunity. Other approaches [7][8] aim at identifying readiness/preparedness for collaboration assessment procedures, in order to determine if a potential VBE member has the needed elements to collaborate and participate in a collaborative network such as a VBE or a VO. In this approaches, it is substantially assumed that the long-term CNO type is a VBE. The same assumption is done in [9], where a structured approach for implementing a VBE is illustrated and applied to a case study in the Mold and Die sector in Brazil. The perspective adopted in our framework is different, because the particular form of the long term CNO has not yet been defined, and the definition of the long term CNO type represents the very objective of the decision process.

This work presents the results of a study commissioned by the ICE (the Italian Institute for Foreign Trade) and by a local industrial association (Confartigianato Terni) to the University of Perugia, in order to investigate how the companies belonging to an industrial cluster of the metal-mechanic industry in Italy could be aggregated in an innovative way. The starting point is representative of many industrial environments in Italy and other countries, where a long-term alliance among a group of companies already exists (in the form of a consortium named CON.ART), but is facing some difficulties. The participants asked for the evolution of the actual form toward a more innovative collaboration form. Facing the difficult task of indicating which is the right way to do it, it is important to elaborate approaches that suitably balance theoretical abstraction and practical applicability, considering also that companies are Small and Medium Enterprises (SMEs), and they often cannot provide structured data to be analysed.

The paper is organized as follows: in section 2, a synthetic summary of the proposed framework is reported; in section 3, the tools utilized to perform the analysis are described and consolidated results are discussed; in section 4 the selection of the most appropriate CNOs is discussed and in section 5 conclusions are drawn.

2 The Framework

How already illustrated in [1], to define the most appropriate network mission for a potential pool of partners, three steps are required.

1) The definition of some types of networking collaboration forms: three possible collaborative networks forms, taken as representative of long term collaboration forms with different integration degree, are considered: VBE, VDO and T-Hodling.

2) The classification of strategic objectives a generic CNO can be based on. The strategic objectives (SOs) have been classified in SOs of "primary" type (i.e. to create new Business Opportunties, BOs, and new Core Process Opportunities, CPOs) and SOs of "secondary" type (i.e. to create new Supporting Process Opportunities, SPOs). The three collaboration forms considered are then assessed on the basis of their ability to satisfy the different types of strategic objectives, both in a stable and in an occasional manner (Figure 1).

		VBE	VDO	T-Holding
Business Opportunities (BOs)	Stable	+	+++	++
	Occasional	++	+	+
Core Process Opportunities (CPOs)	Stable	+	++	+++
	Occasional	++	+	+
Supporting Process Opportunities (SPOs)	Stable	+++	+	+++
	Occasional	+++	++	+

Fig. 1. Assessing CNOs forms on the basis of different strategic objectives

3) The definition of the analysis dimensions through which assess a potential pool of companies in order to evaluate the possibility that their aggregation brings to new BOs, CPOs and SPOs, that is, to fulfill the strategic goals that have been defined in the previous step. The dimensions identified are: Segments of Business [12], Primary and Supporting Activities [13], Critical Resources [14], Financial statements analysis [15] (see Fig. 2).

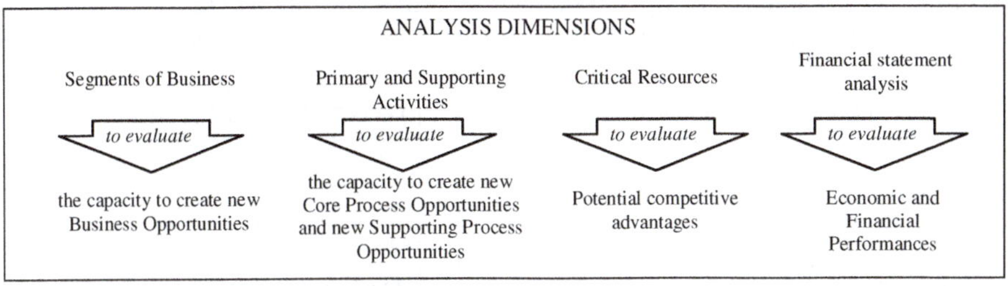

Fig. 2. Analysis dimensions

3 A Case Study: The Application of the Framework

The proposed framework has been applied to the case study described in the introduction. On a total of 19 companies constituting the actual consortium, 9 companies adhered to the project and provided information for our study. The questionnaire is the survey tool that has been utilized to collect information on qualitative and quantitative variables, and consists of three distinct sections, each one related to one of the analysis dimensions defined in the previous section. The first section concerns the analysis of the "competitive dimension" of the company (its markets, its customers, its suppliers, its competitors) and is mainly dedicated to the definition of Segments of Business of each company. The second one, dedicated to define companies Primary and Supporting Activities, considers its "organizational dimension", which expresses the organizational and operational arrangements through which the company currently carries out its activities (logistics processes, manufacturing, purchasing, human resources, etc.). The third section covers the survey of the so-called company's critical resources. Data provided by the questionnaires have then been integrated trough economical and financial data provided by the companies' balance sheets.In the following, results provided by the three section of the questionnaire (1-3) and by the financial statements analysis (4) are discussed.

1) *The Competitive Dimension (Segments of Business).* The results obtained from the questionnaires (some of which are reported in Figure 3) show that the market is primarily at a regional level (66%) and to a lesser extent at national level. It is simple to deduce that the companies work for local customers, so they do not have the opportunity to meet the challenges and opportunities from a national and international competitive environment. Customers appear to be mostly big companies. The respondents confirms that their economic activity is mostly induced by ThyssenKrupp's industries, i.e. their revenues greatly depend from the German multinational of the steel industry. The survey shows that companies operates in different mechanics's fields, and consequently have a different work's specialization among them. There are no internal competitors among the examined companies and the degree of overlap of products and services offered is very limited. Machinery and equipment have a high degree of diversification and a medium-high degree of technological updating, which could lead to the creation of innovative and integrated products. Production processes were mainly those typical of the metal-mechanic industry, but characterized by a good degree of diversification. This consolidated set of data point out a high degree of heterogeneity of the strategic segments of business.

Markets: geographical distribution	
Regional	66%
National	33%
UE	1%
ExtraUE	0%
Clients dimension	
Big Clients (>250 employers)	59%
SME	41%
Clients relative dimensions: clients vs. firm	
All bigger	67%
All smaller	0%
Bigger and smaller	33%
Turnover generated by top 10 clients	
0-20%	0%
20-50%	25%
50-100%	75%

Number of direct competitors	4
Competition aggressiveness	
High	66%
Medium	33%
Low	0%
Threat: potential substitutive	
Yes	50%
No	50%
Threat: potential entering	
Yes	60%
No	40%

Fig. 3. Questionnaire results: the competitive dimension

2) *The Organizational dimension (Primary and Supporting activities).* Figure 4 shows some of the results form the Organizational Dimension section of the questionnaire. The number of common suppliers is quite limited, as the different types of products purchased. There is a limited impact of transportation costs, both for the 'inbound' and for the 'outbound' flows. The consolidated result suggests that

Core Processes	
Annual transportation costs (€)	
Inbound	8962
Outbound	21798
Annual cost for plant maintenance (€)	6929
Plants utilization rate	51%
Human resources: n. of workers per area	
R&D	9
Product Design/Quality	23
Commercial	16
Production	147
Administration	10
TOT	210
Annual cost for production workers (€)	234143
Amortization and industrial leasings (€)	40742
After sales/returned management	67%
Customers assistance	83%
Warranties	92%
Annual explicit investments in R&D (€)	80000
Innovation sources (multiple answers allowed)	
Internal research	42%
Collaborations with research centres/institutions	42%
Induced by clients	33%
Induced by internal workers	17%
Other	8%

Supporting Processes	
Accounting	
Internal	42%
External	58%
Leasings	
Amount (€)	129042
Due date (monthes)	38
Long-term budgeting	
Complete	42%
Partial	17%
No	33%
Annual budgeting	
Complete	50%
Partial	17%
No	25%
Periodical reports	
Complete	50%
Partial	36%
No	8%
Financial Planning	
Yes	58%
No	42%

Fig. 4. The organizational dimension: Core Processes and Supporting Processes

a collaboration could benefit of a very limited for new process opportunity, like potential synergies on logistics or on the purchasing process. The R&D area may represent an important synergy area for a network between these companies, because the number of persons employed in new product developments activities related to R&S and Product Design is not negligible on an aggregate basis. Similarly, companies could benefit from potential synergies in some other common activities, such as returned management, customers' assistance, warranties, and facilities maintenance. However, the amount of money involved in such activities is not relevant, and the aggregation could not be based on the sole strategy of achieving these type of synergies. From data collected through the financial section of the questionnaire, it emerges that companies face increasing difficulties to obtain the necessary financing that allow them to develop new products or processes. In Italy, the increasing size of banks brought to a corresponding decreasing fraction of loans directed to small and medium enterprises. Small firms face increasing difficulties in standardizing their unstructured information and transferring it to banks, so that banks consider more onerous the monitoring, the control and the overall management of relationships with entities of smaller size. It is therefore confirmed the role that a network of companies could play in supporting activities related to corporate planning and control, both in order to assess the feasibility of new businesses, both to facilitate the necessary access to credit.

3) *Critical resources.* Critical resources of firms surveyed are mainly technology, relations hips, while the majority of respondents highlight the difficulty of penetrating new markets and introducing innovation. The aggregation should be able to enhance the role of actual critical resources, and at the same time to improve the role of the other resources types that are poorly used until now.

4) *Financial statement analysis.* Following the consistent literature highlighting the importance of accounting on networking strategies [16], the framework design and implementation has been integrated with a financial statement analysis. The result of the consolidation is shown in the figure below (Fig. 4). From the economical perspective the pool of companies considered shows a strong volatility of the sales

process, with an evident growth in 2008 balanced by an heavy decrease in 2009. This demonstrates a strong dependence of the potential partners turnover from the negative trends the market was suffering over the reporting period. With reference to economic ratios, we can firstly observe a satisfactory level of operating profitability (ROI) and economic return on equity (ROE). Examining the financial indicators it is possible to highlit the improvement of the leverage during the observed period. The last phase of financial statement analysis has focused on the study of the performance variability within the sample analyzed, representing an important factor to take into consideration to assess the degree of dynamic homogeneity and the potential integrability of the processes. Comparing the incidence of value added on turnover calculated for each entity with the average level observed, companies tends to show very different performances, both in terms of percentage level and in terms of historical trend. Also analyzing the leverage there is a situation of greater homogeneity, with a significant group of companies that show a level below average, with a good financial position. Finally, considering the relationship between interest expenses and EBITDA, is still present a marked heterogeneity with about half of the companies placed below the average while the other half over that level.

Values in € thousand	2007		2008		2009	
Economic Values	€ Mil	%	€ Mil	%	€ Mil	%
TURNOVER	20,420	100.0%	23,897	100.0%	21,565	100.0%
VALUE ADDED	10,861	53.2%	12,673	53.0%	11,918	55.3%
EBITDA	2,578	12.6%	2,535	10.6%	2,126	9.9%
EBIT	1,227	6.0%	848	3.5%	741	3.4%
INTEREST EXPENSES	(408)	-2.0%	(582)	-2.4%	(481)	-2.2%
NET PROFIT	813	4.0%	425	1.8%	331	1.5%
Financial Values						
NET INVESTED CAPITAL	11,087	100.0%	10,932	100.0%	12,026	100.0%
covered by:						
NET FINANCIAL POSITION	8,979	81.0%	7,243	66.3%	8,205	68.2%
EQUITY	2,108	19.0%	3,689	33.7%	3,821	31.8%
Profitability Ratios						
ROI = Ebit/Net invested capital	11.1%		7.8%		6.2%	
ROE = Net profit/assets	38.6%		11.5%		8.7%	
Financial Ratios						
Leverage = NFP/Equity	4.26		1.96		2.15	
NFP/EBITDA	3.48		2.86		3.86	
NFE/EBITDA	16%		23%		23%	

Fig. 5. Economical and financial performances (consolidated data)

4 Selecting the Network Mission and the Collaboration Form

The results reported in the preceding sections allow to draw the actual situation of the pool, and to define which strategic objectives are most probably reachable and desirable by the new collaboration form that have to be implemented.

From the analysis of consolidated data, it emerges that potential synergies on core processes are very limited. Thus, it is unreasonable to choose a collaboration form, such as T-Holding, that is on the contrary the most appropriate when mainly new Core Process Opportunities are likely to arise (see Fig. 1). At the same time, the high heterogeneity degree of the segments of business, especially due to complementary technologies and scarce products/services overlapping, may be functional to the creation of a network capable of generating new integrated product-services that arise from the integration of the participants' skills. Thus, the creation of new Business Opportunities seems to be an achievable strategic objective. Results also show that the aggregation could also benefit from some Supporting Process Opportunity (such as synergies for corporate planning and control activities and for financing). So, depending on the relative weight of these two components, the choice should be done among the other two models: the VDO, if the stable creation of new BOs are taken as main objective, and the VBE model, if the main objective will be the creation of new SPOs, and, occasionally, of new BOs. Considering the network activities implemented by the actual consortium, the consortium itself represents an earlier experience of VBE. A long term collaboration form in which business opportunities arising in the actual competitive scenario are occasionally caught, and are essentially proposed and managed by the single companies of the consortium. However, the ability to integrate products and services among partners is very limited, as also the ability to plan adequate investments in order to penetrate new markets. Without the possibility to plan investments at a network level, it is very difficult that collaborative actions could bring to a stable creation process of new BOs. This requires constant marketing intelligence, planning and investing activities that only a Virtual Development Office can provide. In this view, even the application of the newest conceptual framework for VBEs (the so called 2nd generation VBEs [4]) seems to provide a limited contribution with respect the actual state of the consortium.

In conclusions, the strategic objective that would bring to the highest benefit for the pool is the stable creation of new BOs. The analysis demonstrated that this objective is potentially achievable, and in this case the best type of collaborative form to achieve this objective is the VDO. The VDO should be able to provide products and services both at a national and at an international level, providing an independent management structure able to adequately plan the network activities, taking advantage of the complementary skills of participants, while paying attention to the financial and economic heterogeneity of the companies. The VDO is a model that provides the foundation of a for-profit company (the VDO itself), that have to find an own economical equilibrium. In pursuing new business opportunities the VDO realizes VOs and VEEs of network members and/or external partners.

The tangible success of the project has been measured by the understanding, by the participating partners, of the basic characteristic of the proposed network model, through which is been possible to give start to a change in the strategic logic of the actual collaboration.

5 Summary

The choice of the strategic goals of a CNO is a crucial phase for determining the most appropriate form of the alliance. In general, when analyzing a pool of company that wants to collaborate, strategic network goals are not defined 'a priori', but should be the result of an assessment of the possible opportunities deriving from the collaboration. The case study is related to the typical situation of an already existing long-term alliance among a group of SMEs, a consortium in the metal-mechanic sector in Italy, which is facing some difficulties, and asks for an evolution from the actual form toward a more innovative collaboration form. The framework provided the assessment of the competitive and the organizational dimensions of the companies, of their critical resources, and of their economic and financial performances. The analysis of the consolidated data allowed identifying which types of strategic objectives are at same time desirable and achievable by the alliance. This in turn allowed determining the most appropriate type of CNOs. The methodology can be replicable to similar case studies, and it is an answer to the need of evolution from traditional towards innovative forms of collaboration.

References

1. Cardoni, A., Saetta, S., Tiacci, L.: Evaluating how potential pool of Partners can join together in different types of Long Term Collaborative Networked Organizations. In: Camarinha-Matos, L.M., Boucher, X., Afsarmanesh, H. (eds.) PRO-VE 2010. IFIP Advances in Information and Communication Technology, vol. 336, pp. 312–321. Springer, Heidelberg (2010)
2. Vallejos, R.V., Lima, C.P., Varvakis, G.: Towards the development of a frame work to create a vrtual organization breeding environment in the mould and die sector. Jorunal of Intelligent Manufactring 5, 587–597 (2007)
3. Camarinha-Matos, L.M.: Collaborative Networked Organizations: Status and trends in manufacturing. Annual Reviews in Control 33, 199–208 (2009)
4. Afsarmanesh, H., Camarinha-Matos, L.M., Msanjila, S.S.: On management of 2nd generation Virtual Organizations Breeding Enviornments. Annual Reviews in Control 22, 209–219 (2009)
5. Baldo, F., Rabelo, R.J., Vallejos, R.V.: A framework for selecting performance indicators for virtual organisation partners' search and selection. International Journal of Production Research 47(17), 4737–4755 (2009)
6. Noran, O.: A decision support framework for collaborative networks. International Journal of Production Research 47(17), 4813–4832 (2009)
7. Rosas, J., Camarinha-Matos, L.M.: An approach to assess collaboration readiness. International Journal of Production Research 47(17), 4711–4735 (2009)
8. Romero, R., Galeano, N., Molina, A.: Mechanisms for assessing and enhancing organisations' readiness for collaboration in collaborative networks. International Journal of Production Research 47(17), 4691–4710 (2009)
9. Baldo, F., Rabelo, J.R.: A structured approach for implementing Virtual Organization Breeding Environments in the Mold and Die sector – A Brasilian case study. In: Camarinha-Matos, L.M., Boucher, X., Afsarmanesh, H. (eds.) PRO-VE 2010. IFIP AICT, vol. 336, pp. 197–203. Springer, Heidelberg (2010)
10. Camarinha-Matos, L.M., Afsarmanesh, H., Galeano, N., Molina, A.: Collaborative networked organizations – Concepts and practice in manufacturing enterprises. Computers & Industrial Engineering 57, 46–60 (2009)
11. Lewis, D.J.: Partnership for profit: structuring and managing strategic alliances. The Free Press, New York (1990)
12. Abell, D.F.: Defining the business: the starting point of strategic planning. Prentice-Hall, Englewood Cliffs (1980)
13. Porter, M.: Competitive Advantage: creating and sustaining superior Performance. Free Press, New York (1985)
14. Rugmann, A.M., Verbeke, A.: Edit Penrose's contribution to the resource based view of strategic management. Strategic Management Journal 23(8), 769–780 (2002)
15. Cavazzoni, G.: Il sistema del controllo di gestione. Strumenti per le decisioni operative aziendali, Giappichelli, Torino (2004)
16. Hakansson, H., Kraus, K., Lind, J.: Accounting in network. Routledge, New York (2010)

Capability Maturity Model for Collaborative Networks Based on Extended Axiomatic Design Theory

Hadi Kandjani and Peter Bernus

School of ICT & Centre for Enterprise Architecture Research and Management, Griffith University, Brisbane, Australia
{h.kandjani,p.bernus}@griffith.edu.au

Abstract. The paradigm of forming and sustaining Collaborative Networks as environments that create Virtual Organisations (VOs) assumes that effective (and efficient) enterprise engineering (EE) capabilities and processes are available. However, these processes are only effective if they produce VOs which have sufficiently limited complexity, because as complexity grows, the VO's behaviour becomes increasingly harder to predict under all circumstances. This paper proposes the use of EE methods based on Extended Axiomatic Design Theory to limit the complexity of VOs – and of the CN itself. We introduce process- and people capability maturity levels, whereupon higher maturity implies higher probability of success of CNs in creating and maintaining VOs, and success of the VOs themselves, and formulate strategies for capability-improvement, intended to achieve higher levels of EE maturity.

Keywords: Extended Axiomatic Design Theory, Process and People Capability Maturity Models, Concurrent Collaborative Networks Engineering.

1 Introduction

The establishment of Collaborative Networks which serve to create dynamic responses to market opportunities (through the creation of virtual organisations) emerged as a new paradigm for doing business [4]. The field raised a number of research questions, one of these (complexity management) is addressed below.

Two Collaborative Networks (CNs) with the same objectives and requirements may apply the same design methodology, but may still develop different virtual organisations (VOs), in terms of quality of models, processes, etc. as well as 'systemic' properties of the VOs. We argue that this is (at least partially) due to the difference in levels of enterprise engineering (EE) capability/maturity of the two CNs. Thus the same design methodology and requirements may lead to different results (a property called multifinality [6]).

Management literature calls this form of non-determinism 'path dependency' which arises because the result also depends on decisions that were made along the way of evolutionary history prior to the present state (see Liebowitz and Margolis *et al.* [13,14]). Part of this path dependency / multifinality is due to the evolutionary history of the CN which led to the present EE capability that is a determining factor in

L.M. Camarinha-Matos et al. (Eds.): PRO-VE 2011, IFIP AICT 362, pp. 421–427, 2011.

the CN's (and its VOs') effectiveness. Conversely, CNs as open systems need to be assumed to follow the principles of equifinality (or 'convergence'), *i.e.,* finding equally valid alternative ways of attaining the same end state if starting from a given initial state (or from different initial states) (see von Bertalanffy [3]). The principle applies to open systems when a given end state is reached by many potential means. The intention of developing a (process and people) EE capability maturity model for CNs is to improve the understanding and to inform and direct the evolution of CNs.

The Software Engineering Institute's Capability Maturity Model Integration (CMMI) [4,19] is a process improvement reference model informing enterprises wishing to improve their process capabilities and organisation (and through it their performance). CMMI integrates multiple bodies of knowledge developed separately (software engineering, systems engineering, acquisition,...)[5]. (ISO/IEC 15504:2007 defines 'process capability' as "...the capability of a process to meet its purpose ..." [20].) In our case, the purpose of the EE processes (ISO 15704:2000 [8,10]) is to design (and maintain for life) the CN and its VOs through their stages of evolution.

An important problem facing a CN is complexity, because uncontrolled complexity can cause undesired CN- and VO characteristics. A number of relevant complexity measures may be considered: (according to Lloyd [15] and interpreted by the authors [11]) these can be classified as those characterising the difficulty to describe a) the function, behaviour, and states of the system, b) the architecture (relationship between physical and functional structure), and c) the process to create the system. Categories a) and b) measure the complexity of the CN and of its VOs, and c) measures the complexity of VO creation and CN creation projects.

Axiomatic Design (AD) [18] claims to codify in a discipline-independent way what a 'best design' is, aiming to avoid unnecessary complexity. Li and Williams [11] refer to the possibility of using AD in EE, but to avoid complexity of category (c) we extended AD by introducing the Recursion Axiom stipulating that the system that designs the system must also obey the axioms of AD. The question arises: how to maximise the probability of the success of the EE practice used to design VOs/CNs?

Many EA researchers and practitioners fail to recognise that they are in fact applying methods and models derived from laws and theories of cybernetics. Cybernetics is a pluralistic theory (and interdisciplinary movement) of generic laws and theories of information processing. We observe that applied cybernetic laws and theories in EA lack harmony and our aim is to introduce *EA Cybernetics* as a field of EA research that harmonises, formalises and synthesises the results of cybernetics and demonstrate their applications in EA practice.

Stafford Beer [1] was perhaps the first person to apply cybernetics to management. However, EA [2] not only embraces the application of models, methods and theories of management & control, it also incorporates models, methods and theories of the service, engineering and production to design an effective enterprise, including resources, organisation, products etc. of the enterprise. Therefore, EA cybernetics is distinct from Management Cybernetics, but considers the management & engineering views of enterprises and demonstrates how to apply cybernetic laws and theories in Enterprise Architecture. EA is a discipline that invokes other disciplines to analyse, design, construct, maintain and evolve an enterprise throughout its life history to accomplish the enterprise's short and long term aims. One such worthy aim is of course long term viability and sustainability (threatened by untamed complexity).

This is why the authors situate the presented analysis as a contribution to EA Cybernetics (aimed at building EE capability to reduce unnecessary complexity) – the kind that helps EE steer the enterprise to viable futures.

2 Axiomatic Design and Enterprise Engineering in Collaborative Networks

Axiomatic Design (AD) is a theory of complex systems (that can not be predicted for sure to always satisfy their functional requirements [18]). AD explains reasons of emerging complexity, and offers a formal design theory and two design axioms that system designs must satisfy to minimise complexity (measured by the probability that the structure always performs the function (category b)).

Axiom I: Independence Axiom [18]**.** 'The independence of Functional Requirements (FRs) must always be maintained.' (An FRi is independent of others if there exist 'design parameters' [DP] so that if changing one FRi only one DPi must change, whereupon [FR] = [[A]] * [DP]**.** Here [FR] is the vector of FRs, [DP] is the vector of DPs and [[A]] is the matrix mapping DPs to FRs. If [[A]] is diagonal matrix then the design is uncoupled (full independence is achieved). If [[A]] is triangular then the design is decoupled (the implementation process is 'serialisable'). Otherwise the design is coupled (the implementation process of DPs is not 'serialisable').

Axiom II: Information Axiom [18]. 'Out of the designs that satisfy Axiom I that design is best which has the minimal information content.' (Suh defined information content (IC) as the negative logarithm of the 'probability of success'.)

We see Axioms I and II as intending to minimise the complexity of the system's architecture (complexity type 'b') and can be used to design less complex CNs and VOs. We observe that complexity type 'c' (of CNs and VOs) is not automatically addressed by using AD into EE practice, so we recently proposed [12] that Axioms I & II must also be applied to projects creating Vos / changing the CN. This is expressed in a 'recursion' axiom: change projects (as a system of systems) not only must follow Axioms I & II, but they themselves need to be 'axiomatically designed'.

Axiom III: Recursion Axiom [12]**:** 'The system that designs a system must satisfy the two Axioms of design.' NB**:** systems that satisfy Axioms I & II do not necessarily satisfy Axiom III: while at a given moment in time in its life history a system may be considered moderately complex, this system may be very hard to create or change.

Example: Denote three consecutive stages of an evolving CN as S_1, S_2 and S_3. In stage S_1 the CN is operating and has a design satisfyingi Axioms I & II. Let S_2 be the stage of change (S_2 is the original CN extended by a change project P). The task of P is to create S_3. When S_1 creates P it can mandate that P *use* Axioms I & II to design S_3. However, P (and thereby S_2) may not satisfy Axioms I & II, so P can be more complex than necessary; even if its mandate is to design S_3, the likelihood of success of this endeavour may be less than desired, *i.e.* P does not satisfy Axioms I & II (even if it applies them to design S_3). Axiom III states that S_1 not only must mandate that P use Axioms I & II, but S_1 must design P *using* Axioms I & II (in the interest of successful evolution). NB. the change system of systems is called the set of 'supporting systems' in ISO 15288 [9]. Thus, "among the design processes that apply axioms I & II to design a system, that is best which *itself* satisfies axioms I & II" [12]. If a CN wishes to reduce its own complexity and to subsequently maintain reduced complexity through life, it may wish to adopt AD as a strategy. Therefore it is legitimate to ask whether the CN is ready to use such practices and to increase the probability of success (i.e., what is its 'AD process maturity'). A model of such maturity is a type of 'EE Capability Maturity Model'. To differentiate this from other CMMs the authors abbreviate it as EE-AD-CMM. Given the equifinality and multifinality properties of enterprises, we do not claim that such maturity model would be useful for CNs that have no desire to apply complexity reduction measures or use AD practices. The value of this EE-AD-CMM is that untamed complexity is a dangerous phenomenon that may put at risk not only the VOs but the CN itself.

3 Enterprise Engineering Maturity Based on Extended Axiomatic Design Theory

Several authors have developed Capability Maturity Models and formulated strategies to increase the level of engineering capability and maturity of the enterprise. Hintersteiner and Zimmerman [7] developed an Axiomatic Design Capability Maturity Model to provide a roadmap for implementing AD practices in systems engineering. What this paper is proposing is two qualitatively different additional capabilities: 1) the enterprise (in this case the CN) not only has to design 'systems' (such as VOs), but it also has to design, or re-design, itself, *i.e.* the CN needs *self-design capability*, and 2) the CN also has to have the *capability to obey the third design axiom.*

Our proposed model extends the set of necessary EE capabilities and associated maturity levels, and the model is intended to help enterprises to avoid complexity of categories b) and c). Importantly, category c) complexity of CNs and VOs has not been addressed in previous maturity models. Note: category a) complexity can only be mitigated, but not avoided, unless we change what functions we expect from the systems of interest (i.e., the CN or its VOs).

3.1 Enterprise Engineering Process Maturity

Level 0: Not Performed (AD is not applied anywhere)

Level 1: Informal (non-institutionalised practice or pilot project applying AD) This is the starting point of CN-level intention to practice AD in designing CN entities. Pilot projects help reduce the risk of failure and the impact on the CN and help create best practice.

Level 2: Defined (a program is defined to apply AD in all VO design projects) Here there is commitment of CN management (or of participants) to apply AD principles (projects observe AD principles when developing the CN and designing VOs). The practice is *mandated* (ensuring to include experts / staff, resources and appropriate processes and tools to support AD). This level is process-following: AD is followed, but not in a tacit manner.

Level 3: Recursively-Defined On Level 3 there is awareness by CN participants of ineffectiveness and inefficiencies of existing CN and VO design practice. Thus the CN is in a stage of aiming at self-improvement.

Level 4: Established Extended AD practice A well-defined CN and VO design methodology is used in all VO design projects, and all CN change projects.

Level 5: Continuously Improving On Level 5 the performance of the current AD-based CN design methodology is monitored and continuously improved.

3.2 Enterprise Engineering People Maturity

The CN and its participants can not acquire, attain, practice and institutionalise AD capability and achieve higher levels of maturity in one day, so we introduce the AD based People CMM. Each level of the model focuses on developing enterprise environment and culture supporting distributed design process in EE practice.

Level 0: No AD Competency An enterprise at Level 0 has no AD competency in the network or in participating organisations.

Level 1: AD Competency Acquisition and Outsourcing At Level 1 there is awareness of AD and its advantages by a subset of network participants. The CN may use a pilot project to assess CN-wide adoption possibilities. Some AD skills & competencies may have to be acquired from outside of the CN.

Level 2: AD Competency Training At Level 2 the CN may be in training mode and use a CN-wide education program to develop AD-competencies of key staff. Projects may use mentors to monitor and manage the new type of design processes.

Level 3: AD Competency Building At Level 3 the CN runs projects to gain CN-wide experience of AD processes.

Level 4: AD Competency Improvement Here the CN benefits from empowered and experienced workforce openly collaborating and having mastered AD-based EE processes. The CN at this level still needs dedicated AD experts and a reward- and motivation system for the rest of the workforce to successfully manage enterprise engineering practices.

Level 5: AD Tacit Competency / Continuous Improvement At Level 5 enterprises do not need enterprise engineering experts to manage and control enterprise engineering practice: advantages of AD-based CN design methodology are obvious to the entire enterprise and all workforce throughout the CN, its members have experienced them and tacitly apply them in a collaborative and distributed way. This means that while practitioners' knowledge of this methodology is available in explicit form, when practicing it, the methodology if followed in a tacit way. From an external observer's point of view practitioners appear to be following a methodology most of the time, but the behaviour does not appear to be strictly following a process as practitioners can adjust, optimise, or tailor the methodology without diverting from its original intent and principles: the workforce at this level is self-motivated and self-organised in AD.

4 Concurrent Enterprise Engineering: Ability to Self-design and Self-organise

Pennell and Winner [16] describe concurrent engineering as "*a systematic approach to the integrated, concurrent design of products and their related processes, including, manufacturing and support. This approach is intended to cause the developers from the very outset to consider all elements of the product life cycle, from conception to disposal, including cost, schedule, quality and user requirements.*" In other words, concurrent engineering is an approach in which all phases of engineering potentially operate simultaneously. Product and process design run in parallel and design processes are closely coordinated to achieve optimal matching of requirements for cost, quality, and effective delivery.

The concept can be applied to CN design: when moving towards level 5 of the EE process CMM. At the same time, Level 5 of the EE people CMM emphasises collaboration and teamwork as an integral part of concurrent EE. At this level, all components of the ability to self-organise in terms of team cooperation are visible (*cf.* 'the 7Cs of collaboration in concurrent engineering' [17]):

- flexible, unplanned and continuous **c**ollaboration,
- **c**ommitment to meet the goals,
- **c**ommunication (exchange of information),
- ability to make **c**ompromises,
- **c**onsensus in spite of disagreement,
- **c**oordination (managing interdependencies between activities), and
- **c**ontinuous improvements in order to increase productivity and reduce process times.

5 Conclusion

This article proposed a Capability Maturity Model based on extended axiomatic design for the use of capability assessment and strategy making for Collaborative Networks. This maturity model includes both Process- and People maturity levels. The model is based on the promise of Extended Axiomatic Design Theory which aims at guaranteeing the probability of success of CNs and of the virtual organisations which emerge from the CN. These models may be used as a roadmap for incorporating extended axiomatic design practices and techniques into enterprise engineering in general and into the practice of Collaborative Networks and its member enterprises.

Part of the maturity model includes the ability of the CN to self-design / improve as it ascends to higher levels of maturity. According to this model, a CN ultimately attains process capabilities to simultaneously maintain, manage or change the CN design methodology itself, as well as to apply the methodology to all CN entities (including the CN itself). Based on the maturity model proposed in this paper, dedicated AD-based enterprise engineering staff and resources are no longer needed as on Level 5 the AD-based enterprise engineering methodology is well-entrenched and consistently performed by everyone in the CN.

We incorporated the extension of axiomatic design theory to CN design practice and the results were demonstrated in terms of 6 different maturity levels – each with different levels of process and people capability / maturity. For future research we suggest the verification and validation of these developed models through empirical applications, case study and other relevant methods. In the final section, the article also briefly introduced the notion of concurrent CN engineering process capability but details have been relegated to future research.

References

1. Beer, S.: Cybernetics and Management. English Universities Press, London (1959)
2. Bernus, P., Nemes, L., Smidt, G. (eds.): Handbook on Enterprise Architecture. Springer, Berlin (2003)
3. Bertalanffy, L.: General Systems Theory: Foundations, development, applications. Braziller, New York (1968)
4. Camarinha-Matos, L.M., Afsarmanesh, H., Löh, H., Sturm, F., Ollus, M.: A Strategic Roadmap for Advanced Virtual Organizations. In: Camarinha-Matos, L., Afsarmanesh, H. (eds.) Collaborative Networked Organizations, pp. 289–312. Springer, Berlin (2004)
5. Chrissis, M., Konrad, M., Shrum, S.: CMMI Guidlines for Process Integration and Product Improvement. Person Education, Boston (2003)
6. Hanson, B.: General systems theory beginning with wholes. Taylor & Francis, London (1995)
7. Hintersteiner, J., Zimmerman, R.C.: Implementing Axiomatic Design in the Systems Engineering Process: An Axiomatic Design Capability Maturity Model. In: Proc. ICAD 2000, pp. 9–17. Axiomatic Design Inc., Cambridge (2000)
8. IITForce. GERAM: Generalised enterprise reference architecture and methodology (V1.6.3) (1999); Also in Handbook on Enterprise Architecture, pp. 22–64. Springer, Berlin (2003)
9. ISO15288:2008. System Life Cycle Processes. ISO, Geneva (2000, rev. 2008)
10. ISO15704:2000, Industrial automation systems – Requirements for enterprise-reference architectures and methodologies. ISO Geneva (2000, Amd 1: 2005)
11. Kandjani, H., Bernus, P.: Engineering Self-Designing Enterprises as Complex Systems Using Extended Axiomatic Design Theory. In: Proc. 18th IFAC World Congress (to appear)
12. Li, H., Williams, T.: A formalization and extension of the Purdue enterprise reference architecture and the Purdue methodology. TR 158 Purdue Lab. of Applied Industrial Control. Purdue University, West Lafayette (1994)
13. Liebowitz, S., Margolis, S.: Path dependence, lock-in, and history. Journal of Law Economics & Organization 11(1), 205–226 (1995)
14. Liebowitz, S., Margolis, S.: Encyclopedia of Law and Economics. E Cheltenham (2000)
15. Lloyd, S.: Measures of complexity: a nonexhaustive list. IEEE Ctrl. Sys. Magazine 21(4), 7–8 (2000)
16. Pennell, J., Winner, R.: Concurrent engineering: practices and prospects. In: Proc. Globeco 1989, pp. 647–655. IEEE, Los Alamitos (1989)
17. Prasad, B.: Concurrent engineering fundamentals- Integrated product and process organization. Prentice Hall, New Jersey (1996)
18. Suh, N.P.: The Principles of Design. Oxford Univ. Press, New York (1990)
19. Team, CP. CMMI for Development, version 1.2. Preface, SEI, CMU (2006)
20. Van Loon, H.: Process Assessment and ISO/IEC 15504: a Reference Book. Springer, Berlin (2007)

Drivindus Case Study: Choosing an e-Business Solution

Oihab Allal-Chérif

BEM Management School Bordeaux France,
680 cours de la Libération 33400 Talence France
oihab@bem.edu

Abstract. Over time, Drivindus has become one of the world's leading manufacturers of automotive parts. This industrial group is present in 20 countries, employing 50,000 persons from 50 different nationalities and running around 100 factories and 40 research centers. It generates annual revenues of nearly €10 billion. The firm's General Management has noticed that productivity reserves still exist within its purchasing management function. The company has therefore decided to invest in an e-sourcing project. This case study describes this project which has been inspired from a real one and shows how an electronic marketplace has been designed to reach all the objectives. This case study takes between 4 and 6 hours to be solved by post graduate management students. They may be organized in groups of 4 and the instructor can go from one group to another to help them progress, according to their capacities, in answering the 5 questions. A PowerPoint presentation and teaching notes are provided to help in the animation of the case which has been tested and optimized in three different accredited management schools before its publication. It's ideal to illustrate purchasing management evolution and information systems management.

Keywords: Procurement function, Information Systems, e-business, project management.

1 Presentation of the Company and the Purchasing Function

The French group Drivindus is born out of the progressive merger of a number of smaller firms, some of which are at least 100 years old. Only French firms were involved at first, followed by European ones. Over time, Drivindus has become one of the world's leading manufacturers of automotive parts. This industrial group is present in 20 countries, employing 50,000 persons from 50 different nationalities and running around 100 factories and 40 research centres. It generates annual revenues of nearly €10 billion. The group organisation is a decentralised structure comprised of 10 branches (B1 to B10) corresponding to its commercial product lines. It has 15 main customers (C1 to C15). The organisation has evolved constantly to match customer demands. The group has a three-pronged structure, featuring an:

- *Operational organisation* shadowing each branch, materialising in divisions organised into autonomous profit centres. These are the key entities in the overall organisation and group several production sites specialised by product or system.

L.M. Camarinha-Matos et al. (Eds.): PRO-VE 2011, IFIP AICT 362, pp. 428–435, 2011.

- *Functional organisation* encompassing cross-departmental functions like financial control, human resources, legal services, product marketing, R&D, quality and purchasing. These cross-departmental functions implement the group strategy. They develop and apply its methods and procedures; disseminate information; monitor the main investment projects; and supervise the realisation of objectives.
- *Geographic organisation* watching over group interests worldwide and managing relationships with automakers' headquarters.

Drivindus has always cooperated with its suppliers in the development of new components. This is a high-tech company where imagination and the invention play a considerable role in letting Drivindus partner its customers, who view the company as a valuable advisor and as a source of competitive advantage. The company's €10 billion in revenues are divided as follows: Europe: 70%, North America: 18%, Asia and Africa: 8%, South America: 4%. Sales growth has regularly been in double digits. The main explanation has been Drivindus's dynamism and acquisition of innovative smaller firms. The company operates in a very competitive sector but has succeeded in generating operational earnings of €500 million. R&D spending equals 6% of sales, or an investment of more than €600 million.

Purchases amount to 60% of total turnover, or more than €6 billion. In other words, this is very strategic activity at Drivindus since it is both the basis of the company's cost structure and a key innovation driver. Saving 1% on purchasing costs corresponds in profitability terms to a 10% increase in sales. Purchasing is not only a major profit and innovation centre but also the department responsible for ensuring the quality of the components that Drivindus buys from its own suppliers, thus the quality of the sub-assemblies that it manufactures itself.

The Purchasing function has evolved thusly:

- Pre-1975: Purchasing was not yet considered a key function. Suppliers were not integrated into company operations but mainly chosen based on price. They had to compete intensively each and every time an order was renewed. All in all, this was a 'cost out' system characterised by limited and very short-term relationships.
- Between 1975 and 1985: The beginning of a delocalisation process that was a direct result of the group's very strong growth. Purchasing volumes rose considerably and total quality became more important than price alone. It was during this era that the company shifted from a 'cost out' to a 'value in' outlook.
- Between 1985 and 1995: The group started to internationalise and focus on innovation. Product life spans shortened, creating a need for partnerships with networks of highly innovative privileged suppliers, so as to foster and maintain competitive advantage. This was an era of long-term relationships, with Drivindus positioning itself as the leader of teams of suppliers working together.
- Since 1995, the group has been entirely geared towards global partnerships. This has led to an intense and systematic search for information, with Drivindus - together with its suppliers – constantly analysing the possibility of developing new products on a project basis. The notion of 'co-makers' has appeared.

Purchases can be broken down as follows:

- Natural and synthetic raw materials. The constraints in this market mainly involve localisation questions and speculation-driven price volatility.

- Production components like electronic or mechanical parts. These are purchases from a range of very different markets, some of which are competitive and others more oligopolistic in nature. Prices are negotiated to varying degrees. Moreover, these purchasing segments require a great deal of strategic monitoring;
- Purchases relating to outsourcing contracts, like parts in complex systems requiring many exchanges of documents that can be voluminous and complex;
- General administrative (overhead) items like paper, office supplies or furniture. Suppliers rarely compete in these fields. Once chosen, they are asked to agree framework contracts specifying transaction conditions over a certain period of time;
- Purchases of services like maintenance (cleaning) or security, all of which are very localised. There are great disparities between the services offered in the different countries where Drivindus operates. Price differentials can also be significant;
- Logistics costs incurred when transporting goods;
- Engineering purchases, i.e. during the construction of a new plant;
- IT, including hardware, software and maintenance.

Drivindus has decided to cut costs by globalizing purchasing volumes. Suppliers can be categorised thusly:

- Local (often regional) suppliers who are usually quite small in size and work out of a single site. Volume effects are not possible with this kind of supplier;
- National suppliers with more extensive activities than local counterparts and greater responsiveness than international ones;
- International suppliers with whom the company can work in more than one country. These actors often possess a specific know-how that makes then indispensable. They transact enormous volumes, reducing the importance of any one customer;
- Low-cost suppliers with whom the company specifically works for this one reason. Turnover is quite rapid in this category, which presents quality and delivery risks.

2 Description of the 'e-Business Project'

The e-business project is very ambiguous and potentially headed in different directions, largely because it is driven by a variety of Drivindus managers, not all of whom have the same conceptions. Each views the project through the prism of very different realities. In short, Drivindus's e-business project has heterogeneous goals - which makes it hard to find a global solution and explains why the project has had to be run over two phases. After appointing Mrs. Biz to manage the e-business project, Senior Management asked her to achieve the following objectives:

- Cut acquisition and procurement costs significantly (O1);
- Reduce the number of suppliers without endangering their autonomy, or indeed Drivindus's (O2). This is referred to as Purchasing globalisation;
- Homogenise the tender bid processes and the technical specifications communicated to suppliers worldwide (O3);
- Improve the company's general knowledge of its suppliers' competencies, means of production, financial structures or customer bases (O4);
- Track supplier performance on both a day-to-day and global basis (O5);

- Accelerate and raise the quality of dispute resolution mechanisms to solve any production incidents as quickly and efficiently as possible (O6);
- Help buyers leverage their knowledge and implement internal benchmarking (O7). Buyers must possess a tool that will allow them to engage in technological and strategic watch activities and share anything they learn with one another.

Senior Management is ready to invest in solutions that will give it a decisive competitive advantage by raising productivity and developing new partnerships with innovative suppliers.

Mrs. Biz has decided to call her e-business project E@SI, which stands for *E-business at Supplier Integration.* As a concept, *Supplier Integration* is one of Drivindus's five strategic axes. The project is set to run over two phases: an initial stage mainly devoted to the standardisation, optimisation and globalisation of transactions and marked by significant cost-cutting efforts; and a second, more qualitative stage revolving around problems like the management of supplier relationships, establishment of new forms of collaboration, and leveraging of purchasing-specific knowledge and know-how. After exploring which tools and solutions are on offer in the e-business package markets or different electronic marketplaces, Mrs. Biz noted that none of them fully satisfies Drivindus's expressed needs and decided to initiate a series of sub-projects that she delegated to different project managers. Thus, it is not one but four e-business projects that will run concurrently, with a two-year gap between the transaction and cost phase versus the relationship and knowledge phase.

- The first sub-project (P1) involves online bidding and uses a reverse auction system for certain kinds of purchases. The project will run during phase 1 and start in 2006.
- The second sub-project (P2) involves web-procurement, i.e. purchases from standardised electronic catalogues. It runs during phase 1 and also starts in 2006.
- The third sub-project (P3), called SUMO for SUpplier MOnitoring, establishes a supplier referencing package. It will run during phase 1 and starts in early 2007.
- The fourth sub-project (P4) involves Supplier Relationship Management (SRM) and mainly manages quality disputes and supplier incidents through its Incident Management System (IMS) solution. This collaborative extranet project will run during phase 2 and start in 2008.

3 Simplified Specifications

Drivindus has very precise specifications for this first project. The tool must be simple and user-friendly yet provide very high value added. Reverse auctions have a mystique but also a relatively negative reputation. Many people have preconceptions about them, meaning that there is a strong possibility that Drivindus buyers could reject them. Drivindus considers it crucial that auctions do not deprive buyers of their role as negotiators and purchasers. Quite the contrary, the buyers' mission will become increasingly complex meaning that their workload will increase instead of being reduced. The goal is to gain time on tasks that generate little value added – and to spend this time on improving the fit between people's needs and the products and services that the company purchases. This project has priority and will be the first launched during e-business project phase 1.

At the beginning of the project, Drivindus observed a certain immaturity on the part of solution designers in terms of their knowledge of the Purchasing function. Specifically, there seemed to be a lack of awareness of what people expect in terms of procurement management and performance measurement. The company would like to develop certain functionalities leading to a standardisation of technical specifications, globalisation of purchases, development of framework contracts and above all, access to new reporting tools. Web catalogue solutions offer basic 'meta-catalogue' functions (or catalogue catalogues) that homogenise formats and offer comparisons of similar products offered by different suppliers. Drivindus would like to develop its marketplace in conjunction with a service provider who has a sufficiently open mind to be willing to listen to requests from the Project Manager – and whose vision of the Purchasing function is similar to the group's. This project will be launched in parallel with the online bidding project, i.e. during phase 1 of the e-business project.

The monitoring tool must be capable of measuring suppliers' service quality, viability, innovation potential, asset value and key competencies. As such, it will subject suppliers to a financial audit (financial solidity, cost structure, profitability, etc.), industrial audit (production capacities, equipment maintenance, staff training, etc.) and technological audit (R&D investment, number of innovations over a given period of time, number of partnerships with lower tier suppliers, etc.). These criteria will be periodically analysed to determine which suppliers should be certified and feature on a short list - or blacklist - and monitored for future developments. Towards this end, there needs to be a supplier database replete with SAP codification and interfacing (since this is the integrated management package used throughout the Drivindus group). The project will complement the two preceding projects and will be launched at the end of period 1, before the beginning of period 2.

Drivindus would like to design a highly strategic tool that is specific to the particular relationships it has developed with suppliers. Two applications will have to be designed and developed internally with the help of external providers, mainly consultants. The first is a tool for managing supplier quality incidents, one that should facilitate monitoring, improve problem-solving and keep malfunctions from recurring. The system should, for example, contain different alert levels requiring suppliers to act with various degrees of urgency. The second application shares the main performance indicators with those suppliers who have a more consolidated vision of their role as value creators working on Drivindus's behalf. The SRM project will be launched in 2008, i.e. during phase 2 of the e-business project, at the same time as the Intranet platform.

4 Presenting Solutions

After testing several platforms, Drivindus signed in April 2006 a partnership with Freemarkets, a marketplace specialised in reverse auctions. The agreement covered the management of $300 million worth of supplier deals for a period of two years. These purchases mainly involved capital equipment like electronic or mechanical components, chemical products or organic matter. Freemarkets seemed very willing to listen to Drivindus's wishes. The principle of electronic auctions is that participants can monitor the price action and adjust their own bids in real time. Drivindus is supposed to allocate contracts based on a supplier's overall performance, with price being only one aspect of the decision. Price competition only occurs after suppliers have been pre-selected for their ability to work to some very rigorous specifications. The goal is not only to save money but also to reduce and rationalise the company's shortlist of suppliers. If a firm already working with Drivindus takes part in an auction and wins the contract, it will have to satisfy the company's minimum product quality and service conditions.

Drivindus has also got together with IBM Business Consulting, chosen to serve as integrator of the Commerce One electronic catalogue solution. This is a software structure that standardises catalogues and customises them to fit different needs. Commerce One is not only able to define a standard but can also achieve a large enough critical mass in a sufficiently short period of time to recoup the costs incurred developing the solution. This also means that Commerce One has had some major financial problems and is in a weak bargaining position when dealing with customers. Drivindus has suggested to Commerce One then it invest in the latter company's solution. An opportunity arose for the group in 2007 in the form of an 'Escrow Agreement', i.e., a contract enabling it to obtain exclusive ownership of the core application's Java source code. Using this core, IBM Business Consulting can supplement existing functionalities with new ones specific to Drivindus. This allowed the company to design a customised solution after receiving advice from IBM experts – and to do this at the lowest possible cost, since it could start with a solution that already exists.

It was on the basis of a product specification determined by Drivindus's P3 Project Manager that the monitoring solution was developed to remedy the present lack of satisfactory solutions. Because the stakes are so high, Drivindus has invested in a single platform whose design has been subcontracted to a small software consultant before being passed on to Cap Gemini. This supplier referencing package has been built on a module-via-module basis, i.e., functionality-by-functionality, to enable a progressive installation and optimise the management of its particularly high investment costs. The customisation advantage is entirely realised by Drivindus, which has kept a close eye on the project all throughout, validating each step by rigorously applying its specifications before moving onto the following step. Drivindus does not hesitate to finance all of the developments needed to obtain certain functionalities that may be entirely specific to its line of business.

The first application of the SRM solution is a supplier quality incident management platform called IMS (Incident Management System) that is supposed to encourage, structure and accelerate the processing of any incidents. If one occurs, the quality manager records it on IMF and creates a file with photos and recordings done using measurement and control tools, before transmitting everything to the supplier involved. The supplier will then have very short period of time to respond, step-by-step, via a method called QRQC (Quick Response Quality Control):

- In fewer than 24 hours, the supplier will have to implement conservational actions, i.e. suggest an immediate action plan addressing any defects and preventing any new defective goods from reaching Drivindus.
- In fewer than five days, the supplier will have to provide analysis of the causes of the incident and explain why are the defect appeared and why it was not detected on the supplier's premises before Drivindus noticed it. The group's preference at this

level is to get suppliers to act autonomously and take responsibility for their own quality and not leave this to Drivindus.
- After a further five days, the supplier must confirm that it has adopted an action plan aimed at avoiding any recurrence of the incident – and that is able to use statistical data and all necessary documentation to prove that the action plan will be both efficient and effective.

SRM is a very visual tool that ties KM relating specifically to the incidents in question to information shared with all of the divisions in the Drivindus group, thereby accelerating business or sectorial level problem-solving, even if the incident occurs in another division.

5 Stages of Deployment

This tool, which is very destabilising for both buyers and suppliers, has become standard. It is associated with a communications plan and also an intensive training programme for each buyer. Suppliers (especially French ones) continue to view this practice as abusive and anti-competitive, simply because it leaves them exposed to global competition. Other suppliers see it as an opportunity to increase their market share at Drivindus. As time goes by, the platform will be used by almost 800 of the 1,000 buyers who currently work with Freemarkets and manage all of the auction phases for which they are responsible. The buyers in question are mainly those working in branches like administrative costs, engineering, transportation and raw materials. All buyers receive training supervised by the 'key users' who have led the platform's testing and debugging process, with Freemarkets maintaining responsibility for preparing the auction. Subsequently, the buyers themselves will manage all of the stages and, once they start to master the tool, assume an advisory role. Within a few years, this solution will be used for nearly 20% of all purchasing volumes, or the equivalent of more than €1 billion. This amounts to a total cost reduction of between 9 and 12%.

The idea here is to have a custom-made package that will be hosted internally, and not to use an external marketplace. The problems experienced with Commerce One ultimately became an opportunity for Drivindus, which after appropriating the core of their marketplace is now able to build its own tailor-made portal. The web catalogue solution was launched in 2006 and deployed on all sites worldwide from 2008 onwards. Catalogues were only used on 10% of all non-production-related purchasing at the time, but Drivindus does have the possibility of organising its calls for tender online and hopes to increase the overall percentage of work done in this way to 50% by the year 2010. Despite being highly supportive of the solution at first, buyers subsequently felt quite disappointed, if only because their early expectations were too high. This kind of marketplace is a victim of its own success, with technical limitations having bothered users to such an extent that a new version was installed in 2009 – since when users and suppliers alike have been very satisfied with its performance. The time needed to process a tender bid has been divided by a factor of three and internal customers' satisfaction levels have risen noticeably.

Performance monitoring has mainly focused on production-related purchases. This allows people to have a global and segmented vision of the purchases that Drivindus makes across the world, while tracking leading indicators like quality, cost and delays. Its extension to non-production-related purchasing will be organised over the course of 2009. When it was first set up, this tool was considered quite restrictive insofar as it needed to be systematically updated on a monthly basis. Over time however, it has become a key information source for managing suppliers. Its main weakness remains the reliability of the information it provides, which can be incomplete, redundant and even obsolete. There is still some room for improvement in the sense that users need to be more rigorous in updating the tool with whatever information they acquire.

After two months testing the Covisint solution - a specialist automotive sector electronic marketplace created by General Motors, Ford and Daimler Chrysler - Drivindus was unconvinced by the experience and initiated the development of a dedicated solution. Contrary to the cumbersome nature, technical complexity and rigidity of Covisint - which has become increasingly difficult to implement - Drivindus has been looking for a very simple and ergonomic solution requiring little training and featuring only functionalities that are strictly necessary. Of course, the upfront costs of designing this kind of collaborative platform were extremely expensive, but Drivindus's project manager has decided to devote a lot of time and energy to its relatively long functional design phase and remains intransigent. The initial functionalities were implemented very quickly in 2008 after the arrival of a new Quality Manager. This extranet tool has a very good reputation among buyers and suppliers alike. In turn, this has led to the implementation of a standardised quality incident resolution process, which has considerably facilitated and accelerated the resolution of any and all incidents.

References

1. Beukers, M., Versendaal, J., Batenburg, R., Brinkkemper, S.: The Procurement Alignment Framework: Construction and Application. Wirtschaftsinformatik 48(5) (2006)
2. Brousseau, E.: The Governance of Transaction by Commercial Intermediaries: an Analysis of the re-engineering of intermediation by electronic commerce. International Journal of the Economics of Business 9(3) (2002)
3. Carter, C.R., Ellram, L.M.: Thirty-five years of the Journal of Supply Chain Management: where have we been and where are we going? Journal of Supply Chain Management 39(1) (2003)
4. Cousins, P.D., Lawson, B., Squire, B.: An empirical taxonomy of purchasing functions. International Journal of Operations & Production Management 26(7) (2006)
5. Davila, A., Gupta, M., Palmer, R.: Moving procurement systems to the Internet: The adoption and use of E-procurement technology models. European Management Journal 21(1) (2003)
6. Kaplan, S., Sawhnay, M.: E-Hubs: the new B2B Marketplaces. Harvard Business Review (May-June 2000)
7. Le, T., Rao, S., Truong, D.: Industry-Sponsored Marketplaces: a Platform for Supply Chain Integration or a Vehicle for Market Aggregation? Electronic Markets 14(4) (2004)

Part XVI

VO Formation

A Methodology for Logistics Partners' Selection to Compose Virtual Organizations Based on KPI

Omir Correia Alves Junior[1] and Ricardo J. Rabelo[2]

[1] Dept. of Computer Science,
State University of Santa Catarina, Brazil
omalves@gmail.com
[2]Dept. of Automation and Systems Eng.,
Federal University of Santa Catarina, Brazil
rabelo@das.ufsc.br

Abstract. This paper presents an exploratory and qualitative work of a novel model for the selection of the most adequate logistics providers that will compose a virtual organization. It includes a performance measurement model and a supporting methodology that considers the intrinsic dynamics, autonomy and temporality of Virtual Organizations, involving both intra and inter-organizational indicators at strategic levels. The model is flexible in terms of both allowing performance indicators' weights relaxation and being adapted according to the organizations' governance model.

Keywords: virtual organization, logistics partners' selection, performance indicators, AHP method, performance measurement.

1 Introduction

The Globalization is a trend that favors the expansion of logistics partners. New markets and new products have been increasingly created all over the world and proper logistic providers should be hired. The cleverer this activity is done the greater visibility, improved customer service, better planning and cost savings will be supported [1]. When companies work in more volatile strategic networks, the difficult of selecting the most appropriate logistic providers is even higher. This works focuses on the *Virtual Organization* (VO) type of network.

Part of such difficulty is due to the intrinsic nature of a VO, which is a temporary and dynamic strategic alliance of autonomous, heterogeneous and usually geographically dispersed companies (often SMEs) created to attend to very particular business opportunities [2-4], sharing costs, benefits and risks, acting as it was one single enterprise [5, 6]. After ending all legal obligations a VO is dismissed.

Differently from traditional supply chains, logistics providers (responsible for handling material and cargo transportation) are not known in advance, as this depends on the business, on the client, on the country or region's regulations, etc. Therefore, the collaboration among involved industrial partners (who produces some part of the good) and logistic providers are crucial to be augmented [7, 8] as a way to fulfill temporal and quality requirements of this unique business opportunity as well as to

L.M. Camarinha-Matos et al. (Eds.): PRO-VE 2011, IFIP AICT 362, pp. 439–449, 2011.

differentiate in the market as long as they create value in this chain [9, 10]. Considering this tighter collaboration, logistics providers are seem as logistics *partners* (LP) and a business opportunity is as a *collaboration* opportunity (CO).

Most of the works found out in the literature tackled this problem usually calling it as *partner's search and selection*, but with the focus on the selection of *industrial* partners (IP) instead of on *logistics* partners. Besides that, the works on logistics in VOs essentially considers performance indicators basically at operational level, neglecting the also important strategic level. Yet, they do not consider other relevant dimensions when autonomous and collaborative companies do business together, such as governance and trust. Finally, the large majority of the works try to apply an automatic approach when selecting partners. We argue that the selection of LPs in a VO scenario is so complex and full of particularities that making this automatically is perhaps unrealistic as well as it prevents involved companies' managers from properly putting in practice their experience.

This work proposes a novel model that complements other contributions about IPs' selection, supporting the suggestion of adequate *LPs* for given VO.

This paper is organized as following: section I introduced the problem; section 2 details the problem and contextualizes it within the collaborative networks area; section 3 presents the supporting methodology for LP suggestion; section 4 provides an example of the model usage; and section V provides some preliminary conclusions about the model.

2 Logistic Network Problem

A VO is one type of a diversity of Collaborative Network Organizations (CNO). However, a key aspect when considering VOs is that all of its members come from another type of CNO, which is the so-called *Virtual organization Breeding Environment* (VBE). A VBE is a long-term alliance of companies whose ultimate goal is to be the basis for the creation of VOs. Likely VOs, VBE members are also composed of autonomous, heterogeneous and geographically dispersed companies. Regarding that they share principles and working methods, the creation of VOs from a VBE becomes much faster, more effective and less complex to manage [11, 12]. A typical VO is generally composed of LPs and IPs, creating a logistics and value chain network, as illustrated in Figure 1.

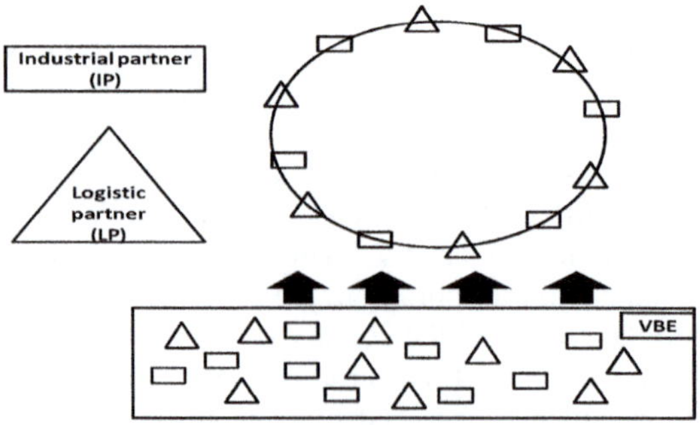

Fig. 1. VO composed of LPs and IPs

The reference process for a VO creation consists of seven steps (Figure 2) [13]. Adopting a performance measurement approach, in [14] partners' search and selection step is extended introducing key performance indicators (KPI) as a first task to be made to filter IPs. This paper follows the same approach, adapting it to LPs and restricting the model to the *suggestion* stage. This is a complex task because LPs will work collaboratively in a VO and their selection should consider particular aspects of a VO and VBE, such as:

- LPs can only be identified after knowing the particular CO in details;
- A repeated CO will be rarely composed of the same set of VBE members;
- VO's LPs and IPs not necessarily will have worked together in previous COs;
- COs are usually unique or one-of-a-kind;
- KPI and/or their weights vary from one CO to another;
- LPs usually have different information system, semantics and performance measures;
- The final handshake among IPs and LPs should be carried out as fast as possible;
- Each VBE has its particular governance model.

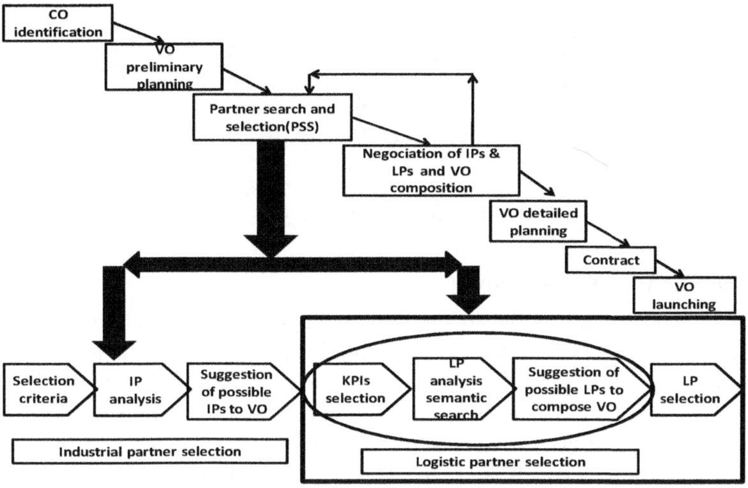

Fig. 2. Extended framework for the VO creation

A literature survey about this showed that there are several approaches based on performance measurement and KPIs for evaluating companies [15]. However, few of them address the problem of KPI models for LPs in VOs. For example, in [16] a generic methodology based on balanced Scorecard (BSC) indicators is proposed, but without any support for governance and trust issues. The methodology proposed by [17] assigns performance indicators for each partner but does not provide criteria for analyzing the collaboration level of partners to compose VOs. In [18] the complexity of structuring a methodology for VO partners' selection is identified and a hierarchical methodology based on multiple attribute decision making is proposed. However this work has focused only on intra-organizational performance indicators.

3 Proposed Methodology

In order to tackle this issue of suggesting adequate LPs for a given VO a methodology is proposed (Figure 3). Two important assumptions are considered. Firstly, all LPs are members of a VBE. Secondly, there is a global coordinator of the process, which is called *VO Coordinator*. An additional role is taken by a logistic specialist, who permanently audits the LPs' KPI values.

A. CO Identification

In this first methodology stage the CO is verified in order to identify the logistics itineraries that have to be carried out. A CO, besides other information, is composed of logistics-related data showed on section 4. This set of information was based on a VO information reference model [19] [14] and extended for this work.

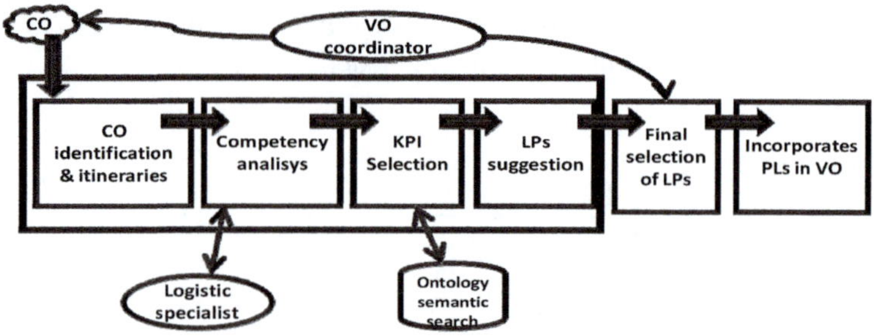

Fig. 3. LP selection steps

B. LP competency skills analysis

In a first round of analysis the methodology checks the technical LP's competences against to every single CO itinerary. If a given LP is pre-selected then it is moved to a suggested list for further VO coordinator decision. After an analysis on the logistics discipline [20], seven attributes were elicited to represent LP competences showed on section 4. The formal competency skills analysis is performed using the set theory. Two sets are considered: *R* and *M*. *R* represents the whole set of specific CO requirements *(R={1,...,r})*. *M* represents the set of LP's competencies *(M={1,..,m})*. The problem is to find a match between *R* and *M*, which will then define the pre-selected PLs for the given CO. This is provided by the function *G(i,j)*, which represents the intersection of *R* and *M* sets:

$$G(i,j) = |\, Ri \cap Mj \,|,\ \ \forall i\ \epsilon R\ \wedge\ \forall j\ \epsilon M \tag{1}$$

Where:

i=number of PLs; j=number of COs.

C. Identification and selection of KPIs

The third step of the methodology aims at selecting the most appropriate KPIs that will be applied over every CO's itinerary to filter the pre-selected LPs. This process is aided by an *ontology*, which links the semantic of CO's attributes with the KPI model (Figure 3). It is used to provide a formal representation that can be used and reused to facilitate understanding of all involved concepts and relationships between them in a specific domain [21]. The developed KPI model comprises fifteen KPIs (see section D). More than one KPI can be applied to evaluate a given CO itinerary. LPs will be selected after this set of KPI evaluation. This strategy has been inspired from [14]. With the selected list of KPIs and LPs, the methodology determines the level of collaboration (LC) (see section G) of each pre-selected LP for each itinerary. The LP to be finally suggested is the one with the highest LC value or with the highest coefficient of regression. VO coordinators evaluate the suggested list and assign one LP to the given itinerary and then this LP becomes member of the VO. The method repeats until the end of the CO itineraries, i.e. when there is one or a set of LPs selected to link all the involved (and previously defined) VO's industrial partners.

D. KPI model

A crucial element in the methodology is the KPI model. Regarding this, two general requirements were necessary to cope with. Firstly, the set of KPIs should consider both intra and inter organizational perspectives. Secondly, they should also consider indicators at strategic level. After a literature review, several KPI models were found out (e.g. [22-25]). However, none of them were neither comprehensive enough to cope with those requirements nor were devoted to logistics in dynamic alliances (e.g. VOs). The devised KPI model has considered some existing models (e.g. SCOR [26]) and complemented with a literature overview. It is composed of fifteen KPIs:

- *ROE* (return-on-equity): The amount of net income returned as a percentage of shareholders equity;
- *Cash flow*: focusing on the cash being generated related to how much is being generated and the safety net it provides to the LP;
- *Cost Control*: controls the cost reduction of LPs;
- *Customer satisfaction*: measures the customer perception related to delivered services;
- *Susceptibility*: the elapsed time between customer purchase order and product(s) delivery;
- *Commitment*: measures the level of commitment between the LPs;
- *Collaboration*: measures the LPs level of collaboration;
- *IT maturity*: measures if the LP's IT objectives are aligned to its business strategies;
- *Governance*: measures how is the code of conduct and cultural issues of each LPs;
- *Flexibility*: measures the LP flexibility to adapt to changes along VO operation;
- *Environmental performance*: measures how the LP copes with environmental practices;
- *Availability*: measures the level of LP availability;
- *Effectiveness*: measures if resources (e.g. labor) are properly allocated;
- *Trust*: measures the level of trust between the LPs;
- *Communication*: measure the level of effective communication among LPs' members.

Each KPI is seen as a strategic dimension, which is divided into a subset of individual and operational/lower level performance indicators (PIs). When computed as a whole, they provide the value of the KPI itself. For example, KPI *Cost Control* is calculated considering the PIs *cost of warehousing, reverse cost* and *labor cost.*

E. Assigning weights to KPIs

The methodology applies the AHP method to assign weights to the fifteen KPIs. AHP was proposed in [27] to solve multiple criteria problems in a hierarchical structure. In

AHP, criteria related to the goal are distributed at lower levels from the top of the KPI weight structure (Figure 4).

The LC calculation (see section G) uses this hierarchical structure to distribute weights (i.e. their importance) of KPIs and hence to suggest the most suitable LPs. All KPIs are weighted. By default, the methodology assigns the higher weights to KPIs with makes a semantics matching with the CO, whereas lower weights are assigned to those without matching. The VO coordinator is in charge of assignment weights to KPIs. If necessary, weights can be redefined along the process.

F. Assign values to KPIs

As the model works also based on historical data, the VBE database should be updated with the applied KPIs values after the VO dissolution. This is done by all the involved VO's companies via electronic questionnaires. Likert scale [28] is used to normalize KPI values, defining values from zero to five. These values are calculated from the set of tactical performance indicators that composes each (strategic) KPI.

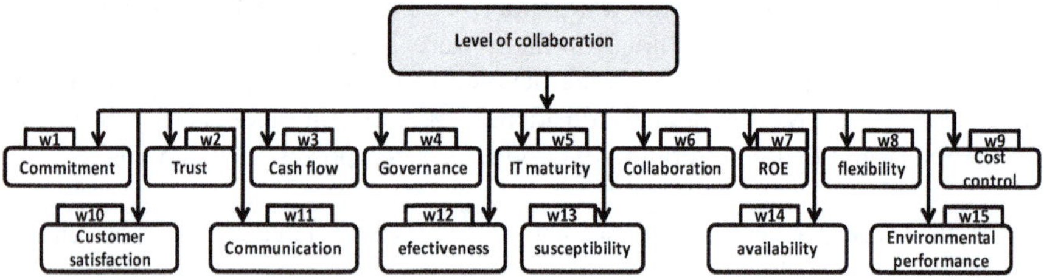

Fig. 4. Using AHP with the KPIs

G. Level of collaboration (LC)

The final decision about which LPs will compose a VO is determined by a last filter, which is LC. LC is a value calculated for each LP that was selected by the competence analysis. It is represented by a vector of collaboration (VC), which is formed by the historical collaboration of each pre-selected LP in past VOs (Figure 5).

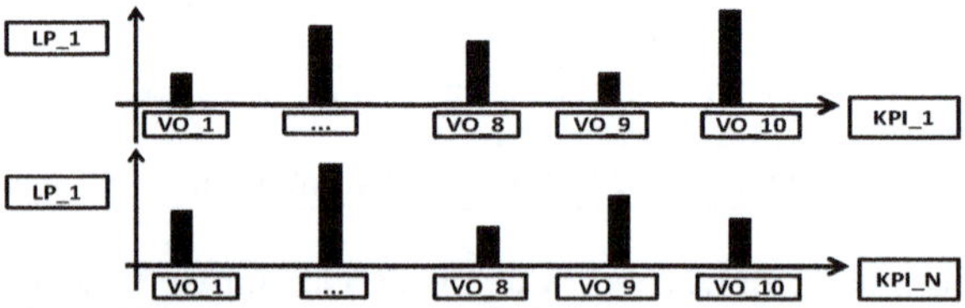

Vector_Collab_LP1=
= V[(AA_KPI_1 - S1)*W.kpi1, (AA_KPI_2 - S2)*W.kpi2, ..., (AA_KPI_N - Sn)*W.kpin] (2)

AA_KPI_1 = represents the arithmetic average of the last N values of KPI_1
W.kpin = represents the weight of each KPI assigned by the method AHP
Sn = represents the standard deviation of KPIn for PL1

Level_collaboration_LP_1 = LC_LP1
LC_LP1 = ((AA_KPI_1 - S1)*W.kpi1 + (AA_KPI_2 - S2)*W.kpi2 + ...+ (AA_KPI_N - Sn)*W.kpin) (3)

Fig. 5. Value of KPIs and level of collaboration formula

LC is composed of a set of "positions" (KPIs), where each position is calculated multiplying the average of the historical values of each KPI minus the standard deviation for each KPI by its respective weight. The determination of the LC is applied to all LPs, as follows:

- *Get past KPI values (from the VBE database) from each pre-selected LP associated to their previous VOs;*
- *Determine the time horizon to be applied upon the LPs. Depending on the VO or the VBE policy, this can vary from a number of past VOs (e.g. the last ten participations) or period of time (e.g. the participation in the last two years);*
- *Calculates Vector of Collaboration (VC), where each vector field is the arithmetic average of the last values minus the standard deviation multiplied by the respective KPI's weight for each KPI. The weight is represented by the variable W.idn, and it is calculated using the AHP method;*
- *Determine the total LC for each LP by the sum of the indices of the respective KPI VCs;*
- *Determine the straight line for the range of last n LC values for each LP and its coefficient, using the regression theory and the minimum quadratic method. (Figure 6);*
- *Suggests the LP for each CO's itinerary according to the highest LC and/or the positive coefficient of regression of the straight line. The positive coefficient means that, historically, after each VO the KPIs values of a LP are increasing.*

The formula for VC and LC calculation is given by:

$$VC(i,j,k)=(AA\_KPI(i,j,k) - S(i,j,k))*W(i,j,k) \tag{4}$$

where:

i = amount of KPIs; j = number of LPs per itinerary; k = number of itineraries within a CO;

AA_KPI = arithmetic average of historical values of the KPI i, referring to PL j, which is associated with the itinerary k;

W(i,j,k) = weight assigned to KPI i by AHP;

S(i,j,k) = standard deviation of KPI i, LP j, and itinerary k;

$$LC(j,k) = \sum_{i=1}^{13} VC(i,j,k) \tag{5}$$

where:

i = number of KPIs; j = number of LPs by itinerary; k = number of itineraries of the CO;

VC (i,j,k) = Vector of collaboration from KPI i to partner j, related to itinerary k;

LC (j,k) = level of collaboration of the PL j to itinerary k;

LC_a(j,k) = represents the LC of the PL j to itinerary k considering its coefficient of regression value;

$$LC(k) = [Max(LC(j,k)) \text{ or } Max(LC\_a(j,k))] \tag{6}$$

where:

LC(k):represents the greatest value for the LC or for the LC with the highest coefficient of regression to itinerary k.

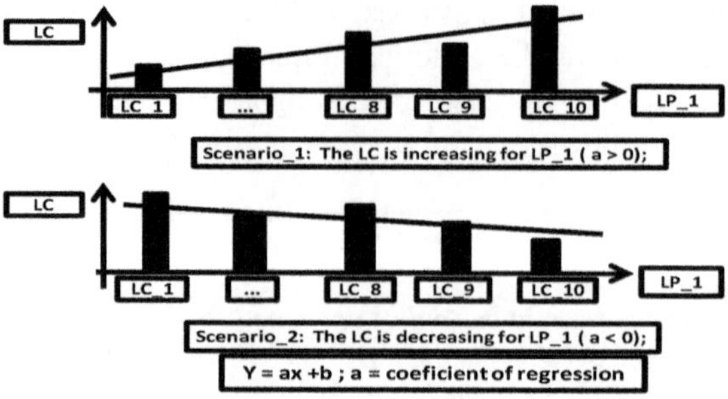

Fig. 6. Linear regression analysis for LC

4 Example of the Methodology Usage

Figure 7 generally illustrates an example on how the proposed model can be used. The given CO refers to a transportation of some good from the location A to B, with three legs in between: A-C, C-D and D-B. Each leg is represented by a CO's itinerary and they require up to three LPs to deliver the involved parts to the industrial partners. A LP may even get all the three itineraries, depending on its LC. CO's details are:

- *Place of origin: A;*
- *Place of destination: B;*
- *Departure Date: 01-31-2011;*
- *Delivery Date: 02-04-2011;*
- *Service Modal: plane and train;*
- *Cargo Type: shoes;*
- *Quantity: 1,20 tons;*
- *CO itinerary: itinerary_1: AC; itinerary_2: CD; itineray_3: DB;*
- *Technical skills for itinerary_01;*
  - ✓ *geographic coverage at source: A;*
  - ✓ *geographic coverage at the destination: C;*
  - ✓ *transportation of different types of loads: nill;*
  - ✓ *modal: plane;*
  - ✓ *realization consolidated shipments: mandatory;*
  - ✓ *response time: 12 hours;*
  - ✓ *cost: 1,200 dollars;*
- *Technical skills for itnerary_02;*
  - ✓ *geographic coverage at source: C;*
  - ✓ *geographic coverage at the destination: D;*
  - ✓ *transportation of different types of loads: nill;*
  - ✓ *modal: plane;*
  - ✓ *realization consolidated shipments: mandatory;*
  - ✓ *response time: 1day;*
  - ✓ *cost: 1,500 dollars;*
- *Technical skills for itinerary_03;*
  - ✓ *geographic coverage at source: D;*
  - ✓ *geographic coverage at the destination: B;*
  - ✓ *transportation of different types of loads: mandatory;*

- ✓ *modal: train;*
- ✓ *realization consolidated shipments: mandatory;*
- ✓ *response time: 1 day;*
- ✓ *cost: 1,800 dollars;*

- *Level of Collaboration (LC): 5,1.*

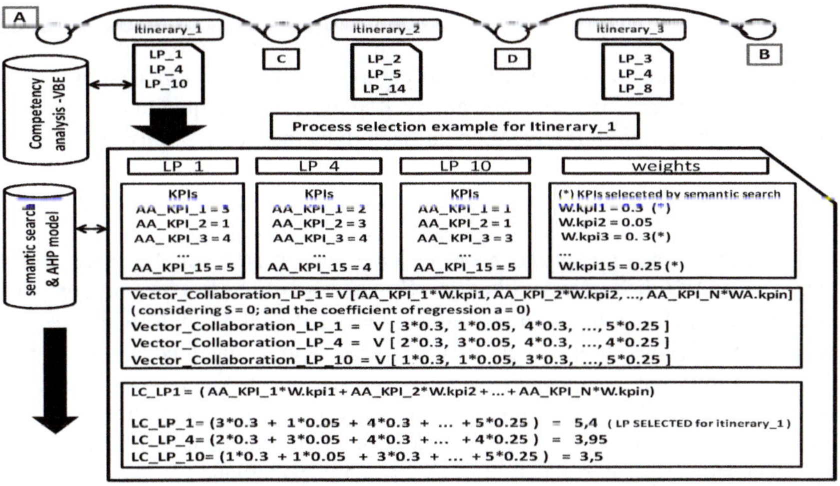

Fig. 7. Example of LP selection

As explained in Section 3, the selection of the set of LPs to be suggested to VO coordinator to compose VO related to the given CO is carried out along five phases:

- Phase 1: the actor who gets the CO (e.g. the VO coordinator, a VBE broker or the industrial partner who was directly contacted by the customer, depending on the VBE operating rules checks the itineraries associated with the CO;
- Phase 2: for each CO's itinerary the VBE database is consulted and LPs are pre-selected based on their competencies. In the example, *LP_1, LP_4* and *LP_10* would be pre-selected for *itinerary_1*;
- Phase 3: Semantic search selects KPIs which are related to the OC, and weights are assigned to them (using AHP method);
- Phase 4: calculation of: i) the arithmetic average for each KPI; ii) the standard deviation for each KPI (in this example, $Sn = 0$, and so $a = 0$); iii.) the VC for each LP; iv) the final LC for all LPs previously selected;
- Phase 5: For each itinerary the LP with the highest LC is suggested to compose the VO. For example, *LP_1* would be selected for *itinerary_1* with the score *5.4*;

The process repeats for all OC's itineraries (*2* and *3* in this case). In the case of problems during the VO execution (or before its effective starting) that cause the need for a LP replacement, the second (and so forth) LP of the list is contacted to see if it is still available. If none of them is available or the VO coordinator considers that they are no longer useful, the methodology is started again from the competence analysis phase on. In the worst case, if none LP is found out, the client should be contacted to see at which extent some relaxations (e.g. in the delivery time) are allowed. Otherwise the VO should be cancelled.

5 Conclusions

This paper has presented a novel model and supporting methodology for the selection of the most adequate logistics partners to compose a Virtual Organization (VO). It corresponds to an ongoing and essentially exploratory and qualitative work. The complexity of the problem refers to the intrinsic dynamics, temporality and autonomy of VO, whose partners (including logistics ones) can only be identified when the business opportunity is got. Therefore, it is of extreme importance to not only make this process faster but also with more quality and confidence.

A new performance model has been presented and it is devoted to cope with the singularities of VO. It is composed of 15 KPIs and it is used to compare companies' competences, which can be flexibly assigned via AHP method. A formal ontology to establish the relation among requirements, KPIs and competences was specially conceived so mitigating semantic problems. The set of logistics partners are selected based on their level of collaboration, also considering their past performance.

So far the model has been verified in a controlled environment and close to a small group of logistics operators in the form of general questionnaires. Next main steps include the development of a decision support system prototype that implements the whole model's environment, and testing it in near real scenarios.

References

[1] Mentzer, J.T., Konrad, B.P.: An efficiency/effectiveness approach to logistics performance analysis. J. of Business Logistics 12(1), 33–62 (1991)

[2] Camarinha-Matos, L.M., Afsarmanesh, H.: Collaborative Networks: A New Scientific Discipline. J. of Intelligent Manufacturing 16(4), 439–452 (2005)

[3] Mowshowitz, A.: Virtual organization. Com. of the ACM 40(9), 30–37 (1997)

[4] Katzy, B.R., Obozinski, V.: Designing the virtual enterprise. In: Proceeding of ICE 1999, 5th Int. Conf. On Concurrent Enterprising, pp. 11–20 (1999)

[5] Sandberg, E.: Logistics collaboration in supply chains: practice vs. theory. The Int. J. of Logistics Management 18(2), 274–293 (2007)

[6] Camarinha-Matos, L., Afsarmanesh, H.: Collaborative Networks: Reference Modeling. Springer, New York (2008)

[7] Skjoett-Larsen, T.T., Andresen, C.: Supply chain collaboration Theoretical perspectives and empirical evidence. Int. J. of Physical Distribution and Logistics Management 33(6), 531–549 (2003)

[8] Whipple, J.M., Russell, D.: Building supply chain collaboration: a typology of collaborative approaches. Int. J. of Logistics Management 18(2), 174–196 (2007)

[9] Rafele, C.: Logistic service measurement: a reference framework. J. of Manufacturing Technology Management 15(3), 280–290 (2004)

[10] Esper, T.L., Williams, L.R.: The value of collaborative transportation management (CTM): its relationship to CPFR and information technology. Transportation Journal 42(4), 55–65 (2003)
[11] Rabelo, R.J., et al.: Smart Configuration of Dinamic Virtual Enterprises. In: Fifth IFIP Working Conference on Virtual Enterprises, pp. 193–204 (2004)
[12] Afsarmanesh, H., Camarinha-Matos, L.M.: A Framework for Management of Virtual Organization Breeding Environments. In: Sixth IFIP Working Conference on Virtual Enterprises, pp. 35–48 (2005)
[13] Camarinha-Matos, L.M., et al.: Towards a Framework for Creation of Dynamic Virtual Organizations. In: 6th IFIP Work. Conf. on Virtual Enterprises, pp. 69–80 (2005)
[14] Baldo, F., Rabelo, R., Vallejos, R.V.: Modeling Performance Indicators' Selection Process for VO partners' Suggestion. In: 8th IFIP International Conference on Information Technology for Balanced Automation Systems, pp. 67–76 (2008)
[15] Seifert, M.: Collaboration formation in Virtual Organisations by applying prospective performance measurement. Phd Thesis, University of Bremen (2009)
[16] Westphal, I., Thoben, K., Seifert, M.: Measuring collaboration performance in virtual organizations. In: 8th IFIP Working Conf. on Virtual Enterprises, pp. 33–42 (2007)
[17] Bititci, U.S., et al.: Measuring and managing performance in extended enterprises. Int. J. of Operations & Production Management 25(4), 333–353 (2005)
[18] Sarkis, J., Talluri, S., Gunasekaran, A.: A strategic model for agile virtual enterprise partner selection. Int. J. of Operations & Production Manag. 27(11), 1213–1234 (2007)
[19] Camarinha-Matos, L.M., Afsarmanesh, H.: Elements of a base VE infrastructure. Computers in Industry 51(2), 139–163 (2003)
[20] Gunasekaran, A., Patel, C., Tirtiroglu, E.: Performance measures and metrics in a supply chain environment. Int. J. of Operations and Production Management 21(1/2), 71–87 (2001)
[21] Berners-Lee, T., Hendler, J., Lassila, O.: The semantic Web. Scientific American 284(5), 28–37 (2001)
[22] Saiz, J.J.A., Bas, A.O., Rodríguez, R.R.: Performance measurement system for enterprise networks. Int. J. of Productivity and Performance Management 56(4), 305–334 (2007)
[23] Westphal, I., Thoben, K.D., Seifert, M.: Measuring Collaboration Performance in Virtual Organizations. In: 8th IFIP Work. Conf. on Virtual Enterprises, pp. 33–42 (2007)
[24] Kim, D.H., Kim, C.: A generic framework of performance measurement in networked enterprises. In: Camarinha-Matos, L.M., Paraskakis, I., Afsarmanesh, H. (eds.) PRO-VE 2009. IFIP AICT, vol. 307, pp. 259–265. Springer, Heidelberg (2009)
[25] Seifert, M., Wiesner, K., Do, T.: Prospective performance measurement in virtual organizations, pp. 319–326 (2008)
[26] Supply-Chain Council, Supply Chain Operations Reference Model (2006)
[27] Saaty, T.L.: How to make a decision: the analytic hierarchy process. European Journal of Operational Research 48(1), 9–26 (1990)
[28] Linacre, J.M.: Optimizing rating scale category effectiveness. J. Appl. Meas. 3(1), 85–106 (2002)

Risk Assessment in the Formation of Virtual Enterprises

Sri Krishna Kumar and J. Harding*

Wolfson School of Mechanical Engineering, Loughborough University, UK
J.A.Harding@lboro.ac.uk

Abstract. A Virtual Enterprise (VE) is considered as a temporary consortium of member enterprises formed to pool their core competencies and exploit the market opportunities. Although a VE has many phases, such as business opportunity identification, formation and partner selection, operation and dissolution. The partner selection phase is considered to be of the utmost importance and care should be taken to assess all the risk factors. This paper examines the partner selection problem by considering three types of risks, individual performance risk, collaborative performance risk and network risk. Based on the information provided by the potentially collaborating enterprises, a mathematical model has been developed for calculation of all three types of risks.

Keywords: Virtual Enterprise (VE), risk analysis, partner selection, performance risk, network risk.

1 Introduction

With the introduction of a global economy and drift towards customized products, enterprises are seeking new paradigms, such as lean production, agile manufacturing, and virtual enterprises (VEs), to grasp market opportunities in a competitive global environment. A VE can be considered as a temporary coalition of globally distributed independent enterprises which share resources, skills, and costs, through the support of Information and Communication Technologies (ICT). A VE is formed when a market opportunity is realized and is dissolved when the opportunity or goal is achieved. In a VE, members of the alliance keep their own independent business processes and contribute their 'core competencies' in different complementary areas.

A VE operates in different phases as (1) opportunity identification, (2) VE formation and partner selection (3) operation and (4) dissolution. It is arguable, that of all the phases of a VE's lifecycle, partner selection is the most difficult task as it not only requires integration of core competencies but must also address different management styles and corporate cultures within the potential partners. A review of research literature reveals cases of the failure of VEs due to improper partner selection. According to [1] 60-70% of VEs are disbanded prematurely and identified trust, cultural differences, and different levels in the use of information as reasons for VE failure.

* Corresponding author.

L.M. Camarinha-Matos et al. (Eds.): PRO-VE 2011, IFIP AICT 362, pp. 450–455, 2011.

Although member enterprises of VEs, are capable of overcoming some of their individual limitations due to the advantages coming from being small (i.e they tend to be reactive, proactive and so forth), nonetheless collaborating within a VE brings a higher degree of risk than is experienced by individual enterprises. Due to such peculiarities, risk in VE formation requires a dedicated study.

In literature risk has been defined as "the variance of probability distribution of outcomes" [2]. The achievement of objectives realized by a VE depends on individual partners' capabilities and their cooperative relationships. This produces the multi-dimensional risk associated with a VE and can negatively affect the desired outcomes of the VE. In an early study of risk factors, [3] defines risk as emerging from eight different perspectives. [4] studied the collaborative or network risk and divided the risk factors into performance and relational risks, where consideration of another dimension of risk, i.e. of accessing and managing risks rather than identifying them, [5] proposed a supply network risk tool to identify, assess and manage risk to support the single partner decision making process concerning network evaluation. According [6], when a network is chosen to run a business the consequent risk is higher than the risk related to the same business run by a single company. It is obvious from the findings of researchers that, although, return of investment, opportunities and risk sharing abilities are higher in VEs, they still operate in higher risky environments than single enterprises and therefore care must be taken in the formation (including partner selection) of VEs as it plays an important role in their success.

In the formation of a VE, the whole project is divided into subprojects and for each subproject a single enterprise is selected. In this study, the overall risk in the VE has been divided into three categories (as shown in figure 1) individual performance risk, collaborative performance risk and network risk.

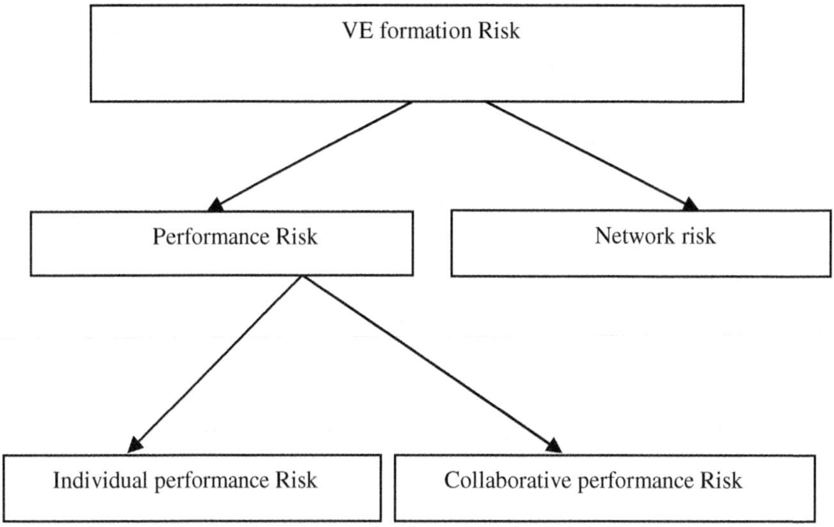

Fig. 1. VE formation risk

To clarify the proposed VE risk decomposition the overall risk can be considered as a combination of performance and network risk. Performance risk can be further subdivided into individual and collaborative performance. Individual risk is associated with and quality constraints. Collaborative risk is the measure of member enterprises' capability to undertake the project. Network risk is related to lack of trust, inaccurate information sharing and asymmetry in reciprocal position that hinders the effective collaboration [7].

This research aims to support risk management during the formation of VEs, firstly through the quantitative estimation of the overall risk and then through the evaluation of the overall risk associated cost. This approach will help decision makers to find the best possible consortium.

2 Quantitative Measure of the Risk in the Formation of a VE

The partner selection problem can be described as follows: A project **N** is divided into subprojects which are indexed n, $n \in \{1,2,....,N\} = \mathbf{N}$. m_i is the set of enterprises bidding for the subproject i, $i \in \mathbf{N}$. Every enterprise, bidding for the subproject provides information about its ability, capacity, technology, competency and other related information. Based on the information provided, individual performance risk is calculated, which is related to the enterprise's ability to finish the subproject, in terms of time, quantity, quality and other aspects. In most cases, with improper and incomplete information, individual risk can be given by interval values as: $[Lr_i^k, Ur_i^k]$, where L and U corresponds to the lower and upper limit of the individual performance risk associated with k^{th} enterprise and i^{th} subproject. Depending upon the optimism present in the partners this risk can vary between its lower and upper limit and can be taken as: $\mathbf{r}_i^k = \alpha Lr_i^k + (1-\alpha)Ur_i^k$, with $\alpha \in [0,1]$ defining the degree of optimism. Hence, a more optimistic network will have a lower risk value when compared to a pessimistic network.

The decision variable $x_i^k \in \{0,1\}$, determines the subproject and enterprise relation with respect to the constraint that a subproject cannot be awarded to more than one enterprise. If c_i is the cost of subproject i, then after considering the individual performance risk the estimated cost of the subproject will be: $E[c_i] = \sum_k (1 + \mathbf{r}_i^k x_i^k) c_i$.

2.1 Collaborative Performance Risk

Collaborative performance risk analyses the risk level for each enterprise due to the presence of the other member enterprises in the VE. Based on the collaborative performance risk factor, an individual enterprise can decide whether to join the consortium. Collaborative performance risk ( ) can be calculated as:

$$\mathbf{R}_i^k = (1-\mathbf{r}_i^k)x_i^k[1 - \prod_{i' \neq i} \prod_{k' \neq k} (1-\mathbf{r}_{i'}^{k'})x_{i'}^{k'}]$$

The first part of the formula calculates the probability that the kth enterprise will be successful for ith project (if assigned) and second part calculates the probability that at least one of the other subprojects will fail. The collaborative performance risk will increase the expected cost of the operation for each enterprise as the higher the risk in the environment, the higher will be the risk of return of investment. So now the cost of operation, considering the collaborative risk factor can be given as:

$$E'[c_i] = \sum_k [1 + (\mathbf{r}_i^k + \mathbf{R}_i^k) x_i^k] c_i$$

2.2 Network Risk

The first two types of risk, discussed above were related to individual risk factors and their consequences on the other partners. However, in a VE, where partners need to be seamlessly interoperable and cooperative, lack of communication, social, technological or cultural factors may hinder the desired output. This type of risk has been categorized as network risk in a VE, and this can be defined as: $nr_i^k = \sum_{k',k'\neq k} \sum_{i',i'\neq i} (\gamma^{kk'}/2) x_i^k x_{i'}^{k'}$ where $\gamma^{kk'}$ = risk of collaboration between two enterprises, with $\gamma^{kk'} \in [0,1]$ and $\gamma^{kk'} = 0$ if $k=k'$. In order to avoid double calculation we have divided the factor by 2.

The value of $\gamma^{kk'}$ will determine the affinity of collaboration between two enterprises (k and k') in the VE. If the value is closer to 0, higher will be the affinity of collaboration due to low risk factor.

The total network risk can be given as: $\mathbf{NR} = \sum_k \sum_i nr_i^k$

Mathematically, partner selection problem with risk analysis can be given as:

$$\text{Min} \sum_i E(c_i) + \{\sum_i c_i\} \mathbf{NR} \tag{1}$$

$$\text{Subject to } \sum_i \sum_k x_i^k = 1 \tag{2}$$

Equation (1) defines the objective function which minimizes the performance risk (first part) and network risk (second part). Constraint (2) determines that only one enterprise will be selected for each project.

3 Numerical Experiment

For numerical analysis, this paper considers a project which can be divided into four sub projects. The cost of each subproject is taken between 15,000 - 25,000. Three enterprises are bidding for the each subproject and their lower and upper limit for the individual performance risk are generated randomly between 0.1 and 0.2. The degree of optimism has been taken as 0.5 i.e. the mean of lower and upper value of the risk. Network risk between the enterprises is generated randomly between 0 to 1. The experiment result obtained has been shown in table 1. The first column in the table depicts the optimal network according to the all three risk factors taken separately and corresponding rows depicts the monetary value of the risk factor.

Table 1. Cost associated with risk factors

Optimal Network	IR cost	CR cost	NR cost	TR cost
Individual risk(IR)	85500	38074	172500	296124
Collaborative risk (CR)	87350	33721	135000	256070
Network risk(NR)	88800	34095	120000	280395
Total risk (TR)	86100	34795	125000	245895

IR: Individual risk, CR: Collaborative risk, NR: Network risk, TR: Total risk

From Table 1 it is clear that the optimal network is not the optimal for any of the risk factors. In determining member enterprises for VE, this risk analysis will help in determining optimal network which will have lowest possible risk.

4 Conclusion

This paper considers the risk associated with the formation or partner selection of the virtual enterprise (VE). [8] had studied the performance and relational risk in the lieu of direct and indirect risk for the Network. However, individual risk and collaborative performance risk plays an important role along with network risk. As, the risk factors discussed in this paper not only help in forming optimal consortium for VE, but also provide useful information regarding risk and its associated cost for individual enterprises, which will help them in decision making regarding joining the consortium.

References

1. Wildeman, L.: Alliances and networks: the next generation. International Journal of Technology Management 15(1/2), 96–108 (1998)
2. March, J.G., Shapira, Z.: Management perspective on risk and risk taking. Management Science 33(11), 1404–1418 (1987)
3. Baird, I.S., Thomas, H.: What is risk anyway? In: Bettis, R.A., Thomas, H. (eds.) Risk, Strategy, and Management, pp. 21–52. JAI Press, Greenwich (1990)
4. Das, T.K., Teng, B.: A risk perception model of alliance structuring. Journal of International Management 7, 1–29 (2001)
5. Harland, C., Brencheley, H., Walker, H.: Risk in supply network. Journal of Purchasing and Supply Management 9(2), 51–62 (2003)

6. Link, P.: risikomanagement von Innovationskooperationen. Doctoral Thesis, Nr. 14240, ETH Zurich, Zurich (2001)
7. Ojala, M., Hallikas, J.: Investment decision-making in supplier networks: management of risk. International Journal of Production Economics 104, 201–213 (2006)
8. Lo Nigro, G., Abbate, L., Bruccoleri, M., Perrone, G.: How risk consideration can affect inter-organization relationship decisions. In: Proceedings of 19th International Conference on Production Research, Valparaiso (Chile), July 29-August 2 (2007)

Business Process Driven Matching of Partner Profiles to Resource Requirements

Maik Herfurth[1], Thomas Schuster[1], and Peter Weiß[2]

[1] FZI Forschungszentrum Informatik, Haid-und-Neu-Str. 10-14, 76131 Karlsruhe, Germany
{herfurth,schuster}@fzi.de
[2] ISS International School of Service Management, Hans-Henny-Jahnn-Weg 9, 22085 Hamburg, Germany
weiss@iss-hamburg.de

Abstract. Based on recent research in business process modeling and management enhanced integration of resource management can be beneficial. In this context appropriate resources can be identified by matching their profiles with business process requirements. Requirements may be generated from business process models as competence profiles, if advanced modeling techniques that enable detailed modeling are being used. Matching generated profiles to profiles of internal resources (typically maintained by human resource departments) or external business partners (organizations as well as individuals) requires profile descriptions at a similar level of detail. In order to enable sound matching of resource profiles between supplicants and suppliers in collaborative networks, we suggest modeling and system architecture that can handle these challenges. As one main pillar we will present a framework that allows formal description of competence profiles as well as their aggregation to common job profiles; we will outline this approach for the sector of information and communication technology (ICT). Formal description is accomplished by building profiles with the Resource Modeling Language (RML). Regarding architecture we focus on exchange and processing of profile description models. The practical application of our approach is demonstrated by formalization of competence descriptions given by the European e-Competence Framework (eCF).

Keywords: Collaborative Resource Management, Business Process Management, Resource Allocation, Resource Profile Aggregation.

1 Introduction

In many economic sectors the accumulation of company consortia in order to manage projects is fostered by emerging worldwide markets and broader access to foreign products, services, companies, and workforces. With the advent of enhanced communication technologies, the competition of companies in these global markets is increased. As a suitable response to these circumstances, companies need to adjust and improve their business processes continuously [3,9]. Throughout this competition

L.M. Camarinha-Matos et al. (Eds.): PRO-VE 2011, IFIP AICT 362, pp. 456–464, 2011.

partners and staff in formed collaborative business networks change fluently, which raises the need for finding and selecting new and appropriate partners. The increased interconnectedness of the markets furthermore strengthens the comparability of offers. As a result, business partner selection is one success key that companies need to manage [12]. Appropriateness of new partners can be measured in several dimensions such as reliability, performance, or quality of service.

Recent research investigated several metrics of the dimensions mentioned before for competence profiles [6,10]. In this context three research questions need to be addressed: (1) Which requirements have to be fulfilled by the new partners? (2) Which partners are capable to meet these requirements? (3) And how can these partners be found and contracted? An efficient identification of the requirements has to be based on the underlying business processes, available resources, and demanded competences. Thus competence based requirements (in this context often also referred to as profiles) can be identified and the difference to available resources can be calculated. In order to identify partners that meet these requirements a sound method to match offers with derived demands is needed. Apart from the calculation methods and models a similar level of abstraction and concept description in the models of bidders and buyers is needed to ease comparability. Finally, a platform that fosters a global view on market offers is needed. Today a multitude of platforms does exist, however, several different description methods are used and none of the existent platforms does offer a meta search concept.

2 Modeling Resource Profiles

Modeling of resource profile is related to two disciplines: business process management and human resource management. Common research approaches often foster the differentiation of business process and competence-based resource management. As a result both disciplines have utilized different modeling techniques with a minimal overlap. While this strict differentiation is also common in modeling and management techniques, several research studies [16,10,12] state that both disciplines are affected by each other. The additional strengths of an enhanced alignment of business process modeling and resource management (as mainly driven by human resource departments) have been outlined in [12]. The identification of appropriate resource requirements, such as needed competences, can be driven by an analysis of business processes managed by organizations. In this context the increased interdependence and continuous changes in business processes have to be considered.

2.1 Modeling Requirements

Resource-based analysis is subject of related research in collaborative networks [14]. Since resource requirements can only be identified in business processes if tasks contain quantitative and qualitative requirements; these requirements enclose properties of resources which may be assigned to tasks [10,11]. Yet the vast majority of business process driven resource classification schemes is based upon two dimensions only: role models and organizational hierarchies. Since the formulation and derivation of resource requirements tend to be tremendously complex, these two dimensions are insufficient to cover requirements of modern resource management (especially regarding scheduling mechanisms). Thus multidimensional, formal and machine readable approaches to business process modeling and resource description are required.

Resource description is primarily addressed by (human) resource management, hence a variety of standards describe possible attributes of (human) resources. These standards, however, either do not cover important properties necessary to describe resource requirements in business processes or are not well formalized and structured. One approach that covers the description of human resource competences is the European e-Competence Framework (e-CF), which is a result of an initiative at European level that succeeds several earlier approaches [5,4,15,1,2]. The framework currently describes 36 categories of competences for jobs in the information and communications technology sector. Nevertheless precise and formal definitions are not included. Other approaches to describe data related to human resource planning and competences such as HR-XML [7] and RCD [8] are XML-based languages.

Their data definitions are given by a set of XML schemas, thus these languages have an improved structural architecture. However these descriptions are restricted to certain aspects. Most organizational characteristics and different types of resources (non-human) are not reflected. Also on the subject of competence descriptions a distinction between the concepts skill, knowledge and competence is missing. In order to overcome these drawbacks of current approaches RML (Resource Modeling Language) as fine grained resource description approach fosters formalization [10]. RML is a precise and extensible language conforming to existing standards of competence descriptions.

2.2 Sound Modeling of Resource Profiles

The resource modeling language (RML) is a modeling approach that fulfills the described design requirements [10]. RML is based on a MOF-compliant meta model called resource meta-model (RMM). RMM is a multi-part meta model consisting of a specialized human resource meta-model (HRMM) and a competence meta-model (COMM). Existing standards such as RCD and HR-XML [8,7] have influenced the conceptual model of RMM, thus a transformation of existing descriptions in these standards can be transformed to RML. A detailed description of RML is beyond the scope of this paper, see [10] instead.

RML allows describing resources and reusable competence descriptions, similar to RCD or HR-XML. However RML enables modeling of details not covered by these standards, especially distinction of competences, skills and knowledge, as well as description of relationships and dependencies between concepts. This can be seen as particular advantage of RML. RML also enables linking of competence related information not only to personnel resources but also to role descriptions. Furthermore RML allows modeling of various organizational aspects (such as projects, groups, hierarchies or privileges). Figure 1 shows an example of a formal competence description represented in RML. The illustrated competence is called Solution Deployment 2 (compare to competence B.4 in [5]), directed connection means implies, therefore the competence shown in Figure 1 implies a set of skills, skills again imply several knowledge objects.

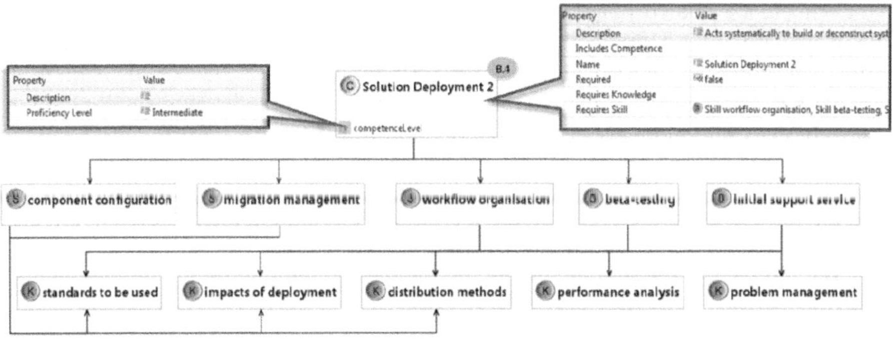

Fig. 1. RML Instance Solution deployment

Many details of RML model elements cannot be part of the graphical model, they are modeled as properties instead (see annotations left and right of the competence element shown in Figure 1). According to its MOF-compliant meta model, the RML editor stores this information in an XML-Format (which is XMIcompliant). An organizational description exemplified as RML model is depicted in Figure 2. In following example, properties of human resources (here Joe Smith) are outlined. In shown example model Joe Smith is working for an organizational unit (IT-Department) in an organizational group (SOATeam). He possesses one role (EntrepriseDeveloper) and works currently in a project (AgileCoupling). For simplicity not all details of the illustrated model elements are covered, instead properties of Joe Smith (shown in the box left to the element) are set.

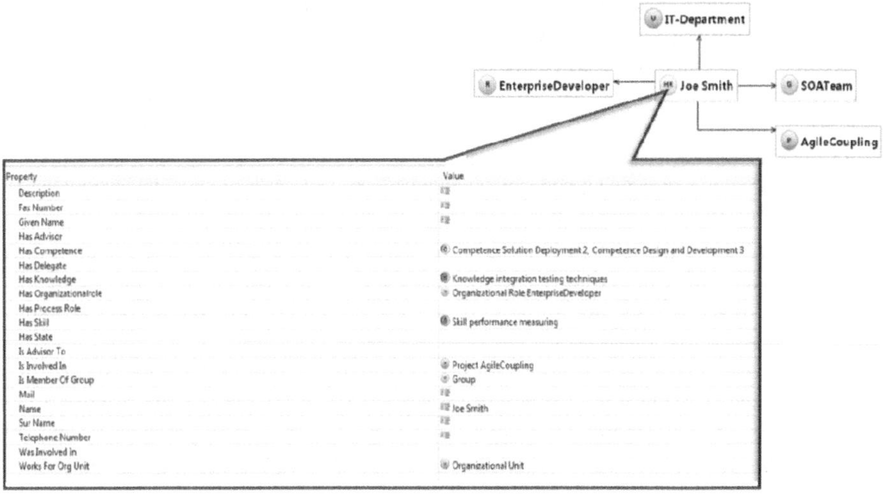

Fig. 2. Linking competence description to organizational resources

Competence related concepts are looked at particularly. According to introduced RML meta model human resources can possess set of competences, skills and knowledge besides those determined by the roles assigned. Described relationships are defined as properties shown in the box left of referred model element "Joe Smith". Thus, besides requirements of assigned organizational role (EnterpriseDeveloper) Joe Smith possesses in addition competence "Solution Deployment 2" (which we outlined in Figure 1).

3 Job Profiles in ICT

Under the umbrella of CEN/ISSS Workshop on ICT Skills, an expert group is currently working on a project named "Towards e-Job Profiles" which elaborates job profiles based on the European e-Competence Framework (e-CF) [13,19]. Standardized ICT job profiles are seen to facilitate required level of interoperability imposed in the context of collaborative networks. Standardized descriptors and common modeling languages are needed and considered to be an enabler. Job profiles help building position descriptions and career paths within an organization or collaborative network. Various views and applications can be identified in connection with job profiles.

According to [24] two concepts lay the foundations to describe job profile descriptions, namely required competences and desired results/deliverables. The latter refers to the competence definition of [17]: "Competence is demonstrated ability to apply knowledge, skills and attitudes for achieving observable results". Attitudes equate with cognitive and relational capacity. Learning outcomes referring to knowledge and skills are seen as link to qualification systems (European Qualification Framework (EQF)). Job profiles are classified into groups using criteria as customer contact (relational capacities), technical skills and domains (cognitive capacities), and required proficiency or associated hierarchy level (e.g. associate, technician, expert, principal, etc.). Thus job profiles are mostly composed of the following elements: title and short definition, tasks overview, behavior, deliverables, competences, required resources, performance indicators, dependencies and interfaces. List of ICT profiles can be found in [20,21,22]. Applications are spanning from provision of students with information concerning possible career paths to assistance of HR managers in analyzing and planning competence requirements or development of ICT curricula for training and qualification measures. Standardized ICT job profiles support bi-directional and flexible communication with business partners forming company's ecosystem. Make-or-buy decisions can be better planned and based on company's strategy and business processes.

Business processes or activities can be outsourced or contracted in short or longer term. This necessitates transparency of requirements and competences needed to run types or classes of business processes. The European e-Competence Framework differentiates four dimensions which deliver descriptors reflecting levels of business and resource planning requirements. Dimension 1 addresses competence areas referring to typical ICT business process phases within an ICT organization, namely plan, build, run (or operate), enable and manage [13]. Job profiles are supported through an online tool developed within the e-CF project. However, the e-CF does not offer or use a formal model or representation language allowing transformation of competence descriptions. Competence-based professional profiles aim defining and exchanging information about respective professional or performance standards. Profiles describe set of competences required to operate business processes, render and deliver services or refer to a specific position or role as part of a working team or project. Competence based profiles are built without any particular reference to an individual or employee [22,23]. Job profile description given as natural language description can be formalized by means of RML [10]. In conjunction with standardized profile descriptions the use of RML can result in sound calculations to determine appropriate business partners as well as new employees.

Table 1. ICT Profiles of AITTS [22]

Group	Profiles
Administrator	Administrator
Customer Advisor	IT Sales Advisor IT Service Advisor IT Trainer
Coordinator	IT Project Coordinator IT Quality Management Coordinator IT Security Coordinator
Software and Solution Developer	Digital Media Developer IT Solution Developer IT Tester Software Developer
Technician	Component Developer Industrial IT Systems Technician Security Technician

4 Information Exchange in Collaborative Scenarios

In collaborative networks (compare Fig. 3) a multitude of stakeholders is involved in the execution of inter-organizational business processes. Thus in order to ensure appropriate communication standardized message formats and service interfaces may be used. In order to identify appropriate business partners, profiles and requirements need to be described in a similar way: by the same description language and on a similar level of abstraction. Thus implementation of collaborative networks requires availability of standards to support business interactions. [19, p. 151] describe capabilities of companies to maintain partnerships and sustain strategic ecosystems supporting business transformations and "servicization" as driving force of "value chain redesign".

Business partner relationship management requires organizational structures with abilities to self-manage, self-configure and self-optimize besides the necessary culture "[...] semantic-informed self-organizing structures [...]" [23, p.8]. Semantics of profile data has to be made explicit or based on shared standards. Thus a set of competences is proposed as extension in form of a view or additional section of the concept of Business Partner Profiles (BPP) introduced by [24]. Formal representation of competence descriptions as suggested in section 2 would allow applying techniques such as information retrieval to collect information from network partners.

In our opinion continuous analysis of company's business processes reveals competence gaps and supports strategic decisions and planning concerning make-or-buy-decisions. In figure 3 for instance a collaborative business process can be automatically supported by a broker – process requirements can be met by suggested suppliers (see process step competence requirements), if requirements and profiles are provided adequately. Thus business processes analysis and modeling should in future take into account competence requirements. Furthermore information of competence requirements has to be exchanged amongst business partners forming the value chain. This necessitates a common language or formal representation allowing exchange of information or data stored in respective HR-systems. Typically, systems do fulfill required interoperability because data models do not match [17]. Secondly means of a service oriented platform can address data exchange itself, however a bunch of issues (e.g. security and confidentiality) has to be solved by such a platform.

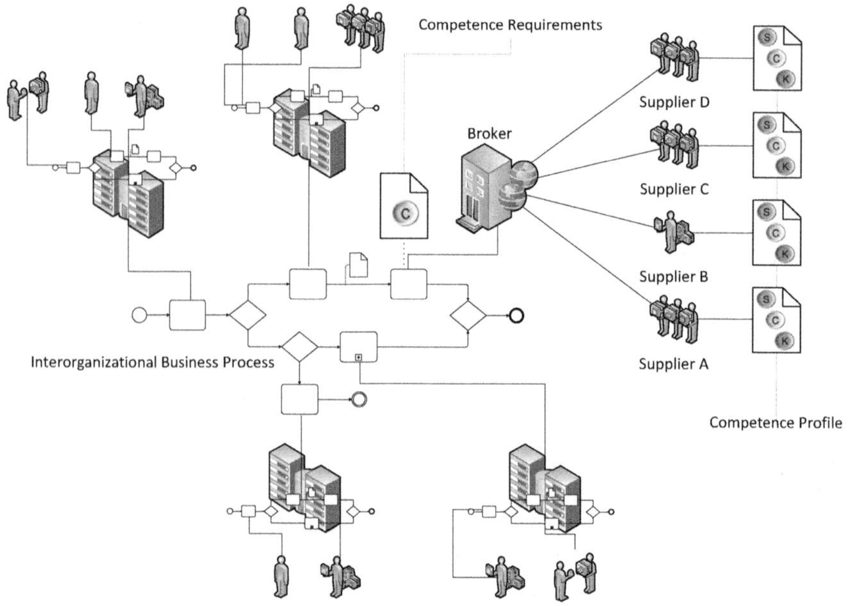

Fig. 3. Collaborative Network Scenario

5 Conclusion

In collaborative networks data exchange between participating actors and the challenge to match available information of resource profiles comes to the fore. Standards to ensure exchange of competence requirements and definitions between organizations are needed. On basis of the presented modeling language and method interoperable resource profiles can be described and analyzed. The presented resource modeling language (RML) demonstrates the potential of the combination and extension of known concepts in resource modeling, competence modeling and business process management. Competence and resource models of human resource departments can be re-used for the modeling of business process relevant requirements to resources. Furthermore existing competence models can be adapted to the actual business process requirements. In network scenarios organizations can create and exchange comparable resource models by employing the out method of goal oriented modeling guidelines.

Therefore models can be used to improve sound recruitment of new partners. To extend concepts outlined in this paper, we plan to develop mechanisms for competence gap analysis and automatic aggregation of competence profiles. Finally we strive to generate resource models automatically from existing data by the usage of transformation rules in regard to the goal oriented modeling guidelines. In order to validate the given theoretical approach and future calculation methods the evaluation in a service oriented broking scenario will be desirable.

References

1. CEN Workshop Agreement. CWA 14925: Generic ict skills profiles for the ICT supply industry—a review by CEN/ISSS ICT-skills workshop of the career space work (2004)
2. CEN Workshop Agreement. CWA 15893-1: European e-competence framework (2008)
3. Doubrovski, V., Grundler, J., Hogg, K., Zimmermann, O.: Service-oriented architecture and business process choreography in an order management scenario: Rationale, concepts, lessons learned. In: OOPSLA 2005, San Diego (2005)
4. eCCO. A european e-skills meta-framework. Technical report, AICA, Federcomin, Fondazione Politecnico di Milano. Draft Proposal (2005)
5. European e-Competence Framework 2.0. A common European framework for ICT Professionals in all industry sectors. Technical report, CEN (2010)
6. Hlaoittinun, O., Bonjour, E., Dulmet, M.: Managing the competencies of team members in design projects through multi-period task assignment. In: Camarinha-Matos, L., Boucher, X., Afsarmanesh, H. (eds.) Collaborative Networks for a Sustainable World. IFIP AICT, vol. 336, pp. 338–345. Springer, Boston (2010)
7. HR-XML Consortium, Competencies (2007/2009)
8. IEEE Learning Technology Standards Committee. RCD: Draft standard for reusable competency definitions (RCD) (2006)
9. Lenz, K., Oberweis, A.: Interorganizational business process management with xml nets. In: Ehrig, H., Reisig, W., Rozenberg, G. (eds.) Petri Net Technology for Communication-Based Systems. LNCS, vol. 2472. Springer, Heidelberg (2003)
10. Oberweis, A., Schuster, T.: A meta-model based approach to the description of resources and skills. In: Proceedings of 16th Americas Conference on Information Systems, AMCIS 2010 (2010)
11. Russell, N., van der Aalst, W.M.P., ter Hofstede, A.H.M., Edmond, D.: Workflow Resource Patterns: Identification, Representation and Tool Support. In: Pastor, Ó., Falcão e Cunha, J. (eds.) CAiSE 2005. LNCS, vol. 3520, pp. 216–232. Springer, Heidelberg (2005)

12. Schuster, T., Weiß, P.: A new approach to competence-based business partner profiles for collaborative business process management. In: Camarinha-Matos, L., Boucher, X., Afsarmanesh, H. (eds.) Collaborative Networks for a Sustainable World. IFIP AICT, vol. 336, pp. 356–363. Springer, Heidelberg (2010)
13. The European e-Competence Framework. CEN workshop agreement (CWA 15893 (part 1 & 2)). Technical report, CEN (2008)
14. van der Aalst, W.M.P., Kumar, A.: Xml-based schema definition for support of interorganizational workflow. Information Systems Research 14(1), 23–46 (2003)
15. Winterton, J., Delamare-Le Deist, F., Stringfellow, E.: Typology of knowledge, skills and competences: clarification of the concept and prototype. In: Cedefop 2005 (2005)
16. zur Mühlen, M.: Organizational management in workflow applications—issues and perspectives. Information Technology and Management 5, 271–291 (2004); Appendix: Springer-Author Discount
17. Povalej, R., Stucky, W., Weiß, P.: Conceptual Data Model for Data Interchange between HR Information Systems. In: The 11th International Conference on Informatics and Semiotics in Organisations, IFIP WG8.1 Working Conference (ICISO 2009): Information Systems in the Changing Era: Theory and Practice, IFIP WG8.1 Working Conference Proceedings. IFIP WG8.1, IEEE Press and submitted for index by INSPEC, EI (Compendex) and ISTP, April 11-12, Oral Session 11: Information Systems (4) (2009)
18. Weiß, P., Klink, S.: Collaborative services to maintain electronic business relationships. In: Camarinha-Matos, L., et al. (eds.) PRO-VE, Band Establishing The Foundation of Collaborative Networks, IFIP TC 5 Working Group 5.5 Eighth IFIP Working Conference on Virtual Enterprises, Guimarães, Portugal, Seiten 435442, Boston, September 10-12. IFIP. Springer, Heidelberg (2007)
19. CEN/ISSS Workshop on ICT Skills: Towards e-Job profiles based on the European e-Competences Framework, `http://www.cen.eu/CEN/sectors/sectors/isss/activity/Pages/wsict-skills.aspx` (last visited April 14, 2011)
20. ICT Careers Portal, Australian Computer Society, `http://www.acs.org.au/ictcareers/` (last visited April 14, 2011)
21. EUCIP Elective Profiles, `http://www.ecdl.org/files/eucip/docs/20080527022608_Intro_%20EUCIP%20Professional%20v2.4.pdf` (last visited April 14, 2011)
22. AITTS (Advanced IT Training System), 14 specialist profiles, `http://www.cert-it.com/en/it-specialists/the-14-profiles/` (last visited April 14, 2011)
23. Camarinha-Matos, L.M., Afsarmanesh, H.: Processes and Foundations for Virtual Organizations. In: IFIP TC5/WG5.5, Proceedings PRO-VE 2003 (2003)
24. Weiß, P., Klink, S.: Collaborative Services to Maintain Electronic Business Relationships. In: Proceedings of Eighth IFIP Working Conference on Virtual Enterprises, September 10-12. Springer, Boston (2007)

Aggregate Collaborative Planning in Non-hierarchical Business Networks

Ricardo Almeida, César Toscano, Luis Carneiro, and Américo Azevedo

INESC Porto, Rua Dr. Roberto Frias, 378, 4200 - 465 Porto, Portugal
ralmeida@inescporto.pt

Abstract. The last decade has been characterized by times of change, including increasing levels of globalization and competition. Collaboration allowed SMEs to respond effectively to the development of new complex products and services but presented new barriers concerning the management of their business processes and relations with partners. This paper presents a new collaborative aggregate planning for non-hierarchical business networks, where SMEs collaborate in the selection of partners and definition of the operations plan required to specify, manufacture and distribute a custom made products. The proposed approach is based on negotiations undertaken by the partners in order to promote the creation of alternative operations plans and allow a multi-criteria evaluation of the involved costs and delivery dates. The proposed approach promotes the reduction of communication between partners, a reactive analysis of changes to planning and associated impact, enhancement of trust (since all partners have the same weight on the decision process).

Keywords: Collaborative, virtual organization, aggregate, planning.

1 Introduction

Manufacturing companies are facing one of the most difficult periods after Industrial Revolution. The worldwide crisis has reduced significantly the levels of market consumption, having a high impact on the resellers' orders increasing even more competition levels. On the other side, market demand for innovative and complex products and services, require more agile organizations, leading to unique opportunities for SMEs.

This new business reality required a higher flexibility for companies and forced them to focus on business processes integration (internal and external to their organization), aiming to reduce the effort on virtual organization's management (like setup and delivery times, changes' control and associated impact evaluation to the planning, etc). Companies searched for methods and tools which could help on the support of sustainable decisions and become more reactive to market uncertainty.

This research work addresses particularly the collaborative aggregate planning of operations that takes place during the formation of non-hierarchical business networks, supporting the definition of lead times and costs for custom made and complex products.

L.M. Camarinha-Matos et al. (Eds.): PRO-VE 2011, IFIP AICT 362, pp. 465–474, 2011.

This work presents (on the first two chapters) the scope and areas of research, which resumes the methodology applied and definition of concepts related with collaborative networks. The next chapters focus on the possible approaches for collaborative planning and the proposed solution to deal with aggregate planning (which derives from a high-level product design phase). Finally, this work ends with the major conclusions and future works.

2 Background

This research was developed under the European RTD project Net-Challenge [Ref.: FP7-CP-FP229278-2], whose goal is to design and develop an integrated framework to support SMEs implement new business models and establish dynamic and non-hierarchical business networks for complex products manufacturing.

The scope definition and requirements for this research work were extracted from the analysis of the six companies involved in the project; two belonging to the textile and garment sector, two from the shoe industry and the last two from the machine tool industry.

Some authors [3] resumed these requirements and proposed, as methodology for non-hierarchical collaboration networks, two main levels to be considered: management of the Business Community activities and management of the temporary Virtual Organization. Regarding answering to these two levels, the author presented four major phases: Build, Form, Operate and Dissolve. The first and last phases to respond to the first level; and the second and third phases to respond to the last level.

During the Form phase, partners collaborate to specify the product, find solution for the customer needs and set up a price and lead-time to manufacture the production batch. For this research work, the focus has been dedicated to this phase, concerning to collaborative planning and partner's quotation evaluation, which requires ICT tools to support managers in decision making.

3 Related Research Areas

A collaborative network (CN) is constituted by a variety of entities (organizations and people) that are largely autonomous, geographically distributed and heterogeneous in terms of their operating environment, culture, social capital and goals [1]. Usage of computer networks to support collaborative networks and the shared belief of a win-win relationship to achieve a goal which would never be possible working individually are some of their major characteristics. When integrating such kind of networks, companies aim to build a new organization of larger dimension, access new markets and produce new products and services, share risks, develop synergies for investigation and supply a wider service (upstream and downstream) for their customers. These kinds of networks are characterized by an intensive exchange of detailed data with its suppliers and customers who may consider, for example, actual and future load of machines, availability of resources, forecasting and orders' progress.

Considering governance model, business networks can be hierarchical or non-hierarchical [4]. The hierarchical relationship (hierarchical network) is characterized by the existence of one leading partner that controls the network and settles the operational rules. It is the superior partner that makes the rules and dictates. In a non-hierarchical network, all partners have the same status, that is to say, no one has a special position or leads the network. Therefore, all decisions affecting the partnership are mutually agreed upon. In this type of networks, one partner may assume the coordination responsibilities, but has no dominant status over the other partners.

4 Collaborative Planning Approaches

Production planning is one of the most critical business processes on traditional industrial companies and assumes the same importance on CNs. The major challenge of production planning on CNs arises of how to link and coordinate planning between the different parts that comprise the network. The need for a process of negotiation (coordination scheme between two or more parties) was detected by several authors, to ensure the synchronization between production plans from distinct organizations.

Planning as a negotiation process

Some authors defined a coordination scheme, through which plans of two or more decision-making units are aligned [5]. This scheme requires all members to adapt their individual plans in order to be developed an overall planning acceptable by all supply chain members, and refusing to follow any centralized planning approach that do not consider an active contribution of all partners. The same author defined Collaborative Planning (CP) as a joint decision making process of individual ("local") production plans (supply chain partners), with the aim of achieving coordination to create an overall optimized solution for a business opportunity. CP might also be defined as a connection of planning processes; local to their planning domains, but that collaborates in order to create a common and mutually agreed upon plan [7]. This collaboration is achieved through an exchange of relevant information. Thus, input data is updated faster and planning results become more accurate.

Collaborative planning involves activities by means of which individuals coordinate their planning processes [6]. Individuals predominantly plan according to the goals of their own department, but in cooperative relationships they additionally try to create possibilities for the optimization of others' planning. Thus, CP includes aspects that enable the other person to recognize how individual plans should be adapted, according to which criteria the planning can be optimized, and which restrictions in the common planning must be accepted. In short, CP describes how individuals are able to orient their plans towards each other to reach a joint optimization of the planning across departmental boundaries.

Centralized and decentralized planning approaches

The choice of applying a collaborative approach has revealed several challenges to organizations. One of the most challenging is the idea of a centralized planning that must be followed and achieved to guarantee the overall success. Some authors presented some doubts about the appropriateness of a centralized planning approach [8]. Some of the constraints pointed by these authors are the multi-network involvement of partners (since they participate on several networks, the probability of interference on their planning activities is extremely high) and unwillingness to share information (most of the time, companies are not available to share information about resources and capabilities).

When working on a centralized planning approach, all decisions lead to an optimal solution at a first try, since the calculation is provided by a unique entity, based on the theoretical capacity of each partner. A lack of transparency of the overall decision-situation leads to poor coordination in decisions involving several of these intra-organizational planning domains [8]. To establish coordination in this situation, centralized collaborative planning solutions provide remedy by offering decision models and processes. The delivery time calculation is performed using traditional sequence algorithms, assuming each partner as a local resource that is fully available. Such kind of planning approaches are only possible when the supply chain partners belong to the same group of companies or when partners have a dedicated capacity (which is assumed from the beginning of the business opportunity). This approach was defined as hierarchical organized coordination [9].

When working with actual and complex business scenarios (like the textile sector, for instance), the centralized approach presents several constraints, like the loss of local autonomy, which is not accepted by most companies. Supply chains are most commonly planned and controlled on a decentralized basis, which are less advantageous and profitable than the centralized approach [8]. The coordination required for this planning approach is provided via bilateral negotiations with relevant partners on the supply chain [9]. The authors assume that the first step should be the definition of the best planning for the organization; then, it should only depend on the direct customers and direct suppliers. This could reduce drastically the conflicts and the loss of confidential information.

5 Aggregate Collaborative Planning

5.1 Scope and Major Requirements

Business companies have revealed that a daily major concern is dedicated to manage the articulation between their local productions planning with the requirements of their customers, especially when depending on partners' responses about their own availability [2]. According to key-users of these companies, this is one of the most expensive processes due to the high number of activities dedicated for control and communication (considered as non-value added activities) as well the required number of iterations to achieve a common agreement (between the internal production plan and partners' availability).

Another important issue presented by these key-users [2] was the need of a quick and accurate response to customer's requirements about delivery date and cost, which occur in two different moments. The first moment is triggered after the contact of the customer with one company, where the business opportunity is presented and a first prediction on delivery dates and costs is requested from the company. Usually, the company analyses the business opportunity and (when doesn't have enough knowledge about all manufacturing phases) requests some help to other companies to define the major product design phases and to calculate the needed time for each operation. The next step includes the definition of precedence between all operations and, finally, a rough plan is developed according to the theoretical capacities of each company (defined at the beginning of each year), to calculate the delivery time. Regarding prices, the cost of all operations are summarized. Finally, the proposal is sent to the final customer.

The second moment is triggered when the company receives the customer order. The business case company requests the participation of the other companies (contacted on the first moment) in order to validate if the previous agreements (considering cost and availability) remain valid for the customer order. A detailed approach is performed, taking the product design phase to lower levels of the product structure, defining detailed bill-of-materials and routings. A high number of technical documents are exchanged requiring many activities of control and communication. Also the availability of each partner is validated in this moment, asking for each partner to confirm their capacity and propose new dates if necessary. Every change (to the defined plan) needs to be evaluated (since each company analysis the new proposal on their local planning) requiring a great effort for to achieve a common understanding. Also, since this planning is not visible to all companies, it's very difficult to work for an optimal global solution, increasing the number of iterations to achieve a final agreement. The same situation occurs anytime a change is requested by one partner, for example, due to a delay of his raw material supplier. In this case, the partner will not follow the predicted plan, and all members need to re-adjust their plans.

The choice of the best alternative plans was also referred by key-users as a difficult activity, due to several aspects. One of the presented arguments was related to the criteria used (and the associated indicators) which differ from the type of business, the company's goals and even the type of business opportunity. Besides this complex approach, it was also referred the different types of data assumed for each indicator and the high number of possible plans (due to the combinations of different partners for each operation) which make almost impossible, for key-users, to select the best proposal without using empirical techniques. Key-users are aware of the uncertainty of empirical decisions and desire an effective method to help them on this type of decisions.

5.2 Multi-criteria Planning Methodology

Net-Challenge's project designed a collaborative aggregate planning based on a negotiation process, as a response to the needs of the first phase of the production planning (described on the previous chapter). The term "aggregate" was used to express the definition and planning of major operations (and not detailed operations planning for shop floor control) which are assigned to partners in the virtual organization (VO) being formed, leaving the operation's details for partner's own management. This approach is based on a decentralized negotiation model, which allows partners to propose new delivery dates and costs, represented graphically at Image 1.

The proposed approach for aggregate collaborative planning includes two steps:

- The customer presents the business opportunity requirements to the Broker (company that identified the business opportunity and is responsible for the interaction with the customer). After the elicitation of the major requirements on the required custom made product, the product concept/design is defined by the Broker and by the new partners that are invited to join the VO, based on their specific competencies and availability [3]. These partners are called "core partners" since they integrate Product Design activities and share some risk in responding to the overall business opportunity. In this context, the necessary main operations of the virtual organization are defined by the Broker and core partners, with its sequence and timing restrictions (start, finish and leading times), taking into account the due date specified or expected by the customer and theoretical capacities defined on each partner's profile.

- In the beginning of the planning process the criteria for partner selection are defined and agreed by core partners.
- Additional partners (called "potential partners") are invited to participate on several operations. Their selection is performed according a criteria (for example, certification or feedback from previous negotiations) previously defined by the Broker and core partners. This gives rise to a first operations "rough" plan that the Broker proposes to all the members in the VO;
- Partners receive the first "rough" plan and a set of requests for quotations, one for each operation allocated to him. Each partner proceeds then to a local analysis of their local production capacity to evaluate if it is possible to accept the proposed dates and lead time for the indicated quantity. A quotation is then formulated, accepting the proposed plan or proposing an alternative for the request.

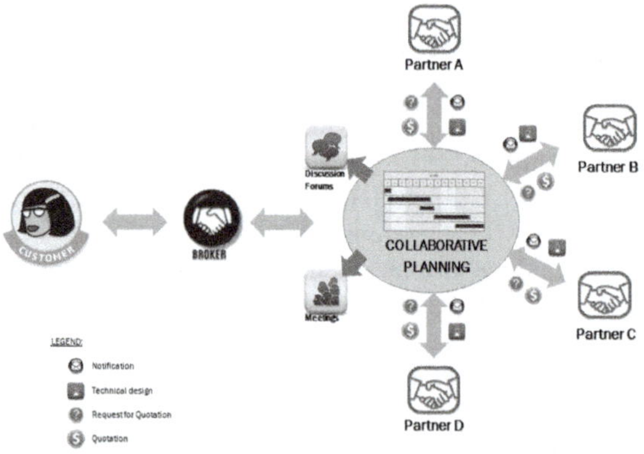

Fig. 1. Aggregate planning approach

This approach, although centralized when considering the supporting ICT architecture (for the graphical view and management of requests and quotations), promotes a decentralized approach on the definition of the VO's planning, since each partner is capable of proposing and participating actively on the characterization of each required operation and to request from any other partner a change on the plan (through the creation of a request for quotation).

The major characteristic is the inexistence of a major partner imposing a plan to the others; every core partner has the same "weight" on the decision process over the operations planning of the network (major condition for non-hierarchical networks). The Broker has the responsibility to coordinate this process and promote the resolution of any conflicts. Major advantages can be resumed as follows: reduction of the "traditional" communication, like e-mails and phone calls, between partners (since the planning is shared and available for any partner in the VO); accurate control of any change and evaluation of the associated impact, with the ability to apply the necessary events to handle those changes; enhancement of trust, due to the increased visibility and to the fact that core partners have the same weight on the decision process. Each change proposed by any member in the VO will create new possible plan which, after been analyzed and accepted by the involved partners, will create a new (accepted) plan which will be evaluated following common criteria (defined in the very beginning of the process); this topic is explained on the next chapter.

5.3 Solutions Quality Evaluation

Each partner can propose new delivery dates, lead times and costs, directly on a web-based planning graphical tool which is available and shared by all VO's partners. Every time a partner proposes a change on a given operation, he is (in fact) asking the affected partner to accept this change (and declare its cost) or to make a counter-proposal. Each negotiation round correspond to a pre-defined time period (for example, 2 days) available to discuss/negotiate delivery times and costs, allowing partners to present quotations for each request-for-quotation (RFQ) performed by other partners. For each change proposed (which "triggers" RFQs to all involved partners), it is asked to the partners to present quotations which might answer, integrally, to the asked RFQ or even suggest new changes. When a proposal has 100% agreement of all partners ("no pending notifications") it will be considered a plan; although it still allows to be changed by any VO's partner, as long as the negotiation time period doesn't expired. This plan is serialized according multi-criteria (previously defined by the Broker and core partners). If the negotiation time period expires and some changes are still waiting for partner's quotations, they will be avoided and it will only be invoked the "effective" plans. Image 2 presents a flowchart representing the steps taken to create a plan. An overall scheme is presented on Image 3, representing a negotiation round.

The criteria to be used are, collaboratively, defined by the Broker and core partners in the initial setup of the VO, thus specifying the criteria that will support subsequent decisions in the process. For each of these criteria, it's possible to define a degree of importance, using a percentage score as a final weighting factor, which will used for calculate the best partner proposal. So each criteria considered do not have the same importance but each has an importance expressed by a ranking system. One of the major concerns of the criteria definition is to include criterions which maximize the probability of gain of the customer's proposal and not only the internal efficiency of the network. This is an important step to assure the requirements of non-hierarchical networks.

The requirements analysis carried out with business case companies confirmed the two criteria are considered is most situations: **price** and **delivery date**. However, in the model proposed, it is included additional criteria to promote a wider approach and business application.

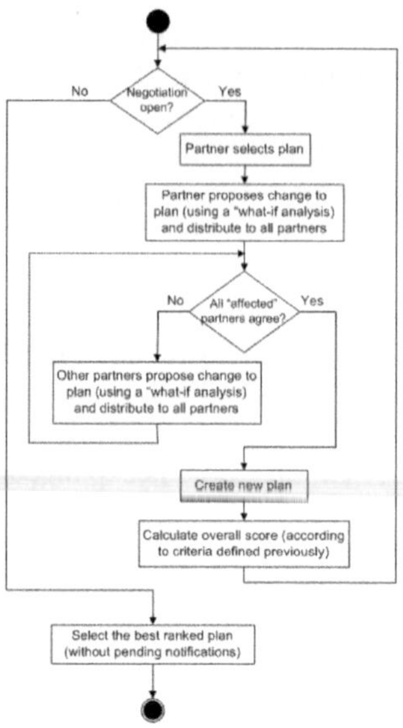

Fig. 2. Creation of an alternative plan

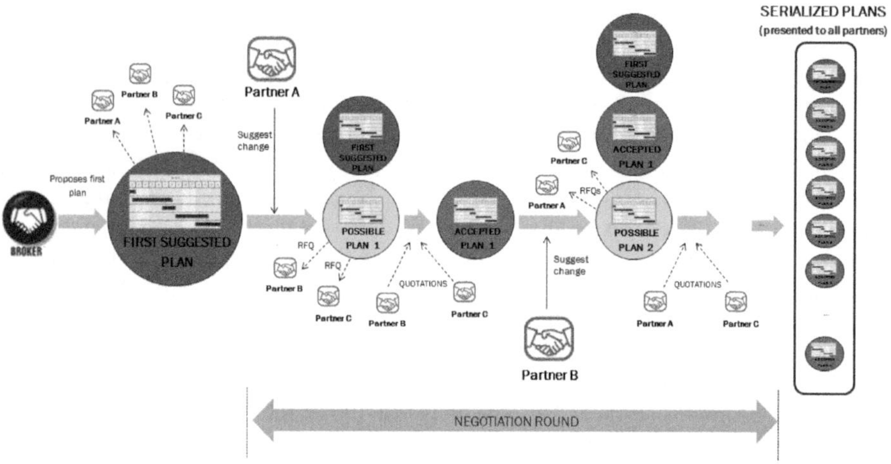

Fig. 3. Negotiation round

In order to perform a multi-criteria analysis and assist in decision making, normalization criterion must be defined and used. For the case in question, linear normalization was selected. The basic principle for this standardization was the definition of minimum and maximum values, and assignment of simple formulas for the normalization of attributes for benefits and costs. For each indicator, it must be defined if it's considered a cost or benefit, in order to apply different formulas (presented on Image 4).

$$\textbf{Costfunction} \quad \sum \frac{\frac{1}{value}}{\frac{1}{minimum}} * weightfactor$$

$$\textbf{Benefitfunction} \quad \sum \frac{value}{maximum} * weightfactor$$

Fig. 4. Formulas used for attributes' normalization

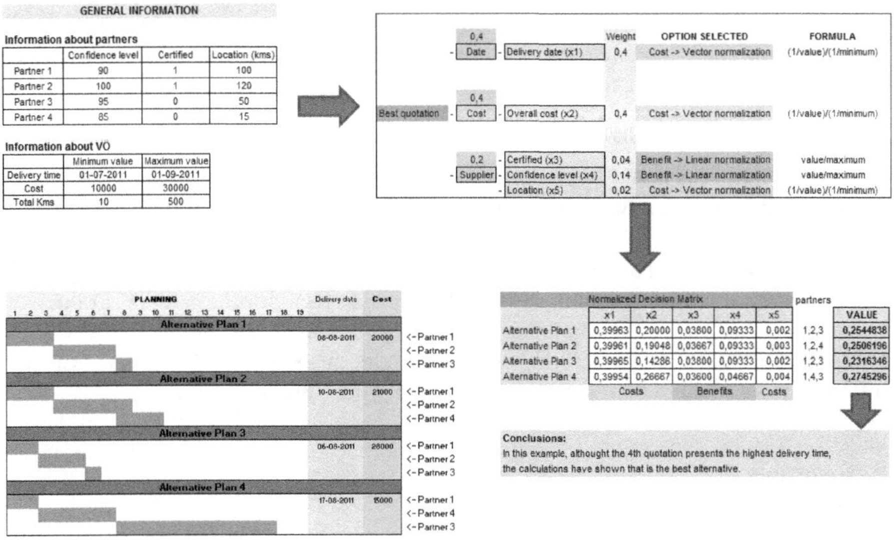

Fig. 5. Example of algorithm calculation for evaluation of alternative plans

All values are summed (costs and benefits), resulting in a value between 0 and 1, which represents the score of the alternative plan (closest to 1, the better result).

Image 5 shows an evaluation of four alternative plans, considering five criteria elements: delivery date, cost, confidence level, partner's certification and location. The tables presented on the left side of Image 5 present the indicators and the Gantt charts of the four possible plans being evaluated. The tables on the right side of the same image resume the formulas used (for benefit and costs) and the calculation for the normalization process. The algorithm is responsible for data normalization (applying the related formulas) and applies the weight factor for the indicators of each alternative plan. As final operation, the algorithm sorts the results, defining the best plan to the higher result retrieved (closest to 1).

6 Conclusions and Further Developments

In this research work, it has been studied several concepts related with virtual business networks and collaborative planning processes. Integrated on the Net-Challenge European project it proposes an innovative collaborative planning approach, based on a truthful concept of negotiation between partners. It includes the definition and organization of operations and a concrete set of activities, with the goal of defining and organizing the operations that are required by the product's high level design, and given the customers' specific requirements (delivery date and price among others). The proposed approach reveals several major advantages, like the reduction of the traditional communication means (since all information is centralized and shared by all partners), ability of partners to suggest new delivery dates in a decentralized negotiation model, evaluations of alternative plans based on multi-criteria and a guarantee of partner's data privacy, since other partners don't access to partner's local planning information. This approach assumes a major role for managers to provide sustainable decisions on their companies. At the moment, the presented approach is being developed by Net-Challenge's partners and will be tested on the business case companies described.

As future work, it's expected to validate the proposed approaches on several industries and evaluate the possibility of including new capabilities of integration with local information systems (in order to allow managers for an automatic production capacity validation with their local production planning).

Acknowledgements. The authors would like to acknowledge the co-funding of the European Commission within NMP priority of the Seventh RTD Framework Programme for the Net Challenge project (Innovative Networks of SMEs for Complex Products Manufacturing). The authors also acknowledge the valuable collaboration provided by the project team during the research work.

References

[1] Camarinha-Matos, L.M., Abreu, A.: A contribution to understand collaboration benefits. In: Emerging Solutions for Future Manufacturing Systems. IFIP, vol. 159, pp. 281–298 (2005)

[2] Carneiro, L., et al.: An innovative framework supporting SME networks for complex product manufacturing. In: Collaborative Networks for a Sustainable World, vol. 336, pp. 204–211 (2010), doi:10.1007/978-3-642-15961-9_24

[3] Kankaanpää, T., Shamsuzzoha, A., Carneiro, L., Almeida, R., Helo, P., Fornasiero, R., Ferreira, P.S., Chiodi, A.: Methodology for non-hierarchical collaboration networks for complex products manufacturing. In: Collaborative Networks for a Sustainable World. IFIP AICT, vol. 336, pp. 204–211 (2010), doi:10.1007/978-3-642-15961-9_24

[4] Pisano, G.P., Verganti, R.: Which kind of collaboration is right for you? Harvard Business Review (USA) 86(12), 78–86 (2008)

[5] Stadler, A.: A framework for collaborative planning and state-of-the-art. Springer, Heidelberg (2007)

[6] Windischer, A., et al.: Characteristics and organizational constraints of collaborative planning. Springer, Heidelberg (2007)

[7] Kilger, C., Reuter, B.: Collaborative Planning. In: Supply Chain Management and Advanced Planning, Concepts, Models, Software and Case Studies, pp. 259–278 (2005)

[8] Breiter, A., et al.: Coordinarion in Supply Chain Management - Review and Identification of directions for future research. In: Logistik Management, Systeme, Methoden, Integration, pp. 11–42. Springer, Heidelberg (2009)

[9] Fischer, J.-G., Gneiting, P.: Collaborative Planning Processes. In: Build to Order - The Road to the 5 Day Car. Springer (2008)

Part XVII

Networks in Crisis and Emergency Scenarios

Towards a Collaborative Network Paradigm for Emergency Services

Ovidiu Noran

Griffith University, Australiia
O.Noran@griffith.edu.au

Abstract. The rate and intensity of large scale disasters, natural and induced by humans via deforestation, carbon emissions, terrorism etc appears to be steadily increasing. At the same time, mankind appears to create increasingly complex systems to sustain its survival, quality of life and evolution. Ensuring that the people and their vital systems survive and cope with the natural disasters require proper preparation, response and recovery. Unfortunately, often the organisations put in place to deliver emergency services operate in a sub-optimal way due to a plethora of factors, with a prominent role played by the lack of proper inter-operation and collaboration. This paper proposes the use of Collaborative Networks (CN) concept in Emergency Services from an Enterprise Architecture (EA) perspective so as to take advantage of the wealth of knowledge accumulated in these domains. Following an introduction and a brief review of the state-of-the-art, the paper justifies the adoption of the CN paradigm and demonstrates the use of an EA approach previously tested for the CN domain, in the Emergency Services area.

Keywords: Disaster Management, Emergency Service, Enterprise Architecture, Collaborative Networks.

1 Introduction

Natural and man-made disasters appear to affect mankind in a more profound way than ever before. Globalisation, climate change and the increasing complexity of the systems ensuring our well-being and survival are a few crucial factors. Due to historical, administrative and geographical reasons, the organisations put in place to prepare for and assist the society in coping with the consequences of disaster events have evolved independently. The result is a heterogeneous collection of emergency services worldwide that often have significant difficulties in cooperating and interoperating in order to achieve a much needed synergy – as typically, handling disaster events require resources and capabilities beyond those of any individual organisation, whether local, state or national.

This paper proposes the use of a Collaborative Network (CN) approach in order to tackle some of the causes that cannot be addressed in the short amount of time available to respond to a disaster event. It argues that the interoperability-related issues must be addressed in advance and in a holistic manner – so that when a disaster event occurs, an efficient, collaborative task force can promptly be put together.

L.M. Camarinha-Matos et al. (Eds.): PRO-VE 2011, IFIP AICT 362, pp. 477–485, 2011.

2 Collaborative Disaster Management – The Problems

Emergency Services cooperation is often mandated by laws and frameworks at state, national and international level (e.g. [1-4]). However, simply mandating / coercing organisations into cooperation and using high-level generic frameworks does not bring true collaboration and / or interoperability. Consequences include extended response time, confusion / dispute as to who is in charge and when, difficulty in coordinating with other teams / systems due to incompatibilities in infrastructure and delays in validating and using the inevitable flood of information generated by a disaster event. For example, lack of agreement on the type and delivery format of warning messages may result in a lack of / delay in warnings or in the saturation of the intended audience with ambiguous/irrelevant warnings, leading to delayed or no preventive / evacuation action from the recipients and subsequent injury and life loss.

The typical approaches taken in trying to eliminate the above-mentioned problems have been either leaning towards centralisation / hierarchical command or towards the federalisation of emergency services. However, both alternatives have been criticised by authors and community response [5-7] because irrespective of the approach used, proper emergency response and cooperation has still not been achieved. The lack of preparedness and readiness appears to be caused by inadequate information and knowledge flow and quality between the participants [8, 9], lack of trust, organisational confusion and even misguided perception of competition. An alternative approach [10] proposes the use of military operations-inspired network-enabled capabilities as the backbone of disaster management. However, the authors recognise that this model works only as a component of the overall disaster management effort and could lead to excessive reliance on the infrastructure alone.

In finding a solution to this apparent conundrum, it must be recognised that true, prompt and efficient collaboration requires that organisational cultures, processes and resources of the participants must display the required preparedness [11]. This requires access to a plethora of interdisciplinary information and knowledge not always obvious or readily available to planners and disaster managers.

The above-described situation is significantly similar to that of commercial enterprises that need to cope with a global business environment requiring them to tackle projects beyond their own resources and knowledge. A typical response to this problem in the commercial domain is to set up or join Collaborative Networks (CNs) that act as 'breeding environments' for Virtual Organisations (VOs) that can be promptly created in order to bid for, win and complete projects requiring combined resources and know-how.

3 Adopting a Collaborative Network Approach

Calls to set up and improve cooperation through various collaborative artefacts are common in medical / emergency response reports, conferences and journals; unfortunately, the actual implementation of such recommendations is still limited.

Firstly, it is often difficult to even achieve stakeholder consensus (common image) on the present (AS-IS) situation, which hinders progress towards defining the optimal future (TO-BE) state of affairs. This is often accompanied by lack of agreement on an optimal roadmap to achieve the TO-BE caused by the various ways of 'getting things done' used by the participants, showing organisation, culture and even language gaps that result in a semantic interoperability barrier between the participants especially at middle and upper management level. Interoperability is paramount in the efficiency and survival of a CN – therefore it has been (and still is) extensively researched with aspects and dimensions identified and partial solutions proposed (e.g. [12, 13] and many others). The difficult area of organisation and culture has also been tackled (e.g. [14]). This wealth of interoperability knowledge could be applied to the disaster management area under the CN paradigm.

Secondly, it appears that there is insufficient emphasis laid on the life cycle / life history aspect of the participant organisations, potential network and other relevant entities - including the disaster event(s). The interactions required to collaborate and interoperate must be considered in this context because all entities of interest are continuously evolving.

Adopting a CN approach for disaster management / emergency response organisations would result in multiple benefits. Technical (infrastructure) and syntactic interoperability aspects could be addressed in the beginning. However, importantly, the participants will also have the time to address the organisational / cultural interoperability aspect by getting to 'know each other' and thus build trust. Such human-related processes cannot be rushed and thus be successfully performed during the very limited set-up time or the operation of the disaster management task force (when all efforts and resources should be focused on the disaster event).

Enterprise Architecture (EA) is a change management approach bridging management and engineering best-practice. An EA perspective, by means of artefacts such as EA frameworks and an EA-based guiding methodology would complement the CN approach by facilitating common understanding among all stakeholders and formulating methods to set up / operate Disaster Management Collaborative Networks (DMCNs) covering all aspects relevant to the envisaged emergency response tasks.

3.1 Specific Features of the Disaster Management Collaborative Network

A DMCN would have some specific features that must be observed in order to achieve a working model. Thus, the time available for set-up of a Disaster Management VO (DMVO) is significantly shorter than that available for a project bidding process. In addition, the DMCN, its participants and the DMVO(s) produced would operate under tighter / legislated operational guidelines set by the relevant Governments and national / international frameworks. The commercial and competitive motivations of the typical CN participants would be transformed into the efficiency / interoperability motivation translated into lives and physical / intellectual property rescued. Thus, the classic decision processes to create / join / remain / leave the CN for most partners would be mandated from outside. Partial (reference) models should be abstracted out of the lessons learned from past disasters and used to speed up VO creation. They could be classified on type reflecting the location (e.g. flooding, tornadoes, wildfires, severe storms in Australia [15]) and customised to allow for specific intensity, duration, side-effects and consequences.

The DMVO produced by the DMCN will not bid for projects, but rather be created for and assigned a specific one, namely the management of the disaster event. The management structure, communication infrastructure, and other organisational interoperability issues would have been sorted out in advance, ensuring prompt response (readiness) and thus addressing a frequent weakness of crisis management. Human-related aspects requiring time such as trust, culture, and recognition (the latter featuring prominently in volunteer-based organisations [16, 17]) could be more specifically tackled using the concept of an 'emergency services academy' with local (state based) branches providing training based on a unique interstate curriculum (see [18] for an early initiative).

The 'lead' (initiating) partner(s) within the DMCN could be the major government bureaus / agencies (e.g. Attorney General's Office, Federal Emergency Management Agency etc) while normal partners could be local and volunteer-based emergency services, contractors and other relevant third parties.

In conclusion, while significant challenges in the domains of CN [19] and Enterprise Interoperability [14, 20] remain, adopting the CN paradigm allows to use tested research results and more mature artefacts. The EA perspective adds the life cycle dimension and ensures a whole-system, consistent approach as further shown.

4 Using Enterprise Architecture Artefacts in the Approach

In order to test the concept, in this research we have selected a reference Architecture Framework (AF) obtained by generalising several other AFs and thus potentially expressive enough to contain all the elements necessary to express all relevant disaster management aspects using EA artefacts. This AF is GERAM (Generalised Enterprise Reference Architecture and Methodology), described in ISO 15704:2005 [21]. Among others, GERAM has been used in practice to guide EA projects [22], assess other enterprise AFs [23-25], build a structured repository of AF elements for a project management decision support system [26] and to define an Environmental Management approach for CNs [27]. The main component of the reference architecture of GERAM is a MF (called GERA) containing an extensive set of aspects including life cycle, management, organisation, human and decision, corresponding to various stakeholder concerns [28]. For more details on GERAM and GERA see [21].

Subsets of GERA MF can and have been used towards modelling formalisms used in the creation of life cycle-based business models. For example, Fig. 1 shows on the left hand side a high level representation of a disaster event, taking into account its relevant life cycle phases and possible relations to other events. The typical GERA 'Detailed Design' and 'Implementation' life cycle phases can designate particular features of the event(s) – e.g. earthquake time, epicentre and duration, or tsunami epicentre, spread, wave speed, height etc. Note that the detail of the diagram is limited as a high level business model and some irrelevant life cycle phases have been omitted (shown dashed in the figure).

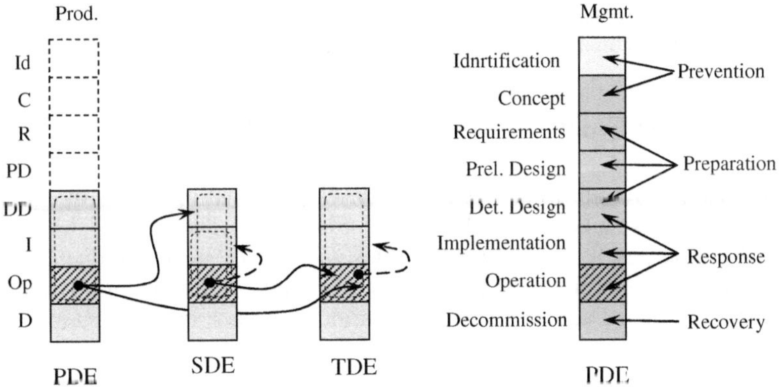

Legend:

PDE: Primary Disaster Event; SDE: Secondary Disaster Event; TDE: Tertiary …
▯ : Production view ▯ : Management view ●–> : Possible scenario

Fig. 1. Disaster event mapping and modelling using a GERA-based formalism

Using this kind of representation, it can be conveyed for example that a Primary Disaster Event (PDE) can trigger / influence other events (SDE, TDE). For example, an earthquake event (PDE) can trigger a tsunami (SDE) that can in turn trigger a partial nuclear meltdown (TDE). However PDE can also influence TDE directly. The diagram also shows that events can influence themselves (see arrows from Operation to Implementation within same entity) e.g. in the case of chain reactions etc. The right hand side of Fig. 1 shows how the life cycle phases of a disaster event can be mapped to typical disaster management activities [2]. Such graphical diagrams are useful in getting all the stakeholders to grasp a common understanding of disaster event aspects and help overcome the 'fuzzy' cultural / linguistic semantic interoperability barriers.

The paper argues that an EA approach can also provide an overarching life cycle-based approach in setting up and operating an emergency management CN aiming to produce emergency response VOs dealing with disaster events. In order to test this assumption, the author has used a 'method to build methods' applicable for specific types of EA tasks (projects), based on an original approach abiding by EA principles and tested in several case studies (e.g. [26, 29]). In a first step, the user is prompted to create a list containing entities of interest to the project in question, including project participants and target entities (organisations / systems being created). A second step comprises the creation of business models showing the relations between the previously identified entities in the context of their lifecycles, i.e. illustrating how entities influence each other during their life histories. The third and final step assists the user in inferring the set of project activities by reading and interpreting the previous representations for each life cycle phase of the project and other target entities. The resulting activities can be decomposed to a level deemed suitable for the intended audience. Due to its scope and to space limitations, the paper will cover only the first and second meta-methodology steps, focusing on the benefits of creating business models showing all relevant aspects of the participating entities. For comprehensive details on all meta-methodology steps see [29].

5 Modelling the Emergency Services CN and VO

Fig. 2 shows a possible business model of the creation and operation of a DMCN using a modelling formalism derived from the GERA MF. The level of detail in the figure has been purposely kept low (life cycles and management / production views only) so as to avoid confusion and to promote common understanding. If required, several diagrams may be added, focusing on various aspects – in which case attention must be paid to maintaining information consistency across models.

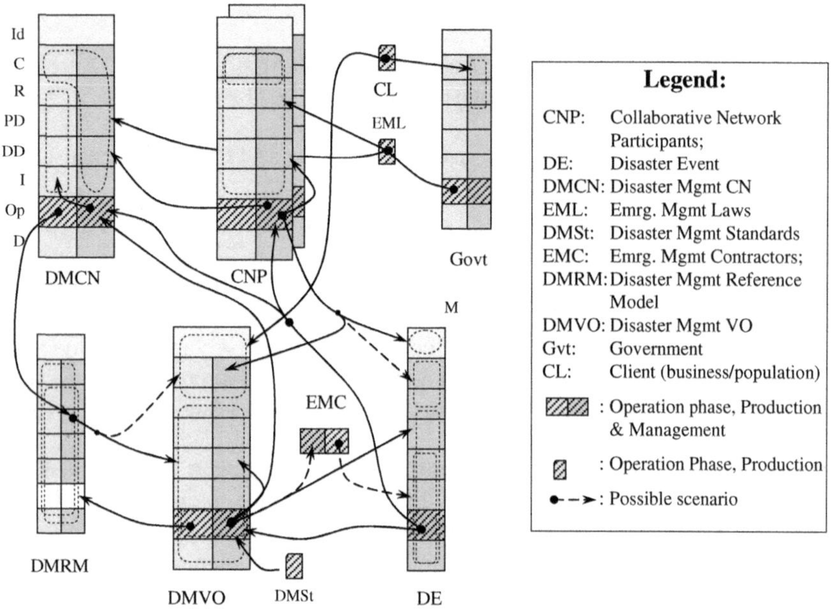

Life cycle phases: Id: Identification; C=concept; R=requirements, PD=preliminary design, DD=detailed design, I=implementation, Op=operation, D=decommissioning. *Other aspects:* P=Production / Service, M=management

Fig. 2. Life cycle-based business model of DMCN and DMVO creation / operation

The figure shows how a disaster event DE can be managed by a DMVO which is quickly put together by a DMCN, using suitable reference model(s) DMRM (if applicable). As can be seen, the DMVO would manage only the 'urgent' life cycle phases of DE (i.e. short-term preparation, response and recovery), while prevention and long-term preparation phases would be managed by the DMCN and possibly also by individual network members (CNP). Due to the importance of disaster management, significant parts of the CNP and DMCN life cycles are influenced directly by the local / federal Gvt and by national / international laws and treaties.

The 'clients' (CL in Fig. 2) are businesses and population that are being assisted in case of DE and who provide feedback used to improve Gvt and DMVO in the future. Emergency management contractors EMC (or other third parties such as foreign rescue teams etc) contribute to DE management. While not necessarily part of the DMCN or DMVO, they must coordinate their efforts with the DMVO (arrow from DMVO operation to EMC management).

The arrow from DMVO's Management side of the Operation life cycle phase to some of its upper phases represents a very important 'partial redesign' capability, showing a need for the DMVO to be *agile* and adapt in real time in the face of rapidly changing conditions on the ground that are typical of some disaster events. Any major redesign will involve the DMCN, CNP, and Gvt and will be reflected in the subsequent DMVOs being created. Lessons learned in the operation of the DMVOs should be used towards building a repository of reference models (DMRM) that will help accelerate DMVO creation and thus improve emergency services readiness.

6 Conclusions and Further Work

Collaboration and interoperation are necessary and required in disaster management. Unfortunately, this often occurs in a sub-optimal manner due to the typical difficulties encountered when attempting to put together a heterogeneous task force in a very limited time. Lack of trust, different organisation / geographic cultures, diverse communication infrastructures and a limited or missing life cycle-based perspective of the disaster event(s) and of the participants' roles are decisive factors that can be addressed by prior preparation in a suitable environment. This paper has argued that emergency response organisations could significantly benefit by adopting a CN paradigm applied from an EA perspective to ensure a whole-system approach and has attempted to support this hypothesis by providing a high-level example involving EA artefacts. Further work is required to validate the proposed approach in several case studies involving various types of disaster events so as to triangulate the findings.

References

1. Government of South Australia. Emergency Management Act, 2004 (2004), http://www.legislation.sa.gov.au/LZ/C/EMERGENCY_MANAGEMENT_ACT2004.aspx (March 30, 2011)
2. Australian Government. Attorney's General's Office - Emergency Management in Australia (March 2011), http://www.ema.gov.au/
3. Federal Emergency Management Agency. National Response Framework (2011), http://www.fema.gov/pdf/emergency/nrf/about_nrf.pdf (March 30, 2011)
4. United Nations International Strategy for Disaster Reduction Secretariat (UNISDR). Hyogo Framework for Action 2005-2015: Building the resilience of nations and communities to disasters (March 2011), http://www.preventionweb.net/1037_hyogoframeworkforactionenglish.pdf
5. Clark, J.: Practical aspects of federalizing disaster response. Critical Care 10, 107–113 (2006)

6. Wiese, C.R.: Organizing Homeland Security after Katrina: is adaptive management what's missing? Public Administration Review 66(3), 302–318 (2006)
7. 't Hart, P., et al.: The Politics of Crisis Management: Public Leadership under Pressure. Journal of Homeland Security and Emergency Management (2005)
8. Wickramasinghe, N., von Lubitz, D.K.J.E.: Knowledge Based Enterprises: Theories and Fundamentals. Journal of Homeland Security and Emergency Management 5 (2007)
9. Prizzia, R., Helfand, G.: Emergency preparedness and disaster management in Hawaii. Disaster Prevention and Management 10(3), 163–172 (2001)
10. von Lubitz, D.K.J.E., Beakley, J.E., Patricelli, F.: Disaster Management: The Structure, Function, and Significance of Network-Centric Operations. Journal of Homeland Security and Emergency Management 5(1), Art 42 (2008)
11. Kapucu, N., Arslan, T., Demiroz, F.: Collaborative emergency management and national emergency management network. Disaster Prev. and Management 19(4), 452–468 (2010)
12. Chituc, C.M., Azevedo, A.: Multi-perspective challenges on collaborative networks business environment. In: Camarinha-Matos, L., Afsarmanesh, H., Ortiz, A. (eds.) Collaborative Networks and Breeding Environments, pp. 25–32. Springer, Heidelberg (2005)
13. ATHENA State of the art of Enterprise Modelling Techniques and Technologies to Support Enterprise Interoperability. Deliv D.A1.1.1 (2004), http://www.athena-ip.org (cited March 30, 2011)
14. Whitman, L., Panetto, H.: The Missing Link: Culture and Language Barriers to Interoperability. Annual Reviews in Control 30(2), 233–241 (2006)
15. Ellis, S., Kanowski, P., Whelan, R.: National inquiry into bushfire mitigation and management. Commonwealth of Australia, Canberra (2004)
16. Esmond, J.: Report on The Attraction, Support and Retention of Emergency Management Volunteers (2011), http://www.ema.gov.au/www/emaweb/emaweb.nsf/Page/Volunteers2 (cited March 2011)
17. McLennan, J.: Issues Facing Australian Volunteer-Based Emergency Services Organisations 2008 – 2010 (2008), http://www.ema.gov.au/www/emaweb/emaweb.nsf/Page/Volunteers2 (March 30, 2011)
18. Queensland Government. Queensland Combined Emergency Services Academy, QCESA (2011), http://www.safecom.sa.gov.au/site/emergency_management.jsp (March 2011)
19. Camarinha-Matos, L., et al.: Collaborative networked organizations - Concepts and practice in manufacturing enterprises. Computers and Industrial Engineering 57(1), 46–60 (2009)
20. Molina, A., et al.: Enterprise Integration and Networking: Challenges and Trends. Studies in Informatics and Control 16(4) (2007)
21. ISO/IEC, Annex C: GERAM, in ISO/IS 15704:2000/Amd1:2005: Industrial automation systems - Requirements for enterprise-reference architectures and methodologies (2005)
22. Bernus, P., Noran, O., Riedlinger, J.: Using the Globemen Reference Model for Virtual Enterprise Design in After Sales Service, in Globemen. In: Karvoinen, I., et al. (eds.) VTT Symposium, Helsinki / Finland, vol. 224, pp. 71–90 (2002)
23. Noran, O.: A Mapping of Individual Architecture Frameworks (GRAI, PERA, C4ISR, CIMOSA, Zachman, ARIS) onto GERAM. In: Bernus, P., Nemes, L., Schmidt, G. (eds.) Handbook of Enterprise Architecture, pp. 65–210. Springer, Heidelberg (2003)

24. Noran, O.: An Analytical Mapping of the C4ISR Architecture Framework onto ISO15704 Annex A (GERAM). Computers in Industry 56(5), 407–427 (2005)
25. Saha, P.: A Synergistic Assessment of the Federal Enterprise Architecture Framework against GERAM (ISO15704:2000 Annex A). In: Saha, P. (ed.) Enterprise Systems Architecture in Practice, pp. 1–17. IDEA Group, Hershey (2007)
26. Noran, O.: Discovering and Modelling Enterprise Engineering Project Processes. In: Saha, P. (ed.) Enterprise Systems Architecture in Practice, pp. 39–61. IDEA Group, USA (2007)
27. Noran, O.: Towards an Environmental Management Approach for Collaborative Networks. In: Camarinha-Matos, L., Boucher, X., Afsarmanesh, H. (eds.) Collaborative Networks for a Sustainable World, pp. 17–24. Springer, Berlin (2010)
28. ISO/IEC, ISO/IEC 42010:2007: Recommended Practice for Architecture Description of Software-Intensive Systems (2007)
29. Noran, O.: A Meta-methodology for Collaborative Networked Organisations: Creating Directly Applicable Methods for Enterprise Engineering Projects (2008); VDM Verlag. Dr. Mueller

Gathering, Structuring and Modeling Business Process Knowledge of the Response to a Nuclear Crisis: Towards a Simulation Platform for Better Coordination

Aurélie Charles, Matthieu Lauras,
Anne-Marie Barthe, and Frédérick Bénaben

Université de Toulouse, Mines Albi,
route de Teillet, 81013 Albi cedex, France
{aurelie.charles,matthieu.lauras,
anne-marie.barthe,benaben}@mines-albi.fr

Abstract. This paper illustrates how nuclear crisis are managed in France. It proposes IT solutions dedicated to event management that could help to resolve such a crisis by facilitating coordination between actors and increasing situational awareness. This study has been conducted as part of the European project PLAY. Requirements have been collected from different stakeholders through reviews of the literature, internal reports and websites, and interviews. Our proposal consists in the construction of a simulation tool to validate the complex-event processing architecture and the associated platform. The aim is to show the potential added value from the PLAY platform in the context of the response to a nuclear crisis.

Keywords: Complex-event processing, distributed systems, crisis management, modeling, collaboration.

1 Introduction

A large quantity of radioactive substance is accidentally released in the atmosphere, due to a critical accident in a French nuclear plant. To resolve this crisis, a lot of heterogeneous actors may be involved. The services provided by these actors are also diverse and varied, ranging from psychological assistance to traffic duty. This heterogeneity is probably the main cause of the difficulty to manage such a crisis situation. But there are many other difficulties to cope with. For instance, there are a lot of critical dependencies between the actions of these heterogeneous actors. A decision to evacuate will depend on the actual level of radioactivity measured, but also on weather forecasts and assessments of the situation in the nuclear plant. Collaborative processes describe the chronology of activities but also how activities might be pre-condition or post-condition for each other's. Besides, crisis situations are obviously the kind of context where agility, especially reactivity and flexibility, is one critical point. It is crucial that workflows and actions remain perfectly adapted to the situation and its possible changes. Japan's last disaster provides many examples of the vital importance of timely and accurate diffusion of information between actors, but also toward population.

L.M. Camarinha-Matos et al. (Eds.): PRO-VE 2011, IFIP AICT 362, pp. 486–493, 2011.

To help to resolve such a crisis, our research work consists in developing IT solutions that could facilitate coordination between actors. We have chosen to develop a simulation tool that should be used with the complex-event processing architecture and the associated platform designed and built within the framework of the ongoing European project PLAY [14]. The main benefit of using the platform built for PLAY is that the management of the crisis would be facilitated by the increased situational awareness provided by the platform. In addition to that, the platform would ensure a timely and adequate diffusion of information to relevant actors. All these characteristics make this nuclear use case an accurate illustration for Internet of Services, although it is not easy to imagine this context as a strongly computed environment where services could easily send their events to the clouds.

To reach this goal, we have developed a two-step approach. The first step is to gather knowledge about the current situation and to propose a structured analysis of the situation, as it would be if PLAY platform was used to facilitate the management of the crisis (process description and analysis). The second step is to build a tool to simulate various collaborative workflows, actors' behavior, and event production.

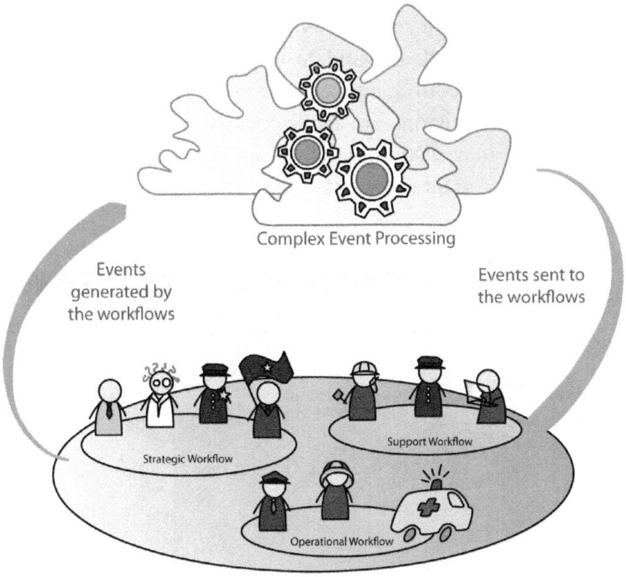

Fig. 1. Nuclear Crisis Use Case, Actors and Events

This article develops this approach in order to turn the whole "natural language" use case description into a set of relevant, representative and usable business process models containing the numerous pieces of information, interactions and events to take into account in such a situation. In order to build a simulation tool dedicated to run the nuclear crisis example use case, we have to identify and characterize all the involved services and the events generated by these services from heterogeneous partners. At this condition, we will be able to experiment the elastic and reliable architecture for dynamic complex event driven interaction of the PLAY proposal.

Concretely, the purpose of this part of the research work is to collect data and identify the processes of realization, in order to identify specific requirements for each of them. Specifically, this analysis will identify the strengths and weaknesses of the current situation in order to successfully acquire end-user requirements. But as many stakeholders are involved in the crisis management process (see. Figure 1), discussions with IRSN, France's public service expert in nuclear and radiation risks as well as with Nuclear plants technical experts or field actors such as firemen are undergoing. A review of the literature, available reports and websites has also complemented those discussions. See [11] [4] [2] [5] among others.

2 The Nuclear Crisis Cell: A Need for a Interoperable IT Platform

To resolve the crisis, many stakeholders are involved. The crisis cell, in charge of operation, is managed by the prefect (representative of the national authority), outside the nuclear plant. Inside the nuclear plant, the company in charge of the plant is managing operations. Delegates of each actor are present in the crisis cell. Firemen, policemen, and any other actor involved in the response processes has one representative in the crisis cell, to validate the feasibility of decisions, link with the field and ensure communication between actors. Consequently, this crisis cell is distributed. Most of the decisions are made locally, where prefect and delegates are gathered, but decisions may also come from the national authority, local or national responsible of the nuclear plant or experts. (See. figure 2).

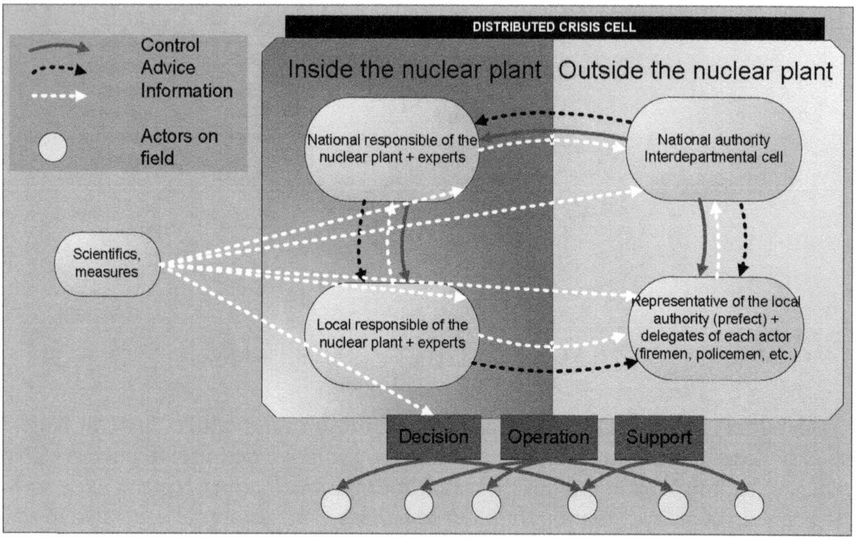

Fig. 2. Distributed crisis cell and actors

This distributed cell, combined with the lack of a proper IT system to ensure timely and accurate exchange of information often results in delays or inconsistence at many levels. No one has a clear awareness of the situation or a precise knowledge of all latest information. For example, mid-March 2011 in Japan, many dysfunctions regarding communication of information have been deplored. "Employees confirmed a second blaze at the reactor, but it took another 35 minutes for them to inform a fire station in nearby Tomiokamachi" [13]. "Complicating matters, a lack of phone service meant that they had little input from upper management" [3]. Japan's prime minister deplored that "though there was a direct broadcast of explosions on national TVs, it took [TEPCO, the electric power company] more than an hour to inform the government." [8] A few days later, communication had not improved. For example, it took nine hours between the publication of an sky-high level of 134 iodine, which created panic among international experts, and the communication of corrected values, without any information on the new number, except that it was "under the limit" nor any explanation on why the first figure was wrong. [1]

3 Step 1: Gathering and Structuring Knowledge

We have chosen to follow a Business Process Modeling approach to implement our research work. Consequently, in this first step, our objective consists in transforming the three classical levels of business processes that exist in any system (decisional, operational and support processes) in workflows in order to support the agility of both orchestration (internal business processes) and choreography (interactions between actors) of the coordination.

Concretely, to resolve the nuclear crisis described in introduction, seven sub-processes have been identified and divided into the three levels evoked before (see. figure 1).

- 1. Strategic level - To manage nuclear crisis: This first level is dedicated to present the decisional part of the process cartography. It concerns decision taking during the crisis management.
- 2. Operational level - To resolve nuclear accident and its consequences: This second level deals with the concrete operational part of the process cartography. It concerns mainly the actions performed on the crisis site.
- 3. Support level - To support nuclear crisis response: This last level concerns the supporting activities dedicated to provide means to other processes and to ensure logistic aspects of the crisis management.

From the seven business processes identified during the global analysis, we decided to focus our attention only on the five that concentrate the main coordination problems. Concretely, those business processes concern activities that occur outside the nuclear plant. Moreover, decisions and operations within the plant are not managed by the same authority than the rest of the crisis. They also depend on the nuclear plant itself, and the technology it uses. Furthermore, those operations are really technical, not always available, and does not affect the rest of operations (radioactive measurements and previsions are sufficient).

Those business processes are as follow:

1.2 To plan and control relief process and means (Decisional)
2.2 To protect population (Operational)
2.3 To provide aid to employees and population (Operational)
3.2 To back relief operations (Support)
3.3 To assess situation (Support)

From these five business processes, we detailed sixteen sub-processes, as described in figure 3.

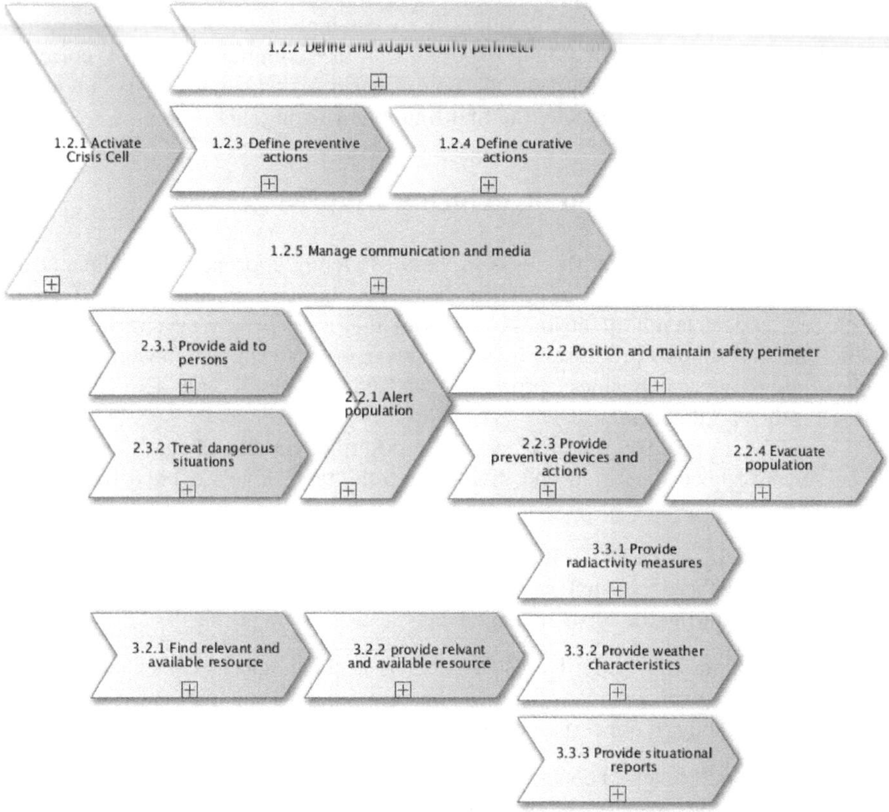

Fig. 3. Low-level structure: 16 sub-processes identified

4 Step 2: Supplying the Simulation Platform with Events

In our case of nuclear crisis management, the scenario is very complex and as explained before, a lot of sub-processes are involved. We plan to simulate this use case through a demonstration platform able (i) to run all these sub-processes in a Service Oriented Architecture (SOA) context, and (ii) to simulate the CEP platform.

Implementing a real exercise implying all the expected actors, services and events is not an easy task. The simulation tool compensates this difficulty and enables the validation of the complex-event processing architecture. We suppose that a business service matches with a single technical operation (i.e. a single operation of a WebService).

The demonstration platform provided will be based on SOA principles [10] and on the ESB PETALS [7]. Such a technical infrastructure requires describing processes as workflows in a runnable language (for instance BPEL, Business Process Execution Language [6]). In order to make that task easier and to ensure coherence into the whole approach, all the sub-processes will be described with BPMN language (Business Process Modeling Notation) [9][12]. Furthermore, this language is not only strongly aligned with computer implementation of workflows but also structurally event-oriented (events are represented through circles and can be typed). BPMN is so perfectly at the intersection between PLAY project specificities (event-based) and technical requirements of the demonstration platform to be provided (proximity between BPMN and workflow language). Figure 4 shows one of the BPMN built for this project.

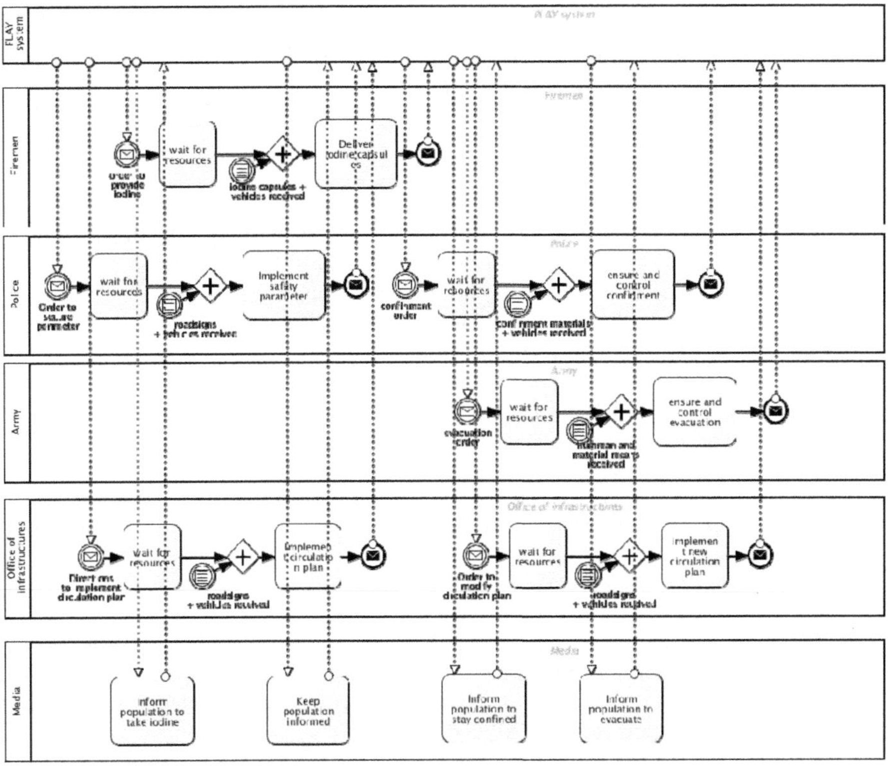

Fig. 4. One example of BPMN – To protect population

5 Motivations

Three main elements make this use case a relevant illustration for Internet of Services, although it is not easy to imagine this context as a strongly computed environment where services could easily send their events to the clouds:

- The heterogeneity of actors is taken into account. Actors involved operate with their own information system, which may already use web services, but may also be fairly basic.
- High volumes of heterogeneous information is exchanged
- Changes in orchestration (internal business processes) or in choreography (interactions between processes) are possible, and driven by events

With its complex-event processing architecture, European project PLAY can contribute significantly. The management of the crisis would indeed be facilitated by the increased situational awareness provided by PLAY's platform for event processing. In addition to that, PLAY would ensure a timely and adequate diffusion of information to relevant actors.

Acknowledgements. This study is part of a project, PLAY, supported by the European Commission through the Seventh Framework Programme. We would like to thank all the partners for their involvement.

References

1. Ané, C.: Tepco accumule les erreurs de communication. LeMonde.fr (2011), http://www.lemonde.fr/japon/article/2011/03/28/tepco-accumule-les-erreurs-de-communication_1499820_1492975.html
2. ASN. Les situations d'urgence - Autorité de sûreté nucléaire, http://www.asn.fr/index.php/S-informer/Dossiers/Les-situations-d-urgence
3. Belson, K.: Panic and Heroism Greeted Crisis at Japan Nuclear Plant. The New York Times (2011), http://www.nytimes.com/2011/03/31/world/asia/31workers.html?_r=1&src=recg
4. IRSN. CODIR-PA Présentation de deux scénarios d'accident affectant une centrale nucléaire française (2007)
5. IRSN. IRSN - Expert in nuclear and radiological risk, http://www.irsn.fr/EN/Pages/home.aspx
6. Jurič, M.B., Mathew, B., Sarang, P.: Business Process Execution Language for Web Services. Packt Publishing Ltd. (2006)
7. Konstantas, D., Bourrières, J.-P., Léonard, M.: Interoperability of enterprise software and applications. Springer, Heidelberg (2006)
8. Mesmer, P.: Tepco, une entreprise trop sûre d'elle-même. LeMonde.fr (2011), http://www.lemonde.fr/japon/article/2011/03/16/tepco-une-entreprise-trop-sure-d-elle-meme_1493754_1492975.html
9. OMG. BPMN, http://www.omg.org/spec/BPMN/2.0/PDF/

10. Touzi, J., Benaben, F., Pingaud, H., Lorré, J.P.: A model-driven approach for collaborative service-oriented architecture design. International Journal of Production Economics 121(1), 5–20 (2009)
11. Trémeur, M., Lencznar, V.-A.: Communes et agglomérations face aux risques naturels et technologiques. du Papyrus (2006)
12. White, S.A., Miers, D.: BPMN Modeling and Reference Guide: Understanding and Using BPMN. Future Strategies Inc. (2008)
13. Shimbun, Y.: Firefighters struggle to find effective tactics. Daily Yomiuri Online (2011), http://www.yomiuri.co.jp/dy/national/T110316004482.htm
14. PLAY Project, http://www.play-project.eu/

Procurement Information Systems: Collaboration to Fight against Crisis

Oihab Allal-Chérif

BEM Management School Bordeaux France
680 cours de la Libération 33400 Talence France
oihab@bem.edu

Abstract. The length and sheer scale of the current economic crisis has surprised managers, who were completely unprepared to deal with such an unanticipated situation. Standing at the heart of their businesses and providing a link between executives and employees, these managers need to limit the impact of the crisis in an environment in which various constraints, unexpected events and social tensions are on the increase. Restructuring and cost-killing are the first port of call, which makes buyers very busy people. However, some buyers are pioneering a new kind of collaborative management which, instead of increasing the pressure on suppliers and reducing risk-taking to a minimum, advocates taking new initiatives that are not aimed solely at maximising profits in the short-term. This article offers an overview of this new, foresight-based Procurement practice. After highlighting recent Procurement function developments, which were largely responsible for the consequences of the crisis, our constructivist methodology proposes to interview 12 buying experts in order to develop scenarios and identify the features of the Collaborative Procurement. The final section then presents: (1) new forms of internal and external collaboration; (2) the roles and specific skills of this type of the "buyer of the future"; and (3) how the globalised economy is becoming an increasingly community-based, collaborative virtual environment.

Keywords: Procurement function, Economic crisis, Collaboration, Collaborative Buyer, Foresight.

1 Introduction

As firms have refocused on their core business there has been a rapid, significant increase in the importance of managing the Procurement function. This increase in purchasing volumes automatically puts greater pressure on the control of costs, quality and lead-times (Ballaz, 2002). It is accompanied by a new development in the Procurement function whereby buyers, in addition to managing supplies, listen to the market in order to detect new trends and technical progress resulting from technological innovation (Allal-Cherif, 2007). The 2009 economic crisis has put businesses, and especially Procurement departments, in a particularly difficult situation. Faced with dwindling order books and significant financial losses, the initial reaction is to embark on a drastic policy of cost-killing and procedural restructuring.

L.M. Camarinha-Matos et al. (Eds.): PRO-VE 2011, IFIP AICT 362, pp. 494–503, 2011.

Objectives are all scaled down, investment projects and recruitment are frozen and output is slowed or even stopped in some cases.

Buyers are the first levers in cost reduction, particularly in industrial companies such as Caterpillar, Schneider Electric, Nestlé, Thales or PSA, where they manage over 65% of turnover. However, the Procurement function is faced with a dilemma: it needs to reduce spending significantly without increasing the pressure on suppliers that are already on the verge of bankruptcy. Buyers therefore need to manage risk and prepare for the end of the crisis by implementing root and branch changes to business practices and consolidating the competitive advantages deriving from better management of supplier relations. The major multinationals have thus realised that the reason some of their suppliers have completely disappeared is not for the want of customers, but rather a lack of cash-flow; these suppliers are often paid 60, 90 and even 120 days after the billing month (Benassy-Quéré et al, 2009). Despite their order books being full, many of them had accepted trading conditions that were too dangerous for their financial stability, which the crisis ended up undermining.

This paper presents a new, "collaborative buyer" approach to the management of the Procurement function, as applied by 12 Procurement Directors or Managers in their companies. During the course of our interviews a new approach to managing the Procurement function emerged, with different objectives and new methods. In the first part, traditional Procurement practices will be analysed in light of the current crisis in order to underline their limitations and the need for innovative approaches to internal and customer-supplier relations. The second part will present the two-pronged research methodology: occupational foresight and the scenario approach. The profile of the "Procurement experts" interviewed and the interview guide will be described. The third part will present several hypothetical scenarios that have been co-constructed, along with recommendations for best Procurement practice.

2 Procurement and the Economic Crisis

2.1 Polymorphic Management of the Procurement Function

Over the past 15 years, the Procurement function has evolved significantly: it has played an increasingly important role in the life of firms and has become highly strategic. This traditionally low-profile function involving between 2% and 5% of employees in multinational firms has emerged as a key profit centre that is managed meticulously by head office (Lurin and Beloeuvre, 2005). In addition to their normal tasks, i.e. to maximise quality while minimising costs and optimising lead-times, buyers create value by identifying their suppliers' new techniques, developments or inventions (Vlcek, 2002). They are at the heart of the innovation process because they are best placed to know the suppliers that they might bring into a potential partnership to work together on a new product or new technology (Teece et al. 1997). Buyers now work proactively: they find solutions through strategic alliances involving several links of the same industrial value chain, enabling them to access resources, technologies and levers which the firm would not be able to access alone. They can see how the talents of several companies may be combined to produce key competitive advantages (Rodriguez Ruiz, 2005).

After a long period lasting until the late 1990s in which buyers tended to be recruited for their expertise in reducing costs and streamlining the supply chain, they are now much more likely to be selected for their ability to anticipate market changes and to propose new development projects rather than in response to any accounting concerns. Cost and lead-time optimisation quickly reaches a ceiling which technological progress can ignore and it is in this race for innovation than most companies are now seeking a technological advantage (Calvi and Barreyre, 1997). Groupings – whether between competitors or between customers and suppliers – are on the increase, in order to secure financial, material and human resources and greater expertise. The teams subsequently set up systematically involve buyers who use information and communications technology to improve business intelligence, information sharing, collaboration, knowledge capitalisation and project management (Bressler and Grantham, 2000; Schubert and Ginsburg, 2000; Brousseau, 2002).

2.2 A Strategic Function That Needs to Develop Significantly Before Being Mature

In the 1990s, despite early studies showing the strategic role of the purchasing function, most buyers were acting as "cost-killers", their main role being to minimise supply costs. Fierce pressure was exerted on prices and suppliers, which gave rise to unfair trading conditions accompanied by destabilising manoeuvres and bargaining tactics. These harmful approaches were often approved by management, with its inadequate knowledge of the business of Procurement and managing customer/supplier relations. Outsourcing an activity was considered like outsourcing the problems related with this activity and companies didn't want to know about it. The emergence of sustainable development in companies with a focus on ethical, fair and environmentally-friendly trading has changed the rules of the game and radically altered buyers' behaviour (Carter et al., 2007).

Today, purchasing is considered as a key function, involved in the global strategy of a firm and contributing to the creation of sustainable value and decisive competitive advantage (Cavinato, 1999). However, this function as to be structured by specific processes, competencies and tools to reach a high level of maturity and develop its full potential (Cousins and al., 2006). The economic crisis is an opportunity to improve and to have a new vision of the way to do business: it's time to accept that suppliers have their own expertise, that maybe it would be a good thing to adapt the organisation to their schedule, and that they need money to invest in improving production and creating new technology (Tassabehji and Moorhouse, 2008). Buyers have to build strong long term partnership with their most strategic suppliers and to develop collaboration and knowledge management (Ordanini, 2006). They even have to protect their suppliers from financial difficulties by helping them in paying them faster and investing in their projects to get exclusivities. The trust relation is essential to share the risks and work together to reach ambitious objectives (Ratnasingam and al., 2005).

2.3 The Future of Procurement: The Cooperative Management Approach

There are several factors behind the current radical rethink of traditional management methods. An accelerating economy leads to a frantic race to innovate in a bid to be the "first mover" to exploit a killer technology. Globalisation requires a much more highly-developed, sophisticated competitive intelligence, capable of detecting faint signs of opportunities or threats at a very early stage. The rise of Information and Communication Technologies (ICT) has helped to strengthen horizontal communication and opportunities for coordination between players within and outside the company. The new Generation Y now accounts for 20% of the workforce, but should rise to 40% within 5 years (INSEE). The economic crisis has shown the limitations of the traditional models of managing the Procurement function by revealing the interdependence of companies operating in the same market and the risks ensuing from stiff competition between competitors or when the customer/supplier power relationship is heavily skewed.

Thus, the cooperative management approach to the Procurement function is only present in a few pioneering companies with a high level of maturity such as Schneider Electric, IBM and Nestlé. This method has gained many followers since the beginning of the economic crisis, both in terms of internal and external collaboration. Internally, it can be achieved through: (1) synergies between Procurement and other functions such as Research and Development or Marketing; (2) co-decisions between hierarchical levels; (3) buyer-led cross-project management. Externally, the main forms of cooperative management of the Procurement function involve: (1) technological co-development and product co-design with suppliers; (2) sponsorship of innovation; (3) assisted production planning; (4) integration of information systems; (5) automation or outsourcing part of the Procurement function; and (6) collaborative strategic management (Allal-Cherif, 2007).

3 A Constructivist Methodology: Foresight and Scenario Method

3.1 Procurement Foresight: towards Structural, Functional Anticipation

This paper aims to carefully co-construct a common picture of the future of the Procurement function, based on interviews with twenty experts (Thamain, 2009). This "anticipation, however imperfect, of changes, discontinuities, contingencies" of the Procurement function is not covered by managerial foresight (Boyer and Scouarnec, 2009). Given the increasingly sustained, violent turbulence affecting the business world, foresight has become essential for companies to prepare to challenge their competitors, who are also trying to look ahead and find their place in the world of the future. Preparing to adapt will always be much more effective than reacting to the unexpected and it is through the use of foresight to identify potential problems that solutions are most likely to be found and implemented in time (Julien et al., 1975).

"Occupational forecasting is an approach that involves anticipating possible futures in terms of the skills, activities and responsibilities of an occupation. It enables us to envision the knowledge and qualifications, expertise or professional know-how and the attitudes and social skills that might, in future, best serve the individual and the organisation. To achieve this, the experts in the occupation/s under analysis need to co-construct a picture of the potential future of that occupation or those occupations. It therefore involves reflecting on the individual occupation and the way work is organised." (Boyer and Scouarnec, 2009).

3.2 Selecting the Procurement Experts and the Interview Protocol Used

In order to carry out this foresight study, we chose 12 experts in the field, working in various sectors such as Textile, IT or energy and from heterogeneous size. This diversity allows for a sufficient variety of viewpoints to cover most of the buyer's skills, activities and responsibilities being studied. In order to minimise the effects of any subjectivity and interpretation, only half of these experts were previously known to the interviewers. However, even those experts who were unknown to the interviewers before the survey were approached by the researchers, following a recommendation, in order to promote the climate of trust and confidence required by the nature of the research. Table 1 summarises some of the characteristics of the Procurement experts and assigns them a code which will be referred to when quoting verbatim.

Table 1. Panel of Procurement Managers/Directors interviewed

Buyer code	Position	Size of firm (employees)	Turnover	Sector
A1	Procurement Manager	400 000	€104 billion	IT
A2	Procurement Manager	270 000	€75 billion	Foodstuffs
A3	IT Procurement	200 000	€19 billion	Electricity
A4	Procurement Director	120 000	€180 billion	Energy
A5	Procurement Manager	100 000	€40 billion	Machinery
A6	Buyer	70 000	€20 billion	Cosmetics
A7	Procurement Manager	55 000	€10 billion	Distribution
A8	Procurement Director	9 000	€5.1 billion	Telecoms
A9	Procurement Director	8 000	€2.5 billion	Textiles
A10	Procurement Director	1 400	NA	Public Health
A11	CEO	47	€200 million	Equipment
A12	CEO	20	€50 million	IT consulting

3.3 The Interview Guide and Method

The interview guide was based on a review of the literature by the authors, all Procurement function professionals for between 10 and 30 years, and ten contact interviews used to present the project to the experts. Noting the individual interests and specialisations of each expert, we tailored the interview guide to reflect their experience and style. A first round of informal exploratory talks was conducted with the 12 Procurement experts in order to identify development pathways for the Procurement function. During these initial interviews, no reference was made to the responses given by other interviewees. A second round of semi-structured interviews was then held to confirm and expand on the previous interviews. These were conducted in reverse order so as to revisit all the pathways identified and to get a more accurate picture of the views of the experts.

The purpose of these interviews was to get respondents to express their views and their vision of the future straightforwardly and with a certain amount of risk on their part. The first non-structured part of the information gathering exercise thus consisted of conversations in which the interviewers did not attempt to guide the interviewees but did prompt them to give further information (Thiétart et al, 2007). A semi-structured interview guide specifically tailored to each expert was then designed in order to obtain additional information and examples. This second interview not only allowed each interviewee to clarify his point of view but also to comment on the views expressed by others.

4 A More Collaborative Buyer, Both Internally and Externally

4.1 More Internal and External Collaboration: Creating a Competitive Advantage

A1 says that the role of the *project buyer*, the *cross-buyer* and the *purchasing coordinator* will grow considerably at the expense of *product buyers* or *national buyers.* Buyers will assist project leaders and in some cases even replace them, from one project to the next. "The same person will source all the components for the project and then move on to the next one." This method differs significantly from that most commonly used, in which one person sources a class of products or services for a large number of different projects. Furthermore, the *project buyer* organises all the Procurement activity for his projects, whereas the *product buyer* is part of a very rigid hierarchy, having to report to several higher levels and being responsible for the tasks delegated to the lower levels. The buyer of the future will therefore need to have a much broader vision of the company. This is borne out by current trends in the internal interfaces with which he has to operate. Rather than imposing new constraints, these actually constitute new prerogatives for buyers. A8 is concerned, however, about the need to manage them with the utmost care, given that there is considerable potential for drift.

Sustainable, responsible and ethical Procurement will also become a standard feature of all supply operations rather than merely a side-line of this function. New forms of collaboration between customers and suppliers are emerging, such as in the automotive, electronics or food processing industries, where supplier integration is increasingly a key factor in strategic success. When it achieves a high level of maturity, the Procurement function has a major influence on the adoption of sustainable practices. Stable partnerships and the need to promote innovation and develop new projects are prioritised over economic calculations. Unilateral decisions in the interests of a single link in the supply chain are no longer made; instead, collective decisions are taken in a bid to consolidate the whole venture.

When the whole process is taken into account, sustainable value is created – and not just an ad hoc basis. It can therefore be argued that the members of the logistics chain gradually establish partnerships by pooling their resources, risks and profit. The relationships thus established are extremely complex. Information, goods and capital flows need to be managed scrupulously. Collaboration and anticipation yield considerable reductions in transportation costs as the logistical synergies emerge. A2 says that in his firm, the "road map is modelled on the road map used by our suppliers. We adapt to their pace and organise ourselves around their projects and the innovations they can bring to us. If we have no overview of their business, then we have no overview of our own."

4.2 Managing Procurement Expertise: Lead Project Buyer and Talent Manager

The buyer recruitment procedure is highly elitist. Employers are looking for specialists with 5 years of post-high school education in either engineering or business. Experience is less important than the initial training, which must be solid and enable young graduates to avoid the traps laid in heated negotiations. Buyers are becoming a pro-active force: by forming strategic alliances between different links in the same value chain, they can access resources, technologies and levers which the firm would not be able to access alone. C4 highlights the creative side of the buyer: "The character of the buyer is increasingly important: the best buyers are the most forceful and resourceful. They have to think outside the box and come up with original solutions. They need to shape, from the countless items at their disposal, the most appropriate response to the needs of their firms. They have an element of intuition that a computer cannot replicate."

The foresight skills of the buyers of the future, identified together with the Procurement experts we interviewed, are as follows: the ability to operate in virtual environments and to detect faint signs of opportunities or potential threats; the use and optimisation of information and communication technology, especially collaborative platforms, social networks and the virtual communities of practice that constitute strategic intelligence tools, as well as benchmarking, management of expertise, collaboration and facilitation of professional networks; being a global responsibility activist by combining sustainable development, fair trade and ethical work; the ability to bring suppliers on board and secure exclusive innovations; flexibility and multi-tasking, naturally dipping in and out of several projects or cultures; highly mobile, etc; highly creative and spontaneous: questioning existing solutions and with a strong ability to innovate; strong leadership with senior management potential.

For A6, "the new people think that our firms are still living in the Stone Age." This view is shared by most of the experts we interviewed. In their opinion, firms are lagging behind society. In some cases, it is no longer the private sector that innovates for the public sector, but the public sector that innovates for the private sector. Firms take some time before adopting the new practices: "they are increasingly lagging behind". A gap is also gradually emerging, but more quickly between traditional buyers and those of the Internet generation: they don't use the same methods, tools, or even the same language. Given that one side is under the impression that the other side is trying to push them out of the door, we can imagine the tensions and problems involved in managing such a wide variety of profiles.

4.3 Towards a Virtual, Community-Based Collaborative Economy

A5 says that "the crisis made us realise that we needed to treat our suppliers better. We decided to be just as concerned about them as we are about ourselves because we are interdependent. We changed our payment policy and we now settle our invoices in 8 days instead of 3 months." Companies thus prefer their money to be with their suppliers so that it can be used to innovate and keep them going rather than being parked in the bank to earn interest. Consequently, investment and long-term gains are prioritised over structured finance. Some companies even go as far as paying their suppliers' suppliers, so that their business will not be put at risk by financial difficulties. The spate of bankruptcies which the financial crisis has produced in a huge domino effect has induced buyers to pay more attention to their strategic partners. However, this type of chaperone policy may be seen as interfering and as a perverse way of extending control, with over-intrusive concern for the way a sovereign company manages its finances.

A3 stresses the importance of modern means of communication, which also play a key role in the new relationships between firms. Companies are gradually organising themselves as professional virtual communities that share the same values and cooperative closely on a wide range of activities. This type of "meta-company" requires a "meta-network", an intelligent network enabled by the new information and communication technologies. It allows member companies to pool their intelligence, their technical expertise and some of their business costs. It also gives them three precious gifts: ubiquity, omnipresence and omniscience. The more responsive, more flexible joint ventures will have a considerable advantage over individual companies as they are able to share costs and expertise simultaneously. "In a virtual universe of exchange networks, we now need to optimise value added chains between partners" and "roll out new forms of cooperative business." The fact that these potential suppliers are grouped together in the same community, making it possible to submit problems and directly compare the solutions proposed by each of them, provides incalculable gains in terms of time, money and quality.

5 Conclusion

Traditional Procurement practices were an aggravating factor in the consequences of the financial crisis of 2009. They caused value chains to be weakened and called supplier relationship management practices into question. Some firms ended up weakening themselves by overshadowing and oppressing respected players in their own market and which they helped to eliminate. Cooperative management, which is still at the experimental stage, has become a much more credible alternative to the drastic policies of cost-cutting and fierce competition achieved through radical, automated sourcing methods. The Procurement function thus acts as a pioneer in developing new forms of internal and external collaborations and adopting a partnership approach with all key suppliers in order to address the economic crisis and prepare to emerge from it. There is still some scepticism surrounding these new methods, which the drastic situation has helped to highlight and make more popular. However, in large multinational companies, the profile of buyers has changed dramatically. Their role is no longer confined to satisfying internal needs and automatically reducing costs: it now involves maximising the sustainable value created jointly with their partners. From initially managing transactions and then information, they have now moved on to relationship management, which calls for very specific skills. They have replaced a confrontational, systematically comparative approach with a process of association and coordination. Buyers are no longer content to meet current needs; they now try to anticipate future ones. They run projects in which they need to combine complementary talents in order to co-build a key competitive advantage. The buyer's buying role is increasingly less important: they are becoming mediators who ensure a healthy market; watchmen who anticipate dangers and look out for opportunities; and project managers who prepare for the future of the company and ensure its long-term survival.

References

1. Allal-Cherif, O.: An economic model for electronic marketplaces, PhD thesis in Management Sciences, University of Grenoble 2, UPMF (May 2007)
2. Bakos, J.Y.: Reducing buyer search costs: implications for electronic marketplaces. Management Science 43(12), 1676–1692 (1997)
3. Ballaz, B.: Le management des achats et de la chaîne intégrée clients-fournisseurs: le rôle clé du système d'information. In: Castagnos, J.-C., Retour, D. (eds.) Le management des achats, pp. 87–109. Presses Universitaires de Grenoble (2002)
4. Boyer, L., Scouarnec, A.: La Prospective des métiers. EMS (2009)
5. Bressler, S.E., Grantham, C.E.: Communities of Commerce. McGraw Hill, New York (2000)
6. Brousseau, E.: The Governance of Transaction by Commercial Intermediaries: an Analysis of the re-engineering of intermediation by electronic commerce. International Journal of the Economics of Business 9(3) (2002)
7. Calvi, R., Barreyre, P.Y.: La participation des Services achats au développement des produits nouveaux: une approche organisationnelle. Colloque International de Génie Industriel, Albi, 3, 4 et 5 septembre (1997)
8. Carter, P.L., Carter, J.R., Monczka, R.M., Blascovich, J.D., Slaight, T.H., Markham, W.J.: Succeeding in a Dynamic World: Supply Management in the Decade Ahead, p. 138. CAPS Research (2007)
9. Cavinato, J.L.: Fitting purchasing to the five stages of strategic management. European Journal of Purchasing and Supply Management 5, 75–83 (1999)
10. Cousins, P.D., Lawson, B., Squire, B.: An empirical taxonomy of purchasing functions. International Journal of Operations & Production Management 26(7), 775–794 (2006)
11. Julien, P.-A., Lamonde, P., Latouche, D.: La méthode des scénarios, une réflexion sur la démarche et la théorie de la prospective. In: Travaux et Recherche de Prospective, coll. Schéma général d'aménagement de la France, vol. (59). La documentation française, Paris (1975)
12. Lurin, F., Beloeuvre, F.: Valeur de Croissance ou Le directeur des Achats. Lettre Stratégie 22, Bearing Point (2005)
13. Ordanini, A.: What drives market transactions in B2B exchanges? Communications of the ACM 49, 89–93 (2006)
14. Rodriguez Ruiz, J.A.: European study about e-purshasing. Master Thesis in Strategy and International Affaires, ESSEC Business School (2005)

15. Schubert, P., Ginsburg, M.: Virtual communities of transaction: the role of personalization in electronic commerce. Electronic Markets 10, 45–55 (2000)
16. Teece, D.J., Pisano, G., Shuen, A.: Dynamic Capabilities and Strategic Management. Strategic Management Journal 18(7), 509–533 (1997)
17. Thamain, J.-L.: Anticiper en GRH, prévision et prospective, un diagnostic des pratiques et des représentations. Management et Avenir, Juin 25 (2009)
18. Thiétart, R.-A., et al.: Méthodes de recherche en management, Paris, Dunod (2007)
19. Ratnasingam, P., Gefen, D., Pavlou, P.A.: The Role of Facilitating Conditions and Institutional Trust in Electronic Marketplaces. Journal of Electronic Commerce in Organizations 3(3), 69–82 (2005)
20. Tassabehji, R., Moorhouse, A.: The changing role of procurement: developing professional effectiveness. Journal of Purchasing and Supply Management 14, 55–68 (2008)
21. Vlcek, J.: Le profil de la fonction d'acheteur et les défis du futur. European Center for Research in Purchasing and Supply, Vienne (November 2002)

Part XVIII

Benefits Analysis

Computational Results of Membership in R&D Cooperation Networks: To Be or Not To Be in a Research Joint Venture

Duarte Leite[1,2], Pedro Campos[1,2], and Isabel Mota[1,3]

[1] FEP (Faculty of Economics, University of Porto)
[2] LIAAD – INESC, LA (Laboratory of Artificial Intelligence and Decision Support)
[3] CEF-UP (Center for Economics and Finance at UP)
Rua Dr. Roberto Frias, 4200-464 Porto, Portugal
{100421015,pcampos,imota}@fep.up.pt

Abstract. In this study, we analyze firms' membership in R&D (Research and Development) cooperation networks trough simulation methods. Our main research hypothesis is that the membership in cooperation networks is related to the degree of the knowledge spillover. The approach has two scenarios: cost symmetry and cost asymmetry. We first develop an analytical model with three stages: firstly, firms decide whether to participate in a cooperative research network; secondly they simultaneously choose the level of R&D output, and finally they choose the level of output. Then we proceed with computational simulations to verify our hypothesis. From our results, we were able to conclude that cooperation leads to an improvement on RJV firms' position in the market as they produce more than others with the same production conditions. Additionally, cooperating firms have to spend fewer resources on research, which turns the network a tremendous success on the productive efficiency level.

Keywords: R&D, cooperation, networks, spillover; simulation, RJV.

1 Introduction

In recent years, cooperation networks are one of the most appealing topics to study, gathering researchers from different scientific fields, such as biology, economy, management and computer science.

It is generally recognized that R&D activities have some public good features, as firms cannot fully appropriate the returns of their R&D investments, due to the existence of R&D spillovers. As a result, R&D expenditures are usually less than socially optimal. For this reason, R&D cooperation frequently emerges, so as to internalize spillovers.

Cooperation in R&D is usually identified with research collaboration and it is often investigated in the context of two-stage oligopoly models in which firms make their R&D decisions in a first pre-competitive stage and their quantity/price setting in a second stage. The most influential article on R&D cooperation is due to [8], who assumed that there are spillovers in R&D output. Another prominent work is [10],

L.M. Camarinha-Matos et al. (Eds.): PRO-VE 2011, IFIP AICT 362, pp. 507–516, 2011.

which proposed spillovers in R&D expenditures and allowed for different R&D organization models that may involve R&D expenditures cartelization and/or full information sharing. Since these starting articles, a lot of scientific models emerged around the topic of R&D cooperation, providing numerous extensions to those original models (e.g. [12] and [11] on oligopolistic markets; [13] and [1] on R&D spillovers; [7] and [9] on absorptive capacity; [3] and [4] on spillovers asymmetry; [6] on welfare). In this study we analyze the membership and profitability of cooperation networks. Our main research hypothesis is that the membership in a cooperation network is associated with the degree of R&D spillovers.

This approach tries to extend existing literature on R&D cooperation networks by focusing on an oligopolistic scenario with asymmetric production costs and a previous membership stage. The work has been conducted in two parts, each of them divided in two steps. In the first part, we assume that firms are symmetric in what respects the marginal cost of production, R&D costs and the spillover outside the network. In the second part, we consider that firms may have different marginal costs of production. As for the steps, we propose developing (i) an analytical model, followed by (ii) a computational approach.

The main conclusions reached driven us to the fact that firms prefer R&D cooperation. Principally when there is cost asymmetry, we find that a network, for some level of spillover, would arise, containing some of the companies in the market. These companies benefit from higher profits and from R&D from other companies which reduced their production costs. The number of firms keeps stable as the firms inside the RJV did not allow new companies to enter. This may allow us to infer that cooperation networks play a great role on firms' interaction and benefit some of them by giving a way to improve efficiency of companies that joined the RJV through a positive impact on internal productive

2 Part I: R&D Cooperation under Symmetric Marginal Costs

By extending the model of [8] to an oligopolistic scenario with partial-industry agreements between cost-symmetric firms, we develop a three-stage game where firms decide about entering in the R&D cooperation network, then about its R&D expenditures and afterwards they compete in the output market.

There are n firms that produce a homogeneous output, whose inverse demand function is given by:

$$P = a - bQ \ . \tag{1}$$

where the parameter a captures the market size and b is a constant. Q is the total output given by the expression:

$$Q = \sum_{i=1}^{n} q_i \quad (a,\ b>0 \text{ and } Q \leq a/b) \ . \tag{2}$$

As it is typical in R&D cooperation models (e.g. [8]), we assume that R&D output is cost reducing through an additive formulation, that is:

$$c_i = \overline{\alpha_i} - x_i - \beta \sum_{j \neq i}^{n} x_j \ . \tag{3}$$

where c_i is firm i's marginal cost of production, $\overline{\alpha_i}$ accounts for stand-alone marginal costs ($0 < \overline{\alpha_i} < a$), x_i measures firm i's R&D output and β is the spillover ($0 \leq \beta \leq 1$). Additionally, and as in [8], we consider a specific functional form for the R&D cost function:

$$C(x_i) = 0{,}5\gamma x_i^2 \ . \tag{4}$$

where $\gamma > 0$ represents the R&D cost. The profit of firm i is then given by:

$$\pi_i = (P - c_i)q_i - C(x_i) = (a - b\sum_{j=1}^{n} q_j - \overline{\alpha_i} + x_i + \beta \sum_{j \neq i}^{n} x_j)q_i - 0{,}5\gamma(x_i)^2 \ . \tag{5}$$

where q_i is firm i's output. The game is organized in three stages, as follows:

(i) In the first stage (*membership stage*), firms decide whether to participate (or not) in a cooperative research network. For simplicity, we will assume that within the cooperative network, the degree of information sharing is set at its maximum level ($\beta=1$), a structure known as the *Research Joint Venture* (RJV) [10]. Additionally, we will consider that insiders can obstruct the entry of an additional firm if it reduces their profits, while an outside firm will join the RJV only if it increases its profits. The conditions are defined according to those usually adopted in the literature (e.g. [11]; [2]): the conditions are the following, for a RJV of size m:

$$\pi_i^m(m) \geq \pi_i^m(m-1) \ . \tag{6}$$

$$\pi_i^m(m) \geq \pi_i^{n-m}(m-1) \ . \tag{7}$$

$$\pi_i^m(m) \geq \pi_i^m(m+1) \text{ or } \pi_i^{n-m}(m) \geq \pi_i^m(m+1) \text{ or both} \ . \tag{8}$$

where π_i^m (t) represents the profit of an insider and π_i^{n-m} (t) the profit of an outsider when the RJV is of size t. π_i^m (m) represents the average profit of firms in network of size m and π_i^m (m-1) represents the average profit of firms in network of size m, not taking into account one specific firm.

(ii) In the second stage (*development stage*), firms simultaneously choose the level of R&D output, independently or under cooperation. If firms cooperate, then they will coordinate R&D output in order to maximize their joint profits.

(iii) At last, in the *production stage*, firms simultaneously choose the level of output through Cournot competition.

Due to the complexity of the analytical solution for the equilibrium R&D output, we use numerical simulations to model the game described before. We were able to arrive to some interesting conclusions regarding the behaviour of companies in terms of network formation. Simulation results are presented in Table 1.

Table 1. Results of the simulation for n= 5 firms and for different values of Beta (β)

Marginal cost=50 and R&D cost (γ)=50						
Beta (β)	-	0.2	0.4	0.6	0.81	0.91
RJV Profits	48.90	49.58	50.09	50.42	50.58	50.59
Non-RJV profits	24.75	24.92	25.06	25.17	25.25	25.28
RJV R&D output	0.05	0.11	0.11	0.11	0.11	0.11
Non-RJV R&D output	0.14	0.11	0.09	0.07	0.05	0.04
Marginal cost=50 and R&D cost (γ)=90						
Beta (β)	-	0.2	0.4	0.6	0.81	0.91
RJV Profits	49.34	49.75	50.05	50.25	50.35	50.35
Non-RJV profits	24.85	24.95	25.03	25.10	25.15	25.17
RJV R&D output	0.03	0.07	0.07	0.07	0.07	0.07
Non-RJV R&D output	0.08	0.07	0.06	0.04	0.03	0.02

Firstly, we may observe that all firms outside the RJV want to make part of the network and, simultaneously, insiders do not obstruct the entry of those additional firms. There is stability when all firms are inside the network and therefore there is no entrance or exit of firms to and from the RJV. Whatever is the number of companies in the market and for every spillover levels, companies will sooner or later enter in the RJV and there will be a huge cooperation network between all companies in the market, after interaction starts.

From our computational exercise, we first observe that there is a direct relationship between the R&D spillover outside the network (β) and firms' profit (Figure 1). In fact, we may conclude that an increase of the R&D spillover outside the RJV will make firms to benefit from other firms' knowledge, and, therefore, to increase its profits. And this is true for both RJV and non-RJV firms, while in the first case, profits are higher due to a maximum spillover among cooperating firms. A correlation coefficient of 0,997 between the spillover and firms' profit was found to be statistically significant.

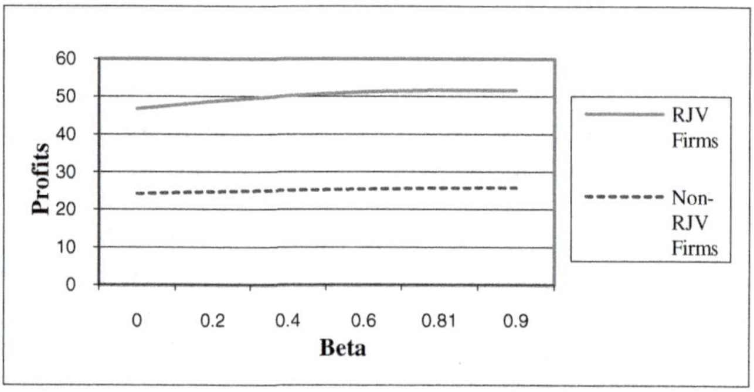

Fig. 1. Profits evolution with the spillover between non-cooperating firms (beta)

Additionally, when we focus on the R&D investment, we observe that it is higher for non-cooperating firms when compared with cooperating firms, except for a high degree of information sharing among non-cooperating firms (Figure 2). At the same time, we observe that for non cooperating firms, there is an inverse relationship between the level of knowledge spillover and the investment in R&D. This result is rather intuitive: higher degree of information sharing means lower appropriateness of R&D efforts and, therefore, lowers R&D investments.

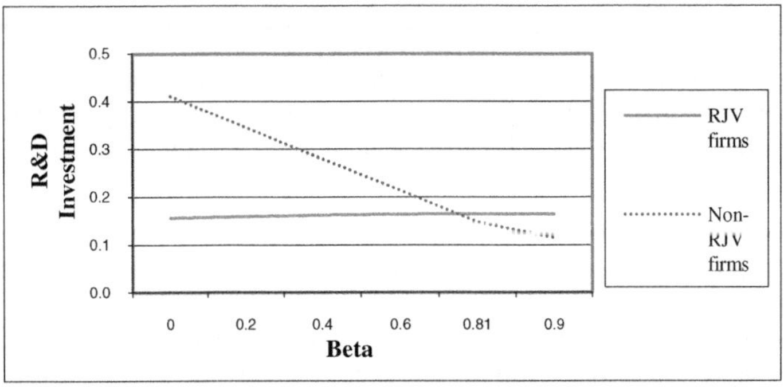

Fig. 2. R&D output evolution with the spillover between non-cooperating firms

We can also see that whenever we repeat the simulation for different number of firms in the market (n), we observe that as n increases, the R&D output decreases. This fact can be explained by the inverse relationship between the R&D output and the spillover. Therefore, as the number of firms in the market increases the R&D output decreases due to the fact that the spillover is greater for larger number of firms in the market and the need for R&D output is inferior.

3 Part II: R&D Cooperation under Asymmetric Marginal Costs

The results given in the previous simulation were very interesting and gave some insights on the behaviour of firms. However, it seems worthwhile to consider a more appealing framework where there is cost asymmetry between firms, giving literature a better perspective through simulation.
So, now we considered both equations 1, 2 and 3, that have been introduced in part I, while equation (3') captures the existence of diverse marginal costs of production between firms:

$$c_i = \alpha_i - x_i - \beta \sum_{j \neq i}^{n} x_j . \tag{3'}$$

where α_i accounts for stand-alone marginal costs ($0 < \alpha_i < a$), x_i measures firm i's R&D output and the R&D spillover has the same properties, $\beta \in [0, 1]$. As written before, it will be assumed that there are diminishing returns to R&D expenditures, that is, $C'(x_i) > 0$ and $C''(x_i) > 0$.

The profit function has changed so that it reflected the differences on marginal costs of production between firms:

$$\pi_i = (P - c_i)q_i - C(x_i) = (a - b\sum_{j=1}^{n} q_j - \alpha_i + x_i + \beta\sum_{j \neq i}^{n} x_j)q_i - 0{,}5\gamma(x_i)^2 \, . \qquad (5')$$

The same three-stage game used in Part I is proposed: firms decide about cooperation membership, R&D and then about the output. However, and in order to find different structures and the responses of network formation to these types of frameworks, we assume three different decision criteria on the members' decision of letting non-members enter or not the network. Each one of these three options is used to find out how network formation can show different features by changing this condition. Following the literature (e.g. [11]; [2]), we add these new three criteria:

(1) The average profit inside the network increases with the entrance of a non-member firm;
(2) The profit of the firm that will enter is higher than the network's average profit;
(3) The profit of the firm with highest income (a kind of "leader" firm) remains the same or increases with the entrance of a new member.

From the simulation considered in Part II we could observe several aspects that differ from the previous simulation in Part I. As regarding firms' cost asymmetry, it is possible to say that, in general, firms with low marginal production costs have higher profits, produce more output and are those who do more research, which means that they have higher R&D output. We then test some combinations of firms, with different marginal costs of production, in order to evaluate if there are some changes in the firms within the network. Not in all combinations but in most of them, network stability occurs for low levels of spillover. This means that when the spillover reaches a lower level, firms prefer to join the R&D network in order to benefit from a total share of research output and then have less production costs and so higher profits, contrasting with same background firms. The network advantages make possible firms with same marginal costs of production have different profits, as the ones inside the RJV reduce more their production costs due to R&D output spread between them. That is why their profits are normally superior.

A relevant fact is that some networks are formed by a mix of firms with better and worse production skills. Therefore, with some exceptions, cooperation takes place not only between firms with high or low efficiency, but they are formed by middle marginal cost companies or joint "extreme marginal cost" firms where the ones with the lowest production efficiency are the most benefited by cost reduction. On the profits issue, we can state that they tend to diminish with the fall of the spillover since the marginal production costs are not so reduced by efficiency achievements. Only if the firm belongs to the RJV then its profit increases in the first moment when the company joins the network. From the example in Table 2, where we show one of the simulation results, we see that firms that enter the RJV increase greatly their profits, while the others that have the same level of profits maintain that level and watch them decreasing when spillover increases. Mostly important, we also observe that firms with different levels of marginal costs (reflected in the different levels of profits), join together to form a strong and beneficial network. As we can see, from the three groups of firms here, we have in the network, for a spillover of 0.27, one firm from the first group and two from the third group.

Table 2. Firm's profits determined on the simulation experiments made

	Firms								
Spillovers	1st	2nd	3rd	4th	5th	6th	7th	8th	9th
075	419	421	419	110	110	110	649	649	649
0,5	417	419	417	109	109	109	646	646	646
0,3	416	416	416	109	108	108	645	645	645
0,29	415	415	415	**112**	108	108	**655**	**655**	644
0,27	415	415	**426**	107	107	107	**657**	**657**	643
0,1	412	412	**428**	106	106	106	**659**	**659**	640
0,03	412	412	**428**	106	106	106	**660**	**660**	639

These results are confirmed by empirical literature. [5] study the effects of incoming spillovers and appropriability on having cooperation. Using data from Belgium they found that incoming spillovers have a positive and significant effect on the probability of firms cooperating. They also find that the higher appropriability, the higher the probability of network cooperation. However, they show that it may depend on the kind of partners firms deal with. In addition, some non-spillover determinants of cooperation are also examined, and they found that larger firms are more likely to cooperate, which is partially confirmed in our study as the results show that firms with lower marginal costs usually engage easily in cooperation.

Statistical tests were used in order to corroborate the relationships and the effects of the variables in the experiments. One–way ANOVA has been computed, considering the effect of several values of the marginal cost (here used as a factor/qualitative variable), over the profit of the firms. The overall null hypothesis has been rejected, meaning that different marginal costs produce different levels of profits in the firms. Post-hoc multiple comparisons tests (Tuckey HSD) have been performed and we were able to conclude that lower marginal costs are associated with higher profits.

We have also compared the profits between networked and non networked firms. The result of the Mann-Whitney test is that statistically significant differences exist between those kinds of firms: firms in networks have higher profits than those not in networks.

Concerning R&D output, we can notice that it has a propensity to increase as a result of a diminishing spillover (Table 3). Nevertheless, if some firms start to cooperate and their R&D output decreases, as a result of the full knowledge sharing benefit that the network agreement provides. As they will share all the research they make, they will not spend so many resources on R&D and then their private R&D output decreases. Continuing using the previous example, we see that R&D output decreases with the entrance in the network but it still increases if the spillover decreases outside the network. This happens because firms will have to invest more so that they can maintain themselves producing in the market, and also because their investment will almost not flow to other firms outside the network. Since the spillover is lower, which decreases free riding behavior, firms outside the network need to increase their R&D output.

Table 3. Firm's R&D output determined on the simulation experiments made

	Firms								
Spillovers	1st	2nd	3rd	4th	5th	6th	7th	8th	9th
0,75	0,06	0,06	0,06	0,03	0,03	0,03	0,08	0,08	0,08
0,5	0,10	0,10	0,10	0,05	0,05	0,05	0,13	0,13	0,13
0,3	0,14	0,14	0,14	0,07	0,07	0,07	0,17	0,17	0,17
0,29	0,14	0,14	0,14	**0,06**	0,07	0,07	**0,13**	**0,13**	0,17
0,27	0,14	0,14	**0,11**	0,07	0,07	0,07	**0,14**	**0,14**	0,17
0,1	0,17	0,17	**0,13**	0,09	0,09	0,09	**0,16**	**0,16**	0,21
0,03	0,18	0,18	**0,14**	0,09	0,09	0,09	**0,18**	**0,18**	0,22

Finally, regarding the output or production level (q), we see that it depends on the type of firms existing in the network, more precisely, the asymmetry between firms' marginal cost of production. In fact, when there are firms with different levels of efficiency, those who are more productive normally tend to increase their output, while the less efficient ones see their output being reduced. However, this situation changes if a network arises: in this case, cooperating firms produce more than in a non-cooperation scenario, mainly if compared with other firms with the same parameter profile.

Concerning the interactions between network formation and stability, we know that companies inside the network have, in this algorithm, the last word on letting or not outside firms to enter in it. Three different entering criteria were defined that turned different numerical results mostly significant on network stability, as it was explained (Figure 3). Considering the above mentioned criteria, the second one, where outsiders enter the network if their initial profit is higher than the average profit, originates the highest frequency of networks. It contrasts with all other criteria, where the last criterion is the one with worse results in what respects network formation.

Generally it is possible to visualize which criterion is more flexible, making the entrance easier to new companies inside the RJV. As we can see in Fig. 3, the spillover necessary to build a network is higher for criterion 2, followed by criterion 1 and then 3, the least advantageous criterion. Considering the third criterion, only in four experiments a network was formed. On the other hand, in the experiments with the second criterion there is always a network formed. Therefore, as explained above, circumstances necessary to generate a RJV are less tough in the second criterion than for the other possible criteria.

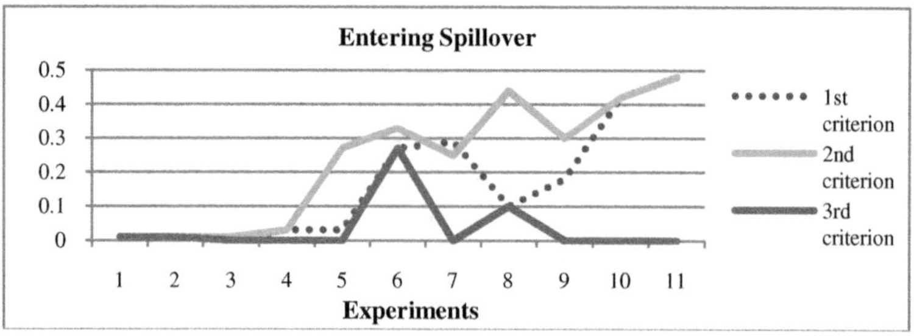

Fig. 3. Spillover value needed to form a network for each criterion

4 Final Remarks

In this study, we analyzed the membership in R&D cooperation networks and its impact on some economic indicators. Our main research hypothesis was that the membership in cooperation networks is related to the degree of the knowledge spillover. We first developed an analytical model where we considered that production costs were symmetric between all companies in the market. We then used numerical simulations to verify our hypothesis. The conclusions obtained were that the profit of firms in the network is higher than the corresponding profit outside the network. We also observed that as the number of firms in the market increases the R&D output decreases due to the fact that the spillover is greater for larger number of firms in the market and the need for R&D output is inferior.

However, all firms entered in the network independently of the environment they faced in the market. So, in order to get close to the reality, a new approach was attempted by introducing cost asymmetry. By doing this we could find that a network, for some level of spillover, would arise but without all companies entering it. Only some would be able to join together and benefit from R&D cooperation and then benefit from higher profits and from R&D of other companies which reduced their production costs. The number of firms kept stable as the firms inside the RJV did not allow new companies to enter, maintaining cooperation benefits just for them.

Nevertheless, networks also depended on how companies manage the RJV. The formation and maintenance of a network depended on what were the entrance and exit decisions defined by firms. As seen before, there were types of decisions that leaded to easier network formation and others did not, depending on what were the minimum requirements for companies to belong to the network. By comparing the two approaches we reached the conclusion that the second was more close to reality. In both cases the number of firms in the network kept stable but on the first model companies entered into the network regarding any kind of situation while in the second model there was entrance only for some levels of spillover and in only some circumstances making the simulation more alike to reality.

But, whatever the approach was, the gains to companies that joined the network were higher. And its impact on profits was showed vital to their performance on the model.

References

1. Amir, R., Wooders, J.: One-Way Spillovers, Endogenous Innovator/Imitator Roles, and Research Joint Ventures. Games and Economic Behavior 31(1), 1–25 (2000)
2. Atallah, G.: Information sharing and the stability of cooperation in research joint ventures. Economics of Innovation and New Technology 12(6), 531–554 (2003)
3. Atallah, G.: Research Joint Ventures Cartelization with Asymmetric R&D Spillovers. Economics Bulletin 12(18), 1–11 (2005)
4. Atallah, G.: Research Joint Ventures with asymmetric spillovers and symmetric contributions. Economics of Innovation and New Technology 16(7), 559–586 (2007)
5. Cassiman, B., Veugelers, R.: R&D Cooperation ans Spillovers: Some Empirical Evidence from Belgium. The American Economic Review 92(4), 1169–1184 (2002)

6. Cellini, R., Lambertini, L.: Dynamic R&D with Spillovers: Competition vs cooperation. Journal of Economic Dynamics & Control 33(3), 568–582 (2009)
7. Cohen, W.M., Levinthal, D.A.: Innovation and Learning: The Two Faces of R&D. Economic Journal, Royal Economic Society 99(397), 569–596 (1989)
8. d'Aspremont, C., Jacquemin, A.: Cooperative and Noncooperative R&D in Duopoly with spillovers. American Economic Review 78(5), 1133–1137 (1988)
9. Kamien, M.I., Zang, I.: Meet me halfway: research joint ventures and absorptive capacity. International Journal of Industrial Organization 18(7), 995–1012 (2000)
10. Kamien, M.I., Muller, E., Zang, I.: Research Joint Ventures and R&D Cartels. American Economic Review 82(5), 1293–1306 (1992)
11. Poyago-Theotoky, J.: Equilibrium and Optimal Size of a Research Joint Venture in an Oligopoly with Spillovers. Journal of Industrial Economics 43(2), 209–226 (1995)
12. Suzumura, K.: Cooperative and Noncooperative R&D in an Oligopoly with Spillovers. American Economic Review 82(5), 1307–1320 (1992)
13. Vonortas, N.S.: Inter-firm cooperation with imperfectly appropriable research. International Journal of Industrial Organization 12(3), 413–435 (1994)

Towards Achieving Benefits of IT Utilization in Collaboration Networks

Iris Karvonen

VTT Industrial Systems, P.O. Box 1000, 02044 VTT, Finland
Iris.Karvonen@vtt.fi

Abstract. Information technology, with the recent developments towards Future Internet, creates expectations for enterprises and collaboration networks about ease of use and high business benefits. However, the benefits are not an automatic outcome of an IT system take-up. In addition to technical aspects, organizational implementation is needed, with user participation and enterprise collaboration in the process. This paper discusses the challenges and barriers of IT implementation in collaborative networks, with the aim to identify success factors for achieving the benefits. The study is based on previous research and uses the experience of collaboration business cases of COIN project (EU FP7 ICT 216256).

Keywords: Collaboration networks, IT utilization, interoperability, SMEs.

1 Introduction

Most SMEs today operate in some kind of collaboration networks, offering efficiency, flexibility and access to knowledge, capabilities and customers which they could not reach alone. There are different forms of cooperation, from the long term collaboration networks to short term consortiums or virtual organizations (VO) [20]. The long term networks may have different levels of preparedness [31], from more sustainable and prepared "VO breeding environments" [3] to less tight business ecosystems [24]. Today collaboration is spreading increasingly from traditional manufacturing to other areas like co-creation, product development and service provision, to support the whole product lifecycle.

Information and communication technology systems and services are not only support but also enablers for collaboration. Efficient information exchange with supporting infrastructure is not any more a competitive edge but a necessity for SMEs. Especially globally distributed operations, requiring enterprise collaboration and interoperability, benefit from Information technology (IT) services. IT, developing towards Future Internet systems, enables also SMEs to participate in global activities as part of supply chains, collaborative networks or business ecosystems. Advanced platforms, tools and services to support Enterprise collaboration and interoperability have been developed for example in past EU-funded research projects ECOLEAD and ATHENA and recently in COIN (Collaboration and Interoperability in networked Enterprises) [5]. This paper is based on the work performed in COIN. The development in COIN has been performed in

L.M. Camarinha-Matos et al. (Eds.): PRO-VE 2011, IFIP AICT 362, pp. 517–526, 2011.

continuous interaction with 6 end user organizations, representing collaboration networks (CN), supply chains (DC) or business ecosystems (BE) in different industrial fields, including automotive, aerospace, aeronautics, pulp& paper engineering, healthcare and ICT-industry . These organizations which have been involved in the development from requirements to testing are called COIN end users in this paper.

Recently, supporting business innovation has been seen to become an important objective for future enterprise systems [10]. The visions in Future Internet Enterprise Systems and cloud computing foresee services to be available "on-fly", with low cost and with more flexible configuration, scalability and openness [9]. The services will be available through generic service platforms and the need for local technical software set-ups will decrease. Thus, the technical barriers for IT utilization are envisaged to decrease. The availability of low cost services should also remove some economic constraints, at least for "mass-services".

However, showing the full benefit of the ICT requires that not only technology but organizational aspects, how to use the technology in the organization and between organizations, are taken into account in the take-up process. It is foreseen that "the power in the development of future enterprise systems will progressively move from IT specialists to business experts" [10]. As the technology is expected to evolve into easier and more usable systems and services, the significance of the organizational take-up process will increase.

2 IT Implementation Challenges

Information technology providers claim remarkable gains when using their services. However, for companies, especially SMEs, it may be challenging to achieve the expected benefits by IT take-up. It is often difficult to understand how to use the technology, what are the objectives behind and how the processes should be changed. The high resources, knowledge and capabilities required for the take up seem to restrain the adoption of IT in SMEs: "Often small and medium-sized companies will not have the knowledge or resources available to carry out the configuration, adaptation, or integration work by themselves" [8]. "The actual implementation of use of ICT in business processes, especially those involving customers and suppliers, remains limited." [9] Especially SMEs suffer of unfinished IT projects, unrealized savings, delays and exceeding the take-up costs. Experiences gained in earlier implementation projects affect the future user's attitudes for a new implementation project [19] and may hinder the will to start new implementations.

Lack of awareness of the possibilities and benefits that ICT could offer is also considered as one barrier for ICT adoption by SMEs [9]. The technology and vendors with approaches from onsite to cloud-based solutions make many SMEs confused and willing to wait until the market settles down [29]. On the other hand, when always following others' the enterprises cannot be in the lead, gaining the potential competitive advantages [22].

Additionally, there is the problem of sharing the benefits: Some manufacturing SMEs see that the benefits of IT utilization do not come for them but accumulate at the end of the manufacturing process [32]. A similar observation can be seen on user level [7]: "the value may be obvious at the level of an enterprise but not as evident at the individual level". This decreases the motivation for change which is needed at the end user level, to make success at the company or network level.

The barriers are familiar also for enterprises interested in innovative solutions. The six end users of COIN project [5] identified the following main obstacles: not knowing about the potential and the benefits clearly enough, the benefits going to someone else, high costs, additional work, risks, resistance to change, too complex implementation, not believing in security, not knowing the sustainability of the solution etc. To overcome these obstacles they suggest strategic approach, success stories and demonstration of benefits as well as service provider support. Also customers requiring the take-up of novel solutions would contribute to the implementation of new solutions and processes.

The benefits created by technology are of course dependent on its usability. However, the same IT solution does not necessarily give the same advantages in different companies. The same system may not fit all the cases and the main question often is, how the technology is used in the organization. The decisions are made and realized in the organizational implementation process. That is why, in addition to software usability, the implementation process is important [15]. It does not only affect the costs or schedule of the start-up of the system, but also how the system is used in the long run and how the processes of the organization are modified, the roles defined etc. [18].

In the take up process the organizations must be able to determine which goals they wish to reach with the system [28], often the processes need to be re-defined and the individual end users need to be committed to the system use. The implementation project has proved to be challenging. Some previous studies have shown failure in about half to two-thirds of information system projects [28]. Even business losses have been reported [34, 17]. For complex IT systems, like ERP (Enterprise Resource Planning), the failure percentage has been assessed to be even higher: in early take-ups in 1990's about 90% of the implementation projects were reported to fail at the first attempt [12] or "three quarters of ERP system installations were judged unsuccessful by the companies paying the bills" [13]. Still in 2000's "Many ERP implementation projects are geared towards failure, out-of-budget deployments, implementations unable to deliver the expected functionality or, in the best case, delays." [2]. Because of the challenges, the IT implementation success has become a relevant research issue, not only in the ERP field, but also in e-Business, enterprise portals, web applications etc [for example 2,4,23,26]. The need for organizational implementation has been identified.

IT implementation is defined as "the entire process from needs analysis and choice of technological solution, to the realization of the full benefits from the technology" [25]. Other terms used for the task are system roll-out and system transition [16]. The starting point is as soon as the decision about the IT implementation has been made and the focus is on the implementation in the organization, not in software development.

As seen above, the take-up of complex IT systems is challenging already in one organization. In collaboration networks, in an inter-enterprise environment the challenges of IT take-up are even higher:

- The partners are independent enterprises, they have greater autonomy [25] and the decision-making is distributed. It may be difficult to reach a common decision about the IT take-up and understanding about the new processes. Take-up of systems or services supporting collaboration is not fully successful if all partners are not interested and capable of using them.
- The systems or services are not always as beneficial for each enterprise – for some they may create benefit, while for some others the system may mean only additional work.
- Inter-enterprise environment has additional complexity because of more units, functions, and locations.
- There are more differences in concepts, cultures, processes, practices, skills and management styles between network partners.
- Openness is not always accepted between organizations. Thus more careful specification of access rights is needed than inside one organization.
- Companies may collaborate within several networks. They are not willing to take up and use many parallel systems.

Thus, the organizational implementation process needs to be extended to an inter-organizational process. Inter-organizational ICT implementation may be defined as the process and actions required to adopt the ICT tools & services into operational use in the network, including the necessary process changes and end user participation.

3 Development Approach

As described in the previous sector, the availability of an IT solution does not guarantee the business benefits when taking it into use. Thus, from the research point of view, it is not enough to develop new technology. It is important also to consider how the technology could be best utilized and through which processes and actions each organization and network can achieve the benefits. One way to approach this is to identify the best practices or critical success factors for take-up of EC & EI solutions. They could serve as guiding principles or a check list of actions, processes or conditions that need to be fulfilled to achieve the expected results in an inter-enterprise environment.

This paper focuses on the identification of critical success factors for the context of Enterprise Collaboration (EC) and Enterprise Interoperability (EI) services. As a starting point research about IT adoption, organizational implementation and conditions for enterprise system success has been reviewed. Critical success factors of IT implementation identified in previous research were reviewed and consolidated to a list of 17 items. This is described in chapter 4.1. The research base was enriched and adapted using the experience of COIN end users. The preliminary views of the end users were collected by interviews and survey templates and discussed in workshops. The list was added with specific factors relating to the context of inter-organizational collaboration, coming from the observations of the end users. The resulting list of 23 factors is presented in chapter 4.2.

Finally, to validate the critical success factors in the context of EC & EI take up, the list was developed into a questionnaire to the end users. The questionnaire asked the end users to assess for each factor:

- the importance of the factor in the context of IT supporting collaboration and interoperability (with scale not important.. highly important),
- the current level of practice: Is the factor currently considered and put into practice in the network/ ecosystem of the end user organization when taking up IT solutions (always-often-sometimes-seldom-never)?

The questionnaire was distributed to COIN end users. Because of the project internal use only, the group of respondents was, of course, quite small but on the other hand, the replying end users especially represented enterprises for which collaboration is important. The results are described in chapter 4.3.

In addition to the identification of the importance of the presented factors the results can be used to indicate which factors (processes, practices) have the largest gaps within this group of end users. The gaps have been measured for each factor as the ratio of average importance rating and the average current usage:

Gap = average importance rate / average current level of practice,

where

the average importance rate is the average of different users' assessments given with scale from 1..5 (not important .. very important) and the average current level of practice is the average of the users' assessments given also by 1..5 (with never-seldom-sometimes-often-always).

Thus the gap "indicator" should identify the factors which are important but seldom taken into account in the organizations and which would thus need more attention. The results can be used to emphasize both the important and the usually ignored practices and for developing guidance for end users when taking up EC & EI services.

4 Critical Success Factors (CSFs) for EC and EI Take Up

4.1 Previous Research of CSFs in IT Implementation

To support successful implementation, IT research has identified best practices as critical success factors, guiding the activities of organizations in the implementation process. Critical success factors (CSF) are defined as "the limited number of areas in which results if they are satisfactory, will ensure successful competitive performance of the organization" [27] or "key areas of performance that are essential for the accomplishment of a mission or project, i.e. the fields in which satisfactory results ensure the attainment of goals". [2] Thus CSFs describe the activities and conditions for success, not only being in time and budget but also achieving the expected benefits. IT research has reviewed the CSFs for ERP implementation, e-commerce or enterprise portals, mainly for single organizations [27, 33]. The focus has been in organizational change [21], measuring the relevance of CSFs with benefits based on case experiences [14,23,30], studying the interrelations [1], timing of CSFs in different phases of the implementation [11], in different types of organizations [2] etc. The factors given in different sources are largely similar and overlapping, even if their order of importance may be different for different application areas [27].

4.2 Adaptation for Inter-organizational Environment

Critical success factors of EC & EI implementation represent the factors that are needed to ensure the success of EC & EI solution take-up. To define the CSFs for EC & EI context the factors presented in previous research were collected and consolidated together into a list of 17 success factors, classified into 6 groups.

In a collaboration environment the success is not dependent alone of one company but may require the participation of several organizations. Thus some of the factors were modified because of the inter-organizational aspect. Based on the preliminary discussions with COIN end users also 6 factors relevant for collaboration environment were added (marked with * below). This resulted to the following list of 23 potential factors:

1. Management and vision:
   1.1 Top management support, participation, commitment and involvement
   1.2 The vision of the collaboration is clear and shared*
   1.3 The take-up has clear goals and objectives.
   1.4 Common decision of the take-up*
2. Solution selection
   2.1 Selection with minimal customization
   2.2 Sustainability of the service*
   2.3 Service offering future innovation*
   2.4 The solution business model & prizing clear and acceptable*
3. Organization of take-up
   3.1 Take-up team has sufficient competencies and skills.
   3.2 Excellent Take-up Project management
   3.3 Consideration of multi-site issues - Local champions.
4. System and process adaptation
   4.1 Adaptation of existing practices, identify inter-organizational processes affected
   4.2 Readiness of organizational culture for cooperation, change and participation
   4.3 Take into account balance of power and homogeneity
5. Practices towards end users
   5.1 User involvement into the take-up process
   5.2 Collaboration maturity*
   5.3 Adequate training program
   5.4 Strong communication inwards and outwards
   5.5 Creation of incentives for collaboration, participation and information sharing
6. Take-up phases
   6.1 Time box philosophy
   6.2 Phased take-up approach
   6.3 Analyze the interfaces with legacy/other systems
   6.4 Managing post-implementation process.

The content of the factors and their sources have been described more in [6].

4.3 Results of End User Assessment

This list, with supporting descriptions, was used as the basis for the identification of their relevance in the EC & EI context, using a questionnaire to the end users [6], as described above. The responding group was quite small; with six end user organizations of which seven replies were received. Thus the results should also be assessed with this restriction; they are not telling the final importance of the factors but give anyway some preliminary information from users knowing well the EC & EI domain challenges. The results of the questionnaire showed that all the success factors which were considered critical in previous IT research, were assessed important also in this group of collaborating enterprises: they all had the average rate above 3,5 (scale 1..5) and most of them had an average rate above 4. All the additional factors relating to collaboration had the average rate above 4. Within this group of enterprises the following factors were seen most important:

- Having or creating a *clear and shared vision of collaboration*: The partners in the CN/BE/SC need to understand the benefits and goals of collaboration and have a common vision of the future.
- Using *time box philosophy* in the take up: take-up plan offering benefits at different stages. Performance measures of benefits should be followed.
- The services should offer *future innovation*, possibility for scaling up and further development.
- The take-up team must have *sufficient competencies and skills*, including knowledge from past deployments and technology readiness. Multifunctional/organizational team is recommended.
- The take-up should be supported by *excellent project management* at the CN/BE/SC level, depending on the take-up size and scope. Purposeful planning with formalized project plan, project monitoring and controlling, use of steering committee, risk management, competent project manager are recommended.
- *Collaboration maturity* of the participating organizations, including trust, should be at sufficient level in the network. Previous experience of collaboration is needed.

Thus, according to this group, these practices and conditions are the most important to take into account when taking up EC & EI solutions in a collaborative environment. However, their importance is not highly different from the other factors. Thus the list should not be “cut” but all the factors should be taken into account. A more detailed presentation of the observed rates of importance within COIN end user group is presented in [6].

Even if all the factors were generally identified important, the companies are not usually following these practices. The rate of practice or factor usage was below 3,2 for all the factors and for most factors less than 3 (meaning that the practice is sometimes applied). Thereby it seems that these practices are not commonly taken into practice even if the enterprises recognize them important and belong to the group of enterprises interested in innovation. Thus there is a need for this type of guiding list to support enterprises in their take up processes.

When comparing the importance and the usage with the “gap indicator” (as described in chapter 3) the largest gaps were identified for the following factors:

- The end users would like to be able to *select the solution/ service business model*, for example as a service or as a utility. The prizing is clear and acceptable. Currently they are not able to do this.

- The organizational change management, *adaptation of existing practices*, designing to-be processes, identifying inter-organizational processes affected and aligning the functionality with the business processes are considered important but not sufficiently considered in practical take-up cases of collaborating organizations.
- According to the end users the take-up teams do not usually have *sufficient competencies and skills*.
- The *multi-site / multi-organization* issues are not considered sufficiently. Local champions, translating the take-up vision into reality from the local viewpoint and solving problems, is recommended to support the take-up in a distributed organization / different organizations.
- The *balance of power and homogeneity,* group cohesion and social capital are not sufficiently handled in organizations and networks within the take up. Psychological safety and recognition decrease the resistance and increase motivation of users.

Three of these gaps come from low level of usage (seldom) and only one of the factors assessed in the six most important belong to this group. The full list of the values of the gap indicators is presented in [6].

5 Conclusions

This paper discusses the challenges of IT implementation in inter-enterprise environment, in the context of Enterprise Collaboration and Enterprise Interoperability services. The main focus is in the identification of critical success factors for EC & EI service take up. Based on previous research and COIN end user experience critical success factors were identified, organized and finally validated by industrial end users participating in COIN project.

The analysis within this group of six networked end user organizations showed that all the criteria defined for the single organizations were relevant also for inter-organizational take up, but additionally six factors coming from the EC & EI context were needed. These consider, for example, collaboration maturity, common vision of the collaboration, common decision of the take up and offer for future innovation and scalability. Furthermore, the application of the different practices or principles behind the critical success factors was studied within the end user group. The result was that the common level of application or usage was low for most factors. This is partly due to underestimating the resources needed to create common understanding about the future concept which the IT is aimed to support. A measure of "gap indicator" was defined as the ratio of average importance rating and the average current usage of a factor. The gap indicator is able to reveal factors or practices that are not taken into practice sufficiently even if they are recognized important.

The analysis was in this phase restricted in quite a small, COIN internal group. In future it would be interesting to extend it to larger user groups to see if there are differences in the importance or in the current practices between application fields. The reasons behind the gaps should be analyzed more in the future. Within the development towards Future Internet Enterprise Systems, which are expected to offer more ease of technical take up, it is important to increase the awareness of both end users and the supporting software providers about the organizational requirements of IT implementation. Future Internet research should also include a topic about IT innovations, from the end user viewpoint, taking into account user-oriented and user-involved development.

Acknowledgement. This work has been partly funded by the European Commission through ICT Project COIN: Collaboration and Interoperability for networked enterprises.

References

1. Akkermans, H., van Helden, K.: Vicious and virtuous cycles in ERP implementation: a case study of interrelations between critical success factors. European Journal of Information Systems 11, 35–46 (2002)
2. Araujo, I.: Critical Success Factors for ERP Deployments in International Federation for Information Processing. In: Tjoa, A.M., Xu, L., Chaudhry, S. (eds.) Research and Practical Issues of Enterprise Information Systems, vol. 205, pp. 319–324. Springer, Boston (2006)
3. Camarinha-Matos, L.M., Afsarmanesh, H., Ollus, M. (eds.): Methods and Tools for Collaborative Networked Organizations. Springer, New York (2008)
4. Carneiro, L., Alves, A., Carneiro, D., Wolf, C., Macey, J., San Martin, F., Ballester, F.: Methodology for the implementation of e-Business solutions in SMEs. In: Stanford-Smith, B., Chiozza, E. (eds.) E-work and E-commerce. Novel Solutions and Practices for a Global Networked Economy, vol. 1, pp. 106–112. IOS Press, Amsterdam (2001)
5. COIN project (EU-FP7-216256), `http://www.coin-ip.eu/`
6. COIN: COIN (EU-FP7-216256) Deliverable D64.1b EC &EI inter-organizational implementation methods (to be published, 2011)
7. EC: Value Proposition for Enterprise Interoperability ref version 3, 3. EC (December 2007), `http://cordis.europa.eu/ist/ict-ent-net/isg.htm`
8. EC: eBusiness Guide for SMEs. eBusiness Software and Services in the European Market. European Communities 2008 (2008), `http://ec.europa.eu/enterprise/e-bsn/ebusiness-solutions-guide/docs/eBusiness_Guide_for_SMEs.pdf`
9. EC: FInES Position Paper. Final version 1.9.2009. Future Internet Enterprise Systems (FInES) Cluster. European Communities (2009)
10. EC: FInES Position Paper on Orientations for FP8. A European Innovation Partnership for European Enterprises. Final Version 18.3.2011. Future Internet Enterprise Systems (FInES) Cluster. European Communities (2011)
11. Esteves, J., Pastor, J.A.: Organizational and technological critical success factors behavior along the ERP implementation phases. In: Enterprise Information Systems VI, pp. 63–71 (2006)
12. Donovan, R.M.: Why the controversy over ROI from ERP. Mid-range ERP (2000), `http://www.midrangeERP.com`
13. Griffith, T., Zammuto, R.F., Aiman-Smith, L.: Why New Technologies Fail. Industrial Management 41(3), 29–34 (1999); ABI/INFORM Global
14. Hong, K.-K., Kim, Y.-G.: The critical success factors for ERP implementation: an organizational fit perspective. Information & Management 40, 25–40 (2002)
15. Hyötyläinen, R.: Implementation of technical change as organizational problem-solving process. Management of user activities (VTT Publications 337). Espoo: Technical Research Centre of Finland. Academic dissertation (1998)

16. ITIL. An Introductory Overview of ITIL® V3. Best Management Practice. itSMF; The IT Service Management Forum (2007), http://www.itsmfi.org/files/itSMF_ITILV3_Intro_Overview_0.pdf
17. Jeffery, B., Morrison, J.: ERP. One Letter at a Time. September 1, 2000 Issue of CIO Magazine (2000), http://www.cio.com
18. Karvonen, I.: SMEs and the implementation of information systems: how to succeed. In: Stanford-Smith, B., Chiozza, E. (eds.) E-work and E-commerce. Novel Solutions and Practices for a Global Networked Economy, vol. 2, pp. 1138–1144. IOS Press, Amsterdam (2001)
19. Koskinen, M.: On the Role of Interpretation Schemes in Organizational IS Implementation. In: Proceedings of the 39th Hawaii International Conference on System Sciences (2006)
20. Kurumluoglu, M., Nostdal, R., Karvonen, I.: Base concepts. In: Camarinha-Matos, L., Afsarmanesh, H., Ollus, M. (eds.) Systems and Practices Virtual Organizations, pp. 11–28. Springer, Heidelberg (2005)
21. Lanning, H.: Planning And Implementing Chang In Organisations – A Construct For Managing Change Projects. Dissertation at Helsinki University of Technology (2001)
22. Li, M.-S.: Enterprise activity in the Future Internet Assembly. FInES cluster meeting, June 2 (2010), http://cordis.europa.eu/fp7/ict/enet/fines-meeting-20100602_en.html2.7.2010
23. Lin, H.-F.: Empirically testing innovation characteristics and organizational learning capabilities in e-business implementation success. Internet Research 18(1), 60–78 (2008)
24. Moore, J.: Predators and Prey: A New Ecology of Competition. Harvard Business Review (May/June 1993)
25. Munkvold, B.E.: Challenges in IT implementation for supporting collaboration in distributed organizations. European Journal of Information Systems 8, 260–272 (1999)
26. Nicolaou, A.I., Bhattachary, S.: Organizational performance effects of ERP systems usage: The impact of post-implementation changes. International Journal of Accounting Information Systems 7, 18–35 (2006)
27. Remus, U.: Critical success factors for enterprise portals. A comparison with ERP implementations. Business Process Management Journal 13(4), 538–552 (2007)
28. Scheer, A.-W., Habermann, F.: Enterprise resource planning: making ERP a success. Communications of the ACM 43(4), 57–61 (2000)
29. silicon.com: The practicalities of unified communications and collaboration (2009), http://www.silicon.com/special-features/unified-communications/2009/11/17/unified-comms-what-it-needs-to-succeed-39653038/
30. Sun, Y.T., Yazdani, A., Overend, J.D.: Achievement assessment for enterprise resource planning (ERP) system implementations based on critical success factors (CSFs). International Journal of Production Economics 98, 189–203 (2005)
31. Tolle, M., Vesterager, J.: VEM: Virtual Enterprise Methodology. In: Karvonen, et al. (eds.) Global Engineering and Manufacturing in Enterprise Networks (GLOBEMEN), VTT Symposium, vol. 224, pp. 53–70 (2003)
32. TT: Electronic Business in Finnish industry. TT - The Confederation of Finnish Industry and Employers (2000), http://www.tt.fi/english/publications/tehoa.pdf
33. Umble, E.J., Haft, R.R., Umble, M.M.: Enterprise resource planning: Implementation procedures and critical success factors. European Journal of Operational Research 146, 241–257 (2003)
34. Wheatley, M.: ERP Training stinks. June 1, 2000 Issue of CIO magazine (2000), http://www.cio.com

Cooperation of SMEs – Empirical Evidences After the Crisis

Jens Schütze, Heiko Baum, Martina Ganß, Ralica Ivanova, and Egon Müller

Chemnitz University of Technology,
Institute of Industrial Management and Factory Systems,
Department of Factory Planning and Factory Management,
09107 Chemnitz, Germany
{jens.schuetze,heiko.baum,martina.ganss,ralica.ivanova,
egon.mueller}@mb.tu-chemnitz.de
http://www.tu-chemnitz.de/mb/FabrPlan/Englisch/

Abstract. Cooperation is a key success factor for small and medium enterprises (SME) in most of the countries. At the beginning of the 2000s, a large European study has analysed the extent and the effect of cooperation between SMEs. However, how successful have been cooperation of SMEs during the economic crisis of the last years? Has the cooperation rate decreased or increased? What are the drivers and obstacles of SME cooperation? Based on an empirical study in a SME-rich region in Germany, which was finished in January 2011, these and further questions will be answered in detail.

Keywords: Cooperation, Small and Medium Enterprise, Empirical Study, Collaborative Network, Virtual Breeding Environment.

1 Introduction

SMEs are a crucial economic factor in nearly every country in this world [1]. This fact has been recognized by the European Union at an early stage. In order to improve the monitoring of the economic development of SMEs and consequently to offer political support for the SME-sector, which is important in terms of economic policy, but also has a weak lobbying, the *Observatory of European SMEs* has been created in December 1992 by the European Commission, and replaced in 2008 by the *SME Performance Review*.

However, the effort of this analysis of the SME-sector is enormous. Due to the legal form and the size only limited statistical data on SME are available (e.g. from business registers and tax authorities), SME-analyses are often conducted in the form of interviews with the companies. For example, in the *2007 Observatory survey* more than 17,000 SMEs were interviewed over the telephone within one month EU-wide [2].

Although the scientific discipline of the *Collaborative Networks (CN)* has been well established in the meantime [3] and cooperation is considered essential especially for SME [4], only little empirical data on cooperation in SMEs is existent. In 2003, the extent and the effect of cooperation between European SMEs were

L.M. Camarinha-Matos et al. (Eds.): PRO-VE 2011, IFIP AICT 362, pp. 527–534, 2011.

analysed in a large-scale study [5]. Unfortunately, this research line was not continued. Most of the following empirical analysis by the *Observatory of European SMEs* and the *SME Performance Review* have not reflected cooperative aspects. In addition, other SME-analyses, like the British *CBR SME Survey* [6] or the Canadian *Stats Link SME Report* [7], hardly allowed any conclusions on cooperative questions in SMEs. The only reliable access to empirically based data marks case studies in collaborative networks of SME (e.g. [8], [9]).

In light of this, it appeared meaningful to conduct a survey on cooperation in SMEs and especially to include the experiences during the global economic and financial crises of 2007 to 2010. In the following, a survey about German SMEs will be presented dealing with this problem.

2 The SME*flex* Survey

SME*flex* is a German collaborative research project dealing with the stability-conducive use of flexibility strategies in SME.[1] The project started in autumn 2009 and first gained a wide range of established flexibility approaches, which are mentioned in the literature. 50 internal and 74 external flexibility instruments had been identified and were clustered in seven groups. One of these flexibility groups comprised all kinds of cross-company collaboration.[2]

The survey was carried out from September 2010 to January 2011 in 131 SMEs. It was designed as a multi-hour personal interview with the company owner, the executive board or the upper management level (e.g. chief financial officer). The surveyed enterprises belong to the following industrial sectors and regions:

- Mechanical and plant engineering in the region East Germany
- High performance composite materials in the federal state of Saxony-Anhalt
- Precision technology and precision engineering in the federal state of Saxony
- Renewably energies in the federal state of Berlin-Brandenburg

All size ranges of SMEs were surveyed[3]: (1) micro-enterprises with a maximum of 9 employees and an annual turnover of up to 2 million Euro, (2) small enterprises with a maximum of 49 employees and an annual turnover of up to 10 million Euro as well as (3) medium-sized enterprises with a maximum of 249 employees and an annual turnover of up to 50 million Euro (balance sheet total of up to 43 million Euro). Due to country-specific characteristics and on the basis of the SME definition given by the German Institute for SME Research [13], additional another size range of SMEs was surveyed: (4) medium-sized enterprises with a maximum of 499 employees and an annual turnover of up to 50 million euro (balance sheet total of up to 43 million Euro). For comparative purpose, two large scale enterprises (LSEs) were surveyed too. The questionnaire was tested and improved in all four sectors and regions.

---

[1] The research agenda of the project is described in [10].

[2] Details on the flexibility groups can be found in [11]. The present article focuses only on cross-company collaboration.

[3] According to the EU definition of SMEs [12].

3 Empirical Results

3.1 Extent of SME Cooperation

As the EU-study of 2003 [5] already stated, the extent of cooperation is subject to considerable country-specific differences. Whilst nearly 70% of all SMEs in Finland cooperated, it was only 10% in Portugal. The cooperation rate in German SMEs totalled at less than 30% according to this study [5:24].

Compare to that, the SME*flex* survey of 2010/11 shows a strong increase in the cooperation rate since 2003 – 72% of the surveyed SMEs stated that they are cooperating. It is striking that the extent of cooperation correlates with the enterprise size. Whilst only up to 46% of the micro-enterprises participate in cooperation, already up to 67% of the small enterprises and up to 82% of the medium-sized enterprises act likewise. The cooperation rate in medium-sized enterprises with more than 250 employees (German SME definition, see chapter 2) and large scale enterprises, mounted up to 100% (figure 1).

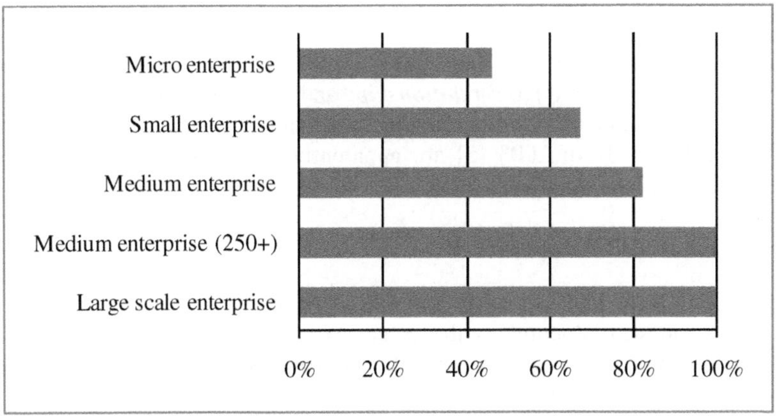

Fig. 1. Cooperation rate in German SMEs (n=131+2)

3.2 Objectives of SME Cooperation

The objectives enterprises associate with cooperation are exceedingly multifaceted. Table 1 outlines the pursued objectives. Altogether, a large percentage of SME cooperation aims at economic aspects: By cooperating, 61% of the SMEs aim at improving their profitability, 59% at using synergies, 51% at achieving cost reductions and 47% at saving time. Market-oriented objectives are in second place: By cooperating, 56% of the SMEs would like to enter new markets, 42% want to create new market strengths or improve their negotiating position and 24% target on overcoming market and mobility barriers. Further objectives like representation of interests and risk splitting only play a subordinate role.

Table 1. Reasons for SME cooperation (n=94)

	Percentage of SMEs*
Improve profitability	62%
Use of synergies	61%
Entering new markets	55%
Realising qualitative competitive advantages	54%
Cost reduction	51%
Optimisation of the value-added chain	49%
Time-savings	48%
Taking up activities not realisable by the power of a single enterprise	46%
Create market strength/improve negotiating position	43%
Representation of interests	35%
Changing market and mobility barriers	24%
Risk splitting	19%
Remedying competitive situation	17%
Prestige reasons	15%
Unification and standardisation of inter-company procedures	13%
Others	15%

* Multiple answers allowed

A *better qualification of the employees, development of new products, improve customer loyalty, creating fixed relationships* and *gaining information on trends and tendencies of the industry at an early stage* were named as other aims. The categories used in the EU-study of 2003 [5] are apparently not sufficient to cover the entire range of cooperation objectives.[4]

3.3 Drivers of SME Cooperation

Which factors have had a positive influence on the cooperation with other SMEs? This central question documents the actual experiences made by the SMEs whilst cooperating (Table 2) and is a major factor in providing support for Virtual Breeding Environments and finally CN creation [14].

The achieved know-how profit is pointed out as a positive effect by 54% of the enterprises. When cooperating, already existing business relationships are considered advantageous by 51% of the SMEs and 43% associate an improved corporate image with cooperation. Likewise, 43% of the surveyed SMEs improved their market position by cooperating, whilst 31% observed rationalisation effects and 21% a more efficient business organisation in their enterprises. If there is no existent business relationship between the cooperating partners so far, 27% found it advantageous to have a structural similarity between the partners and 16% preferred a similar organisational culture. A reduced risk of non-productive time could be observed by 11% of the SMEs. Only 2% of the surveyed SMEs were not able to detect any positive factors occurring out of cooperation. *Confidence, a reduction of the processing time* and *an advance in new technologies* were named as other drivers.

[4] The following objectives were differentiated: access to new and bigger markets, to expanded procurement options for products, access to know-how and technologies, additional production capacities, lower costs, access to labour, access to capital and others [5:19].

Table 2. Enhancers of SME cooperation (n=94)

	Percentage of SMEs*
Achieving know-how profit	55%
Already existing business relationships	51%
Improved image of the own company	43%
Improved market position	43%
Rationalisation effects	32%
Structural similarities of the partners	28%
More efficient business organisation	21%
Similar business culture	16%
Reduced risk of non-productive time	12%
Others	15%
No enhancers	2%

* Multiple answers allowed

3.4 Obstacles to SME Cooperation

Of course, it is important as well to name those factors that could negatively affect cooperation or maybe even avoid their initiation. The answers documented in Table 3 exclusively result from companies that already took part in cooperation, i.e. have own experiences. The apprehensions of non-cooperating SMEs are not included.

Basically, two important categories can be recognised: organisational and confidence barriers. The following barriers can be counted among the category *organisation*: 31% of the surveyed SMEs considered the organisational effort emerging from cooperation to be negative and 20% stated longer decision-making times because of the cooperation. The category *confidence* is considerably more multifaceted: 25% of the companies rated arising dependencies as a barrier, 22% had difficulties in finding appropriate cooperation partners, 20% were afraid to lose know-how, 10% feared unequal power distribution between the cooperation partners, 8% worried about an opportunistic behaviour of a cooperation partner, 8% criticised a lack of communication and 7% a lack of confidence. 18% of the surveyed SMEs

Table 3. Barriers to SME cooperation (n=94).

	Percentage of SMEs*
Organisational effort	31%
Arising dependencies	25%
Difficulties in finding appropriate cooperation partners	21%
Fear of losing know-how	20%
Longer decision-making times	19%
Fear of unequal power distribution between the cooperation partners	11%
Fear of opportunistic behaviour of a cooperation partner	9%
Lack of communication	9%
Lack of confidence	7%
Unclear advantage of the cooperation	7%
Others	4%
No barriers	18%

* Multiple answers allowed

observed no cooperation barriers and the advantage of the cooperation was not clear to 7% of the companies. In comparison to the EU-study *"SME and cooperation"*, a similar categorisation of the cooperation barriers could be detected, even though the prioritisation of the factors is, to some extent, considerably varying [5:36].

3.5 SME Cooperation and Competitive Strength

In the SME*flex* survey, it was attempted to evaluate how the competitive strength of an SME is influenced by cooperation. *"The measurement of the relationship between SME co-operation and competitive strength is complex, ambiguous and difficult"* [5:33] already found the ENSR Survey 2003.

Thus, in a first step the SMEs were asked according to their satisfaction in relation to introduction, achievement, employee acceptance, business benefit and crisis aptitude (Figure 2).

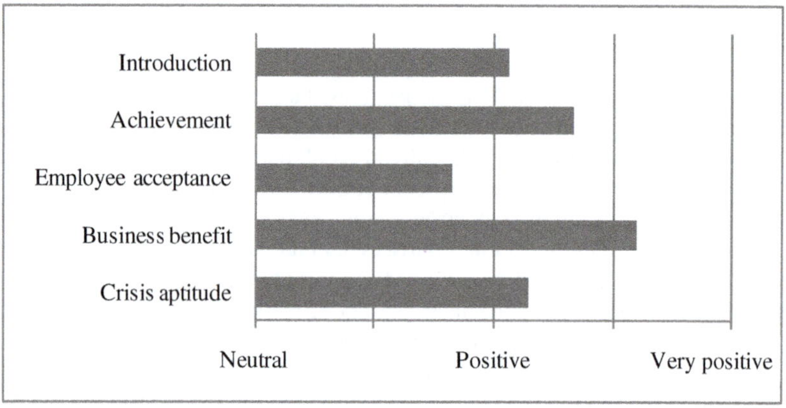

Fig. 2. Satisfaction with cooperation (n=94)

Since these statements are subjective and tends to be too positive after recovery from crisis, additionally the staff acquisition was analysed. As shown in Figure 3, the percentage of SMEs with staff inflow in 2009 was in the cooperating enterprises significantly higher than in those without staff acquisition (76% vs. 52%).

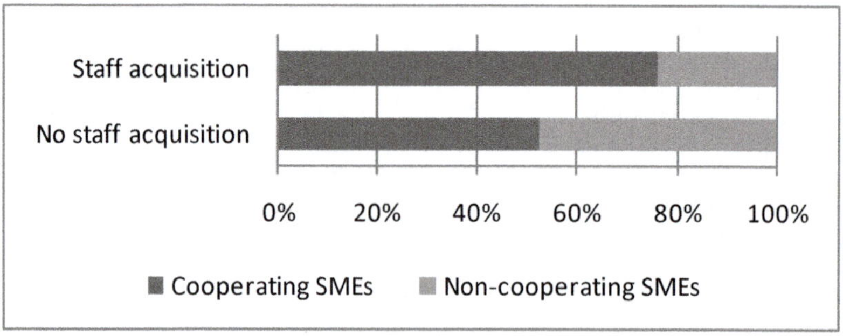

Fig. 3. Staff acquisition in SME during 2009 (n=116)

4 Conclusions

This report provides an overview of the current (post-crisis) situation in the SME sector of East Germany. It could only be given a brief outline. However, even these few empirically-based data show the importance of cooperation for SMEs and what factors contribute to help or hinder the creation process of cooperation. A consolidated view indicates that the smaller the company, the more potential there is for cooperation.

Therefore, the creation of a cooperative milieu, particular in regions with a high share of SMEs[5], is crucial to their economic survival. The approaches from the European FP6 ECOLEAD project or the German Collaborative Research Center 457 „Non-hierarchical Regional Production Networks" provide a sound base for this but need a stronger policy support.

A deeper analysis of the empirical data with multivariate statistics is envisaged as the project continues.

Acknowledgments. This work has been supported by the German Federal Ministry of Education and Research (BMBF) and the European Social Funds (ESF) under grant number 01FH09147. It has been developed in the scope of the German research project SME*flex* (www.smeflex.info) and the European WORK-IN-NET Coordination Action (www.workinnet.org). The authors also thank the contributions from their partners.

References

1. Ayyagari, M., Beck, T., Demirguc-Kunt, A.: Small and medium enterprises across the globe. Small Business Economics 29, 415–434 (2007)
2. European Commission: Flash Eurobarometer 196 – Observatory of European SMEs. Analytical Report, The Gallup Organization, Brussels (2006)
3. Camarinha-Matos, L., Afsarmanesh, H.: Collaborative networks – a new scientific discipline. Journal of Intelligent Manufacturing 16(4-5), 439–452 (2005)
4. Müller, E. (ed.): Ergebnisbericht des Sonderforschungsbereiches SFB 457 "Hierarchielose regionale Produktionsnetze" (Final report of the Collaborative Research Center CRC 457 "Non-hierarchical Regional Production Networks"), Chemnitz University of Technology (2007)
5. European Commission: Observatory of European SMEs No. 2003/5 "SMEs and Co-operation", Office for Official Publications of the European Communities, Luxembourg (2004)
6. Cosh, A., Hughes, A., Bullock, A., Milner, I.: SME finance and innovation in the current economic crisis: The 2008 Survey. Centre for Business Research, University of Cambridge (2009)
7. White, J.: 2009 SME Check-up – Surviving the Crisis, GDSourcing – Stats Link Canada (2009)

[5] Just like East Germany.

8. Baldo, F., Rabelo, R.J.: A Structured Approach for Implementing Virtual Organization Breeding Environments in the Mold and Die Sector: A Brazilian Case Study. In: Camarinha-Matos, L.M., Boucher, X., Afsarmanesh, H. (eds.) PRO-VE 2010. IFIP AICT, vol. 336, pp. 197–203. Springer, Heidelberg (2010)
9. Botarelli, M., Taticchi, P., Cagnazzo, L.: The Virtual Development Office Framework for Business Networks: A Case Study from the Umbrian Packaging District. In: Camarinha-Matos, L.M., Picard, W. (eds.) Proceedings of 9th IFIP Working Conference on Virtual Enterprises, Pervasive Collaborative Networks, Poznan, Poland, September 8-10, pp. 611–618 (2008)
10. Schütze, J., Baum, H., Müller, E.: Flexibility Strategies in Small and Medium Enterprises – Discussion of Research Perspectives. In: Proceedings of the 20th International Conference on Flexible Automation and Intelligent Manufacturing – FAIM 2010, July 12-14, pp. 364–370. California State University, Oakland (2010)
11. Müller, E., Schütze, J., Baum, H., Ganß, M., Ivanova, R.: Business Flexibility in Small and Medium Enterprises – An Empirical Study. In: Proceedings of the 21th International Conference on Flexible Automation and Intelligent Manufacturing – FAIM 2011, Taichung, Taiwan, June 26-29 (accepted, 2011)
12. European Commission: Commission Recommendation (2003/361/EC) of 6 May 2003 concerning the definition of micro, small and medium-sized enterprises, Official Journal of the European Union, L 124/36, Brussels (2003)
13. Günterberg, B., Wolter, H.J.: Unternehmensgrößenstatistik 2001/2002 – Daten und Fakten (Company size statistics 2001/2002 – Facts and Figures). In: Institut für Mittelstandsforschung Bonn (ed.): IfM-Materialien Nr. 157, Bonn (2003)
14. Galeano, N., Guerra, D., Irigoyen, J., Molina, A.: Virtual Breeding Environment – A First Approach to Understand Working and Sharing Principles. In: Konstantas, D., Bourrières, J.P., Léonard, M., Boudjlida, N. (eds.) Proceedings of INTEROP-ESA 2005, Interoperability of Enterprise Software and Applications, Geneva, Switzerland, February 23-25, pp. 99–110 (2006)

A Review of Factors Influencing Collaborative Relationships

María-José Verdecho, Juan-José Alfaro-Saiz, and Raúl Rodríguez-Rodríguez

Department of Business Organization, CIGIP,
(Research Centre on Production Management and Engineering),
Universitat Politècnica de València, Camino de Vera, s/n, 46022, Valencia, Spain
{mverdecho,jalfaro,raurodro}@cigip.upv.es

Abstract. Collaboration is a term commonly used to refer to a type of inter-organizational relationship. However, in real business assessments, many collaborative relationships fail due to the lack of understanding of the factors influencing collaboration sustainability. For this reason, enterprises, prior to engage to a collaborative relationship, need to understand further which the main factors influencing collaboration relationships are, how they are structured and how they interact so that decision makers that desire to engage in a collaborative relationship/network focus not only on improving performance indicators but also on the factors that influence the results of those performance indicators. The purpose of this paper is to present a critical literature review of factors influencing collaborative relationships in order to perform a comparative study of the works for identifying main strengths and gaps for future research.

Keywords: Collaboration, collaborative networks, conceptual issues.

1 Introduction

In the current complex business environment, enterprises adopt different strategies and business models to remain competitive in the marketplace. In order to be efficient, enterprises focus on their own core competencies and rely on other enterprises for developing activities that are related to non-core competences. In fact, enterprises engage in diverse types of relationships that differ in their scope and broadness ranging from transactional type (punctual relationship) to collaborative relationship (long-term relationship). Enterprises must know which type of relationship they need to engage as not all types of relationships are suitable for all the business purposes. For example, in [1], it is presented a classification of four types of relationships among organizations depending on the degree of interaction: networking, coordinated networking, cooperation and collaboration. From a global perspective, collaboration relationships are the ones that involve the greatest degree of interaction and, for that reason, are the most complex. Collaboration involves two or more independent enterprises working together to align their processes with the goal of creating value to end customers and stakeholders with greater success than acting alone [2]. However, collaborative relationships may fail if they are not properly

L.M. Camarinha-Matos et al. (Eds.): PRO-VE 2011, IFIP AICT 362, pp. 535–542, 2011.

managed [3-4]. The Supply Chain Management Review and Computer Science Corporation [5] performed a survey and observes that collaboration is cited as the single most important topic; but how to achieve it is not well understood. The survey showed that 44 percent of the organizations in the sample have functions specifically for supplier and customer collaboration. However, only about 35 percent of the collaboration initiatives turned out to be even moderately successful. As [4] suggest, perhaps, it is because not all participants in every supply chain have embedded collaborative values. In [6], it is indicated that the lack of understanding of collaboration structure and dynamics is considered the main cause of failure of collaborative initiatives. Then, it seems important that enterprises that desire to engage into a collaborative relationship understand the complexity of collaboration, which are the main factors influencing collaboration, how they are structured and how they interact so that so that decision makers that desire to engage in a collaborative relationship/network focus not only on improving performance indicators but also on the factors that influence the results of those performance indicators.

The aim of this paper is twofold. The first purpose is to provide a literature review of works that analyze factors influencing collaborative relationships (section 2). The second purpose is to perform a comparative study of the works reviewed for identifying main strengths and gaps for future research (section 3 and 4).

2 Literature Review

In this section, it is presented a review of works that deal with inter-organizational and collaborative relationships in order to analyze the factors that influence inter-organizational relationships (in general) and collaborative relationships (in particular). It has to be noted that inter-organizational relationships embed all types of relationships, as collaborative relationships are the most complex type involving the greatest degree of interaction. From the literature review, a typology composed of three groups has been defined (see Fig. 1).

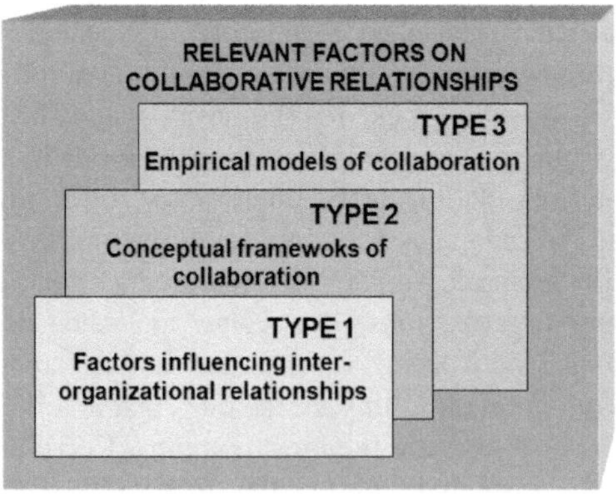

Fig. 1. Relevant factors influencing collaborative relationships: a typology

The first group consists of works that identify factors influencing inter-organizational relationships (type 1). The second group present works that propose conceptual frameworks of collaboration (type 2), and finally, the third group is composed by works that present empirical models of collaboration (type 3). The typology is then structured from a lower to a higher degree of interaction among factors (type 1 only describe some conceptual interaction among factors, type 2 structures the interaction among factors under a conceptual framework and type 3 structures the interaction among factors under a framework and quantifies their relationships empirically).

2.1 Works That Identify Factors Influencing Inter-organizational Relationships

There are numerous works in literature that deal with inter-organizational relationships. It is out of the scope of this paper to review all these works, but a selection has been performed with the aim of identifying the main factors influencing inter-organizational relationships. Within this group of the typology, we have considered two main subgroups of works. One subgroup consists of works that present classifications of inter-organizational environments according to the level of maturity reached in different aspects of their relationships, i.e. they present supply chain evolutionary models (from lower to higher level of collaboration). Within this subgroup, in [3], it is presented a supply chain classification depending on two main aspects: strategic value of the relationship and technology used to support it. From a process perspective, in [7], it is developed a model to classify supply chains based on the maturity of their processes. Each level is characterized according to different factors such as alignment of processes, organizational structure, cooperation, process performance and trust. In [8], a typology for supply chain characterization related to Fiske [9] social relationships theory and the interdependence concept is exposed. In [10], it is presented a classification of supply chains according to the presence of three factors in the CPFR (Collaborative Planning, Forecasting and Replenishment) process: collaboration form, ICT and coordination mechanisms. In [1], organization relationships are classified into four groups depending on four types of factors: communication and information shared; complementary, compatible and/or joint objectives; activity alignment and joint responsibility. In addition, the authors highlight the need of measuring collaborative performance and importance of relationships attributes such as trust.

The second subgroup comprises works that identify the main factors influencing partnerships. In [11] it is considered five factors of inter-organizational relationships: degree of absolute and relative commitment, symmetry of rewards, extent of uncertainty, degree of mutual trust, and length of the relationship. [12] identifies seven factors for partnering contexts: business processes, people, trust, technology, structure, financial resources and culture. [13] analyzes eight factors from different disciplines of theory (marketing, economy, strategy and management) that may influence the evolution on supply chain management. The eight factors are: trust, power, dependency, economy, collaboration, assets, risk and communication.

From the review, we can group the key factors influencing inter-organizational relationships into: strategic value of the relationship and goal congruence; information shared; ICT and Information Systems (IS) role; joint decision-making, activities and problem solving; process approach and management levels; relationship attributes such as trust, commitment, interdependence and coordination; equity or symmetry of investments, risks and rewards; and performance measurement.

2.2 Conceptual Frameworks of Collaboration

In this work, a conceptual framework that characterizes collaboration is defined as *'the set of elements that organized and interrelated allow the representation of the collaboration relationships within inter-organizational environments in a generic manner'*. [14] proposes a conceptual framework that associates variables of relationships (commitment, cooperation, interdependence/power, technology, trust, mutual goals, etc.) to different stages in relationship process (partner selection, defining purpose, setting relationship boundaries, creating relationship value and relationship maintenance). It exposes the interaction among some of the variables describing how they may evolve when an event happens during the different stages. Nevertheless, the work could be further extended by including collaborative processes and performance measurement.

In [15], it is developed a conceptual framework for cross-enterprise collaboration that identifies processes, competencies and capabilities. Key process performance objectives for each process are established. In this sense, the inclusion of performance objectives for the leadership process sustained by the 'relationships' competence is noticeable. However, the relationships competence does not consider important relational attributes e.g. trust.

[16] presents a conceptual framework structured in three levels: strategic, collaborative and cultural elements. The framework considers inter-organizational process alignment through the organizations, performance indicators for the whole SC, the connection between SC performance indicators and the cultural elements, and identifies technology as strategic factor. However, the connection among some of the elements is not explicit. For instance, there is no direct connection between performance indicators and joint decision-making.

Other works reviewed are [17], [18], [19], [20] and [21]. From the review, we can conclude that although the reviewed conceptual frameworks present some aspects that can be extended, they are a foundation for understanding which are the main factors and interrelations influencing collaborative relationships. Therefore, these works facilitate to analyse further the connection of these collaborative factors although they do not use quantitative techniques that allow measuring the degree of influence among the different factors what is reviewed on the next type of works.

2.3 Empirical Models of Collaboration

The works presenting empirical models have gained attention in the literature in the last years as they test relationships among variables (factors) based on real data. [22] develop a model of commitment-trust theory suggesting that trust and commitment are mediating variables between other factors such as cooperation, conflicts, communication, opportunism and benefits.

[23] identify from an empirical study the characteristics that contribute to successful partnerships: relationship attributes (coordination, commitment, and trust),

communication behaviour (participation, and communication quality) and joint problem solving techniques.

The works [24], [25], [26] and [27] expose models with trust as a key factor to increase commitment in relationships as well as a mediator between commitment and the other collaboration factors. The authors suggest that commitment improves with a higher degree of adaptation, shared values, communication, satisfaction and cooperation. [28] presents a model with interdependence, commitment and trust factors. This work details that there is two types of commitment, calculated and affective, and analyze to what extent they are influenced by interdependence and trust in the supply chain. [26] also distinguish types of commitment: affective, continuity and normative. The work aims to study the impact of affective and continuity commitment in supply chain integration and increases coordination among partners. On the other side, normative commitment allows establishing objectives and shared values. Other works, [29] and [30] do not include in their works the commitment factor but they consider trust an essential factor of collaboration. [29] analyze the impact of three factors: trust, ICT, and information network on the joint efforts (planning and conflict resolution). In [30] trust is a mediator factor between other factors such as participation, communication, learning capability, and ability to share knowledge to finally obtain inter-organizational knowledge share. Other works reviewed include [31] and [32].

After analyzing the works it is observed that there is not a consensus reached among the authors regarding what are the main factors of collaborative relationships and which are the influences among them. In fact, there are some factors, e.g. trust that is modeled in two different manners (mediator variable and dependent variable). It has to be noted that the most modeled factors are trust, commitment and communication. Each work establishes different objectives for their models but the most commonly used dependent variable are joint action, trust and commitment. This means that this type of models mostly try to analyze the effects of the other collaborative factors on these three factors in order to achieve sustainable relationships.

3 Comparative Study

Table 1 presents a comparative study of the works reviewed. For that purpose, eight most commonly cited factors have been considered so that different perspectives of enterprises are covered: strategic, process, culture, communication infrastructure and performance measurement (management). This is because the works that integrate different enterprise perspectives constitute a sound basis for understanding collaboration relationship dynamics. The reviewed factors are: common strategy (S), collaborative processes (P), collaborative culture (in general) (CC), trust (T), commitment (C), information shared (IS), ICT and performance measurement (PM). The criteria established to compare the works ranges from absence of the factor (blank) to high degree of consideration (++).

Table 1. Comparative study of the works reviewed

Tip.	References	S	P	CC	T	C	IS	ICT	PM
	Birnbirg (1998)			+	++	++		+	+
	Boddy et al. (2000)	+	+	+				+	+
	Sabath and Fontanella (2002)	++	+	+			+	++	
	Handfield and Bechtel (2004)	+		+	++		++		+
1	Lockamy and McCormack (2004)	+	++	+	+		+		+
	Lejeune and Yakova (2005)	+		+	++		++		
	Danese (2006)	+		+			+	++	
	Camarinha-Matos et al. (2009)	++	+	+	+	+	+	+	+
	Wilson (1995)	+		+	+	+	+	+	+
	Bowersox et al. (2003)	++	++	+		+	++	++	+
	Barratt (2004)	+	++	+	+	+	+	+	+
	Min et al. (2005)	++	++	+			++	+	+
2	Simatupang and Sridharan (2005)	++	++	+	+	+	++	++	+
	Burgess and Singh (2006)	++	++	+	+		++	++	+
	Giannakis (2007)	++	++	+	++	++	+	+	
	Gruat La Forme et al. (2007)	+	++	+			++		+
	Morgan and Hunt (1994)	+		++	++	++	++		+
	Mohr and Spekman (1994)			++	++	++	++		+
	Geyskens et al. (1996)			+	++	++			
	Zineldin and Jonsson (2000)	+		++	++	++	++		+
	Coote et al. (2003),			++	++	++	++		
3	Wu et al. (2004)	+	++	++	++	++	++		
	Handfield and Bechtel (2002)	+		+	++		++		+
	Kwon and Suh (2005)			+	++	++		++	
	Pimentel et al. (2006)			+	++		++		
	Matopoulos et al. (2007)	+	++	+	+		++	++	
	Cheng et al. (2008)	+		+	++		++	+	

4 Conclusions and Research Implications

From the table, the main conclusion obtained is that there is not a consensus regarding what are the main factors of collaborative relationships and which are the influences among them. First, the different groups present different insight into the factors. For example, type 2 and 3 provide more insight than type 1. However, type 2 and 3 differ on the factors treated. Type 2 deepens more on strategy, processes, information shared and ICT while type 3 deepens more on collaborative culture, trust, commitment and information shared. It has to be noted that other factors such as performance measurement are only treated in low detail in these works. Thus, one future research line is to analyse how performance measurement frameworks developed for collaborative enterprises can be connected to the conceptual frameworks and empirical models reviewed in this work to conceptualize further and measure factors influencing collaborative relationships.

Second, the interrelations among collaborative elements identified by the different works of type 2 and 3 of the typology differ and only cover some of the factors. Even in the type 3, there are some factors, e.g. trust that is modeled in two different manners (mediator variable and dependent variable). Further research is needed to model all the factors influencing collaborative relationships, establishing the interactions among them and quantifying under the same model all the existing influences. It may seem that complex models do not capture the essence of what is analysed. However, simple models do not capture the dynamics of complex phenomena. Further research should encounter a balance of both aspects for the different situations.

Third, some interactions among factors have been analysed in more detail e.g. trust and commitment, while other interesting interactions have been less treated e.g. strategy and trust or strategy and performance measurement. Further research should consider these issues into their scope. Finally, it is important to note that it will be interesting to analyse combinations of all types of factors as all of them influence each other in a collaborative relationship.

References

1. Camarinha-Matos, L.M., Afsarmanesh, H., Galeano, N., Molina, A.: Collaborative networked organizations - Concepts and practice in manufacturing enterprises. Computers & Industrial Engineering 57, 46–60 (2009)
2. Simatupang, T.M., Wright, A.C., Sridharan, R.: Applying the theory of constraints to supply chain collaboration. Supply Chain Management: An International Journal 9(1), 57–70 (2004)
3. Sabath, R.E., Fontanella, J.: The Unfulfilled Promise of Supply Chain Collaboration. Supply Chain Management Review (July/August 2002)
4. Kampstra, R.P., Ashayeri, J., Gattorna, J.L.: Realities of supply chain collaboration. The International Journal of Logistics Management 17(3), 312–330 (2006)
5. Supply Chain Management Review (SCMR) and Computer Sciences Corporation, CSC (2004); The second annual global survey of supply chain progress, `http://www.csc.com/`
6. Busi, M., Bititci, U.S.: Collaborative performance management: present gaps and future research. International Journal of Productivity and Performance Management 55(1), 7–25 (2006)
7. Lockamy, A., McCormack, K.: The development of a supply chain management process maturity model using the concepts of business process orientation. Supply Chain Management: An International Journal 9(4), 272–278 (2004)
8. Lejeune, M.A., Yakova, N.: On characterizing the 4 C's in supply chain management. Journal of Operations Management 23(1), 81–100 (2005)
9. Fiske, A.P.: Relativity within Moose ("Mossi") culture: four incommensurable models for social relationships. Ethos 18, 180–204 (1990)
10. Danese, P.: Collaboration forms, information and communication technologies, and coordination mechanisms in CPFR. International Journal of Production Research 44, 3207–3226 (2006)
11. Birnbirg, J.C.: Control in interfirm co-operative relationships. Journal of Management Studies 25(4), 421–428 (1998)
12. Boddy, D., Macbeth, D., Wagner, B.: Implementing collaboration between organizations: an empirical study of supply chain partnering. Journal of Management Studies 37(7), 1003–1018 (2000)

13. Handfield, R.B., Bechtel, C.: Trust, power, dependence, and economics: can SCM research borrow paradigms? International Journal of Integrated Supply Chain Management 1(1), 3–32 (2004)
14. Wilson, D.T.: An integrated model of buyer-seller relationships. In: Working Paper, Institute for the Study of Business Markets. The Pennsylvania State University, State College (1995)
15. Bowersox, D.J., Closs, D.J., Stank, T.P.: How to Master cross-enterprise Collaboration. Supply Chain Management Review (July/August 2003)
16. Barratt, M.: Understanding the meaning of collaboration in the supply chain. Supply Chain Management: An International Journal 9(1), 30–42 (2004)
17. Min, S., Roath, A.S., Daugherty, P.J., Genchev, S.E., Chen, H., Arndt, A.D.: Supply chain collaboration: what's happening? The International Journal of Logistics Management 16(2), 237–256 (2005)
18. Simatupang, T.M., Sridharan, R.: An integrative framework for supply chain collaboration. The International Journal of Logistics Management 16(2), 257–274 (2005)
19. Burgess, K., Singh, P.: A proposed integrated framework for analysing supply chains. Supply Chain Management: An International Journal 11(4), 337–344 (2006)
20. Gruat La Forme, F., Botta Genoulaz, V., Campagne, J.: A Framework to analyse Collaborative Performance. Computers in Industry 58, 687–697 (2005)
21. Giannakis, M.: Performance Measurement of Supplier Relationships. Supply Chain Management; An International Journal 12(6), 400–411 (2007)
22. Morgan, R.M., Hunt, S.D.: The Commitment-Trust Theory of Relationship Marketing. Journal of Marketing 58, 20–38 (1994)
23. Mohr, J., Spekman, R.: Characteristics of partnership success: Partnership attributes, communication behavior, and conflict resolution techniques. Strategic Management Journal 15(2), 135–152 (1994)
24. Zineldin, M., Jonsson, P.: An examination of the main factors affecting trust/commitment in supplier-dealer relationships: an empirical study of the Swedish wood industry. The TQM Magazine 12(4), 245–256 (2000)
25. Coote, L.V., Forrest, E.J., Tam, T.W.: An investigation into commitment in non-Western industrial marketing relationship. Industrial Marketing Management 32, 595–604 (2003)
26. Wu, W.T., Chiag, C.Y., Wu, Y.J., Tu, H.J.: The influencing factors of commitment and business integration on supply chain management. Industrial Management & Data Systems 104(4), 322–333 (2004)
27. Kwon, I.K., Suh, T.: Trust, commitment and relationships in supply chain management: path analysis. Supply Chain Management: An International Journal 10(1), 26–33 (2005)
28. Geyskens, I., Steemkamp, J.B., Scheer, L.K., Kumar, N.: The effects of trust and interdependence on relationship commitment: A trans-Atlantic study. International Journal of Research in Marketing 13, 303–317 (1996)
29. Pimentel Claro, D., Borin de Oliviera Claro, P., Hagelaar, G.: Coordinating collaborative joint efforts with suppliers: the effects of trust, transaction specific investment and information network in the Dutch flower industry. Supply Chain Management: An International Journal 11(3), 216–224 (2006)
30. Cheng, J.H., Yeh, C.H., Tu, C.W.: Trust and knowledge sharing in green supply chains. Supply Chain Management: An International Journal 13(4), 283–295 (2008)
31. Matopoulos, A., Vlachopoulou, M., Manthou, V., Manos, B.: A conceptual framework for supply chain collaboration: empirical evidence from the agri-food industry. Supply Chain Management: An International Journal 12(3), 177–186 (2007)
32. Handfield, R.B., Bechtel, C.: The role of trust and relationship structure in improving supply chain responsiveness. Industrial Marketing Management 31, 367–382 (2002)

Part XIX
Sustainability Issues

Green Virtual Enterprise Breeding Environment Reference Framework

David Romero and Arturo Molina

Tecnológico de Monterrey, México
david.romero.diaz@gmail.com, armolina@itesm.mx

Abstract. A Green Virtual Enterprise (GVE) is an emerging sustainable manufacturing and logistics networked enterprise model focused on offering, delivering and recovering green products to/from the market, under a lifecycle thinking and supported by its source network. In this paper, a GVE Breeding Environment Reference Framework is proposed as a common architectural framework offering a clear approach for conceiving sustainable and fully flexible forward and reverse supply networks, within a breeding environment context, based on a set of five building blocks: targets, main actors, operating principles, lifecycle and supporting technologies, to create and manage GVEs.

Keywords: Collaborative Networked Organizations, Green Virtual Enterprises, Breeding Environments, Sustainable Supply Networks, Industrial Ecology, Industrial Symbiosis, Sustainable Industrial Development.

1 Introduction

The Green Virtual Enterprise phenomenon is nowadays gaining attention worldwide, be it in the form of sustainable supply chains, finding its way as a promising paradigm in manufacturing and service industries to help enterprises to cope with the challenges of turbulent market conditions in the context of economic, environmental and social pressures to achieve a sustainable industrial development model. However, traditional sustainable supply chain practices tend to value innovations that are incremental in nature. As a result, current sustainable supply chain strategies are appropriate to make the supply chain "more sustainable", rather than "fully sustainable", as a fully sustainable approach may require a complete re-engineering of the whole supply chain. In this sense, the Green Virtual Enterprise (GVE) initiative [1] aims a radical value innovation approach as a response to the difficulties of dynamically creating and managing different but integrated flexible forward and reverse supply networks, better known as 'closed-loop supply networks', to address the market dynamic changes and divergent customers' buying behaviour in a sustainable way. By enhancing the traditional sustainable supply chain practices [2] with the dynamic VE principles [3], the GVE Breeding Environment (GVBE) Reference Framework goal is to support the creation and management of short-term and dynamic coalitions of green enterprises, that may be tailored within a GVBE, to respond in a sustainable way to collaboration (business) opportunities, by integrating the green skills or core-

L.M. Camarinha-Matos et al. (Eds.): PRO-VE 2011, IFIP AICT 362, pp. 545–555, 2011.

competencies and resources required to meet or exceed the quality, time and cost frames expected by the customer, striving always the triple bottom line.

In this paper, a GVBE Reference Framework is proposed as a common architectural framework offering a clear approach for conceiving sustainable and fully flexible forward and reverse supply networks, within a breeding environment context, based on a set of five building blocks: targets, main actors, operating principles, lifecycle and supporting technologies, to create and manage GVEs.

2 Green Virtual Enterprise Breeding Environment Base Concepts

For a complete understanding of the GVBE Reference Framework building blocks it is important to first define the following base concepts:

Green Enterprise – is an enterprise that strives to meet the triple bottom line by ensuring that all products, processes, manufacturing and logistics activities in its business operation address the sustainable principles [1].

Green competencies – are those environmentally conscious business practices and strategies such as [1]: *For forward supply networks:* Design for the Environment (DFE), Green Product Lifecycle Management (G-PLM) and Lifecycle Analysis, Lean Manufacturing, Total Quality Environmental Management (TQEM), Environmental Management Systems (EMS), Green Supply Chain Management (G-SCM), Green Logistics, ISO14000 series' requirements. *For reverse supply networks:* inspection, diagnostic and recondition techniques to obtain the most value from a recovered product through a re-use (e.g. spare parts), refurbish (e.g. repair or re-manufacturing), recycling (e.g. scrap) and/or safe disposal (e.g. hazardous wastes treatments) strategy.

GVE Breeding Environments (GVBEs) – are long-term strategic alliances of green enterprises and their related support institutions aimed at offering the necessary conditions (human, financial, social, infrastructural and organisational) to support the rapid and fluid configuration of GVEs. GVBEs act as closed-loop systems where material, energy, information and technology among their members are recycled or shared to achieve a sustainable efficiency strategy (e.g. industrial symbiosis). GVBEs are intelligent networks for competencies and resources management from different green enterprises aiming to combine their green capabilities and capacities to deploy innovative and cost-effective green technologies and practices to promote a sustainable industrial development through F-GVEs and R-GVEs creation [1] [4] [5].

GVEs as dynamic forward supply networks (F-GVEs) – are temporary alliances of green enterprises that come together in order to better respond the market demands through the most efficient use of their complementary skills or core-competencies and shared resources, for developing and delivering in a sustainable way new products to the customer with a minimal environmental impact - within a GVBE [1] [4] [6].

GVEs as dynamic reverse supply networks (R-GVEs) – are temporary alliances of green enterprises that come together in order to better respond a business opportunity based on a sustainable reverse logistics and end-of-life manufacturing approach for recovering products, parts, subassemblies and/or scrap through the most efficient use of their complementary skills or core-competencies and shared resources for their direct-use (re-use), repair, re-manufacture, recycle or safe disposal - within a GVBE [1].

3 GVE Breeding Environment Reference Framework

A *Green Virtual Enterprise (GVE)* is an emerging sustainable manufacturing and logistics networked enterprise model focused on offering, delivering and recovering green products to/from the market, under a lifecycle thinking and supported by its source network. As shown in Fig. 1, the GVBE Reference Framework can be described based on five building blocks to create and manage GVEs in their both modalities: forwards and reverse supply networks.

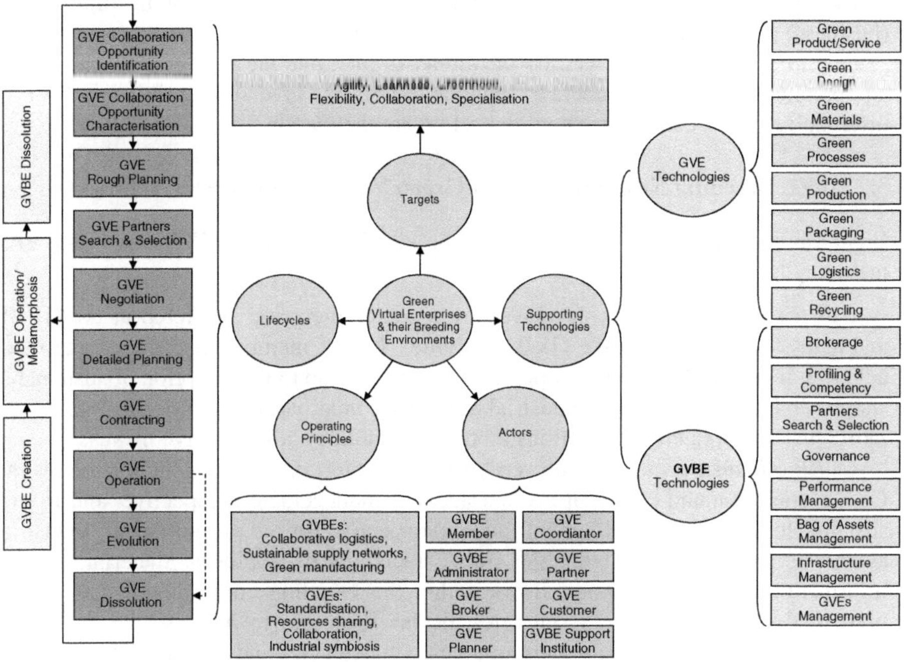

Fig. 1. GVE Breeding Environment Reference Framework

3.1 GVE Breeding Environment and Green Virtual Enterprises Targets

The GVBE model potential, to target the achievement of sustainable and fully flexible supply networks, resides in its ability to dynamically configure forward and reverse supply networks (e.g. GVEs), according to the needs and opportunities of the market and keep them operational as long as these opportunities persist, suggesting a number of sustainable benefits, among which the following can be emphasised [see also 3]:

Agility – represented by the ability to react in a short time to a competitive market opportunity through the rapid configuration of a GVE - within a GVBE.

Leanness – represented by the ability to focus on efficiency and lowest cost-to-serve by searching, assessing and selecting the most suitable green enterprises (GVE partners) according to different sustainable quantitative and qualitative metrics [7] in order to reduce production and logistics costs, and environmental impact.

Greenness – represented by the ability to minimise the environmental impact by integrating different green competencies and technologies available in several green enterprises (GVBE members) within a GVE.

Flexibility – represented by the ability to offer and/or respond with "unlimited" capabilities and capacities to the market demand variations and picks by adding either more green enterprises with complementary competencies to enhance engineering capabilities and/or more green enterprises with the same resources to increase production capacity to a GVE.

Collaboration – represented by the ability to share costs and integrate resources and capabilities from multiple green enterprises in a GVE to exploit collaboration (business) opportunities in the most sustainable way.

Specialisation – represented by the ability to integrate the best green technologies and practices (core-competencies) available in multiple green enterprises in a GVE to offer, deliver and recover green products to/from the market.

3.2 GVE Breeding Environment and Green Virtual Enterprises Actors

Eight kinds of actors or stakeholders can be identified within a GVBE and its GVEs, including [5] [8]:

GVBE member – basic role played by a green enterprise registered at the GVBE and ready to participate in the GVBE activities. GVBE members are green enterprises adhering to a base long-term cooperation agreement and to the adoption of sustainable supply chain practices and 'industrial symbiosis' approaches in order to make their individual and collective operations more sustainable by collaborative means.

GVBE administrator – role played by a green enterprise responsible for the overall GVBE operation and evolution from a network management perspective, and from a sustainable industrial development model perspective for the promotion of 'industrial symbiosis partnerships' among the GVBE members by exploring material, energy, information and/or technology flows within the breeding environment that can be used to find resources-based synergies, devise strategies to increase the cycling of resources, and identify gaps in current green competencies and resources management and solve them by searching and recruiting new green enterprises into the GVBE.

GVE broker or simply *broker* – role played by one or more GVBE members responsible for the identification and acquisition of new collaboration (business) opportunities in the market (e.g. green products development and/or green services provision) by marketing the GVBE green competencies to potential customers, and for the identification and development of new complementary businesses for existing GVBE members' activities or creation of new ones based on core-competencies and resources synergies. GVE brokers should assess each opportunity based on its technical feasibility, economic advantage and environmental impact.

GVE planner or *business integrator* – role played by a green enterprise responsible for a GVE creation in any of its two modalities: F-GVE or R-GVE. GVE planners are responsible for the identification of the necessary green competencies and capacities, as well as the GVBE members that possess those competencies (potential GVE partners) to deliver and/or recover a green product to/from the market.

GVE coordinator – role played by a green enterprise responsible for the GVE operation, following the sustainable principles in all its sourcing, production and distribution/logistics activities, in order to achieve the GVE goals in a sustainable way.

GVE partner – basic role played by a green enterprise (GVBE member) involved in a GVE (in any of its two modalities), contributing with its green capabilities and capacities to the GVE goals achievement.

GVE customer – role played by a green consumer that may be an individual or an organisation with an environmental conscious and interested in purchasing green products and/or services from the GVBE by triggering the formation of GVEs.

GVBE support institution or *service provider* – a green service provider offering complementary services, supporting tools and/or mechanisms to the GVBE, such as: environmental certifications, eco-labels and/or green standards to support the GVBE sustainable industrial model.

3.3 GVE Breeding Environment and Green Virtual Enterprises Operating Principles

At GVBE level, some main operating principles to be considered are:

Standardisation – GVBE members will adopt common working and sharing principles, common interoperable infrastructures and a common ontology in order to reduce the barriers towards successful collaborations [8].

Resources sharing – GVBE members will create a resource pool (bag of assets) with different tangible and intangible shared resources in order to eliminate redundant assets within the GVBE and manage their ownership costs in an efficient way [8].

Collaboration – GVBE members will share information, resources, responsibilities, risks and rewards to jointly plan, implement and evaluate sustainable initiatives [9].

Industrial symbiosis – GVBE members will follow a cooperative approach to a sustainable industrial development model and sustainable supply networks involving links/exchanges/sharing of material, energy, information, technology and other tangible and intangible assets and by-products based on a collaboration strategy supported by shared use of assets, logistics, expertise and knowledge transfer [1] [10].

At GVE level, some main operating principles to be considered are:

Collaborative logistics – GVE partners (shippers, carriers and suppliers) will create a green logistics network to reduce the costs and environmental impact related to the transportation of raw materials, components and products by sharing logistics services assets such as trucks, trailers, warehouses and/or containers [11].

Sustainable supply networks – GVE partners will integrate/adopt the sustainability principles into their forward and reverse supply networks, from product design (green designs and green products), to material sourcing and selection (green materials and green suppliers), to manufacturing processes (green production), to the delivery of the final product to the customer (green packaging and green logistics/transportation), as well as into the end-of-life management of the product after its useful life (green recycling) [1] [2].

Green manufacturing – GVE partners will attempt to reduce the environmental impact of their manufacturing activities without sacrificing product quality and cost by focusing on the adoption of those green materials, green processes and green technologies that reduce waste, pollution and energy consumption [12].

3.4 GVE Breeding Environment and Green Virtual Enterprises Lifecycles

GVBEs lifecycle scenario:
All GVBEs will go through the following lifecycle stages [1] [5] [8]: (a) *creation* – planning the creation of a new breeding environment by identifying potential areas for eco-industrial networking among the potential GVBE members, defining the GVBE business model targeting specific industry sectors with sustainability benefits and potential GVBE members with a competitive (green) differentiation, and establishing the business processes, (ICT) infrastructures and governance model for populating and launching the GVBE; (b) *operation/metamorphosis* – GVBEs will operate striving for the diversity of green- enterprises, materials, processes, technologies, products and services that may enhance the industrial symbiosis partnerships within the breeding environment, promoting the creation of truly dynamic and sustainable supply networks (GVEs) offering, delivering and recovering green products and/or services to/from the market, and creating the necessary (common interoperable) infrastructures to facilitate the linking, exchanging and sharing of tangible and intangible assets and by-products as part of the GVBE industrial symbiosis strategy [10] [13]; and (c) *dissolution* – in the case of a GVBE closing, a knowledge transfer of best practices and lessons learned should be made to other GVBEs (see Table 1).

Table 1. GVBE Detailed Lifecycle Stages [1] [5] [8] [13] [16]

Lifecycle Stages		Description
Creation	Initiation & Recruiting	Identification of the potential industry sectors and (green) enterprises that could be involved in the GVBE. Modelling the GVBE to reveal potential collaboration (business) opportunities to build-up symbiotic industrial networks (GVEs). Identification of the infrastructures and support services to be provided by the GVBE to enable effectiveness and efficient in doing green businesses and collaborating in industrial symbiosis initiatives.
		Recruitment of the right mix of industries and green enterprises to achieve a critical mass to create successful industrial symbiosis partnership (GVEs).
	Foundation	Establishment and set-up of the business processes, infrastructures and governance model needed to support the GVBE members' industrial symbiosis partnerships (GVEs).
Operation		General management of all activities needed to support the GVBE smooth operation such as: strategic and marketing management; financial, accountability and resources management; governance management; bag of assets management; value systems management; ontology management; ICT management; support institutions management; membership and structure management; profiling and competency management; trust management; performance management; etc. [16]
Metamorphosis		GVBEs as natural ecosystems, or properly said industrial ecosystems, will adapt their strategies, business processes and structure to tactically respond to new sustainable market changes and trends.
Dissolution		If a GVBE may cease to exist, knowledge and technology transfers' initiatives such be promoted as part of a meta GVBEs' industrial symbiosis network.

GVEs lifecycle scenarios:
All GVEs, in their forward or reverse supply network modalities, will go through the following lifecycle stages within a breeding environment [1]: (a) *creation* – a new green business opportunity will be identified (by a GVBE member acting as broker) and will trigger a F-GVE formation for a new green product development or a R-GVE

formation for a product repair, re-manufacturing, recycling and/or safe disposal; managing both kind of supply networks within a GVBE makes possible to achieve real closed-loop supply networks in any manufacturing industry; (b) *operation/ evolution* – F-GVEs will operate following sustainable engineering, manufacturing and logistics principles in order to offer and deliver green products to the market, and R-GVEs will operate following sustainable logistics, end-of-life manufacturing and safe disposal principles in order to recover (green) products from the market in order to re-use, re-manufacture, recycle and/or make a safe disposal of them; operating in this way as truly sustainable supply networks supports the journey to a sustainable industrial development model; and (c) *dissolution* – since F-GVEs and R-GVEs were created within a breeding environment, after the product delivery or recovery, the GVBE will continue with its industrial symbiosis [10] strategy, acting as a closed-loop system, in where any surplus and/or abandoned resources/scrap after a F-GVE

Table 2. F-GVE Detailed Lifecycle Stages [1] [6] [14] [15] [16]

Lifecycle Stages		Description
Creation	Collaboration Opportunity Identification	Identification of a collaboration (business) opportunity for manufacturing a green product and/or offering a green service to a customer. A collaboration opportunity can be detected by a green broker or promoted as part of the GVBE strategy to introduce new green products and/or services to the market.
Creation	Collaboration Opportunity Characterisation	Identification of the main features of the collaboration (business) opportunity, including the green competency requirements and opportunity constrains: (a) *green product manufacturing* – needed green design, materials and process for designing, engineering and manufacturing a green product or (b*) green service* – needed green knowledge and skills to offer a green service.
Creation	Rough Planning	Identification of the required F-GVE partners competencies and capacities, as well as the F-GVE possible configurations (supply network topologies) to respond in a sustainable way to a collaboration (business) opportunity.
Creation	Partners Search & Selection	Identification of the potential F-GVE partners and their assessment and selection based on their green degree. F-GVE partners will be evaluated based on their green capabilities (design, materials, processes, technologies and logistics) to design, produce, supply or distribute a green product or service.
Creation	Negotiation	Interactive process to integrate the most suitable F-GVE partners in a dynamic sustainable supply network to produce and/or offer the required green product and/or service by the customer or demanded by the market.
Creation	Detailed Planning	Definition of the final F-GVE topology and its F-GVE partners' activities schedule, including tasks assignments, budget allocation and green performance indicators (clean production and forward logistics).
Creation	Contracting	Formulation of the F-GVE contract, paying special attention to the environmental regulations (laws, trades, taxes, fines).
Operation		F-GVEs will operate following all sustainable principles in order to reduce the environmental impact of their manufacturing and logistics activities.
Evolution		In case of unexpected events or disruptions during the F-GVE operation, the F-GVE coordinator will re-configure and/or re-schedule the F-GVE partners and their activities (tasks, budget) in order to try to keep the original production and/or offering plan for the promise product and/or service.
Dissolution		As part of the GVBE industrial symbiosis strategy, any resource that could have a secondary usage will be placed in the GVBE bag of assets for any possible usage. Additionally, as part of the F-GVEs product stewardship other GVEs may be launched in order to provide after-sales services to the customer/market.

Table 3. R-GVE Detailed Lifecycle Stages [1] [6] [14] [15] [16]

Lifecycle Stages		Description
Creation	Collaboration Opportunity Identification	Identification of a collaboration (business) opportunity for a green product recall based on a reverse logistics and an end-of-lifecycle manufacturing strategy.
	Collaboration Opportunity Characterisation	Identification of the main features of the collaboration (business) opportunity, including the green competency requirements and opportunity constrains for: (a) *product re-use* – dealing with the direct-use of product components as spare parts, (b) *product re-manufacturing* – dealing with the product for restoring or rebuilding, (c) *product recycling* – dealing with the product for reclaiming the valuable of its raw materials, or (d) *product safe disposal* – dealing with the product hazardous wastes.
	Rough Planning	Identification of the required R-GVE partners competencies and capacities, as well as the R-GVE possible configurations (supply network topologies) to respond in a sustainable way to a collaboration (business) opportunity.
	Partners Search & Selection	Identification of the potential R-GVE partners and their assessment and selection based on their green degree. R-GVE partners will be evaluated based on their green capabilities (receiving, separating, dismantling, sorting, testing) to handle the end-of-life of a product.
	Negotiation	Interactive process to integrate the most suitable R-GVE partners in a dynamic sustainable supply network to recover a green product from the market.
	Detailed Planning	Definition of the final R-GVE topology and its R-GVE partners' activities schedule, including tasks assignments, budget allocation and green performance indicators (end-of-life manufacturing, reverse logistics, hazardous wastes management).
	Contracting	Formulation of the R-GVE contract, paying special attention to the environmental regulations (laws, trades, taxes, fines).
Operation		R-GVEs will operate following all sustainable principles in order to reduce the environmental impact of their reverse logistics and end-of-life manufacturing activities.
Evolution		In case of unexpected events or disruptions during the R-GVE operation, the R-GVE coordinator will re-configure and/or re-schedule the R-GVE partners and their activities (tasks, budget) in order to try to keep the original end-of-life manufacturing plan.
Dissolution		As part of the GVBE industrial symbiosis strategy, any resource that could have a secondary usage will be placed in the GVBE bag of assets for any possible usage. Additionally, as part of the R-GVEs hazardous wastes management activities, a specialised GVE may be tailored for their safe disposal.

dissolution will be placed in the GVBE bag of assets for its direct-use (re-use), repair, re-manufacture, recycle and/or safe disposal, and any output after a R-GVE dissolution will take two possible paths: to be returned immediately, if possible, as an input to active F-GVEs within the GVBE or will trigger a GVE formation specialised in hazardous wastes disposal.

3.5 GVE Breeding Environment and Green Virtual Enterprises Technologies

GVBEs supporting technologies (as concepts, methods or tools) [see 16 for more]:

Brokerage – Set of management activities and supporting tools that will support the identification of new collaboration (business) opportunities in the market that will trigger the formation of new GVEs and/or inside the GVBE that will lead to industrial symbiosis opportunities and/or collaborative investments (shareable infrastructures, joint purchases > better negotiation power, joint promotion > green marketing, etc.).

Profiling and competency management – Set of management activities and supporting tools for creating and maintaining the GVBE and its members' profiles.

Partners search and selection – Set of management activities and supporting tools to identify, assess and select potential GVBE members and GVE partners.

Governance – Set of management activities and supporting tools that will facilitate any approach to collaboration (principles, rules, bylaws, values) and will guarantee the sustainability and correct behaviour/performance of all GVBE stakeholders.

Performance management – Set of management activities and supporting tools for planning and monitoring the GVBE strategies and rating and rewarding the GVBE actors' actions towards the GVBE goals achievement.

Bag of assets – Set of management activities and supporting tools to administrate a common virtual and physical warehouse to make easier the share of tangible and intangible assets between the GVBE members for different collaborative purposes [1].

Infrastructure management – Set of management activities and supporting tools for handling the GVBE infrastructures (ICT-based and physical-based) that will allow GVBE actors to interoperate and collaborate for different collaborative purposes.

GVEs management – Set of managing activities and supporting tools to manage the GVEs during its lifecycle [14] [15].

GVEs supporting technologies (as concepts, methods or tools):

Green product/service – refers to a product or service whose manufacturing or offering, purchase and use allows a sustainable economic development.

Green design – refers to a product or service design that puts special consideration into its environmental impact during its whole lifecycle.

Green materials – refers to a material that preserves natural resources and reduces the environmental impact, including those materials composed of recycled materials or can be recycled at the end of its lifespan.

Green processes – refers to a process that eliminates the environmental burden in its resources input, energy consumption, and outputs impact.

Green production – refers to a production system that puts a strong effort to lessen its environmental impact by conserving raw materials (using more recycled and/or renewable materials), minimising energy use and emissions, and wastes.

Green packaging – refers to the use of green materials in packaging, comprising recycled content, or reusable or degradable packaging materials to minimise landfill waste and transportation costs.

Green logistics – refers to any environmental friendly logistics strategy such as: commuting and shipping products together, using alternative fuel vehicles, reducing overall packaging, sharing warehouses and containers, etc.

Green recycling – refers to any of the 5R strategies: repair, re-manufacture, recycle, re-use or re-generated to reduce environmental impact.

4 Conclusions and Further Research

Defining a comprehensive *reference model* for GVBEs is a long-term endeavour, nevertheless based on the significant empirical knowledge (frameworks, models, concepts, methods and tools) and existing (eco-) industrial cases from the *Industrial Ecology* and *Collaborative Networks* scientific disciplines, it was realistic for the authors of this paper to try to design the first steps for a gradual definition of a "GVBE reference model". Future looks for sustainable industrial development models and current technological advances are leading to the formation of strategic alliances of enterprises that are geographically distributed, but work together to increase economic gains and minimise their environmental impact. Further research aims to work on a detailed model and management framework for GVEs and their breeding environments.

Acknowledgments. The research presented in this document is a contribution for the ECOLEAD Project (FP6 IP 506958), for the S-MC-S Project (FP7 NMP-ICT-FoF 260090), and for the ITESM, Campus MTY & CCM, Research Chairs.

References

1. Romero, D., Molina, A.: Green Virtual Enterprises and their Breeding Environments. In: Camarinha-Matos, L.M., Boucher, X., Afsarmanesh, H. (eds.) PRO-VE 2010. IFIP AICT, vol. 336, pp. 25–35. Springer, Heidelberg (2010)
2. Srivastava, S.K.: Green Supply-Chain Management: A State-of-the-Art Literature Review. International Journal of Management Reviews 9(1), 53–80 (2007)
3. Camarinha-Matos, L.M.: Virtual Organizations in Manufacturing: Trends & Challenges. In: 12th International Conference on Flexible Automation and Intelligent Manufacturing, pp. 1036–1054 (2002)
4. Camarinha-Matos, L.M., Afsarmanesh, H.: A Framework for VO Creation in a Breeding Environment. Annual Reviews in Control 31(1), 119–135 (2007)
5. Romero, D., Molina, A.: Virtual Organisation Breeding Environments Toolkit: Reference Model, Management Framework and Instantiation Methodology. Journal of Production Planning & Control 21(2), 181–217 (2009)
6. Camarinha-Matos, L.M., et al.: A Framework for Computer-assisted Creation of Dynamic Virtual Organisations. International Journal of Production Research 47(17), 4661–4690 (2009)
7. Verdecho, M.J., Alfaro-Saiz, J.J., Rodríguez-Rodríguez, R.: An Approach to select Suppliers for Sustainable Collaborative Networks. In: Camarinha-Matos, L.M., Boucher, X., Afsarmanesh, H. (eds.) PRO-VE 2010. IFIP AICT, vol. 336, pp. 304–311. Springer, Heidelberg (2010)
8. Afsarmanesh, H., Camarinha-Matos, L.M.: A Framework for Management of Virtual Organization Breeding Environments. In: Camarinha-Matos, L.M., et al. (eds.) Collaborative Networks and their Breeding Environments, PRO-VE 2005. IFIP, pp. 35–48 (2005)
9. Camarinha-Matos, L.M., Afsarmanesh, H.: Collaborative Networks: Value Creation in a Knowledge Society. Knowledge Enterprise, IFIP 207, 26–40 (2006)
10. Chertow, M.R.: Industrial Symbiosis: Literature and Taxonomy. Annual Review of Energy and the Environment 25, 313–337 (2000)
11. Langley, J.: Seven Immutable Laws of Collaborative Logistics. NISTEVO Consulting (2000)
12. Ilgin, M.A., Gupta, S.M.: Environmentally Conscious Manufacturing and Product Recovery: A Review of the State of the Art. Journal of Environmental Management 91(3), 563–591 (2010)

13. Cohen-Rosenthal, E.: Handbook on Codes, Covenants, Conditions & Restrictions for Eco-Industrial Parks. Cornell Center for the Environment (1999)
14. Negretto, U., et al.: VO Management Solutions. Methods and Tools for Collaborative Networked Organizations, 257–274 (2008)
15. Karvonen, I., Salkari, L., Ollus, M.: Identification of Forms and Components of VO Inheritance. In: Camarinha-Matos, L.M., et al. (eds.) Foundation of Collaborative Networks, PRO-VE 2007. IFIP, vol. 243, pp. 253–262 (2007)
16. Romero, D., Molina, A.: VO Breeding Environments & Virtual Organizations Integral Business Process Management Framework. Journal of Information Systems Frontiers 11(5), 569–597 (2009)
17. Chertow, M.R.: The Eco-Industrial Park Model Reconsidered. Journal of Industrial Ecology 2(3), 8–16 (1998)

Remanufacturing System: Characterizing the Reverse Supply Chain

Ana Paula B. Barquet[1], Henrique Rozenfeld[1], and Fernando A. Forcellini[2]

[1] Escola de Engenharia de São Carlos, Universidade de São Paulo,
Rua Trabalhador São Carlense, 400, CEP 13566-590, São Carlos, Brazil
anabarquet@gmail.com
[2] EPS/CTC/ UFSC, Campos Universitário,
Universidade Federal de Santa Catarina, CEP 88040- 970, Florianópolis, Brazil

Abstract. End-of-life strategies, such as remanufacturing, have gained ground in order to promote product reuse, reduce environmental impacts and costs, as well as to win new markets. The remanufacturing process preserves part of the product's raw materials and added value during its manufacturing. This study addresses the system that includes remanufacturing in order to understand it and to define its elements, as well as to characterize the supply chain that permeates and leads to the effective functioning of this system. To this end, a Systematic Literature Review on remanufacturing was conducted. Moreover, the RS proposed was based on the General Systems Theory.

Keywords: Remanufacturing, Reverse Supply Chain, System, Elements.

1 Introduction

Increased competition in the market, environmental concerns, changing customer requirements and the emergence of new laws regarding the products' end-of-life management has led companies to seek new operation models to maintain and expand their market share [1] [2]. Thus, adopting end-of-life strategies for products, as for instance remanufacturing, have become increasingly important in today's business operations.

The remanufacturing process preserves part of the product's raw materials and added value during its manufacturing, which enables productivity and profit gains for the companies [3]. Additionally, due to its environmental benefits, remanufacturing is increasingly gaining ground on the world stage.

However, companies often encounter difficulties in implementing remanufacturing due to the lack of knowledge on the subject [4], the lack of strategic remanufacturing issues [5] and studies that indicate how to implement it [6]. This issue is new to Brazilian companies and is still in the exploratory phase, therefore justifying the importance to conduct a structured literature review on remanufacturing.

Furthermore, the overall outlook on matters relating to remanufacture in an integrated and systematic manner is not an easy task. A system is a set of interdependent elements that interact to reach an objective and perform a determined function [7] and considered to be the elements and the relationships between them which determine how the system works, forming a whole unit that is organized and

L.M. Camarinha-Matos et al. (Eds.): PRO-VE 2011, IFIP AICT 362, pp. 556–563, 2011.

complex [8]. This demonstrates the need to develop a model for the Remanufacturing System (RS). This need particularly falls on the importance of understanding how the supply chain for remanufacturing works, which requires integrating different players and implementing various activities [2] to reach a successful RS operation.

Taking into account the aforementioned facts, it is possible to observe the importance of regarding remanufacturing as a system, as well as its elements, features, players, challenges and practices, in order to assist the implementation of this system into organizations and also to provide an outline of the activities and players that make this system work through the supply chain. Thus, the objective is to identify the elements that comprise this system to then characterize the supply chain associated to it.

Below is the work methodology used to develop this study.

2 Methodology

The study herein was conducted using the Systematic Literature Review [9]. Therefore, articles were searched that addressed the words: Remanufacture; Remanufacturing; Remanufactured; Design for environment; Design for remanufacturing; Reverse logistics; Product recovery; Reverse supply chain; Closed loop; Closed loop supply chain; End of life; Lifecycle, as well as the translation of these words into Portuguese. 223 abstracts of the studies found were read, of which 91 research studies that dealt with practices to implement remanufacturing were selected and 24 were used because they presented remanufacturing practices related to reverse supply chain.

Since these elements are to be presented within a systemic outlook, the General Systems Theory was used, whose objective is to study the elements that comprise a system, as well as the interaction between them [10]. Given that, this interaction is critical to understanding the system as a whole [7].

Thus, after completing RBS on remanufacturing, the organization of concepts was carried out to obtain the definition and characterization of the Remanufacturing System and of the elements inserted into this system, presented below.

3 Remanufacturing System

Based on the literature, the Remanufacturing System (RS) in this study is addressed as a system that encompasses all the elements involved in remanufacturing, from the reverse supply chain steps up to the return of the already remanufactured products to be sold on the market [11]. The elements and sub-elements adopted in this work are:

- Element 1: Remanufacturing Design;
- Element 2: Reverse supply chain (RSC)
  - Sub-element 2.1: Relationship with the supplier of the used product;
  - Sub-element 2.2: Reverse Logistics;
- Element 3: Remanufacturing Operation;
- Element 4: Sales of the remanufactured product;
- Element 5: Information flow in the Remanufacturing System;
- Element 6: Employees' knowledge and skills on remanufacturing.

Figure 1 shows the Remanufacturing System model developed in this research work. The first element is the Remanufacturing Design, a part of the Product Development Process, aimed at facilitating remanufacturing. The Reverse Supply Chain is composed of two sub-elements: acquisition/relationship with the used product supplier and reverse logistics. The main players in this system are the customers who purchased the new product and that become the supplier of the product's end of life, the player responsible for reverse logistics, the company responsible for the remanufacturing and selling of the remanufactured product and the customer who buys such a product.

The information flow in the RS is considered an element that permeates and interconnects all the others. It should also be considered that the employees' remanufacturing Knowledge and Skills are crucial for the system and should be present in all the processes.

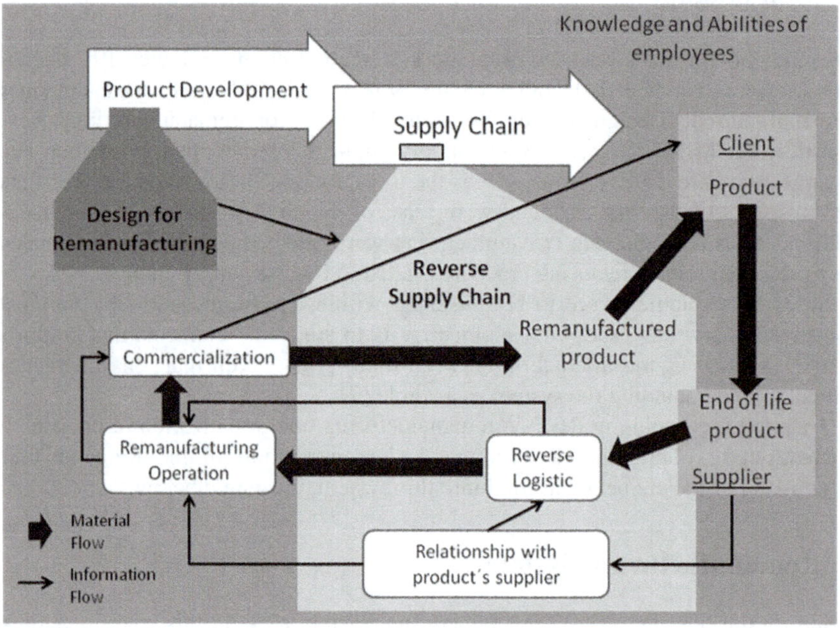

Fig. 1. Remanufacturing System Model

After presenting remanufacturing as a system, the next section focuses specifically on the reverse supply chain as well as on the analysis and description of this element and its sub-elements.

3.1 Reverse Supply Chain (RSC) for Remanufacturing

According to Guide and Van Wassenhove [12], reverse supply chain (RSC) is the set of steps necessary to collect a used product, followed by the desired end-of-life strategy application (remanufacturing, reuse, recycling or disposal) [2]. The RSC begins with the collection of products from customers and/or companies in different links of the supply chain, given that the collection sources tend to be geographically dispersed. Next, there is the inspection stage or the tests performed at the collection site, at a receiving center or place where the product will be recycled and reused. At this point, the fate of the recovered product is decided, which has various reuse possibilities, such as remanufacturing [13].

- **Difficulties and practices**

Leite [14] reports that the RSC stages are treated as a series of independent and isolated steps, without considering their integrated nature. Moreover, with regard to RSC, both in business and in academia, little is being undertaken concerning its strategic issues [2]. Most research studies address technical and operational issues, since focusing on the technical activities is considered attractive for initial investigations [15].

Some of the features of Reverse Supply Chain make it difficult to manage and plan its stages and activities. For example, when a company collects the used products, its provider is usually the final customer, which complicates the access to the appropriate number of products at the time of return. Another complication is that the quality of used products varies, hence requiring efficient inspection [16]. Moreover, there is the need to disassembly the products collected, structure a reverse logistics network and deal with the high processing time variability [17].

Some recommendations to achieve efficiency in the reverse supply chain are: (i) to structure a specialized team to have contact with the supplier of the used product, (ii) to perform demand prediction for the products' return time, using its sales and lifetime as a base and (iii) to align the RSC with the Direct Supply Chain and achieve effectiveness in the activities of the closed Supply Chain Flow [18].

- **Interdependence and interaction with other RS elements**

The degree of structuring of a RSC can be defined depending on the existence of structured organizational practices relating to the return of the used products, the relationships between companies belonging to the reverse chain, as well as the level of resources made available by these companies, as for example, employee skills for remanufacturing [6] [13] [14] [19].

The appropriate management of reverse chains can also serve as an excellent source of information about the customers' habits and expectations [13]. Next, the sub-elements of the reverse supply chain are discussed.

3.1.1 Sub-Element 2.1: Relationship with the Supplier of the Used Product

Sundin [20] cites that the relationship of the remanufacturer with its used products supplier is an important aspect to the effectiveness of the business. If the recovered product is intended for remanufacturing, it is important that before the product is selected to return to the reverse flow, a "pretrial" of its remanufacturing should be performed to prevent it from being transported without the proper conditions to be reused, which would generate additional costs. This trade-off between the potential for reuse and additional costs is difficult to predict and to do this, employees with certain skills and experiences are needed [21]. The large number of small-quantity suppliers of used products and the manifold conditions of these products makes quality control difficult by the companies that receive them for remanufacturing.

There are cases when the raw-material suppliers for Remanufacturing Operations are the consumers themselves, who discard the product due to the end of its useful life or due to other reasons, such as the launching of a more modern product. In this case, there are some problems regarding the lack of incentive these customers receive to return the used products to remanufacturing companies [22], such as the lack of contact the remanufacturer has with the customer [23] and the consumer's lack of information and trust regarding remanufacturing [24], as for instance the economic and environmental advantages of remanufacturing. Thus, companies that desire to have success with remanufacturing need to have strategies that encourage the consumers to return these items [23].

3.1.2 Sub-Element 2.2: Reverse Logistics (RL)

According to the Council of Logistics Management [19], Reverse Logistics is the process of effectively planning, implementing and controlling the flow of components, materials under processing, the final product and related information from the consumption point to the point of origin, with the objective of recovering and adding value or achieving the most appropriate disposal [18]. Adding value can be of various types: economic, ecological, corporate image, among others [14].

RL is a major challenge for RS, due to the difficulty to predict the return volume and timing and the products' quality conditions, making Remanufacturing Operation difficult to plan [1]. Some of the difficulties in implementing RL by businesses are: the lack of a system that integrates direct logistic activities with those of reverse logistics [25], difficulty in measuring the impact and controlling the return of the products and materials and the fact that the reverse flow is considered a cost for companies, thus receiving little or no priority as a business strategy [19]; the lack of studies by companies to assess the impacts of the RL practices in the success of organizations [26]; the relationship between the players involved in the activities of reverse logistics is not very structured; there is low proximity between the factories and suppliers of used products; and the freight costs are higher due to the lower volumes transported [27].

Unlike the distribution in direct logistics, which is designed to carry large volumes of the same product from the producer to a few local clients, in reverse logistics the volume may considerably low. This can set back the economy in the transport. Another aspect to consider is that unlike direct logistics, the used products that are collected are not packaged and are therefore unprotected and at risk of damage, which limits its reuse. Thus, a packaging system is necessary to protect the product [21].

Pires [27] raises other drawbacks to RL, such as the tendency for products to remain longer in the reverse channels, which results in higher inventory, transportation and storage costs, as well as the decrease in revenue due to the possibility of obsolescence and degradation of the product.

According to Lacerda [28], the six major factors to minimize the challenges of reverse logistics activities are:

- good entry and exit controls;
- mapped and formalized processes;
- reduced cycle times;

- accurate information systems;
- planned logistics network and;
- collaborative relationships between customers and suppliers.

Reverse logistic activities require skills to properly execute the transportation, storage and stockpiling of used products, in addition to information on how the product was designed.

4 Conclusions and Contributions

This work enabled to organize the knowledge on remanufacturing through the proposition of the Remanufacturing System concept and the elements included in this system. It was also highlighted the characteristics of reverse supply chain involved in the RS, indicating the related steps, actors, practices and difficulties and the importance of relationship of the remanufacturer with used products users and reverse logistics to the success of the entire system.

When investigating the literature that addresses remanufacturing, no model was found that integrates remanufacturing issues in a system or that broached the elements that are part of a Remanufacturing System. This work consolidated and organized the elements of this system, enabling a better understanding of remanufacturing by highlighting the chain and the main interdependencies between the elements.

Therefore, the RS proposed contributes to an integrated outlook and to the expansion of theoretical knowledge on the subject. Such contributions are intended to facilitate the development of future works in this area, as well as to assist companies that are structuring remanufacturing practices or intend to start them.

Moreover, this work aims to stimulate the development of studies on remanufacturing and the supply chain for remanufacturing in Brazil, since there are few domestic companies that remanufacture and few studies on remanufacturing. Additionally, this work seeks to encourage companies to implement remanufacturing, as this study provides a holistic outlook on the operation of this system with features of its supply chains.

With regards to the supply chain for the Remanufacturing System, some of its features and difficulties were shown. For future works, it is then recommended that the practices that seek to overcome such difficulties should be studied and analyzed. Besides, studies on remanufacturing companies are required to demonstrated the status of remanufacturing in Brazil.

References

1. Kato, P., Laurindo, F.J.B.: Discutindo o Planejamento Integrado de uma Remanufatura em um ciclo fechado de Supply Chain. XXIV ENEGEP (Encontro Nacional de Engenharia de Produção), Florianópolis, SC (2004)
2. Guide Jr., V.D.R., Harrison, T.P., Van Wassenhove, L.N.: The Challenge of Closed-Loop Supply Chains. 33(6), 3–6 (2003)
3. Giuntini, R., Gaudette, K.: Remanufacturing: The next great opportunity for boosting US productivity. Business Horizons (2003)

4. Zanette, E.T.: A Remanufatura no Brasil e no Mundo: Conceitos e Condicionantes. 2008. Monografia (Graduação em Engenharia Ambiental) - Escola de Engenharia de São Carlos, Universidade de São Paulo, São Carlos, SP (2008)
5. Ferguson, M.E., Toktay, L.B.: The Effect of Competition on Recovery Strategies. Technology and Operations Management, INSEAD (2004)
6. Jacobsson, N.: Emerging Product Strategies: Selling services of remanufactured products. Dissertação. The International Institute of Industrial Environmental Economics, Lund University, Sweden (2000)
7. Oliveira, J.P., Portela, L.O.V.: A Cidade Como Um Sistema: Reflexões Sobre a Teoria Geral de Sistemas Aplicada à Análise Urbana. Perspectivas Contemporâneas. Revista eletrônica de ciências sociais aplicadas 1(2), 164–182 (2006)
8. Johnson, R.A., Kast, F.E., Rosenweig, J.E.: The theory and management of systems. International Student Edition, Mc Graw Hill, New York (1963)
9. Biolchini, J., et al.: Systematic Review in Software Engineering. Technical Report Rt – Es 679/05. Rio de Janeiro: Systems Engineering and Computer Science Department, Universidade Federal do Rio de Janeiro (2005)
10. Bertalanffy, V.L.: Teoria Geral dos Sistemas. Vozes, Petrópolis (1975)
11. Östlin, J.: On Remanufacturing Systems: Analysing and Managing Material Flows and Remanufacturing Processes. Dissertação (Mestrado em Administração e Engenharia) – Universidade de Linköping, Suécia (2008)
12. Guide Jr., V.D.R., Van Wassenhove, L.N.: The reverse supply chain. Harvard Business Review 80(2), 25–26 (2002)
13. Leite, P.R., et al.: O papel dos ganhos econômicos e de imagem corporativa na estruturação dos canais reversos. Gestão.Org 4(4) (2006)
14. Leite, P.R.: Logística Reversa: meio ambiente e competitividade. Prentice Hall, São Paulo (2003)
15. Guide Jr., V.D.R., Van Wassenhove, L.N.: The Evolution of Closed-Loop Supply Chain Research. Operations Research 57(1), 10–18 (2009)
16. Guide Jr., V.D.R.: Production planning and control for remanufacturing: industry practice and research needs. Journal of Operations Management 18, 467–483 (2000)
17. Guide Jr, V.D.R., Jayaraman, V., Linton, J.D.: Building contingency planning for closed-loop supply chains with product recovery. Journal of Operations Management (2002)
18. Fioravanti, R.D., Carvalho, M.F.H.: Aplicações de modelos de cadeia reversa em uma operação de serviços: estudo de caso no setor de serviços de impressão. XI SIMPOI (Simpósio de Administração da Produção, Logística e Operações Internacionais) (2008)
19. Rogers, D.S., Tibben-Lembke, R.S.: Going backwards: reverse logistics practices and trends. Reverse Logistics Executive Council, Reno (1998)
20. Sundin, E., et al.: Remanufacturing of Products used in Product Service System Offerings. In: The 41st CIRP Conference on Manufacturing Systems (2008)
21. Ferrer, G., Whybark, D.C.: From Garbage to Goods: Successful Remanufacturing Systems and Skills. Business Horizons (2000)
22. King, A.M., Burguess, S.C.: The development of a remanufacturing platform design: a strategic response to the Directive on Waste Electrical and Electronic Equipment. Proc. IMechE Part B: Journal of Engineering Manufacture 219, 623–631 (2005)
23. Östlin, J., Sundin, E., Björkman, M.: Importance of closed-loop supply chain relationships for product remanufacturing. International Journal of Production Economics (115), 336–348 (2008)
24. Seitz, M.S.: A critical assessment of motives for product recovery: the case of engine remanufacturing. Journal of Cleaner Production 15, 1147–1157 (2006)

25. Daher, C.E., Silva, E.P.S., Fonseca, A.P.: Logística Reversa: Oportunidade para Redução de Custos através do Gerenciamento da Cadeia Integrada de Valor. Brazilian Business Review 3(1) (January/June 2006)
26. Miguez, E., Mendonça, F.M., Valle, R.A.B.: Impactos ambientais, sociais e econômicos de uma política de logística reversa adotada por uma fábrica de televisão: um estudo de caso. XXVII ENEGEP (Encontro Nacional de Engenharia de Produção), Foz do Iguaçú, PR, Brasil (2007)
27. Pires, N.: Modelo para a logística reversa dos bens de pós-consumo em um ambiente de cadeia de suprimentos. 2007. Tese (Doutorado em Engenharia de Produção) – Curso de Pós-Graduação em Engenharia de Produção, UFSC, Florianópolis (2007)
28. Lacerda, L.: Logística reversa, uma visão sobre os conceitos básicos e as práticas operacionais. Centro de Estudos em Logística. COPPEAD, UFRJ (2004)

Sustainable Value Generation through Collaborative Symbiotic Networks Planning

Juliano Bezerra de Araujo, Raphael Pintão, and Cyntia Watanabe Rosa

Axia Value Chain, Avenida das Nações Unidas,
12551, cj1811, 04578-903 Sao Paulo, Brazil
{juliano.araujo,raphael.pintao,
cyntia.watanabe}@axiavaluechain.com

Abstract. Industrial Symbiosis is an important component of Industrial Ecology which studies the collaboration and coexistence of companies to achieve mutual benefits. Its concepts have traditionally focused on eco-efficiency and its direct benefits such as costs reduction, resources optimization and environmental impacts reduction. The paper introduces the use of externalities and collaborative networks as tools to amplify the spectrum of opportunities and, consequently, the potential value of Industrial Symbiosis development. Externalities are related to side effects of companies' decisions and acts. They offer a broader systemic view to Industrial Symbiosis planning and execution. Sustainable value brings up intangible value drivers such as institutional, organizational and relationship capital as well as risk management consideration. It helps companies to visualize the totality of potential value of Industrial Symbiosis.

Keywords: Collaborative Networks, Industrial Symbiosis, Externalities.

1 Introduction

Industrial symbiosis concept has originated from industrial ecology in allusion to the mutualism between living beings, and it has been studied by academics with great impulse since the 1990s. It is an important form of collaboration between companies when considering that the value created by them becomes greater than the sum of the eventual value created by each one individually. Industrial symbiosis traditionally offers three types of opportunities: infrastructure sharing, services sharing and reuse of energy and materials (water and co-products). Their benefits include primarily economies of scale from physical assets, prevention of negative externalities and promotion of positive ones.

Externality denomination was pointed for the first time by economists, and refers to the positive or negative effects of a business decision over those who do not take part in it. It is constructive to apply the externality approach into the searching for symbiotic opportunities between industries or service companies, as it can enhance the potential for generating positive impacts over a larger group of stakeholders.

The goal of this paper is to present externality control and collaborative networks importance for industrial symbiosis development. The collaboration between partners

L.M. Camarinha-Matos et al. (Eds.): PRO-VE 2011, IFIP AICT 362, pp. 564–571, 2011.

from the symbiotic network is able to generate value to a more diverse public. If analyzed from a business perspective, can minimize risks, maximize eco-efficiency, reduce costs, and generate revenue and increase institutional, organizational, relationship and intellectual capital.

2 Industrial Ecology: Concepts and Eco-industrial Parks

The study of industrial systems that operate more like natural ecosystems is known as Industrial Ecology (IE) [13]. The term was coined in the early 1990s, but the current concepts involved have been around for decades. They involve the sustainable philosophies of Reduce, Reuse, Recycle applied toward industry. It is based on environmental awareness and good economic sense.

Industrial Ecology has numerous aspects including pollution prevention, product life cycles, design for environment and green accounting [6]. A key concept is that processes and industries are seen as interacting systems rather than comprising isolated components in a system of linear flows. This provides a basis for thinking about ways to connect different waste-producing processes, plants or industries into an operating web that minimizes the total amount of industrial material that goes to disposal sinks or is lost in intermediate processes. The focus changes from minimizing waste from a particular process or facility (i.e. pollution prevention), to minimizing waste produced by the larger system as a whole, as well as reducing materials inflow [17, 4].

Since the introduction of Industrial Ecology, the Industrial Symbiosis (IS) concept has been put in a new perspective. Chertow [6], defines the concept of Industrial Symbiosis as "(...) part of the emerging field of Industrial Ecology, demanding resolute attention to the flow of materials and energy through local and regional economies. Industrial Symbiosis engages traditionally separate industries in collective approach to competitive advantage involving physical exchange of materials, energy, water, and/or by-products. The keys to industrial symbiosis are collaboration and the synergistic possibilities offered by geographic proximity".

Based on the principles of Industrial Ecology and Industrial Symbiosis, a new concept has been developed. An Eco-Industrial Park, or EIP, is a public/private partnership where the Industrial Ecology and Industrial Symbiosis approach to industry is contained in one development. Cote [8] define EIP as " (...) an industrial system which conserves natural and economic resources; reduces production, material, energy, insurance and treatments costs and liabilities; improves operating efficiency, quality, worker health and public image; and provides opportunities for income generation from use and sale of wasted materials."

The benefit of this arrangement is that the waste material or product of one company can be recycled into the manufacturing process of one or more companies with minimal transportation and production costs. EIPs are designed to produce minimal emissions, minimal noise and ground pollution, and minimal waste. EIP firms are designed to fit the environment instead of adjusting the environment to fit the firm [10].

There are three primary opportunities for resource exchange in EIP: 1) By-product reuse - the exchange of firm-specific materials between two or more parties for use as substitutes for commercial products or raw materials. The materials exchange component has also been referred to as a by-product exchange, by-product synergy, or waste exchange and may also be referred to as an industrial recycling network. 2) Utility/infrastructure sharing - the pooled use and management of commonly used resources such as energy, water, and wastewater. 3) Joint provision of services - meeting common needs across firms for ancillary activities such as fire suppression, transportation, and food provision [5]

These resource exchanges are aimed to avoid disturbing the environment where the companies are located. Relocating the resources reduces the impacts since landfills, pollution and residues are reduced as well as natural resources necessity is reduced due to re-use. These are important tasks in Industrial Ecology and the limit of its development is known as Circular Corporation. According to Yang and Feng "Circular economy is an abbreviation of 'Closed Materials Cycle Economy or Resources Circulated Economy', aiming at the efficient use of resources, taking reducing, reusing and recycling as principles and 'closed materials cycles and recycled use of energy' as features" [20].

Technical reports [12,16] on Eco-Industrial Park show that they differ a lot depending on geographical location, participant companies, government involvement and motivation for establishing it. Independently of how Eco-Industrial Parks are initiated or developed, they have the potential to bring several benefits to communities, environment and business. Some of them are listed in Table 1.

Table 1. Potential benefits from Eco-Industrial Parks [7]

Communities	Environment	Business
Larger tax base	Better resource use	Enhanced market image
Community pride	Reduced waste	Increased employee productivity
Improved environmental health	Increased protection of natural ecosystems	Access to financing
Enhanced quality of life in area near EIP	Innovative environmental solutions	Reduction in disposal costs
Good jobs	Increased protection of natural ecosystems	Income from sale of by-products

3 Business Externalities

Companies referred to as leaders in sustainability are those which bear responsibility on their externalities, Externalities is the term used to signal the "side effects" on the operations of a business, whether positive or negative ones. They are the impacts a business produces in broad terms, be it directly or indirectly, but not being obliged to pay for them, or rather, consider them during their decision-making processes. [16]. "Externalities are those consequences of a production process, imposed on society or the environment, which are not taken into account in the product price. They are produced whenever production processes, or consumers` utility, are affected by variables not controlled by themselves, but by other economic agents. These effects may be positive (external benefits) or negatives (external costs)" [18], p.469.

The activities generating externalities can create positive or negative consequences on the stakeholders (Table 2). If positive, the social benefit provided by the business exceeds the traditional view of economic gain, and creates private social welfare for other stakeholder groups. In contrast, the activities that produce negative externalities end up penalizing different groups without their being able to enjoy any compensatory benefits coming from the activities of the business. As mentioned by Sankar [19] in situations with negative externalities, the social cost of business is higher than the private cost paid by them.

Table 2. List of business externalities [3,9]

Business Area	Activity	Externalities
Power plant	Coal burning	Economic development, job creation, pollution
Casino	Gambling	Job creation, tourism development, urban revitalization, crime, corruption, suicide, bankruptcy
Motor vehicle use	Mobility	Economic development, job creation, trade increase, air pollution, pain, suffering, death

Thus, one can say that economic development has brought a number of problems, or "side effects". According to the guide The Natural Step (TNS), this scenario is known as "the challenge of sustainability." Also according to TNS, the systemic conditions for sustainability depend on four factors: in a sustainable society, nature is not subject to systematically increasing concentrations of substances extracted from soil (1), the accumulation of substances produced by society (2) and physical degradation of natural areas (3). Nevertheless, people should also be able to meet their needs (4) [3].

The systemic view of sustainability proposed by TNS has the role of showing the main lines to be followed by companies so as not to generate negative externalities. The perpetuity of enterprises depends on a positive balance of externalities, since only by ensuring a harmonious coexistence with their environment, may the companies receive a license to continue existing. May any phenomenon happen that make the sustainability of systemic conditions impracticable, negative externalities will emerge. In order to deal with scenarios like these, one shall adopt an approach to control the externalities. Figure 1 shows the main steps to be followed in order to act on the externalities of a business.

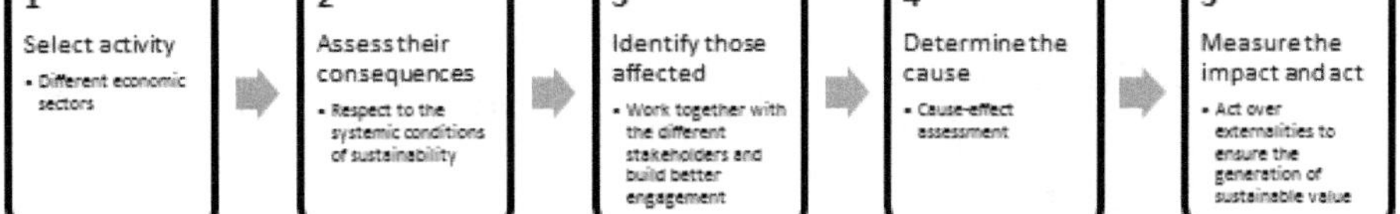

Fig. 1. Way to control business externalities

By using the above approach to deal with externalities, one can enjoy good opportunities, be they represented by tangible gains, i.e. those associated with resource savings, or by intangible benefits, i.e. benefits for the brand and better risk control. Sustainability actions designed to act on some externalities may simultaneously generate both tangible gains and intangible gains.

4 Externalities Control and Facilitating Structures for Symbiotic Collaborative Networks Development

As it is in previous sections, the growth of world industrial production has brought a series of negative developments, or "side effects", also known as externalities. The accumulation of unwanted material into the environment characterizes the industrial system as an open system. An objective of the industrial ecology is to transform the linear character of the industrial system into a cyclic system, in which raw materials, energy and waste will always be reused [14]. According with Beers et al. [1], one way to reduce emissions or disposal of wastes to water and atmosphere is through the realization of industrial symbiosis, also referred to as regional resource synergies. These concern the "capture, recovery and reuse of previously discarded by-products (materials, energy and water) from one industrial operation by other, traditionally separate, industries operating in their close proximity [1], p.831.

The desire to change the material flow from a linear view into another cyclic or circular is the target of the industrial symbiosis. It becomes an appropriate way to contain the generation of negative externalities of industrial activities over the population, respecting, thus, the systemic conditions of sustainability (Figure 2).

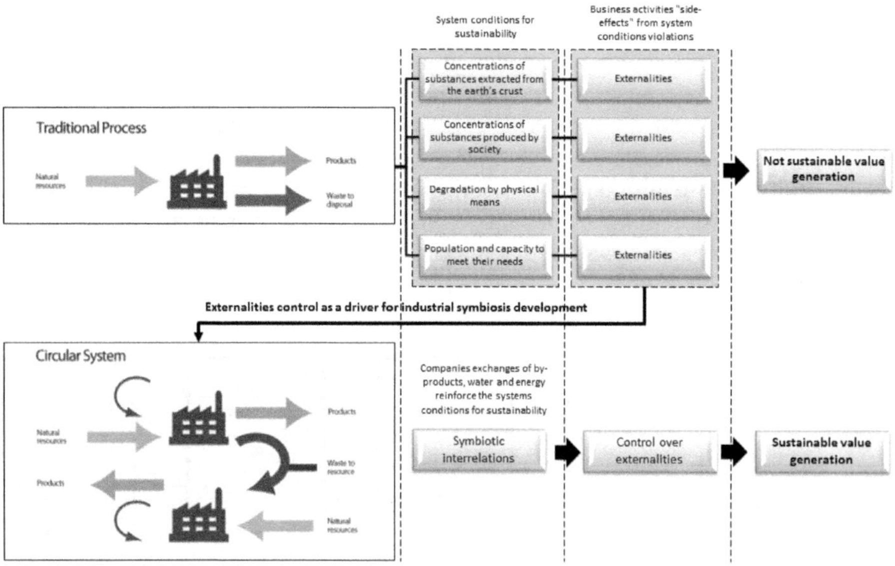

Fig. 2. Externalities control as a driver for industrial symbiosis development

As it is shown in Figure 2, an appropriate way to develop symbiotic relationships between enterprises in different economic sectors is based on the identification of negative externalities which penalize one or more groups of individuals to then enable actions that transform the problem into a new opportunity of revenue generation and intangible gains.

Hence, Table 3 contains real examples of externalities and industrial symbiosis as solution to cope with. This table was constructed following the externalities approach of five steps. The case of the power plant in Denmark, which used to lose some of the heat generated from coal without there being some kind of compensatory benefits for the company and society, is a good example of how industrial symbiosis has come to bring economic, environmental and social benefits to stakeholders. In this case, the company, in partnership with the city of Kalundborg, invested in numerous underground pipes so that the heat that used to be wasted would be taken to the residences in the city, which in turn allowed better energetic efficiency to the burning process. The externality associated with the non-efficient consumption of non-renewable resources has been circumvented, and used to generate additional revenues, reduce the population cost of living and, more importantly, to make disappear the environmental impact of burning fuel oil in residential buildings, no longer existing.

Table 3. Main business externalities and alleviation acts via industrial symbiosis [1,11]

Business	Externality	Symbiosis	Outcome
Mining (Gladstone, Australia)	Use of water from local reserves during drought	8.5 km pipeline so that secondary treated effluent from Gladstone sewage treatment plant could be used for its mud washing process	During drought alumina refinery was able to continue to operate at full production; no need to install tertiary treatment AT Gladstone sewage treatment plant; water source conservation; no city effluents discharged to local waterways
Chemical; production of titanium dioxide (Kwinana, Australia)	Production of contaminated acid water	Hydrochloric acid reuse	Revenue from sale

Common goals and close collaboration are prerequisites to create industrial symbiotic connections among companies in different business sectors. According with Bititci [2, p.7], collaboration is “a process in which organizations exchange information, alter activities, share resources and enhance each other’s capacity for mutual benefit and a common purpose by sharing risks, responsibilities and rewards”. The same author ratify that collaboration arises from the inability of organizations to generate sustainable value working alone, aside from society. Therefore, companies should work mutually to generate positive externalities and to act against negative ones.

To generate a collaborative symbiotic network, third parties should focus not just on externalities control, but also on facilitating structures to speed the transformation process. An approach was constructed based on Harris [15] and described in terms of industry facilitation and provision of technical assistance for symbiosis development (Figure 3).

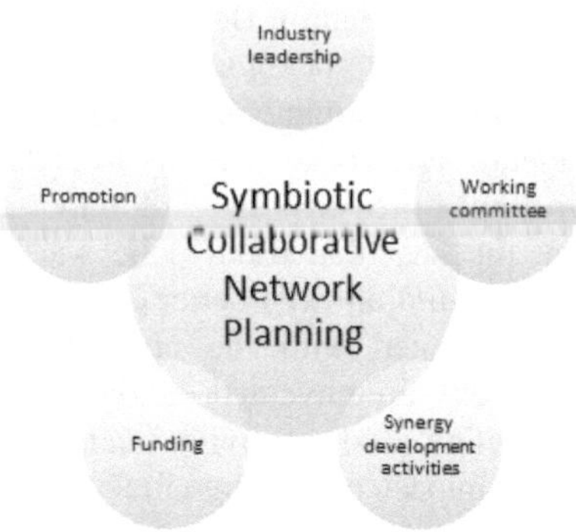

Fig. 3. Facilitating structures to achieve industrial symbiosis

The approach from Figure 3 presented industry leadership from prominent companies as a recommended factor to create synergy among other members. Leadership from local or regional government can also help to create more synergy. Another factor pointed as beneficial is the adoption of an effective symbiosis development process management by means of a working committee with representatives from key businesses, facilitators and other parts providing input to the synergy creation goal. The tasks associated with synergy development ("synergy development activities") are composed by the collection of data from process input and output maps, lists of synergy opportunities and, finally, open workshops to explore good opportunities and concretize this symbiotic exchanges. Provisions are needed to cover the costs for data collection, synergy opportunity identification and screening and industry facilitation, but not necessarily for the actual investment costs for the implementation of any particular synergy project [15].

The symbiosis promotion is also an important part and should be conducted as a facilitating structure. As Harris state [15, p.12], "it is generally beneficial to document and communicate regional synergy achievements to various stakeholders, including local industries (to enhance their participation), community and other stakeholder grouping".

5 Final Remarks

The proposed contribution of this paper was to present two important elements of industrial symbiosis development - externalities control and collaborative networks - and their importance to speed up the symbiotic connections and their effectiveness. Traditional references about industrial symbiosis work mainly on information about by-products exchanges and services sharing. Our intention was to point out externalities control and sustainable value generation as additional information for symbiosis development. Their use can be more attractive for business companies and theirs stakeholders. Collaborative networks are the vehicles where this data can be concretized on symbiotic relations, leading to sustainable value generation.

References

1. Beers, D.V., Corder, G.D., Bossilkov, A., Berkel, R.V.: Regional synergies in the Australian minerals industry: Case-studies and enabling tools. Minerals Engineering 20, 830–841 (2007)
2. Bititci, U.S., Martinez, V., Albores, P., Parung, J.: Creating and managing value in collaborative networks. International Journal of Physical Distribution & Logistics Management 34(3/4), 251–268 (2004)
3. Boisvert, A., Leung, P., Mackrael, K., Park, C., Purcell, M.: Planning for Sustainability: A Starter Guide! The Natural Step, Canada (2009)
4. Brand, E., de Bruijn, T.: Shared responsibility at the regional level: the building of sustainable industrial estates. European Environment 9, 221–231 (1999)
5. Chertow, M.: Industrial symbiosis, The Encyclopedia of Earth. Annual review of energy and the environment 25, 1 (2008)
6. Chertow, M.R.: Industrial symbiosis: literature and taxonomy. Annual Review of Energy and Environment 2(1), 8–337 (2000)
7. Cohen-Rosenthal, E.: Handbook on Codes, Covenants, Conditions, and Restrictions for Eco-Industrial Parks (1999)
8. Cote, R.: Designing eco-industrial parks: a synthesis of some experiences. Journal of Cleaner Production 6(3-4), 181–188 (1998)
9. Delucchi, M.A.: Summary of the Nonmonetary Externalities of Motor-Vehicle Use (1998)
10. Dunn, S.V.: Eco-Industrial Parks: A Common Sense Approach to Environmental Protection. Yale University, New Haven (1995)
11. Ehrenfeld, J., Gertler, N.: Industrial Ecology in Practice. Journal of Industrial Ecology 1(1) (1997)
12. Fleig, A.-K.: Eco-industrial parks - A Strategy towards Industrial Ecology in Developing and Newly Industrialized Countries, http://linkinghub.elsevier.com/
13. Frosch, R.A., Gallopoulos, N.E.: Strategies for manufacturing. Scientific American 261(3), 94–102 (199)
14. Gianetti, B.F., Almeida, C.M.V.B.: Ecologia Industrial: Conceitos, Ferramentas e Aplicações. Editora Edgard Blücher (2006)
15. Harris, S.: Mechanisms to Enable Regional Resource Synergies: Facilitating Structures and Operational Arrangements. Centre of Excellence in Cleaner Production, Bulletin No. 3. Curtin University of Technology, Perth (2008)
16. Meyer, C., Kirby, J.: Leadership in the Age of Transparency. Harvard Business Review (2010)
17. Richards, D.J., Allenby, B.R., Frosch, R.A.: The greening of industrial ecosystems. In: Allenby, B.R., Richards, D.J. (eds.) The Greening of Industrial Ecosystems, National Academy Press, Washington, DC (1994)
18. Sáez, R.M., Linares, P., Leal, J.: Assessment of the externalities of biomass energy, and a comparison of its full costs with coal. Biomass and Bioenergy 14(5/6), 469–478 (1998)
19. Sankar, U.: Environmental Externalities. Madras (2006)
20. Yang, S., Feng, N.: A case study of industrial symbiosis: Nanning Sugar Co., Ltd. in China. Resources, Conservation and Recycling (2008)

Author Index

GPSR Compliance

The European Union's (EU) General Product Safety Regulation (GPSR) is a set of rules that requires consumer products to be safe and our obligations to ensure this.

If you have any concerns about our products, you can contact us on ProductSafety@springernature.com

In case Publisher is established outside the EU, the EU authorized representative is:

Springer Nature Customer Service Center GmbH
Europaplatz 3
69115 Heidelberg, Germany

Batch number: 10837186

Printed by Printforce, the Netherlands